A gathering with an acknowledged bias toward and emphasis on Charles Williams, *The Inklings and King Arthur* offers new insights on the difficult and demanding Arthurian poetry of this least critically studied Inkling. But it has as well an impressive array of essays on all the preeminent Inklings—Tolkien and Lewis and Williams and Barfield—that will be a significant contribution to the study of their Arthurian works in particular and of twentieth-century Arthurian literature in general.

—**Verlyn Flieger**, Author of *Splintered Light, A Question of Time,* and *Interrupted Music*

In recent years, it has become increasingly clear that the Arthurian legends and their world were of vital importance to the writing and thought of the major Inklings. Under Sørina Higgins' enterprising editorship, this adventurous and illuminating volumes offers a wealth of insights—from theoretical, contextual, interpretative, and other viewpoints—which will move the study of Barfield, Lewis, Tolkien, Williams, and their immediate predecessors into new and exciting territory, showing that the Inklings' concern with the 'Matter of Britain' was motivated not by nostalgia but by urgent concern for the present and future.

—**Grevel Lindop**, author of *Charles Williams: The Third Inkling*

Sørina Higgins has performed a wonderful service in opening our eyes to the living presence of King Arthur in the scholarship, imaginative writing, and wartime religious reflection of the major Inklings. With its stellar cast of scholars and interpreters, this volume is an indispensable resource for Inklings and Arthurian studies, and indeed for all who seek to understand the modern mythopoeic imagination.

—**Carol and Philip Zaleski**, co-authors of *The Fellowship: The Literary Lives of the Inklings*

The Inklings and King Arthur: Owen Barfield, C. S. Lewis, J. R. R. Tolkien, and Charles Williams on the Matter of Britain is a powerful collection of essays that fills a gaping hole in Inklings' scholarship. While many readers have long noted the presence of Arthurian motifs and allusions in the works of the Inklings, few are aware of how extensive these connections are. Sørina Higgins has drawn together an impressive group of scholars who offer scholarly yet thoroughly readable essays covering the scope, depth, and influence of Arthuriana in writings of Barfield, Lewis, Tolkien, and Williams. This book should be on the shelf of all Inklings readers.

—**Don W. King**, Montreat College, author of *C. S. Lewis, Poet*

The Inklings and King Arthur is a very significant addition to serious study of the Inklings circle of C. S. Lewis, J. R. R. Tolkien, and their friends. It distinctively focusses upon the group rather than only on Lewis, Tolkien, or other members individually, as has often been the case. The circle is represented convincingly in featuring four of the shaping members, all important writers, and their common interest in King Arthur and the Matter of Britain as a living and breathing tradition. This theme is demonstrated to be an important key for unlocking the heartbeat of the informal group, and dispels the persistent myth that the Inklings were not part of, nor relevant to, the concerns of modernist writers after World War I. This deeply researched, sharply up-to-date, and well-unified collection of essays provides a wealth of discoveries for the reader and opens many doors for further Inklings' study.

—**Colin Duriez**, author of *The Oxford Inklings: Lewis, Tolkien and Their Circle*, *J.R.R. Tolkien and C.S. Lewis: The Gift of Friendship*, and other books relating to the Inklings

Taken as a whole, the essays in this collection lead to the surprising but inescapable conclusion that it is in their Arthurian works that the Inklings' thoughts and writings are most intertwined, not only with each other, but with the wider currents of the twentieth century. This book is essential reading, not only for scholars of fantasy literature, but for all those interested in understanding how traditions and writers shape each other.

—**Michael D. C. Drout**, Wheaton College

Just when serious students of C.S. Lewis' writing think there is nothing new to be said about his work—at least nothing original and significant—Sørina Higgins has edited *The Inklings and King Arthur*. In short, this is an important book. Every contributor's essay is fascinating. I intend to recommend it to my students.

—**Lyle Dorsett**, Beeson Divinity School, Samford University

The historical, legendary, and literary King Arthur lay at the heart of much of what the Inklings wrote—sometimes explicitly, sometimes concealed as deeply as the Isle of Avalon itself, and always filtered through the unique interests and interpretations of the authors as individuals, as Higgins' introductory essay demonstrates. This ground-breaking collection presents new scholarship on topics as diverse as violence, historicity, gender, medievalism, ecology, mysticism, and personal biography at the nexus of Arthuriana and Inklings studies. Especially exciting is the inclusion of some of the first published criticism on Tolkien's *The Fall of Arthur* and its unique re-visioning of the Matter of Britain. Those interested in the Inklings or in modern interpretations of the Arthurian mythos will find much thought-provoking material in these pages.

—**Janet Brennan Croft**, editor of *Mythlore: A Journal of J.R.R. Tolkien, C.S. Lewis, Charles Williams, and Mythopoeic Literature*

Sørina Higgins collects twenty essayists' discussions of twentieth-century British Arthuriana, primarily but not quite exclusively that written by the Inklings. Some essays compare thematic aspects of Charles Williams', C. S. Lewis', J. R. R. Tolkien's, and Owen Barfield's Arthurian writings; other essays give historic backgrounds, consider the Inklings' treatments of gender, or discuss the religious significance of the Holy Grail (that is, discuss mainly Charles Williams' treatments of the "Graal"). Some readers will think the lengthy focus on the Inklings' Arthuriana too restrictive, but these writers' continued-and-growing critical acceptance as exponents of types of Christian Romanticism that survived through Modernism(s), and seem to be doing better than some Modernists through Post-Modernism, means that the Victorian fragmentation of the literary culture is still the basic truth. Here are discussed some fascinating cultural shards.

—**Joe Christopher**, Professor Emeritus, Tarleton State University

This book identifies a very important thread in the intellectual curiosity, creative work, and spiritual convictions of the Inklings. For students of the Arthurian tradition, it will reveal an under-appreciated chapter of the Arthur story from the early twentieth century. For Inklings enthusiasts, it will unfold a fascination they might never have known that the Inklings shared.

—**Corey Olsen**, President of Signum University, author of *Exploring J.R.R. Tolkien's* The Hobbit

This is such a good idea for a book that it's surprising no one thought of it before. It's hard to overstate the degree to which the world the Inklings grew up in was permeated by the Arthurian story. Just going by names alone, think of Tolkien's father (Arthur Tolkien), Lewis's best friend (Arthur Greeves), Williams's mentor in occult studies and ritual magic (Arthur Edward Waite), and one of the Inklings himself (Barfield, who went by his middle name, but whose full name was Arthur Owen Barfield).

—**John Rateliff**, author of *The History of* The Hobbit

This volume follows Arthurian leylines in geographies of myth, history, gender, and culture, uncovering Inklings lodestones and way markers throughout. A must read for students of the Inklings, particularly those interested in Charles Williams.

—**Aren Roukema**, Birkbeck, University of London

This is a wonderfully rich and long overdue examination of a theme in the Inklings that has never had the attention it deserves—a theme that locates them firmly within the mainstream of the British imagination. These studies are theoretically sophisticated, lively and original, and will be of the greatest interest to students of English literature in general as well as Inklings enthusiasts.

—**Dr. Rowan Williams**, Master of Magdalene College, Cambridge

Apocryphile Press
1700 Shattuck Ave #81
Berkeley, CA 94709
www.apocryphilepress.com

Cover Art & Design by Emily Austin
www.emilyaustindesign.com

Please join our mailing list at
www.apocryphilepress.com/free
and we'll keep you up-to-date on all our new releases
—and we'll also send you a FREE BOOK.
Visit us today!

The Inklings and King Arthur

J. R. R. Tolkien, Charles Williams, C. S. Lewis,
and Owen Barfield on the Matter of Britain

edited by Sørina Higgins

Dedication

I dedicate my work on this volume to my mother,
who taught me to love learning and literature
and whose life is a light on the spiritual quest.
—SH

Contents

Introduction—Present and Past: The Inklings and King Arthur

Sørina Higgins

Inspiration for and Purpose of this Volume

The *Fall of Arthur* by J. R. R. Tolkien was published in May of 2013. As I read it, three truths quickly became evident. The first was that Tolkien's only Arthurian work is an important text worthy of rigorous study. It is a poem whose elements of craft—alliterative meter, diction, imagery, balance of the lines, and so forth—show some level of sophistication. It is a significant document in the history of Tolkien's legendarium, revealing ideas that he entertained and then later discarded about how to integrate the story of King Arthur into his own evolving mythology. John Garth wrote in his review of *The Fall of Arthur* that "any addition to the Arthurian tradition by a major author is welcome; this one is also exciting because of what it adds to our picture of a great modern imagination" (Garth, "The Road").[1] Indeed, Tolkien's addition to the Arthurian tradition is not only one more document that provides evidence of his writing methods, ideas, and creative evolution—it is also exciting because of what it adds to our knowledge of twentieth-century British Arthuriana.

This leads to the second truth that *Fall of Arthur* revealed to me, one that is continually reinforced by further study: it is one work among many Arthurian writings composed in Great Britain in the period of the two World Wars, which suggests that Tolkien participated in his culture's use of Arthurian symbols for social or spiritual experiences. Many important writers in the early twentieth century composed important Arthurian works. I became curious, then, about the material conditions and cultural contexts that fostered an Arthurian upsurge in Britain in the period from around 1914 to 1945. As I discuss below, Arthur was a powerful figure of social cohesion, moral rectitude, and military might during the terrible conflicts in

---

[1] Full bibliographical citations for this introduction have been absorbed into the works cited for chapter 1, which can be found on page 55.

which Britain was engaged.[2] Mainstream and minor writers alike participated in this revival or continuation of Arthurian appropriation. Several of the Inklings' literary predecessors, teachers, colleagues, students, and friends were similarly engaged: George MacDonald (1824–1905), William Morris (1834–96), A. E. Waite (1857–1942), Arthur Machen (1863–1947), G. K. Chesterton (1874–1936), Roger Lancelyn Green (1918–87), and John Heath-Stubbs (1918–2006)[3] each wrote Arthurian works.

The third truth I realized while reading *The Fall of Arthur* was that the time had arrived for a study of the Inklings' Arthuriana. Each of the major members of this gathering of Oxford Christian writers—C. S. Lewis, J. R. R. Tolkien, Charles Williams, and Owen Barfield—wrote letters, poetry, fiction, or performance pieces with Arthurian elements.[4] As highly educated men of letters, several of whom taught literature at Oxford or Cambridge, these authors provide an essential dual insight into Arthurian texts. Their professional knowledge of medieval and Renaissance literature gave them the ability to read earlier Arthurian materials with a level of accuracy, detail, and interpretive depth not available to the average reader—or writer. Yet they were focused not on a revival of the past, but on the present's need for redemption; as soldiers, office workers, and creative professionals, the Inklings wrote Arthurian works that contain incisive critiques of their own times and visions of utopian or dystopian futures evolving out of contemporary decisions.

One purpose of this volume, then, is to fill a sizable hole in the field of Inklings studies. There has never been a comprehensive study of their Arthurian works. In 1960, Charles Moorman published *Arthurian Triptych: Mythic Materials in Charles Williams, C. S. Lewis, and T. S. Eliot*. That book, of course, could not take *The Fall of Arthur* into account, nor did it consider Chesterton and MacDonald as predecessors of, or Barfield as contributor to, the Inklings' Arthurian vision. Several Arthurian encyclopedias have devoted entries to one or another of the Inklings, but these hardly constitute in-depth studies. There are important articles examining either Tolkien and Arthur, Williams and Arthur, or Lewis and Arthur[5]—but again, no book-length study. In addition, then, to serving as the first sizable study of Inklings Arthuriana, this book also aims to be the first full-length, peer-reviewed book to consider *The Fall of Arthur*.[6] To those ends, *The Inklings and King Arthur* considers the four major Inklings together, with a focus that enables close comparison and contrast of some of their most important works and ideas.

---

2   This topic is taken up by Taylor Driggers in chapter 10, "The Stripped Banner: Reading *The Fall of Arthur* as a Post-World War I Text."

3   Heath-Stubbs's important Arthurian poem can be considered a direct descendant of Charles Williams' works, as Joe Christopher discusses in his three-part essay "John Heath-Stubbs' *Artorius* and the Influence of Charles Williams." *Mythlore* 13.2 (1986): 56–62; 13.3 (1987): 51–57; 13.4 (1987): 51–56.

4   See pages 15–22 for an inventory of Inklings Arthuriana.

5   such as those by Bradbury, Carter, Cavaliero, Christopher, Curtis, Fimi, Finn, Flieger, Garth, Göller, Grimaldi, Hanks, Hannay, Higgins, Huttar, Martin, McClatchey, Moynihan, Rateliff, Ryan, Schneider, and Zemmour; see the Bibliography of Secondary Studies on pages 515–26.

6   There are individual articles examining this Tolkien text, including Verlyn Flieger's "*The Fall of Arthur* by J. R. R. Tolkien" and Taylor Driggers's "Modern Medievalism and Myth: Tolkien, Tennyson, and the Quest for a Hero." There are also several book reviews.

Furthermore, the present collection endeavors to usher the field of Inklings studies into more rigorous theoretical territory and to bring recognized writers into dialogue with newer, emerging voices. There are chapters by students and by professors, by both emerging and established scholars. There are varied approaches, including historical contextualization, gender studies, postcolonial criticism, examinations of intertextuality, and theological perspectives.

Another goal of *The Inklings and King Arthur* is to demonstrate the ongoing relevance of both Arthurian legends and the works of the Inklings. Most of the works of literature under discussion are alive and well in the twenty-first century, living and breathing in the minds of new readers, teachers, and scholars; in their resonance with current events and ideas; and in numerous adaptations and permutations in a wide variety of media. King Arthur has returned and is always returning.

Organization of this Volume

The Inklings and King Arthur is not structured according to some obvious principle, such as chronologically or by author. Such simplistic categorization is, in fact, contrary to the nature of the kinds of examination the chapters in this volume pursue. Many of the articles are large survey essays, considering Lewis, Tolkien, Williams, and Barfield all at once, or reviewing the historical, cultural, or philosophical landscape in which they worked. Many follow a theoretical or ideological theme through multiple works, providing a broad-and-deep approach to the texts in question. Several chapters are in dialogue with each other, offering variant perspectives on the same or similar questions.

Texts and Intertexts

The book begins, therefore, with a sizable section on questions of intertextuality: What is an "Arthurian text"? What constitutes the body of Arthurian work that preceded the Inklings? How do their writings interact with those of their predecessors and with each other? In this section, I begin in chapter 1, "The Matter of Logres: Arthuriana and the Inklings," by defining terms and providing an overview of the adaptability of cultural appropriations of Arthur throughout his palimpsestuous history. I then set the stage for the chapters to follow by giving a brief summary of each of the major Inklings' Arthuriana; of particular note is my discussion of Owen Barfield's only thoroughly Arthurian work, *The Quest of the Sangreal*. Holly Ordway follows this with a brief history of the major medieval Arthurian texts. Her focus is "on the sources that are most widely recognized as influential or important and that are also significant in some way to the Inklings' writings" (62), and she also notes that "the Arthurian legendarium provided fruitful material for commentary on current events" (65). The nature of Arthuriana as a cultural gloss is a theme throughout this volume.

Once the source texts have been presented, Brenton D. G. Dickieson's chapter, a study of intertextuality in Lewis' Ransom cycle, introduces the complicated ways that the Inklings' Arthurian texts interacted not only with their literary ancestors, but also with each other. In this groundbreaking exploration, Dickieson calls for deeper theoretical approaches to these writers and demonstrates how such critical moves can be made. After surveying critical diction relevant to discussions of Inklings intertextuality, Dickieson offers a new valence for the term "hyperlink" in our Internet age. Throughout, he argues that Lewis anticipated later critical approaches to intertextuality.

With this theoretical foundation in place, Charles Huttar's meticulous examination of "the idea of Avalon" essentially begins the project for which Dickieson calls: applying global concepts of intertextuality to particular elements of discourse. These two chapters dovetail nicely, providing some insightful overlap, then moving in different directions. Huttar investigates a particular intertextual moment: the point of contact among "houses of healing," the idea of "Avalon," and *Sehnsucht*, or western longing. In positioning the Inklings, Huttar points out that "Avalon was but one ingredient among many from a range of myth, legend, and imagery" (116), and he examines the result of these layered influences in the ways each of our authors came to a well-established Arthurian tradition and transformed it, particularly in regard to this central idea of longing for a paradise in the West, which is connected with King Arthur's mysterious departure for Avalon.

Christopher Gaertner next takes up another large point of conceptual overlap: one that is less tied to instances of specific diction or topicality, but rather looking at the influence of Owen Barfield's belief in the evolution of consciousness (itself derived from the teachings of Rudolf Steiner) on the Inklings' views of language, consciousness, and meaning, including the ways that they shaped geography, archetypes of wise characters, and trajectories of humanity's future in their works. Gaertner's discussion of Barfield's novella *Night Operation* is particularly valuable, as Barfield often gets short shrift in Inklings studies.

Histories Past

Once this volume has established that the Inklings were *bricoleurs*, as well as adapters and myth-makers, it can move "From Myth to History and Back Again": looking historically at the past that shaped the Inklings' present and then at the historical space in which they lived and worked. Yannick Imbert begins this process with his survey chapter on "Inklings Arthuriana in Historical Context," revealing how the Inklings were responding to a Victorian Arthur who represented social cohesion, domesticity, political conflicts, rapid urbanization, and industrialization. Like every writer in this collection, Imbert recognizes that Arthurian literature has always been "a vehicle for social and cultural discourse" (179). He provides the primary discussion in this book on the vexed issue of Arthur's historicity—or, more accurately, how the Inklings were interested in that question—but argues that the more interesting inquiry is how myth and history interact with and inform one another. Williams, for instance, wrote that "history is itself a myth; to the imaginative, engaged in considering these things, all is equally myth" ("Figure" 264).[7] The Inklings, Imbert suggests, saw no war between the mythological and the historical.

Neither did G. K. Chesterton, an important influence on the Inklings, whom J. Cameron Moore discusses next. Chesterton saw the Arthurian legendarium as a kind of national fairy tale, as he saw England itself as an expression of fairyland. This is similar to Tolkien's approach in *The Fall of Arthur*, as Tolkien was attempting a "cultural recovery" similar to the ideas of Recovery, Escape, and Consolation that he lays out

---

7   See the list of abbreviations on p. 13.

in "On Fairy-stories." In "The Elegiac Fantasy of Past Christendom," Cory Grewell argues that Tolkien employs a medievalism relevant to twentieth-century modernism.

Histories Present

This brings us to the context in which the Inklings were working. In their survey article "Spiritual Quest in a Scientific Age," Jason Jewell and Chris Butynskyi cover scientism, Darwin, Marx, Nietzsche, Freud, and eugenics to provide a clear picture of the ideological climate in which the Inklings worked and to which they responded. The data they present challenges the "secularization thesis" and shows the Inklings combating declining religiosity. The least specifically Arthurian of all the chapters, Jewell and Butynskyi's covers a large period of time and a vast array of important social elements, setting the stage for the cultural analysis to come. These include Taylor Driggers' historically grounded reading of *The Fall of Arthur* "as a Post-World War I text," Jon Hooper's comparison of Arthurian Waste Lands in the works of T. S. Eliot and C. S. Lewis, and Benjamin D. Utter's examination of Charles Williams' gendered, Christian imperialism in the light of postcolonial critique.

Driggers' chapter, "The Stripped Banner," offers a "critical analysis of the role of violence within Tolkien's stories" (266) that has hitherto been lacking in Tolkien scholarship. In comparing Tolkien with Tennyson, Driggers reveals ways that Tolkien subverts imperialism by showing violence as a distraction: "To Tolkien, Arthur's vastly misguided attempt to resurrect past glories that belong to Other Time within his own present represents a gross perversion of the desire that Faërie awakens in author and reader" (273). Reading this chapter (10) against Grewell's (8) provides a fascinating conversation between two variant interpretations of *The Fall of Arthur*, particularly its attitudes toward its own past and present.

Jon Hooper's analysis of Lewis' Narniad places these seven children's stories firmly in their modernist context, in dialogue with Eliot's barren landscape—which may have been, according to the scholars Hooper surveys, either "an expression of modern chaos" (281) or "a symbol of the lack of religious values in the modern world, contrasting a spiritually healthy past with a spiritually impoverished present, through symbols of fertility and sterility" (281). Either way, there are both kinds of waste lands in the Narnian chronicles, but there are also "places that offer respite from the waste land, versions of the *locus amoenus*" (293), Edenic pastoral settings. These connect to the westward longing toward Avalon that Charles Huttar examined in chapter 4.

Continuing and expanding the postcolonial conversation, Benjamin Utter's chapter closes this section. It is entitled "'What Does the Line along the Rivers Define?': Charles Williams' Arthuriad and the Rhetoric of Empire." As Rouse and Rushton wrote in 2013: "Arthurian scholars have increasingly begun to read the Arthurian history of Britain as a postcolonial narrative, as a story of multiple ruptures through conquest and repeated attempts to rewrite both history and the landscape in order to legitimatise the invader or to provide consolation to the invaded" (218–19). Utter's piece is a direct response to this turn, providing both a postcolonial reading of Williams' poetry and a rejoinder to that reading.

Geographies of Gender

Utter's work on Williams' rhetoric of empire is the perfect transition piece between "history" and "gender," as racism/imperialism and sexism/misogyny are often interimplicated—especially in Williams' mythological map, which is both colonized and feminized. Thus bodies are landscapes, and geographies are gendered. This is especially relevant in an Arthurian England, as "England has a kind of mythical geography, a network of associations and oppositions" (Shippey, "Winchester" 18). This is not a modern phenomenon:

> For medieval writers, the locating of Arthurian geography within the actual landscape of the British Isles was not merely of antiquarian interest: rather, it was often a serious matter of political, cultural and institutional importance .... The Arthurian tradition plays an important role in the construction and articulation of this mythical landscape, interweaving the aura of the age of Camelot into the palimpsest that is the British landscape. (Rouse and Rushton 218)

The geographical setting of fantastical places has long been important. Sir Thomas More's *Utopia* had a map in 1516, as did Jonathan Swift's *Gulliver's Travels* in 1726 and Robert Louis Stevenson's *Treasure Island* in 1883; "in modern fantasy, especially high fantasy, maps are considered common enough to be almost obligatory, mainly because of the maps J. R. R. Tolkien included in *The Lord of the Rings*" (Ekman 14). The Arthurian situation is more complex: the maps are those of both real places and imaginary places, worldly and otherworldly realms. This is a stratigraphic approach, in which the imagined is layered on top of the material: "Through this accretive process, Arthurian geography becomes a complex grafting of fictional, sometimes allegorical, places onto the real topography of the British Isles" (Rouse and Rushton 219).

Tolkien did not include a map in the unfinished *Fall of Arthur*, but Williams did in *Taliessin through Logres*—and it is a map of Europe superimposed with the figure of a nude woman. There could hardly be a more startling or more explicit image of the problematic associations of Arthuriana, Christianity, imperialism, and patriarchy. Alyssa House-Thomas establishes the groundwork for a textually rich, historically rooted approach to gender studies in her analysis of Guinever in *The Fall of Arthur*, and then Andrew Rasmussen takes up these controversial, apparently misogynistic aspects of Williams' poetry. This important section on gender concludes with Benjamin Shogren's substantial contribution: "Those Kings of Lewis' Logres: Arthurian Figures as Lewisian Genders in *That Hideous Strength*." Shogren examines the two names that Elwin Ransom takes on in *That Hideous Strength*—"Pendragon" and "Fisher King"—and associates them with Lewis' concepts of masculinity and femininity.

These seven chapters—four from a historical perspective, three through the lens of gender studies—comprise a significant contribution to the critical rigor of Inklings studies. They provide varying approaches to some of the most crucial questions facing literary studies in our time, leaving a forceful impression (on this reader at least) of the relevance and importance of Lewis, Tolkien, and Williams in their century, in ours, and in our culture's constantly shifting values regarding war, science, race, class, religion, geopolitics, and gender.

Cartographies of the Spirit

The Inklings would be among the first to argue for stable, unchanging, timeless values: love, service, humility, work, order, ceremony, sacrament. The final section of *The Inklings and King Arthur* takes up these eternal themes. In "Servant of All: Arthurian Peregrinations in George MacDonald," Kirstin Jeffrey Johnson looks back at an important literary ancestor of the Inklings and examines what his Arthurian novels have to teach about true knighthood—a knighthood that is particularly English, but also transcends a specific cultural or historical setting.

The final three chapters are devoted to the works of Charles Williams. This should not be surprising, as he wrote by far the largest number of completed, thoroughly Arthurian works of all the Inklings. It could be argued that his life was centered on the Holy Grail. These three chapters take up the modes in which he engaged with the king and the quest: his early plays in "Camelot Incarnate" by Bradley Wells, his novel *War in Heaven* in "Any Chalice of Consecrated Wine" by Suzanne Bray, and his final volumes of poetry— *Taliessin through Logres* (1938) and *The Region of the Summer Stars* (1944)—in "The Acts of Unity" by Andrew Stout. A picture of Williams' complexity emerges: thoroughly Christian, deeply hermetic, saintly and sadistic, his mysticism and praxis meet in these examinations of his visionary Arthuriana.

Finally, then, Malcolm Guite's conclusion—"Once and Future: The Inklings, Arthur, and Prophetic Insight"—relies upon and reinforces Roger Simpson's claim in 2003 that "we remain inextricably involved in an Arthurian world" (Simpson 85). In chapter 2 in this volume, Holly Ordway claims that

> the Arthurian tradition is a living one, which not only provided material for medieval writers and poets, but continues to inspire authors to the present day. The earlier texts are not mere relics of the past, but the productions of authors who, like modern-day authors, felt the need to retell an important story in their own way. (77)

Similarly, in his conclusion Malcolm Guite answers critics by saying that "far from refusing the challenges of Modernism, the Inklings were dealing with those challenges in a far-reaching and prophetic way" and that "the very way they handle and rework the Arthurian material ... was itself a powerful and helpful response to the deepest currents of modernism" (494). He goes on to provide specific examples of how Charles Williams speaks to the recent (and ongoing) financial crisis, how J. R. R. Tolkien offers a critique of warmongering, and how C. S. Lewis is relevant for deep ecology and for combating what Guite calls the "deep evils and deadly tendencies inherent in amoral reductivism and moral subjectivism" (503).

As you read this book—straight through or in an order of your own devising—you will perform your own acts of comparison and contrast. What the Arthuriana of four major Inklings had in common is one fascinating study; how those works differed is another. As Alyssa House-Thomas writes in her chapter: "The Inklings, clearly, did not respond to Arthur with one voice" (362)—and their varied voices ask and sometimes answer many of the same questions that are still asked today.

Bibliographical Explanations

At the end of each chapter, you will find "Works Cited" pages with references for all the resources cited in that individual chapter. The sources for this introduction have been absorbed into the Works Cited for chapter 1. At the end of the book, you will find three bibliographies:

1. Bibliography of Arthurian Sources. This contains citations for all non-Inklings Arthurian works referenced throughout the volume. Editions are those used by the various chapter-writers throughout the text, which means that they are not "original" publications (this is, of course, a vexed question for older texts in any case) and that there are multiple editions listed for several of the works.

2. Bibliography of Works by the Inklings. This contains citations to first editions of all works by C. S. Lewis, J. R. R. Tolkien, Charles Williams, and Owen Barfield referenced throughout the volume, as well as works by others who attended Inklings meetings, according to Humphrey Carpenter (even though such a rigid definition of an "Inklings" is admittedly problematic) and by George MacDonald and G. K. Chesterton.

3. Bibliography of Secondary Studies. This contains citations for the scholarly works on either Arthurian literature or the writings of the Inklings referenced throughout the volume. Articles contained in essay collections are not listed individually unless there is one article of significance in an otherwise unused volume; articles in periodicals are retained.

The selectivity of these three bibliographies means that some works, such as classical sources, volumes of nineteen-century philosophy and twentieth-century literary theory, etc., do not appear in these bibliographies, but only in the Works Cited of the chapters in which they are referenced. There has been no attempt to standardize editions among the authors of chapters in this book, especially because digital versions of many texts are readily available. Contributors have chosen what editions to use, and these are identified in the Works Cited of the individual chapters.

After this introduction, there are two helpful lists:

1. Abbreviations for works most commonly referenced throughout this volume (pp. 13–14).

2. Inventory of Inklings Arthuriana: information about works by Barfield, Tolkien, Lewis, and Williams that have Arthurian connections (pp. 15–22).

Permissions

The editor would like to thank the copyright holders of works quoted in this book, as well as all those who have assisted in the process of securing permissions. Excerpts from *Beowulf: A Translation and Commentary* by J. R. R. Tolkien copyright © 2014 by The Tolkien Trust. Excerpts from *The Fall of Arthur* by J. R. R. Tolkien copyright © 2013 by The Tolkien Trust. Excerpts from *Sauron Defeated: The History of the Lord of the Rings*, part 4 by J. R. R. Tolkien copyright © 1992 by Frank Richard Williamson and Christopher Reuel Tolkien as Executors of the Estate of J. R. R. Tolkien. Excerpts from *The Lord of the Rings* by J. R. R. Tolkien, edited by Christopher Tolkien, copyright © 1954, 1955, 1965, 1966 by J. R. R. Tolkien; copyright © renewed 1982, 1983 by Christopher Tolkien, Michael H. R. Tolkien, John F. R. Tolkien, and Priscilla M. A. R.

Acknowledgements

There are many people and organizations to thank in a collection of this scope. I am very grateful to Douglas A. Anderson, Owen A. Barfield, Devin Brown, David Llewellyn Dodds, Diana Glyer, Verlyn Flieger, Grevel Lindop, John Rateliff, Elizabeth Sklar, and Ralph Wood for the advice, reading, commentary, suggestions, critiques, and references they provided at various stages of the process of collecting and editing this book. Charles Huttar gave generously of his time and expertise to guide me in many ways. Thank you to Marjorie Lamp Mead and Laura Schmidt at the Marion E. Wade Center at Wheaton College for advice about several matters, especially permissions, and for checking archival details. Devin Brown (again), Charlie Starr, Carol Zaleski, and Philip Zaleski gave great encouragement at a crucial point in the process when we shared a panel at the 2017 CSLIS conference in Tulsa, Oklahoma, as did Joe Ricke and all the fine folks at the Taylor Colloquium in 2016 and Corey Olsen and my dream team at Signum University along the way and especially at Mythmoot IV. My Baylor colleagues Clayton McReynolds and Andrew Rasmussen and my Signum colleague Richard Rohlin assisted with checking citations. Other wise scholars and readers have earned gratitude, including Stephen Barber, Kevin Belmonte, Joe Christopher, Kelly Cowling, Janet Brennan Croft, Jan Curtis, Alice Deegan, Lyle Dorsett, Colin Duriez, Helen Fulton, Kevin Hensler, Brian Horne, Carl Hostetter, Crystal Hurd, Todd Jensen, Bruce Johnson, Don W. King, Nadine He, Trish Lambert, William O'Flaherty, Michael Paulus, Walter Raubicheck, Eric Rauscher, Joshua Reichard, Richard Rohlin, Katherine Sas, John Rateliff, Aren Roukema, Tom Shippey, Leigh Smith, Michael Ward, Richard West, Michael Wodzak, and Victoria Holtz Wodzak.

Many people joined in the conversation about "The Inklings and King Arthur" as these ideas were tested out online (especially on my Charles Williams blog, *The Oddest Inkling*, and on Brenton Dickieson's *A Pilgrim in Narnia*), at conferences, and in conversation. All of the writers and I are grateful to the organizers of conferences and events, editors of periodicals, and members of faculty who have given their permission, time, expertise to this project. To everyone who has ever commented on a blog post, shared a conversation, or socialized around an Inklings conference with us, thank you. You are the community that gave birth to this book and for whom (primarily) it is intended.

An army of warriors from the West rallied with specific support for the GoFundMe campaign to meet permissions fees, including Janet Croft, Matthew DeForrest, Jack Elmy, Verlyn Flieger, John Garth, Ron Griggs, Curtis Gruenler, Diana Glyer, James Hart, Andrew Higgins, Joe Hoffman, Penelope Holdaway, Carl Hostetter, Charles Huttar, Kirstin Johnson, Matt Kirkland, David Lenander, David Maddock, Joel Miller, Franny Moore-Kyle, Katherine Neville, Carolyn Priest-Dorman, John D. Rateliff, Eric Rauscher,

Richard Rohlin, Cynthia Smith, Jason Smith, Kris Swank, Amanda Taylor, Charles Wells, Roger White, Shawn White, Carol Zaleski, and the others who wish to remain anonymous.

Grateful thanks are due to the staff of the Marion E. Wade Center at Wheaton College; the Bodleian Library at Oxford University; King's College, London; John Rylands Library, Manchester; Beinecke Library, Yale; and the many other libraries where the chapter-writers and I did our research. I would like to express particular appreciation to Lona Beitler, librarian at Lehigh Carbon Community College, and the librarians at Baylor University, who performed more than their usual duties in procuring sometimes obscure items through interlibrary loan.

I received much assistance in compiling the "Inventory of Inklings Arthuriana." Paul J. Spaeth, Director of the Library at St. Bonaventure University, has a very helpful website of Williams' Arthuriana. Likewise, Arend Smilde's *Lewisiana* site, especially the page on Lewis' short prose writings, was a great aid, as was *C. S. Lewis—An Annotated Bibliography and Resource* by P. H. Brazier (Wipf and Stock, 2012). Members of my social media networks and followers of *The Oddest Inkling* contributed ideas, suggestions, and references. Owen A. Barfield, David Llewellyn Dodds, John Matthews, Nicholas J. Perry, Gabriel Schenk, Jonas Zeit-Altpeter, and the contributors to this volume suggested additional entries, which I have happily incorporated.

Finally, as editor of this volume, I would like to thank my family and friends—in particular Eve Droma, Sharon Gerdes, Jennifer Raimundo, Rebecca Tirrell Talbot, and my colleagues at Baylor University—for their enthusiasm about this project, for good conversations, and for mutual inspiration. My husband Gary has given more than mortal gifts and sacrifices to support every aspect of my career and work. May all these wise and kind people receive passage from the Grey Havens to the port of their heart's desire.

—Sørina Higgins

List of Abbreviations

C. S. Lewis

AMR	*All My Road Before Me*
AoL	*The Allegory of Love*
CL	*The Collected Letters of C. S. Lewis*
CP	*The Collected Poems of C. S. Lewis*
CR	*Christian Reflections*
DI	*The Discarded Image*
Dock	*God in the Dock*
DT	*The Dark Tower and Other Stories*
FSE	*Fern-Seed and Elephants*
GD	*The Great Divorce*
HHB	*The Horse and His Boy*
I&I	*Image and Imagination*
LB	*The Last Battle*
LWW	*The Lion, the Witch and the Wardrobe*
MC	*Mere Christianity*
MN	*The Magician's Nephew*
NP	*Narrative Poems*
OHEL	*English Literature in the Sixteenth Century, excluding Drama.* Oxford History of English Literature 3
OSP	*Out of the Silent Planet*
OTOW	*Of This and Other Worlds*
OW	*Of Other Worlds*
Per	*Perelandra*
PC	*Prince Caspian*
PCon	*Present Concerns*
PPL	*A Preface to* **Paradise Lost**
PR	*The Pilgrim's Regress*
Reh	*Rehabilitations and Other Essays*
SB	*Spirits in Bondage*
SbJ	*Surprised by Joy*
SC	*The Silver Chair*
SL	*The Screwtape Letters*
SLE	*Selected Literary Essays*

SMRL	*Studies in Medieval and Renaissance Literature*
TAP	*They Asked for a Paper*
THS	*That Hideous Strength*
TWHF	*Till We Have Faces*
VDT	*The Voyage of the "Dawn Treader"*
WA	"Williams and the Arthuriad" in *Arthurian Torso*
WG	*The Weight of Glory and Other Addresses*

J. R. R. Tolkien

FoA	*The Fall of Arthur*
Letters	*The Letters of J. R. R. Tolkien*
LotR	*The Lord of the Rings*
LR	*The Lost Road*. The History of Middle-earth 5
LT	*The Book of Lost Tales*. The History of Middle-earth 1–2
MR	*Morgoth's Ring*. The History of Middle-earth 10
OFS	"On Fairy-stories"
SD	*Sauron Defeated*. The History of Middle-earth 9
Silm	*The Silmarillion*
UT	*Unfinished Tales*

Charles Williams

AHE	*All Hallows' Eve*
AP	*Arthurian Poets: Charles Williams*
Beatrice	*The Figure of Beatrice*
DiH	*Descent into Hell*
Dove	*The Descent of the Dove*
"Figure"	"The Figure of Arthur" in *Arthurian Torso*
HCD	*He Came Down from Heaven*
Image	*The Image of the City and Other Essays*
ORT	*Outlines of Romantic Theology*
RSS	*The Region of the Summer Stars*
TtL	*Taliessin through Logres*
WiH	*War in Heaven*

Inventory of Inklings Arthuriana

What follows reflects an attempt to compile a complete list of works by the four major Inklings that engage with the legends of Arthur, the Knights of the Round Table, or the Quest for the Holy Grail. These are not complete bibliographical citations, as those are found in the Bibliography of works by the Inklings at the end of the book. Instead, they are short descriptions of the nature of each composition. The dates, where possible, indicate the year in which the works were originally written or presented. The purpose of this list is to give readers an idea of how many Arthurian works, of what sorts, each Inkling composed. Readers are invited to send additional entries to inklings. arthur@gmail.com.

Owen Barfield

1931	"Ballade." A poem, probably written in 1931. It is available on www.owenbarfield.org, transcribed from the typescript at the Bodleian Library. In the last stanza, there is a reference to "when the time comes to seek entry / Where Uther's Son and Alfred sleep."
1935–47?	*The Quest of the Sangreal.* A sixteen-page adaptation of Grail episodes from Chrétien and Malory. It is a work of Eurythmia, composed for use at the London School of Eurythmics. It remains unpublished and is in the Bodleian library. This assigned date range is speculative.
1935–47?	Annotations in Sir Thomas Malory's *Morte d'Arthur.* This is a copy of the Everyman's Library edition that was originally published in 1906 and reprinted in 1934 (volume two) and 1935 (volume one). The exact dates of Barfield's notes and annotations are unknown but probably predate Vinaver's 1947 edition of the Winchester MS of Malory.
1947	The *Mark vs. Tristram* letters. Comedic correspondence between Barfield and Lewis. 11–20 June 1947.
1975	*Night Operation.* A dystopian novella whose plot is a "Grail" story.

C. S. Lewis

1915–16	Letters to Arthur Greeves, whom he calls "Galahad." Published in *CL.*
1916	"The Quest of Bleheris." An Arthurian prose tale sent to Arthur Greeves. It remains unpublished and is in the Bodleian library (see Downing, "The Dungeon of his Soul" 37–54).
1919	"Victory." A poem in *Spirits in Bondage,* based on Laȝamon.
1919	A lost poem, possibly entitled "Decadence," "Retreat," or "Venusberg." See King, "Lost but Found," and Christopher, "C. S. Lewis' Lost Arthurian Poem."
1930s?	"Launcelot." Narrative poem. *NP.*

1935   "The Alliterative Metre." Essay. It refers to an "alliterative poem" by Tolkien, which JRRT said was probably *The Fall of Arthur*. *Reh* and *SLE*.

1936   *The Allegory of Love: A Study in Medieval Tradition*. An academic analysis of the courtly love tradition and chivalry. Includes chapters on Chrétien and *The Faerie Queene* and much discussion of the "matter of Britain." Argues that "in the hands of a great poet, the Arthurian story, treated in terms of courtly love, produced the first notable examples of psychological or 'sentimental' fiction" (142).

1939   "A Sacred Poem: Charles Williams, *Taliessin through Logres*." Review of *TtL*. *I&I* 125–36.

1940   "The Necessity of Chivalry." Essay. Comparison of Malory and modern times. *PCon*.

1940   "Why I am Not a Pacifist." Talk given to a pacifist society in Oxford. Claims that "If I am a Pacifist, I have Arthur and Aelfred, Elizabeth and Cromwell ... against me." *WG*.

1941   "On reading *The Faerie Queene*." Essay. *SMRL*.

1942   "Psycho-Analysis and Literary Criticism." Essay. In a discussion of Jungian archetypes, Lewis mentions those who have discovered "behind the Arthurian stones some far off echo of real happenings in the thick darkness of British history" (298). *SLE*.

1944   "Is English Doomed?" Essay. Contains a few references to Launcelot. *PCon*.

1945   Obituary for Charles Williams. Published in *The Oxford Magazine*, vol. 63 (*I&I* 147; here, the date 24 March 1945 is given, but as Williams did not die until 15 May, it must mean 24 May 1945).

1945   "Addison." Essay. Contains some discussion of the culture of courtesy in *Sir Gawain and the Green Knight*. *SLE*.

1945   "The Funeral of a Great Myth." Essay. Puts the death of Arthur in the context of grand, tragic endings in many myths. *CR*.

1945   *That Hideous Strength*. Final novel of the Ransom cycle. Merlin features as an important character, and Ransom is the Pendragon.

1946   "Charles Williams, *Taliessin through Logres*." Another review of *TtL*. *I&I* 137–46.

1947   "The *Morte Darthur*." Review of Vinaver's edition. *SMRL*.

1947   The *Mark vs. Tristram* letters. Comedic correspondence between Barfield and Lewis. 11–20 June 1947.

1948   "Williams and the Arthuriad." Commentary on CW's *TtL* and *RSS*. Based on CSL's course of lectures at Oxford, fall 1945. Printed with Williams' "The Figure of Arthur" in *Arthurian Torso*.

1950   "The Literary Impact of the Authorised Version." Essay. Discusses Malory as source and influence for Tennyson. *TAP, SLE*.

1952   "Hero and Leander." Essay. Talks about the composite nature of Malory's *Morte*. *SLE*.

1954   *English Literature in the Sixteenth Century, Excluding Drama* [OHEL]. Lewis' most exhaustive academic work, it includes a sizable section on Sidney and Spenser.

1954   "Edmund Spenser, 1552–99." Essay. *SMRL*.

1954   "The Gods Return to Earth." Review of *The Fellowship of the Ring*. Reprinted as "Tolkien's *The Lord of the Rings*." Contains a comparison of JRRT's sense of depth to Malory's.

1950s   "De Audiendis Poetis" ("How to study poetry": title after Plutarch). Book chapter. In discussing the value of historical research for reading poetry, CSL mentions the possible connections between Sir Gawain and a sun-god legends; he also responds to the anthropological hypotheses of Frazer and Weston. *SMRL*. On dating its composition, see Hooper's introduction (*SMRL* vii).

1955   "On Science Fiction." Essay. Includes "some of Malory (but none of Malory's best work)" in the "marvelous" category of science fiction. *OW, OTOW*.

1956   "Imagination and Thought in the Middle Ages." Two-part lecture series. In analyzing medieval thought, CSL uses examples from the *Brut*, tracing sources back through Geoffrey to Apuleius and Plato. *SMRL*.

c.1958–60   "The Genesis of a Medieval Book." A draft chapter for a book that CSL did not end up writing (Hooper, *SMRL* viii). Contains a fifteen-page section on Laȝamon's *Brut*. *SMRL*.

1959   "Modern Theology and Biblical Criticism," also called "Fern Seeds and Elephants." Essay. One brief reference: "We may without disgrace believe in a historical Arthur." *CR, FSE*.

1960.   "Arthuriana." Book review of *Arthurian Literature in the Middle Ages: A Collaborative Study*, ed. R. S. Loomis. First published in *The Cambridge Review*, vol. 81, 13 February 1960, p. 355, 357. *I&I*.

1960s   *Spenser's Images of Life*. Lecture notes. Compiled by Alistair Fowler and published posthumously in 1967.

1961   "Neoplatonism in the Poetry of Spenser." Review essay of a book with that title by Robert Ellrodt. Discusses Ellrodt's perspective on Arthur and Gloriana. *SMRL*.

1962   "The Anthropological Approach." Essay. Uses Gawain and the Grail as examples of the uselessness of some anthropological "explanations" of literary phenomenon. *SLE*.

1962–63   *The Discarded Image: An Introduction to Medieval and Renaissance Literature*. Lectures, published posthumously as a book.

1963   "The English Prose *Morte*." Essay. *I&I*.

1963   Introduction to *Selections from Laȝamon's* Brut, edited by G. L. Brook and published by the Clarendon Press. See Huttar's note 32 in chapter 4 of the present volume.

J. R. R. Tolkien

1914   "The Kalavala." Typescript of a talk given at the Corpus Christi College Sundial Society on
            22 November 1914 and again to the Exeter College Essay Club in February 1915. See Verlyn
            Fieger's edition of *The Story of Kullervo*, 63–65, 91. JRRT says that there is nothing in the *Kalavala*
            like "the catalogue of the heroes of Arthur's court" (108).

1916/17–
late 20s?   *The Book of Lost Tales* 2. "The History of Eriol" introduces a character named Éadgifu, "a maiden
            from the West, from Lionesse as some have named it since" (*LT* 2 313). Lyonesse is "one of
            those enchanted places of Arthurian romance, usually associated with Tristran or Galahad"
            (Fimi, "Celtic" 54).

1925   *Sir Gawain and The Green Knight*. An edition of the fourteenth-century Middle English poem,
            edited by JRRT and his colleague E. V. Gordon.

1926   *Beowulf: A Translation and Commentary together with Sellic Spell*. Throughout the commentary, Tolkien
            compares Hrothgar's court at Heorot to Arthur's court at Camelot. Published posthumously
            in 2014.

1925–27   *The Lay of Leithian*. A metrical version of the Beren and Lúthien story. Thingol's kingdom is in
            Broceliande/Broseliand (see Fimi, "Celtic" 63).

1925–27   *Roverandom*. A children's story. There is a character known as "The White Dragon in the Moon."
            The narrator tells the reader that this is the same dragon who fought the Red Dragon in Merlin's
            time. Also, as Charles Huttar notes in his chapter (131), "in a context suggestive of Avalon,
            he wrote 'King Arthur's death,' but then altered 'death' to 'disappearance'" (*Roverandom* 33,
            97–98).

1930   "The Lay of Aotrou and Itroun." A poem set in Broceliande, probably influenced by the *Lais*
            of Marie de France (see Shippey, *Road* 277; Fimi, "Celtic" 53). Written in 1930 and published
            in 1945.

1930s?   *The Fall of Arthur*. An unfinished poem in alliterative meter. Published posthumously in 2013.

1937–38   *The Lost Road and Other Writings*. The History of Middle-earth 5. Contains one indexed reference
            to King Arthur; one to Camelot; and an overt association between Avallon and Tol Eressëa,
            with eleven indexed references. Avalon was very important to Tolkien in this period of the
            development of his legendarium; see Huttar, chapter 4 below.

1938   "On Fairy-stories." There are four Arthurian references: the first claims that the Arthurian
            legends are fairy-stories even though the main characters are not "diminutive elves or fairies"
            (41); the second states that Arthur is one of the ingredients in the great Pot of Story—and,
            interestingly, that Arthur was "once historical (but perhaps as such not of great impor-
            tance)" (55); the third, in the same paragraph as the second, calls Hrothgar's court at Heorot
            "Arthurian" (in quotation marks; 55); and the fourth mentions stories that he liked as a child,

including tales of "Red Indians," but "the land of Merlin and Arthur was better than these" (63). There were additional Arthurian references in the draft manuscript that did not make it to publication (see Flieger and Anderson, *Tolkien on Fairy-stories*, and Hanks 55).

1945   *The Notion Club Papers*, in The History of Middle-earth 9. Contains six indexed references to "Arthur, King," one to "Camelot," and fifty-two to "Avallon" and related terms. See chapter 4 by Charles Huttar in this volume.

1949   Foreword to *Farmer Giles of Ham*. One brief reference to a description "as historians of the reign of Arthur tell us" and a statement that the story takes place before Arthur (66).

1951   Letter to Milton Waldman. JRRT writes: "To Bilbo and Frodo the special grace is granted to go with the Elves they loved—an Arthurian ending, in which it is, of course, not made explicit whether this is an 'allegory' of death, or a mode of healing and restoration leading to a return." This sentence is not in the excerpt(s) in *Letters* (No. 151) but is given by Christopher in *SD* 1.9.

1950s   *Sir Gawain and the Green Knight*. Tolkien's translation, written in the early 1950s and broadcast by the BBC in 1953. Published posthumously.

1953   "Sir Gawain and the Green Knight." The W. P. Ker Memorial Lecture at the University of Glasgow, 15 April 1953.

1955   "English and Welsh." Essay. Mentions "the great company of Arthur in the hunting of the Twrch Trwyth."

Charles Williams

1912   *The Chapel of the Thorn*. Dramatic poem. While this play is not overtly Arthurian, it about a conflict over the possession of a sacred relic: one of the Hallows of Christ's passion. Published posthumously in 2014.

c.1912–

16? 23?   *The Arthurian Commonplace Book.* A scrapbook of notes and clippings relating to the Matter of Britain, especially the Grail. It remains unpublished and is in the Bodleian library.

1917   *Poems of Conformity.* Arthurian poems in this collection include "Inland Travel," "Quincunque Vult," "The Assumption," "The Wars," and "Invocation." "Black-Letter Days" also refers to the "hallows." In addition to clear references to Arthurian people and places, there are themes of Affirmative Theology, the City of God, and the spiritual quest that accord with CW's mature Arthuriana.

1920   *Divorce.* Arthurian poems in this collection include the title poem, "Divorce," as well as "Ballade of a Country Day," "Celestial Cities," "Ballad of Material Things," "Invitation to Early Communion," "Christmas," many poems about "the City" that evoke a vision of Sarras without naming it, and several with a Grail-like sacramental view of love, church, and everyday life.

1924	*Windows of Night.* Arthurian poems in this collection include "Domesticity," "To Michal: On Bringing her Breakfast in Bed," "For a Child I: Walking Song," "Honours," and "To the Protector, or Angel, of Intellectual Doubt."
c.1924	*Outlines of Romantic Theology.* Prose study, published posthumously. Contains a section on Malory.
1929	*The Masque of Perusal.* A play. Contains a "Grail procession" with objects from the publishing industry.
c.1929–31	*The Advent of Galahad.* Unpublished poems. Latter collected in Dodds, *Arthurian Poets: Charles Williams* (1991).
1920s–30s	"Notes on the Arthurian Myth." Rpt. in *Image*, 169–75.
1930	*Heroes and Kings.* A collection of poetry. Arthurian poems in this volume: "Tristram's Song to Iseult," "Palomides' Song to Iseult," "Lamoracke's Song to Morgause," "Percivale's Song to Blanchfleur," "A Song of Palomides," "Taliessin's Song of a Princess of Byzantium," "The Song of the Riding of Galahad."
1930	*War in Heaven.* A Grail novel.
1931	*Many Dimensions.* It is possible that the Stone of Suleiman in this sequel to *War in Heaven* is an allusion to Wolfram von Eschenbach's Grail Stone (see A. E. Waite's *The Hidden Church of the Holy Graal*, 1909, and *Secret Doctrine in Israel*, 1913); also, later in *TtL*, the Grail goes to Sarras on the Ship of Solomon, which may suggest another thematic connection.
1931	"Percivale's Song" and "Taliessin's Song of Lancelot's Mass." Poems. Collected in an anthology entitled *New English Poems: A Miscellany of Contemporary Verse Never Before Published*, ed. Lascelles Abercrombie. 340–46. Rpt. in *TtL*.
1931	*Three Plays.* Arthurian poems interspersed between the plays in this volume: "Taliessin's Song of Logres," "Taliessin's Song of Byzantium," "Taliessin's Song of the King's Crowning," "Taliessin's Song of the Setting of Galahad in the King's Bed," and "Epilogue in Somerset: A Song of the Myths."
1937	*Henry VII* discusses Prince Arthur, who died before there could ever be an historical King Arthur of England.
1938	"Prelude," "Taliessin's Return to Logres," "The Vision of the Empire," and "The Calling of Arthur." Poems. *Christendom* 8 (March). 19–30. Rpt. in *TtL*.
1938	*Taliessin through Logres.* A volume of twenty-four Arthurian poems.
1939	*The Descent of the Dove: A Short History of the Holy Spirit in the Church.* Discussion of Arthuriana in chapter 5.
1939	"Divites Dimisit." Poem. An early version of "The Prayers of the Pope" (*RSS*). *Theology* 39 (December). 421–24.
1940	"The Coming of Palomides." Poem. Originally published in *TtL*. Reprinted in an anthology entitled *Modern Verse* ed. Phyllis Jones.

1940s   Notes about *TtL* for C. S. Lewis: lists and brief glosses on characters, images, etc. They are preserved in three typescripts at the Marion E. Wade Center (CW/MS-2, CW/MS-166, CW/MS-415; see Rateliff, "Lost Letter"). MS-2 contains additional extended descriptions not included in the others. In 1965, Glen Cavaliero published CW's notes as "Charles Williams on *Taliessin through Logres*" in *Gnomon* 1, 37–45. Much of the information from these MSS was included, along with notes from other sources, in the 1991 booklet *The Taliessin Poems of Charles Williams* by "Various Hands," edited by Anne Ridler and published in the quarterly newsletter of the Charles Williams Society between 1977 and 1986, then again by Apocryphile in 2010.

1941   "Taliessin in the Rose Garden." Poem. *Dublin Review* 208 (January). 82–86. Rpt. in *RSS*.

1941   "Dinadan's Song." Poem. *Time and Tide* 22 (March 15). 210.

1941   "The Making of *Taliessin*." Essay. *Poetry Review*, April 1941. Rpt. in *Image*, 179–83.

1941   "Charles Williams on *Taliessin Through Logres*." Article. *Poetry Review* 32 (March/April), 77–81. Some of the content of this article is similar to the notes for C. S. Lewis, rewritten to explain the poems to a general audience.

1942   "The Chances and Changes of Myth." Book review in *Time and Tide* of *La Grant Ystuire de Monsignor Tristan Li Bret*, ed. F. C. Johnson. Rpt. in *Image*, 183-85.

1942   "The Queen's Servant." Poem. *Poetry* 2. 38–41. Rpt. in *RSS*.

1942   "The Vision of the Empire." Poem from *TtL*. Rpt. in *An Anthology of Religious Verse Designed for the Times*, ed. Norman Nicholson. 79–82.

1943   *The Figure of Beatrice: A Study in Dante*. Theology/literary criticism. Contains one reference to Galahad (101).

1944   "Malory and the Grail Legend." Essay. *Dublin Review* 214 (April). 144–53. Rpt. in *Image* 186–94.

1944   *The Region of the Summer Stars*. A volume of eight Arthurian poems.

1940s   *The Noises that Weren't There*. Unfinished fragment of a novel; the protagonist's uncle is "Bishop of Caerleon," and the male lead's name is Challis. Published posthumously in *Mythlore* 6 (Autumn 1970), 7 (Winter 1971), and 8 (Winter 1972).

1948   "The Figure of Arthur." Unfinished prose study of Arthurian legends. Printed with Lewis' "Williams and the Arthuriad in *Arthurian Torso*.

1948   "The Calling of Arthur." Poem from *TtL*. Rpt. in the *Penguin Anthology of Contemporary Verse*, ed. Kenneth Allot. 73–74.

1953   "Mount Badon" and "Taliessin's Song of the Unicorn." Poems from *TtL*. Rpt. in *The Faber Book of Twentieth Century Verse*, ed. John Heath-Stubbs and David Wright. 336–39.

1958   *The Image of the City, and Other Essays*. Short articles and essays, ed. Anne Ridler. This collection contains many important prose pieces about the Arthurian legends and their meaning to Williams, listed individually above. See esp. lviii–lx and section 4, "On the Arthurian Myth" (169–94).

1991   *Arthurian Poets: Charles Williams*. Arthurian Studies 24, ed. David Llewellyn Dodds. This two-part
            collection contains "Part 1: The published poems" and "Part 2: Uncollected and unpublished
            poems," including some not published in *RSS* that might have been written after that volume
            was completed.

N.B.   Of course, there are additional references to Arthur, the Grail, and other elements of
            Arthuriana throughout Williams' letters, unpublished fragments, lectures, etc.

Texts and Intertexts

1

The Matter of Logres: Arthuriana and the Inklings

Sørina Higgins

Every scholar of Arthuriana has to ask and answer one fundamental question: What is an "Arthurian" work? I had to ask that question in order to decide what works to include on the Inventory of Inklings Arthuriana (15–22); all of the authors of the chapters in this volume asked this question either in preparation for writing or in the course of their arguments. Norris J. Lacy writes that the criterion for inclusion in his 1986 *Arthurian Encyclopedia* was simply "the question: 'Is this a genuine Arthurian text?'" (viii). While this tautology is not very helpful, he goes on to add that it must be "an actual recasting of the legend" (viii) rather than, for instance, a mere passing use of imagery.

But to which "legend" does Lacy refer? There are myriad texts that contain legendary material related to Arthur, yet not one can claim originary status. There is an even larger body contained within "The Matter of Britain," a term that appears around 1200 to distinguish "the subject matter of the romances concerned with the Arthurian legends ... from those concerned with classical stories (the matter of Rome) or with Charlemagne and his circle (the matter of France)" (Drabble 654). But the matter (or "Matter") is not so simple: the term "Matière de Bretagne (Matter of Britain) ... is a convenient and accepted label if something of a misleading oversimplification.... The usual, but not exclusive, subject of much of the Matter of Britain is Arthur" (Lacy, *Encyclopedia* 378). This implies that an Arthurian work does not have to contain King Arthur himself as a character. Indeed, "much of Arthurian literature is only marginally, if at all, about Arthur" ("Arthur, Character of" 19). If it can be Arthurian without Arthur, then what distinguishes it?

If Arthur does not have to appear in a work, is it admissible if Merlin alone makes an appearance, as in C. S. Lewis' *That Hideous Strength*? Does Gandalf count as an Arthurian character, since he may be based on Merlin (Hanks 54)? Should a work be included if its protagonist is one of the famous knights or ladies from the tradition, even if Arthur is absent? That is circular reasoning, as establishment of "the tradition" from which the list of permissible characters may be drawn is the very question under discussion. Are tales of Grail quests included, such as *Night Operation* by Owen Barfield, even when they are metaphorical or the objective is intangible? What if the quest is not to gain, but to lose, some object, such as the One Ring in *The Lord of the Rings*? Does the whole scope of chivalric literature fall into the "Arthurian" category? If so, how thoroughly medieval does the tale need to be, or does the thin layer of chivalric romance in *The Chronicles of Narnia* allow them to qualify? The questions proliferate. Should the vast wealth of modern adaptations count: books, music, movies, and works of visual art that use the story line from a traditional tale—such as a fatal love potion or a kitchen boy who becomes a hero—in a contemporary setting? And finally, what about works that merely depict some of the iconography, or the innumerable references and allusions to the trappings of Arthur's tale, such as Camelot, Carbonek, Excalibur, the Round Table, or the Lady of the Lake?

In his 2009 article "The Arthur of the Twentieth and Twenty-first Centuries," Lacy adds to his earlier, simplistic standards "four admittedly imprecise and oversimplified categories: retellings, updated narratives, the use of Arthurian themes as metaphor or structure, and 'revisionist' views that reinterpret the Arthurian story irreverently or even cynically" (122). This list is more helpful.

Retellings of earlier Arthurian source materials—reiterations of the same plot patterns with the same named characters or identifiable substitutions—are clearly Arthurian. Owen Barfield's *The Quest of the Sangreal*, Tolkien's *The Fall of Arthur*, and Charles Williams' *Taliessin through Logres* and *The Region of the Summer Stars* are all examples of such derivations in spite of their vast differences of technique, style, and tone. Other easy candidates are "updated narratives," which place the same plots and characters, perhaps with different names, in the author's own historical, social, and technological context. Charles Williams' *War in Heaven* is an updated narrative, as it transports the Grail quest to a country parish in twentieth-century England.

"The use of Arthurian themes as metaphor or structure" is more dubious: Lacy goes on to admit that "some of the most productive modern approaches to Arthurian composition involve the appropriation of an element—a motif or an episode—of the legend … to structure a text that may not be explicitly Arthurian at all" (Lacy, "Twentieth" 127). Indeed, the mere presence of a motif or pattern that *could* be mapped onto an earlier Arthurian text by an ingenious scholar means that almost any work can be included (see my discussion below of Barfield's *Eager Spring*, p. 38). The two most common elements, Lacy adds, are "the quest (whether for the Grail or another goal) and the waste-land theme." These two motifs are readily identifiable in many works by the Inklings and their contemporaries.

"Revisionist" approaches are far less common in the Inklings; in looking through the Inventory of Inklings Arthuriana on pages 15–22, I find that only the *Mark vs. Tristram* letters (Barfield and Lewis, 1947) and *Farmer Giles of Ham* (Tolkien, 1949) are irreverent, and then in fun rather than mockery. Three works have a cynical tone: "Victory," a poem by Lewis in *Spirits in Bondage* (1919), Barfield's "Ballade" (1931?), and Tolkien's unfinished *The Fall of Arthur* (1930s).

Arthuriana is clearly a very broad category indeed; clever contortions might allow the whole body of work by all the Inklings into the present volume. In fact, the inquiry "What is an Arthurian work?" was precisely the first question each of the chapters in this volume had to address. Each author had to ask him- or herself: In what ways were the Inklings interacting with materials that might be considered "Arthurian"? If some interaction with Arthuriana is discernable, what are the nature and significance of that interaction? Do these authors share the sensibilities of their times, or do they react against prevailing ideologies? How far are their "Arthurian" works similar to one another, and in what ways do they differ? This, then, means that the current volume examines most of the Inklings' *oeuvre*, asking of each text whether it takes up questions of kingship, statehood, empire, quest, conquest, consciousness, chivalry, and hierarchy in ways that are in fruitful relationship with an Arthurian past, present, and future. The result is a rich conversation among the various Inklings, between the Inklings and their culture, and between the Inklings and ourselves.

Arthur's Evolving Popularity

While "the Arthurian legend seems one of the most permanent fixtures of the imagination of the English-speaking peoples" (Merriman 3), its popularity has waxed and waned. Yet it does not disappear: Arthur "has remained a presence, sometimes more, sometimes less dominant in literary and cultural history" (Lupack, "The Old Order" 209). Holly Ordway, in chapter 2, provides an admirable survey of the most significant Arthurian texts from the early Latin chronicles until Malory's *Morte* (1485). Here, I want to pick up on a claim made by Alan Lupack: "It is commonly accepted that the high points of the Arthurian legend are the late Middle Ages, the Victorian Age, and the twentieth century" ("Sixteenth to Eighteenth" 340). I would like to show, briefly, how this was the case.

The Middle Ages saw the first flourishing of Arthur's popularity, as he appeared in historical texts, legends, and romances. In some of them, Arthur is a warlord. In others, magic and mystery are attached to his person or his court. Toward the end of the High Middle Ages, Camelot becomes the center of chivalry, courtly love, and romance.

Another fertile period of Arthurian literature in England is often overlooked: the time of the Tudors and Stuarts. Arthur suddenly reemerged as "numerous English kings sought to appropriate his legacy for political and propaganda purposes" (Rouse and Rushton 219) and Arthur became "central to Tudor royal propaganda" (White 34). Henry VII named his heir Arthur. Henry VIII engaged in colorful Arthurian imagery, "traced his lineage and his claim to the throne back to Arthur and reinterpreted the legend so that not Arthur himself but his descendant, in the person of Henry VII, was said to have returned at a time of need" (Lupack, "Sixteenth" 340–41). Elizabeth I's coronation was rich with knightly, chivalric, and Arthurian pageantry (Lupack, *Guide* 43; White 34). Edmund Spenser's epic *The Faerie Queene* (1590, 1596) deploys Arthur and his knights in an allegory dedicated to Queen Elizabeth.

While Shakespeare apparently never wrote an Arthurian drama, Phillip Henslowe records that the Lord Admiral's Men performed "at least five that relate to King Arthur and the Knights of the Round Table" throughout the 1590s; these plays "were part of the widespread popularity and political interest in what we might call 'Arthurianism,' which may have peaked in the last decade of the sixteenth century" (White 33). Playwright Thomas Hughes wrote *The Misfortunes of Arthur* (1587. Ben Jonson's masque *The Speeches at Prince Henries Barriers* (1610) includes the Lady of the Lake and Merlin flattering James I's son Henry. William Rowley wrote *The Birth of Merlin* (c. 1620), and Milton considered taking Arthur as the topic of his epic (see, for instance, Kennedy xxxii n78). John Dryden collaborated with Henry Purcell on a "dramatic opera" entitled *King Arthur* for Charles II in 1684 (Lupack, "Sixteenth" 346–47; Merriman 49). Clearly, the Early Modern period witnessed a high point in Arthur's history.

The next monarch who drew on Arthur's mythic appeal was Queen Victoria. In chapter 16 of this book, Kirstin Jeffrey Johnson paints a vivid picture of the Arthurian culture of the second half of the nineteenth century in England. During Victoria's reign, visual artists and writers produced some of the most powerful and enduring Arthurian works. The Pre-Raphaelite brotherhood found Arthurian themes inspirational and depicted them in many works in the 1850s and onwards, including James Archer's "The Death of King Arthur" (1860) and Arthur Hughes's "The Lady of Shalott" (1863). There were other important instances of Arthuriana, such as William John Montaigne's "Prince Arthur at the Battle of Caerbadon," which was exhibited to much acclaim at the Royal Academy in 1848; William Morris's "Defence of Guenevere" (1858) and "La Belle Iseult" (1858); and William Dyce's "Hospitality: The Admission of Sir Tristram to the Fellowship of the Round Table" (1864), which was in Queen Victoria's robing room. Finally, the jewel of the age appeared: Alfred, Lord Tennyson's *Idylls of the King* was published between 1859 and 1885, and it was "a kind of literary second coming of Arthur, a resurrection in Victorian England of the long sequence of Arthuriads extending back centuries before Malory and forward through Spenser, Dryden, Scott, and Tennyson" (Rosenberg 228–29).

Scholars disagree about whether there has been another Arthurian revival since Tennyson. Yet a great number of important Arthurian texts proliferated in English in the period of the two world wars—many of which were written by the Inklings. The Inklings are not often categorized as "war poets" or "war writers," but that is what they were, to a great extent.[1] The wars deeply affected these men: Owen Barfield, C. S. Lewis, and J. R. R. Tolkien, as well as other Inklings Nevill Coghill, Hugo Dyson, Warren Lewis, and R. B. McCallum all served actively in World War One; J. A. W. Bennett, Roy Campbell, Robert "Humphrey" Havard, Colin Hardie, Warren Lewis (a career military man), and Christopher Tolkien served in World War II. Lewis and Tolkien each served at the Somme. Lewis was wounded; Tolkien contracted trench fever. Many of their closest friends died. Charles Williams was not fit for active service; he stayed in England, where "he dug trenches in Hyde Park, London, and did civilian war work at St. Albans" (Hadfield 23); however, his two closest friends, Harold Eyers and Ernest Nottingham, were killed. At least partly in response to their loss, which he felt had been a sacrifice in place of his own death, Williams developed his idea of Exchange or Substitution, writing poetry in which he dealt with survivor guilt.

All of the Inklings, then, were deeply influenced by the horrors of the First World War. Tom Shippey writes that "it is possible to see Tolkien as one of a group of 'traumatized authors,'" including not only the Inklings but also George Orwell, William Golding, Kurt Vonnegut, T. H. White, Joseph Heller, and Ursula Le Guin, "all of them extremely influential … , all of them tending to write fantasy or fable" (Shippey, *Author* xxix–xx). They were all shot at, wounded, bombed, or had friends and family members who were. "They were bone-deep convinced that they had come into contact with something irrevocably evil" (Shippey, *Author* xxx). And yet, they used fantasy, medievalism, and Arthuriana to speak to the traumas of the present and to warn against a fearful future.

---

1   Works that do consider the Inklings and the world wars include Robert S. Blackham's *Tolkien and the Peril of War* (2011); Janet Brennan Croft's *War and the Works of J. R. R. Tolkien* (2004); John Garth's *Tolkien and the Great War* (2003); Joseph Loconte's *A Hobbit, A Wardrobe, and a Great War* (2015); and, to some extent, *The Fellowship* by Philip Zaleski and Carol Zaleski (2015).

There were not many Arthurian works published in England during World War I—but there were many significant ones during the 1920s and 30s. Then, during World War II, knightly and chivalric sentiments were used in military propaganda and in poetry, some of it romantically patriotic, some skeptical of chivalric and military glory. Arthurian works of the 1920s, '30s, and '40s include T. S. Eliot's *The Waste Land* (1922); Thomas Hardy's *Tragedy of Isolde* (1923),[2] John Masefield's *The Midnight Folk* (1927), *Midsummer Night and Other Tales in Verse* (1928), *The Box of Delights* (1935), and many short poems;[3] John Cowper Powys's *A Glastonbury Romance* (1932) and *Porius* (1951); David Jones's *In Parenthesis* (1937) and *The Anathemata* (1952); James Joyce's *Finnegans Wake* (1939),[4] Ezra Pound's *Section: Rock-Drill: 85–95 de los cantares* (1955),[5] and T. H. White's *Once and Future King* (1938–58). Arguably, Arthurian works by the Inklings were among the most popular and influential of their period.

All of this historical contextualization, this discussion of when Arthur was popular in British literature, serves to show that the Inklings were not "dinosaurs" (as Lewis called himself in his inaugural lecture at Cambridge University, "De Descriptione Temporum" 13–14). They were not dusty artifacts left over from an earlier era, whose only use was to provide archeological facts about previous, extinct, obsolete civilizations. On the contrary: they were up-to-date, forward-thinking individuals, whose teaching, writing, and speaking engaged in dynamic ways with their own culture. They were part of an Arthurian revival—or continuation—that spoke directly to the concerns of their own times. What is more, as Malcolm Guite argues in his lucid conclusion to this volume, they possessed uncanny insights into the future development of culture in Europe and North America, with the result that their works—Arthurian and otherwise—continue to resonate today.

The Adaptability of Arthur

Applicability is a particularly conspicuous feature of Arthurian legends throughout time, largely because of their adaptable nature. Why is this so? Why do writers, artists, filmmakers, and video game designers draw from the deep well of "The Matter of Britain," generation after generation? One reason is "Umberto Eco's disarmingly simple 1986 dictum in *Travels in Hyperreality* that 'people seem to like the Middle Ages'—or, at least, what they think of as the Middle Ages" (Harty 139). Another reason is the organic relationship between this complex of stories and the past of many of the people who have retold it: "it drew not only on the legends about historic persons but also on the mythic history of the Irish and British races" (Loomis, "The Oral Diffusion" 52). But the legend quickly traveled beyond the British Isles. As Holly Ordway writes

---

2   This is a dramatic work, *The Famous Tragedy of Isolde, Queen of Cornwall at Tintagel in Lyonesse* (see Goodman 93–94).

3   Collected in *Arthurian Poets: John Masefield.* Ed. David Llewellyn Dodds. Woodbridge, Suffolk: Boydell Press, 1994.

4   If one counts *Finnegans Wake* as a Tristan-and-Isolde story, as Norris Lacy does in "The Arthur of the Twentieth and Twenty-first Centuries" 127.

5   In this section of the *Cantos*, Pound "pillaged Laʒamon's *Brut* ... to comment on vanishing British traditions and the changing role of the poet in the modern world" (Goodman 103).

in her important survey, chapter 2 in this volume, "it moved from being a strictly Welsh and then British tradition to becoming a favorite theme on the continent" (68), and many of the most prominent versions are French. In America in the twentieth and twenty-first centuries, "Arthur's story is probably more popular than it is in Britain" (Lupack, "The Old Order" 217). John Steinbeck wrote in 1976: "These stories are alive even in those of us who have not read them" (xiii). They are part of a collective consciousness.

A third reason for Arthur's ongoing popularity is that the Matter of Britain is enormous, many-limbed, and lithe with variety. It is a gallimaufry of characters, events, images, and emblems: what Lupack calls "its large cast of characters and its complex of fascinating narratives" ("The Old Order" 209). In his significant 1959 study, R. S. Loomis wrote: "Consistency, harmony, fixity are not its outstanding qualities" (*Arthurian Literature* xvi) and that "the astonishing disharmony, the consistent inconsistency ... is one of several reasons why the subject of the Grail so piques the curiosity of modern men of letters and so exercises the ingenuity of scholars" (Loomis, "The Origin" 274). This is true not only of the Grail thread, but of the entire Arthurian tapestry: Holly Ordway writes that "there is no single 'story of King Arthur.' Rather, the Arthurian legends include many stories, by various authors, over a long span of time: tales that were complex and often contradictory, fusing historical, traditional, and purely literary elements" (61). As there is no urtext, so there is no definitive narrative: "the Arthurian legend is many stories at the same time that it is one story.... The legend is comprised of a complex of stories" (Lupack, "The Old Order" 209). It is so various, so changeable, that each reader is able to find some fold of the fabric that fits.

But the final, most significant reason for its popularity, is its adaptability. The Arthurian complex has proven itself astonishingly flexible, able to take on the concerns of many cultures. "Stories remain vital by changing," claims Alan Lupack, "and no story is more adaptable than that of Arthur" ("The Old Order" 209). In her seminal study of adaptation theory, Linda Hutcheon wrote that "like living beings, stories that adapt better than others (through mutation) to an environment survive" (167). Adaptations are also appropriations: each new storyteller uses the court at Camelot or the knightly quest as a vehicle for political, religious, or economic discourse: "In part, it is this 'transposability' of the legend that explains, or at least permits, its popularity" (Lacy, *Encyclopedia* vii). Arthurian adapters might use the material to condemn hypocrisy or to promote syncretism. They might alter it for or against a particular nationalism or patriotism; in Geoffrey of Monmouth and the Alliterative *Morte*, Arthur goes to attack Rome in an attempt to become emperor, while in Tolkien's *Fall of Arthur*, he is "defending the Roman realm from ruin" (Rateliff, "Fatal" 19). They might shape it in support of the monarchy (Spenser's *Faerie Queene*) or in praise of democracy (Mark Twain's *Connecticut Yankee*). Each transformation "reflects the way in which a particular author and his or her audience thought to fashion their own conceptions of the past, so as to benefit their own positioning in the present" (Higham 3).

All of this is to say that the multipartite Arthurian story has evolved dramatically throughout the millennium-and-a-half of its existence. New characters appear and become essential to the legend; Lancelot, for instance, was not introduced until the twelfth century. Antagonists become protagonists, and vice versa; Morgan le Fay is notorious in this regard. Entire narrative elements become inextricable to the overall plot; the Quest for the Holy Grail is one such addition that developed in the high middle ages. The ending may be catastrophic or eucatastrophic: in some retellings, Arthur dies at the end, while in others, he is taken to Avalon to be healed. Several of them prophesy his eventual return. In short, the whole story is tailored to suit the times: "there have been many Arthurs: each age, each culture found in him an iconic figure embodying something significant for its society" (Barron 47) and "the Arthurian past is always open to further layers of both change and preservation according to the positions, temporal and ideological, from which it is seen by each new 'conservator'" (Eckhardt 208).

To some readers, the idea of endless revision may imply infidelity to a source text. Compare this to the experience of many logocentric moviegoers, who experience sharp disappointment or anger when the film adaptation of a beloved book appears to them to be a travesty of the author's work. If there is so much variation in the content of medieval and (especially) post-medieval Arthuriana, surely that must imply that many of them are mutilations of their original(s)?

Yet this is not the case. On the one hand, from a twenty-first-century vantage point that labors under significant suspicion of textual authority, readers can discern an endless slippage in the body of Arthurian material, such that originary meaning is constantly deferred from one text to another. For example, as Holly Ordway writes, Malory "draws on a range of earlier Arthurian romances" (75); any analysis of Malory's story(ies), then, must defer to those earlier tales. But those tales rely upon earlier Breton and Welsh accounts, and Bede and Nennius draw from Gildas, for instance. Beyond these, oral traditions probably predate written works, and even further back again beyond these lurks the question of any "historical" Arthur, with all the doubts that raises about historical accuracy, the selectivity in supposedly historical narrative, and the building of legends upon actual events. There is, then, no urtext for Arthur. I suggest that this is yet another reason for Arthur's perennial popularity: without an urtext, without a source text behind each adaptation, none of the adaptations can be condemned for lack of fidelity to a source text. They are all richly intertextual—all texts are intertextual, of course, but this body of legends is so in more obvious and entangled ways. This is a liberating concept that allows for fertile reproduction and permutation of the materials.

On the other hand, there is little consensus about methods of judging adaptation in relation to their source texts. It is no longer a truism that they should be judged by their supposed fidelity to prior material. A more common conviction is the belief that each adaptation, no matter what it alters, should be evaluated on its own aesthetic terms, because form changes content so significantly that each adaptation is a new work of art: "In many cases, because adaptations are to a different medium, they are re-mediations, that is, specifically translations in the form of intersemiotic transpositions from one sign system (for example, words) to another (for example, images)" (Hutcheon 16).

This, then, is exactly what was going on in Britain in the first half of the twentieth century, when the Inklings joined the respectable tradition of adapters of Arthuriana: the offices of war propaganda were using Arthur as an icon of military might and the preservation of particular visions of civilization, while T. H. White was discovering that on the contrary "the central theme of *Morte d'Arthur* is to find an antidote to war" (qtd. in Gallix 283). The Winchester manuscript of Malory was discovered in 1934 and published by Eugène Vinaver in 1947, which reinvigorated scholarly interest in Arthurian subjects. The Inklings were nearly all veterans and nearly all scholars, so both academic and military approaches to Arthuriana met in their persons and their work. And there was a third reason that they were drawn to adapt these materials:

as Christians, they had concerns about the secularization and materialization of European culture, and the deep spirituality of many Grail narratives and the warning of waste land imagery lent themselves naturally to commenting on spiritual deadness and dearth. They were able to use these tales to question cultural assumptions. For these three reasons, then—military, academic, and religious—the Inklings drew together many of the Arthurian threads from their culture and wove them into new, colorful, lasting designs.

Arthurian Works by the Inklings

Why did the Inklings choose King Arthur as a frequent character among the many stories they told? In *A Theory of Adaptation*, Linda Hutcheon argues that "adapters' deeply personal as well as culturally and historically conditioned reasons for selecting a certain work to adapt and the particular ways to do so should be considered seriously by adaptation theory" (95). What, then, were their cultural and historical reasons for doing so? How did they change these tales from what had gone before? To round out this chapter, I discuss some of the overarching themes of each of the four Inklings' interactions with King Arthur. I hope that this summary serves as a foundation for what follows in the many chapters of *The Inklings and King Arthur*, as the writers in this collection confirm, deny, expand upon, nuance, and contradict my claims.

Barfield

Owen Barfield (1898–1997) composed the fewest Arthurian works of the authors under consideration, and none of them were published during his lifetime. Two of them remain unpublished as of the writing of this chapter. Arguably, of the five listed in the "Inventory," only one—*The Quest of the Sangreal*—is a genuinely Arthurian piece of literature. What is interesting about his approach to Arthur and the Grail is that he uses these tales, as he uses many others both established and original, as subtle vehicles of spiritual meaning. In many of his writings, "Barfield, like his fellow Inklings, creates a medievalist world of romance wherein Christian spiritual ideals and truths are illustrated and presented as providing a superior alternative to the modern world of materialism" (Grewell 16). Even when the secondary world is not quasi-medieval, it still frequently illustrates or embodies such spiritual alternatives. Lewis summed up Barfield's approach neatly in a letter to Daphne Harwood about "the points on which anthroposophy is certainly right—i.e. the claim that it is possible for man, here and now, in the phenomenal world, to have commerce with the world beyond" (*CL* 2:107). This may be the meaning Barfield attempted to convey in all of his writings: that it is possible for temporal humans to communicate with transtemporal reality.[6] But Barfield's few Arthurian works are certainly not pieces of blatant anthroposophist or Christian propaganda. Indeed, their methods of communicating meaning are extremely understated. They are political, pragmatic, academic, comic, or fantastic rather than religious. Yet a closer examination reveals the shrewd ways they are constructed as vehicles of significance.

6   Jason Jewell and Chris Butynskyi explore this topic in all four writers in their chapter, "Spiritual Quest in a Scientific Age," pages 237–63.

Barfield's first Arthurian work is "Ballade," a poem that was "probably written in 1931" (Owen Barfield Literary Estate, "Poetry, 1930s"). It is a short, sharp piece of political satire, with a refrain taken from a news article: "Goods must be modern, bright, and cheap." In it, the narrator mocks a king for repeating this refrain while his subjects are starving. Then, suddenly, there is an unexpected Arthurian *Envoi*:

> Prince, when the time comes to seek entry
> Where Uther's Son and Alfred sleep,
> Fear nothing! Tell the startled sentry:
> *"Goods must be modern, bright, and cheap."*[7]

The implications of these four short lines are many and various. There is, of course, the strong political and economic statement condemning materialism and the alienation caused by mechanized labor. But more surprisingly for our purposes, there is the suggestion that all kings and princes (at least of England) come to Avalon (rather than to the pearly gates of Heaven?) and ask for admittance. This creates the image of a mythic resting-place for all past rulers of England, or at least those who are worthy to join Arthur and Alfred in that sleep, presumably awaiting either a return to England in a time of need or the Last Judgment. This brief analysis shows that Barfield was directly engaged in current events and contemporary political concerns, and yet even so, commented on them through the lens of legend with an eye to their spiritual significance.

Barfield's second Arthurian work, *The Quest of the Sangreal*, may also come from the 1930s or from the 1940s. This is his most extensive and unambiguous work of Arthuriana, arguably his only truly Arthurian work.[8] It is a sixteen-page typescript, housed in the Bodleian Library, Oxford.[9] This is the work that I called "pragmatic" above, and its practical purpose was for use in an anthroposophist education. It is a prose adaptation, in an archaic style, which Barfield claims is from Malory. However, several of the incidents are not from Malory, but from Chrétien, the *Mabinogion,* and other sources.[10]

Barfield's narrative retells the major incidents of the Quest for the Holy Grail. Its narrative structure interlaces stories of Galahad with those of Perceval. It recounts Launcelot's love of Guinevere and his siring of Galahad. This is interwoven with Perceval's life: the death of his father and his mother's attempts to keep him from finding out about knighthood, then the time he spent learning from elves, from one of King Arthur's knights, from his uncle, and from a castle full of witches. Meanwhile, many knights set out "upon

---

7 The italics are original, as are the quotation marks.

8 *The Quest of the Sangreal* was not available to the authors of the chapters in this collection while they were writing; I gained access to it in the Bodleian Library's Special Collection with the kind permission of Owen A. Barfield (the grandson of the Inkling) in June of 2015, when this volume was well underway.

9 Barfield, Owen. *The Quest of the Sangreal.* TS. Dep. c. 1101. ml#barfield.C.1. Bodleian Library, Oxford University. Oxford, UK.

10 Gabriel Schenk pointed out to me that it is more accurate to say this is an adaptation of "the Perceval story from Chrétien de Troyes and the *Mabinogion*" in addition to Malory and that it also shows evidence of influence from other French sources.

the quest of the Sangreal" (8). Perceval is knighted by King Arthur, then goes to the Castle Carbonek, where he sees the Grail procession. It consists of "a spear of mighty size, with three streams of blood flowing from the point to the ground" and "a large salver ... in the which was a man's head surrounded with a profusion of blood" (8). Perceval fails to interrupt his host's conversation to ask questions about these strange objects, and so is called "Perceval the Recreant" for his "craven silence," which is responsible for keeping King Pelles's kingdom in danger. Later, Perceval, Bors, and Galahad return to the castle, where they and a few other knights see "the hallows" and "the holy meat," in language lifted almost exactly from Malory:

> There they saw angels, and two bare candles of wax, and the third a towel, and the fourth a spear which bled marvellously that three drops fell into a box .... Right so the man took an obley [wafer] which was made in the likeness of bread. And at the lifting up there came a figure in the likeness of a child and the visage was as red and as bright as any fire, and smote himself into the bread, so that they all saw it that the bread was formed of a fleshly man; and then he put it into the holy vessel again, and then he did that longed to a priest to do to a mass. (16)

After that, "there entered into the hall the Holy Greal covered with red samite," which passes through the hall and out again. Then Galahad heals the wounded king, and Joseph of Arimathea tells the three Grail knights to set sail for the city of Sarras.

In one sense, then, Barfield's *Quest of the Sangreal* is standard Arthurian fare, a pastiche of some of the main Grail texts. In another way, however, it is unique in the history of Arthurian literature and a locus of some of Barfield's most distinctive literary and educational practices. These distinctives are revealed not in the text itself, but in a letter that precedes *The Quest of the Sangreal* in its folder in the Bodleian library. This typed letter was written to Inkling Cecil Harwood and is dated 6 July 1968. Harwood was a fellow anthroposophist whose second wife, Marguerite Lundgren, was founder of the London School of Eurythmy. In the letter, Barfield writes that he is happy to think that this work will continue "to be performed as eurythmy."

Eurythmy is a kind of interpretive movement that is often used in Steiner and Waldorf education. According to Rudolf Steiner, the founder of anthroposophy, "Eurythmy is a singing through movement; it is singing. It is not dancing; it is not mime" ("Eurythmy as Visible Singing," Lecture 7). In this art form, a musical selection is played or a narrator reads a written text, and the performers listen for significant sounds. They move in prescribed ways, using expressive gestures, in response to those significant sounds.

In the letter to Harwood, Barfield insists that he wants

> to assign the copyright to the London School of Eurythmy in consideration of an undertaking by the School to use its best endeavors, so long as the copyright lasts, to ensure that it is used solely for the purposes of Eurythmy, and particularly that it is not at any time published or duplicated and distributed so as to become available as reading matter.

Harwood signed it on behalf of the school, guaranteeing that it would not be published nor read alone, only performed, as long as the School held the copyright.

This text, therefore, is a performance piece, not a work of literature. Indeed, Barfield laments what he sees as its poor literary quality in that same letter, as he apparently looks back at it after some time, saying: "Considered exclusively as a literary composition however I feel it has certain notable defects." Its performative nature may be a clue to the educational and philosophical ideas that underlie the text, just as the selections Barfield chose to include also give evidence about the purpose of this text.

There is another clue to the ideas that underlie *The Quest of the Sangreal*: there are four musical interludes scattered throughout *Quest*, four times that "(music)" is written in parentheses. The first occurs right after Perceval first meets the Fisher King and "Perceval rode to the palace and the door was open, and he entered the hall" (7). The second occurs the next morning, after he has failed to answer the questions and awakens to an empty castle, "Whereupon he turned his horse's head, and, full of musing, rode deep into the forest" (9). The third follows a scene when a witch called Domna tempts Perceval to betray King Arthur, "But Perceval gainsaid her" (11). The fourth is almost at the very end of the piece, after the three knights have seen the Grail, and "Then prayed Galahad to every each of them, that if they come to King Arthur's court that they should salute my lord Sir Launcelot, my father, and of them of the Round Table; and prayed them if that they came of that part they should not forget it" (16). The music seems to be associated with moments of magic or of high metaphysical significance; in eurythmic performance, the music would serve to heighten these moments.

The Quest of the Sangreal, then, is a simple story, but an adaptation with a life beyond the page. It carries a dramatic message about the power of language, speech, and movement, as all of these would be emotionally moving and potentially revelatory in a live performance. It also relies upon Steiner's teaching, so central to all of Barfield's work, about the evolution of human consciousness: the educational method in which eurythmy is used relies upon the child as his or her own best teacher based on the divine spirit inside each (hence a kind of free, uninhibited performance). A teacher in a Waldorf school

> holds the conviction that what he meets in the child from week to week, from year to year, is the expression of a divine spiritual being that descends from purely spirit-soul existence and evolves here in physical-bodily existence between birth and death .... [The teacher] has tremendous reverence for the growing person who, from the first day of his existence in a physical body, shows how his inner soul nature is revealed in his features, in his first movements, utterances of sound, and first beginnings of language. (Steiner, *Education as an Art* 23)

Based on this philosophical foundation, eurythmy is a means by which that divine spiritual being can express itself through movement, sound, and language. The selection of moments of high mystical significance in *The Quest of the Sangreal*, then, punctuated by music and embodied in physical gesture, makes it a distinctively anthroposophist text. What appeared to be a simple adaptation from Malory and Chrétien turns out to be far subtler and more significant than that.

There is no certain information about when Barfield wrote *The Quest of the Sangreal*. However, its composition history is connected with that of his third Arthurian work: a series of marginal notes and annotations in his copy of the Everyman's Library edition of Malory's *Le Morte D'Arthur*. These notes have been transcribed by Angela Grimaldi; she analyzes them in a 2010 article. Grimaldi writes that "the exact dates of Barfield's notes and annotations are, unfortunately, unknown." But some textual comparison suggests that both these notes and *The Quest of the Sangreal* were made between 1935 and 1947. His Everyman's edition "was originally published in 1906 and reprinted in 1934 (volume two) and 1935 (volume one)" (Grimaldi). This provides a *terminus post quem* for the marginal notes, at least: he could not have started marking up this book before it was published in 1935. It is reasonable to suppose that he would have exchanged this edition for Vinaver's in 1947, especially since he engaged in correspondence with Lewis over the appearance of Vinaver's book. Furthermore, the passages Barfield marked in his Malory appear to me to be significant for the composition of *The Quest of the Sangreal*; perhaps he was marking the *Morte* as he planned and worked on *Quest*.

For these reasons, then, and others, I propose that both the annotations and *Quest* were composed between 1935 and 1947. The annotations look as if he marked his Everyman copy when he was working on *The Quest of the Sangreal*, as they appear to be interested in the same characters and episodes. He is already very familiar with the *Morte* when he writes the *Mark vs. Tristram* letters to Lewis in 1947 (discussed below). *Quest* is already quite old when he writes about it to Cecil Harwood in 1968.

This brings us to the fourth of Barfield's Arthurian works: his comedic *Mark vs. Tristram* correspondence with C. S. Lewis. Lewis and Barfield exchanged a series of parodic letters between 11 and 20 June 1947.[11] Eugène Vinaver's magisterial *Works of Sir Thomas Malory* was just being published, and Lewis had reviewed it in *The Times Literary Supplement*. In his review, Lewis discusses how foreign the morality of the *Morte* is to its twentieth-century audience and ends with this sentence: "But how different such nobility may be from the virtues of the law-abiding citizen will appear if we imagine the life of Sir Tristram as it would be presented to us by King Mark's solicitors" (*CL* 2:780). Barfield, a lawyer, took up the challenge: "using the notepaper of his firm, Barfield and Barfield, and acting as if for King Mark of Cornwall, [he] led off with the first letter to Messrs Inkling and Inkling. Lewis replied as the solicitors Blaise and Merlin, representing Sir Tristram" (Hooper, *CL* 2:781).[12]

These letters are a delightful and hilarious example of the kind of friendship that Barfield and Lewis enjoyed: in them, the friends banter back and forth, employing many registers of humor from simple insults to sophisticated literary witticisms. Barfield creates a particular type of absurdity (not entirely dissimilar from Mark Twain's method in *Connecticut Yankee*) by restating elements of the medieval text in contemporary legal jargon. The last letter in the series, by Lewis, is in mock Middle English, and its tone of erudite jocularity contrasts pleasingly with the buffoonery of its content.

---

11   These were originally published in *Mark vs. Tristram: Correspondence between C. S. Lewis and Owen Barfield*. Ed. Walter Hooper. Cambridge, MA: The Lowell House Printers, 1967. The relevant letters are also in Lewis, *CL* 2:780–86.

12   The story of Tristram or Tristan is a tragic love triangle (or quadrangle). Tristan is a knight in the service of King Mark of Cornwall. King Mark sends him to collect the lovely lady Isoud or Iseult, who is to marry the king. Tristan and Iseult drink a potion and fall in love, with much resultant suffering to all parties (including Tristan's wife, who also happens to be named Iseult). The tale of Tristan and Isoud may date as far back as the sixth century (Lupack, *Encyclopedia* 371). It occupies over one third of Vinaver's *Works* of Malory and has been one of the central tales for Arthurian adaptation.

More importantly for the present purpose: this epistolary joke reveals quite a bit about Barfield's interaction with Arthuriana. To begin with, they show that he was very familiar with the legends in general and with Malory in particular. Barfield is conversant with the names of people and places, and with terminology such as "garboils."[13] But there is a deeper kind of understanding revealed in the following extended quotation: King Mark's solicitor advises a potential jury

> to take into consideration such facts as (a) the previous long and close personal association between our respective clients (b) the fact that your client was at the time employed in a fiduciary capacity in a matter of the utmost delicacy (c) that your client owed to ours at the time not merely the loyalty of an old friend but the allegiance of a tried and trusted subject and (d) the unwritten law of chivalry and the obligation imposed thereby on your client, as the only person of equestrian status on board a small vessel carrying a female passenger of noble rank. (CL 2:782)

This is seriously funny. But it also touches on some important elements of medieval romance literature, showing that Barfield had a deep understanding of the values that undergirded, if not a historical chivalry, at least the literature of chivalry.

When Barfield refers to "the unwritten law of chivalry," he evokes a whole field of study, and one in which C. S. Lewis was intimately involved. Chivalry and courtly love were significant topics of conversation among members of the Inklings, as evidenced by many of their letters and published works. In 1936, Lewis had published *The Allegory of Love: A Study in Medieval Tradition*, in which he wrote extensively of "courtly love": the "love religion of the god Amor" or "erotic religion [that] arises as a rival or parody of the real religion and emphasizes the antagonism of the two ideals" (AoL 18). That same year, Lewis had engaged in a debate on this topic with Charles Williams in the first three letters they ever exchanged (11, 12, and 23 March 1936; CL 1:183–86). Lewis does not approve of the "blend of erotic and religious feeling" that Williams describes: "Put briefly, there is a romanticism which finds its revelation in love, which is yours, and another which finds it in mythology (and nature mythically apprehended) which is mine" (CL 1:185–86). Lewis denigrated "the Religion of Love" as idolatrous; Williams praised it as a Way to God and went so far as to claim that "Infidelity to love consists in the deliberate preference of some other meaner motive and occupation to love, and the identification of love in marriage with Christ involves something very like the identification of infidelity with Antichrist" (ORT 52).[14] While there is nothing to suggest that Barfield read these letters between Lewis and Williams, it is extremely likely—based on the works they were writing, reading, reviewing, and teaching at the time—that chivalry, courtly love, and romantic theology were among the frequent topics of conversation at meetings of the Inklings in the 1940s. Lewis explored the nature of chivalry in *The Allegory of Love, The Discarded Image,* and in the Narniad; Williams wrote about his particular "Romantic Theology" in his early poems, most of his works of literary criticism, and the posthumously published *Outlines of Romantic Theology*. Tolkien engaged with the chivalric world in various parts of *The Lord of*

---

13   The *OED* defines "garboils" as "Confusion, disturbance, tumult; … a brawl, hubbub, hurly-burly."

14   I have written about this previously; see Higgins, "Double Affirmation" 69–70.

the Rings and the fragmentary *Fall of Arthur*.[15] Barfield was clearly aware of these subjects of conversation and well-read on the topics of chivalry and courtly love.

As a side note, it is worth remaking that chivalry is also an important topic in another work of Barfield's that is not Arthurian, yet reveals some of his ideas about literature, the environment, and relationships between the sexes. This is *Eager Spring*, Barfield's last work of fiction. Owen A. Barfield (the author's grandson) calls it an "eco-novella" ("Selected Works"). In it, a student of medieval allegory becomes involved in an environmental movement; the novel ends with an embedded tale, a *conte*, written by the main character as an allegory of her experiences (see Blaxland-de Lange 107–12). Themes of chivalry and courtly love run through her story, making the whole novella "a story about the trials and tribulations of romantic love" (Karlson; cf. Rateliff's introduction vii). While *Eager Spring* is not Arthurian, it does contain some of Barfield's thoughts on courtly/chivalric love—which he was thinking about forty years earlier in these letters to Lewis.

Another important point in the *Mark vs. Tristram* letters is the "fiduciary capacity" in which Sir Tristram relates to King Mark, acting on his behalf as if in financial matters, but here matters of the heart are in question. Tristram is a sworn knight; Mark is his king, his lord, his sovereign. There is an essential hierarchy implied here as well as ethics of permanent loyalty and selfless service. These are continued in "the allegiance of a tried and trusted subject." Again, this shows Barfield's familiarity with the stories of Tristram and the ethical codes that had developed in medieval literature about knightly culture. This discussion of the *Mark vs. Tristram* letters, then, shows that Barfield was thoughtfully engaged with Arthurian materials, even though his literary interactions with them were infrequent, and that he quickly got to the heart of the story and to deeper ethical matters beneath the admittedly chaotic surface of Malory's tale(s).

Barfield's final "Arthurian" work was written in 1975 (Hipolito ix). *Night Operation*, a work of dystopian speculative fiction, raises questions about what to include and what to exclude from the canon of Arthurian literature, discussed above. But this novella, in which the three main characters have a kind of mystical "Grail" encounter, explores ideas of human consciousness and communication with the transtemporal similar to those prompted by a performance of *The Quest of the Sangreal*. Christopher Gaertner discusses *Night Operation* in detail in chapter 5, pages 154–56. Gaertner writes that "the story provides a setting in which

---

15   On the question of whether Barfield attended meetings of the Inklings in the 1940s, see Tolkien's *Letters* 103. The passage is so good I am moved to quote it at length:
> ... a great event: an evening Inklings. I reached the Mitre at 8 where I was joined by C. W. and the Red Admiral (Havard), resolved to take fuel on board before joining the well-oiled diners in Magdalen (C. S. L. and Owen Barfield). C. S. L. was highly flown, but we were also in good fettle; while O. B. is the only man who can tackle C. S. L. making him define everything and interrupting his most dogmatic pronouncements with subtle *distinguo*'s.

On the other hand, Carpenter notes that Williams and Barfield "never found the opportunity for a lengthy conversation" (169n3). Grevel Lindop writes that Barfield and Williams "did meet sometimes" and that once, "Williams, knowing nothing of Barfield's beliefs, announced 'I have just been talking to someone who told me I was an Anthroposophist.' Sadly, the conversation was diverted, and a potentially fascinating discussion lost" (Lindop, *Third Inkling* 308).

Barfield's views on human consciousness are manifest. The story also shows how his views are a response to the intellectual issues of the Inklings' day, and how his views speak to an interpretation of the collective Arthurian works of the Inklings" (154).

Indeed, Barfield's fiction, like that of the other Inklings, is pertinent to our own times. In particular, like many dystopian works, *Night Operation* is uncannily prophetic in its warnings about the reduction of human life to biological function and the ways the human race avoids communication with the divine. It has many other areas of applicability, too. Cory Grewell writes in an article about Barfield's *Studies of Meaning*:

> Barfield's apologetic defense is directed primarily at the scientific materialism, Modernist frag-
> mentation, and logical positivism that by turns dominated much of academic thought in the West
> in the twentieth century. Its implications are just as important, however, for much of today's aca-
> demic culture in the West, dominated as it often is by materialist politics and Postmodern relativ-
> ism (though much of Barfield's thought, particularly his theories of language, are quite compatible
> with Postmodernism). (Grewell 29–30)

Grewell goes on to state quite practical ways Barfield's thought applies to "the university, the arts, and the evangelical church"—and I would add that Lewis', Tolkien's, and Williams' ideas can also be used for the regeneration of these institutions in the twenty-first century.

In the largest and most important ways, then, Barfield's Arthuriana are like those of his friends. They all strive to communicate metaphysical truth; they are engaged in what Yannick Imbert calls "the quest for a common consciousness" (180). They all use speculative fiction and visions of the fantastical to speak into their own times. And they all observed and analyzed the movements of their lifetimes and projected warnings into our own.

And yet, of course, Barfield is distinctive. Lewis had a habit of picking up everything that interested him at the moment, including bits and pieces of Arthuriana, and incorporating them into whatever his current project was at the moment. Tolkien was much more methodical, gathering all the myriad threads of literature and history that he could hold, including Arthur, and weaving them into his own ever-growing legendarium. Charles Williams did just the reverse: he took everything else and wove it into his Arthurian myth. But Barfield only used the Grail a handful of times, as a vessel of anthroposophist ideas.

Lewis

Clive Staples Lewis (1898–1963) was a prolific Arthurian, and his output covers poetry, fiction, and academic work.[16] I do not need to give a survey here, as Brenton D. G. Dickieson provides an overview of "Lewis' Arthuriana in four identifiable periods," pages 81–86 below, in his chapter on intertextuality in the Ransom cycle. It is worth noting, however, how important this story was to Lewis' thought. It was not the one story onto which he tried to map his life and all of his most important writing, as it was for

---

16   Again, see the Inventory on pages 15–22 for an extensive list.

Williams, but it was a story to which he returned again and again. He tried writing it in poetry and prose, as he did with the story of Psyche and Cupid, and (again, like that myth) finally turned to the novel as his preferred means of expression. Yet *That Hideous Strength* and *Till We Have Faces* could hardly be more different, and their contrasts reveal how the Arthurian story functioned in Lewis' imagination differently than the tale of Psyche and Cupid did. This in turn is due to the nature and history of the two stories and to who was influencing Lewis at the time of composition and in what ways.

That Hideous Strength is a deeply intertextual novel. As Dickieson and Huttar discuss in their chapters in this volume, Lewis brought into it elements from the writings of his friends Tolkien and Williams, as well as from older sources. This novel has received a great deal of criticism. George Orwell, in reviewing it, wrote that "it would probably have been a better book if the magical element had been left out" and "one could recommend this book unreservedly if Mr. Lewis had succeeded in keeping it all on a single level" (Orwell, "The Scientists"). Sanford Schwartz calls it—albeit affectionately—"an outsized amalgam of medieval legend and modern mayhem" (91; cf. Ward 8–11). This critique, of course, is similar to the objection Tolkien lodged against the Narniad: that it was made up of disparate mythologies insufficiently unified. While these critiques are wildly overstated and *That Hideous Strength* follows its own logic of coherence, it is true that there is a larger variety of intertextual procedures followed in this novel than in *Till We Have Faces*.

I propose that the greater intertextuality is due in part to the varied nature of the Arthurian material, discussed above. Once an author chooses to open the door to the Knights of the Round Table, it is hard to shut it again. Material from across a fifteen-hundred-year period could come in, from Welsh, French, or German sources, bringing late Roman or high medieval or Victorian trappings with it—or Byzantine, if Charles Williams is one of the sources. Williams was a direct source for Lewis, as was Tolkien, which partially explains why conventions of Gothic horror jostle against the notion of an Elvish paradise in the West, and both with biblical materials and a modernist setting.[17]

Till We Have Faces is quite different in tone and texture. It is a clean, streamlined myth, a retelling of one story, with as low a reading on the intertextuality meter as is reasonable for an adaptation. It lives entirely in its own secondary world; there are very few moments of metalepsis. This is not a value judgement either way, nor an attempt to claim that one novel is somehow "better" than another; merely an observation of the levels of intertextuality in each and a glance at their respective lineages. Lewis was trying to accomplish so many things in *That Hideous Strength*—wrap up the Ransom storyline that dates as far back as drafts of *The Screwtape Letters*,[18] satirize college politics, warn against technocracy and violations of bioethics, lay down standards for gender roles and marital hierarchy,[19] bring in Williams' ideas about co-inherence and community, promote Tolkien's (supposedly) forthcoming *Silmarillion*, resuscitate Merlin in the modern world, embody planetary influences, illustrate God's action through people in this world—that the novel feels overstuffed and heterogeneous. But so does Malory. There, a narrative interlace structure weaves

---

17   On the point about the Gothic genre, see Schwartz 92–97.

18   See Dickieson, "The Unpublished Preface."

19   See Benjamin Shogren's chapter, "Those Kings of Lewis's Logres: Arthurian Figures as Lewisian Genders in *That Hideous Strength*," pages 387–412.

the plot lines together in a complex, counterintuitive manner. In *That Hideous Strength*, the narrative is fairly straightforward (although there are shifting character perspectives), but the theological implications are many and various.

And indeed, the theological implications are much the same as those in the Arthuriana of his fellow Inklings: Lewis believed that there was meaning beyond the material universe; there was a supernatural realm that gives meaning to the natural one. In *That Hideous Strength*, the Heavens carry this meaning down to earth.[20] Buckman and Ross argue that Merlin "became a metaphor for Lewis' understanding of fantasy, the genre that has to overcome our understandable incredulity in the face of the extraordinary. Lewis' ambitious novel attempts to bring Arthurian values directly into the modern world" (Buckman and Ross 5). These are values of human dignity, mutually reciprocal relationships, hierarchy, community, environmental stewardship, and—when necessary—violent resistance to tyranny. They are timeless values, and *That Hideous Strength* is as apposite now as when it was written.

Tolkien

John Ronald Reuel Tolkien (1892–1973) wrote only a very small number of works that can be considered even marginally Arthurian and only one (unfinished) actual retelling. He approached this legend as he did most elements of English literature: he looked for the gaps, the lacunae where explanations were missing, and he wrote into those empty spaces, filling them up and connecting them with material of his own making so that these stories all came into his legendarium, his history of everything.

This process began when he encountered the Anglo-Saxon poem *Crist* by Cynewulf, probably in the spring of 1914. The *Crist* contains these lines:

> Hail Earendel, brightest of angels,
> above the middle-earth sent unto men,
> and true radiance of the sun,
> bright above the stars ...[21]

There is very little else about Earendel (or Eärendil, as Tolkien came to spell the name) anywhere in extant English literature,[22] so this was a gap in English literature: an unexplained name. Who was Earendel? How

---

20 This is also a Williamsian move. The novels of Charles Williams are not set in some other time and place, either the Middle-earth of an imagined past or a Narnian universe reached by magic or the inhabited planets of the Ransom cycle. Instead, they occur on earth, in quite ordinary twentieth-century surroundings. Instead of having the characters travel to a supernatural or magical realm, archnature invades the natural and disturbs the normal. This is what happens in *That Hideous Strength*.

21 For discussions of the dating of this encounter, see Garth, *Great War* 44–45, Carpenter 72, and *SD* 236. Carpenter supplies this translation (and Garth quotes the first two lines of it).

22 It does appear in the Anglo-Saxon *Blickling Homilies* (Garth, "The Road" 14). There are cognate references in other works, and "Earendel-references appear in several Germanic languages" (Shippey, *Road* 246) and works of literature, such as the *Prose Edda*, *Orendel*, the Heldenbuch tradition, *Chronicon Lethrense*, and

could he be both an angel and a star? Tolkien resolved to create the back-story that would explain this mystery. By 24 September 1914, he had composed a forty-eight-line poem called "The Voyage of Éarendel the Evening Star" (Garth, *Great War* 45). Eventually, Eärendil evolved into Tolkien's half-elf, half-human hero who sails into the West, seeking a lost paradise.

This method of writing into the gaps, of drawing existing literature into his own evolving Elvish mythology, catalyzed his great work of inventing Elvish languages, legends, and history, which eventually led to *The Hobbit, The Lord of the Rings, The Silmarillion,* and the histories of Middle-earth. Tolkien tried this approach again with *Beowulf,* drawing that story into his own via another Eärendil-like character. *Beowulf* opens with the history of Scyld (or "Shield"), "the eponymous ancestor of the *Scyldingas,* the Danish royal house to which Hrothgar King of the Danes in this poem belongs" (Tolkien, *Beowulf* 137). Here are the opening lines, in Tolkien's own translation:

> Lo! the glory of the kings of the people of the Spear-Danes in days of old we have heard tell, how those princes did deeds of valour. Oft Scyld Scefing robbed the hosts of the foemen, many peoples, of the seats where they drank their mead, laid fear upon men, he who first was found forlorn ... a good king was he! (Tolkien, *Beowulf* ll. 1–5, 9)

This same King Scyld had come mysteriously to the Danes: one day, they found a boat on the shore with a baby inside. In the boat with the child was a mysterious, beautiful, golden grain. When the child grew up, they made him their king. So Scyld was to them a culture hero: the good king, the victorious warrior, the bringer of corn. When he died, his people put him in a boat and sent him off as he had come:

> With lesser gifts no whit did they adorn him, with treasures of that people, than did those that in the beginning sent him forth alone over the waves, a little child. Moreover, high above his head they set a golden standard and gave him to Ocean, let the sea bear him. Sad was their heart and mourning in their soul. None can report with truth, nor lords in their halls, nor mighty men beneath the sky, who received that load. (33–40)

Tolkien believed that the *Beowulf*-poet was taking previous material about a warrior-ancestor and about a culture god "and adding to it a mysterious Arthurian departure, *back into the unknown*" (Tolkien, *Beowulf* 138–39, emphasis original), making a "suggestion ... that Scyld went back to some mysterious land whence he had come" (*LR* 106). Notice that he specifically calls it an "Arthurian departure"; this makes all mysterious voyages across the sea into the West iterations of the motif of King Arthur going to Avalon.[23]

Saxo Grammaticus's *Gesta Danorum.* Tolkien would probably have used Jakob Grimm's *Teutonic Mythology* and *Grundriss der germanischen Philologie* edited by Hermann Paul to learn about these cognates and stories of Earendel/Orendel (Garth, "The Road" 14). For a complete study of this topic, see Hostetter.

23   This is the topic of chapter 4 in the present volume, "Houses of Healing: The Idea of Avalon in Inklings Fiction and Poetry" by Charles A. Huttar.

Tolkien decided to follow this same method again, the method that the *Beowulf*-poet used of combining pre-existing story materials with his own new ideas, seeking out hidden significance, and weaving it all into a much larger whole. To that end, Tolkien used King Sheave in his own *Lost Road* and *Notion Club Papers* projects, retelling the story in both prose and verse (*LR* 96–106; *SD* 273–76). In Tolkien's version, Sheave is not dead, but dying, when his men put him on a ship:

> and they thrust him forth to sea, and the sea took him, and the ship bore him unsteered far away into the uttermost West out of the sight or thought of men. Nor do any know who received him in what haven at the end of his journey. Some have said that that ship found the Straight Road. (*LR* 95)[24]

In Tolkien's view, the *Beowulf*-poet took "rustic legends of no great splendor" and connected them "with a glory and mystery, more archaic and simple but hardly less magnificent than that which adorns the king of Camelot, Arthur son of Uther" (*LR* 105–06). This is essentially what Tolkien himself is doing throughout his work, and he probably learned this method from the *Beowulf*-poet: "as often, Tolkien took the hints, but felt he could improve on them" (Shippey, *Author* 37).

Tolkien took one other hint from the beginning of *Beowulf* and used it openly in his works, connecting it to Eärendil. There is a sense that some mysterious beings sent Scyld to the Danes when he was a baby. Through a complicated and ingenious bit of creative philology (which Shippey traces in *Author* 286), "Tolkien was prepared, rather daringly, to identify the *osas/Æsir* [the pagan gods of Norse myth] not with demons, but with the demi-gods or archangels or Valar of his own mythology" and also seems to identify the mysterious beings who sent Scyld forth with his own Valar, too (Shippey, *Author* 286; Shippey, "Welcome to Beowulf"). This means that Scyld is an Eärendil-figure; a mysterious, possibly superhuman, hero who comes from the West and goes off mysteriously into the West, sent by the Valar and received by them again.

Note, however, that all the Scyld/Shield/Sheave material I have been talking about was unpublished in Tolkien's lifetime. Most of it is in notes for projects he never finished, such as *The Lost Road* and *The Notion Club Papers*. Some of it, the material about *Beowulf*, he did discuss in his Oxford lectures on the poem, but he is unlikely to have made the connection with his own Valar explicit in that context. Therefore, this connection is not part of his official published works—the works that he himself completed and made public during his life—nor is it present in *The Silmarillion*.

This is also the case with Tolkien's Arthur-Eärendil connection: It is not part of the works he published during his lifetime—which brings me at last to *The Fall of Arthur*, Tolkien's only unequivocally Arthurian work. Throughout *The Inklings and King Arthur*, the chapter-writers deal with many important aspects of this poem's context, content, and implications; here, I will briefly comment on its Eärendil connection, which is found in notes Tolkien left about how he intended the fragmentary *Fall of Arthur* to continue. Christopher

---

24 "The Straight Road" runs across the sea "to the Isle of Eressëa in Elvenhome" (*SD* 280), to the land of the Elves, heading toward the land of the Valar. Tolkien thought that Sheave came from the gods in the West to begin with and that "his true name was in tongue unknown of a far country, where the falling seas wash western shores" (*SD* 275; cf. *LR* 99, where this is rendered into verse).

Tolkien includes the following details in his editorial matter about how the story could have shared narrative continuity with the larger legendarium.

Tolkien's notes reveal that, had he finished *The Fall of Arthur*, he planned to have Mordred mortally wound Arthur, Arthur kill Mordred, and Arthur be carried away to the West for healing. Lancelot, arriving too late, would set sail into the West, searching for his king, never to return. Tolkien wrote:

> Lancelot gets a boat and sails west and never returns. Eärendel passage.... Lancelot parts from Guinevere and sets sail for Benwick but turns west and follows after Arthur. And never returns from the sea. Whether he found him in Avalon and will return no one knows. (*FoA* 136, 37)

In other words, had the poem been finished, Lancelot would have functioned somewhat like Eärendil, the mariner who used the Silmaril to sail into the Uttermost West and reach the Undying Lands. Both Lancelot and Eärendil sail into the West, seeking a lost paradise. Tolkien tried to unite the westering legends about islands of the blest with Arthur and with his own elvish mythology in *The Fall of Arthur*.

At around this same time, Tolkien wrote a fragment of a poem about Eärendel's Quest, including these lines:

> Eärendel goeth on eager quest
> to magic islands beyond the miles of the sea,
> past the hills of Avalon and the halls of the moon,
> the dragon's portals and the dark mountains
> of the Bay of Faery on the borders of the world. (*FoA* 137–38)

And then another fragment about Arthur's grave:

No mound hath Arthur	in mortal land
under moon or sun	who in ___ ___
beyond the miles of the sea	and the magic islands
beyond the halls of night	upon Heaven's borders
the dragon's portals	and the dark mountains
of the Bay of Avalon	on the borders of the world.
up[on] Earth's border	in Avalon ~~sleeping~~ biding. (*FoA* 138)

Here he makes the identification of Avalon with Faërie and with Valinor plain. While I will not dwell on this identification, as it is only in discarded drafts, I merely use it to point out the way in which Tolkien tried, at one time, to draw Arthur into his own Elvish legendarium, in what Dimitra Fimi describes as an ongoing "continuation of the blending of traditions of the British Isles in Tolkien's work" (58). The motif of King Arthur going to Avalon, then, is seen again and again, subtly, throughout Tolkien's work, in the longings and journeys of many a mariner into the West.

I see one other possibly Arthurian resonance in Tolkien's legendarium. In *The Lord of the Rings*, Galadriel tells Frodo that, with Celeborn, "together through ages of the world we have fought the long defeat" (1:462; 2:7). *The Silmarillion*, the Histories of Middle-earth, and the other texts of the legendarium tell the tale of one long defeat: it is the cyclical story of "one brief shining moment"[25] always followed by disaster, war, horror, and fading. This happens for the Valar in Almaren, then in Valinor; for the Elves in Cuiviénen, then in Tol Eressëa; for Men in Númenor, then Arnor, then Gondor, and so forth. Each began as a place of beauty and a race of great wisdom and power, but each was destroyed or isolated by the withdrawing, failing, or fading of its bliss. This is comparable to the trajectory of many works of Arthuriana, especially in the twentieth century: Arthur (and, often, Merlin) establishes a righteous kingdom in Logres, but then it fades, fails, and is destroyed. "In our time," writes D. Thomas Hanks in an article on Malory and Tolkien, "the upshot for Malory has been to convert his serious comedy of eucatastrophe to a reader's perception of tragedy, lost love, and lost life" (60). I find a sense of inevitability in both story-complexes, but the fated nature of the defeat does not rob it of any of its poignancy. I read both the Arthurian legends and Tolkien's legendarium as heart-breaking tales of the long defeat that mortals fight here in this realm, always destined to enjoy new heroes in every generation, always fated to fail. It is, arguably, the tragedy of the Christian story: The Fall has rendered all human endeavors futile. That is the message I read in these two tales—but I must note that both are also touched with the eucatastrophic hope of a blessed return, a future joy. As Hanks says, with intentional anachronism: "Malory has written a Tolkienian happy ending—but a happy ending which at the same time reminds one that along with eucatastrophe come tears and earthly loss" (61). The Tolkienian kind of happy ending—whether of *Beowulf* or a fairy tale or an Arthurian retelling—includes fading, diminishment, and loss. Ye, each of these tales is incorporated into his own totalizing, theological mythology, with its hope of a future eucatastrophe.

In short, Tolkien saw his elvish legendarium as the primary narrative, while Arthur was secondary. This is the opposite of Williams' method, as Williams tried to draw everything else into his composite Byzantine Arthuriana. For Williams, at least by the end of his life, the Grail story was primary and all of his other ideas were secondary components of it. Yet both of them, like Lewis and Barfield, were interested in using this collection of stories—and all other stories that were to their taste—for the communication of spiritual truth.

Williams

Charles Walter Stansby Williams (1886–1945) was the most serious Arthurian author of the four. Indeed, he took the legends of King Arthur so seriously as to shape many areas of his personal and professional life after his vision of the Arthurian myth. Whereas Barfield took one or two oddments from the story of the Grail to serve his own anthroposophist didacticism, Tolkien tried to draw Arthur into his own mythology for England, and Lewis cut convenient elements out of their original context and pasted them into his

---

25   To quote the lyrics to *Camelot*, the musical by Alan Jay Lerner and Frederick Loewe based on T. H. White's *The Once and Future King*.

modernist Mere Christian fairy tales, Williams viewed many aspects of his life and thought—love, religion, work, history, geography, anatomy, politics—*sub specie Arthuriana*. As Alyssa House-Thomas writes:

> Williams' Arthurian poetry collections *Taliessin through Logres* and *The Region of the Summer Stars* are also medievalist and syncretic in technique, yet to a much higher degree than Tolkien they demonstrate a source-independent approach, rather than concern for imitation. Their handling of mystical and occult themes owes as much to Williams himself as to the old authorities. (362)

For these reasons, as well as because he wrote the fullest, most complete Arthuriad, he is treated at greatest length in this volume.

Williams began exploring Arthuriana as the story of his life perhaps as early as 1908, when evidence suggests he was discussing his plans for Arthurian poetry with his office mate Fred Page (Lindop, *Third Inkling* 2). He certainly was working on it in 1912, when he began keeping a "Commonplace Book" of notes that he hoped to use in his later poetic cycle (Dodds, "Arthurian Commonplace Book"). He wrote and published Arthurian poetry throughout his working life, in anthologies and periodicals as well as his own collections, and even included Arthurian poems in odd places (such as distributed among the theatrical works in *Three Plays*, 1931). In the 1920s, he wrote dramas for his co-workers to perform, one of which involved a Grail procession.[26] In the late 1920s or early 1930s, he wrote a collection of poems originally entitled *King Arthur* and later *The Advent of Galahad* (Lindop, *Third Inkling* 161, 226); it remained unpublished until David Llewellyn Dodds brought these verses together with others in his 1991 *Arthurian Poets* edition. Williams wrote one novel that is a Grail quest in a modern setting, *War in Heaven* (1930).[27] Then in 1931, he published *Heroes and Kings,* which contains seven highly personal Arthurian poems. He explored his ideas in nonfiction format in essays on his own poetry, on Malory, on the French romances,[28] and on the history of Eucharistic practices.[29] And, finally, he poured his soul into his life's work: two volumes of Arthurian poetry, *Taliessin through Logres* (1938) and *The Region of the Summer Stars* (1944). He was working on another volume, to be entitled either *Jupiter Over Carbonek* (Cavaliero 124) or *The Household of Taliessin* (Dodds, *Arthurian* 6),[30] at the time of his sudden death in 1945. There is evidence that he planned to revise all the previous poems (including some published only in periodicals) into one consistent, coherent, narrative whole, completing his totalizing myth (Dodds, *Arthurian* 5–6).

Williams differs from Lewis and Tolkien in several ways and is perhaps closer to Barfield in at least one aspect of his vision. Williams was a high-ranking initiate in A. E. Waite's occult secret society, The Fellowship of the Rosy Cross. He remained in this Rosicrucian society for ten years, climbing rapidly up the grades and

---

26   See chapter 17, "Camelot Incarnate: Arthurian Vision in the Early Plays of Charles Williams" by Bradley Wells, pages 435–58, for a full discussion of these dramas.

27   Suzanne Bray's "'Any Chalice of Consecrated Wine': The Significance of the Holy Grail in Charles Williams's *War in Heaven*," chapter 18, pages 459–71, explores this novel in its ecclesiastical context.

28   See the many essays on these topics collected in *The Image of the City*, edited by Anne Ridler.

29   For which see chapter 19, "The Acts of Unity: The Eucharistic Theology of Charles Williams's Arthurian Poetry" by Andrew C. Stout, pages 473–92.

30   Dodds quotes a letter from Williams to Raymond Hunt of 29 Nov 1941.

participating enthusiastically in the rituals, which he memorized. He served as Master of the Temple three times (Roukema 43) and rose to the highest order, "where he received a summons to generate symbolism with which the Secret Tradition could be communicated" (Roukema 47). Aren Roukema demonstrates how Williams fulfilled this charge in his novels, producing in both fiction and poetry "a bricolage of symbolism that exhibits the modern occult passion for blending the widest possible array of esoteric images and traditions" (48). This is also true in his poetry, which shows the direct influence of A. E. Waite's 1909 book *The Hidden Church of the Holy Graal* and involves a complicated layering of systems of hermetic symbolism. Even after he left the F. R. C., occult matters remained important to Williams. There is evidence that suggests he may have been involved in an offshoot from the Order of the Golden Dawn (the Stella Matutina), or at least a group of initiates who discussed and perhaps practiced those rituals (Lindop, *Third Inkling* 63–66; cf. Roukema).[31] Another author, "One of the mystery writers of the Golden Dawn period, Arthur Machen, may have inspired Williams to the idea of a modern *parousia* symbolized by the grail. His story *The Great Return* (1915) is an account of the Grail and its effect on a modern Welsh parish church" (Göller 466). Williams also took ideas from the Zohar, the Bible, Dante, and a great deal of disparate English poetry. His Arthuriad is certainly the most complicated of all the Inklings' and the most infused with hermetic imagery and ideas.

Williams' vision of the Grail quest also resulted in the highest-quality poetry any of the Inklings ever produced. On the level of sheer mechanical skill, I believe that Williams was the best writer of the group, although he certainly lacked Tolkien's storytelling and world-building skills and Lewis' clarity. His efforts are marred by obscurity[32] and by a layering of systems of symbolism without a key, but Lewis was only exaggerating slightly when he assessed *Taliessin through Logres* and *The Region of the Summer Stars* "both for the soaring and gorgeous novelty of their technique and for their profound wisdom, to be among the two or three most valuable books of verse produced in the century" (Preface to *Essays* vi–vii; *pace* Rateliff, "Lost Letter" 13). Granted, Lewis was a personal friend of Williams', one of many who fell under the enchantment of his charms—but even Norris Lacy writes that Williams is "among modern English poets, the foremost reshaper and recreator of Arthurian mythology" (*Encyclopedia* 630). Williams brought many fresh insights and startling innovations to his Arthuriad, both in narrative changes and, especially, a spiritual depth at once orthodox and occult. Many of his ideas are discussed throughout this volume,[33] but I will discuss some of his innovations here.

The characterological perspective in Williams' Arthurian poetry is unique. While it is not new to approach the story through a character other than King Arthur himself, Williams' use of Taliessin, the king's poet and captain of horse, provides a particularly poetic insight. The place and power of poetry are very high indeed in *Taliessin through Logres* and *The Region of the Summer Stars*, and the creative impulse is connected to victory in war and to the formation of spiritual households. His use of Galahad, too, is startling and vivid: The High Prince is the product of a sinful union, yet is used as the means of salvation and as a

---

31   David Dodds also discussed this possibility with me by email in 2012 ("Re: reference? (II)").
32   See Lewis' "Williams and the Arthuriad" for a detailed discussion of kinds of obscurity and the degree to which Williams is guilty of each.
33   Especially in the chapters by Suzanne Bray, Andrew Rasmussen, Andrew C. Stout, Benjamin D. Utter, and Bradley Wells.

type of Christ in the poetry. Percivale, also, takes an important poetic, musical, and spiritual role. These three, along with Bors as the example of happy domestic love and Lancelot as the faithful/unfaithful lover, are all practitioners of various aspects of Williams' Affirmative Theology.

Perhaps his greatest Arthurian innovation is the degree to which he made the Grail essential to the story and unified it with the tales of Arthur and the Knights of the Round Table: The Grail "must take the central place. Logres then must be meant for the Grail" ("Figure" 267), he asserted. In Chapter 19 of this volume, Andrew Stout writes: "While earlier versions of the myths focused on Arthur's kingship or the romance of Lancelot and Guinevere, Williams brought the quest for the Grail and its spiritual power to the forefront" (481). There had been other authors who had focused on the Grail to some degree, but comments throughout Williams' *Arthurian Commonplace Book* and his prose study "The Figure of Arthur" reveal that he did not think any previous author had seen the essential spiritual unity—perhaps an occult unity— between those two halves of the narrative complex. There are moments in the legends when Arthur comes very close to "the mystery" of the Grail, but does not quite achieve it. In discussing *The High History of the Holy Grail*, Williams complains that this romance "does not entirely unite the Arthur theme and the Grail theme, and this is the more disappointing because it starts off as if it were going to do precisely that" (258–59), and he is disgusted with Tennyson's "treatment of the Sacred Lance as a jumping-pole" ("The Making of *Taliessin*," *Image* 180). In an essay entitled "*The Morte darthur*," Lewis praises Williams' *Taliessin through Logres* and *The Region of the Summer Stars* for their vitality, the centrality they give the Grail, and the inevitability of their concluding tragedy (Lewis, "Morte" 08). Williams has given the Arthurian world "a dynamic orientation toward a new spiritual centre" (Göller 471): the unification of all the elements of the vast, sprawling Matter of Britain in the object of the Grail. In these poems, the Holy Grail is a synecdoche for all objects and actions of Christ's passion: "Almost any article connected with the Act served for its symbol," Williams wrote in "The Figure of Arthur" (206), meaning that any object associated with the Crucifixion could be used in commemorating it. Whether Williams himself finally achieved this poetic unity himself is a matter for debate.

The Holy Grail is traditionally associated with Christ's passion, as it was either the cup from which Jesus and the apostles drank at the Last Supper, and which Joseph of Arimathea subsequently used to catch blood from Jesus' side, or it was the platter or plate on which Jesus ate bread for the last time before His crucifixion. Clearly, then, the Grail is at least symbolically connected with the ritual Lord's Supper that Christians practice regularly in remembrance of Him. In "Figure," Williams traces the history of the doctrinal developments in the Christian Church related to the Eucharist. He reveals his wide knowledge of ecclesiastical, literary, and historical sources and casually refutes "cauldron of plenty" theories. These hypotheses, put forward by such writers as Sir James Frazer and Jessie Weston, claim that the Grail is merely a common archetype and that our idea of it evolved from earlier Celtic stories about a great magical pot that could provide endless food or raise the bodies of the dead that were flung into it.[34] Williams gracefully disposes of these theories of primitivism: at the beginning of his chapter entitled "The Grail," he writes about "that Cup which in its progress through the imagination of Europe was to absorb into itself

---

34   See chapter 11 in the present volume, "Lilacs Out of the Dead Land" by Jon Hooper, for a discussion of James Frazer and Jessie Weston.

so many cauldrons of plenty and vessels of magic" (197). At the end of the study, he gives a summary of the Frazer-and-Weston school of thought, then asserts again that if the Grail

> swallowed up its lesser rivals, it did so exactly because it was greater. The poetic inventiveness of Europe found itself presented with the image of a vessel much more satisfying to it—merely as an image—than any other ... the Grail contained the very Act which was related to all that existence. Of course, it absorbed or excluded all else; *sui generis*, it shone alone. (207)

Later on, in his chapter on Chrétien and the French romances, entitled "The Coming of the Grail," he claims that in the evolution of Arthurian literature, the Grail "became particular and the grand material object of Christian myth" (244). He traces the Grail's path through poetry, as it becomes more and more closely related to high and holy mysteries.

Williams' purpose in his own Arthurian poetry was to unite the episodic, knightly tales of King Arthur and his court with the spiritual quest for the Holy Grail in a relationship closer than had ever been done in literature. In *Taliessin through Logres* and *The Region of the Summer Stars*, he makes the Grail the sacred object that serves to reveal the spiritual condition of each character and serves also as the apex of the narrative arc. He does this in his poetry by a structure of narrative interlace and by using the Grail as a catalyst of spiritual disclosure. Characters' responses to it are revelatory of their eternal salvific or damnatory condition. It functions much the way the crime does in many murder mysteries: as the detective investigates, the reader learns many dark secrets in the pasts of all of the characters, bringing them all under suspicion. The crime reveals their true natures. Similarly, the Grail itself functions this way in Williams' Arthuriad: knights and ladies are able to approach the Grail when their souls are in right relationship with God, while those who have turned away from righteousness are unable to achieve it. The Grail itself is a symbol, or even a sacrament, of the same kind as the elements of the Lord's Supper and of the same kind as Galahad in Williams' poetry: all are visible signs of Christ's presence; in "Taliessin in the Rose-Garden," "the altars of Christ everywhere offer the grails" (l. 159). Men's approach to romantic and domestic love is also a Grail quest, for in

> women's flesh lives the quest of the Grail
> in the change from Camelot to Carbonek and from Carbonek to Sarras,
> puberty to Carbonek, and the stanching, and Carbonek to death.
> Blessed is she who gives herself to the journey. (165–68)

Blanchefleur/Dindrane, then, gives her body to a journey of celibacy, taking "vows ... for the sake of Christ" and in spite of "the sword of schism that pierced her lord" Taliessin's heart, because he loves her ("The Departure of Dindrane" 51–52, 53). Elayne, Bors' wife, does the same by being "the mistress of a household" ("The Departure of Dindrane" l. 42). Each of these affirms "the Grail" by submitting herself in service to God.

In his prose study, Williams gives a literary history of King Arthur, then discusses his own contributions to the myth. He states "that the centre of the myth must be determined" (267)—meaning that he had to determine what the center would be in his adaptation—and then immediately determines it: "The problem is simple—is the king to be there for the sake of the Grail or not?" That is the center of Williams' poetry: will characters serve themselves, or will they serve God and the kingdom, revealing this service by their submission to the Grail? As David Dodds wrote about *The Chapel of the Thorn*: "to use violence to secure a Hallow is to misuse your powers and to be improperly disposed toward It," and this is the case throughout Williams' writings (Dodds, "*Chapel*" 173). The Grail itself, and the characters' attitudes and actions toward it, comprise "the central matter of the Matter of Britain," Williams boldly claims (267). It is certainly the central theme of his life's literary work.

This theme reveals itself over and over again through the cycle, as characters face moments of decision. In each case, they must decide whether to satisfy their own self-turned desires or to serve something larger than themselves. On the day of his crowning, Arthur "stood to look on his city: / the king made for the kingdom, or the kingdom made for the king?" ("The Crowning of Arthur," *TtL*, ll. 62–63). This is the question he asks himself on the first day of his rule: Will I serve the kingdom, or will I use the kingdom to serve me? He answers the question wrongly, and this act of rebellion, of setting up himself against God (much like Satan's in *Paradise Lost*), is the first of many such decisions that cause the destruction of the Empire.

Many of Williams' character make this fatal mistake. Members of the Court gather to partake of the Lord's Supper. Arthur and Lancelot are there among the others, but "the king in the elevation beheld and loved himself crowned; / Lancelot's gaze at the Host found only a ghost of the Queen" ("The Star of Percivale" 33–36). Arthur and Lancelot look at the elements of the Lord's Supper, the bread and wine, but they do not discern the Body of Christ. Instead, each sees his own object of idolatry. Arthur sees himself; Lancelot sees Guinevere. They suffer greatly for their sin, but something immeasurably worse than personal grief also occurs: the very Kingdom of Logres is lost, and then follows the most dreadful catastrophe that could possibly befall the human race: "Against the rule of the Emperor the indivisible / Empire was divided; therefore the Parousia suspended / its coming, and abode still in the land of the Trinity" ("The Prayers of the Pope" 145–47). The sins of Arthur and his kingdom have postponed the second coming of Christ![35]

The postponement of the Parousia by means of human actions is one of Williams' more important Arthurian innovations. Another is the nature of Logres in his poetry. "Logres" is a name for Arthur's kingdom, "sometimes applied to Britain in Arthurian romance" (Lupack, *Encyclopedia* 457). It can be traced back to Geoffrey of Monmouth. In many versions of the tales, it is a kind of ephemeral, Edenic dream-kingdom: the ideal of what Arthur's kingdom could be if all were ordered aright. But Williams took the concept of "Logres" further than did his sources. He developed the idea of two kingdoms coexisting simultaneously: Britain (earthly, worldly, natural, political) and Logres (heavenly, theocratic, arch-natural, spiritual). These are analogous to—or more than analogous to: perhaps even sacramentally related to—the Christian

---

35   I discuss this topic more fully in my introduction to Charles Williams' early play *The Chapel of the Thorn*. Williams commented upon the Dolorous Stroke in his *Commonplace Book*, asking "does this mean the use of sacred things for 'temporary' ends — the use of personality for (created by the Eternal Generation) for its own purposes, personality guarding itself in its own selfhood, instead of yielding itself completely up? — as Balin used the lance for his own welfare" (142; also partially qtd. in Dodds "*Chapel*" 135).

doctrine of the Old Man (the sinner) and the New Man (the saint). In each kingdom, as in each person, the sanctifying spirit strives against the sin-enslaved self. In chapter 3 of this volume, "Mixed Metaphors and Hyperlinked Worlds," Brenton D. G. Dickieson expands upon this definition of Williams' Logres and shows how Lewis took up this idea and deployed it in *That Hideous Strength*.

Williams, then, posited a spiritual reality coexisting behind the geopolitical one—and pushed that principle to a logically extreme application. In his *Encyclopedia*, Lacy wrote that the two volumes of Williams' poetry take varying perspectives on their subject matter:

> *Taliessin through Logres* portrays the establishment, growth, and fall of the realm of Arthur. In a sense it shows the progress through the earthly kingdom. The poems of *Region of the Summer Stars* (the "third heaven" of poets and lovers) take up the same themes, but from a perspective *sub specie aeternitatis*. (631)

While this is partly correct, it would be more nearly accurate to say that both books investigate the relationship of the natural and the arch-natural in Arthur's kingdom(s). Heinz Göller praises this innovation: "Williams gives the story of King Arthur an entirely new slant .... Charles Williams provides us with a completely different concept of the Arthurian myth. The major innovation consists in the exclusion of an antithetical opposition of Logres and Rome .... The result of dropping the rivalry between Logres and Rome is a denationalisation of the Arthurian myth" (Göller 466–67). Both are provinces of God's kingdom on earth, represented in Williams' poetry as the Byzantine Empire.

If individuals' decisions in the geopolitical realm are also actual occurrences in the spiritual, it follows that failure in the one is disaster in the other. So when Arthur uses the kingdom as a mere tool for his own pleasure, when Lancelot replaces worship of Christ with idolatrous adoration of Guinevere, when "Balin and Balan fell by mistaken impious hate. / Arthur tossed loves with a woman and split his fate" ("Lamorak and the Queen Morgause of Orkney," *TtL*, 49–50)—Balin killed his brother and struck the Dolorous Blow against Pelles, when Arthur slept with his sister Morgause and fathered Mordred—when all of these people chose self above service, the kingdom of Britain fell.

But with it fell the spiritual kingdom of Logres. In Williams' myth, Arthur was made king (from the point of view of Providence) in order to prepare a place for the coming of the Grail. Then, once the Grail was established in Logres, Jesus' Second Coming would occur. When the chief actors in the Arthurian drama sinned, they rejected the Grail, so it left the shores of England and was hidden away in Sarras, the land of the Trinity, a mysterious island in the west across the sea. And then the Parousia itself was postponed.

This is a terrifying, startling innovation. To suggest that human decisions could wreck the plans of God is an extreme application of the doctrine of Free Will, but one that is perfectly in harmony with Williams' usual practice of pushing a teaching to its limits and discovering new perspectives on the truth there. Whether those farthest shores were always within the bounds of orthodoxy is an open question.[36]

---

36   Indeed, it is exactly the question Richard Sturch asked in his article "CW as Heretic?" and did not answer conclusively.

All of his ideas are interrelated in an unusually consistent, if idiosyncratic, system of thought. Not only is Arthur's Britain shadowed by the heavenly (or Platonic) Logres; it is also a province of a Byzantine Empire of his own invention. This creative geopolitical entity is the product of layered historical conflation[37] and hermetic imagery. In his Arthuriad, Williams conflates events from as early as c. 500 AD with those as late as 1453 (and, arguably, some references that are contemporary to his own time as well).[38] I will not go into this topic in detail here, as I have done so elsewhere,[39] and as aspects of this vision of empire are covered with insight and panache by Benjamin Utter and Andrew Rasmussen in their chapters in this volume. Suffice it to say that he lays the figure of a woman's body over a map of Europe, then layers astrology, the Sephirotic tree, the Roman empire, the Byzantine empire, church history, and political history into a complicated, self-consistent system of symbolism worthy of William Blake. It is a difficult symbolic system to decode, but its riches of imagery and meaning fully reward the diligent cryptographer.

Really, though, Williams was his own only decoder. He was the only one who held all the documents, all the keys, in his mind, hidden yet deployed in his poetry and his personal life. Perhaps the most startling aspect of his Arthuriana is the extent to which he required his friends, co-workers, and associates to participate in the system he had set up. He drew together autobiography and myth in a way that is perhaps unprecedented. This alone makes his life a worthy topic of literary study, as, if anyone committed the biographical fallacy, it was Williams himself. Just as he drew no distinctions between the natural and the supernatural, so he drew none between work and life, between the literary and the living. Brenton D. G. Dickieson calls him a "praxis theologian" (103); he endeavored to shape his life and the lives of those around him after the pattern of his own mythology, which frequently took an Arthurian form. One young disciple of his wrote that after first reading some of the poems that would later appear in *The Region of the Summer Stars*, "I was, not surprisingly, confused and bemused by the way in which the 'Company' [in 'The Founding of the Company'] appeared to be at the same time the 'household' of the King's poet in Charles' own highly original version of the Arthurian myth, and the circle of his own personal friends" (Lang-Sims 38). Throughout his life, "increasingly, he would become Taliessin; and many of those he knew would be drawn into the myth" (Lindop, *Third Inkling* 232).

Williams may be unique in the degree to which he united his theology, literary criticism, and Arthurian adaptations with his personal life. He carried on a life-long master-slave affair of extreme emotional intensity with a coworker named Phyllis Jones. (This relationship was perhaps not fully consummated but was certainly sexual in nature.) In many of his Arthurian poems, "Williams meditated upon Phyllis'

---

37   As I argue in "Double Affirmation."

38   Although Simpson warns historically-curious readers that

even where he ostensibly indicates contemporary matters—such as when the octopod tentacles of the oriental P'o-l'u extend menacingly along the coast of Burma, and a reader may leap to interpret this threat as the Japanese advance of 1942—both Williams and C. S. Lewis assure us that no such meaning was intended. his lines had preceded the military campaign. (Simpson 83).

Simpson cites Williams, "Notes on the Way." *Time and Tide* 23 (28 February 1942): 170–71 and Lewis, WA 185.

39   Higgins, "Double Affirmation."

body, making it in turn a written text, a source of power through erotic constraint, and a microcosm of the Arthurian world" (Lindop, *Third Inkling* 157). His fusion of Christian doctrine and occult practice is unusual, and his use of magical ritual to transmute sexual energy into poetic creativity sets him apart from the other Inklings, to be sure. Indeed, the contrast between the two halves of his life is so sharp that it prompted John Rateliff to write recently: "I would say that a man may either lay claim to being the great Christian theological poet of his time .... Or he can write, and publish, illustrated bondage poetry. But not both" ("Lost Letter" 9–10). Of course, he can—and did—do both, but the impact of either is muted by coexistence with the other. Now, Williams' private life might not be relevant to his poetry except for the fact that he translated his own experiences into the verses themselves, often enacting private practices on the pages of his books. Thus, his biography is often one of the wards on the multipartite key that is needed to unlock his symbolic code.

Some of Williams' attempt at synthesis are described and analyzed by Bradley Wells in chapter 17 of this volume, which deals with the early plays. Several of these dramas were enacted in his workplace, the London Offices of Oxford University Press at Amen House, where Williams gave mythological names to his co-workers, wrote plays for them to perform, and behaved toward them on a daily basis as if they were all participants in a high and holy ceremony. In his personal relationships, he gave his "disciples" nicknames taken from a variety of literary sources, then treated them according to the roles he had given them, such as slave, disciple, master, servant, etc. These were not all Arthurian, but as one such servant-disciple wrote: "In his mythical world [his workplace] was sometimes Byzantium, sometimes Camelot (the one being an extension of the other in the Taliessin poems)" (Lang-Sims 27). In one play, *The Masque of Perusal*, his co-workers processed through the library of Amen House in a publishing company's Grail procession, carrying an inkpot, a pen, pieces of type, paper, and periodicals: he brought the Grail into his workplace.[40]

All of this is to say that the Arthurian legend, according to the way in which he remade it, was essential to Williams' life. Tolkien and Lewis brought the Arthurian legend into their works, but Williams brought everything else into his Arthurian legend. To him, it was truth: biblical, spiritual, historical, mythological, occult, personal, and apocalyptic. It told the tale of the meaning of things from the Fall of humanity through Christ's earthly passion and to the end of times: The Second Coming, the final achievement of the Grail and all it stood for. It was his one story. It was his metanarrative.

---

40 I do not want to overstate this point. David Dodds pointed out to me in correspondence that this mythologization of his life was neither always Arthurian nor universal. Most of the nicknames were not Arthurian at all ('Lalage' for Lois Lang-Sims comes from Horace's *Odes*; the 'Phillida,' 'Colin,' 'Dorinda,' and so forth of the Masques are pastoral); and 'Celia,' another nickname for Phyllis Jones, comes from Latin literature, the pastoral tradition, a poem by Ben Jonson, and Shakespeare's *As You Like It*. He also mentioned that while Williams did cause his colleagues to conform to his vision of a theological, ceremonial workplace, the majority of them were not his "disciples" (Phyllis Jones certainly was, and Alice Mary Hadfield may have been), and that the Inklings appeared to remain outside of any of these kinds of re-imaginings on Williams' part.

Conclusion

This chapter has in many ways imitated the moves that matter in the Matter of Britain: intertextuality, source-dependence, palimpsestuosity, and indeterminacy. In it, I have relied as much on the works of my fellow chapter-writers in this volume as on anything that came before, making it a kind of contemporary conversation. I have layered their thoughts and my own on top of the works of other scholars, who in turn participate in a complex stratigraphy (not a simple linearity) with the works of literature on which they comment. In yet another kind of relationship, those works of literature respond to both each other and to scholarly analyses of one another. This is how Arthurian writers have almost always worked and how the Inklings lived, taught, and wrote. I hope, therefore, to have both demonstrated and enacted the lively, dialogic nature of Arthuriana.

I also hope that this chapter and all those that follow raise as many questions as they answer. For instance (and it is a sizeable instance), this volume does not directly address the question: "Were the Inklings' Arthurian works more largely similar to one other, or more disparate and contrasting?" While similarities tend to be emphasized slightly, especially their common concern with addressing what they saw as the bankrupt nature of scientistic materialism and with offering a metaphysically-rich alternative, their differences of genre, tone, and style should be apparent, as well as the vastly varying ideas, themes, genres, technical mechanisms, and emphases of their works.

Yet I will close with one final similarity, springing from the question: Is the story-complex of Arthur ultimately tragic or comedic? John Rosenberg, in surveying Arthurian works up to and including Tennyson, comments on "The Passing of Arthur" from *Idylls of the King*. He writes that he sometimes believes "the great world of Arthurian myth came into being solely to memorialize this primal scene of loss" (221). The knights are at war with one another, the kingdom is torn, lovers are separated, and virtue is lost. The king is gone. The Round Table is dissolved. There was once hope of a kind of new Eden on earth, but that hope has faded. The last faithful knight, Bedivere, "watches Arthur dwindle to a mere speck on an empty horizon, his death-pale, death-cold king departing for a paradise that can never be, in the faint hope of returning to a kingdom that never was" (Rosenberg 225). This may well be. Perhaps the entire appeal of Arthuriana, the one quality that has kept it alive for a millennium and a half, is ultimately its hopelessness. If all of those wildly different works have a theme in common, perhaps it is loss: the passing of the one bright and shining moment when Camelot approached Logres.

If that is true, then there is one characteristic that unites the Inklings and sets them apart from all those others: Hope. They agree with Rosenberg that such an Edenic kingdom "never was," but they stoutly refuse to accept that it is "a paradise that can never be." Certainly, on this earth Arthur falls. His body sails away across the sea where few can follow and from whence none return. Elwin Ransom, the Pendragon, the Fisher King, sails away into the heavens, never to return. In the midst of apparent victory, even when thinking of "children," his people must still think "of pain and death" (382) and go on fighting "the long defeat" (*LotR* 2:462). "Logres was withdrawn to Carbonek; it became Britain" (Williams, "The Last Voyage" 125). The Grail withdraws to Sarras, and the Second Coming of Christ is postponed.

But that is in this world. The Inklings believed that though the Grail was taken away, "ye shall see it in the city of Sarras in the spiritual place" (Barfield, *Quest* 16). Although the Parousia may be postponed, it has not been cancelled. The real Once and Future King will return; "let the Company pray for it still" (*TtL* "Taliessin at Lancelot's Mass" 60).

Works Cited

"Arthur, Character of." *The Arthurian Encyclopedia*. Ed. Norris J. Lacy. NY: Garland, 1986. 19. Print.

Barfield, Owen. "Ballade." www.owenbarfield.org.

——. *Eager Spring*. Barfield Press UK, 2009. Print.

——. *Night Operation*. Barfield Press UK, 2009.

——. *The Quest of the Sangreal*. TS. Dep. c. 1101. ml#barfield.C.1. Bodleian Library, Oxford University. Oxford, UK.

Barfield, Owen, and C. S. Lewis. *Mark vs. Tristram: Correspondence between C. S. Lewis & Owen Barfield*. Cambridge: Lowell House Printers, 1967. Print. Cf. Lewis, *CL* 2:780–86.

Barron, W. R. J. "*Bruttene Deorling*: An Arthur for Every Age." *The Fortunes of King Arthur*. Ed. Norris J. Lacy. Cambridge: D. S. Brewer, 2005. 47–65. Print.

Blaxland-de Lange, Simon. *Owen Barfield: Romanticism Come of Age: A Biography*. Forest Row, UK: Temple Lodge Publishing, 2006. Print.

Brazier, P. H. *C.S. Lewis—An Annotated Bibliography and Resource*. Eugene, OR: Wipf and Stock, 2012. cslewisandthechrist.net. Web. 6 February 2016.

Buckman, Ty, and Charles Ross. "An Arthurian Omaggio to Michael Murrin and James Nohrnberg." *Arthuriana* 21.1 (2011): 3–6. *Project Muse*. muse.jhu.edu. Web. 15 November 2013.

Cavaliero, Glen. *Charles Williams: Poet of Theology*. Eugene, OR: Wipf and Stock, 1983. Print.

Christopher, Joe R. "C. S. Lewis' Lost Arthurian Poem: A Conjectural Essay." *Inklings Forever* 8 (2012). 1–11. Print.

——. "John Heath-Stubbs' *Artorius* and the Influence of Charles Williams." *Mythlore* 48–50 (1986–87): 56–62, 51–57, 51–57. PDF file. Email correspondence with Sørina Higgins. 16 March 2015.

Dickieson, Brenton D. G. "The Unpublished Preface to C. S. Lewis' *The Screwtape Letters*." *Notes and Queries*. Oxford UP, 23 April 2013. oxfordjournals.org. PDF file. 24 April 2013.

Dodds, David Llewellyn. Introduction. *Arthurian Poets: Charles Williams*. Arthurian Studies 24. Ed. David Llewellyn Dodds. Rochester, NY: The Boydell Press, 1991. Print.

——. "*The Chapel of the Thorn*: An unknown dramatic poem by C. Williams." *Inklings Jarbuch* 5 (1987): 133–52. Rpt. in *Chapel of the Thorn*. Ed. Sørina Higgins. Berkeley: Apocryphile Press, 2014. 123–39. Print.

——. "Charles Williams, Arthurian Commonplace Book." Unpublished introduction. Email correspondence with Sørina Higgins. 5 June 2013.

——. "Re: reference? (II)." Email correspondence with Sørina Higgins. 28 June 2012.

Drabble, Margaret, ed. "The Matter of Britain." *The Oxford Companion to English Literature*. 6th ed. Oxford UP, 2000. 654. Print.

Driggers, Taylor. "Modern Medievalism and Myth: Tolkien, Tennyson, and the Quest for a Hero." *Journal of Inklings Studies* 3.2 (2013): 133–52. inklings-studies.com. Web. 5 February 2016.

Eckhardt, Caroline. "Reconsidering Malory." *The Fortunes of King Arthur*. Ed. Norris J. Lacy. Cambridge: D. S. Brewer, 2005. 195–208. *Google Books*. Web. 18 August 2015.

Ekman, Stefan. *Here Be Dragons: Exploring Fantasy Maps and Settings*. Wesleyan University Press, 2013. Print.

Fimi, Dimitra. "Tolkien's '"Celtic" Type of Legends': Merging Traditions." *Tolkien Studies* 4 (2007). 51–71. *Project MUSE*. Web. 6 October 2015.

Flieger, Verlyn, and Douglas A. Anderson, eds. *Tolkien on Fairy-Stories*. NY: HarperCollins, 2014. Google books. Web. 17 October 2015.

Gallix, François. "T. H. White and the Legend of King Arthur: From Animal Fantasy to Political Morality." Kennedy 281–98.

"Garboils." *OED*. oed.com. Web. 19 August 2015.

Garth, John. "'The Road from Adaptation to Invention': How Tolkien Came to the Brink of Middle-earth in 1914." *Tolkien Studies* 11 (2014): 1–44. *Project MUSE*. Web. 27 August 2015.

——. *Tolkien and the Great War: The Threshold of Middle-earth*. Boston: Houghton Mifflin, 2003. Print.

——. "Tolkien's Unfinished Epic: 'The Fall of Arthur.'" *The Daily Beast* 23 May 2013. thedailybeast.com. Web. 28 August 2015.

Göller, Karl Heinz. "From Logres to Carbonek: The Arthuriad of Charles Williams." *The Grail: A Casebook*. Ed. Dhira B. Mahoney. NY: Garland, 2000. 465–504. Print.

Grewell, Cory. "'It's All One': Medievalist Synthesis and Christian Apology in Owen Barfield's Studies of Meaning." *Journal of Inklings Studies* 3.2 (2013): 11–40. Print.

Grimaldi, Angela. "Owen Barfield's Marginalia in Sir Thomas Malory's *Le Morte D'Arthur*." *Renascence: Essays on Values in Literature*. The Free Library. 22 September 2010. Web. 28 May 2015.

Hadfield, Alice Mary. *Charles Williams: An Exploration of His Life and Work*. Oxford UP, 1983. Print.

Hanks, D. Thomas Jr. "'A Far Green Country Under a Swift Sunrise': Tolkien's Eucatastrophe and Malory's *Morte Darthur*." *Fifteenth-Century Studies*. Vol. 36. Eds. Barbara L. Gusick and Matthew Z. Heintzelman. Rochester, NY: Camden House, 2011. 49–64.

Harty, Kevin J. "Review of Gail Ashton and Daniel T. Kline, eds., *Medieval Afterlives in Popular Culture*." *Arthuriana* 24.1 (2014): 139–41. *Project MUSE*. Web. 26 August 2015.

Higgins, Sørina. "Double Affirmation: Medievalism as Christian Apologetic in the Arthurian Poetry of Charles Williams." *Journal of Inklings Studies* 3.2 (2013): 59–96. Print.

Higham, N. J. *King Arthur: Myth-Making and History*. NY: Routledge, 2002. Print.

Hipolito, Jane. Introduction. *Eager Spring*. By Owen Barfield. Barfield Press UK, 2009. ix–xii. Print.

Hostetter, Carl F. "Over Middle-earth Sent unto Men: On the Philological Origins of Tolkien's Eärendil Myth." *Mythlore* 17.3 (1991): 5–10.

Hutcheon, Linda. *A Theory of Adaptation*. NY: Routledge, 2006. Print.

Karlson, Henry. "Vox Nova At The Library: Owen Barfield's *Eager Spring*." *Vox Nova: Catholic Perspectives on Culture, Society, and Politics*. vox-nova.com. Web. 19 August 2015.

Kennedy, Edward Donald. *King Arthur: A Casebook*. London: Routledge, 2013. Print.

Lacy, Norris J. "The Arthur of the Twentieth and Twenty-first Centuries." *The Cambridge Companion to the Arthurian Legend*. Ed. Elizabeth Archibald and Ad Putter. 120–36. Cambridge Companions Online. Cambridge UP, 2013. universitypublishingonline.org. PDF file. 15 November 2013.

——, ed. *The Arthurian Encyclopedia*. NY: Garland, 1986. Print.

Lang-Sims, Lois. *Letters to Lalage: The Letters of Charles Williams to Lois Lang-Sims*. Kent State UP, 1989. Print.

Lewis, C. S. *The Allegory of Love: A Study in Medieval Tradition*. London: Oxford UP, 1936. Print.

——. *The Collected Letters of C. S. Lewis*. Ed. Walter Hooper. 3 vols. NY: HarperSanFrancisco, 2004–07. Print.

——. "De Descriptione Temporum." Inaugural Lecture from the Chair of Mediaeval and Renaissance Literature at Cambridge University. Cambridge UP, 1954. *Internet Archive*. archive.org. Web. 26 August 2015.

——. "The Morte Darthur." *Studies in Medieval and Renaissance Literature*. Cambridge UP, 1998. *Google Books*. Web. 27 August 2015.

——. Preface. *Essays Presented to Charles Williams*. Ed. C. S. Lewis. London: Oxford UP, 1947. v–xiv. Print.

——. *That Hideous Strength: A Modern Fairy-Tale for Grown-Ups*. 1945. NY: Macmillan, 1977. Print.

——. *Till We Have Faces*. NY: Harcourt, 1956. Print.

——. "Williams and the Arthuriad." *Taliessin through Logres; The Region of the Summer Stars; Arthurian Torso*. By Charles Williams and C. S. Lewis. 1948. Grand Rapids, MI: Eerdmans, 1974. 275–384. Print.

Lindop, Grevel. *Charles Williams: The Third Inkling*. Oxford UP, 2015.

Loomis, Roger Sherman, Ed. *Arthurian Literature in the Middle Ages: A Collaborative History*. Oxford UP, 1959. Print.

——. "The Oral Diffusion of the Arthurian Legend." Loomis 52–63.

——. "The Origin of the Grail Legends." Loomis 274–94.

Lupack, Alan. "The Old Order Changeth: King Arthur in the Modern World." *The Fortunes of King Arthur*. Ed. Norris J. Lacy. Cambridge: D. S. Brewer, 2005. 209–24. Print.

——. *The Oxford Guide to Arthurian Literature and Legend*. Oxford UP, 2007. Print.

——. "The Arthurian Legend in the Sixteenth to Eighteenth Centuries." *A Companion to Arthurian Literature*. Ed. Helen Fulton. Chichester, West Sussex: Blackwell, 2009. 340–54. Print.

Merriman, James Douglas. *A Study of the Arthurian Legend in England between 1485 and 1835*. UP Kansas, 1973. Print.

Orwell, George. "The Scientists Take Over." *Manchester Evening News* 16 August 1945. Rpt. *The Complete Works of George Orwell*. Ed. Peter Davison. Vol. 17. London: Martin Secker & Warburg, 1998. 250–51. *Lewisiana*. http://www.lewisiana.nl/orwell/. Web. 17 September 2015.

Owen Barfield Literary Estate. "Poetry, 1930s." *Owen Barfield: Poet, Philosopher, Author, Thinker, Sage: The First and Last Inkling*. www.owenbarfield.org/books/. Web. 18 November 2015.

——. "Selected Works by Owen Barfield." *Owen Barfield: Poet, Philosopher, Author, Thinker, Sage: The First and Last Inkling*. www.owenbarfield.org/books/. Web. 19 August 2015.

Rateliff, John D. Introduction. *Eager Spring*. By Owen Barfield. Barfield Press UK, 2009. ix–xiii. Print.

——. "The Lost Letter: Seeking the Keys to Williams' Arthuriad." *Mythlore* 34.1 (2015). Email correspondence with Sørina Higgins. 7 September 2015.

——. "'That Seems to Me Fatal': Pagan and Christian in *The Fall of Arthur*." Unpublished. Email correspondence with Sørina Higgins. 19 June 2015.

Rosenberg, John D. "Tennyson and the Passing of Arthur." *The Passing of Arthur: New Essays in Arthurian Tradition.* Ed. Christopher Baswell and William Sharpe. NY: Garland, 1988. 221–34. Print.

Roukema, Aren. "A Veil that Reveals: Charles Williams and the Fellowship of the Rosy Cross." *Journal of Inklings Studies* 5.1 (2015): 22–71. Print.

Rouse, Robert Allen, and Cory James Rushton. "Arthurian Geography." *The Cambridge Companion to the Arthurian Legend.* Ed. Elizabeth Archibald and Ad Putter. 218–34. Cambridge Companions Online. Cambridge UP, 2013. universitypublishingonline.org. .PDF file. 15 November 2013.

Schenk, Gabriel. "blog note." Message to Owen A. Barfield, forwarded to the author. 23 Jun 2015. Email correspondence.

Schwartz, Stanford. *C. S. Lewis on the Final Frontier: Science and the Supernatural in the Space Trilogy.* Oxford UP, 2009. Print.

Shippey, Tom. *J. R. R. Tolkien: Author of the Century.* Boston: Houghton Mifflin, 2000. Print.

——. "Welcome to Beowulf." LITD5304: Beowulf Through Tolkien, and Vice-Versa. Signum University Online. 19 January 2015. Lecture.

Simpson, Roger. "King Arthur in World War Two Poetry: His Finest Hour?" *Arthuriana* 13.1 (2003). 66–91. *JSTOR.* Web. 21 October 2013.

Smilde, Arend. "C. S. Lewis' essays, short stories and other short prose writings." *Lewisiana.* www.lewisiana. nl. Web. 6 February 2016.

Spaeth, Paul J. "Charles Williams, 1886–1945. Publications on 'The Matter of Britain': The Arthurian Poems and Other Writings." St. Bonaventure University. www.sbu.edu. Web. 6 February 2016.

Steinbeck, John. *The Acts of King Arthur and His Noble Knights.* NY: Farrar, Straus, and Giroux, 1970. Print.

Steiner, Rudolf. *Education as an Art.* 1970. Great Barrington, MA: SteinerBooks, 1988. Print.

——. "Eurythmy as Visible Singing." 1924. Rudolf Steiner Archive. wn.rsarchive.org. Web. 26 August 2015.

Sturch, Richard. "Charles Williams as Heretic?" *Charles Williams Quarterly* 136 (2010): 7–19. Print.

Tolkien, J. R. R. *Beowulf: A Translation and Commentary together with Sellic Spell.* Ed. Christopher Tolkien. Boston: Houghton Mifflin Harcourt, 2014. Print.

——. *The Book of Lost Tales Part Two.* Ed. Christopher Tolkien. Boston: Houghton Mifflin, 1984. Print.

——. *The Fall of Arthur.* Ed. Christopher Tolkien. London: HarperCollins, 2013. Print.

——. *Farmer Giles of Ham.* London: Allen & Unwin, 1949.

——. *The Lord of the Rings.* 1954–55. NY: Ballantine, 1986. Print.

——. *The Lost Road and Other Writings.* The History of Middle-earth 5. Ed. Christopher Tolkien. NY: Random House/DelRay, 1987. Print.

——. "On Fairy-stories." *Essays Presented to Charles Williams.* Ed. C. S. Lewis. 1947. London: Oxford UP, 1947. 38–89. Rpt. Grand Rapids, MI: Eerdmans, 1981. Print.

——. *Sauron Defeated.* The History of Middle-earth 9. Ed. Christopher Tolkien. Boston: Houghton Mifflin, 1992. Print.

——. *The Story of Kullervo.* Ed. Verlyn Flieger. London: HarperCollins, 2015. Print.

Ward, Michael. *Planet Narnia: The Seven Heavens in the Imagination of C. S. Lewis.* Oxford UP, 2008. Print.

White, Paul Whitfield. "The Admiral's Men, Shakespeare, and the Lost Arthurian Plays of Elizabethan England." *Arthuriana* 24.4 (2014) 33–47. *Project MUSE*. Web. 26 August 2015.

Williams, Charles. *Arthurian Commonplace Book*. MS. Eng. e. 2012 (as "Notes on the Holy Grail"). Bodleian Library, Oxford, UK.

——. *The Chapel of the Thorn: A Dramatic Poem*. Ed. Sørina Higgins. Berkeley, CA: Apocryphile Press, 2014. Print.

——. "The Figure of Arthur." *Taliessin through Logres; The Region of the Summer Stars; Arthurian Torso*. By Charles Williams and C. S. Lewis. 1948. Grand Rapids, MI: Eerdmans, 1974. 189–245. Print.

——. *Taliessin through Logres; The Region of the Summer Stars; Arthurian Torso*. By Charles Williams and C. S. Lewis. 1948. Grand Rapids, MI: Eerdmans, 1974. Print.

2

Medieval Arthurian Sources for the Inklings: An Overview

Holly Ordway

Nearly all readers of the Inklings' work are aware that Lewis, Tolkien, and Williams drew on medieval sources; the importance of *Beowulf* and the Norse sagas for Lewis and Tolkien, and the late-medieval poetry of Dante for Williams, is well known. However, when we come to considering the way that these three authors interacted with the "Matter of Britain," as the Arthurian legends were called, most readers know only the broad outlines of their source material, largely because these sources are comparatively obscure, and are widely varied in literary genre as well as language (Latin, Welsh, French, English).

Lewis and Tolkien, as professional medievalists, read and studied the original texts as part of their academic work, while Williams explored the medieval Arthurian corpus as a dedicated amateur. Not only did they have deep roots in the material, they could expect many, if not all, of their readers at the time to have at least a passing familiarity with it as well. However, today, when a thorough study of Old and Middle English texts—or any study of them at all—is no longer a standard part of the English literature curriculum in the U. K. or America, most readers lack the context that contemporary readers had for these works.

Although it is impossible for a non-specialist even to approach the level of knowledge that Lewis or Tolkien had of medieval literature, it is possible to become familiar with the lay of the land, as it were, so as to appreciate the ways that the Inklings used, responded to, and adapted the Arthurian legendarium. An acquaintance with their medieval sources will serve us well, helping us to be more sensitive readers and critics.

For one thing, we will be reminded that there is no single "story of King Arthur." Rather, the Arthurian legends include many stories, by various authors, over a long span of time: stories that were complex and often contradictory, fusing historical, traditional, and purely literary elements. The stories of Arthur have different audiences, different rhetorical purposes, and different literary forms. Furthermore, medieval writers did not view creativity and originality in precisely the same way that we do today. What they did with their source materials seems surprising or even shocking to modern sensibilities fed on the value of "originality": the medieval writers assimilated, adapted, refined, modified, re-purposed, and added to the authors they read. With these differences in mind, we will be able to better appreciate that Lewis, Tolkien, and Williams were not simply "using" bits of the Arthurian legends to flavor a story, but were intentional participants in an ongoing story-tradition.

The "Matter of Britain" brings with it the particular challenge that it refers to the overall content of the stories rather than a particular form or even a particular language. From the medieval to the early modern period, the Arthurian corpus includes Welsh triads, Latin historical chronicles, French rhymed stanzas, English alliterative verse, and prose romances in both French and English. Even the characters and plots range widely: not just Arthur and his rise and fall, but stories of the Grail Quest, the affair of Tristan and Iseult, and the adventures of knights from Gawain to Owein. In literary terms, we have not only apples and oranges, but also tomatoes, walnuts, and pretzels. In this very brief survey of medieval Arthurian literature, I have of necessity been highly selective and therefore have omitted many texts and passed over many threads of the narrative. My focus has been on the sources that are most widely recognized as influential or important and that are also significant in some way to the Inklings' writings.

My intention here is to set the stage, and therefore I have deliberately refrained from analysis of the material. Identifying sources can tempt us to move too quickly to analysis and thereby lead us to place too much emphasis on surface features or fail to recognize that the author may be responding to themes, images, or techniques that appear in multiple source texts. I present the material in roughly chronological order, beginning with the earliest Latin chronicles and ending with Malory. I have attempted to sketch out the content and genre of the various Arthurian texts, with attention to the notable features of each work in the larger context of the legendarium. I have focused on British works (in Latin or English) with the inclusion of some Welsh and French texts, but I freely admit that many important texts have been excluded by the necessity of keeping this essay a readable length.

For Lewis, Tolkien, and Williams, "old books" were a living and vital part of their intellectual and emotional lives, side by side with works from later centuries. We should be careful not to allow a chronological consideration of the literature to trick us into viewing the Arthurian corpus as linear, with each succeeding author steadily improving on his predecessors' work. It is often the case that successive authors bring a newly invented form to a higher degree of artistry by learning from and building on what has been done before, but different forms are favored by different times. We should appreciate what makes a good chronicle, a good alliterative poem, or a good romance; then we can value each for what it is, as a good or bad example of its kind. My goal here is to paint, with broad strokes, the medieval literary background, so that critics may look with fresh eyes on the twentieth-century works in the foreground.

Historical accounts

"Did King Arthur really exist?" This question comes naturally to many readers and students of the Arthurian legendarium. In one sense, the answer is an easy "No, and the medieval authors knew that as well as we do": the great court at Camelot in the full flowering of medieval courtly love and chivalry is a literary invention. However, that is not the best approach to the answer, as the distance in time between ourselves and the medieval audience can be misleading. The high medieval trappings of the Arthurian legends were contemporary for authors like the Gawain-poet and Chrétien de Troyes. The readers who enjoyed their literary accounts of a very modern and up-to-date Arthurian court would have been aware that no such men lived among them in their own day.

What about the so-called "historical Arthur," the man on whom the later stories were built? Here the question becomes more difficult to answer. The early medieval chroniclers present him as a historical figure, but specific details are hard to come by, and the interlacing of the supernatural, the legendary, and the purely fictitious into historical accounts poses an interpretive challenge for modern literary critics.[1]

In any case, something, or someone, prompted the first chroniclers and poets to write about a heroic war-leader in fifth-century Britain; what happened? Perhaps the most straightforward, if not simplest, answer is: "A man like him probably did great deeds that planted the seeds of the Arthurian story." Certainly this is what the earliest medieval accounts of Arthur suggest. Historians and archaeologists will, of course, be interested in sifting and weighing the evidence, but their concerns are not the same as those of the literary critic. It may be that this tower has a historical base, just as the story of *Beowulf* includes historical elements; but for literary critics, what is of greatest interest is the way that the medieval authors built on these foundations (historical or not).

The early Latin chronicles

Gildas, a British monk, wrote *On the Downfall and Conquest of Britain* (*De excidio et conquestu Brittaniae*) around AD 547 as a denunciation of the sins of the British. He laments, in his Preface, "the general destruction of every thing that is good, and the general growth of evil throughout the land" (295). He begins with the account of the Roman invasion and occupation of Britain and then the withdrawal of the Romans from Britain, leaving the people vulnerable to invasion from the northern tribes. Gildas recounts the disastrous decision of Vortigern to hire Saxons to fight the northern tribes: "Then all the councillors, together with that proud tyrant Gurthrigern [Vortigern], the British king, were so blinded, that, as a protection to their country, they sealed its doom by inviting in among them (like wolves into the sheep-fold), the fierce and impious Saxons, a race hateful both to God and men, to repel the invasions of the northern nations" (310). The Saxons, seeing the island relatively undefended, turned against their hosts and began to conquer and settle in Britain.

---

1   For a discussion of the Inklings' view of an "historical Arthur," see chapter 6 by Yannick Imbert, pages 189–99. [Editor's note]

The Arthurian portion of the chronicle relates the exploits of one Ambrosius Aurelianus, "a modest man, who of all the Roman nation was then alone in the confusion of this troubled period by chance left alive" (312). Leading the remnants of the British, Aurelianus has some success: "After this, sometimes our countrymen, sometimes the enemy, won the field, to the end that our Lord might in this land try after his accustomed manner these his Israelites, whether they loved him or not, until the year of the siege of Bath-hill [Mt. Badon]" (313). Gildas' chronicle may not do much to authenticate Arthur himself, but he does establish the circumstances of the origin of Arthur's legend, in the temporary victory against the Saxons. Here we also see that the earliest reference to Arthur places him in a Christian context.

A similar account appears in the Venerable Bede's *Ecclesiastical History of the English People* (AD 731); Bede appears to draw heavily on Gildas in his brief account of the battles of Ambrosius Aurelianus.

The Welsh monk Nennius's chronicle, *The History of the Britons* (*Historia Brittonum*), written around 800, is longer and more detailed than Gildas' and begins to include material of a more folkloric or legendary kind. One element of note is the appearance of a background story for the figure who would be known as Merlin in later developments of the legendarium. Vortigern attempts to build a citadel but finds that each time construction begins, the materials vanish overnight. Querying his counselors, he finds that he must sacrifice "a child born without a father" (402) on the foundations. Such a child is found, called Ambrose, who displays preternatural knowledge in uncovering a pool that contains a tent within which are sleeping serpents, one red and one white, who wake and fight. Ambrose declares that

> The pool is the emblem of the world, and the tent that of your kingdom: the two serpents are two dragons; the red serpent is your dragon, but the white serpent is the dragon of the people who occupy several provinces and districts of Britain, even almost from sea to sea: at length, however, our people shall rise and drive away the Saxon race from beyond the sea. (403)

Nennius presents the same events as Gildas, but names "the magnanimous Arthur" (408) as the war leader responsible for driving back the Saxons and elaborates on the circumstances by describing twelve important battles, ending at Mt. Badon where, according to Nennius, "nine hundred and forty fell by his hand alone, no one but the Lord affording him assistance" (409). The twelve battles most likely come from Welsh heroic poetry rather than twelve historic battles (Wilhelm, "Latin Chronicles" 5). No more is said of Arthur in the main chronicle, but in a later chapter, Nennius includes two local legends of Arthur. One describes a heap of stones with the footprint of Arthur's dog Cabal on it; according to the story, Cabal stepped on the stone while hunting the boar Troynt, and Arthur made the pile beneath it. The imprinted stone always reappears on the pile even if taken away. The other Arthurian legend in Nennius' chronicle is attached to a tomb that supposedly contains the body of Anir, Arthur's son, who was killed by Arthur. The tomb is said to change size each time it is measured (Nennius chapter 73; qtd. in Wilhelm, *Romance* 5). Here we have a hint of familial tragedy already being attached to the figure of Arthur.

In the twelfth century, we begin to see diversification of the Arthurian legends. In William of Malmesbury's *The Deeds of the English Kings* (ca. 1125), a figure called Ambrosius is identified as "the lone sur-vivor of the Romans who ruled after Vortigern" but he is distinguished from "the heroic Arthur" (qtd.

in Wilhelm, *Romance* 7). William notes with some disapproval that Arthur is already becoming a legendary figure, but that he is "surely worthy of being described in true histories rather than dreamed about in fallacious myths" (7). In William's description of the Battle of Mt. Badon, he adds the important detail of Arthur's devotion to the Blessed Virgin: "Finally at the siege of Mt. Badon, relying on the image of the Lord's mother, which he had sewn on his armor, he dashed down nine hundred of the enemy in an incredible massacre" (7). Later in his account, William also mentions a legend associated with "Walwen [Gawain], who was the by no means degenerate nephew of Arthur through his sister" (7). This is the first appearance of Gawain in the Arthurian literature, already with a reputation for heroic prowess.

Geoffrey of Monmouth

Geoffrey of Monmouth's *The History of the Kings of Britain* (*Historia Regnum Britanniae*), completed around 1138, is one of the most influential Arthurian texts.

Geoffrey was presumably born in Monmouth, a town in southeast Wales. The use that the *History* makes of Welsh sources, both those that have been identified, such as Nennius, and others that are only presumed, supports the idea that Geoffrey was familiar with Welsh literature and tradition. However, it is likely that Geoffrey's family came from Brittany. Geoffrey shows an interest in the doings of the Britons in his work, and in the Arthurian section he adds the entire continental campaign to Arthur's achievements, which in earlier versions had been limited to Britain. This combination of a familiarity with Welsh stories and a connection to the Norman culture of Brittany is an important element in the *History*.

Geoffrey brought this material to the eyes of the Norman cultured class, the recent conquerors of Britain, showing that their new territory had an antiquity reaching back to the time of Rome, and he presented a literary model of a kingdom similar to the Norman empire. Arthur's kingdom fell, to be sure, but Geoffrey celebrates its existence and uses the prophecies of Merlin to suggest its future renewal. We can see already, with Gildas and Geoffrey, that the Arthurian legendarium provided fruitful material for commentary on current events.

Geoffrey claims to have used a book written in the British language given to him by his friend the archdeacon Walter. However, no trace of this book has survived, leaving the possibility that it was lost, that it never existed in the first place, or that the "book" refers to some source or sources that have not yet been identified. Many sections of the *History* are fiction rather than historical fact, yet it is not possible to simply dismiss the *History* entirely as fabrication, as many verified historical events, people, and places are included in his story, alongside references from verifiable sources.[2] To what extent the rest is based on an unidentified source and to what extent the "ancient book" was Geoffrey's way of supplying authentication for his own invention are unknown; likewise, we have no way to know for certain whether any of the seemingly fabulous stories have bits of historical fact embedded in them. What we can say is that Geoffrey seems to be moving from straight chronicle to a more literary form, expanding and inventing as he goes.

---

2   See Lewis Thorpe's introduction to *The History of the Kings of Britain*.

Several important elements appear in the Arthurian body of legends for the first time in the *History*. Most striking is the enhanced role of Merlin, now named as such for the first time.[3] Geoffrey adopts the account of the prophetic boy from Nennius's chronicle, dramatically extending the prophecy spoken by him, unites this character with that of the Welsh prophetic poet Myrddin, and makes him an important figure in the reigns of Vortigern and Arthur. Most notably, Geoffrey recounts the passion of Uther Pendragon for Ygerna [Igraine], with Merlin responsible for bringing Uther, magically disguised, into Ygerna's bed. Geoffrey, however, provides a different ending for the story than later authors. Learning that Ygerna's husband Gorlois has been killed in battle, Uther "returned to Tintagel Castle, captured it and seized Ygerna at the same time, she being what he really wanted. From that day on they lived together as equals, united by their great love for each other; and they had a son and a daughter. The boy was called Arthur and the girl Anna" (Geoffrey, *History* 208).

Geoffrey develops the reign of Arthur in detail, complete with dialogue and circumstantial detail. The Christian elements are reinforced, alongside elements that have a Welsh flavor: in battle, Arthur carries

> a circular shield named Pridwen, on which there was painted a likeness of the Blessed Mary, Mother of God, which forced him to be thinking perpetually of her. He girded on his peerless sword, called Caliburn, which was forged in the isle of Avalon. A spear named Ron graced his right hand: long, broad in the blade and thirsty for slaughter. (217)

Arthur marries Guinevere and goes to war; Geoffrey is the first to give a detailed account of Arthur's continental campaigns. In the *History*, Arthur then sets up court at Caerleon in a fashion that is a precursor to the courtly depictions of Camelot in later writings. "Britain had reached such a standard of sophistication," Geoffrey writes, "that it excelled all other kingdoms in its general affluence, the richness of its decorations, and the courteous behavior of its inhabitants ... The women became chaste and more virtuous and for their love the knights were ever more daring" (229).

In a further extension of Arthur's military exploits, Geoffrey recounts that Lucius, Procurator of the Roman Republic, demands that Arthur come to Rome to be tried for his crimes of military aggression and refusal of tribute. Arthur does not come quietly, and much fighting ensues, with the Romans defeated and Lucius killed in battle. Here the story takes its tragic turn. While he is headed for Rome, "news was brought to him that his nephew Mordred, in whose care he had left Britain, had placed the crown upon his own head. What is more, this treacherous tyrant was living adulterously and out of wedlock with Queen Guinevere, who had broken the vows of her earlier marriage" (257). Arthur returns and fights Mordred; Guinevere flees and, we are told, "took her vows among the nuns, promising to lead a chaste life" (259). We can see, then, that Guinevere's betrayal of Arthur and later repentance appears very early in the stories, though at this point Mordred is an ordinary nephew, not (as later versions would make him) Arthur's son.

---

3   Geoffrey alters the Welsh name of Myrddin to Merlin. The Latinized version of 'Myrddin' would be 'Merdinus,' likely to be unintentionally humorous for Geoffrey's readers (as the Latin word 'merda' means 'excrement').

In the battle at the River Camblam,[4] Mordred is killed and Arthur is mortally wounded, though simply in the normal course of battle, not by each other. Geoffrey closes the story of Arthur by noting that Arthur "was carried off to the Isle of Avalon, so that his wounds might be attended to. He handed the crown of Britain over to his cousin Constantine, the son of Cador Duke of Cornwall: this in the year 542 after our Lord's Incarnation" (Fulton 45–46).

Around 1150, Geoffrey composed another work on Merlin, the *Vita Merlini* (*The Life of Merlin*). This poem purports to be a biography of Merlin, filling out the little that Geoffrey told of him in the *History*, although the events of the poem do not align particularly well with the events of the *History*, as the two accounts of Merlin place him in two different centuries (Fulton 45–46). The story features Merlin as a Welsh king and prophet who, when his brothers are killed in battle, goes mad with grief and runs off to live in the woods as a wild man. He continues to be a prophet, is visited by Taliessin and holds learned discussions with him. Eventually he is cured of his madness, but continues to live in the woods. Here we see the inclusion of the "wild man" motif that appears in British legend and would appear in various iterations of the later Arthurian stories as well.

Williams refers to the Latin chroniclers Gildas, Nennius, and Geoffrey of Monmouth in "The Figure of Arthur," the incomplete study of the Arthurian legends that Lewis paired with his own study of Williams' poetry as *Arthurian Torso*. The figure of Taliessin is of course significant in Williams' Arthurian poetry, while Merlin appears as a character in Lewis' *That Hideous Strength*.

Welsh sources

We must now take a step back in time to trace the appearance of the first vernacular Arthurian literature, which appears in Welsh. In early Welsh poetry, we can see a growing depiction of a heroic Arthur: an intriguing figure who is realistic in some respects but fantastic in others. Probably the earliest reference is an allusion in the poem *Y Gododdin,* where another hero's bravery is celebrated, "though he was not Arthur" (qtd. in Dunbar 86); here we see Arthur presented as a standard of comparison for other heroes.

The story of Culhwch and Olwen, found in the *Mabinogion*, is the earliest vernacular Arthurian prose text from Wales, probably composed around the end of the tenth century, though it has survived only in manuscripts of the fourteenth century. In this story, the young man Culhwch, who is Arthur's first cousin, must complete a series of tasks in order to win his bride, Olwen. Culhwch goes to Arthur's court to ask for help in finding, and then winning, Olwen; Arthur sends some of his men to help him, including Kei (Kay) and Bedwyr (Bedivere). Although Arthur has a minor role here, it is interesting to note the way that his story is already intersecting with folklore and other story traditions in interesting and imaginatively fruitful ways. Here we see Arthur as part of a decidedly fantastical Celtic story, with both court and characters sketched larger than life—sometimes literally, as with Kei, of whom it is said that "he could be as tall as the tallest tree in the forest when he pleased" (*Mabinogion* 149).

---

4   Spelling varies; some sources have 'Camblan.'

Another appearance of Arthur in Welsh literature is in the triads, where he seems to have been "absorbed into the native Welsh folk tradition" (Fulton 90). The triads are threefold groupings of names or events, referring to stories that would have been known to the poet and his audience. The earliest manuscripts of the triads are from the thirteenth century, but many of the triads themselves are products of a much older oral tradition, composed by court poets or bards. In this oral tradition, the Welsh bards used these triple groupings of names of important heroes or incidents to classify and transmit their body of legends, literature, and history. The three names in a triad are all related to each other in some way, so that remembering one element aided in remembering the other two; the names are also frequently accompanied by a short summary of or reference to associated stories. In this way, the triads served as a way to remember and refer to the vast bulk of stories in the tradition. For instance, Arthur appears as a warlord, one of the "Three Red Ravagers of the Isle of Britain" and as a fourth and higher example of the "Three Generous Men of the Island of Britain" (*Mabinogion* 91).

Tolkien knew the *Mabinogion*, and in an early draft of the lectures that would become "Beowulf: The Monsters and the Critics," he contrasts *Beowulf* to "old Celtic tales," noting that they are very different in flavor (*Beowulf and the Critics* 51). Williams mentions the *Mabinogion* in "The Figure of Arthur."

French vernacular sources

Wace

Wace is notable for producing the first French rendition of the Arthurian story, around 1155, in his *Roman de Brut*, a verse translation of Geoffrey's Latin history into Old French. Born on the island of Jersey, Wace lived most of his life in Normandy and holds a key place in the development of the Arthurian legends in that he is the first known writer to introduce the Arthurian matter into French literature, where it would flourish.[5] His mention of Breton storytellers helps indicate the path that the Arthurian matter was taking as it moved from being a strictly Welsh and then British tradition to becoming a favorite theme on the continent. In terms of the development of the legends, Wace is notable for the first mention of the Round Table.

Chrétien de Troyes

Once the Arthurian legendarium took root in France, it began to develop in new ways, most notably by adding the element of courtly love and also, as we will see, by developing the story of the Grail. Chrétien de Troyes stands out as an exemplar of the "courtly" strain in Arthurian literature.

Chrétien wrote around the end of the twelfth century, probably between the 1150s and 1190, but he is difficult to date precisely, and we know little about him except the fact that, in an age of mostly anonymous

---

5   An earlier Latin source, *The Legend of St Goeznovius* (1019), does make a connection with Brittany. The saint in question is a Breton, and the Arthurian section refers to Arthur's victories in both Britain and Gaul (Wilhelm, *Romance* 6).

writers, he signed his name to each of his works: *Erec et Enide*, *Cligés*, *Lancelot*, *Yvain*, and *Perceval*. The dedication of *Lancelot* to Marie de Champagne indicates that he was associated with her court around the 1170s; the dedication of his last work, *Perceval*, to Count Philip of Flanders may indicate a change in patronage at some point.

Chrétien's sources are an interesting (and highly debatable) topic. There is no extant text that can be seen as a direct source for any of Chrétien's romances, yet even in his own work he acknowledges that he has worked from a source. Certainly, he would have been aware of Geoffrey of Monmouth's *History* and Wace's *Brut*, which provided the outline of the Arthur story and showed a move toward a view of Arthur's world as a courtly one.

A more difficult issue comes in the relation of Chrétien and Welsh literature. The Welsh *Mabinogion* contains the stories *Gereint and Enid*, *Owein*, and *Peredur*, which tell the same stories as *Erec et Enide*, *Yvain*, and *Perceval*. The earliest manuscript of parts of the *Mabinogion* dates to 1225, the earliest complete version to 1400, but undoubtedly the tales were in existence before then; how much earlier depends on interpretation, ranging from 1000 and 1250. With such a wide range of possible dates of composition, it becomes difficult to assess what role the *Mabinogion* tales and Chrétien's romances played in each other's development. It is possible that the *Mabinogion* is a reworking of French sources, including Chrétien; that Chrétien and the *Mabinogion* drew on common Welsh sources; or that there were common sources, but they were one step further removed, being French versions of Welsh material. Leaving aside the details of exactly how the particular texts came into being, it is at least evident that Chrétien's romances use material that comes, by one route or another, from Wales.

Chrétien's *Lancelot* is not one of the tales directly reflected in the *Mabinogion*; Lancelot himself is a character foreign to Welsh Arthurian literature and is essentially Chrétien's invention. Nonetheless, *Lancelot* still shows the influence of Celtic material. The main action of the story revolves around Guinevere's kidnapping by the knight Meleagant, a structure that bears a strong resemblance to the Celtic *aithed* or bride-abduction tale. The usual pattern of the *aithed* is for a married woman to be kidnapped by a stranger and rescued by her husband, although in the case of *Lancelot* it is Guinevere's lover rather than her husband who rescues her. An interesting aspect of this possible basis for the plot of Lancelot is that Meleagant's kingdom has striking similarities to a Celtic otherworld. Anyone who wishes to may enter Meleagant's kingdom, Lancelot is told, but they may not leave (Chrétien 213). Later, Lancelot frees all the inhabitants of the kingdom by winning his own freedom to leave (237).

Chrétien uses the same overall organization in several of his romances: the main character commits some fault against the principles of courtly love or chivalry and must undergo a series of adventures in which he eventually understands his error and redeems himself. In *Lancelot*, this sequence begins when Lancelot hesitates for two steps before humiliating himself by riding in a cart on the way to rescue Guinevere. She blames him for putting his reputation above his duty to her, even for a moment. In the remainder of the story, Lancelot must redeem himself by consistently putting his duty to serve women above any personal desire for glory and recognition; in a tournament, Guinevere requires him to humiliate himself for her by performing badly.

Chrétien's romances took the Arthurian legends along different lines than they had taken in previous versions. Building on hints in Geoffrey of Monmouth and Wace's chronicles, Chrétien makes the world of Arthur one of courtly love, romantic adventures, and chivalry. The adventures of the various knights radiate out from the center and example formed by Arthur's romance court. Unlike previous writers, his treatment of the Arthurian world focuses not on conquest and martial prowess, but on love. The delicate balance between the requirements of courtly love and those of chivalry is a frequent issue: in *Erec et Enide*, we are given a knight who neglects his public duties in favor of spending time with his wife; in *Yvain*, the knight pursues adventure to such an extent that he neglects his wife; and of course, in *Lancelot*, the most famous of all knights is at the beck and call of Guinevere.

Chrétien's role in the development of the Arthurian legends on the continent is significant. Not only did he transform the legends from the material of history and chronicle to that of fictional romance narrative, his treatment of the story also introduces elements that are swiftly incorporated into the body of Arthurian tales. While Guinevere's infidelity to Arthur had been an element in earlier Arthurian material, in his *Lancelot* Chrétien introduces Lancelot as Guinevere's lover and develops Lancelot's character, forming the base for much elaboration of the topic by later authors. Chrétien also innovates in *Perceval* by developing a story centered on the Grail, though it is not yet the Holy Grail, as at this point it is simply a mysterious vessel associated with the wasteland and the Fisher King, with decidedly Celtic overtones.

The Vulgate Cycle

Another significant group of Arthurian romances is the set of French prose narratives collectively called either the "Vulgate Cycle," because they are written in French (the vernacular, or vulgar, language), the *Prose Lancelot*, or the Lancelot-Grail cycle. The cycle comprises *Lancelot*, *La Queste del Saint Graal*, and *La Mort le Roi Artu*.

La Queste del Saint Graal (*The Quest of the Holy Grail*), ca. 1190, is perhaps the most interesting of the three prose romances in this cycle. Here we have a significant development of the Grail story, as the mysterious Grail becomes the *Saint Graal*, the Holy Grail. Here the author of the *Queste* draws on a romance of Robert de Boron, who identifies the Grail as the dish used by Jesus at the Last Supper and connects this dish (not a cup) with England and Glastonbury via Joseph of Arimathea, who is traditionally held to have brought it with him as the first apostle to Britain (Matarasso 11–12). The *Queste* is notable as well for being a consistent and full-fledged allegory of the spiritual life; the Grail becomes a "symbol of divine grace" (16), and Lancelot's adultery is incorporated into the story not as an admirable expression of courtly love, but as a sin of which he must repent and which will prevent him from achieving the Grail quest.

In addition to adding a Christian dimension to the Grail story, the author of the *Queste* also develops some of the characters of the Arthurian legendarium in interesting ways. Most notably, he invents Galahad, a character not previously found in any of the earlier Grail or Lancelot stories (Kennedy 209). Perceval remains an important figure, but becomes secondary to Galahad as the epitome of knighthood. Gawain, who in the earlier Arthurian stories is shown as an ideal knight, is given a subtle revision here. The *Queste* shows that he "epitomizes the courtly ideal ... and then sets out to show their bankruptcy in the spiritual order" (Matarasso 19). Gawain not only fails on the Quest for the Grail, he ends up bogged down in violence and killing his own companions.

Williams' fascination with the Grail (or as he called it, the Graal) is rooted in the French sources, particularly the various parts of the Vulgate Cycle, but also the romances of Chrétien de Troyes. Lewis addresses Chrétien in *The Allegory of Love*, as well.

Middle English sources

Laȝamon's Brut

The Arthurian legends had a roundabout route into the vernacular in England: passing from Britain to Wales and then to France before returning to England. Laȝamon's *Brut* is the first appearance of the Arthur story in English. This massive sixteen-thousand-line poem, composed sometime between 1189 and 1204, tells the history of Britain, emphasizing "the noble deeds of Englishmen ... what they were named and whence they came" (qtd. in Bennett and Gray, 70).

Laȝamon is for the most part translating and expanding Wace's *Roman de Brut*, but in so doing he deliberately avoids adopting Wace's French style wholesale. While he does include some use of rhyme—a French literary technique—it is incorporated into an overall style that is very English. The *Brut* is written in alliterative verse in the style of earlier Anglo-Saxon (Old English) heroic poetry: "Almost half of his verses follow the Old English pattern of two half-lines with two stresses in each, linked by alliteration, and with a varying number of unstressed syllables" (Bennett and Gray 71). This Anglo-Saxon emphasis can be seen in Laȝamon's handling of the subject as well; whereas Wace, like Geoffrey of Monmouth, suggests the courtly tradition that would fully develop in the French Arthurian literature, Laȝamon's Arthur is more violent, hearkening back to the Celtic war leader rather than the French king.

Laȝamon adds several elements to the Arthurian legendarium, including some "fantastic" elements: for instance, at Arthur's birth he is given gifts by the elves, and his sword "Calibeorne" is elf-made (86). He also adds detail to the downfall of Arthur, including a grim prophetic dream and—most notably—a prophecy by Merlin that Arthur will come again (87–88).

The Stanzaic Morte

In the stanzaic *Le Morte Arthur*, c. 1350, we see an intersection between French and English literary and narrative traditions for the Arthurian stories. The author draws on the *Mort Artu* from the Vulgate Cycle, but compresses the story significantly (Stone 169) and converts the prose into poetry. The form is eight-line rhyming stanzas, which owes a great deal to French literary style and to English and Scottish balladry (170), but the poet makes effective use of alliteration as well.

The poet strips away or naturalizes many of the fantastic elements of the Arthurian story; for instance, three women do arrive in a boat to retrieve the wounded Arthur, but they take him for a conventional burial, not for safekeeping on the Isle of Avalon. Because of this approach, the Stanzaic *Morte* provides a glimpse of which of the fantastic elements have by this time become essential (or nearly essential) parts of the legendarium, to be included even by a more realistic-minded poet. For instance, the poet includes the scene of Arthur instructing Bedivere to throw Excalibur into the lake, with Bedivere hesitating to do so (and lying about it) on the first two attempts. On the third occasion:

> He thought it best to obey the King,
> And so with the sword he went
> And flung it far, and closely watched
> To see what sign would be sent.
> Out of the water there came a hand
> Which brandished it as if to break it;
> Then gleam-like glided away. (Stanzaic *Le Morte Arthur* 3486–93)

The narrative of the Stanzaic *Morte* picks up after the Grail quest is finished and focuses on Lancelot and Guinevere, the consequences of their adultery, the blood-feud that erupts between Lancelot and Gawain, and the treason of Mordred. Most readers would have been familiar with the larger context of the events that are retold here, but even for those who were not, the poem would work well on its own: the fast-paced narrative, with its emphasis on relationships gone wrong, has much of the feeling, as well as adopting some of the literary form, of a ballad. The result is a dramatic, vivid rendition of the Arthurian tragedy.

The Alliterative Morte

Alliterative poetry had been a part of the Anglo-Saxon (Old English) literary tradition, but as Latin and French took precedence after the Norman Conquest, the old alliterative tradition was left to popular and oral channels; Laȝamon's *Brut* marks the end of the original period of alliterative poetry in English. In the fourteenth century, however, an "alliterative revival" brought this tradition back into written literature, but with further development. The long narrative poem *Morte Arthure* is one of the fruits of this revival. Composed by an unknown author around 1400, it begins with Arthur's continental campaign against the Emperor Lucius, before moving to the now-familiar events of his downfall at home through the treachery of Mordred. Lancelot, however, does not play a part in this story, though Guinevere does, since Mordred marries her as part of his coup.

On New Year's Day, a messenger comes from Lucius, the emperor of Rome, declaring that Arthur owes homage and tribute to Rome. Arthur refuses and declares he will fight Lucius, heading off to war while leaving Mordred in charge of the kingdom. Along the way, Arthur defeats a giant at Mont St. Michel, before defeating Lucius in France and then marching onward, laying waste to the countryside as he goes. The Pope sends a message for him to come to Rome to be crowned king, which prompts one of the most notable elements of the poem: Arthur's dream that he is cast down on the Wheel of Fortune and will be crushed, which his philosophers interpret to mean that he has achieved his highest fortune and will achieve no more; they advise him to repent of his deeds and ask for mercy. This image of the Wheel of Fortune is an important one in medieval art and literature; it is a recurring reminder to princes that they do not hold their power and wealth through their own merit and that the Wheel may turn and bring them low just as it raises up others.

The *Morte* concludes with Arthur returning to England to fight Mordred, whom he learns has taken over the kingdom and married Guinevere (here called Waynor). Gawain is killed, Guinevere becomes a nun in fear of what will happen to her, and Arthur kills Mordred in battle and is mortally wounded by him. Arthur is brought to Glastonbury, to the isle of Avalon, where he realizes that he will not recover; he bequeaths the crown to Constantine, his cousin, and orders that Mordred's children be killed, before he dies and is buried at Glastonbury.

The Alliterative *Morte* hearkens back to Anglo-Saxon literature in its tone as well as its verse form; it has a sprawling, almost epic feeling to it. However, this is still very much a poem in the tradition of Arthurian romance, and Arthur as a character is considerably developed: "Arthur's role in the poem is much fuller, and more dynamic, than in any earlier Arthurian text. He is presented as one of the Nine Worthies, a world conqueror on the scale of an Alexander, closer to a Beowulf than to the courtly king of *Libeaus* or *Gawain*; and his humour is like the grim humour of *Maldon*" (Bennett and Gray 185).

Sir Gawain and the Green Knight

The most notable of the poems of the alliterative revival is *Sir Gawain and the Green Knight*. Indeed, *Sir Gawain and the Green Knight* is not merely the most notable of this particular revival, but the finest flower of medieval romance in general, and one of the gems of English literature:

> the gulf between the poem and its congeners is as great as that between the novels that Jane Austen read and her own. Its author has mastered all the poetic techniques and narrative devices of his pre-decessors, but he has also taken elements from various genres of romance, including chronicle, and welded them to form a vehicle for new values and more subtle suggestions. (Bennett and Gray 202)

It is worth taking a detailed look at this important poem.

Sir Gawain and the Green Knight comes from a single manuscript dating from 1400; the poem itself is usually considered to have been written in the last quarter of the fourteenth century. The author is unknown; he is likely to have also written the poems *Pearl*, *Purity*, and *Patience*, which appear in the same manuscript, but this is not conclusive. The dialect of the poem is from the Northwest Midlands, and although the poet was a contemporary of Chaucer, his English is very different from Chaucer's, and for non-specialists today is impossible to read except in translation. The poem consists of passages of alliterative verse followed by a "bob and wheel": a rhymed quatrain attached to the alliterative section by a truncated rhyming line. The need for translation poses a particular challenge for appreciating the poem, because of the complexity of its meter and form combined with the use of specialist vocabulary, especially in the hunting scenes, and the Gawain-poet's brilliant grasp of both sound and shades of meaning in his word choice. He is a master of both dialogue and description.

The poem is divided into four parts, or "fits." In the first, we are introduced to Arthur's court in full celebratory swing at Christmastide. They are seated for a feast on New Year's Day when a strange knight rides in: a giant, green-haired and green-garbed, carrying a green axe, riding a green horse. He challenges one of the knights there present to a "game": an exchange of blows, in which he will take the first hit. Gawain accepts the challenge and lops off the knight's head, at which point the now-headless giant retrieves his severed head and reminds Gawain that he is now pledged to come to the Green Chapel in a year and a day to take his turn.

In the second fit, Gawain tarries at the court until All Saints' Day (1 November) before setting off to find the Green Chapel. If the first fit highlighted the otherworldliness of the story, this one brings into focus Gawain's faith and his particular devotion to Mary, the Mother of God. The scene in which he is armed for his send-off includes a long passage describing the device painted on his shield: the pentangle, a "bytoknyng of trawth" ("a token of fidelity"; *Sir Gawain* 626) that indicates Gawain's virtues and Christian faith, centered on the five wounds of Christ on the cross. Furthermore, the poet notes that Gawain has an image of Mary painted inside his shield to bolster his courage. After wandering in the wilderness for weeks, on Christmas Eve Gawain prays that he will be guided to a house where he can hear Mass on Christmas Day. With that in mind, he prays his "pater and ave / and crede" (Pater Noster, or Lord's Prayer; Ave Maria, or Hail Mary; and the Apostles' Creed; 757–58). He then comes across a great castle where he is welcomed with abundant hospitality. The host, when he learns of Gawain's errand, tells him that he can lead him to the Green Chapel, and so Gawain can stay and enjoy himself until New Year's Day. What's more, he makes a pact: Gawain will stay in the castle and enjoy himself while his host goes hunting; at the end of each day, they will swap what they have gained.

The third fit juxtaposes Gawain's activities in the castle with the host's hunting. Each morning, the lady of the house visits Gawain while he is still lying in bed and attempts to draw him into declaring his love for her. (Readers familiar with the Lancelot-Guinevere element of the Arthurian stories would be well aware that such a declaration would not be innocent.) Here we see the tension of courtly love and Christian morality put front and center. As a chivalrous knight, Gawain is bound to oblige the lady; yet as a Christian, it would be a mortal sin to do so. During the three days of the game, he attempts to hold the lady at bay without an outright refusal, which would offend her; thus, on the first two days, his "winning" is a kiss, given in exchange for the spoils of the hunt. The hunting scenes are described vividly and effectively and provide a thematic counterpoint to the testing of Gawain. Finally, on the third day of the game, Gawain is forced to rebuff the lady more strongly, and in turn she presses on him a gift of a ring, which he refuses, and then a girdle (or belt), which again he refuses, until she reveals that it offers magical protection against any blow. He accepts—but then does not own up to this "winning" in the final exchange with his host.

The fourth fit finds Gawain being taken to the Green Chapel, where he encounters the Green Knight and bares his neck to the blow. He flinches as the knight lifts the axe, for which the knight reproaches him, but then holds still as the knight swings a second time—but stops before striking. On the third occasion, the Green Knight finishes the blow, but in such a way that he only nicks the skin on Gawain's neck. At that point, with the game completed, the Green Knight reveals that he is the same as the host—and that the three blows were for the three exchanges of winnings, with the nick on the third blow from Gawain's withholding of the girdle. As it happens, the lady was part of the host's plan to test Gawain, who has thus proved to be a faultless knight, except for a certain lack of loyalty. However, the host notes, it is "for ye lufed your lyf—the lasse I yow blame" ("you loved your own life; so I blame you less"; 2368). Gawain is terribly embarrassed and declares that he will now wear the girdle as a token of his cowardice. He returns to Arthur's court, where he is welcomed back with great joy and where the company adopts a green sash in imitation of him. The tone of this final passage is gently humorous—Gawain is just as excitable in his newfound humility as he was in his readiness to take the Green Knight's challenge—but also warm. The poem has come to a genuine resolution of the tension between the courtly and Christian ideal by firmly placing the courtly ideal in service to Christian morality, not on the same level.

Sir Gawain and the Green Knight is thus both deeply Christian and imbued with a deep sense of the fantastic, of Faërie; it presents the height of the culture of courtly love, but does not, as other writers had done, ignore or brush aside the tensions between the worldliness of chivalry and the moral claims of Christianity. Thanks to the skill of the Gawain-poet, these different elements appear in a work that is both morally and imaginatively integrated: "It is this fusion of chivalry, magic, and a firmly held orthodoxy that gives Gawain its special flavour" (Bennett and Gray 213). The poem ends with a prayer that comes naturally from the entire ethos of the poem: "Now that bere the croun of thorne, / He bryng uus to his blysse! AMEN" ("Now let our Lord, thorn-crowned, / bring us to perfect peace. AMEN"; 2329–30).

Williams mentions Wace and Laȝamon in "The Figure of Arthur," but seems more interested in the French than the English versions of the Arthurian story. In contrast, the Middle English poems are significant sources for Tolkien's Arthurian work—most notably in that he translated *Sir Gawain and the Green Knight*. Christopher Tolkien's supporting materials for his father's unfinished *The Fall of Arthur* shows the importance of Laȝamon, the Stanzaic *Morte*, and the Alliterative *Morte* as sources for that poem.

Thomas Malory

Our examination of major medieval Arthurian sources comes to its natural conclusion with Sir Thomas Malory, who is the single most influential of all the medieval writers of Arthurian literature. He draws on a range of earlier Arthurian romances, rendering them into prose while also re-shaping and developing the story as he goes.

Malory's Arthurian tales mark the transition from the medieval to the early modern period, in part by their language—Malory can be read in the original with relative ease and needs at most to be modernized in spelling and punctuation, not translated—but mainly because this is the first time that Arthurian romances appear in print. Working from a now-lost original manuscript, the printer William Caxton produced the book known as the *Morte Darthur* (or *Le Morte D'Arthur*) in 1485: as a single, massive tome with twenty-one "books," each sub-divided into chapters. From that date until 1934, Caxton's edition was the only known version of Malory's text. However, in 1934 a new manuscript, substantially different from Caxton's, was discovered. Known as the "Winchester Manuscript," this version of Malory's work presents a significantly different version of the material, as well as more information about Malory himself. It is not an original manuscript, but the material evidence indicates that it is a very early copy, and the textual evidence shows that it is not the same as that used by Caxton to prepare his printed edition.

From 1934 to 1947, scholars knew of the existence of the Winchester manuscript, but it was not widely available for study until Eugène Vinaver published his complete edition. In titling the edition the *Works of Malory*, Vinaver indicates his view that Malory's authorial intent was to write individual stories and that the assembly of them into one book is Caxton's editorial intervention. It is possible that the revisions may have been Malory's own, done in collaboration with Caxton or on his own, resulting in the now-lost manuscript that Caxton used for his print edition, but this seems unlikely, not just because the book was not published until after Malory's death, but also because Caxton's division into chapters does not always follow the logic of the narrative, as we would expect the author's divisions to do (Chambers 185).

The Winchester manuscript is divided into eight tales, each based primarily on a single source and ending with an author's *explicit*. However, considering the book as an assortment of tales rather than as a unified work has its difficulties. It is manifestly not as separate as, say, Chrétien de Troyes' various Arthurian tales. Malory himself called the entire production *The Whole Book of King Arthur and of His Noble Knights of the Round Table*, which suggests a certain unity, and taken as a whole, it tells one story, albeit with certain discrepancies and lapses of continuity. We start with Arthur's birth, work our way through the doings of the knights of the Round Table, and end with the tragic fall of the kingdom.

Whatever one's views on Malory's intention for the whole book, however, the structure of the sections in the Winchester manuscript is useful in considering Malory's use of sources.

The first of the eight tales in the Winchester manuscript is *The Tale of King Arthur*, comprising Books 1–4 in Caxton's version, which includes the story of Arthur's begetting and early rule as king and includes Merlin in a prominent role. Here, Malory's French source is primarily the prose romance *La Suite du Merlin*, from a cycle known as *Le Roman du Graal* (Vinaver 729).

It is followed by *The Tale of the Noble King Arthur and the Emperor Lucius* (Book 5 in Caxton), which the text of the Winchester manuscript shows to be drawn from the Alliterative *Morte*. Malory follows his source closely, even reproducing many alliterating lines, but still makes important changes. He softens the character of Arthur; he stresses the character of Lancelot whenever possible, though he leaves out any hint of the courtly role Lancelot will play later; and he radically alters the ending, choosing instead a successful ending for Arthur's wars that makes it possible for him to have further adventures. Within the context of the tale itself, there is no longer the tension between Arthur's glory as a conquering king and his immediate downfall; the tale ends on a rising note, with Malory reserving the tragic aspects of the tale to work into later events.

Next are various episodes of Arthurian adventures: *A Noble Tale of Sir Launcelot du Lake* (Book 6), for which Malory draws on the French *Prose Lancelot* (744); *The Tale of Sir Gareth of Orkney* (Book 7), for which no immediate source has been identified; and *The Book of Sir Tristram de Lyones* (Books 8–12), which is based on the French *Prose Tristan* (749). *The Quest of the Holy Grail* is, as the title suggests, a version of the French *Queste del Saint Graal*, from the Vulgate Cycle. It comprises Books 13–17 of Caxton's edition.

The final two tales, containing much of what captured the imagination of later writers, are *The Book of Sir Launcelot and Queen Guinevere* (Books 18–19) and *The Tale of the Death of King Arthur*, which comprises Books 20 and 21 in Caxton's edition. For both of these, Malory drew heavily on the French *Mort Artu* and the English stanzaic *Le Morte Arthur*.

Throughout his work, Malory tends to compress his sources, or he is selective in his use of episodes from longer works, though he not infrequently adds details of his own as well. He adapts as needed to make his stories fit into the larger arc, for instance by changing the ending of the Alliterative *Morte*, and to bring about a more consistent characterization, for instance in depicting Lancelot more favorably than some of his sources did. As a general rule, Malory de-emphasizes the "interlacing" effect (*entrelacement*) that is so characteristic of the French stories, but he does not remove it entirely.

The scene of Arthur and the giant at Mont St. Michel illustrates both Malory's adaptation of his sources and Caxton's editorial work on Malory's text. In the Alliterative *Morte*, the poet leads up to the confrontation with a full description of Arthur arming himself, followed by about ten lines of the beautiful scenery that he and his companions pass through on the way to the mountain; once they arrive and confront the giant, the poet gives about thirty lines of graphic description of the giant before starting the battle. Malory's treatment of the same scene leads him to condense the arming of Arthur slightly, but not much, to reduce the landscape description to "And than they trotted on stylly togedir over a blythe contray full of many myrry byrdis" (Malory 120), and to compress the description of the giant to about six lines of text. Caxton cuts down the scene even more, removing Malory's one line about the scenery and reducing the entire description of the giant to calling him a "glutton" (Malory, *Le Morte D'Arthur* 175).

Overall, Caxton's edition uses a more modern style, particularly in *The Tale of King Arthur and the Emperor Lucius*, where Caxton has smoothed out the alliteration considerably; the corresponding section in the Winchester manuscript is significantly longer and is heavily alliterated, corresponding with Malory's close use of the Alliterative *Morte* as a source. Certainly, the now-familiar title drawn from Caxton's colophon is not representative of the whole: *Le Morte Darthur* refers only to *The Death of Arthur*, the eighth of Malory's tales.

From a literary-historical perspective looking forward at Malory's later influence, Caxton's edition is perhaps more significant, because it is that version that fired the imagination of so many authors following. However, the differences between the two editions are overshadowed by the fact that both display Malory's work in the same basic text, albeit in slightly different forms. The *Morte Darthur* is the single work (however organized) that brings together the largest range of Arthurian stories and characters, and as such, it has had more impact on the literary scene than any other individual Arthurian work.

Lewis engages directly with Malory, most notably contributing an essay on the "English Prose Morte" to the edited volume *Essays on Malory* in 1963. This essay is reprinted in *Image and Imagination*, along with several other reviews of books related to Middle English Arthurian texts. With regard to Tolkien, Verlyn Flieger argues convincingly that "the Winchester Manuscript was the model for the book Sam Gamgee conjures in the conversation about stories on the Stairs of Cirith Ungol" (Flieger 49).

Conclusion

The Arthurian tradition is a living one, which not only provided material for medieval writers and poets, but continues to inspire authors to the present day. The earlier texts are not mere relics of the past, but the productions of authors who, like modern-day authors, felt the need to retell an important story in their own way.

Appreciating the way that the medieval authors worked with, drew on, expanded, revised, and adapted the Arthurian legends, changing both form and content, focusing and expanding as they wished, will help guard against a narrow "source-hunting" or "influence-hunting" approach to the Inklings and King Arthur, while also helping readers to appreciate how much connection there is between these sources and the Inklings' work. Williams was a voracious reader and avid amateur scholar of the Arthurian legends; Lewis and Tolkien were professional academics specializing in medieval literature. It is difficult to overstate the depth of knowledge of, and familiarity with, the medieval texts that Lewis and Tolkien, in particular, had. This recognition, combined with an awareness of the complexity and depth of the Arthurian legendarium itself, should encourage the reader and scholar to expect complexity, subtlety, and depth.

Works Cited

Alliterative *Morte Arthure*. Trans. Valerie Krishna. Wilhelm 491–527.

Bennett, J. A. W., and Douglas Gray. *The Oxford History of English Literature: Middle English Literature: 1100–1400*. Oxford: Clarendon Press, 1986. Print.

Chambers, E. K. *The Oxford History of English Literature: English Literature at the Close of the Middle Ages*. Oxford: Clarendon Press, 1945. Print.

Chrétien de Troyes. *Arthurian Romances, including Perceval*. Trans. D. D. R. Owen. London: J.M. Dent & Sons (Everyman), 1987. Print.

Dunbar, Helen. "Arthur and Merlin in Early Welsh Literature." *A Companion to Arthurian Literature*. Ed. Helen Fulton. Chichester, West Sussex: Wiley-Blackwell, 2012. Print.

Flieger, Verlyn, ed. *Green Suns and Faerie: Essays on Tolkien*. Kent State UP, 2012. Print.

Fulton, Helen. "History and Myth: Geoffrey of Monmouth's *Historia Regnum Britanniae*. *A Companion to Arthurian Literature*. Ed. Helen Fulton. Chichester, West Sussex: Wiley-Blackwell, 2012. 45–46. Print.

Geoffrey of Monmouth. *The History of the Kings of Britain*. Trans. Lewis Thorpe. NY: Penguin, 1966. Print.

——. *Vita Merlini*. Trans. Basil Clarke. Cardiff, U of Wales P, 1973. Print.

Gildas. *The Works of Gildas. Old English Chronicles*. Ed. J. A. Giles. London: George Bell and Sons, 1901. 293–380. Print.

Kennedy, Edward Donald. "The Grail and French Arthurian Romance." Wilhelm 202–17.

Layamon. *Layamon's Arthur: The Arthurian Section of Layamon's* Brut *(lines 9229–14297)*. Ed. and trans. W. R. J. Barron and S. C. Weinberg. Essex: Longman Group UK Limited, 1989. Print.

Matarasso, P. M. Introduction. *The Quest of the Holy Grail*. Trans. P. M. Matarasso. Harmondsworth, Middlesex: Penguin, 1969. 11–12. Print.

The Mabinogion. Trans. Jeffrey Gantz. NY: Penguin, 1976. Print.

Malory, Sir Thomas. *Le Morte D'Arthur*. Vols. 1 and 2. Ed. Janet Cowen. NY: Penguin, 1969. Print.

——. *Works*. Ed. Eugène Vinaver. 1947. 2nd ed. London: Oxford UP, 1971. Print.

Nennius. *Nennius' History of the Britons. Old English Chronicles*. Ed. J. A. Giles. London: George Bell and Sons, 1901. 381–416. Print.

The Quest of the Holy Grail. Trans. P. M. Matarasso. Harmondsworth, Middlesex: Penguin, 1969. Print.

Sir Gawain and the Green Knight. Trans. Simon Armitage. NY: Norton, 2007. Print.

Stanzaic Le Morte Arthur, King Arthur's Death: Alliterative Morte Arthure and Stanzaic Le Morte Arthur. NY: Penguin, 1988. Print.

Stone, Brian. Introduction. *Stanzaic Le Morte Arthur*. King Arthur's Death. Trans. Brian Stone. NY: Penguin, 1988. Print.

Thorpe, Lewis. Introduction. *The History of the Kings of Britain.* By Geoffrey of Monmouth. Trans. Lewis Thorpe. NY: Penguin, 1966. 17–19. Print.

Tolkien, J. R. R. "Beowulf and the Critics." *Beowulf and the Critics*. Tolkien. Ed. Michael Drout. Tempe, AZ: Arizona Center for Medieval and Renaissance Studies, 2002. Print.

Wace. *Roman de Brut* (excerpts). Wilhelm 96–108.

Wilhelm, James J. "Arthur in the Latin Chronicles." Wilhelm 5.

—, ed. *The Romance of Arthur: An Anthology of Medieval Texts in Translation*. NY: Garland Publishing, 1994. Print.

Vinaver, Eugène. Notes. *Works.* By Thomas Malory. Ed. Eugène Vinaver. 1947. 2nd ed. London: Oxford UP, 1971. Print.

3

Mixed Metaphors and Hyperlinked Worlds:
A Study of Intertextuality in C. S. Lewis' Ransom Cycle

Brenton D. G. Dickieson

On a first encounter, a reader would not know how important the whole Arthurian world was to C. S. Lewis. A glance at my bookshelf suggests that Lewis' only immediately identifiable Arthurian story is *That Hideous Strength*. If, however, I consider unpublished pieces, his literary criticism, and literature evocative of Arthur, the shelf begins to fill out. In looking at the whole body of Lewis' work, including his Arthuriana, there is good reason to see his approach to writing in more fluid ways than the work of the solo genius drawing his inspiration from the unaffected images in his imagination (see Glyer 135–66). Few would deny that *The Chronicles of Narnia* are something new from the forge fire and that Lewis' work in second-generation science fiction, demonic epistolary fiction, and myth re-telling shows a great deal of originality; however, Lewis' most popular fiction demonstrates how indebted he is to the stories that have come before. C. S. Lewis is a deeply "intertextual" author—a writer who finds his inspiration in the characters, romances, myths, legends, and tropes of his favorite authors and brings them into his own fictional worlds. Indeed, C. S. Lewis was reflective about this process. In his 1963 essay "The Genesis of a Medieval Book," Lewis offers a theory of intertextuality that anticipates later critics.[1] The metaphors Lewis used, combined with subsequent theories of intertextuality, offer a framework for approaching his own intertextual habits—his instinct for drawing other texts into his own.

As Lewis is invested in intertextuality to such a great degree, I will focus on how the King Arthur tales, early and late, find their way into his work. First, I will briefly sketch Lewis' Arthuriana in four identifiable periods. I will then set a context for looking at Lewis' own critical consideration of intertextuality by placing

---

1   Cf. "collage" in Hollander 124. Hollander also links this metaphor to cubist painting (124) and to Hegel's "hieroglyph of a thought" (125).

his criticism in conversation with the work of Claude Lévi-Strauss, Gérard Genette, Harold Bloom, and John Hollander. From this conversation, I draw out a number of metaphors that are helpful in considering intertextuality, using contemporary culture to add depth to these images. When we consider the Ransom cycle as an experiment in intertextuality, Lewis' Arthurian turn in *That Hideous Strength* (1945) provides an opportunity to apply these critical metaphors to a text. As a case study, I will explore how Lewis draws the Arthurian-permeated speculative worlds of J. R. R. Tolkien (Númenor) and Charles Williams (Logres) into *That Hideous Strength*. I hope to demonstrate that Lewis' fiction does not merely quote from or allude to other texts, but draws together various fictional universes, linking them in evocative and suggestive ways within his own subcreated worlds. From this study, I propose that we can discern an approach to Lewisian intertextuality that can be applied to his project more broadly.

King Arthur Stories in Lewis' Writing

There are three identifiable periods in which Lewis' Arthurian adoration produces Arthurian work, and one more in which the grand Arthurian universe leaks into the literature he is working on.

Stage One: 1915–1925

The first Arthurian period was in Lewis' late teens. He discovered Malory while being tutored in preparation for Oxford entrance (Sayer 98–104). Some Arthurian imagery finds its way to his intertextually rich poetry of the era. *Spirits in Bondage* (1919), poems collected at the close of World War I, contains the best of his schooltime and wartime poetry. The poetry is filled with Greek, Irish, and Norse mythology, with echoes of Homer, Beowulf, the *Edda*, and the Matter of France. Faërie and the medieval world haunt *Spirits in Bondage*, and twice Arthur is evoked openly. The first is a Twilight of the Gods poem, "Victory," in which "Roland is dead, Cuchulain's crest is low" (l. 1). Helen and Iseult turn to dust, the fairy woods are empty, Tristan has abandoned the seas, and "Arthur sleeps far hence in Avalon" (8). Avalon is evoked elsewhere in "the mists apart" ("Irish Nocturne" 17) and more overtly as the "Isle of Apples" ("Death in Battle" 3) and "I dare not go / To dreaming Avalon" ("The Hills of Down" *CP* 229, ll. 7–8).

These references that bookend *Spirits in Bondage* match the *Götterdämmerung* tone of "Decadence," an unpublished poem of Lewis' from around Christmas 1916, when he was eighteen. Don W. King, curator of Lewis' poetic project, has posthumously published this most specifically Arthurian extant poem of the period. It begins:

> Oh Galahad! My Galahad!
> The world is old and very sad,
>   The world is old and gray with pain
> And all the ways thereof are bad ("Lost but Found" 181, ll. 1–4).

If King's date is correct, "Decadence" reflects not only the insatiable war that was consuming Europe and would soon vie for Lewis' future—captured in titles of poems with Arthurian romance references like

"Victory" and "Death in Battle"—but also a literary death that Lewis was mourning at the time: the death of Bleheris.

During Easter holidays in 1915, sixteen-year-old Lewis began calling his childhood friend Arthur Greeves by the gallant, religious-tinged name "Galahad" (*CL* 1:115). On 12 October 1916, Lewis wrote to Arthur-Galahad, saying that "As to Bleheris, he is dead and I shan't trouble his grave" (*CL* 1:232). This "Bleheris" is a reference to "The Quest of Bleheris," an Arthurian prose tale written in disciplined four-page chapters and sent to Arthur throughout Lewis' eighteenth year (1916).[2] The serial epic is intentionally constructed in archaic English, and it tells the tale of a young man adrift in his appointed social station who is then suddenly thrust into a real quest. Lewis finally buried "Bleheris"—a book that had been suffering for some time—after seventeen chapters. He promised Arthur-Galahad that he would write something soon, though he warned that he was "rather taken up with verse at present" (*CL* 1:232). *Spirits in Bondage* emerged out of the turn to verse, though none of the poems sustain a long-form narrative. Lewis' narrative poem *Dymer* (1926), written in the years following the war, has little explicitly Arthurian material, though it is evocative of medieval allegorical romances.

Stage Two: 1928–1935

Lewis' first Arthurian period resulted from his discovery of Malory and the other Arthurian authors in his teenage years; his second Arthurian period was coincidental with his relationship with J. R. R. Tolkien. Lewis' Arthurian works in this period are the incomplete verse narrative "Launcelot" (*NP* 93–101) and the academic volume *The Allegory of Love* (complete in 1935). *The Pilgrim's Regress* (1933) is Arthurian in flavor to the extent that it shares features of romance, allegorical imagery, and knightly valor with its urtext, Bunyan's *The Pilgrim's Progress*.

Because Lewis abandoned "Launcelot" early in its formation—it ends at line 296 in a moment of mounting suspense—it is difficult to know the extent of the narrative. What remains is a plot that builds upon Malory and Tennyson's characters, but with new elements to the quest (King, *Poet* 140–45). After a long delay and Guinever's anxious waiting for Launcelot, first Gawain and then Launcelot return, but they are changed. The most interesting aspect of the poem may be the promising exploration of post-traumatic stress disorder—or "shell shock"—though it is possible that it is not war specifically that causes the psychologically problematic trauma.[3]

The twentieth century introduced a golden age of Arthurian studies. While not lacking in critical reflection about the Arthuriad, previous generations were most important for their reworking of Arthurian romances and figures into their own art and literature. By the time *The Allegory of Love* was

---

2   The incomplete and unpublished MS. of "The Quest of Bleheris" is available at the Bodleian. MS. Eng. lett. c. 220/5. Secondary literature on "Bleheris" is thin: Downing, "The Dungeon of his Soul" 37–54; King, "*The Quest of Bleheris* as Poetic Prose" 36–40; Walsh, *Literary Legacy* 126–28; James, "Early Schooling" 51; Ward, *Planet Narnia* 19, 240; Sayer, *Jack* 110–11; Green and Hooper, *Lewis* 47.

3   See Charles Huttar's chapter 4, in which he notes that both Tolkien's incomplete *The Fall of Arthur* and Lewis' "Launcelot" have the Launcelot character in a break with Guinevere (p. 32 n. 62).

released in 1936, the academic conversation was underway,[4] and Lewis was at the beginning of a renewal in modern scholarship taking Spenser's *Faerie Queene* seriously.[5],[6] In addition to Spenser, *The Allegory of Love* considers Arthurian stories throughout, as it discusses medieval courtly love literature, including the works of Chrétien de Troyes, Thomas Usk, Malory, and the authors of the *Roman de la Rose* and *Sir Gawain and the Green Knight*.

Stage Three: 1936–1947

That second period of Arthurian-connected work of the late 1920s through the mid-1930s did not immediately produce definitively Arthurian fiction; it emerged out of Lewis' friendship with Arthur Greeves and his discovery of Malory, while the second period coincides with his friendship with Tolkien and his academic work in courtly love poetry. Lewis' third Arthurian period was connected with his friendship with Charles Williams, which began when *The Allegory of Love* was going to print in 1936, and with his discovery of the value of science fiction in telling worldview-laced stories.

Charles Williams first captured Lewis' imagination with his supernatural thriller, *The Place of the Lion*. Over the next decade, until Williams' death, Lewis became intimate with Williams' incomplete Arthuriad, specifically in the poetry of *Taliessin through Logres* (1938) and *The Region of the Summer Stars* (1944), in supernatural novels like *War in Heaven* (1930), and in didactic form in the unfinished *Arthurian Torso*—edited and published posthumously by Lewis himself, who provided a commentary to the difficult text.[7] I will discuss Williams' work on the Matter of Britain below, and its connection with *That Hideous Strength*, Lewis' most overtly Arthurian tale in print.

---

4   See, for example, Margaret J. C. Reid, *The Arthurian Legend: Comparison of Treatment in Modern and Mediæval Literature*, a 1938 publication of a doctoral thesis. E. K. Chambers, Arthur C. L. Brown, and R. S. Loomis had begun their work. In the late 1920s, Eugène Vinaver had started the Arthurian Society in Oxford and their publication, *Arthuriana*—its name was changed to *Medium Aevum* in 1948. Vinaver's edition of the Winchester Manuscript of *Morte d'Arthur* was not complete until 1947, but the Manuscript was discovered in 1934. This gap, Lewis said, left Malory scholars in great suspense for the thirteen year interval ("The 'Morte Darthur'" 103).

5   Pauline Parker notes in her 1960 study, *The Allegory of The Faerie Queene*, that "Numerous valuable books have been written on Spenser in the last thirty years, more it would appear than in the three preceding centuries" (1). Parker references Lewis' *AoL*.

6   Indeed, Lewis remained interested in Spenser's Arthurian allegory throughout his life. He devoted a full chapter of *The Allegory of Love* and a half chapter in his Oxford History of English Literature volume (1954) to *The Faerie Queene*. He also wrote essays on Spenser in 1931, 1954, 1961, and 1963, and used Spenser as a case study in both *The Discarded Image* and *Studies in Words*. In 1967, Alistair Fowler drew together and completed C. S. Lewis' Cambridge lectures on Spenser (*Spenser's Images of Life*).

7   Williams also wrote a number of Arthurian poems in the 1920s; Lewis does not take these into account in "Williams and the Arthuriad." I would argue that *The Chapel of the Thorn*, Williams' 1912 dramatic poem only recently published, is a kind of grail story, and thus in the spectrum of Arthurian tales. See *The Chapel of the Thorn*.

Stage Four: 1949–1954

This final period I have set aside from the other three because it does not produce specifically or identifiably Arthurian work. The period covers the publication of *English Literature in the Sixteenth Century* and *The Chronicles of Narnia*. Arthur and the Matter of Britain are considered throughout, as Lewis spent fifteen to twenty years studying sixteenth-century texts, many of which evoke courtly themes and Arthurian tales either implicitly or explicitly. Lewis describes how the rise of humanism and Protestantism in the sixteenth century transformed and reacted to the medieval worldview. King Arthur's court was in danger of imaginative death, but was rescued by authors like John Bale and John Leland, who painted Arthur in Protestant colors. There was space, then, for Spenser and Milton.

By 1949, a number of features coalesced for Lewis: his work in the sixteenth century generally and Spenser specifically, the editorial and commentary work on Williams' Arthuriad, a new reading of Malory's *Morte Darthur* with the release of Eugène Vinaver's production of the Winchester manuscript in 1947, a lifetime of reading tales about chivalry, and a struggle to work out a children's fairy tale. This context allows for a particular consideration of the Narnian chronicles, written between 1949 and 1953. Doubtless, they are tales of chivalry. At least three of them are structured like knight's quests, and the characters have opportunities to show knightly valor in each of the seven chronicles. All of them are royal tales (though not all occur in court) with elements of "'high style' diction reminiscent of Sir Thomas Malory" (Ward 4). Without going deeply into the tales, a few examples will highlight the Arthurian quality of Narnia.[8]

Chivalric themes of knightly behavior and speech occur throughout the Narnia chronicles. The high diction peaks at various points, particularly at the close of *The Lion, the Witch, and the Wardrobe* (1950), during the scenes in the Calormene court in *The Horse and His Boy* (1954), and in moments of pomp and circumstance. Peter, Edmund, Caspian, Rilian, and (probably) Tirian are knight-kings, like Arthur. The example of knights is held up throughout the chronicles by dwarfs and talking beasts, as well as humans. The pilgrims in *The Silver Chair* (1953) are not surprised to meet a Lady and a Knight upon the road, and the scoundrel Rabadash is held to a knight's standard when his case is weighed by King Lune: "you have proved yourself no knight, but a traitor, and one rather to be whipped by the hangman than to be suffered to cross swords with any person of honour" (*HHB* 164).

The Horse and His Boy is one of the quest tales that partakes of chivalric lore. Shasta is clearly the hero, yet the title notes Lewis' inversive humor. Since the horse, Bree, is a decorated war horse and a Narnian of honor, the title may also hint at the idea of Shasta as Bree's squire, a relationship evocative of Malory's tales. The hero Reepicheep, a member of the Most Noble Order of the Lion (along with the Pevensie kings), defines honor in chivalrous terms and even challenges the hapless Eustace—doubtless better at economics than swordplay—to a duel. Indeed, Reepicheep takes chivalry to such a degree that his chess game suffers when he sacrifices his knight or castle to save the queen, as a courtly mouse is bound to do

---

8   See also chapter 11 by Jon Hooper, pages 279–98, which explores Arthurian and quest imagery in the
     Narniad in great detail. [Editor's note]

(*VDT* 55). Though occasionally fierce, he was not unkind. When the bedragoned Eustace feels low because of his failure, Reepicheep stays with him, telling him that

> if he had Eustace at his own house in Narnia (it was really a hole not a house and the dragon's head, let alone his body, would not have fitted in) he could show him more than a hundred examples of emperors, kings, dukes, knights, poets, lovers, astronomers, philosophers, and magicians, who had fallen from prosperity into the most distressing circumstances, and of whom many had recovered and lived happily ever afterwards. (*VDT* 81–82)

No other quotation, perhaps, captures the breadth of the Narnian Arthurian narrative landscape better than this one. Reepicheep's impetuous chivalry can create trouble, as does the hasty honor of King Tirian and the unicorn Jewel in *The Last Battle* (1956). Moreover, Narnia is almost completely devoid of courtly love tales, with the exception of the parody of one at the Tashbaan court in *The Horse and His Boy*. In general, however, the moral universe of Narnia is ordered by chivalric honor—or at least as much of chivalry as Lewis' readers are sure to know.

Quest tales abound in the Chronicles. *The Magician's Nephew* (1955) is the least Arthurian of the chronicles; *The Voyage of the "Dawn Treader"* (1952) is the most influenced by the Matter of Britain. While the goal of the *Dawn Treader* is to search for lost kings, Sir Reepicheep is bound in his heart by a quest to the world's end. The quest is evocative of the search for the Holy Grail, especially when Reepicheep tosses away his superfluous sword at the end of the quest: it lands upright in the sea, a moment that evokes the bookends of King Arthur's career. Also in *The Voyage of the "Dawn Treader,"* Lucy is drawn into a task to save the Dufflepuds from their invisibility. As she flips through a magic book, she comes to a spell "for the refreshment of the spirit" (121). She reads the loveliest story she's ever encountered, but when tempted to reread it, she finds she is unable to go back to the first page. And when she tries to remember the story, it fades from page and memory: "And even this last page is going blank. This is a very queer book. How can I have forgotten? It was about a cup and a sword and a tree and a green hill, I know that much. But I can't remember and what shall I do?" (121). It is, perhaps, a grail story that she has forgotten—and perhaps the grail story that connects the Arthurian Hallows with the Golgotha of history and Aslan's How of Narnia.[9] These were the kinds of links that Lewis liked to make. At the beginning of *The Voyage of the "Dawn Treader,"* thinking back to the martial tale *Prince Caspian* (1951), the narrator says: "Consequently, when the Pevensie children had returned to Narnia last time for their second visit, it was (for the Narnians) as if King Arthur came back to Britain, as some people say he will. And I say the sooner the better" (15).

---

9   Green and Hooper (252) note "the plenteous riches of the Arthurian Cycle" in the table and the stone knife on Ramandu's island. They also add that Ramandu's kingdom is patterned after the Fisher King's castle. In reading a draft of this chapter, Charles Huttar noted that Walter Hooper records a conversation in which Lewis said that Aslan's "brightness and a sweet odour" found their source in medieval grail descriptions (*Past Watchful Dragons* 97).

Arthurian Critical Work

Across these four life stages, Lewis wrote essays and lectures on Arthurian-related topics throughout his life. *The Discarded Image*, published posthumously, is a collection of Lewis' "Prolegomena" lectures, which he gave almost yearly at Oxford between 1931–32 and his departure for Cambridge in 1954 (Hooper, "The Lectures of C. S. Lewis" 447–53). Arthur is one of the topics both in the prolegomena and in the medieval poetry that *The Discarded Image* introduces. There are several Arthuriana essays and reviews in *Image and Imagination*, written during World War II (125–36; 137–46) and in 1960–63 (217–22; 223–32; 248–76). Much of *Studies of Medieval and Renaissance Literature* references Arthur or focuses on Arthurian texts—typically written in the periods of WWII, 1954–56, and 1960–63—some of which I discuss below. "The Anthropological Approach" fits also into this latter period and tests a modern literary approach upon medieval texts, including some in the Arthuriad. Lewis also frequently used King Arthur, Arthurian literature, or the Arthurian world as examples in his popular essays.

There is, perhaps, a discernable pattern of Arthurian influence in Lewis' life: his reflection on the topic precedes the imaginative work that emerges from it. Lewis encounters Malory as a teenager and immediately begins trying to write an Arthurian tale (stage one). Lewis befriends Tolkien while he is working on a history of medieval love poetry, and Lewis again struggles to capture his own Arthurian story in narrative form (stage two). Lewis befriends Williams, writes critically about Williams' Arthuriad, and then writes his own explicitly Arthurian tale (stage three). With the death of Williams, Lewis' focused work on his OHEL volume, and the publication of Vinaver's *Morte D'Arthur* in 1947, Lewis creates a world very much patterned after the best of Arthurian romances (stage four). As there is a new concentration of Arthurian academic work in 1960–63, following his marriage and subsequent bereavement, it could be that we may have seen some further Arthurian work emerge in the mid-1960s, had he lived (cf. Green and Hooper 292–93).

Arthur in Lewis' Poetry?

What about Lewis' poetic project? While Arthur was an important feature of Lewis' creative development, he primarily draws from other wells in his poetry. Don King is right that "Merlin is absent in Lewis' poems" (King 140). While there are numerous references to the medieval worldview, his poetry has relatively few Arthurian hints. "The Nameless Isle" of the early 1930s has some parallels with the Mordred-Guinevere storyline in the Arthuriad, but only in that they share the characters of an intimate usurper and a resourceful Queen on the run. There are Arthurian references in poems like "Re-adjustment" and "Old Poets Remembered," as well as in some of his teenage poetry like "The Hills of Down," "Ballade of a Winter's Morning," and, at least in courtly evocation, "Sonnet: To Sir Philip Sidney." Instead, Lewis' poetic inspiration is really the first of all muses: The Greek world. Its mythology, legends, and themes are the single most consistent world that Lewis draws from. The odyssey or travelogue informs his fiction from *The Pilgrim's Regress* through the Ransom cycle, *The Great Divorce* (1945), the Narnian quest tales, and *Till We Have Faces* (1956).

Intertextuality

That C. S. Lewis is an intertextually rich author is beyond doubt. As Sørina Higgins discusses in chapter 1 above, any Arthurian tale will be intertextual in form, but Lewis both draws the Arthurian worlds into his own and also thinks critically about what he is doing as an intertextual writer. It is helpful, then, to look briefly at the critical conversation about intertextuality.

For an accessible introduction to theories about intertextuality, see Graham Allen, *Intertextuality*. The complex paths of "intertextuality" move from poststructuralist conversations and "The Death of the Author" (Julia Kristeva and Roland Barthes) through meaning–determined structuralist responses (Gérard Genette and Michael Riffaterre). There are also mediated positions, such as Harold Bloom's work, or reactionary positions like William Irwin's. Irwin, who wrote "Against Intertextuality," begins his critique with what he considers the problematic nature of the term's fluidity: "The term intertextuality was coined by Julia Kristeva in 1966, and since that time has come to have almost as many meanings as users, from those faithful to Kristeva's original vision to those who simply use it as a stylish way of talking about allusion and influence" (227). Certainly, "intertextual" is often used simply to indicate how an author or text uses other authors or texts. While Irwin criticizes the lack of precision of the term "intertextuality," it could be that the value of the term is demonstrated in its very elasticity: "intertextuality" is a term that draws varying conversations back to the question of textual relationships in literature.

Within this complex and diverse conversation, Gérard Genette attempted to bring terminological clarity through an approach to structuralism informed by the poststructuralist critique. Despite his neologistic tendencies, or perhaps because of them, Genette was able to create a functional narratological taxonomy, especially in the conversation on intertextuality. In his 1964 essay, "Structuralism and Literary Criticism," Genette expands on the "now classic *La Pensée sauvage*," in which "Claude Lévi-Strauss defines mythical thought as 'a kind of intellectual bricolage'" (*Figures* 3; see esp. Lévi-Strauss 16–33). Lévi-Strauss' image of *bricoleur* blends two different French images, as his terms so often do, borrowing from the world of visual arts and capturing the figure of the "odd-job man" for whom there is no precise English term. A *bricoleur*/artist engages in the project of creating a new work of art by using bits and pieces of previous works. The *bricoleur*/odd-job man uses any tool at hand to do a particular job. In both cases, the *bricoleur* uses what is left over, what is lying around, to create. Literature, Genette says, is the "oddments left over" (*Figures* 5).

This image of bricolage was foundational for structuralist and poststructuralist conversations about literature in the 1960s. Genette later refined it in a book named after another intertextual metaphor, *Palimpsests*, evoking the image of the washed and reused manuscript that betrays two or more generations of text. Adding to the metaphors of *bricoleur* and palimpsest, Genette borrows the metaphor of pastiche to explore stylistic imitation among the playful genres ("régime ludique"). The opposite of pastiche in relation to the text it is imitating is the parody, which inverts and degrades the urtext (*Palimpsests* 16, 98–105, 397). Thinking of Genette's metaphorical exploration of intertextuality, I argue that C. S. Lewis is a palimpsestuous[10] author, a literary *bricoleur*, an odd-job man—not just in particular books, but in his entire project of building speculative universes.

Lewis as Literary Critic

C. S. Lewis was one of a few twentieth-century popular authors who were literary critics in their own right. Though he had already published three books, Lewis was a relatively unknown author when his first critical monograph was published in 1936. *The Allegory of Love* is a history of ideas, exploring medieval allegorical love poetry and setting out themes that Lewis would explore throughout his career, including the Arthurian tradition. *The Allegory of Love* contains a nascent theory of the development of speculative fiction, in some ways predicting and paralleling Erich Auerbach's great work, *Mimesis* (1946). Throughout his career as a critic, Lewis produced dozens of essays and several books, often with metacritical or theoretical implications.

Lewis' essay "The Genesis of a Medieval Book" (1963) anticipates Claude Lévi-Strauss's metaphor of bricolage by presenting a working theory of intertextuality. In the first place, while discussing Laȝamon's *Brut*, Lewis attempts to deconstruct the post-Enlightenment idea of the individual author, the sole poetic genius. He admits that although we do not have Laȝamon's manuscripts of Wace and do not know what other sources Laȝamon used nor in what ways, and although this is discouraging to academic investigators, yet the very inability to tie down authorial elements with precision is itself educational. There is no one authorial voice controlling all the material, and that is part of the point. Being forced to leave our post-romantic ideas of authorship behind compels us to examine Middle English literature from within its own cultural perspective instead of from outside ("Genesis" 22, 36). While Lewis is dealing specifically with the complex near-far relationship of the medieval writer and his sources,[11] and he is implicitly critiquing the "cult of originality," his argument may have further implications. In *A Map of Misreading* (1975), Bloom developed the idea of the belated poet as "misreader" of the text rather than the poet as autonomous generator of art. In this way, Lewis' ideas rhyme with Bloom's when he says that medieval poets "are sometimes most indebted to the originals where they most improve them" ("Genesis" 37). Therefore, "… we might equally well call our medieval authors the most unoriginal or the most original of men. They are so unoriginal that they hardly ever attempt to write anything unless someone has written it before" (37).

Practically speaking, Lewis argues (and Bloom agrees) that the object of critical attention should be texts, not authors; the "Author-Book unit" does not work for medieval texts ("Genesis" 38). Lewis attempts a number of metaphors to capture this reality. Lewis moves beyond allusion to use the vocabulary

---

10   Phillippe Lejeune (not Gérard Genette) created this neologistic adjective (*Palimpsests* ix).

11   Note that, when speaking precisely, Lewis makes a distinction between "source" and "influence": "A Source gives us things to write about; an Influence prompts us to write in a certain way. Homer is a Source to Lydgate, but Homer was an Influence on Arnold when he wrote *Sohrab* and *Rustum*. Firdausi's *Shah Nameh* was Arnold's Source, but not an Influence on that poem. Malory was both a Source and an Influence in Tennyson's *Morte d'Arthur*; elsewhere in the *Idylls* a Source but perhaps hardly an Influence" ("Literary Impact" 133).

of "echo" (34), a relatively common term I explore below. The images of a "commune" or the story of a painter touching up or completing another's work are evocative (38). Ultimately, though, Lewis lands on the metaphor of a cathedral:

> A cathedral often contains Saxon, Norman, Early English and Perpendicular work. The effect of the whole may be deeply satisfying. Yet we have no one artist to thank for it. None of the successive architects foresaw or intended it .... It is the work of men, though not of a man. We may find it helpful to regard some medieval literature as we regard such cathedrals. Indeed the books may be in one way easier to accept than the buildings. Each reviser may improve or correct (and of course misunderstand) his predecessor (39).

A cathedral captures the intertextual project in the way that bricolage does: an architect/artist/writer uses what is previously there—the oddments left over—to create his or her work of art. The roles of architect and *bricoleur* are slightly different in the degree of continuity with previous work, but we can see how Lewis and Lévi-Strauss are trying to capture the same idea.

Lewis wrote "The Genesis of a Medieval Book" near the end of his life, in 1963; it is thus roughly contemporary with Claude Lévi-Strauss's metaphor of bricolage.[12] However, in a much earlier *Times Literary Supplement* review of—perhaps more than coincidentally—Vinaver's *Morte D'Arthur* in 1947, Lewis had already used the cathedral metaphor. He compared Malory's masterpiece to Wells Cathedral, which is a composite work built, altered, and expanded over time by many architects, rather than designed and executed all at once by a single person. It is thus, Lewis claims, somewhere between artifice and natural growth ("The 'Morte Darthur'" 110).

The image of collective or evolutionary architecture as metacritical metaphor was alive in Lewis' imagination before he developed it in "The Genesis of a Medieval Book."

In his critique of the cult of originality and his focus on the text as the ground of the critic's work, Lewis anticipates later postmodern scholarship. As with later critics, his concern was to destabilize the contemporary reader, challenge prejudices, and re-contextualize reading projects. This deconstructive instinct is evident in *The Discarded Image* (1964), a lecture series that was published posthumously (see Hooper's "The Lectures of C. S. Lewis"). Lewis' decentering of the reader is highlighted in its epilogue, which emphasizes the symbolic nature of any scientific model (222). While he denies this metanarrative ultimacy as the vocation of any one individual, Lewis also says that no model of the universe "is a mere fantasy." David C. Downing captures Lewis' project well: "Like Derrida, Lewis emphasizes that all analysis is situated, that there is no position of utter objectivity from which one may think about thinking itself"

---

12   It is unlikely—though possible—that Lewis read *La Pensée sauvage* in French in 1962 or 1963. Of continental criticism, he had read Auerbach's *Mimesis*, which he discussed in a 1959 letter with Vinaver (*Letters* 3.1079). In addition to the critical distance between the two figures and also Lewis' distrust of the efficacy of anthropological approaches to literary criticism (see his "The Anthropological Approach"), Lewis was quite ill in this period (Sayer 397–411).

("Among the Postmodernists"). Jacques Derrida's critique of our access to ultimate reality is more radical than Lewis'. Lewis believed in ultimate realities in the sense that he was a theist; he believed that a personal God is related to all stories ("Among the Postmodernists"). But Lewis recognized that even if individuals could see the entirety of reality—"the infinity of events"—and even if they could discern the pattern of reality, there is still the basic fact of their own individual places within reality. The observer is inherently limited in perspective ("Historicism" 50–51).

Critics after Lewis attempted to fully deconstruct the reading standpoint and to produce doubt about the Author-Text unity. In his classic 1969 *Archaeology of Knowledge*, for example, Michel Foucault challenges the unity not only of the medieval book, but of the "book" of any age. "The book is not simply the object that one holds in one's hands," Foucault argues; "… its unity is variable and relative" (23). The "book" is always an intertextual project:

> The frontiers of a book are never clear-cut: beyond the title, the first lines, and the last full stop, beyond its internal configuration and its autonomous form, it is caught up in a system of references to other books, other texts, other sentences: it is a node within a network. (Foucault 23; cf. I. M. Higgins 18–19)

Lewis chose to allow for the foundationalist-decentering tension in his understanding of texts and is therefore outside the diverse conversations about deconstruction that define the critical revolution of the 1960s. He does, however, anticipate Lévi-Strauss's conversation about bricolage with the image of the cathedral. Both scholars also used the metaphor of the painter to stimulate the conversation about how texts use other texts (*The Savage Mind* 24; "Genesis" 38).

Around 1947, Lewis also used a gardening metaphor while referencing Charles Williams' Arthurian project. In his commentary on Williams' Arthuriad, Lewis again rejects the modern authorial myth in favor of a more integrated understanding of authorship:

> There is no question here of a modern artist approaching the old material as a quarry from which he can chip what he pleases, responsible only to his own modern art. It is more a "dove-like brooding," a watching and waiting as if he watched a living thing, now and then putting out a cautious finger to disentangle two tendrils or to train one a little further toward the support which it had almost reached, but for the most part simply waiting. (WA 279)

Characteristically, in discussing intertextual instincts, Lewis echoes Milton's invocation of his own muse: "Dove-like satst brooding on the vast Abyss" (*Paradise Lost* 1.21). The waiting metaphor then shifts to the gardening image. It is an organic metaphor of the poet that has both intriguing synchronicities and continuing tensions with the image of the cathedral builder.

The danger of mixing metaphors is perhaps inevitable as these thinkers try to discern the shape of intertextualities. While there is value in the metaphors of garden, painting studio, and commune, I will focus on Lewis' and Lévi-Strauss's metaphors of bricolage and cathedral building. In the time since Lewis and Lévi-Strauss were writing of the *bricoleur*-architect in the early 1960s, the conversation on intertextuality has developed. Of these developments, I will briefly explore two that are helpful in looking at Lewis' intertextuality project: the echo and the hyperlink. I will then test these approaches by reading *That Hideous Strength* for its transtextual concerns, narrowing the lens to focus on the Arthurian project in action. Finally, I will return to Lewis as world-builder, widening the lens once again to see how the close-up informs the entire picture for suggestive possibilities.

Echo Beyond Allusion

The images of bricolage and cathedral are enhanced in Lewis and Lévi-Strauss in the metaphor of an "echo"— a concept that occurs in each critic ("Genesis" 37; *The Savage Mind* 174) though it remains undeveloped in each. "Echo" is not a technically precise metaphor. According to the OED, the idea of the "echo" as an early metaphor for imitation of a writer's thoughts or style developed from a mythological figure—the mountain nymph, Echo—as well as an artifice in verse. Lewis uses it as a teenager to describe how one author evokes another author without definite reference (*CL* 1:92; cf. *CL* 2:1115). Indeed, in a later letter to the editor of *Delta: The Cambridge Literary Magazine*, Lewis agrees with the lamentation that "many modern undergraduates know the Bible and the Classics so little that they miss many allusions and conscious echoes" (*CL* 3:1231; cf. Auerbach 181, 207, 314, 479). Lewis speaks of Jane Austen echoing New Testament language ("A Note on Jane Austen" 183) and admits the unconscious or subconscious use of echoic allusions, mixing aural and visual metaphors to speak of a picture having an echo ("Dante's Similes" 65).[13] Throughout his essay "Imagination and Thought in the Middle Ages," Lewis uses the metaphor of echo to capture how previous mythologies are evoked in later ones. He also allows the possibility that Arthurian stories are distant echoes of factual historical events in Britain's past (298).

It is unlikely that Lewis is trying to turn an everyday literary metaphor into a technical term. Lewis was a poet who played with words and likely knew he was mixing metaphors when he spoke of pictorial echoes. Lewis moved the metaphor into everyday life: "with things like Bread, Wine, Honey, Apples ... are all the

---

13   "In fact, mythographers would be painting more than sound" (Hollander 9). Hollander explains how the Latin poet Ausonius used sound and image together. It does not seem that Lewis ever references Ausonius, though he was reading him as a student in 1922 (*AMR* 109). Hollander also traces the idea of "echo" in the modern poets from Milton and Cowley, to Wordsworth and Hopkins, to Thoreau and Frost (17–22). Wordsworth, too, mixes imagistic and aural metaphors:

> Ye voices, and ye Shadows
> And Images of voice—to hound and horn
> From rocky steep and rock-bestudded meadows
> Flung back, and; in the sky's blue caves, reborn—
> On with your pastime! till the church-tower bells
> A greeting give of measured glee;
> And milder echoes from their cells
> Repeat the bridal symphony (Wordsworth 569; cf. Hollander 19).

echoes of myth, fairy-tale, poetry, & scripture" (*CL* 3:583).[14] Others, however, find value in moving beyond the idea of "allusion" and using "echo" as a critical term. In *The Figure of Echo: A Mode of Allusion in Milton and After* (1981), John Hollander contrasts "poetic echo with modes of more overt allusion" (ix). Although Hollander would like to "exhume" the older terms "metalepsis" and "transumption" (113–32, 133–50), both would require some extension to function in poetics as intertextual critical terms. His focus on "echo" has value. Far from the "systematic taxonomy of allusive echoic patterns"—a project like Genette's—Hollander argues that poets "seem to echo earlier voices with full or suppressed consciousness," and that the "revisionary power of allusive echo generates new figuration" (ix).

As "echo" is a term used by our critical authors, and specifically by Lewis himself, it is useful to retain it. In the analysis of *That Hideous Strength* below, I will ask the question of how the story echoes other Arthuriana in thought and style. I will also explore how the echoes resonate at the deeper level of world building.

Hypertext → Hyperlink

A second new development of conversation about intertextuality comes out of Genette's system. Doubtless, some readers struggle with some of the critics mentioned here. Derrida, Kristeva, and Barthes are performance artists. Their texts are often difficult to read and have as their object an ontology of texts. Genette's approach is much different. In literary terms he is not creator, but Edenic namer. He is a taxonomist rather than a laboratory scientist. Using the Greek prepositions ὑπέρ and ὑπό—meaning "above" and "under," often transliterated in English as "hyper" and "hypo"/"hupo"—Genette draws our attention to literary relationships in spatial terms: "By hypertextuality I mean any relationship uniting a text B (which I shall call the *hypertext*) to an earlier text A (I shall, of course, call it the *hypotext*), upon which it is grafted in a manner that is not that of commentary" (*Palimpsests* 5).[15] This definition of "hypertext" was refreshingly simple in its generation, but has come to take on a fuller meaning in popular usage.

Little could Genette have known what changes the World Wide Web would perform upon our understanding of the spatial reality of texts. Linearity no longer suffices as the sole organizing principle of relational textuality. Bloom speaks of Poet and Belated Poet, Genette of Hypotext and Hypertext. The metaphors of bricolage (Lévi-Strauss), pastiche (Genette), echo (Lewis' elastic or Holland's technical usage), and palimpsest (Genette) all remain evocative. All of these images are entrenched in linearity: they have a source and then a second movement after the source. A palimpsest is a text upon a text. Pastiche is the imitation of a source text. An echo always has a single source: the voice that shouts into the canyon. Lévi-Strauss'

---

14   This quotation is evocative of Tolkien's conversation about "the potency of words" (OFS 81). David Downing uses the metaphor to consider the "Models, Influences, and Echoes" in the Ransom cycle (*Planets* 121–39).

15   It is unclear if Genette intended the broader sense of the prepositions: ὑπέρ in Greek means both "above" (or "after" in this setting), and "on behalf of"; ὑπό means "under" (or "before" here) as well as "by"—it is the most common preposition for passive verb constructs. Hyper as "on behalf of" has intriguing possibilities. Note also the use of "grafting"—gardening—imagery, such as Lewis used of Williams' Arthuriad.

metaphor of bricolage and Lewis' image of a cathedral are helpful in that they capture successive inter-relationships, as well as the possibility of nostalgic returns to earlier themes, as a belated architect mimics or blends with a previous one. But there is still a starting place: the earliest literary oddments.

None of these images sufficiently captures the explosion of text-relational possibilities that followed the invention of the Internet and its extension into everyday life. Because of the sheer scope and complexity of its web-nature, the Internet demonstrates traditional linear relationships, but also reveals adaptive relationships (where texts can link to previous texts using evolving and "learning" algorithms), mimetic evolutions of ideas, and the vast possibilities of spontaneous generation. Even in the relatively simple world of transferring text to e-text, we discover that books can now contain within the "text" a number of features: video previews, digital links to quotations and allusions, pop-up definitions or factoids, moving illustrations, automatic updates, podcasts of author interviews, soundtracks, and even alternative versions. Writing is now akin to a Hollywood production. We are in an age of three-dimensional readership.

We must ask what this new sense of space does for our metaphors. As we are reading Lewis, there is no critical problem in rooting ourselves in linearity. The metaphors that we have used—garden, echo, bricolage, hypertext, cathedral, palimpsest, communal painting—are still useful. Now, in the age of the Internet, we can add a transformed version of Genette's metaphor of "hypertext" to include the hypertextual nature of the Internet. This transformation enhances the echoic qualities of Genette's understanding of transtextuality. In particular, we should consider the "hyperlink."

While most readers in the digital generation use "hyperlink" often, it is helpful to define the term. Here is one such attempt: a hyperlink is "a link from a hypertext file or document to another location or file, typically activated by clicking on a highlighted word or image on the screen" (Aitken 78). This definition shows that the idea of "hyperlink" is both textual (file/document) and geographical (location), yet remains pictorial (image). In Genette's synchronistic brain, he might call the opposite of the "highlight" a "lowlight," and he uses a similar neologism that evokes "above" and "below" in using hypertext and hypotext. Most use the term "destination" more often in everyday speech.

Searching for the definition of "hyperlink" in Google is both instructive and performative. As part of a Google search, I was able to see a graph of the number of times the word "hyperlink" occurs in its databank of books and online text. I discover in a Google Ngram search that although the word "hyperlink" existed in text form before this generation, it suddenly exploded in popularity, growing exponentially in usage between the late 1980s and the early 2000s, when it was finally normalized. The Google Ngram search instructs us in the way the word is used, but it is also performative: my search of "hyperlink definition" contributes to data that Google uses in providing the next generation of user—even seconds later—with information.

In an almost Derridian way, hyperlink works both prescriptively and descriptively. It can also be a way of transforming Genette's hypertext metaphor without transgressing it, filling it out with a meaning that he could not have anticipated. In terms of intertextuality, we see how the hypertext uses a hypotext through plagiarism, quotation, or allusion.[16] If we encounter a Shakespearean quotation on a blog, the blog is the

16   Genette sets aside commentary.

hypertext and Shakespeare is the hypotext. In Bloom's terms, the blogger is the belated poet who is mis-reading Shakespeare, the poet. A digital hyperlink can easily highlight the quotation, and when clicked, transport the reader to the text of the Shakespearean play.

The potential for complexity here is endless. Shakespeare himself was a belated poet. He used all of the canonical texts available to him, and his works are especially rich in classical, biblical, and medieval intertextuality. His use of these hypotexts is not just verbal. Certainly he quotes, misquotes, alludes to, and echoes Homer, the Psalms, Ovid, folktales, romances, and the like. But he also explores themes, uses and reinterprets characters, retells narratives, and adopts metrical experiments. Even further, Shakespeare takes up the "worlds" of previous texts: the ground rules of reality are different in *A Midsummer Night's Dream* than in *Henry IV*, and these in turn reflect the different ground rules of reality of their different source text-worlds (romances vs. histories). Even more subtly, the moral ground rules may change depending on whether Shakespeare was writing a comedy or tragedy, or whether the courtly backdrop was Rome or Great Britain. When we click on a blogger's hyperlink, then, it does not simply bring us back to a Shakespearean quotation. It takes us back to all that Shakespeare encompasses in the text. The link from the belated poet (blogger) brings us to the belated poet (Shakespeare), who includes various poets in his work.

It is helpful here to return to the idea of echo to fill out the metaphor of hyperlink. I discussed above how Lewis imagined that a textual echo may include not just an allusion to a previous text, but a reference to the textual world or mythological framework of the hypotext. As I am reading the blogger quoting Shakespeare, clicking the hyperlink brings me not just back to the original Shakespeare quotation, or even just the texts that Shakespeare draws into his text. But the hyperlink actually brings me back to an original context filled with complex relationships. As I read that text-in-context, I experience the mythological framework of the text—whether it is fantasy or realism, historically referential or rejuvenated legend, comedy or tragedy, etc. Now in a new context, a hyperlink has the power of evoking for the reader the entire symbolic universe of the linked text or image.

This point is demonstrated poignantly in Aldous Huxley's *Brave New World* (1932). The title is from *The Tempest* (5.1.181–84). Huxley's protagonist, the "savage" John, learns to speak English by reading Shakespeare. Taken from his tribe, he arrives in a futuristic civilization. John's cry—"O wonder! … Oh brave new world" (Huxley 113–14)—is like a hyperlink to Shakespeare's text. But the quotations and echoes are not merely referential: John's entire worldview is Shakespearean. In the end, he cannot live in this new world so devoid of chivalry, honor, and love. When we "click" on Huxley's highlighted texts, we move back to Shakespeare's symbolic universe, his worldview, including the various ur-texts/hypotexts and, if I can use the terms, the "ur-worlds"/"hypoworlds" that he draws into his work.

Returning to the Shakespearean blogger, we recognize that a digital hyperlink trail could be almost endless: the Shakespearean text could contain hyperlinks to the many texts and textual worlds that Shakespeare draws upon. In turn, those texts could refer back to their hypotexts, and so on. The movement need not only be backwards. A hyperlinked Shakespearean text could also refer forward, linking to Shakespearean critics from Ben Jonson to the blogger I first encountered.[17]

Rather than an endless downward spiral or an impossible explosion of possibilities, each of these explorations gives readers an opportunity to experience a new layer of richness in a text. The Internet and e-texts allow us to make these sorts of links for the reader, but the principle of hypertextuality remains true in paper texts. Readers of paper texts may or may not perform this function of thinking hypertextually, but the opportunities are there for them to do so. For example, C. S. Lewis' title, *That Hideous Strength*, is drawn from a sixteenth-century David Lyndsay poem about the Tower of Babel: "The shadow of that hyddeous strength / Sax myle and more it is of length." Some readers, perhaps, would immediately see the hypertextuality of the phrase "That Hideous Strength"; mentally clicking that hypertext allows readers to make the connection to Lyndsay. In doing so, readers will see how Lewis, by quoting this poem, in turn evokes its hypotext and the whole conceptual context it evokes: The Tower of Babel. The Curse of Babel that Merlin releases upon the assembly of N.I.C.E. in *That Hideous Strength* has its context triangulated by the ancient poem evoked in the title.

Granted, not many readers would be able perform this task with regard to *That Hideous Strength*, and publishers have included the hypotext as an epigraph. In e-textual production, whether online or in an ebook format, a hyperlink could provide a link to the original poem, giving the reader the chance to follow the links in the chain Lewis was making, and perhaps also link to Lewis' conversation about Lyndsay in OHEL (80, 100–05).

The illustrative value of this conversation for us, however, is not in technological possibilities, but in rethinking how Lewis made worlds and told stories in these worlds. Lewis, as we will see in the analysis below, is a hyperlink-type writer: he uses little images, allusive echoes, and avatar-like references to link a reader back—not just to a previous text, but to previous textual worlds.

Conversations about Lewisian Intertextuality

With these critical metaphors of "echo" and "hyperlink" combined with *bricoleur*-architect as aids in exploring Lewis' intertextual project, we turn to Lewis' work. We see in Lewisian scholarship a building interest in C. S. Lewis as *bricoleur*. Commentaries on Lewis' work are more common than comparative readings, but the latter are growing in frequency, such as Alf Seegert's 2010 environmental alignment of Lewis' *The Great Divorce* and Faulkner's *The Bear* ("Harsh to the Feet of Shadows" 167–94), among others. Emerging scholars are beginning to step back from the idea of source text as only text and instead to apply critical analysis to Lewis' work where the hypotext is the larger cultural imaginarium or mythological framework. For example, Valerie Estelle Frankel's "The Double-Sided Wardrobe" (2010) takes Joseph Campbell's approach to the classic hero journey and uses it to consider the heroine journey in Narnia. These newer critics are

---

17   This has recently become possible with JSTOR's "Understanding Shakespeare" project, which allows a reader to click on any line of any Shakespeare play in the digital text editions from the Folger Shakespeare Library and see a list of scholarly articles that reference that line. [Editor's note]

building upon the work of scholars like Downing, whose *Planets in Peril* (1992) puts Lewis' Ransom cycle into its historical context, including literary and cultural layers behind the stories. Downing is invested in the question of intertextuality and describes the Ransom cycle using two more metaphors of "recovered" or "rehabilitating" literature (*Planets* 63).

On this view, the Michael Ward *Planet Narnia* debate is also an exploration of Lewisian intertextuality, in this instance focusing on Lewis' use of medieval cosmology in shaping the Narniad. As Ward points out, Lewis believed that understanding medieval cosmology was essential to understanding the literature (see *The Discarded Image*). From this, Ward argues that this same cosmology is also the framework for *The Chronicles of Narnia*. Further, this medieval cosmology is not merely an imaginative framework for Narnia, but also a conceptual one. The cosmology is not merely an influence, or a "recovery" as in Downing's analysis, but is an architectural pattern of Narnia, where each of the *Chronicles* is patterned after the mythological characteristics of one of the seven medieval heavens.

Not all are satisfied with Ward's project (e.g. Barrett or Brown), though all recognize that Lewis includes many historical texts in his writing. Most would agree that Ward has the imaginative scope of Narnia correct; the debate is over questions of detail, refinement of method, and authorial intention. Regardless of one's conclusion on the matter, the *Planet Narnia* discussion itself highlights the importance of Lewis' intertextual project.

However, not all see Lewis' "intertextually rich" tendency as entirely positive. Humphrey Carpenter has evoked Tolkien's own sentiments to critique Lewis' project, arguing that he borrowed "indiscriminately from other mythologies and narratives," including Tolkien's own mythology, throwing in "any incident or colouring that struck his fancy" (*Inklings* 224–27; cf. Sayer 312–13, Green and Hooper 241). It is doubtful that Lewis' project of drawing other worlds into his own—his use of mythologies and narratives—is truly indiscriminate. Carpenter's critique presumes a negative view of pastiche and a preference for the "original" author that Lewis seeks to undercut. Leaving aside the value judgement that Carpenter presumes, it is still clear that Lewis thought critically about intertextuality and applied that theory to his fictional projects.

Intertextuality in the Ransom Cycle

Whatever Tolkien's precise criticism of Narnian intertextuality truly was, the more evocative and puzzling echo of Tolkien in Lewis' fiction is the use of Númninor in *That Hideous Strength*. It is not the only surprising world-echo. Charles Williams' idea of Logres seems to move the Ransom books into a new category—as does the larger Arthurian world in the puzzling appearance of Merlin. Clicking on the hyperlink of these unusual Arthurian moments in *That Hideous Strength* can be instructive.

Though *That Hideous Strength* is Lewis' most overtly (published) Arthurian tale, the stock elements of Arthurian legend are absent. If Tolkien's Middle-earth corpus is in some way an Arthurian retelling (S. Higgins 1–8; *FoA* 125–68), both Tolkien and Lewis take up the legend in their mythopoeic projects in much more sophisticated and subtle ways than other twentieth-century retellers, such as T. H. White and Roger Lancelyn Green. They are different again from Williams' enigmatic and also incomplete Arthuriad. We see among these three friends three very different approaches to Arthurian transtextuality.

The Ransom Cycle

That Hideous Strength is part of Lewis' WWII-era fictional project of five books, at the center of which is Dr. Elwin Ransom, a Cambridge philologist. The first book, *Out of the Silent Planet* (1938), is an unapologetic inversion of H. G. Wells's interstellar corpus (see Schwartz). In the narrative, Dr. Ransom is kidnapped by colonizing scientists and taken to Malacandra (Mars) to be offered by his misinformed kidnappers as a sacrifice by the indigenous people. After all expectations are turned upside down, the reader discovers at the end of *Out of the Silent Planet* that Lewis (the secretary) and Ransom (the pseudonymous hero) are smuggling the true story of an interplanetary counter-conspiracy into the hands of the wider public.

Though the date of *The Dark Tower* is uncertain, it is a Ransom book, and it undoubtedly follows *Out of the Silent Planet* and precedes *Perelandra*.[18] It is also a scientific dystopia, though a failed literary experiment. Lewis and Ransom from *Out of the Silent Planet* are part of a coterie of intellectuals who discover that a "chronoscope"—an instrument for viewing things in other times—is not simply a visual tool but is actually a bridge between time-worlds. This "Othertime" is demonically tinged and in this way predicts *The Screwtape Letters* (1942), *Perelandra* (1943), and *That Hideous Strength* (1945)—each of which has a Satanic focus.

Though *The Screwtape Letters* is not typically included in the Space Trilogy, Lewis originally conceptualized it as a Ransom book. In "The Unpublished Preface to C. S. Lewis' *The Screwtape Letters*," I demonstrate how Lewis thought of Dr. Ransom as the translator of the demonic correspondence.

Next, *Perelandra*—the fourth Ransom book—takes the demonic battle of *The Screwtape Letters* and places it within a neo-Miltonian space opera. Dr. Ransom is transported to the planet of Perelandra (Venus) to fight against a demonic tempter who intends to disrupt the Edenic relational unity that still exists in this newborn world. Dr. Ransom's role in the continued counter-conspiracy from *Out of the Silent Planet* turns to violence. In *Out of the Silent Planet* and *The Screwtape Letters*, Ransom is merely interlocutor, translator, and faint prophetic voice. In *Perelandra*, Ransom becomes a Christ-figure. After a chase through the Dantean hells of Perelandra, Ransom does crush the serpent's head, but not before the serpent strikes his heel (Genesis 3:15). It is a dolorous stroke, leaving Ransom wounded as long as he remains in his earthly form. It is no great surprise, then, that Ransom becomes the Arthurian Fisher King in the next part of the Cycle—quite literally taking the title "Mr. Fisher-King" in *That Hideous Strength*.

Within the Ransom cycle, Lewis triangulates the Arthurian legendarium with classical and biblical mythology. We have a mature Eden-world in *Out of the Silent Planet* and a modernized hell in *The Screwtape Letters*. Hesperides and Eden in *Perelandra* become Avalon-on-Perelandra in *That Hideous Strength*. With the Fisher King role, we can see how Lewis takes up the Arthurian myth. While Downing is unconvinced by the explanation of how Ransom inherited the name Mr. Fisher-King (*Planets* 77)—it is easy to agree that

---

18 In 1978 Kathryn Lindskoog accused Walter Hooper of forging *DT* and carried that accusation forward with a series of books (e.g., *The C. S. Lewis Hoax*). While her instinct to protect Lewis is perhaps understandable, my own work with the original manuscript at the Bodleian (MS. Res. c. 1440) leaves me little room for suspicion. It is not a good story—there is a reason it was abandoned—but it is Lewis' story.

it is not an elegant device—the naming is consistent with the wound Ransom received on Perelandra and carries into the *That Hideous Strength* counter-conspiracy begun in *Out of the Silent Planet*.[19]

Renaming Ransom

The shift of names and titles throughout the series is significant. Ransom begins as the Pedestrian before we discover that he is Dr. Elwin Ransom, philologist. He is the *Hmân*—the man, the human one—to the indigenous Hrossa of Malacandra, and "Ren-soom" or "Small One" to the more intellectual Malacandrians, the Séroni. The Oyarsa or chief Eldil of Malacandra gives him the official designation "Ransom of Thulcandra." Ransom, in *Out of the Silent Planet*, moves from a pedestrian to a key actor in the interplanetary backstory. If Ransom may have been overly conscious of his designation, his first meeting with the Queen-Eve of Perelandra is an antidote to any pride. Tinidril christens him "Piebald" because he is sunburned on one side of his body and chalk-white on the other. The name sticks, so that Piebald is his main designation for much of the book, though its endearing quality fades as the Enemy takes it up to use against Ransom. Tinidril's husband, the King-Adam Tor, dubs Ransom Lord and Father, as well as Friend. In *That Hideous Strength*, Ransom takes on the name Mr. Fisher-King, but he is also the Pendragon, spiritual King of Logres. In his role as Pendragon, he takes on the titles of the Director, Master, and Lord of the House—St. Anne's manor, an eclectic order, a round table collective.

In *That Hideous Strength*, a grand conspiracy is being perpetrated by a bureaucratic group of researchers and politicians. This group, the National Institute of Co-ordinated Experiments (the N.I.C.E.), has begun conquering Britain. Their weapons are not, initially, steel and stones, but officiousness, organization, and a form of proto-Orwellian newspeak. As Pendragon, Ransom must lead a counter-conspiracy, but do so in a way that does not betray the principles of the freedom they are protecting. Mostly the group waits—"Dove-like satst brooding on the vast Abyss"—looking for hints of what is happening in the news, in the environmental shifts around them, and in the protagonist, Jane Studdock the Seer. Ransom, "a respectable Cambridge don with weak eyes, a game leg, and a fair beard" (*THS* 41), is tasked with leading a resistance consisting of a wary Seer, an historian and his barren wife, a sociologist and his wife, a skeptic, a housemaid whose husband is a convict, a great bulgy bear, and a handful of other animals. This is Carbonek and the Round Table. These are the Companions of the Co-inherence. This is the resistance of which Ransom is Director and Master.

As the Ransom cycle develops, Ransom is renamed, and this renaming accompanies the filling of his identity with new meaning (see Downing, *Planets* 120; Glyer 172; cf. Shogren, chapter 15 in the present volume). He has always been "Elwin," but we come to see that this name contains not only the Old English "Elf Friend," but also contains hints at the title of "Eldil Friend": "Powers of Heaven have come down to this house, and in this chamber where we are now discoursing, Malacandra and Perelandra have spoken to me" (*THS* 291). The surname Ransom, too, has deepening significance. As Ransom must face the idea of defeating the Enemy in *Perelandra* by a violence he is clearly unfit to perpetrate, he hears a Voice: "It is not

---

19   Chapter 15 by Benjamin Shogren examines Ransom's names in great detail. [Editor's note]

for nothing that you are named Ransom" (*Per* 147). And later the Voice says, "My name is also Ransom" (*Per* 148). Ransom, whose name means "Son of Ranolf," uncovers the untapped theological significance as he fulfills the redemptive function in Perelandra's Eden. We see in Ransom's titles and names the elastic and evolving nature of his character. This elasticity is key to the power of Ransom's character.

The Arthurian Turn

While WWII was just the time for the myth of Arthur reborn, it is intriguing that Lewis turned to the awakening of Merlin rather than the centralizing of Arthur as warrior-king—what amounts to an inversion of certain characteristics of the legend. In legend, the Fisher King waits to be healed as he guards the grail. In *That Hideous Strength*, Ransom refuses healing by Merlin and links the Fisher King legend to his interplanetary counter-conspiracy while connecting Arthur with biblical characters who "walked with God and ... saw not death" (Gen. 5:24 and Heb. 11:5; *THS* 194–95). Others have outlined the Arthurian nature of *That Hideous Strength* and the complex interlacing of many stories it involves (e.g., Downing, *Planets* 75–82; Lobdell, *Scientifiction Novels* 94–95, 117–23; Hannay; Martin). Tolkien's own Arthuriad is much more nuanced and re-integrated into a new context, and Williams has the richest Arthuriad qua Arthuriad of the Inklings, working it out in an unfinished series of narrative poems. But Lewis does something unusual in how he makes each of his connections with the Arthuriad pay off in more than one way. In *That Hideous Strength*, Lewis brings in both Williams' conceptual framework of Logres and Tolkien's mythic background of Númenor. In looking briefly at Lewis' use of Logres and Númenor—by clicking on these highlighted terms, by paying attention to the intertextual echoes—we can see how Lewis makes use of the Arthurian legend.

Williams' Logres in *That Hideous Strength*

C. S. Lewis wrote a commentary on "the main regions of Williams' poetic universe" (WA 281) that grew out of lectures at Oxford on his friend's poetry: "Williams and the Arthuriad." Though Lewis argues that "the world of [Williams'] poem is a strong, strange, and consistent world" (WA 382), the commentary is welcome to season its strangeness and bring out the flavors of its consistency that are not always evident to all who sit at Williams' table. In addition to this commentary, *That Hideous Strength* may also be regarded as an interpretation of Williams' Arthuriad. For our interest, Williams' idea of Logres emerges in *That Hideous Strength*, forming the speculative framework of a good-evil dialectic in the apocalyptic narrative of this last Ransom chronicle.

   Williams' Arthuriad is difficult to summarize briefly—even as our lens is focused specifically on Lewis' use of Williams' Arthurian world. "The poems *Taliessin through Logres* (1938) and *Region of the Summer Stars* (1944)," Goodrich argues, "form a knotty mystical sequence whose ambiguities and multiple layers of signification readers must sometimes untangle by conjecture" (35). It is the untangling of these that is Lewis' focus in "Williams and the Arthuriad." In his collection of Williams' unpublished Arthurian poems, David Llewellyn Dodds notes that Lewis' interest was in the later poetry of Williams (149). Perhaps *War in Heaven* (1930),

Williams' only overt Arthurian novel, could be added to this canon-within-a-canon as it demonstrates the mystical elements of the Grail legend. While Williams presupposes previous Arthurian authors like Tennyson and Malory, he also remakes them, providing his own theological emphases, quite literally re-mapping the Arthuriad in his particular mystical esoteric myth (McClatchey 55–56; cf. Newman 1–22; Goodrich 35–36). In this mythic re-formation, Williams shifts the point of view to a peripheral charac-ter, the poet-soldier Taliessin, thus "presenting the world with a new Grail hero" (McClatchy 51). While Taliessin does not achieve the Grail, he functions as a kind of spiritual center in the kingdom of Logres, fostering a Company of holy people submitting to the will of the Grail and its Master.

Margaret Hannay notes that there are four elements that Lewis uses of the Arthurian story: the charac-ter Merlin, Dr. Ransom as the Fisher King and Pendragon, the remnant of Logres, and the battle between Logres and Britain (7).[20] There are other possible elements, such as the characterization of Jane Studdock the Seer as Percival, the one who failed to heal the Fisher King because he did not ask the right questions (Downing, *Planets* 77; Schwartz 108). As intriguing as this link is, it is Merlin who is able to offer healing to Mr. Fisher-King in *That Hideous Strength* and not the Percival-Jane character; Ransom refuses the healing, and ultimately it is Jane who is "healed" by Ransom (287). Although Jane is the protagonist of *That Hideous Strength*, it is Merlin who becomes the central Arthurian figure, the individual most specifically linked to the historical Arthurian canon. Lying asleep in a "parachronic" (*THS* 236) state with dormant power that the N.I.C.E. desperately wishes to use, Merlin becomes the focus of a veritable arms race between the leader of the N.I.C.E. on the one hand and Ransom's counter-conspiracy at St. Anne's on the other. In the end, Merlin chooses his own path and submits to what he perceives as the real power-authority: The Pendragon, spiritual descendant of Arthur and true King of Logres.

The first of Hannay's four Arthurian elements is the character of Merlin. Merlin in *That Hideous Strength* is not particularly Williamsian; there is a wild, holy, dangerous, will-centered dynamic of Merlin in the story. Indeed, when Merlin arrives in post-WWII England, he has culture shock and struggles with the morality gap between his world and Ransom's. "It would be great charity," said Merlin, "if you gave order that [Jane's] head should be cut from her shoulders; for it is a weariness to look at her" (279). He is a char-acter from a different time-world; human relationships with the earth and the application of vocation and morality have shifted dramatically since he last awoke. Merlin is equal parts shocking sobriety and intimate humor—a formula that defines Lewis' fiction. Yet even this character may echo previous Merlins: Indeed, the Merlin of Laʒamon's *Brut*, like the Merlin in *That Hideous Strength*, is a shaggy, half-savage man who gives fealty only to the Pendragon, challenges his rivals by asking them riddling questions, and demands that his enemies be beheaded.

The second of Hannay's Arthurian elements, the Ransom-Pendragon character, brings in the third element, the remnant of Logres, which links together two of Williams' Arthurian ideas that have hypertex-tual significance: the idea of Logres as spiritual Britain, and the remnant community. The idea of "Logres"

---

20   Note that Roger Lancelyn Green also uses this Logres-Britain tension in his juvenile retelling, *King Arthur and His Knights of the Round Table* (23–24). Green was one of the Inklings and in Oxford in the 1940s, though Williams' influence is difficult to discern.

in *That Hideous Strength* first emerges not merely as an echo, but as a direct reference to Williams' poetry as one of the literary options in this fictional world (194). This direct hyperlink to Williams should serve as preparation for the reader that the speculative worlds of Ransom and Williams are somehow connected. Once this link is in place, Lewis captures Williams' symbolic universe in the narrative of *That Hideous Strength*.

In the story, the academics in the company who are gathered around Dr. Ransom discover that

> the Arthurian story is mostly true history. There was a moment in the Sixth Century when something that is always trying to break through into this country nearly succeeded. Logres was our name for it … gradually we began to see all English history in a new way. (368–69; cf. Williams and Lewis 194)

The fellowship around Ransom came to realize that what is called "Britain" is always shadowed or haunted by something called "Logres"—a conceptual something trying to break into tactile reality:

> Haven't you noticed that we are two countries? After every Arthur, a Mordred; behind every Milton, a Cromwell: a nation of poets, a nation of shopkeepers; the home of Sidney—and of Cecil Rhodes. Is it any wonder they call us hypocrites? But what they mistake for hypocrisy is really the struggle between Logres and Britain. (369)

The Logres of Arthur's time began with Merlin, and with him "one man and two boys, and one of those was a churl" (292). Through history, a remnant of Logres always survives, a succession of Pendragons in Arthur's line, unbroken into the twentieth century when Ransom became the seventy-ninth after Arthur (369). Each Pendragon draws a company around himself to act in history's "swaying to and fro between Logres and Britain" (370). This is precisely the kind of group that Ransom gathered around himself. When asked who Ransom was, this is the answer: "he is the Pendragon of Logres. This house, all of us here, and Mr. Bultitude [the bear] and Pinch [the cat], are all that's left of Logres: all the rest has become merely Britain" (195). Thus, the character of Ransom draws in the idea of Logres and the importance of the remnant: the last three of Hannay's elements are bound up together.

Some of these Pendragons have disappeared unknown into history, as Ransom and his company would have if Lewis had not recorded the tale; others are known under different names. There are great victories, such as the victory of Merlin and Ransom's company over the N.I.C.E. and its partnership with the Dark Eldila of Earth. But the Britain-Logres tension is not fully resolved except in a future eschatological hope: "When Logres really dominates Britain, when the goddess Reason, the divine clearness, is really enthroned in France, when the order of Heaven is really followed in China—why, then it will be spring" (370–71). Until that springtime, there is a Williamsian principle at play for the defenders of Logres:

> Every Logres fails to receive the Grail and sinks into a mere Britain: Israel, Athens, medieval Christendom, the Reformation, the Counter-Reformation, the Enlightenment …. The movement is not from lovely Titans to still more lovely Gods, but from Augustus to Tiberius, from Arthur to Mordred, from Voltaire to Vichy …. (WA 364; cf. 106)

When readers "click" Logres in *That Hideous Strength*, they are drawn into Williams' spiritual renewal of the idea of Logres, a Britain-within-Britain. The threat of Logres becoming only Britain is alive in Williams' Arthuriad, focused on Arthur's hubris, the Arthur-Lancelot tension, and "the treachery of Mordred the King's bastard son" (*RSS* 118). Because of these infidelities, "Logres is overthrown and afterwards becomes the historical Britain, in which the myth of its origin remains" (*RSS* 118). In *That Hideous Strength*, Lewis uses both the myth and the principle, with the threat centered on the N.I.C.E. and the little counter-conspiracy at St. Anne's.

The counter-conspiracy—the remnant, the household of St. Anne's—is an example of peculiar and poignant Williamsian intertextuality in Lewis. As a praxis theologian, Williams applied the principles in his mythic poetry to his own life. In particular, as Barbara Newman delineates, Williams' romantic theology and his understanding of exchange or co-inherence, combined with his charismatic presence, set the stage for Williams to create the Companions of the Co-inherence, an informal religious order. Newman suggests that the "golden thread that binds virtually all of Williams' fiction, poetry, theology, and spiritual practice into one whole is his idea of co-inherence" (6; cf. Stout). This Patristic term captures the mutual indwelling of the Trinity, or *perichoresis*. "This reciprocity of being, this abiding of every self not in itself but in another, is what Williams means by coinherence" (Newman 6). This theological principle is worked out in human relationships in texts like John 14:11–20 and Gal. 2:19–20. In Romans 12:5, the image of oneness—"one body in Christ"—finds its roots in co-inherence—"members, one of another." This mutual dependence works out into various practical expressions of faith as one member of the Companions will carry the burdens of another. Thus, "Williams cultivated a large circle of female friends and disciples, and it was chiefly these women that he counted as his Companions" (Newman 2). One of these women, Alice Mary Hadfield, records the principles of the Companions of Co-inherence in her memories of Charles Williams. These include the foundational Christian belief that "the Divine Substitution of Messias" is exemplar, that members are to "Bear ye one another's burdens," and that each "shall make a formal act of union" with other members, despite the fact that the "Order has no constitution except in its members" (Hadfield 174; Lang-Sims 30; cf. Roukema on occult syncretistic elements, including Arthurian romance).

There are intriguing synchronicities between the household at St. Anne's in *That Hideous Strength* and Williams' Companions of the Co-inherence, especially when viewed through the lens of Williams' Arthurian poetry. That Williams included "fictionalized versions of the Order of Co-inherence" in his poetry is undoubted (Dodds 267). Williams combines the Companions with the "graces described at the end of St. Mark's Gospel" (Dodds 266) in the poem "Divites Dimisit":

> Only Taliessin, in the west with the king, smiled
> to think how the household had founded a new Order,
> known by no name, least their own,
> grounded in the law of the Empire, the acts of the Throne,
> the pacts of the themes, from rose-lordly Caucasia
> to the sentences sealing the soul through the whole of Logres
> in the mouth of London-in-Logres; their salutation

was everywhere the promulgation of the Co-inherence. (*AP* 277, ll. 55–62)

The Region of the Summer Stars, which could have been named *The Household of Taliessin* (Dodds 267; see 294n17), includes a poem called "The Founding of the Company." This poem echoes the household description in "Divites Dimisit." It also has the idea of a silent, unguided hand in the founding of the Company, the eschewing of a particular name or figurehead, and being "Grounded in the Acts of the Throne and the pacts of the themes" (*RSS* 154, "The Founding of the Company 13). "It spread first from the household of the king's poet" (l. 6), the narrator suggests. And

> it lived only by conceded recollection,
> having no decision, no vote or admission,
> but for the single note that any soul
> took of its own election of the Way. (14–17)

It is focused on worship of the Trinity, the Flesh-taking, the whole manner of love, "the singular and mutual confession / of the indwelling," and living "by a frankness of honourable exchange" in mutual need (26, 43). The remainder of the poem describes the perichoretic doctrine of co-inherence as it plays out in community.

   While Lewis does not develop the principle of co-inherence/substitution or the Eucharistic central-ity of the Grail as significant themes in *That Hideous Strength*, there are aspects of the Company of St. Anne's that are echoes of Williams' poetry. The language of "household" and "company" are used throughout *That Hideous Strength*: "Our little household, or company, or society, or whatever you like to call it is run by a Mr. Fisher-King" (113–14). Returning to Williams' poetry, "The Founding of the Company" begins:

> About this time there grew, throughout Logres,
> a new company, as (earlier) in Tabennisi
> or (later) on Monte Cassino or in Cappadocia
> a few found themselves in common. (1–4)

These four lines capture two aspects of life at St. Anne's: continuity and coinherence. We see, first, the timeless continuity of the remnant, in this case demonstrated by fellowships of monks like Pachomius, Benedict, and the Cappadocian fathers. The importance of this remnant is captured in the discussion on Logres above.

   The second aspect is more complex. Very little survives of *That Hideous Strength* in manuscript form, so it is difficult to know for certain that what we have of rewritten first drafts demonstrates a struggle on Lewis' part to work out the ideas. It is intriguing, however, that the single complete page we have is the most intertextually rich part of *That Hideous Strength*. In file CSL/MS-119/B at the Marion E. Wade Center,[21]

---

21   The original is housed at the Bodleian but was unavailable during my last visit.

there is an unpublished holograph of a rough draft in which Dr. Ransom makes links with Tolkien's legendarium (see below). In this single page, Ransom discusses the founding of the "the order of Logres" at St. Anne's, echoing Williams' poem "The Founding of the Company."

In the case of the Williams echo, the manuscript and the published version are not greatly divergent, differing mostly in language and context. In a crisis of confidence of its members, and challenged by the resident skeptic to dissolve the Company and find new members to perpetrate the counter-conspiracy, Ransom protests: "I have no power to dissolve it" (198). "In that case," the skeptic challenges Ransom, "I must ask what authority you had to bring it together?" (198). In the manuscript, the language is subtly different, suggesting the idea of "power" instead of "authority"—the latter becoming a refined theme in the story as it is published. But the response of the Director is relatively unchanged: "I never brought it together," said the Director. Then, after glancing round the company, he added: "There is some strange misunderstanding here! Were you all under the impression I had selected you?" (198). Indeed, they had been under that impression, as most of them that a company would in fact "collect round [Ransom] ... its head." (114). As in "The Founding of the Company" and Williams' previous poetry, the household is not formed by the charismatic genius—though Ransom, Taliessin, and Williams are each figures of power at the center of an order. Instead, an invisible hand works behind each Company in its shaping and focus.

There is, then, a germ of critical truth in the quip that Green and Hooper quote (without attribution), calling *That Hideous Strength* "a Charles Williams novel written by C. S. Lewis" (174). It is probably true that as Ransom's character developed, the Lewis-Tolkien-Barfield hybrid character of Ransom in *Out of the Silent Planet* looked more like Charles Williams (see Downing, *Planets* 119; Lobdell, "CSL's Ransom Stories" 213; Newman 20). Barbara Newman suggests that Lewis was unaware of the complex, intimate, mytho-sexual rituals in Williams' real life Company (2), though he was aware, if naïvely, of the attraction he had to young women (Lewis, *Essays* x). It would be problematic, then, to transfer the entire Williamsian mytho-sexual cultic perspective into a reading of the Ransom character.

However, there are parallels between Ransom in St. Anne's and Williams' attractive qualities: not of physical beauty—"that face—angel's or monkey's"—but of "immense good" to women and with no interruption to male friendship (Lewis, *Essays* x). We see the household through the eyes of the new initiate, Jane. Upon meeting Ransom, Jane's experience is akin to that of the mystic (cf. Downing, *Region of Awe* 103 and *Planets* 58). She is shaken, and shaking, on the verge of tears. We see that "her world was unmade: anything might happen now .... all power of resistance seemed to have been drained away from her" (143). She discovers in his presence new scruples and an acute sense of her own self-deception, tightening the historic link between mystical experience and ethical self-awareness. The mystical religious elements threaten to overwhelm her. Jane feels "in that room and in that presence, like a strange oriental perfume, perilous, seductive, and ambiguous" (147). Ransom cries, "Stop it!"—though it is unclear whether the command is to Jane or to the otherworldly masters in their midst. Perhaps the ambiguity is intentional. The strong, independent Jane also experiences "schoolgirl" responses more like attraction than reverence—stammering her words, her face flushing red, biting her lip. In *That Hideous Strength*, Ransom inspires rugged comradeship with men, even the skeptic, and a holy awe among the women. This awe is intensified in Jane's experience. Though Ransom divests himself of the admiration, Lewis allows some of the psychosexual tension to remain. The series of ambiguities—attraction and mysticism, an angel's and a monkey's face—are bound up in the hybrid of Charles Williams' chimeric character. Ransom's character—who is haloed at one point in the story (278)—may well be a commentary upon Lewis' view of Williams. As Downing says, "once Ransom has overcome the major spiritual challenges facing him … he comes more to resemble Charles Williams, someone Lewis greatly admired for the quality of holiness in his life" (*Planets* 127). Ransom, then, is a literary hyperlink to the living influence of the text.

The formation of the Company at St. Anne's, its role as a remnant of Logres, and the character of the charismatic centre, when explored hypertextually, reveal evocative and complex "destinations" behind the hyperlinked text, both back to Williams' understanding of the "company" and to his own person.

Tolkien's Núminor in *That Hideous Strength*

With a critical framework in place, we turn very briefly to the second unusual example of intertextuality in *That Hideous Strength*. The preface to *That Hideous Strength* includes this curious statement: "Those who would like to learn further about Numinor[22] and the True West must (alas!) await the publication of much that still exists only in the MSS. of my friend, Professor J. R. R. Tolkien" (7). Besides this preface, there are six references to "Numinor" in four scenes. These scenes are remarkable in that they integrate Tolkien's Númenor with Williams' conception of Logres, as well as the historical Arthurian legend and its Druidic-Roman hybrid background, the story of Atlantis, and the interplanetary beings (Eldila) and language (Old Solar) of the Ransom Universe.

In these scenes we learn that Merlin's magic was something categorically different from "Renaissance magic" (200) or even "primitive Druidism" (265). It was "the last survival of something older and different—something brought to Western Europe after the fall of Numinor and going back to an era in which the general relations of mind and matter on this planet had been other than those we know" (200–01). It was "the last vestiges of Atlantean magic" (201), infused with "Eldilic energy and Eldilic knowledge" (201). This Numinor was in the pre-glacial period (265) and was called the "true West" (272), thus binding together the various speculative histories.

While Ransom's authority as Pendragon is greater than Merlin's, Ransom's assent to this implicit hierarchy comes not merely because he is Pendragon—a designation that alone could win Merlin's allegiance. Nor is it merely because Ransom gives the necessary code-word to a test that Merlin provides; Ransom does not answer Merlin's riddles because they are riddles he can answer—as code-words—but because his answers are simply true. It is Ransom's use of Old Solar, the language of Eden in the Ransom universe, that demonstrates that Ransom has traveled in heaven and spoken to the Oyéresu in a tongue so old it was no longer heard even in Númenor (265).

Even without the preface, the reference to Tolkien's legendarium is obvious. It is no secret that Tolkien had linked Númenor with the Atlantis legend (e.g., see *Letters* 175, 197, 206, etc.)—a link that Lewis was

---

22   Tolkien: "The spelling *Numinor* is due to his hearing it and not seeing it" (*Letters* 224). Lewis was optimistic then that Tolkien's legends would soon appear. They were published a decade later in 1954–55.

aware of at least as early as 1943–44 when he was writing *That Hideous Strength*. In the manuscript fragment of *That Hideous Strength* at the Wade, Dr. Ransom makes the link with Tolkien's legendarium even more specific: "The true reason being that Bragdon is the only centre, which has survived into comparatively modern times, of the original Western Magic brought to this island after the destruction of Numinor—of Atalantë, the fallen, the waste land." In the appendix of *The Silmarillion*, we discover that "Atalantë" is the Quenya word for something that has been thrown down or ruined; it is the name given to Númenor after its fall (381; cf. 376, 347–48). This is an intriguing invention of Tolkien's, because the connection with "Atlantis"—though central to the creation of the myth—is simply a "curious chance" in the evolution of words (Tolkien, *Letters* 347). Clearly, it was a link that Tolkien made early in the development of *The Lord of the Rings*, since Lewis was able to make the link in *That Hideous Strength* in 1943 or 1944. It is unclear why Lewis changed Atalantë to Atlantis in the published manuscript. It may have been because of pressure from Tolkien, who said Lewis' use of Numinor in *That Hideous Strength* was in the spectrum of plagiarism (*Letters* 224). Or perhaps Lewis simply thought the Atlantis connection would be more accessible to the reader. In either case, it demonstrates that Lewis' link between the Ransom world (Field of Arbol) and Tolkien's world (Middle-earth) is greater in his mind than he even allows into his published story.

Analysis: The Metaphors at Play

And that is the striking feature of Lewis' fiction: the complex layers of intertextual echoes, both at the conceptual level in unpublished manuscripts (Arthurian layers in "The Quest of Bleheris" and Ransom in *The Screwtape Letters*) and in their published form (Númenor and Logres in the Field of Arbol). Númenor and Logres are hardly the furthest regions of Lewis' intertextual project. Biblical backgrounds, classical mythology, medieval cosmology, Arthurian romance, Miltonian epic, Shakespeare, Sidney, H. G. Wells, Jules Verne, George MacDonald, and Beatrix Potter—all of these authors with their secondary worlds are drawn into Lewis' original fiction. Our most tempting question to ask is: "Why does he do this?" This is a difficult question to answer with certainty and brevity. Clearly his models were intertextually rich and provided rich possibilities. Virgil echoes Homer, the Old Testament is quoted and echoed in the New (see Hays), and all of these and more are echoed in Milton (see Hollander; Lewis, *PPL*). Diana Pavlac Glyer is convincing in her argument that there is a relational element to Lewis' writing, as he is shaping a reading community for his friends' work (see esp. Glyer chap. 7). The answer, however, to why Lewis draws other worlds into his own might simply be: "It is fun." Lewis may simply have enjoyed that sort of project; he may have loved stretching the speculative possibilities of the fictional worlds he knew best.

   If we return to the critical metaphors, though, we can change the question from *why* Lewis worked transtextually to the preliminary question of *what* he was doing in *That Hideous Strength*. He is not, evidently, completing a painting that another master had begun. Lewis does this with "Williams and the Arthuriad," complementing Williams' incomplete Arthuriad and structuring the reading experience for subsequent generations. In *That Hideous Strength*, however, he transforms Malory, Laȝamon, and Williams, drawing these Arthurian authors into his own speculative universe that had already begun in the person of Elwin Ransom some years before. The metaphors of bricolage or cathedral are more apt than painting for the task of describing Lewis' project. As *bricoleur*, Lewis takes the literary and subcreative oddments he has available to him—including Tolkien, Williams, and the historic Arthuriad—and recreates them in a new piece of work. As cathedral architect, he creates a new architectural-architextual work of art while retaining the historic features that existed before he set to work. These metaphors are helpful in describing Lewisian transtextuality in *That Hideous Strength*.

Pressing further and returning to our critical discussion, we see how an augmented use of a popular metaphor—"echo"—and an adapted consideration of the image of "hyperlink" are helpful together. Lewis sets the allusive context for his use of Williams' Arthuriana by quoting from *Taliessin through Logres* in the narrative. In subsequent uses of "Logres," Williams is not explicitly named. Lewis' Arthuriad evokes Williams' through the literary echo of the word "Logres" and the principles attached to the spiritualized conceptual framework it provides. In critical terms, the word "Logres" works as a hyperlink that connects the reader both backwards and forwards to Williams' (then evolving) project of Arthurian retelling. When we as readers click on the symbolically rich use of "Logres" in *That Hideous Strength*, we are drawn into the rich and complex world of Williams' Arthur, which is a subsequent evocation of the historic Arthurian legend in Laȝamon, Malory, Wace, the Vulgate Cycle, and the rest. In this sense, "Logres" is not simply "a word that contains a story" (Fulford 34); it is a word that contains entire symbolic universes.

In an even more pointed way, when we see the word "Numinor" in *That Hideous Strength*, we are (re) directed to Tolkien's Middle-earth legendarium and the concept of Númenor. Though Lewis pulls back from the explicit and idiosyncratic usage of Atalantë in the published version of *That Hideous Strength*, echoes of Tolkien's mythopoeic project are highlighted throughout the novel. Mythology in Tolkien becomes history in Lewis; an Atlantean and Númenorian period of earth's prehistory is as established as the extraterrestrial and non-human elements that make up the Field of Arbol. Intriguingly, as with Williams, with Tolkien we cannot say we are hyperlinked "back" to the text. It would be some years—decades, actually—before the full history of Númenor and the true West were provided to the public. Instead, Lewis' hyperlink of "Numinor" is dynamic, a "smart link" that updates itself as J. R. R. Tolkien and his subsequent editors continually update the destination: Eä, the world of the Middle-earth legends and their connected mythologies.

Conclusion

In characteristic fashion, Lewis' fiction draws together individual speculative universes, combining worlds where they have the most intertextual possibilities. Moving beyond quotations and allusions to the echoes of other worlds, we see that Lewis uses other subcreated worlds by hyperlinking them into his own narratives. His narratives presuppose not simply the literary canon—the hypotexts that Lewis is evoking—but the cultural, historical, and conceptual framework in the speculative universes of the hypotexts in question. Lewis has little phrases, efficient images, or single words that work as hyperlinks, so that when readers "click" on the highlighted text, they experience not just a quotation from an author, but that previous author's entire speculative world. Lewis is, according to the critical metaphors of Lévi-Strauss and Lewis himself, *bricoleur* and architect-builder, using previously subcreated worlds to create his own little world, cunningly made. But moving beyond these chronologically bound images of art and architecture, we see how adapting Genette's hypertext image to a contemporary metaphor of hyperlink moves us past hypotext-hypertext. In the case of the Arthurian projects of Williams and Tolkien, Lewis echoes them while they are still in formation.

Like the Inklings' Arthuriad, this essay is in some ways incomplete. Looking at Arthurian and Inklings echoes in *That Hideous Strength*, I am merely suggesting an attitude that we might take in reading Lewis—"it is less a matter of method than of sensibility … tuning our ears to the internal resonances" in Lewis' work (Hays 21). This approach, this sensibility, this tuning is the beginning of a larger-scale project of examining intertextual play in C. S. Lewis—both at the textual level and the conceptual level, the symbolic universe of the fictive text.

Works Cited

Aitken, Joan E. *Cases on Communication Technology for Second Language Acquisition and Cultural Learning*. Hershey, PA: Information Science Reference, 2014. Print.

Allen, Graham. *Intertextuality: The New Critical Idiom*. NY: Routledge, 2000. Print.

Auerbach, Erich. *Mimesis: The Representation of Reality in Western Literature*. Fiftieth Anniversary Edition. Trans. Willard Trask. Princeton UP, 2003. Print.

Barrett, Justin L. "Some Planets in Narnia: A Quantitative Investigation of the *Planet Narnia* Thesis." *VII: An Anglo-American Literary Review* 27 (2010): 1–18. Web. 30 September 2015.

Barthes, Roland. "The Death of the Author." *Image Music Text*. Trans. and ed. Stephen Heath. London: Fontana Press, 1977. 142–48. Print.

Bloom, Harold. *The Anxiety of Influence: A Theory of Poetry*. Oxford UP, 1972. Print.

——. *A Map of Misreading*. Oxford UP, 1975. Print.

Brown, Devin. "Planet Narnia Spin, Spun Out." *CSLewis.com: The Official Website of C. S. Lewis*. 13 May 2009. Web. 6 Dec 2014. Print.

Carpenter, Humphrey. *The Inklings: C. S. Lewis, J. R. R. Tolkien, Charles Williams, and Their Friends*. Boston: Houghton Mifflin, 1978. Print.

Dickieson, Brenton D. G. "The Unpublished Preface to C. S. Lewis' *The Screwtape Letters*." *Notes and Queries* 60.2 (2013): 296–98. Print.

Dodds, David Llewellyn, ed. *Arthurian Poets: Charles Williams*. Arthurian Studies 24. Rochester, NY: Boydell & Brewer, 1991. Print.

Downing, David C. "C. S. Lewis Among the Postmodernists." *Books and Culture* November/December 199). www.booksandculture.com. Web. 2 March 2016.

——. "'The Dungeon of his Soul': Lewis' Unfinished 'Quest of Bleheris.'" *VII: An Anglo-American Literary Review* 15 (1998): 37–54. Print.

——. *Into the Region of Awe*. Downers Grove, IL: InterVarsity Press, 2005. Print.

——. *Planets in Peril: A Critical Study of C. S. Lewis' Ransom Trilogy*. Amherst, MA: U of Massachusetts P, 1992. Print.

"Echo, n." *OED Online*. Oxford UP. June 2015. Web. 11 August 2015.

Frankel, Valerie Estelle. "The Double-Sided Wardrobe: The Hero's and Heroine's Journey through Narnia." *Doors in the Air: C. S. Lewis and the Imaginative World*. Ed. Anna Slack. Vitoria, Spain: Portal Editions, 2010. 81–106. Print.

Foucault, Michel. *The Archaeology of Knowledge and The Discourse on Language*. Trans. A. M. Sheridan Smith. NY: Pantheon Books, 1972. Print.

Fulford, Robert. *The Triumph of Narrative: Storytelling in the Age of Mass Culture*. Toronto: Anansi Press, 1999. Print.

Genette, Gérard. *Figures of Literary Discourse*. Trans. Alan Sheridan. NY: Columbia UP, 1982. Print.

——. *Palimpsests: Literature in the Second Degree*. Trans. Channa Newman and Claude Doubinsky. London: U of Nebraska P, 1997. Print.

Glyer, Diana Pavlac. *The Company They Keep: C. S. Lewis and J. R. R. Tolkien as Writers in Community*. Kent State UP, 2007. Print.

Goodrich, Peter H. Introduction. *Merlin: A Casebook*. Ed. Peter H. Goodrich and Raymond H. Thompson. NY: Routledge, 2003. Print. 1–88.

Green, Roger Lancelyn. *King Arthur and His Knights of the Round Table*. Toronto: Everyman's Library Children's Classics, 1993. Print.

Green, Roger Lancelyn, and Walter Hooper. *C. S. Lewis: A Biography*. NY: Harcourt Brace Jovanovich, 1974. Print.

Hadfield, Alice Mary. *Charles Williams: An Exploration of His Life and Work*. Oxford UP, 1983. Print.

Hannay, Margaret. "Arthurian and Cosmic Myth in *That Hideous Strength*." *Mythlore* 2.2 (1970): 7–9. Print.

Hays, Richard B. *Echoes of Scripture in the Letters of Paul*. New Haven, CT: Yale UP, 1989. Print.

Higgins, Iain Macleod. *Writing East: The "Travels" of Sir John Mandeville*. Philadelphia: U of Pennsylvania Press, 1997. Print.

Higgins, Sørina. "Arthurian Geographies in Tolkien, Williams and Lewis." *The Bulletin of the New York C. S. Lewis Society* 45.4 (2014): 1–8. Print.

Hollander, John. *The Figure of Echo: A Mode of Allusion in Milton and After*. Berkeley: U of California Press, 1981. Print.

Hooper, Walter. "The Lectures of C. S. Lewis in the Universities of Oxford and Cambridge." *Christian Scholar's Review* 27.4 (1998): 436–53. Print.

Huxley, Aldous. *Brave New World*. Middlesex: Penguin Books, 1970. Print.

Irwin, William. "Against Intertextuality." *Philosophy and Literature* 28.2 (2004): 227–42. Print.

King, Don W. "C. S. Lewis' *The Quest of Bleheris* as Poetic Prose." *Plain to the Inward Eye*. Abilene, TX: Abilene Christian UP, 2013. 36–40. Print.

——. *C. S. Lewis, The Poet: The Legacy of his Poetic Impulse*. Kent State UP, 2001. Print.

——. "Lost but Found: The 'Missing' Poems of C. S. Lewis' *Spirits in Bondage*." *Christianity and Literature* 53.2 (2004): 163–201. Print.

Lang-Sims, Lois. *Letters to Lalage: The Letters of Charles Williams to Lois Lang-Sims*. Kent State UP, 1989. Print.

Lévi-Strauss, Claude. *The Savage Mind*. U of Chicago Press, 1966. Print.

Lewis, C. S. *The Allegory of Love: A Study in Medieval Tradition*. London: Oxford UP, 1936. Print.

——. *All My Road Before Me: The Diary of C. S. Lewis 1922–1927*. Ed. Walter Hooper. Cambridge UP, 1998. Print.

——. "The Anthropological Approach." *Selected Literary Essays* 301–11.

——. *The Collected Letters of C. S. Lewis*. Ed. Walter Hooper. 3 vols. NY: HarperSanFrancisco, 2004–07. Print.

——. *The Collected Poems of C. S. Lewis*. Ed. Walter Hooper. London: HarperCollins/Fount, 1994. Print.

——. "Dante's Similes." *Studies in Medieval and Renaissance Literature* 64–77.

——. *The Dark Tower and Other Stories*. Ed. Walter Hooper. London: Fount, 1977. Print.

——. *The Dark Tower*. MS. Res. c. 1440. Bodleian Library, Oxford University. Oxford, UK.

——. *The Discarded Image: An Introduction to Medieval and Renaissance Literature*. Cambridge UP, 1964. Print.

——. "Dymer." *Narrative Poems* 1–90.

——. *English Literature in the Sixteenth Century, Excluding Drama*. Oxford History of English Literature 3. NY: Oxford UP, 1954. Print.

——. *Essays Presented to Charles Williams*. 1947. Freeport, NY: Books for Libraries Press, 1972. Print.

——. "The Genesis of a Medieval Book." *Studies in Medieval and Renaissance Literature* 18–40.

——. "Historicism." *Fern-seed and Elephants: And Other Essays on Christianity*. Ed. Walter Hooper. Glasgow: Fontana, 1975. 44–64. Print.

——. *The Horse and His Boy*. 1954. London: Fontana, 1980. Print.

——. *Image and Imagination*. Ed. Walter Hooper. Cambridge UP, 2013. Print.

——. "Imagination and Thought in the Middle Ages." *SMRL* 41–63.

——. *The Last Battle*. 1956. London: Fontana, 1980. Print.

——. "Launcelot." *Narrative Poems* 93–103.

——. *The Lion, the Witch and the Wardrobe*. 1950. London: Fontana, 1980. Print.

——. "The Literary Impact of the Authorised Version." *Selected Literary Essays* 126–146.

——. *The Magician's Nephew*. 1955. London: Fontana, 1980. Print.

——. "The 'Morte Darthur.'" *Studies in Medieval and Renaissance Literature* 103–10.

——. *Narrative Poems*. Ed. Walter Hooper. London: Fount, 1994. Print.

——. "A Note on Jane Austen." *Selected Literary Essays* 175–86.

——. *Out of the Silent Planet*. 1938. NY: Macmillan, 1964. Print.

——. *Perelandra*. 1943. NY: Macmillan, 1965. Print.

——. *The Pilgrim's Regress: An Allegorical Apology for Christianity, Reason, and Romanticism*. 1933. Toronto: Bantam Books, 1981. Print.

——. *A Preface to* Paradise Lost. Oxford UP, 1942. Print.

——. *Prince Caspian*. 1951. London: Fontana, 1980. Print.

——. "The Quest of Bleheris." MS. Eng. lett. c. 220/5. Bodleian Libraries, Oxford University. Oxford, UK.

——. *The Screwtape Letters*. London: Geoffrey Bles, 1942. Print.

——. *Selected Literary Essays*. Ed. Walter Hooper. Cambridge UP, 1969. Print.

——. *The Silver Chair*. 1953. London: Fontana, 1980. Print.

——. *Spenser's Images of Life*. Ed. Alistair Fowley. 1967. Cambridge UP, 2013. Print.

——. *Spirits in Bondage: A Cycle of Lyrics*. 1919. Ed. Walter Hooper. NY: Harcourt Brace Jovanovich, 1984. Print.

——. *Studies in Medieval and Renaissance Literature*. Ed. Walter Hooper. Cambridge UP, 1998. Print.

——. *Studies in Words*. 2nd ed. Cambridge UP, 1967. Print.

——. *That Hideous Strength.* c. 1943–44. MS. CSL/MS-119/B, Marion E. Wade Center, Wheaton College. Wheaton, IL.

——. *That Hideous Strength: A Modern Fairy-Tale for Grown-Ups.* 1945. NY: Collier Books, 1965. Print.

——. *The Voyage of the "Dawn Treader."* 1952. London: Fontana, 1980. Print.

——. "Williams and the Arthuriad." *Arthurian Torso.* Ed. C. S. Lewis. London: Oxford UP, 1948. 91–200. Print.

Lindskoog, Kathryn. *The C. S. Lewis Hoax.* Portland: Multnomah Press, 1988. Print.

Lobdell, Jared. "CSL's Ransom Stories and their 18th Century Ancestry." *Word and Story in C. S. Lewis.* Ed. Peter J. Schakel and Charles A. Huttar. Columbia, MO: U of Missouri Press, 1991. 213–31. Print.

——. *The Scientifiction Novels of C. S. Lewis: Space and Time in the Ransom Stories.* London: McFarland, 2004. Print.

Martin, Thomas L. "Merlin, Magic, and the Meta-fantastic: The Matter of *That Hideous Strength.*" *Arthuriana* 21.1 (2011): 66–84. Print.

McClatchey, Joe H. "Charles Williams and the Arthurian Tradition." *VII: An Anglo-American Literary Review* 1 (1980): 51–62. Print.

Milton, John. *Paradise Lost and Selected Poetry and Prose.* Ed. Northrop Frye. Austin, TX: Holt, Rinehart, and Winston, 1964. Print.

Newman, Barbara. "Charles Williams and the Companions of the Co-inherence." *Spiritus: A Journal of Christian Spirituality* 9.1 (2009): 1–26. Print.

Parker, M. Pauline. *The Allegory of The Faerie Queene.* Oxford, Clarendon Press, 1960. Print.

Reid, Margaret J. C. *The Arthurian Legend: Comparison of Treatment in Modern and Mediæval Literature.* Edinburgh: Oliver & Boyd, 1938. Print.

Riffaterre, Michael. *Semiotics of Poetry.* Bloomington, IN: Indiana UP, 1978. Print.

Roukema, Aren. "A Veil that Reveals: Charles Williams and the Fellowship of the Rosy Cross." *Journal of Inklings Studies* 5.1 (2015): 22–71. Print.

Sayer, George. *Jack: A Life of C. S. Lewis.* 2nd ed. Wheaton, IL: Crossway Books, 1994. Print.

Schwartz, Sanford. *C. S. Lewis on the Final Frontier: Science and the Supernatural in the Space Trilogy.* Oxford UP, 2009. Print.

Seegert, Alf. "'Harsh to the Feet of Shadows': The Wild Landscape of the Real in C. S. Lewis' *The Great Divorce* and William Faulkner's *The Bear.*" *Doors in the Air: C. S. Lewis and the Imaginative World.* Ed. Anna Slack. Vitoria, Spain: Portal Editions, 2010. 167–94. Print.

Stout, Andrew C. "'It Can Be Done, You Know': The Shape, Sources, and Seriousness of Charles Williams' Doctrine of Substituted Love." *VII: An Anglo-American Literary Review* 31 (2014): 9–29. Print.

Tolkien, J. R. R. *The Fall of Arthur.* Ed. Christopher Tolkien. London: HarperCollins, 2013. Print.

——. *The Letters of J. R. R. Tolkien.* Ed. Humphrey Carpenter. London: HarperCollins, 1981. Print.

——. "On Fairy-stories." *The Tolkien Reader.* NY: Ballantine, 1966. 33–99. Print.

——. *The Silmarillion.* 1977. Ed. Christopher Tolkien. London: HarperCollins, 1999. Print.

Walsh, Chad. *The Literary Legacy of C. S. Lewis.* NY: Harcourt Brace Jovanovich, 1979. Print.

Ward, Michael. *Planet Narnia: The Seven Heavens in the Imagination of C. S. Lewis.* Oxford UP, 2008. Print.

Williams, Charles. *The Chapel of the Thorn: A Dramatic Poem*. Ed. Sørina Higgins. Berkeley, CA: Apocryphile
    Press, 2014. Print.

——. *War in Heaven*. London: Faber & Faber, 1930. Print.

Williams, Charles, and C. S. Lewis. *Taliessin through Logres*, *The Region of the Summer Stars*, *Arthurian Torso*. 1948.
    Grand Rapids, MI: Eerdmans, 1974. Print.

Wordsworth, William. *The Poetical Works of Wordsworth, with Memoir, Notes etc*. London: Frederick Warne, n.d. Print.

Houses of Healing: The Idea of Avalon in Inklings Fiction and Poetry. [1]

Charles A. Huttar

When Elwin Ransom takes the name Fisher-King and the office of Pendragon, "Logres" is pitted against "Britain" for the mastery of the island nation, and Merlin is roused from long sleep to be the instrument celestial powers will use in the conflict, then readers of *That Hideous Strength* realize that the Arthurian myth has come to resonate more deeply in C. S. Lewis' creative work than it had before. The first two novels of the Ransom trilogy contain nothing of this sort, and the change no doubt owes something to Lewis' friendship with Charles Williams, with whose mature Arthurian poetry Lewis was deeply familiar. [2] But Lewis too had known and loved the Arthurian legends for years, [3]

1   Portions of this paper appeared in my article "'Deep lies the sea-longing': Inklings of Home." I thank the editor of *Mythlore*, Janet Brennan Croft, for allowing me to recycle them in a new context (correcting some errors).

2   He published two reviews of *Taliessin through Logres* (now reprinted in Lewis, *Image and Imagination* 125–36, 137–42), suggested the title for *The Region of the Summer Stars* (Dodds 6), and gave a course of lectures at Oxford in 1945—based in part on Williams' own explanatory notes—which he proceeded to publish ("Williams and the Arthuriad"), together with Williams' unfinished history of the Arthurian myth's development in tandem with that of the Grail quest, in *Arthurian Torso*.

3   Not long after discovering Malory at age sixteen (Green and Hooper 44), Lewis started addressing his friend Arthur Greeves as "Galahad" (see *CL* 1:115 and note especially the first paragraph of the next letter, 1:118). A year later he wrote several chapters of a projected "romance" (1:181) in which a fledgling knight named Bleheris feels he must undertake a quest to prove himself worthy of his calling, and one adventure he considers is sailing "to 'uttermost lands,' seeking ... 'the isle of Avalon ... the garden of the ladies which are cleped Hesperides'" (Downing, "Dungeon" 43; I have not seen the manuscript, and it is not clear whether the second ellipsis is Lewis' or Downing's).

and of the various Arthurian elements in *That Hideous Strength*, only the symbolic use of the name Logres can be traced with any certainty to Williams' influence.[4]

The element that immediately concerns us, however, is the place of Avalon in Lewis' story. It is first mentioned in chapter 13. Merlin, newly awakened from his chamber beneath Bragdon Wood, finds an England that differs confusingly from the one he had known some fifteen centuries before. On arriving at St. Anne's Manor, he cannot believe Ransom's claim to be "the Master here," this "mannikin" who is dressed "like a slave" (*THS* 319, 321). Ransom's command of the Old Solar tongue, reinforced by his evident knowledge of "Numinor"—not merely the name but also the fact that it is "the true West" (320)—begins to put the two on more equal footing, but Merlin remains suspicious. He asks three test questions. When Ransom gives the correct Old Solar name for the Oyarsa of Saturn, Lurga, and reveals knowledge that Merlin thought he alone possessed—"In the sphere of Venus I learned war.... I am the Pendragon" (322)—Merlin finally recognizes Ransom's superior authority.

Ransom's answer to the second question, that Arthur now dwells "in the cup-shaped land of Abhalljin ... in Perelandra ... till the end of time," brings us to the first place of healing with which this essay is concerned: Avalon. Some readers might consider this puzzling, an arbitrary and unnecessary twist in Lewis' fantasy, to locate Avalon, contrary to all medieval Arthurian lore, in a remote valley on the planet Venus. If so, they must wait until the final chapter of *That Hideous Strength* for more illumination. Twice before, attention was called to the unstanchable bleeding of Ransom's heel (160, 320),[5] the result of that battle on Venus. Now it is revealed that his "wound will only be healed in the world where it was got" and that Ransom, whose year or more on Venus has made his body free of aging and "natural death," will soon be taken to Abhalljin to dwell with Arthur and the other quasi-immortals (440, 441). It looks as if, for the sake of unity in his cosmic myth, Lewis was willing to reshape the myth of Arthur.

Matters are more complicated. As Lewis' reference to "Numinor" suggests,[6] *That Hideous Strength* shows something of the influence of J. R. R. Tolkien as well as that of Charles Williams. But the net must be cast much more widely. In the crucible of Lewis' imagination, Avalon was but one ingredient among many from a range of myth, legend, and imagery that included classical, biblical, Celtic, late antique and medieval Jewish and Christian, Norse, and modern literary texts.[7],[8] Much the same might be said of the way Williams' and

---

4   Indeed, Williams' converting into a symbol what had been a mere place name may have alerted Lewis to the possibilities of Arthurian myth as a framework for his third novel of cosmic conflict. And the presence of Williams is evident in or behind the novel in ways unrelated to Arthurian themes. Both these points are developed in my essay "How Much Does *That Hideous Strength* Owe to Charles Williams?"

5   Both times, simply "My foot is hurt." For the precise nature of the wound, see *Perelandra* 187.

6   See Glyer 98n29. Tolkien as well as others called attention to Lewis' misspelling of the name (probably because he had only heard it read aloud and not yet seen it as Tolkien wrote it, accent mark and all).

7   Writing of Spenser's "concoctive" mind (OHEL 355), Lewis alludes to John L. Lowes's 1927 study of a similar fermenting process in Coleridge's imagination. In his own creative experience, he would have found confirmation for Lowes's theory.

8   For a detailed study of intertextuality in Lewis' writing, see chapter 3 by Brenton D. G. Dickieson. [Editor's note]

Tolkien's imaginations worked, with the addition of Hermetic lore for Williams and Finnish for Tolkien. Tolkien, more than the others, labored to assimilate his sources into his own carefully crafted mythology; he did, however, create at least one work pertinent to our theme, "Leaf by Niggle," that lies outside that mythology. Moreover, as "writers in community" (Glyer's phrase) who were generally sympathetic with one another's ideas, parallels can be observed in their working-out of the theme of Avalon-isles, houses of healing—as well, of course, as significant differences. All three authors draw, as we shall see, on a rich heritage of shared images from the natural world, phenomena of land, sea, and sky. And all three exhibit what Nathan C. Starr calls "the experimental, reconstructive temper of the best modern Arthurians," being not so much interested in retelling tales from the medieval cycles as in "extract[ing] the spiritual core" of the myths (178).[9] It should be no surprise, then, that the Avalon-Venus connection that surfaces in *That Hideous Strength* in 1945 reflects a merging of material from different mythical traditions, which brewed in Lewis' mind over nearly thirty years, and in the process, was also informed by his work as a scholar.

It has deep roots as well in his emotional life, from the time when the daughters of Hesperus,[10] the Hesperides, and their fabled garden at the western edge of the world came to symbolize for Lewis his youthful longings. Several poems written in his late teens use vaguely Hesperian imagery. One, entitled "Hesperus," is more explicit:

> I would follow, follow
> Hesperus the bright,
> To seek beyond the western wave
> His garden of delight. (*CP* 217, ll. 3–6)[11]

---

9   Charles Williams—one of the authors to whom Starr referred—believed that "the greater interpretations were not imagined" in "the love-romances" that came into being around Arthurian themes ("Malory" 191). Nor were they by those like Geoffrey of Monmouth who pretended to be writing history. There was, to be sure, an abundance of what might be called lesser imaginations, of fantastic elements, in the medieval Arthurian tales, whether of history or avowedly of romance. Not that Williams considered history to be merely a matter of recorded or empirical fact: so much is evident from the paradoxical subtitle of his *The Descent of the Dove* (1939), "A Short History of *the Holy Spirit in* the Church" (emphasis added). Similarly, the "haunting" of which Cecil Dimble speaks near the close of Lewis' *THS*—a part of every true history though "lacking in documents" of the archival sort—is the Holy Spirit at work in "secret" (441–42), and "healing" is made possible by "incarnating that ghost" (444).

10   Or, in some ancient texts, of Night; in yet others, of Atlas.

11   First published in *SB* (1919). See also, from the same collection, "Prologue" (*CP* 163); "Song of the Pilgrims" (203–05), where the longed-for gardens, however, are in the North; and "The Roads" (10, 12–14: "the call of the roads is upon me, a desire ... for the lands no foot has trod and the seas no sail has known: ... lands to the west of the evening and east of the morning's birth, / Where the gods unseen in their valleys green are glad at the ends of earth"). In addition, note these early poems: "Laus Mortis" (*CP* 236–37; 29–30: "Cut thy shallop from the shores asunder ... and drift toward the West"), "My Western Garden," and "Sonnet—to John Keats" (both in Don King, "Lost but Found" 167–68, 172–73) .

In a somewhat later poem, "Death in Battle," which reflects Lewis' wartime experience, the speaker longs for "the sweet dim Isle of Apples[12] over the wide sea[']s breast" (CP 223). A similar romantic longing is depicted in John's Island vision in The Pilgrim's Regress, and Lewis the scholar writes of its appeal in his discussion of the garden of medieval allegory (AoL 74–76, 119–20). By then his quest had ended in a more settled sense of discovery (SbJ 238), but as late as 1948, when he was nearly fifty, he could still empathize with (but now critique as well) that Faustian feeling of being drawn on toward a satisfaction never quite to be attained. He has the speaker of "The Landing" tell of a voyage to the Hesperidean isle, glimpsed far off in a telescope, only to find, on reaching the island, not a golden tree but another telescope showing yet another enticing island (CP 41–42).[13] Later still, in Till We Have Faces (9), Lewis has the Fox, the epitome of rationalism, feel uncharacteristically moved by the passage from Euripides's Hippolytus that begins, "Take me to the apple-laden land."[14]

In all of this, Lewis gives expression to that longing which made up one part of his own divided inner life during his early years.[15] Eventually he would understand it as the human hunger for

---

12   This phrase, a standard etymology for Avalon, suggests a possible association forming this early in Lewis' mind between two separate bodies of mythology.

13   Roughly contemporaneous is Lewis' comment on Virgil's portrayal of the refugees from Troy and their "repeated (and always disappointed) belief ... that they have already found" the place where they are destined to resettle, their continuing city—which illustrates the (Augustinian) principle that "the soul cannot know her true aim till she has achieved it" (OHEL 383).

14   Myers provides the identification for this line (Bareface 16), translated by Kovacs as "To the apple-bearing shore of the melodious Hesperides would I go my way" (Euripides 197). In a 1958 letter, Lewis included "some of the choruses of Euripides" among examples of Sehnsucht in ancient poetry (CL 3:996).

15   He wrote in Surprised by Joy that most of his affection was given to mythology, heroes, the Hesperides, Lancelot, and the holy Grail—and yet, he was torn between this love and his conviction that life was nothing more than matter, evolution, and the war (SbJ 174). In one notable instance in the early poems, in the opening section of SB ("The Prison House"), these two sides of Lewis strove and the romantic side lost: the idea that one might "flee away / Into some other country beyond the rosy West" and thus escape "the rankling hate of God and the outworn world's decay" is dismissed as a "cheat" ("Ode for New Year's Day," CP 175; ll. 5–13, 33–34). A similar mood is present in "The Hills of Down" (1915):

> Though
> This world is drear and wan,
> I dare not go
> To dreaming Avalon,
> Nor look what lands
> May lie beyond the last
> Strange sunset strands
> That gleam when day is past
> I' the yearning west. (CP 229–30)

But here the reason for rejection is different—such a journey would entail losing "the goodliness / Of the green hills of Down," themselves a locus for "Joy": the "clean hills" that contrast with industrialized Belfast (CL 1:332).

one's true home beyond this life, believing that if he had a yearning that could not be fulfilled during earthly existence, that was evidence of his *telos* in another realm (see *MC* 121). This outlook is one that Lewis shared with Tolkien and Williams. For them also it took the symbolic form of a fascination with the sea and unknown lands beyond it, demonstrating a remarkable commonality both in the way these writers worked with myths, as makers and not mere students of myth, and in the meanings to which their myths point.

Looking back over the years, Lewis identified his Hesperian fascination as having been "mainly derived from Euripides, Milton, Morris, and the early Yeats."[16] The reference to Milton deserves further attention. In 1917, Lewis wrote to Arthur Greeves about the Attendant Spirit's description in *Comus* of his home "in regions mild of calm and serene air, / Above the smoke and stir of this dim spot / Which men call earth" (ll. 4–6). That last part "always reminds me," Lewis said, "of our walks over the clean hills when we look down into the Nibbelheim below" (*CL* 1:332). He went on to comment on the Attendant Spirit's fuller description toward the end of the masque:

> To the ocean now I fly,
> And those happy climes that lie
> Where day never shuts his eye,
> Up in the broad fields of the sky:
> …
> All amidst the gardens fair
> Of Hesperus, and his daughters three
> That sing about the golden tree .... (*Comus* ll. 976–83)

This passage the young Lewis considered "the best thing of all … so beautifully lonely and romantic" (*CL* 1:333).[17] It is still in his mind at the beginning of his scholarly career, when he explains how Milton used Hesperian imagery ("A Note on *Comus*" 180–81). But even yet he isn't finished with these lines. Years later, when *That Hideous Strength* was at the press, Lewis sent a letter to the *Times Literary Supplement* ("'Above the Smoke and Stir'") in which he argued that the "apparent confusion" in Milton's extraterrestrial location for the Hesperian garden "is not accidental." Rather, Milton was relying on the opinion of seventeenth-century Platonists "that in the upper air is to be found that reality which the myth of the Hesperian garden erroneously located beyond the 'ocean' [*Comus*, l. 976] at the 'green earth's end' [l. 1014]."

---

16 Lewis' preface to the 1950 reissue of his poem *Dymer* (*NP* 4). The whole paragraph (4–5) sheds light on his efforts, while completing *Dymer* in the mid-1920s, to free himself from the what he considered the illusory lure of the Hesperides.

17 The same letter reminds us, in passing, that Lewis was already familiar with the Arthurian legends (*CL* 1:334). In fact, it is clear from several earlier letters that Malory has been among his favorite writers for well over two years. A bit later he's at the university again slogging through Geoffrey of Monmouth in his spare time (1:468), but it's myth—not history, even pseudohistory—that captivates him.

Lewis' concern in this letter is to explain Milton's cosmology, not to expound his own; hence the garden with its golden apples is still within the Moon's orbit—and there, too, is found a place of healing (*Comus*, ll. 998–99).[18] Yet in contrasting "reality" and "myth" Lewis also hints at Venus as he had imagined it in an earlier novel in the trilogy. There, Ransom "opened his eyes and saw a strange heraldically coloured tree loaded with yellow fruits and silver leaves. Round the base ... was coiled a small dragon covered with scales of red gold. He recognized the garden of the Hesperides at once" (*Per* 45). Having had an education much like Lewis' own, he would. And he went on to speculate whether "things which appeared as mythology on earth [were] scattered through other worlds as realities" (45).[19]

Ancient authors disagreed on the exact location of the Hesperian garden. For Hesiod (*Theogony*, ll. 215, 274–75), it lay just outside the Ocean that surrounds the world. Some later poets, perhaps less comfortable with things beyond their ken (or appealing to audiences in a more rationalistic age), put it at the farthest western reaches of the *known* world where, in Euripides's words, a "sacred boundary" is "fixe[d]" by "the pillar held up by Atlas" (197). It is there too, the poets say, that the sun goes down.[20]

But Euripides's choral ode that the young Lewis found so shatteringly evocative (see *SbJ* 217) reflects an imaginative association between this garden and another place of ancient myth, Elysium, which almost by definition had to be out of this world. Whatever route Hercules took by land or sea to pluck the golden apples, reaching the Happy Fields alive required supernatural aid. For Hesiod, this region, too, was outside the encircling Ocean, literally beyond the sunset,[21] and he called it "the Islands of the Blessed" (*Works and Days*, l. 171). There were complicating developments. Some who died were thought to deserve an equally pleasant afterlife. For these, in Plato and Virgil, there would be an Elysium underground, and as Eastern concepts gained influence in Europe this became a place as well for souls awaiting reincarnation (Howatson 210).[22]

Plutarch, renowned for both learning and inventiveness and ever ready to put ancient lore to his own uses, would play both roles: historian and mythographer. Writing of sailors in the early first century

---

18   The Attendant Spirit later identifies the Moon as his abode (line 1017), not—as Lewis goes on to note in his letter—the heavens properly so called. In his poem *The Fall of Arthur*, Tolkien also hints that the place of healing, the fabled Avalon, may be outside Earth (see below).

19   Perhaps Ransom, too, had read the philosopher Henry More, whom Lewis cites in his letter to *TLS*. It should also be noted that Hesperus himself (whose name is also the Greek for 'West') is the evening star, distinct in mythology from the morning star, Phosphorus or Lucifer. Ancient astronomers, however—as the Greeks learned from the Babylonians (Klibansky et al. 136)—recognized that they were the same; and not a star but a planet, namely Venus. For Charles Williams, too, the point had some significance, as we see in a scene that will claim our attention later in this study: "far away on the horizon, [Pauline] half-thought she saw a star—Hesper or Phosphor, the planet that is both the end and the beginning, Venus ..." (*DiH* 163).

20   i.e. (to use today's maps), the coastal mountain range in northwestern Africa that bears Atlas's name. That is the location usually given, but there were others (see Graves 50, 127–30). There and in Frazer's notes in his edition of Apollodorus (1:220, 231), many references to classical texts are provided. For selected quotations from these, see Atsma, "Hesperides."

21   In this he agrees with Homer (*Odyssey* 4.561–68).

22   See also Atsma, "Realm of Elysion," for a compilation of relevant ancient texts.

BCE who had "come back from the Atlantic islands" with reports of their marvelous climate and fertility, he identified them as the storied Islands of the Blest [μακάρων νῆσοι, *makárōn nêsoi*]."[23] But in another work, Plutarch said that those in Elysium live on the unseen side of the moon (*Moralia* 944C, 12:211; cf. 12:17–18, 195–96n*d*, 15:375)—which may help to account for Milton's lines in *Comus*. But it was the other tradition, the impulse to place mythical narratives on real maps, that led Dante to invent a new myth, in which a restless Ulysses launched out past the Pillars of Hercules (Gibraltar and Ceuta), into the unknown sea seeking adventure (*Inferno* 26.90–142). To this quest, Tennyson would add Ulysses' hope of possibly reaching the "Happy Isles" (Tennyson 89, "Ulysses," l. 64). Dante did indeed bring him within sight of the Earthly Paradise (ll. 133–35)—but that was only the island of those not yet, but to be, blest. It is the connection with Paradise, of course, that brings us, by way of Milton's depiction of Eden, where "Hesperian fables [are] true" (*Paradise Lost* 4.250), to the silvery fruit in a hilltop garden in the newly created Narnia.[24] The appeal of such images to Lewis did not depend on location, whether on earth or in the heavens. His "delight" in viewing the stars might evoke a fancy that each star is "a happy isle / Where eternal gardens smile / And golden globes of fruit are seen."[25]

But what have classical myths to do with Avalon and Elwin Ransom? Avalon and the Pendragon spring out of Celtic legend, not Greek. Still, the Irish and the Welsh have their own stories of the Happy Isles and of westward voyages in search of them.[26] Avalon was an earthly paradise in the western seas—akin to the Greek Hesperides—before its final transformation as the place of Arthur's healing. The twelfth-century Welsh bishop and historian Geoffrey of Monmouth, whom Lewis was reading as an undergraduate at University College (*CL* 1:441, 468), called Avalon "Insula Pomorum," the Isle of Apples, apparently deriving the name, not unreasonably, from the Welsh *afal* 'apple'; and Geoffrey added that the island is called "Fortunate" (*Vita Merlini*, l. 908; Chambers 256; qtd. in Williams, "Figure" 35). Some of this may have been in Tennyson's mind when he had Arthur speak of the

> island-valley of Avilion;
Where falls not hail, or rain, or any snow,
Nor ever wind blows loudly, but it lies
Deep-meadow'd, happy, fair with orchard lawns
And bowery hollows crown'd with summer sea,
Where I will heal me of my grievous wound. (Tennyson 67, "Morte" ll. 310–15)

23 Plutarch, *Sertorius* 8.2, in *Lives* 8:20–21. The distances recorded by Plutarch match no existing configuration of islands, but the translator conjectures the Madeiras are meant, with touches of the Canaries in the description (8:21n). These archipelagos, together with the Azores to the north and the Cape Verde Islands to the south, are known to modern geographers as Macaronesia (the Greek name anglicized).

24 Lewis, *Magician's Nephew*, chap. 13. Cf. Christopher, "Mount Purgatory" 68–71.

25 "Song" (*CL* 1:372–73); these lines slightly revised for publication in 1919 (*CP* 206).

26 As modern scholarship, especially in art history and archeology, reveals early contact between Mediterranean and northern Atlantic cultures, it seems likely that such Celtic tales may have contributed to developments in Greek and Roman accounts in late antiquity.

True, the more immediate verbal echoes here are of Homer's *Odyssey* (4.561–68) or later Greek and Latin writings in a similar vein. In fact, the whole question of just how the Celts imaged their Other Worlds is complicated by the probability that Geoffrey was here showing off his classical learning.[27]

Nevertheless, as historian Geoffrey Ashe reminds us, the Celts "had ideas of the paradisal west going far beyond anything Greece could offer" (262). The Celtic *locus amoenus* is not associated with the dead but with the deathless.[28] It resembles the garden of which the Attendant Spirit speaks at the close of Milton's masque, a place of perpetual light and "eternal summer." That is a house of healing as well, where on beds "drenche[d] with Elysian dew … young Adonis oft reposes," attended "sadly" by Venus, "waxing well of his deep wound" (*Comus* ll. 976–77, 987, 995–1001).

Out of such images from a variety of texts, Lewis conceives his Perelandrian Avalon. He goes further, introducing into the mix an important Judeo-Christian allusion. As Ransom explains, the Pendragon Arthur sits in the hall of King Melchisedec, along with Enoch, Elias, and Moses; "for Arthur did not die; but Our Lord took him" (*THS* 322).[29] Unlike the others, Arthur is there to be healed. Lewis had seen that the legends disagree concerning Arthur's fate after the last battle; it is clear which version he prefers. In March 1919, he is reading, in prose translation, Laȝamon's *Brut,* a Middle English poem that owes much to Geoffrey's *History*. He comments to Arthur Greeves that in Laȝamon "the passing of Arthur is really more romantic than in Malory, who … makes Avalon a really existing valley where the great king is buried" (*CL* 1:440). Malory's account is more ambivalent than Lewis' letter allows,[30] but it was Laȝamon's that sparked

27   See Chambers 31. This book is one of three modern Arthurian studies that Lewis recommended (*CL* 2:673).

28   McCulloch 2:692. To a lesser extent, Tennyson's description also echoes a non-Elysian, earthly scene in Homer, the garden of King Alcinous (*Odyssey* 7.110ff). To be sure, the dead also went west, in some Celtic tales, but not into bliss. Cf. Charles Williams' allusions to these tales in "Figure" 80 and "The Coming of Palomides," ll. 24–27 (*TtL* 33).

29   Why this group? The first three of Arthur's companions are stated not to have died (Gen. 5:24; 2 Kings 2:11; Heb. 7:3; 11:5). Although Moses's death is recorded, there are problems associated with it (Deut. 34:5–6; Jude 9), and in apocryphal tradition he too was taken to Paradise (Charlesworth 1:725, 927n1j), whence with Elias he appeared at the Transfiguration (Luke 9:30–31). "Paradise," like "heaven" in 2 Kings 2:11 (AV), does not mean Paradise in Dante's sense. According to one tradition, the deaths of Enoch and Elias were only deferred: they came to be identified by some commentators with the two "witnesses" in Revelation 11 who are slain, then resurrected and taken to Heaven (see Kelly and Livingston 99–100).

30   Malory does relate Arthur's own uncertain hope for healing in "the vale of Avylyon" (but "if thou here nevermore of me, pray for my soule"), and he goes on to take notice of a legend, widespread in England in his time, "that kynge Arthure ys nat dede, but h[ad] by the wyll of oure Lorde Jesu into another place; and men say that he shall com agayne." Malory is skeptical, preferring to accept Sir Bedivere's assertion that the corpse the hermit had just buried "in a chapell besydes Glassyngbyry" was Arthur's. The name Avalon had long been associated with Glastonbury (which also figures in the Grail legend), and it was said that Arthur's sword was forged in Avalon. Long before Malory's time an excavation in the Abbey grounds had turned up a coffin containing, it was claimed, Arthur's bones, and the monks had welcomed an influx of sight-seers. (Laȝamon's poem was written around 1200, soon after that exhumation.) Malory proceeds

Lewis' imagination. Lewis in his letter continues quoting the *Brut*: "They say he abideth in Avalon with Argante [a variant of "Morgan"] the fairest of all elves: but ever the Britons think that he will come again to help them at their need."[31] Lewis adds that he had written a poem based on Laȝamon but couldn't persuade the publisher Heinemann to include it in his forthcoming collection of poetry. That poem is now lost,[32] and we cannot know whether it included Arthur's healing in Avalon, which appears in the *Brut* a few lines before the passage that Lewis quoted (Laȝamon 254) and to which Tennyson, working from Malory, gave such prominence. Arthur's continued life and promised return may be matters of legend—what "the Britons think"—but they are imaginatively real to Lewis. For him, Avalon is not the Virgilian kingdom of dead heroes but a place redolent of Celtic mystery, the abode of those still alive though no longer in our world. In *That Hideous Strength*, Lewis adds another twist, linking Arthur with biblical stories of those mysteriously "translated" (Heb. 11:5, AV) to the heavenly realm without dying. Exactly where to find them only two or three know, presumably instructed by the Oyéresu,[33] for Perelandra is large and "Aphallin" lies "beyond the seas of Lur," a "distant island which the descendants of Tor and Tinidril will not find for a hundred centuries" (*THS* 322, 441).[34]

---

to quote one of the current versions of the inscription found at the tomb, "*Hic iacet Arthurus, Rex quondam Rexque futurus*" (suspiciously rhyming and including alongside its proof of burial an element from the legend implying, possibly by inadvertence, not merely the king's return but his resurrection; or is Arthur, like Lewis' Merlin in Bragdon Wood, in a state of suspended animation?). See Malory 3:1240–42 and Vinaver's commentary (3:1655); Williams, "Figure" 43–45; Chambers 112–17, 217–21. The question of why the monks dug up the coffin in the late 1100s and whether the inscription was a forgery is discussed by the archeologist Alcock (73–80).

31   "And I say the sooner the better," exclaims Lewis' narrator (*VDT* 19). He is using the Arthurian parallel to explain the sudden reappearance of the four children to aid Prince Caspian in setting Narnia to rights, thirteen Narnian centuries since they had first ruled Narnia. Readers have just been introduced to Eustace as the obnoxious product of modern ideas of child-rearing that constitute, in the speaker's view, a crisis that required a comparable rescuing miracle.

32   None of the recently discovered early poems, from a manuscript of c. 1917 (King, "Lost but Found" 195–6n15), fits Lewis' description. The letter to Greeves that mentions this poem was written in 1919, only weeks before *SB* was published. The poem had been part of the book that Lewis submitted, but the publisher cut it out. In his "Conjectural Essay," Joe R. Christopher offers some guesses about its possible contents (4–7). Lewis retained his interest in Laȝamon. In the last year of his life, translating the *Brut* into modern English was a project he was considering (Hooper, Foreword xiii). That never materialized, but in 1963 he did publish a wide-ranging introduction to a book of Arthurian extracts, "the best part" of Laȝamon's long poem (Lewis, Introduction xv). He discussed issues of authorship, sources and Laȝamon's relation to them, the work's merits as poetry, and its prosody compared to that of Old English. His use of the first-person plural at the end (xiv: "We have preferred …") suggests that he may have had a hand in selecting passages to include.

33   Merlin: "In my college it was thought that only two men in the world knew this" (*THS* 322).

34   Lewis' spelling of the place name is inconsistent. The one given here is from p. 441. Distinct from this "cup-shaped land" is another Venusian place of healing, the mountain-top scene of Ransom's recuperation from his fight with Weston and the ensuing underground ordeal (*Per* 184–85).

Two phrases concerning Arthur's destiny invite further exploration: "beyond the seas" and "Our Lord took him" (322). For the first we will turn now to our other two writers. Tolkien and Williams both have a great interest in symbolic geography. Williams' anthropomorphic map of Europe is well known;[35] the map Tolkien imagined is less allegorical but more extensive.[36] In both, the most highly privileged direction is west. The symbolic significance of the setting sun is deeply wrought in our culture. To the west the sun still shines when it has set for us. The defeated Trojans went west to found a new nation; the Greeks called Italy Hesperia, and the Romans gave the same name to Spain. Bishop Berkeley foresaw "empire" taking its course westward; Horace Greeley echoed him in his advice to ambitious youth.[37] In Tolkien, west is the direction that Gondorians face in "a moment of silence" before a meal, looking "toward Númenor that was, and beyond to Elvenhome that is, and to that which is beyond Elvenhome and will ever be" (*LotR* 2:284–85, 4.5). The West is where the Noldor look for the coming of their hope from across the ocean (*Silm* 125, 240).

Yet for Tolkien (and, as we shall see, for Williams too), the western sea is ambivalent, inviting but potentially sinister. When the elf Legolas, born and raised in the forest, first hears seagulls crying, the effect takes him by surprise, yet he finds it natural. He suddenly recognizes, perhaps for the first time, where his true home is. "Deep in the hearts of all my kindred lies the sea-longing" (*LotR* 3:149; 5.9), for the sea is the path to Elvenhome.[38] Early in the fourth millennium of the Third Age, Shire-dwellers begin to notice Elves passing westward toward the Grey Havens. "'They are sailing, sailing, sailing over the Sea, they are going into the West and leaving us,' said Sam, half chanting the words, shaking his head sadly and solemnly" (1:54; 1.2); but others had "sought the Havens long ago" (1:297; 2.3). Frodo is surprised to encounter Gildor Inglorion and his companions, because "not many now remain in Middle-earth, east of the Great Sea"; the elf explains that they are at last going home from "Exile" (1:89; 1.3). Soon after, Frodo dreams, as he has before, of hearing "the Sea far-off; a sound he had never heard in waking life," and he is not, as before, "troubled," but filled with "a great desire" (1:119; 1.5). All these quotations are from *The Fellowship of the Ring*; in this way Tolkien, early in his tale, points forward to the end when two Ring-bearers will join Gandalf and elves in sailing from the Havens.

A similar desire long before had impelled Bilbo as a poet, singing (though without mentioning the sea) of "the hidden paths that run / Toward the Moon or to the Sun" (*LotR* 1:87; 1.3). Moon and Sun are

---

35   *TtL*, end papers. Reprinted in King, *Pattern* 27, and in Dodds's edition, *AP*.

36   Lobdell devotes a chapter to exploring the significance of all the directions in Tolkien's geography (71–93).

37   Within this historical sequence, Lewis detected a shift in mood from the romantic longings of ancient imaginings—which retained their hold on his own imagination—to the increasingly commercial and political motives behind journeys from Columbus onward (OHEL 14–15).

38   Tolkien is here refashioning motifs that had been part of his myth from its earliest stages. In a manuscript dating *c*. 1917, he tells how Tuor encounters seagulls and then becomes "the first of Men to reach the Sea and look upon it and know the desire it brings" (*LT* 2:151). The passage is repeated with only minor changes in a 1951 retelling of the story (*UT* 24–25); see also *Silm* 238. The cry of gulls, we may note, evokes similar feelings in the narrator of Lewis' *LWW* (178).

a significant part of Tolkien's symbolism. Tuor's first sight of the sea (see preceding note) occurs just at sunset, and in succeeding days "on quiet evenings when the sun went down beyond the edge of the sea [his longing] grew to a fierce desire" (*LT* 2:152). Tuor's son Eärendil inherited his "insatiable sea-longing" (Tolkien, *Letters* 386) and, in the earliest form of his adventures, a poem written in 1914, sets forth on his journey from the western shores of Middle-earth "down the sunlit breath of Day's fiery Death" (*LT* 2:268n). In Tolkien's revision of the tale of Tuor, the wording is a little different: "beyond the rim of the world" (*UT* 24–25).

The implications are fleshed out in a story Tolkien made up for his sons while on a seaside holiday in 1925 (on the east coast of England, however, not the west; hence the shift from sunset to moonrise). In the story, from a "house that looked right out over the waves to nowhere" one can see, at moonrise, "the silver path across the waters that is the way to places at the edge of the world *and beyond*, for those that can walk on it" (*Roverandom* 8; emphasis supplied). An enchanted toy dog is carried by a seagull "along the moon's path … straight from the shore to the dark edge of nowhere" (19) and then past the flat world's edge, "where waterfalls … dropped straight into space" (21), and on to the moon. It is pure whimsy, nursery stuff, and yet recognizably cut from the same cloth as the Middle-earth cosmology about which Tolkien took so much greater pains. In fact, he finds a place even in this tale for a glimpse of the "Mountains of Elvenhome" (74). He also tells of a valley where golden apples grow (49).

The cosmology that Tolkien imagines in this story helps us see why Bilbo sings of paths that are "hidden." It is not simply that he knows the general direction to take but not the exact route. By Bilbo's time, the world is no longer flat, and now the way itself belongs to a realm of mystery. For although the sea is a path, it is also a barrier: Galadriel's voice is both "sad and sweet" when, parting from the Nine Walkers, she sings of the "Sundering Seas" that divide her from the longed-for land "beyond the Sun, beyond the Moon" (*LotR* 1:389; 2.8).[39] "Darkness lies on the foaming waves," and she feels the way is "lost" (1:394; 2.8). It is a barrier that betokens, in Tolkien's myth, something akin to the Expulsion from Eden, reversible only with help from a higher power. True, in the Third Age only a minority of the elder race remain exiled in Middle-earth. Most of the Elves have been taken long since to Valinor or Tol Eressëa. Yet when they first came down to the sea, long after their "Awakening," it filled them with fear until, by the music of the god Ulmo, their fear was transformed to desire (*Silm* 48, 54, 57). Even the Ainur could be troubled and restless because of the sounds of the waves; yet, to underscore the ambiguity, the Elves say that fading tones of the original Music of the Ainur can be heard in water Ainur more than in any other part of the created order (19). Desire is uppermost; but to fulfill it is not within one's own power. Valinor has become "hidden," and Eressëa is guarded by Enchanted Isles and Shadowy Seas that defeat even Eärendil without the Silmaril's protection (246–48).

---

39   The idea of locating a paradisal world behind the sun goes back to ancient times: see, for example, Charlesworth 1:168 (2 Enoch 42:4 and note). Tolkien probably also thought of the well-known Norwegian fairy tale "East of the Sun and West of the Moon," or William Morris's verses with the same title in *The Earthly Paradise*. Williams places Sarras beyond sun and stars (see the reference to "beyond the sun" on page 134); Lewis uses the phrase to locate Aslan's country (*VDT* 178, 182, 218).

Tol Eressëa is the Lonely Isle, so called because it was drawn to within sight of the Blessed Realm, Valinor, but no farther, and then fixed in the sea. Nothing ever fades or withers in Valinor (*Silm* 38), and Eressëa too is a place of blessing: itself the object of longing for Legolas, who in verse hears "sweet … voices in the Lost Isle calling, / … / Where the leaves fall not" (*LotR* 3:234; 6.4). Its chief city, on the shore facing west toward Valinor, is called Avallónë (*Silm* 260), a name having the same root as Valar, but on the printed page inevitably striking the reader first as a variant on Avalon.[40] It is here that, by Arwen's "gift," Frodo is sent "until all [his] wounds and weariness are healed" (*LotR* 3:252, 253; 6.6).[41]

Nor is this the only association of the Undying Lands with healing. The *Akallabêth* relates how Isildur was grievously wounded in rescuing a fruit from the tree Nimloth that had come from Eressëa, lay for months near death, and was quickly healed once the seed sprouted and came into leaf (*Silm* 273). Several times in *The Lord of the Rings*, we encounter the healing herb *athelas*. Of its origin we are told only that "the Men of the West brought [it] to Middle-earth" (*LotR* 1:210; 1.12), but it seems reasonable to suppose that it came originally from Valinor.[42] This guess is supported by the account given of its use in the Houses of Healing in Minas Tirith, where ancient lore—"The hands of the king are the hands of a healer" (*LotR* 3:136; 5.8)—validates Aragorn's claim to kingship.[43] When he "cast the leaves into the bowls of steaming water … the fragrance … was like a memory of dewy mornings of unshadowed sun in some land of which the fair world in Spring is itself but a fleeting memory" (3:142; 5.8).[44] I am reminded of lines by a great Catholic poet that may well have come to Tolkien's attention in the early years of his mythmaking. Tolkien returned to Oxford after the war in 1918, the same year that the University Press there issued the first edition of Gerard Manley Hopkins's poetry, in which the use of Old English verse rhythms, in particular, could have aroused Tolkien's interest.[45] "Nothing is so beautiful as Spring,"

---

40   In versions of Tolkien's myth that did not find their way into print during his lifetime, Avallon (which is a common spelling found in Irish legends) is also a name given to Eressëa itself (Tolkien, *Peoples* 144). On the derivation from Valar: Tolkien, *MR* 175n. Tolkien also at one time played with using Avallon as a name for Númenor, but rejected it (*Return of the Shadow* 215).

41   The word "all" is important, since Frodo had experienced times of partial healing during his journey, notably in Rivendell and Lothlórien (a "land where days bring healing not decay," healing for Gandalf as well [*LotR* 2:106; 3.5]) and then with the aid of Galadriel's gifts—but only enough to enable him to continue his task. From Arwen he receives a material gift as well: her gemstone necklace for the healing of his "memory" (3:253).

42   Westernesse came into being only at the beginning of the Second Age, and Elves from Eressëa brought healing herbs with them when they came to Westernesse (*Silm* 263).

43   Jane Chance discusses the significance of this scene (226–27); see also Flieger 133–34. That the healing hands are viewed as a more-than-casual attribute of royalty is evident from the description of Aragorn at his coronation (*LotR* 3:246; 6.5).

44   It was in the dark, "by the scent of its leaves," that Strider found *athelas* growing wild in the thickets below Weathertop and brought it to treat Frodo's wound; its "refreshing" steam "calmed and cleared" the minds of those standing by (1:210, 211; 1.12). The "wise-woman" Ioreth (3:139), though skeptical regarding its healing power, knows "it smells sweet when bruised," or, more accurately, "wholesome" (3:140; 5.8).

45   Charles Williams reports that "the poems were a literary sensation. All the papers reviewed them; everyone who was anyone talked of them" ("Gerard Hopkins" 49).

Hopkins writes, and after seven more lines of luscious description he asks, "What is all this juice and all this joy? / A strain of the earth's sweet being in the beginning / In Eden garden" (142). Valinor and its satellite Eressëa are, in this respect (though not, of course, in relation to humankind), Tolkien's version of the Earthly Paradise.

Frodo is one of only a few mortals who, by special dispensation, were ever permitted to set foot in the blessed lands. One other did so without permission, the renegade king Ar-Pharazôn the Golden, in prideful folly breaking the Ban that the Valar had explicitly pronounced. To summarize how that came about:[46] after the First Age a new home was raised up in the great western ocean to reward the races of Men who had remained faithful. Keen-eyed mariners from this land, Númenor, could see Eressëa in the west (*Silm* 263). But the Ban forbade sailing farther west to within sight of Valinor, which could still be seen with mortal eyes at that time. Númenor flourished for more than thirty centuries, but finally, dreaming of an even greater prosperity beyond the scope of mortals, arrogantly defied the Ban. The king's trespass brought about a massive upheaval of the sea that overwhelmed Númenor. Only a faithful few escaped to found the line of Western kings in Middle-earth. The sea thus demonstrated that, for those whose *desires* were flawed, the more appropriate response toward it would be, indeed, *fear*. Further, this cataclysm turned the world itself, originally flat in Tolkien's mythical cosmogony, into a globe. The Blessed Realm was no longer accessible by any ordinary journeying. Unless specially favored by the Valar, those who sailed west far enough simply came back around to Middle-earth.

Tolkien's nomenclature shows that he, like Lewis, was very much alive to the resonances between his created myth and those of other cultures, and not only in the name Avallonë, already noted. He explains that the name *Númenor* "means Westernesse" or, in "ancient English ... *Westfolde*, Hesperia" (*SD* 305, 303, 309n16; see also *Letters* 151n). The drowned Númenor came to be called, by those who escaped, *Atalantë*, meaning 'the Ruin'—derived, Tolkien explains, from one of his invented languages and only "by chance" (his phrase) resembling the name in Greek legend for the drowned civilization that gives the Atlantic Ocean its name (*Peoples* 158).[47] Yet as he acknowledges elsewhere, the legend of Atlantis is firmly implanted in racial memory and has "profoundly affected the imagination of peoples of Europe with westward-shores" (*Letters* 303)—of no one more than himself.[48] In 1955, *Time and Tide* published his poem "Imram" (rpt. in *SD* 296–99), a work entirely outside the Middle-earth history yet connected with it. Here he reworked something he had composed about ten years before as part of a book he never finished, *The Notion Club Papers*, which also contained an early version of the *Akallabêth*. The poem was labeled then "The Death of St. Brendan" (*SD* 261–64).

The *immram* ('voyage') is one of the classic Old Irish genres, narrating a marvelous ocean journey to wondrous islands such as Tír na nÓg, the Land of Youth. Most of the extant examples reflect a combination

---

46   See the "Akallabêth: The Downfall of Númenor," in *Silm* 259–82.

47   For Tolkien's translation of "the Ruin": *LR* 14. For his alternative translations and etymology, see *LR* 8n, 354 (under DAT-), 390 (under TALÁT-).

48   I have dealt more extensively elsewhere with the grip the Atlantis myth had on Tolkien's imagination and the parallels he saw with stories in Genesis ("Tolkien, Epic Traditions, and Golden Age Myths" 95–96).

of pagan and Christian ideas. The most famous is one that takes motifs from earlier *immrama* and attaches them to the figure of St. Brendan, a sixth-century Irish abbot already known for his travels. The Latin *Navigatio Sancti Brendani* achieved great popularity, being circulated and translated all over Europe and surviving today in well over a hundred manuscripts. This story, instead of giving an account of Brendan's actual journeys, does what is not uncommon in medieval hagiography: it creates a fantastic legend. Brendan and seventeen companions journey by ship for seven years, miraculously nourished, protected through many perils, and visiting sites ranging from the Island of Delights to the environs of Hell. Finally, they pass through a dense darkness to reach the Land of Promise of the Saints. After forty days there, they are told to return home and live out their lives faithfully.

The island of St. Brendan became a standard feature for medieval cartographers. A globe made in 1492 (so much for the popular idea today that before Columbus everyone was a flat-worlder) shows a land mass stretching from the western tip of Africa eastward to China, with various islands offshore on either end. Separating those two ends is a large ocean, and in the middle of that—much like Dante's Mount Purgatory—is an island labeled "Insula de Santi Branden."[49] It rises in splendid isolation just as, in some accounts, the highest bit of Atlantis or the holy mountain of Númenor, Meneltarma (*Silm* 281), might still be seen protruding above the waves.[50]

Adventures like those related in the *Navigatio* helped to shape Tolkien's story of Eärendil in its early development.[51] But when Tolkien tackles the Brendan tale, he writes in verse and leaves out most of the details in the *Navigatio*. Most significantly, he adapts the story to his larger interests.[52] Instead of proceeding in chronological order from the voyage's inception to its end, Tolkien begins with Brendan's return to Ireland, where he is asked to tell

49 See the illustration in Delumeau 69.

50 See Bonnie GoodKnight's drawing on the cover of *Mythlore* 4.2 (1976) and the description of its scenes on p. 2.

51 Many similarities can be seen in the texts assembled by Christopher Tolkien in *LT* 2:254–77.

52 He wants to reveal the deeper meaning in what for his eleventh-century predecessor was only shallowly didactic entertainment with no "glimmer of a perception" of its mythical resonances (*SD* 265). Both Lewis and Williams held similar attitudes toward inherited myths, as noted above. Compare Lewis' reworking of the Cupid and Psyche myth in *TWHF* because "Apuleius got it all wrong" (*CL* 3:590; see Huttar, "What C. S. Lewis Really Did") and Charles Williams' remark quoted above (note 8) about the limitations of the earliest Arthurian storytellers. As for the Victorian poets who wrote of the Grail, none of them, Williams said, "had the full capacity of the mythical imagination." Only Malory presented "the whole grand Myth—or at least much of it," and even he "does not seem altogether to have understood" all the meaning that he suggests ("Malory" 187) or did not "trouble to work out the possibilities" (*TtL* 95; see also Williams, "Figure" 93). There is a hint of this view in Merlin's warning to Taliessin: "Fortunate the poet who endures / to measure in his mind the distance even to Carbonek" (*RSS* 12; "The Calling of Taliessin," ll. 217–18). And we can see Williams, in his poetry, altering his predecessors so as to improve, according to his lights, on the myth—for example, in the immediate onset of Lancelot's madness: see Williams, "Malory" 190, and Lewis, *WA* 158–61.

of islands by deep spells beguiled
         where dwell the Elvenkind:
in seven long years the road to Heaven
         or the Living Land did you find?[53] (*SD* 296; "Imram," ll. 17–20)

In reply, Brendan tells of the only three things he remembers: a cloud, a tree, and a star. Under the cloud rises "a shoreless mountain" (34) that is "grounded in chasms the waters drowned / and swallowed long ago" and that "stands, I guess, on the foundered land / where the kings of kings lie low" (41–44). The manuscript drafts show that Tolkien worked over these lines carefully as he drew the volcano of Brendan's *Navigatio* into his Atlantis myth (*SD* 261, 265, 295). The travelers arrive next at a "hollow isle" (81) where, in a "dale ... like a silver grail / with carven hills for rim" (65–66; in an earlier draft, "a green cup" filled with sunshine [*SD* 263]) there stands

a Tree more fair than ever I deemed
         in Paradise might grow:
its foot was like a great tower's root,
         its height no man could know. (69–72)

There are resonances here of the Tree of Life of Judeo-Christian tradition and the world-tree of Norse myth, Yggdrasil—and imagery of a cup or grail, we may note, resembling that of Lewis' Abhalljin. Brendan mistakenly supposes this is the end of the voyaging, "for no return / we hoped, but there to stay" (79–80). Then Brendan hears a musical voice, neither human nor angelic, and thinks that

maybe ... a third
fair kindred in the world yet lingers
         beyond the foundered land.
But steep are the seas and the waters deep
         beyond the White-tree Strand! (92–96)

If we recall Tolkien's myth in which the Elves are a "kindred" placed between Valar and Men in the chain of being, these lines clearly suggest Elvenhome. Of his third memory, the star, Brendan says, "I saw it high and far / at the parting of the ways, / a light on the edge of the Outer Night" (101–03). Christopher Tolkien sees here an allusion to the apotheosis of Eärendil (*SD* 292n80)—

where the round world plunges steeply down,
         but on the old road goes,
as an *unseen bridge* that on arches runs
         to coasts that no man knows. (105–08; emphasis supplied)

---

53   It is not clear whether the questioner thinks of "Heaven" and "the Living Land" as synonymous, though deriving from Christian and pre-Christian cultures respectively, or as referring to alternative destinations.

Brendan remembers "the breath as sweet and keen as death / that was borne upon the breeze" from those coasts (115–16), but his knowledge ends there. The poem closes with Brendan's death, his final "journey" (in stark contrast to the one reported) "whence no ship returns" (131).

Here, in a framework drawn from the Primary World (though admittedly that world's legends), Tolkien sets ideas he was developing in his Secondary World histories: after the fall of Númenor, sailing west merely brought the mariner around the earth and back to his starting point: the paths of the sea were bent back upon themselves. The Elves, however, were allowed to sail to Avallónë along a straight road over an invisible bridge (*Silm* 281–82).[54] He thus stakes a larger claim for the universality of these ideas.[55]

Tolkien's Arthurian fragment, *The Fall of Arthur*, employs a Primary World geography not so fantastic as that of the Brendan legends. King Arthur, having defeated the heathen marauders who troubled his coastlands, sails *east* and carries the warfare to the European continent, the Saxon homeland, and finally "to Mirkwood's margin" (*FoA* 18–19; I.43, 68).[56] "Mirkwood" is familiar from Tolkien's more fantastic tales, but it was not his invention; he adopted it (see Shippey, *Author* 33–34) from old heroic narratives firmly set in the known world, fictionalized perhaps, but not fantasized. Tolkien adapts that medieval way of storytelling, adding his own eerie touches, such as the ghostly horsemen who ride threateningly in the eastern sky and "phantom foes // with fell voices" (20; I.86–89, 94), and perhaps the uncanny speed of the army's return to Britain when Arthur learns of Mordred's treachery. In the 948 lines that Tolkien wrote, then, we have a straightforward heroic tale based on what might loosely be called the national myth of England, with only the slenderest of ties, the place name Mirkwood, to suggest any connection to the Secondary World that had long been central to Tolkien's imaginative work.

But in the poem as a whole, if Tolkien had completed it in accordance with the sketches and trial verses that he left (though, as the editor points out [*FoA* 141], they are not all mutually consistent), its

---

54 See the upper right medallion in the cover art referred to in n50.

55 Tolkien not only employed the *immrama* for narrative purposes but clearly felt a kinship with the heroes of those adventures; in his poem "Mythopoeia" he takes them as a model for his own aspirations as a "legend-maker" (line 91). First, he praises their vision and courage:

> Blessed are the men of Noah's race that build
> their little arks, though frail and poorly filled,
> and steer through winds contrary toward a wraith,
> a rumour of *a harbour guessed by faith*. (87–90; emphasis supplied)

Then he aligns himself with them:

> I would be with the mariners of the deep
> that cut their slender planks on mountains steep
> and voyage upon a vague and wandering quest,
> for some have passed *beyond the fabled West*. (109–12; emphasis supplied)

56 Arthur's campaign abroad is an essential plot element to enable Mordred's treachery, but, as Christopher Tolkien points out, Tolkien rejected what C. S. Lewis would later call the "tasteless fiction" of the traditional accounts—Geoffrey of Monmouth's "own rather vulgar invention" (*FoA* 74–77; Lewis, Introduction vii)— in favor of a narrative in the older English heroic tradition.

geographical layout would have become more like that of his imagined Arda. Perhaps what he began in quite a different vein was coming under the spell of previously existing conceptions—initially distinct from it but not incompatible—and he suspended the composition so as to work out the best direction to take. He had already, as his son and editor Christopher shows, begun to weave together in his poem rather disparate elements from Arthurian texts while fully rejecting others. Malory, as we have seen, had faced a similar problem of contradictory sources—was Arthur dead and buried, in "Avalon" (Glastonbury) or elsewhere, or healed and living in Avalon?—and he tried to do justice to both sides. The first alternative, Arthur entombed, Tolkien firmly rejected (141).[57] But the matter was complicated for him by a third possibility based in further inventions of his own. The name Eärendel, which appears twice among his jottings (136–37), is the clue to that third option.[58]

Essential to understanding Tolkien is his tendency to view his private mythology, sixty years in the making, as always a work in progress. His famous perfectionism, which resulted in most of his writings being published posthumously, was a matter of substance much more than of style. Thus it is misleading to refer to *The Fall of Arthur* as having been abandoned; as late as 1937 he was still weighing alternatives (*FoA* 155), and twenty years after he suspended work on it he could still say he "hope[d] to finish" it (*Letters* 219).[59] But he did set it aside in the mid-'30s, probably when his mind had become occupied with the time-travel story to which he had committed himself. This involved a new conception: that Eärendil's westward sea journey would become paradigmatic, reenacted several times by father-son pairs across a span of many generations.[60] The Eärendel story had long since evolved from a Brendan-like oceanic adventure into a tale of the hero's redemptive mission and his apotheosis, and it was now developing further to include the destruction of Númenor/Atlantis (*FoA* 151). This was truly a "huge ... perturbation of the existing myth" (154), and the cropping up in Tolkien's mythology of the name Avallon was enough to require a rethinking of where the wounded Arthur was headed when he sailed away from the Cornish shore: somewhere beyond the earthly sphere. Indeed, the need to work out that geographical question in the new larger context may have been one reason for laying aside the Arthurian poem (temporarily, he thought).

In any case, we can guess at his intention (still in flux) by working out as best we can a few lines found among his papers, which place Arthur

---

57   Not long before, he may still have been uncertain. In another fiction, in a context suggestive of Avalon, he wrote "King Arthur's death," but then altered "death" to "disappearance" (*Roverandom* 33, 97–98). In the title of his poem he chose the word "Fall" rather than the "Morte" of his medieval sources.

58   Cf. Shippey's observation that with the story of Eärendil in *The Silmarillion* "Tolkien leaves the mode of heroic chronicle and returns to that of mythology" (*Author* 256).

59   Lewis, in contrast, could readily torch material that dissatisfied him, despite having invested much time in drafting it (see, e.g., *NP* viii–ix). It remained in his mind, however, and sometimes, as with Psyche's story, he would try again much later.

60   Tolkien's work along this line has been laid out and discussed in great detail in two of the "History of Middle-earth" volumes; Christopher Tolkien summarizes it in his new publication (*FoA* 149–54).

beyond the miles of the sea	and the magic islands
beyond the halls of night	upon Heaven's borders
...	in Avalon biding. (*FoA* 139)[61]

The story would continue with Lancelot's arrival, eager to reconcile with both Gawain and Arthur after years of estrangement, but too late. Gawain is dead; Arthur has departed. Christopher Tolkien has called attention to his father's "very original treatment of 'The Legend of Lancelot and Guinevere'" (12),[62] which was to culminate in Lancelot's taking ship and following Arthur's track westward; he "never returns." In another "hastily pencilled note" Tolkien added, "Whether he found him in Avalon and will return no one knows" (136–37). It is hard to guess what thinking lay behind this innovation; doubtless the finished poem would have made it clear. "Never returns" might be taken to mean that he is lost at sea, but the reference to Eärendel that immediately follows, cryptic though it is, negates that reading.[63] A more likely

---

61   The editor finds these "penciled ... verses in the primary stage of composition" to be "of exceptional difficulty" (138). On "magic islands" see pp. 157–58; note, however, that Tolkien's mapping seems not yet quite fixed, since in another draft (138) the "magic islands" are "past the hills of Avalon."

62   See further pp. 164–68. It must be noted that at roughly the same time as Tolkien was working on *FoA*, his close friend C. S. Lewis was writing a poem he entitled "Launcelot" (*NP* 95–103). It too would, after a mere 296 lines, remain unfinished. The story of Lancelot had long been among his favorites (see note 15 above). Walter Hooper dates the period of composition "probably ... in the early 1930s," based on the handwriting (*NP* xii). This judgment seems to be borne out by a letter in March 1932 in which he tells Owen Barfield, "I have written about 100 lines of a long poem in my type of Alexandrine" (*CL* 2:55). No other poem fitting this description is known (though it might, of course, refer to something no longer extant). Tolkien's editor thinks *FoA* was likely begun early in 1932. In 1934, R. W. Chambers read it, though "still far from completion" (*FoA* 11, see also 149); the writing may have continued for another year or two. By 1935, it appears, Lewis also had seen it ("Alliterative Metre" 15n2). But all through the early thirties, Lewis and Tolkien were close friends, and the topic of Lancelot may well have come up now and then in their conversations. I cannot show *influence* in either direction, but the similarities and differences in their handling of the Lancelot story and its larger Arthurian context are worth noting. Both were concerned with the decline and fall of the once flourishing chivalric community. Lewis focuses on the Grail quest, foreseen as disastrous (*NP* 95; ll. 19–26) and ending in failure for most of the knights taking part; Tolkien, on Arthur's misguided effort to turn back time, leading before long to his doom (*FoA* 17, 24; 1.5, 177). Yet common in both accounts is the cooling of Lancelot's passion for Guinevere. In Lewis, it comes about in his two-year absence on the Grail quest (see ll. 69, 94–95, 103–15, and compare ll. 50–61), which one may guess wrought a spiritual change in him that is never explained in the truncated work we have. (Only years later would Lewis discover in Charles Williams—whom he was yet to meet—a similar concern with working out the relationship between Lancelot's Grail quest and his romantic entanglement [see Williams, "Figure" 94].) In Tolkien, the break-up is described in ll. 87–109 of canto 3 (and the depiction in 3.49–62 of Guinevere as a *femme fatale* helps make it credible, as does her self-pity [*FoA* 136]). An immediate result is Lancelot's isolation also from the king (3.140–42), who never reconciles with him, but in Tolkien's projected finish his love for Arthur and rejection of Guinevere are confirmed (*FoA* 136).

63   See the discussion of a related draft passage (137–38, 148–63). I have wondered whether Tolkien might have briefly considered fitting Lancelot into the Eärendil-figure sequence that he was formulating for *LR*, but he seems not to match that pattern in several ways.

meaning is connected, though indirectly, with the second of those lines in *That Hideous Strength* that I chose as springboards for the present discussion: "Our Lord took him."

To understand how that applies to Eärendel and how he fits into the pattern we see developing in our three authors, we should first consider the symbolic meaning of the sea and the West for Charles Williams.[64] Like Tolkien, Williams found symbolic meaning in geography, across the whole sweep of Europe from east to west and beyond. For him, it was a Europe of several centuries ago; for Tolkien, of millennia. We may start with his own succinct statement in the unfinished book on Arthur that Lewis called a "torso": "eastward from Logres" (i.e., Arthur's Britain) is the Christian world of the Empire; "westward from Logres … is the mythical … mysterious forest of Broceliande." Castle Carbonek, where the Grail Hallows are kept, lies within this forest. Still farther west are "the seas on which the ship of Solomon is to sail; beyond them is Sarras" (Williams, "Figure" 80–81).

The first of these westward places can be located on a real map. In Arthur's time, Brocéliande was a vast forest in the northwest corner of France, said to be enchanted.[65] Most of it now has been cleared and goes by other names; judging by the Internet, the name "Brocéliande" survives mainly in the efforts of the tourist industry in Brittany to impart a different sort of enchantment. That dulling of the medieval resonances may be one reason Tolkien emended his name for the northwest region looking out on the great western ocean to "Beleriand" (*Lays* 160, 169). As with Avalon, he wanted his borrowing to be less obvious (and, as we have seen, in the case of Atlantis he denied any borrowing at all). But the enchanted medieval forest represented for Williams the archetypal dark wood found in Dante, Spenser, Milton's *Comus,* and elsewhere, and he gave the name Broceliande a greatly expanded reference:

> Broceliande is somewhere round Cornwall and Devon, to the west of Logres. It is regarded both as a forest and as a sea—a sea-wood; in this sense it joins the sea of the antipodes which lies among its roots. Carbonek is beyond it: or at least beyond a certain part of it; [then comes] the full open sea, beyond which is Sarras. (Williams, "Notes" 179)[66]

Broceliande is the "unpathed" western forest (*TtL* 24; "Bors to Elayne: The Fish of Broceliande," l. 6), a place of potentiality, energy, and creativity; Byzantium, the capital and center of the Empire, is the place

---

64   This section draws mainly on two works by Williams—both of them, like Lewis' "Launcelot" and Tolkien's *FoA,* never completed; in Williams' case, not (we suppose) because of any dissatisfaction but simply because he did not live to finish them. They are his prose historical account "The Figure of Arthur" and his Arthurian poetic cycle, of which two installments were published (*TtL* in 1938 and *RSS* in 1944, each structurally complete in itself yet conceptually part of a larger whole) and a third was in progress. For poems published posthumously and some earlier Arthurian work that the more mature project superseded, see Dodds.

65   Markale 120–23.

66   Lewis included a condensed version of this passage in his commentary (WA 99).

of order; Logres, to thrive, needs both.[67] Indeed, a major theme in Williams' cycle is the co-inherence of these two principles.

But Broceliande is by no means a safe place; its potentiality is for both good and evil. Entering it or even going alongside it is risky: "Dangerous to men is the wood of Broceliande" (*RSS* 9; "The Calling of Taliessin," l. 110). It holds the possibility of enrichment, but also of loss; of salvation—but also of perdition (Lewis, WA 172–73). "Through Broceliande runs the road from earth to heaven"—but also the road to P'o-Lu and hell (WA 99–100). Carbonek, where the Grail and other sacred objects are kept, is "beyond a certain part of it,"[68] but equally Broceliande merges into the ocean that wraps around the earth and that, for Williams as for Tolkien, carries ambivalent significance. On the negative side, the headless emperor and the octopods' grasping tentacles infest the far eastern reaches of the sea (*RSS* "Prelude," ll. 80–84), and Taliessin, traveling alongside the western forest, can see through the woods a threat of "the antipodean ocean … thrusting" into nearby "inlets" under "a dark rose of sunset"; but he also glimpses Merlin's hopeful vision of a time when "the largesse of exchange" is victorious "and the sea of Broceliande enfolds the Empire." "Purpose" may "fail," however (*RSS* 9, 17, 19; "The Calling of Taliessin," ll. 128–30, 349–50, 415–16)—as, in the event, it does, through Arthur's self-centeredness, Mordred's treachery, the Dolorous Stroke, the unasked question, and so on.[69] The Grail, through whose power Carbonek had been for a time a house of healing ("Figure" 67), must depart, taken by Galahad and his companions along "*spiritual* roads / … westward through the trees / of Broceliande" to the Land of the Trinity (ll. 423–25; emphasis supplied).

For, as in Tolkien the roads become bent and there is no longer a navigable route to Valinor, and as in Lewis "Arthur did not die; but Our Lord took him" away to Venus, so in Williams Sarras has been taken out of this world and can be reached only by supernatural means. It is across the western ocean—here again Williams is perfecting the myth, for in medieval tradition Sarras was a city "on the borders of Egypt" ("Figure" 81), and in Malory, ruled by a tyrant who maltreats the Grail-seekers (2:1033). Williams reshapes it into an inaccessible island of granite, located not only beyond the sea, but "beyond the sun" (*RSS* 15; "Calling," l. 310), also called "the land of the Trinity" and "the land of the perichoresis [i.e., the Co-inherence]" (*RSS* 39; "The Founding of the Company," 105). At one stage, he pondered furnishing it with the world-tree of Norse myth, Yggdrasil (Ridler 170). From its "unseen shores" blows a wind, perhaps to be interpreted as the Holy Spirit, and to it against the wind are carried the three lords, Galahad, Percivale, and Bors, and the body of Blanchefleur, in a ship driven not by sail or rowers but by an "infinite flight of

---

67 Cf. Merlin's hopeful prediction (unfulfilled) "that soon / the Empire and Broceliande shall meet in Logres" (*RSS* 12; "The Calling of Taliessin," ll. 209–10).

68 In notes from c. 1930, Williams identifies "Avilion" as "the orchards of Carbonek" ("Notes" 178).

69 In "Figure" (75), Williams traces the connection between the Fisher King's "languishment" and Arthur's aggrandizing inversion of the proper monarchic principle that the king exists for the kingdom's sake (*TtL* 46–47; "The Star of Percivale," ll. 14 and 35).

doves," perhaps also the Holy Spirit; at any rate, "a new-ghosted power" (*TtL* 85, "The Last Voyage," ll. 46, 52).[70] Lewis comments: "we are witnessing apotheosis" (WA 179).[71]

Another poem, "The Prayers of the Pope," tells how they reach Sarras, "the land of the Trinity" located "beyond the summer stars" in "deep heaven," and lie "entranced" for "a year and a day"; meanwhile, the octopods' tentacles become more aggressive until, caught and held by the roots of Broceliande, they and the headless emperor are made "helpless." But "the deep impassable Trinity in the land of the Trinity" "utter[s] unsearchable bliss"; hell is harrowed, even hell must confess and praise God,[72] and "the Empire / revive[s] in a live hope of the Sacred City" (*RSS* 58–61; ll. 234–35, 254, 257–77, 286–87). Williams' myth ends, then, on a note reminiscent of the book of Revelation.

Before the departure of the Grail, one last healing is accomplished: that of the Fisher King's wound. Until Galahad's coming, his bleeding had continued,[73] and in the traditional story the restoration of his barren land was linked to his own healing. Both Lewis and Tolkien with their "Maimed King" figures— Ransom (renamed Fisher-King) and Frodo respectively—significantly alter this part of the myth. As Jeannette Hume Lutton argues, Ransom "*must not be cured*" if he will succeed in defending the land from the "sterility" represented by the N.I.C.E. project.[74] Similarly, at the close of *The Lord of the Rings*, the Shire is well on the way to being made a "desert" and its inhabitants enslaved, but in the campaign to cleanse it from destructive parasites, the wounded Frodo refuses to draw his sword. His only role is to forbid unnecessary killing; he even hopes for Saruman's "cure," if that were possible. Then, while the damaged land does not, as feared, "take long to heal," thanks both to hard but "willing" work and to Galadriel's marvelous gift,

---

70   Lewis quotes the poet's own note identifying the doves as "all that was [left of] Logres and the Empire" (WA 178).

71   Williams contrasts the "pagan" fate of Tristan and Isolde, at "rest" in the "light and sound and darkness of the sea" (Swinburne's phrase), with the riding of Galahad in "the ship that runs over the sea" ("Chances" 185). A similar contrast appears in his novel *Shadows of Ecstasy*. In the penultimate paragraph of this book, Williams combines snatches of poetry about the sea's mysterious transformative power (from *The Tempest* and *Lycidas*) that correspond roughly to the fates of Tristan and Galahad, respectively. These patterns of imagery deserve fuller attention in another study.

72   "Let hell also confess thee, / bless thee, praise thee, and magnify thee for ever." This liturgical formula almost at the end of *RSS* (60) nicely (but more affirmatively) balances one near the beginning of *TtL* (13, in "The Vision of the Empire"):

      if there be wit in the rolling mass of waters,
      if any regimen in marshes beyond P'o-lu,
      if any measurement among the headless places,
      bless him, praise him, magnify him for ever. (ll. 179–82)

73   So too, in a very early version of the Grail story, had that of Christ's body after it was taken down from the cross, when Joseph of Arimathea used the cup of the Last Supper to catch the flow (Williams, "Figure" 70). Williams alludes to the healing in the fourth stanza of "Percivale at Carbonek" (*TtL* 81), but he does not narrate it.

74   Lutton 78, her emphasis; see also p. 83. This is but one way in which, in her view, Lewis improves on T. S. Eliot's handling of the wasteland motif.

Frodo continues to suffer. Sam "will be healed" and become "solid and whole," Frodo promises, and "the Shire ... has been saved," "but I have been too deeply hurt."[75] In both stories, order is restored in the land (albeit never permanently), but the hero's healing must await another time and place.

But healing does not confer immortality. None of those healed at Carbonek were exempt from eventual death. Nor was Faramir, though brought back once from the threshold of death in the Houses of Healing in Minas Tirith, together with Éowyn and Meriadoc, all of them afflicted by the Black Breath. Nor was Frodo, as Tolkien made clear in a 1954 letter. Frodo's "sojourn" in the paradise granted to Elves, for his "healing and redress of suffering," is "strictly ... temporary." He will "'die' ... and leave the world" (*Letters* 198–99).[76] Earlier in the same letter, he explicitly placed "Men, Hobbits, and Dwarfs [sic]" in the category of "mortals" (196). Elves, being by nature immortal, could live on in the Deathless Lands, but something better was in store for the Second Children of Ilúvatar, a fate (hidden from the Elves and even the Valar) that would be made possible by death, that was vouchsafed to them as a gift (*Silm* 41–42, 104–05, 264–65).

But those few mortals allowed into Eressëa may not return to earth.[77] That explains why Tolkien rejected Merlin's prophecy that Arthur would return to Britain in a time of dire need (*Letters* 199). By the same logic, Lancelot, whom Tolkien planned to send west in search of Arthur, must "never return." And, of course, Elves, once they had gone west from Middle-earth, could not go back. But that can hardly be the only parallel Tolkien envisioned between Lancelot and Eärendil Halfelven when he put that cryptic phrase in his notes (*FoA* 136; see above, page 132). Eärendil has his real-world counterpart in St. Brendan, who also loved voyaging, but there is no tradition to support suddenly giving Lancelot the same attribute. What impelled him was love for Arthur. And, so far as we know, Tolkien has nothing more to say about Lancelot;[78] his creative impulse has come to focus on working out Eärendil's place in the whole myth.

Tolkien's notes for continuing his Arthurian poem demand further exploration of Eärendil's story, although it may seem unrelated to Avalon since Eärendil did not go to the Forbidden Lands to be healed;

---

75 *LotR* 3:293 (desert), 285 and 295–96 (sword not drawn, no killing), 299 (Saruman), all in 6.8; 3:302 (long to heal, willing), 304 and 305 (continues to suffer), 306 (Sam), 309 (Shire saved, deeply hurt), all in 6.9. I borrow the designation "Maimed King" from Flieger's extensive analysis (134, 135, 144).

76 The same would apply to Bilbo, Sam, and Gimli, who also were granted a respite outside the now-spherical earth (*LotR* 3:377–78; App. B). The word "sojourn" comes from notes Tolkien wrote in 1967 (*Letters* 386n).

77 Tolkien grants the possibility of "certain rare exceptions" (*Letters* 198). One of these would be the fictional Ælfwine, comparatively a near-contemporary of ours barely a millennium ago, who sails from England to Eressëa (see *LR* 78, 80) and, returning to his own time and his home, brings back tales that were current in the Second Age. A few years earlier, Tolkien appears not to have fully made up his mind about the no-return rule. "To Bilbo and Frodo the special grace is granted to go with the Elves they loved—an Arthurian ending, in which it is, of course, not made explicit whether this is an 'allegory' of death, or a mode of healing and restoration *leading to a return*" (Hammond and Scull, *Reader's Companion* 749, emphasis supplied; from the portion of Tolkien's letter to Milton Waldman that was excluded from the published collection [see *Letters* 160]). My thanks to Richard West for bringing this to my attention.

78 It is not inconceivable that, in a very bold move, he might have considered having Lancelot, if he "found [Arthur] in Avalon" (*FoA* 136), simply stay there with his beloved friend.

but he fits our theme in other ways. He began in the author's mind as a philological puzzle: the name, he felt sure, of a minor Germanic divinity, the Morning Star, more or less parallel to the classical Hesperus or Venus; known, however, only in an eighth-century(?) English poem based on Latin liturgical texts, in which the name is a metonym for Christ.[79] Bringing that name into Tolkien's mythology and its invented language system required slight changes in orthography and gave it a different meaning, 'sea-lover.'[80] That is the role in which Eärendil appears in the 1914 poem "The Voyage of Éarendel the Evening Star," but the astronomical reference is only a metaphor indicating what the poet has turned into a *westward* journey.[81] Many years later Tolkien would still refer to the tale of "Earendil [sic] *the Wanderer*" and imply that the Old English meaning 'ray of light' is merely an irrelevant curiosity (*Letters* 150; emphasis supplied). But in fact he couldn't put that other meaning out of his mind and before long was working out how best to combine them both. In one early note for the story, after reaching "the lip of the world," Eärendil "sets sail upon the sky" (*LT* 2:261). In the full-blown story, he appears finally in the heavens at both morning and evening (*Silm* 250), "a herald star," explicitly Venus (*Letters* 385). For as the tale grew, mere wandering and adventures turned into heroic quest. Like Frodo, who centuries later would be brought to Eressëa after his mission was completed, Eärendil knowingly undertook great risk. Seeking divine aid as a last resort for both of his ancestral peoples, Elves and Men, Eärendil defied the Ban and confronted the Valar in Valinor itself, the forbidden land. This presented them with a dilemma. As a "mortal Man," he must therefore be put to death, but he is also part-Elvish; and his "love of the Two Kindreds" that led him to undertake that "peril" may call for pardon, perhaps even reward.[82] Either way, Man or Elf, he may not return to Middle-earth. The Gordian knot is cut by putting Eärendil back on his ship *Vingilot*, binding again on his brow the recovered Silmaril that had enabled him to sail past the Enchanted Isles and Shadowy Seas and come to Valinor, and sending him in *Vingilot* to the edge of the world to where there are heavenly seas but not stars (*Silm* 250). Thus, Tolkien melds together with his private myth the pre-Christian name that an Anglo-Saxon Christian poet had adapted. The Silmaril Eärendil wears serves not for motive power alone but also for all people to see as a sign of hope—redoubled by the fact of its recovery (249). But Eärendil is not fixed in a star's role. He can return at times to Valinor; in the war against Morgoth, he returns above Middle-earth to play a crucial part; and when Morgoth has been thrust out into the Void, he becomes a guard against that foe's reentry (252, 254–55).

Clearly, Eärendil is unique in his apotheosis, though, like Frodo and all who come to the Undying Lands, he cannot return to earth. Having chosen to join his spouse in an Elvish fate (*Silm* 249), he is made

79   Translating the Latin *Oriens*, a title derived from Luke 1:78 (in the King James Version, "the Dayspring"). See Shippey, *Road* 218–19 for more detail.

80   See *Silm* 325. Evident in Tolkien's drawings and paintings is his own love for the sea: see Hammond and Scull, *Artist* 24–25, 46–47 and Carpenter 70.

81   *LT* 2:267. For another Eärendil poem that reflects Tolkien's love of the sea but has nothing of the fantastic, see "A Secret Vice" 216–17. It is descriptive, not narrative, but ends with "the road going on for ever … to havens in the West."

82   Note that when Eärendil first comes to Valinor, Eönwë hails him as the one they have longed for past the point of hoping (*Silm* 249).

immortal. Yet in that way he differs from Frodo and the other humans who, without dying, are brought to Abhalljin or Avalon or like places in the old Celtic myths. These all await a final home elsewhere.[83]

Charles Williams may have included Galahad in that small Avalonian company. In the Arthurian myth as it came down to him, Galahad dies in Sarras and is buried there, but, having radically altered the place of Sarras in the myth, Williams speaks only of Galahad's "hiding" (*RSS* 61; "The Prayers of the Pope," l. 326). He may not "return to the world ("Figure" 81), but it is not clear whether Williams would share Tolkien's conviction that the path to one's final destiny must always pass through death. Lewis' view on the matter is equally hard to pin down. When Ransom is about to return home from Venus and King Tor proves unable to stop the flow of blood from Ransom's heel, Tinidril wonders whether it will lead to his death. "I do not think so," Tor replies, adding his opinion that a man who has breathed the air and drunk the waters of Perelandra's Holy Mountain "will not find it easy to die"; but then the conversation turns to the longevity of the generations following the expulsion from Eden (*Per* 221).[84] *The Voyage of the "Dawn Treader"* may be Lewis' *immram*,[85] but the story of the chivalrous mouse Reepicheep sheds no light on *human* destiny.[86] His coracle is Brendan's kind of boat, but it also parallels Elias's chariot of fire. After flinging his sword into the water—a glance at Malory?—Reepicheep is driven by an unseen power up and over the thirty-foot wave that marks the flat world's eastern boundary, reaches Aslan's country, "and is alive there to this day" (219).[87] His home, like Tolkien's Eressëa, Williams' Sarras, and Avalon as conceived by both Tolkien and Lewis, is out of this world (though, to be sure, Perelandra is still within the known universe).

---

83   See Kelly and Livingston 87–89.

84   One of Tolkien's characters similarly glances at an old legend among Men about "days when death came less swiftly" (*MR* 313).

85   Downing identifies some of the parallels to the *Navigatio Sancti Brendani* (*LWW* 43–46). Homer's *Odyssey* is another obvious model, but *VDT* has no single epic hero. Once the companions leave the Lone Islands, where the adventure is essentially political in nature, their journey is one of marvels: "it is after the Lone Islands that the adventure really begins" (*VDT* 27), including "new constellations which no one had ever seen in Narnia" or "perhaps ... no living eye had seen at all" (173). Already they have passed into regions unknown. After Ramandu's island ("the beginning of the End of the World" [186]) the way to the Utter East is long, days and miles of which there is no count. Seemingly by magic, the ship is borne across a calm sea inhabited by undersea people (a feature found also in Tolkien's *Roverandom* [59–62]). The seawater is sweet and nourishing (*VDT* 210). The light becomes more and more intense, but so does the voyagers's ability to bear it (207)—a feature Lewis borrows from Dante's *Paradiso*. Finally, nearing the edge of the world, they are able to look "behind the sun" and see a range of unearthly mountains, high yet "warm and green" and sending a breeze laden with fragrance and music. They are "seeing beyond the End of the World into Aslan's country" (218–19).

86   In addition, Lewis' story is what he calls a fairy tale or a supposal. He is not writing an allegory or making a theological statement.

87   The symbolism of "east" in this story, including the word "dawn" in the title and the childhood rhyme that fuels Reepicheep's pilgrimage (25), deserves some reflection in the light of Lewis' fascination with the West that I stressed earlier. Lewis was not alone in this ambivalence; as we have seen, it was as *Oriens* ('rising') that Earendel first came into Tolkien's ken. On a sphere, of course (as John learned in *PR*), East meets West; but Lewis' map is not a globe—his mariners worry about falling over the edge if they go too far. Already in

After Reepicheep has gone, Aslan sends the three children home,[88] first assuring them that "there is a way into [his] country" from their world, too. But it "lies across a river" (VDT 221). Sensitive to their capacity as children, Aslan does not speak explicitly of death, but we understand the symbolism well enough.[89] That is how two of them (in a later tale) do return to Aslan's country. They die in a train wreck in England, as do others who suddenly appear with them in Narnia—bathed in light (here Lewis replaces the river metaphor with the imagery that dominates the final chapter of VDT), and Edmund's sports injury is immediately cured (LB 135, 141). It is a place of healing for Polly and Digory also, or at least of youth restored (137–38).[90] But others are present who have not had to pass through death. They have entered a "pitch-black" stable (69) facing possible death, but it opened instead on a paradisal landscape (139) outside the Narnia they had known. That Narnia is about to undergo its Last Judgment and be brought to an end, but they have come to the "real world" of which "our own world … is only a shadow or copy" (LB 170), "look[ing] cool and fresh," fully cleansed from any marks of battle (136). Even Puzzle the donkey is now "beautiful"; he has at last become "himself" (LB 167).

For healing, more broadly considered, is not limited to the restoration of bodily health alone. That is why Reepicheep, who differs from King Arthur and the Pendragon Elwin Ransom in having no wound to be cured, nonetheless fits so neatly into what we might call the "Avalon" pattern. A moment's reflection on the shared etymology of *health* and *wholeness* will reveal a meaning that applies to spirit as well as body.[91] Aslan's country, where Reepicheep's life-long yearning is fulfilled (VDT 25), is a house of healing in that

his first Narnian tale, before sequels were conceived, he had had Cair Paravel looking eastward to the sea (was this simply a habitual orientation from growing up in northeastern Ireland?); now it was too late to change. But in *The Magician's Nephew*, the earthly paradise, the garden where Digory is sent to fetch an apple with healing power, is to the west. Aslan's Land turns out to be a circular mountain range all round the Narnian world (LB 181 [see also 169]). It is appropriate that Reepicheep should find it behind the rising sun, not the sunset, which is metaphorically associated with death. Tolkien manages a similar fusion of directional imagery. Frodo sails on "the High Sea … into the West" until—as for Brendan, Galahad, and Reepicheep—"sweet fragrance" and music are borne "over the water," and then he catches sight of "white shores and beyond them a far green country under a swift *sunrise*" (LotR 3:310; 6.9; emphasis supplied). Apparently once one has come, by traveling west, to the "Straight Road" and the "bridge invisible," the directional symbolism of our round world with its binary opposition of rising vs. setting is superseded.

88 Aslan's appearance in this scene as (in quick succession) both a lamb and a lion, alluding to Rev. 5:5–6, reminds us that he too has experienced death.

89 Compare the imagery in the final chapter of Lewis' *PR* and the long tradition in hymnody and devotional writing of spiritualizing the story of Israel crossing the Jordan. The medieval story of St. Brendan also emphasizes the need to cross a river in order to reach the Land of Promise.

90 Alongside this may be set the scene near the end of *SC* in which King Caspian, as his funeral is under way down in Narnia, lies in Aslan's Land and his body, wasted by age and grief, is gradually returned by Aslan to its state in his prime (*SC* 213).

91 Compare Charles Williams' observation that in the early stories of the Grail it gave healing and nourishment for the whole person, not the body only ("Figure" 65, 71). An illustration of this is in Malory 2:1028–30, 1033, where the Grail offers both miraculous feeding for forty years (an allusion to the manna of the Israelites' wilderness journey) and the Eucharist.

sense. Lewis and Tolkien are close together on this. Ilúvatar's purpose in giving the gift of death to Men was that they would be restless within the borders of the world, seeking for their true home beyond it (*Silm* 41).[92] True, the mystery that shrouds human destiny can lead to temptation. The kings of Númenor, unwilling to live by trust rather than control, "murmur[ed] … against the doom of Men" to "die and go we know not whither" (264). By trying to seize immortality, they brought destruction on themselves instead, and on their land also. In contrast, King Aragorn, in accepting his impending death—and taking as good news the fact that "we are not bound for ever to the circles of the world"—does not know what lies beyond but is content simply to know that it "is more than memory" (*LotR* 3:344; Appendix A.5).

Whether any of our three authors would allow an exception to the rule that all humans must die, all three do present characters in their fiction who, after death, continue moving toward ultimate salvation.[93] Essential to interpreting Tolkien's story "Leaf by Niggle" are two words that he used to describe it: "allegorical" and "purgatorial" (*Letters* 195). The first of these words he used rather narrowly, viewing the story as an allegory of artistic creation while insisting that the characters were not stand-ins for "any single vice or virtue" (*Letters* 321), but he follows well-established allegorical practice in giving moral force to such tropes as the journey, illness, or lameness. Given the other keyword, "purgatorial," it is best to read the journey not simply as death[94] but as Niggle's whole experience from the end of life on. Thus after his terminal illness ends in his being driven through a "dark tunnel" (96), his first stop is an "Infirmary" (97)—another of Tolkien's houses of healing, which of course brings the story into the orbit of the present study. But it is also a "Workhouse" ("Leaf" 97) where he "is assigned hard labors aimed at correcting his sins and weaknesses" (Kocher 164). From there, he journeys on and encounters his lame neighbor Parish, who has also died. Healing continues; both regain their bodily health over time; together they build

---

92 Cf. George Herbert, "The Pulley" (Herbert 159–60), and the famous prayer that opens Augustine's *Confessions*, "You have made us for yourself, and our hearts are restless until they can find peace in you." It is an explanation for the "gift of death" quite different from that offered by William Morris: "lest we weary of life" (385).

93 Charles Williams can be dealt with briefly. In his last two novels, the earliest stage of an afterlife journey captures his attention. In *Descent into Hell*, Williams tells the story of a despised laborer whose life has come to feel like an endless walking in the gutter. He determines to end it—but ironies accumulate and even in that he is a failure: at the last moment, with a rope around his neck, he becomes aware of an inner impulse *not* to die, but then he falls accidentally and is strangled (31, 118). (Critics sometimes mistakenly refer to this unnamed person as "the Suicide.") His ghost continues to wander the housing estate (32–34, 113–25, 152–56, 164–67) and in this phantasmal state of existence he encounters kindness and is pointed toward salvation and peace (120–23, 159–60, 165–67). *All Hallows' Eve* begins with the stream of consciousness of a woman who has just been killed in a plane crash. Over several days, her ghost encounters others, some dead and some alive, chiefly her husband and two old schoolmates, and she plays a part in undoing the magician Simon's house of fraudulent healing. She learns to grow in love and so finds release to continue her "purgatorial" (77) journey toward "the enlargement of her proper faculties in due time" (188).

94 As in the medieval allegory *Everyman*. Compare also Kent's speech in *King Lear*, "I have a journey, sir, shortly to go. / My master calls me, I must not say no" (5.3.321–22).

a small house and garden that will prove a place of "convalescence" for others—"for many ... the best introduction to the Mountains" ("Leaf" 112) that are the journey's goal.[95]

Worth noting is Tolkien's emphasis on healing (of a sort that may be designated "spiritual growth") and purposeful activity, rather than torment, in his depiction of the purgation that acclimatizes one for Paradise. This seems not far from C. S. Lewis' view.[96] Imagery similar to that found in "Leaf by Niggle" appears in Lewis' dream vision *The Great Divorce*: the distant mountains, extremely high (29), that are called "Deep Heaven" (61);[97] the increasing wholeness, imaged by bodily changes (56), of those who journey upward; and their willing acceptance of the pain that self-fulfillment requires. For the afterlife, in Lewis' conception, is characterized not by stasis but by becoming, as imaged in the Narnians' journey "further up and further in" (*LB* 175), always faster, past the mountain-top Earthly Paradise where Reepicheep greets them, after which they still are only just "beginning ... the real story" in which the chapters keep getting better (183–84). Lewis leaves it at that; wisely, he does not venture to say precisely what "better" might mean.[98] None of us can do more than speculate (and make it clear that is all we are doing). The "endlessly unfolding story" (in Rowan Williams' phrase)[99] is being written by an Artist whose creativity is beyond human imagining.

That leads us to consider one final kind of healing: that of the world itself. The word is not ordinarily used in this connection, but Tolkien uses it in two late writings. He had resumed work on *The Silmarillion*, aiming to clarify its theological underpinnings as regards two interrelated themes: how Ilúvatar will deal with the irreparable ruin resulting from Morgoth's unrelenting interference with Arda (Earth), and the mystery of what happens to humans after they die (*Silm* 105). The Valar in council discuss these matters, and Manwë gives his opinion that Arda is so badly marred it cannot be simply restored, but hope must be centered on a future healing of the world that will make it more beautiful than before (*MR* 245).[100] Then in a new work, a conversation between elf

---

95   Interpreted by Kelly and Livingston as the gateway to "true Paradise" (91). See also Christopher, "Mount Purgatory" 75 regarding traces in the story of Dante's *Purgatory*.

96   See Lewis, *GD* 61, and Derrick 132–33, citing several of Lewis' writings.

97   On the imagery of height—prominent also at the end of Lewis' *VDT* and in other Narnian stories—see chapters 2 and 3 in Bevan (a work whose influence Lewis frequently acknowledged).

98   Nor would Tolkien; but lines from one of his letters may hint at possibilities: "There is a place called 'heaven' where the good here unfinished is completed; and where the stories unwritten, and the hopes unfulfilled, are continued. We may laugh together yet" (*Letters* 55).

99   R. Williams, *Lion's World* 130. He continues: "We could say that, for Lewis, the salient point about death was that it put an end to 'endings' and opened up this perspective of growth without a final horizon" (130–31).

100   In a 1945 letter, Tolkien described the pattern of restoration as spiral, not cyclic: in place of a lost "Eden" will be "something like it, but on a higher plane" (*Letters* 110). Manwë continues the speech quoted: "because of the Marring: this is the Hope that sustaineth." This significant addition points to a thoroughly orthodox belief of Tolkien's which is, however, outside the scope of this study. For now, we may note what is said in Lewis' Great Ode in *Perelandra*—that "the healing what was wounded" results in "a new dimension of glory" (215).

and human, Tolkien adds the speculation that perhaps the healing of Arda, the increasing of the Music of creation, and the fulfillment of the original Vision, with sights beyond what were imagined, might be the job of humans (318): this gives Men a positive role to play and one purpose for Ilúvatar's gift of death.[101]

Behind this "healing," of course, is the ancient vision of a new-made heaven and earth, a doctrine that also fired the imaginations of Lewis and Williams,[102] together with the promise of redeemed humans' sharing in Christ's rule.[103] To say it more explicitly would have been an anachronism in Tolkien's pre-Christian Secondary World. It is important to keep in mind that all of the histories and narratives in his legendarium are cast in the form of ancient writings that reflect the particular viewpoint, including the limited knowledge and the cultural setting, of the putative authors. Therefore, their silence on any point where Tolkien might be supposed to have a distinctively Christian outlook is explained by his principled care to let his authors have their say without intruding notions of his own. Thus, in the dialogue between elf and human already mentioned, he has Andreth speculate on a possibility that readers easily recognize as a core doctrine of Christianity, the Incarnation, but at the same time admit that she is puzzled by it. Among Men, she says, there is a party called the "Old Hope" who hold the view "that the One will Himself enter into Arda, and *heal* Men and all the Marring from the beginning to the end." She wishes she could share that hope but thinks "all wisdom is against them" (*MR* 321, emphasis supplied). Tolkien's personal belief could not be clearer, I think, even though he very properly manages, in the context of First Age metaphysics, to veil it by the device of Andreth's doubt.[104] The elf Finrod in his turn, once informed of that "hope" handed down among Men, is also puzzled. He "cannot foresee" *how* it could happen, how the One who alone has a power greater than Morgoth's could keep his position over and above the created universe yet at the same time carry into it the "medicine for [its] wounds" which "must ... come from without." Yet "if Eru [the One] wished to do

---

101 "Athrabeth Finrod ah Andreth," *MR* 318. The idea was present already in the earliest version of Tolkien's myth, though not so explicitly: "the Sons of Men will after the passing of things of a certainty join in the Second Music" (*LT* 1:59–60; see also *Silm* 42)—that is, in fulfilling that part of the divine purpose which was not revealed to the Ainur at the beginning (*Silm* 15–19), but reserved.

102 See Isaiah 65:17; 66:22; 2 Peter 3:13; Acts 3:21; Revelation 12:1; Romans 8:19–23. The theme was not high on Williams' writing agenda (see *HCD* 1–6, where he is more interested in describing Heaven as a spiritual state than in terms of visual imagery), but he says that the Grail will not return from Sarras "until there is a new heaven and a new earth" ("Figure" 84). It is a central theme in the climactic pages of Lewis' *Miracles* (149, 183–95) and is hinted at in the "real Narnia" that remains after the world the children knew as Narnia has ceased to exist, and which includes the real Earth as well (*LB* 181–82), though this draws as much on Plato as on Scripture.

103 E.g., 2 Timothy 2:12.

104 Christopher Tolkien comments on his father's similar reticence concerning the Christian doctrine of the Fall (*MR* 328).

this … He would find a way" (322). Finrod here is close to intuiting the interrelated doctrines of Incarnation and Trinity but remains incapable of dogmatizing.[105]

Like Avalon as the Inklings understood it, the place of healing—not for a few individuals only but for a broken world and those who dwell in it—is not to be found in *this* world. Christians observe the single season of Advent by noticing two "Comings" that are centuries apart: first the incarnation of God the Son as human, both healer and savior (words with much in common semantically); second, his return to reign: the Not-then, but Future, King.

Works Cited

Alcock, Leslie. *Arthur's Britain: History and Archaeology* AD *367–634*. Harmondsworth: Penguin/Pelican, 1973. Print.

Apollodorus. *The Library*. Trans. and ed. James George Frazer. 2 vols. 1921. Cambridge and London: Harvard UP, 1995. Loeb Classical Library 121–22. Print.

Ashe, Geoffrey. *Mythology of the British Isles*. North Pomfret, VT: Trafalgar, 1990. Print.

Atsma, Aaron J. "Hesperides." *Theoi Greek Mythology: Exploring Mythology in Classical Literature and Art*. theoi.com. Theoi Project 2000–11. Web. 6 February 2015.

——. "Realm of Elysion." *Theoi*. Web. 6 February 2015.

Augustine. *Confessions*. Trans. Rex Warner. NY: New American Library, 1963. Print.

Bevan, Edwyn. *Symbolism and Belief*. London: Allen & Unwin, 1938. Print.

Carpenter, Humphrey. *Tolkien: A Biography*. Boston: Houghton Mifflin, 1977. Print.

Chambers, E. K. *Arthur of Britain*. 1927. Rpt. with supplementary bibliography. Cambridge: Speculum Historiale, 1964. Print.

Chance, Jane. "*The Lord of the Rings*: Tolkien's Epic." 1979. Zimbardo and Isaacs 195–232. Print.

Charlesworth, James H., ed. *The Old Testament Pseudepigrapha*. 2 vols. Garden City, NY: Doubleday, 1983–85. Print.

Christopher, Joe R. "C. S. Lewis' Lost Arthurian Poem: A Conjectural Essay." *Inklings Forever* 8 (2012): 1–11. Print.

——. "Mount Purgatory Arises near Narnia." *Mythlore* 23.2 (2001): 65–90. Print.

Delumeau, Jean. *History of Paradise: The Garden of Eden in Myth and Tradition*. Trans. Matthew O'Connell. NY: Continuum, 1995. Print.

---

105 In his draft "Commentary" on this dialogue, Tolkien says that, in realizing Eru would "have to be both 'outside' and inside," Finrod "glimpses the possibility of complexity or of distinctions in the nature of Eru, which nonetheless leaves Him 'The One'" (*MR* 335). He introduces a fresh metaphor that sheds some light on what puzzled the speakers in the dialogue. Andreth had expressed her doubt using certain art forms as analogies: "How could Eru enter into the thing that He has made …? Can the singer enter into his tale or the designer into his picture?" (322). Tolkien's label for the overall plan in which "Elves and Men … play" different roles is "God's management of the Drama" (329)—an art form involving action—and he develops this figure in the context of the previous quotation (335). It may not be entirely coincidental that C. S. Lewis in his chapter on the Incarnation uses the same metaphor (*Miracles* 150).

Derrick, Christopher. *C. S. Lewis and the Church of Rome: A Study in Proto-Ecumenism*. San Francisco: Ignatius Press, 1981. Print.

Dodds, David Llewellyn, ed. *Arthurian Poets: Charles Williams*. Arthurian Studies 24. Woodbridge, Suffolk: Boydell & Brewer, 1991. Print.

Downing, David C. "'The Dungeon of his Soul': Lewis' Unfinished 'Quest of Bleheris.'" *VII: An Anglo-American Literary Review* 15 (1998): 37–54. Print.

Euripides. *Hippolytus*. Trans. David Kovacs. Loeb Classical Library. Cambridge, MA: Harvard UP, 1995. 115–263. Print.

Flieger, Verlyn. "Frodo and Aragorn: The Concept of the Hero." 1979. Zimbardo and Isaacs 122–45. Print.

Frazer, James George, ed. and trans. *The Library*. By Apollodorus. 2 vols. 1921. Cambridge and London: Harvard UP, 1995. Loeb Classical Library 121–22. Print.

Glyer, Diana Pavlac. *The Company They Keep: C. S. Lewis and J. R. R. Tolkien as Writers in Community*. Kent State UP, 2007. Print.

GoodKnight, Bonnie. *Scene from "Imram." Mythlore* 4.2 (1976): 1–2. Print.

Graves, Robert. *Greek Myths*. 1955. London: Cassell, 1980. Print.

Green, Roger Lancelyn, and Walter Hooper. *C. S. Lewis: A Biography*. New York and London: Harcourt Brace Jovanovich, 1974. Print.

Hammond, Wayne G., and Christina Scull. The Lord of the Rings: *A Reader's Companion*. Boston: Houghton Mifflin Harcourt, 2005. Print.

Herbert, George. *Works*. Ed. F. E. Hutchinson. Clarendon, 1941. Print.

Hesiod. *Theogony, Works and Days, Testimonia*. Ed. and trans. Glenn W. Most. Loeb Classical Library 503. Cambridge, MA, and London: Harvard UP, 2006. Print.

Hooper, Walter. Foreword. *C. S. Lewis' Lost Aeneid: Arms and the Exile*. Ed. A. T. Reyes. New Haven, CT, and London: Yale UP, 2011. xi–xv. Print.

Hopkins, Gerard Manley. "Spring." *The Poetical Works*. Ed. Norman H. MacKenzie. Clarendon, 1990. 142. Print.

Howatson, M. C., ed. *The Oxford Companion to Classical Literature*. 2nd ed. Oxford and New York: Oxford UP, 1989. Print.

Huttar, Charles A. "'Deep lies the sea-longing': Inklings of Home." *Mythlore* 26.1–2 (2007): 5–27. Print.

——. "How Much Does *That Hideous Strength* Owe to Charles Williams?" *Sehnsucht: The C. S. Lewis Journal* 10 (2015): 19–46. Print.

——. "Tolkien, Epic Traditions, and Golden Age Myths." *Twentieth-Century Fantasists: Essays on Culture, Society and Belief in Twentieth-Century Mythopoeic Literature*. Ed. Kath Filmer. London: Macmillan; New York: St. Martin's, 1992. 92–107. Print.

——. "What C. S. Lewis Really Did to 'Cupid and Psyche.'" *Sehnsucht: The C. S. Lewis Journal* 3 (2009): 33–49. Print.

Kelly, A. Keith, and Michael Livingston. "'A Far Green Country': Tolkien, Paradise, and the End of All Things in Medieval Literature." *Mythlore* 27.3/4 (2009): 83–102. Print.

King, Don W. "Lost but Found: The 'Missing' Poems of C. S. Lewis' *Spirits in Bondage*." *Christianity and Literature* 53.2 (2004): 163–201. Print.

King, Roma A. *The Pattern in the Web: The Mythical Poetry of Charles Williams*. Kent State UP, 1990. Print.

Klibansky, Raymond, Erwin Panofsky, and Fritz Saxl. *Saturn and Melancholy: Studies in the History of Natural Philosophy, Religion and Art*. Thomas Nelson, 1964. Rpt. Nendeln (Liechtenstein): Kraus, 1979. Print.

Kocher, Paul H. *Master of Middle-earth: The Fiction of J. R. R. Tolkien*. Boston: Houghton Mifflin, 1972. Print.

Laȝamon. *Laȝamon's Brut: A History of the Britons*. Trans. Donald G. Bzdyl. Binghamton, NY: Medieval and Renaissance Texts and Studies, 1989. Print.

Lewis, C. S. "'Above the Smoke and Stir.'" *Times Literary Supplement* 14 July 1945: 331. Rpt. in *Collected Letters* 3:1560–61. Print.

——. *The Allegory of Love*. 1936. NY: Oxford UP, 1958. Print.

——. "The Alliterative Metre." 1935. *Selected Literary Essays*. Ed. Walter Hooper. Cambridge UP, 2013. 15–26. *Google Books*. Web. 27 August 2015.

——. *The Collected Letters of C. S. Lewis*. Ed. Walter Hooper. 3 vols. NY: HarperSanFrancisco, 2004–07. Print.

——. *The Collected Poems of C. S. Lewis*. Ed. Walter Hooper. London: HarperCollins/Fount, 1994. Print.

——. *English Literature in the Sixteenth Century, Excluding Drama*. Oxford History of English Literature 3. Oxford: Clarendon Press, 1954. Print.

——. *The Great Divorce*. London: Bles/Centenary Press, 1945. Print.

——. *Image and Imagination*. Ed. Walter Hooper. Cambridge UP, 2013. Print.

——. Introduction. *Selections from Laȝamon's* Brut. Ed. G. L. Brook. Oxford: Clarendon Press, 1963. vii–xv. Print.

——. *The Last Battle*. London: Bodley Head, 1956. Print.

——. *The Lion, the Witch and the Wardrobe*. 1950. NY: Collier, 1970. Print.

——. *The Magician's Nephew*. London: Bodley Head, 1955. Print.

——. *Mere Christianity*. 1952. NY: Simon & Schuster, 1996. Print.

——. *Miracles: A Preliminary Study*. London: Bles/Centenary Press. 1947. Print.

——. *Narrative Poems*. Ed. Walter Hooper. New York and London: Harcourt Brace Jovanovich, 1969. Print.

——. "A Note on *Comus*." 1932. *Studies in Medieval and Renaissance Literature*. Ed. Walter Hooper. Cambridge UP, 1966. 175–81. Print.

——. *Perelandra*.1943. NY: Collier, 1962. Print.

——. *The Pilgrim's Regress: An Allegorical Apology for Christianity, Reason and Romanticism*. 1933. 3rd ed. Grand Rapids, MI: Eerdmans, 1958. Print.

——. *The Silver Chair*. London, Geoffrey Bles, 1953. Print.

——. *Surprised by Joy: The Shape of My Early Life*. NY: Harcourt, Brace & World, 1955. Print.

——. *That Hideous Strength: A Modern Fairy-tale for Grown-ups*. 1945. NY: Macmillan, 1946. Print.

——. *Till We Have Faces: A Myth Retold*. 1956. NY: Harcourt, Brace & World, 1957. Print.

——. *The Voyage of the "Dawn Treader."* London: Geoffrey Bles, 1952. Print.

——. "Williams and the Arthuriad." *Arthurian Torso*. Ed. C. S. Lewis. London: Oxford UP, 1948. 91–200. Print.

Lobdell, Jared. *The World of the Rings: Language, Religion, and Adventure in Tolkien*. Chicago and La Salle, IL: Open Court, 2004. Print.

Lowes, John Livingston. *The Road to Xanadu: A Study in the Ways of the Imagination*. Boston: Houghton Mifflin, 1927. Print.

Lutton, Jeannette Hume. "Wasteland Myth in C. S. Lewis' *That Hideous Strength*." *Forms of the Fantastic: Selected Essays from the Third International Conference on the Fantastic in Literature and Film*. Ed. Jan Hokenson and Howard Pearce. Contributions to the Study of Science Fiction and Fantasy 20. New York; Westport; London: Greenwood Press, 1986. 69–86. Print.

Malory, Sir Thomas. *Works*. Ed. Eugène Vinaver. 1947. 2nd ed. Vol. 1 of 3. Oxford: Clarendon, 1967. Print.

Markale, Jean. *Merlin: Priest of Nature*. Trans. Belle N. Burke. Rochester, VT: Inner Traditions International, 1995. Print.

McCulloch, J. A. "Blest, Abode of the (Celtic)." *Encyclopedia of Religion and Ethics*. Ed. James Hastings. 13 vols. NY: Scribner's, 1917–26. 2:689–96. Print.

Milton, John. "A Masque Presented at Ludlow Castle, 1634 [*Comus*]." Ed. John Carey. *Poems*. 168–229. Print.

——. *Paradise Lost*. 1667. Ed. Alastair Fowler. *Poems*. 419–1060. Print.

——. *Poems*. Ed. John Carey and Alastair Fowler. London: Longman, 1968. Print.

Morris, William. *The Well at the World's End: A Tale*. 1896. NY: Ballantine, 1975. Print.

Myers, Doris T. *Bareface: A Guide to C. S. Lewis' Last Novel*. Columbia: U of Missouri P, 2004. Print.

Navigatio Sancti Brendani Abbatis from Early Latin Manuscripts. Ed. Carl Selmer. Publications in Medieval Studies 16. U of Notre Dame P, 1959. Print.

Plutarch. *Lives*. Trans. Bernadotte Perrin. 11 vols. Loeb Classical Library. Cambridge, MA: Harvard UP; London: Heinemann, 1914–26. Print.

——. *Moralia*. Trans. Frank Cole Babbitt et al. 16 vols. Loeb Classical Library. Cambridge, MA: Harvard UP; London: Heinemann, 1927–2004. Print.

Ridler, Anne. "Introductory Note to the Arthurian Essays." Ridler 169–75.

Scull, Christina, and Wayne G. Hammond. *The J. R. R. Tolkien Companion and Guide*. 2 vols. Boston, New York: Houghton Mifflin, 2006. Print.

Shippey, Tom. *J. R. R. Tolkien: Author of the Century*. 2000. Boston: Houghton Mifflin, 2002. Print.

——. *The Road to Middle-earth*. 1982. 2nd ed. London: Grafton/HarperCollins, 1992. Print.

Starr, Nathan Comfort. *King Arthur Today: The Arthurian Legend in English and American Literature 1901–1953*. Gainesville: U of Florida P, 1954. Print.

Tennyson, Alfred. *The Poetic and Dramatic Works*. Boston: Houghton Mifflin, 1898. Print.

Tolkien, J. R. R. *The Book of Lost Tales*. The History of Middle-earth 1–2. Ed. Christopher Tolkien. 2 vols. Boston: Houghton Mifflin, 1984. Print.

——. *The Fall of Arthur*. Ed. Christopher Tolkien. Boston: Houghton Mifflin Harcourt, 2013. Print.

——. *The Lays of Beleriand*. The History of Middle-earth 3. Ed. Christopher Tolkien. Boston: Houghton Mifflin, 1985. Print.

——. "Leaf by Niggle." *The Tolkien Reader* 85–112.

——. *The Letters of J. R. R. Tolkien*. Ed. Humphrey Carpenter. Boston: Houghton Mifflin, 1981. Print.

——. *The Lord of the Rings*. 3 vols. London: Allen & Unwin, Boston: Houghton Mifflin, 1954–55. Print.

——. *The Lost Road and Other Writings*. The History of Middle-earth 5. Ed. Christopher Tolkien. Boston: Houghton Mifflin, 1987. Print.

——. *Morgoth's Ring*. The History of Middle-earth 10. Ed. Christopher Tolkien. Boston: Houghton Mifflin, 1993. Print.

——. "Mythopoeia." *Tree and Leaf*. 3rd ed. London: Unwin Hyman, 1988. 97–101. Print.

——. *The Peoples of Middle-earth*. The History of Middle-earth 12. Ed. Christopher Tolkien. Boston: Houghton Mifflin, 1996. Print.

——. *The Return of the Shadow*. The History of Middle-earth 6. Ed. Christopher Tolkien. Boston: Houghton Mifflin, 1988. Print.

——. *Roverandom*. Ed. Christina Scull and Wayne G. Hammond. Boston: Houghton Mifflin, 1998. Print.

——. *Sauron Defeated*. The History of Middle-earth 9. Ed. Christopher Tolkien. Boston: Houghton Mifflin, 1992. Print.

——. "A Secret Vice." *The Monsters and the Critics and Other Essays*. Ed. Christopher Tolkien. 1983. London: HarperCollins, 1997. 198–223. Print.

——. *The Silmarillion*. Boston: Houghton Mifflin, 1977. Print.

——. *The Tolkien Reader*. NY: Ballantine, 1966. Print.

——. *Unfinished Tales of Númenor and Middle-earth*. Ed. Christopher Tolkien. Boston: Houghton Mifflin, 1980. Print.

Williams, Charles. *All Hallows' Eve*. 1945. NY: Pellegrini and Cudahy, 1948. Print.

——. *Arthurian Poets: Charles Williams*. Arthurian Studies 24. Ed. David Llewellyn Dodds. Woodbridge, Suffolk: Boydell & Brewer, 1991. Print.

——. "The Chances and Changes of Myth." 1942. *Image* 183–85.

——. *Descent into Hell*. 1937. Grand Rapids, MI: Eerdmans, 1965. Print.

——. *Descent of the Dove: A Short History of the Holy Spirit in the Church*. Grand Rapids, MI: Eerdmans, 1939. Print.

——. "The Figure of Arthur." *Arthurian Torso*. Ed. C. S. Lewis. London: Oxford UP, 1948. 3–90, 93–94. Print.

——. "Gerard Hopkins." *Image* 48–51.

——. *He Came Down from Heaven*. 1938. Grand Rapids, MI: Eerdmans, 1984. Print.

——. *The Image of the City and Other Essays*. Ed. Anne Ridler. London: Oxford UP, 1958. Print.

——. "Malory and the Grail Legend." 1944. *Image* 186–94.

——. "Notes on the Arthurian Myth." *Image* 175–79.

——. *The Region of the Summer Stars*. 1944. 2nd ed. London: Oxford UP, 1950. Print.

——. *Shadows of Ecstasy*. London: Gollancz, 1933. Print.

——. *Taliessin through Logres*. London: Oxford UP, 1938. Print.

Williams, Rowan. *The Lion's World: A Journey into the Heart of Narnia*. Oxford and New York: Oxford UP, 2012. Print.

Zimbardo, Rose A., and Neil D. Isaacs, eds. *Understanding* The Lord of the Rings: *The Best of Tolkien Criticism*. Boston and New York: Houghton Mifflin, 2004. Print.

5

Shape and Direction: Human Consciousness in the Inklings' Mythological Geographies.

Christopher Gaertner

Owen Barfield has been commonly referred to as "The First and Last Inkling." Since he resided in London, his presence at Inklings gatherings in Oxford was less regular than that of J. R. R. Tolkien or C. S. Lewis. His influence on the other Inklings, however, was profound. In particular, the influence of his views on human consciousness resounds throughout their works. C. S. Lewis reported that Tolkien, the renowned philologist, said Barfield "modified his whole outlook" on philology (Carpenter, *Inklings* 42). Lewis himself vigorously resisted Barfield's views, but nonetheless called him "the wisest and best of my unofficial teachers" (in the dedication of *The Allegory of Love*).

Barfield asserted that human consciousness has taken an inward course. In many of his works, including *Poetic Diction* and *Saving the Appearances*, Barfield asserts that whereas ancient humanity looked *out* at the world, viewed itself as part of nature, and mythically participated in it, modern humanity has looked inwardly at itself, viewing itself as separate from the world, as a subject that can objectively observe and scientifically analyze the object of Nature. This inward course is evidenced in how humanity has perceived the relationship between thought and speech. Modern language is fragmented, whereas in ancient language meaning and poesy were experienced as a unity.

I am indebted to Verlyn Flieger's work *Splintered Light: Logos and Language in Tolkien's World* (Kent State UP, 2002), which started my own foray into Inklings studies and opened up to me the notion that Tolkien's mythology in *The Silmarillion* is an exploration of light, guided by Barfield's view. Moderns, thinking themselves objective observers of the natural world, split the word into its literal/scientific meaning and its metaphorical/spiritual meaning. But for the Elves (and for the ancients, Barfield would say), there is no such fragmentation of meaning. The Elves are summoned to leave Middle-earth to dwell in Valinor. Some respond fully and go there, others only move closer, and some do not obey the summons at all. These groups' proximity to the physical light emanating from the two trees of Valinor is in direct proportion to their spiritual enlightenment. Flieger also points out how Barfield would say that to the ancients, the *logos* that we now translate into different words or concepts like *word, reason, thought,* or *organizing principle of the universe* would have been experienced as a unity. Later in this chapter, I will explore how this view of unity of meaning influenced the Inklings' Arthurian works.

The Inklings' views on language, consciousness, and meaning were formed and expressed against a backdrop of several centuries of intellectual upheaval. The center of this upheaval was cosmological in nature, characterized by the shift from a geocentric to a heliocentric view of the universe. Closer to the time of the Inklings, scientistic currents of mathematical and biological reductionism and technocratic utilitarianism prevailed. The Inklings' responses to these different points of view reflect the influence of Barfield's view of consciousness, as well as their shared resistance to a scientistic worldview.

In light of the above, this chapter will seek to answer this question: How do the Inklings' Arthurian works fit into the group's shared (and debated) views on the relationships among thought, speech, and human consciousness? Looking for such a fit requires finding a fitting shape that is oriented in a proper direction. This chapter posits that the view of an "inward" direction of movement of human consciousness (whether that view was shared or debated among the Inklings) and the Inklings' aggregate response to cosmological and scientistic issues shaped their mythological geography in two main ways: First, a change in "shape" from Wizard to Pendragon as the proper tension-holder between ancient and contemporary consciousness; second, an "opposite direction," meaning an "outward" course, for the location of Avalon.

The Discarded Image is Lewis' introduction to the study of medieval and renaissance literature. It offers a glimpse of how Lewis, before leading his students into the trees of specific literary works, sought to give them a view of the forest that was the medieval model of the universe. This model, though later replaced by the Newtonian as the accepted scientific model, was of considerable aesthetic and even spiritual value to Lewis. According to this model, the universe consists of concentric spheres, with the earth at the center populated by Man. Luna, the moon, orbits Earth. Inside Luna's orbit is the Sublunary sphere: the realm of transience affected by the Fall of Man. Outside her are the other planets: Mercury, Venus, Sol (the Sun), Mars, Jupiter, and Saturn, which revolve in an un-fallen state and exert influence, even what might be called a personal influence, upon the Sublunary realm. Beyond the planets are the fixed stars, and beyond them, the Primum Mobile, and finally the realm of angels and the abode of God Himself.

In a period of history that has become iconic of the struggle for scientific Enlightenment against the authority of the Church or other tradition, astronomers such Copernicus and Galileo and their findings challenged the scientific veracity of the medieval model. In what is possibly his magnum opus, *Saving the Appearances: A Study in Idolatry*, Barfield explicitly expounds his theory of how humanity's "participation" in the cosmos has evolved over the ages and where humanity's participation in it is heading.

One thing that merits our close attention is that in *Saving the Appearances*, Barfield says that it was not so much the heliocentric model that was challenged by the Church, but how humanity claimed to regard truth. To understand Barfield on this point, it will be helpful to explain what Barfield means by "saving the appearances" in the title of his book. He refers to Plato's three degrees of knowledge: 1. sensory apprehension and observation of objects and events; 2. reasoning from these phenomena into general governing principles; 3. a type of insight into the spiritual nature or "divine idea" of what is observed (46). This third degree is what may most truly be called *knowledge*. Barfield sees these degrees operating in Aristotle's *De Caelo*, which informed the Church's thinking on cosmology for more than a millennium. In the sixth century, the Neoplatonist philosopher Simplicius, in his commentary on *De Caelo*, uses the term σωζειν τα φαινομενα[1] to refer to the second degree of knowledge. It was a way to give a practical model of how the "appearances," the observable objects and events, could be expected to behave.

But the explanation of saving of the appearances was not meant to be understood as ultimate reality. Barfield explains: "all that mattered was, which was the simplest and the most convenient for practical purposes; for neither of them had any essential part in truth or knowledge" (49).

So, in regard to the Copernican revolution, Barfield explains:

> The real turning point in the history of astronomy and of science in general was something else altogether. It took place when Copernicus (probably—it cannot be regarded as certain) began to think, and others, like Kepler and Galileo, began to affirm that the heliocentric hypothesis not only saved the appearances, but was physically true. It was this, this novel idea that the Copernican (and therefore any other) hypothesis might not be a hypothesis at all but the ultimate truth, that was almost enough in itself to constitute the "scientific revolution." .... It was not simply a new theory of the nature of the celestial movements that was feared, but a new theory of the nature of theory; namely that if a hypothesis saves all the appearances, it is identical with truth. (50)

And so through several centuries streamed the question of how we can know what we know, what type of knowledge is valid, and fundamentally, what we are. As regards epistemology (which asks how we know what we know), by the twentieth century, in intellectual circles it was broadly assumed that one arrived at truth only by starting from nothing and accepting only what could be proven empirically and logically (positivism). In ontology, which asks "what are we?" it was also assumed that "all there is" is physical matter and the laws of physics that govern it (materialism). On the level of personhood, the prevailing view was that we are bound to be what we are and do what we do by the chemical reactions in the cells of our own body (biological determinism) and that these processes were governed by an inescapable interaction of mathematical principles (mathematical reductionism).

The Inklings saw this positivist, materialist, and reductionist way of thinking carried to its logical conclusion by the practice of technocratic utilitarianism. Those who developed the most powerful means to subdue nature could throw off any notion of a morality handed down by Authority, in order to achieve what was useful under their invented ideologies. Lewis likened this to the work of the magician:

> For the wise men of old the cardinal problem had been how to conform the soul to reality, and the solution had been knowledge, self-discipline, and virtue. For magic and applied science alike the problem is how to subdue reality to the wishes of men: the solution is a technique; and both, in

---

1   which can be translated "saving the appearances."

the practice of this technique, are ready to do things hitherto regarded as disgusting and impious. (*The Abolition of Man* 88)

The scientific method became the way to "save the appearances." But, in contrast to the former way, the "laws" seen to be offering satisfactory, practical explanation for observable objects and events were now viewed as ultimate reality. In such a universe, the human mind was a passive recipient in observation of phenomena instead of a participant in them.

It is in such a universe that thinkers such as C. K. Ogden and I. A. Richards could attempt to subvert a traditional view of language, words, and meaning, in their works such as *The Meaning of Meaning*. They accused traditional thinking of "language superstition," what Doris Myers calls "the erroneous view that words always imply things corresponding to them" (Myers 5). The nature of metaphor is central to Ogden and Richards' thinking. For them, metaphor is an abstraction. What is most basic is the physical. Metaphors are made by drawing out similarities to something non-physical from something physical. Thus, metaphors belong in a realm of poetic discourse that may bring an emotional effect, but are untrustworthy as basic building blocks of knowledge. Ogden and Richards saw their efforts in explaining the nature of metaphor as something that "will free us from metaphysicians and bishops" and "restore our faith in physicists" (Myers 6).

To return to Barfield's view of ancient semantic unity, to the ancients (or to Tolkien's Elves), light was not, at its most basic, merely a wave/particle scientific phenomenon. It was also spiritual enlightenment. The human who observes it is not just passively receiving a stimulus, but is, as Myers calls it, "an active participant in the very nature of the universe" (7). The wave/particle phenomenon and its scientific description would not be the basis from which a metaphor is abstracted. The relationship with spiritual enlightenment is already there. Our language derives from it and we "participate" in it (7). In other words, our description of scientific laws derived from observation of phenomena like light (our "saving of the appearances") is not ultimate reality. Ultimate reality is found in Plato's third level of knowledge, in the spiritual significance of the relationships between word and meaning and our participation in them.

In *Saving the Appearances*, Barfield divides human consciousness into three eras: 1. original participation; 2. modern consciousness as a detached observer; 3. final participation. In original participation, humankind experienced the world in a mythic way. Every aspect of nature was imbued with mythical significance, and humanity experienced it unconsciously. This experience was reflected in ancient language. The last sentence of the book identifies original participation as paganism. In the modern demythologized era, these myths have died, but in their place a new idolatry has been set up.[2] This idolatry is positivist materialism, mathematical and biological reductionism, and consequently, technocratic utilitarianism. Humanity experiences itself as subject, an inward-turned isolation from the objects in nature. It is now able to consciously reflect upon the self and the self's relationship to the cosmos, whereas in original participation, it is so immersed in the cosmos that there is very little differentiated notion of any "self" that is separate from

---

2   idolatry being the placing of secondary things as ultimate.

it.[3] Barfield wrote "The essence of *original* participation is that there stands behind the phenomena, *and on the other side of them from me*, a represented which is of the same nature as me" (*Saving* 42, emphasis original).

In his book, Barfield repeatedly emphasizes that he in no way advocates a return to original participation, and he sees modern consciousness as a sort of necessary evil to move toward final participation, which he grounds in the Incarnation of the Logos, of Christ. Modern consciousness has provided humanity with individuation, but severed it from an experience of meaning inherent in the universe. This severing is healed in final participation, in which humanity has both a conscious knowledge of the self and a conscious experience of the meaning inherent in the universe and of its Creator. Of the Incarnation's relationship to participation, Barfield wrote:

> We have seen how original participation, which began as the unconscious identity of man with his Creator, shrank, as his self-consciousness increased, and how this was associated with the origin and development of language. We have seen how, in the last few centuries, B.C. it had contracted to a faint awareness of creative activity alike in nature and in man, to which was given the name of the Logos or Word. And then we have seen .... The first faint premonitory symptoms of final participation appearing already in the first centuries of our era.... What in fact happened according to the record? In the heart of that nation, whose whole impulse it had been to eliminate original participation, a man was born who simultaneously identified himself with, and carefully distinguished himself from, the Creator of the world—whom he called the Father .... In one man the inwardness of the Divine Name had been fully realized; the final participation, whereby man's Creator speaks from within man himself, had been accomplished. The Word had been made flesh. (169–70)

Barfield called the Eucharist "the tender shoot of final participation" (170) that the church has acknowledged and protected through two millennia. He also suggested that the proliferation of legends of the Holy Grail shows an increase of a conscious reflection upon the mystery of the Incarnate Word and humanity's relation to Him (173).

I wrote above that Barfield asserted that human consciousness has taken an inward course, but this is really only half the story. Barfield sees it going back outward in final participation. This is not, however, back to where it was before. It is going back outward while retaining the conscious contemplation of the self that it gained in modern consciousness Therefore, it may be most helpful to think of Barfield's view of the course of human consciousness as U-shaped.[4]

Modern thinkers (in Barfield's second stage of consciousness) became increasingly bewildered at old ways of perceiving the universe, ways that would be deemed unscientific, and they included the medieval model. Many wondered how, for so long, humanity could have had such an erroneous view of the structure of the cosmos. However, Barfield writes:

---

3   Many thanks to Kelly Cowling, who suggested this idea after reading a draft of this chapter.

4   This idea also comes from Kelly Cowling.

Possibly the Middle Ages would have been equally bewildered at the facility with which twentieth-century minds are brought to believe that, intellectually, humanity languished for countless generations in the most childish errors on all sorts of crucial subjects, until it was redeemed by some simple scientific dictum of the last century. (*History in English Words*)

This fallacy of seeing ideas as being false simply because their time had passed is what Barfield deemed "chronological snobbery": acquiescence to the assumptions that govern one's own time and an arrogant dismissal of everything pertaining to previous ages (Lewis, *SbJ* 207). Lewis became quite fond of this term as well. Barfield's illumination of it helped convince a young Lewis to turn away from atheism.

My task in this chapter is to show how Barfield's views on human consciousness shaped the Inklings' Arthurian mythological geographies. So, I will start with Barfield's own Arthurian works. Barfield's explicitly Arthurian writings are few. He wrote a piece entitled *The Quest of the Sangreal*, which is unavailable at this time, but is slated for publication and analysis in the near future.[5] The most "Arthurian" work now available is his science fiction novella, *Night Operation*.[6] The story provides a setting in which Barfield's views on human consciousness are manifest. The story also shows how his views are a response to the intellectual issues of the Inklings' day, and how his views speak to an interpretation of the collective Arthurian works of the Inklings.

Night Operation takes place in a dystopian twenty-second-century society that has lived inside of a sewer system for generations. The worldview of this society is biological-reductionistic. Their entire life and framework of meaning revolves around the pursuit and experience of three biological functions known as the "three E's."[7] This society lives in sewers in order to avoid "the Airborne Invasion" (9, 53). Nearly all memory of aboveground civilization has faded. Only a select few are allowed access to the libraries containing books with reference to "Traditional History" (13) and foreign concepts such as marriage, family, courtesy, dignity, honor, the ancient Greeks, gods, and other ideas that the reader likely takes for granted.

The protagonist, Jon, is eventually allowed access to these staggering books and comes to realize the "either/or" thinking that was manifest in the bifurcating tendencies in modern language. As Jon gropes his way toward an understanding about what life was like aboveground, he begins to feel compelled that he must indeed go there, an almost unprecedented experience in that society. Jon persuades Jak and Peet to accompany him.[8]

Once aboveground, as they feared, the three friends encounter an Airborne Invasion. But it is not as they feared: "Huge silky cupolas they seemed, with long inverted cones of pendant strands trailing below them; and they were coming nearer ... 'Parachutes!'" Jon cries (53). These parachutes drop "obviously

---

5   See chapter 1 by Sørina Higgins to understand how *The Quest of the Sangreal*, along with Barfield's intentions
     for the way it was to be performed, is a profound look into his views on language, speech, and movement.
6   *Night Operation* is referred to as a "Grail story" by its editor Jane Hipolito in her introduction (xii).
7   ejaculation, defecation, and vomiting.
8   Hipolito sees "Jak" as alluding to C. S. "Jack" Lewis and "Peet" to fellow Inkling Cecil Harwood (xi).

harmless little spheres" (54) that roll along the ground, then disappear. It is a grail encounter, which approaches them against a backdrop of stars and thence returns.

Afterwards, the three friends discuss the encounter. In their perceptions, each of them describes what they saw as having a "skeleton" and a "body." What they saw differently were the colors. Were the spheres gold, silver, or black? Did they sink into the ground or did they volatilize into the air? They realize that the differences in what they saw were because of the differences in what they were "attending to" (54). Jon says:

> It's possible to see the same thing and be shown different things. But it's also possible to see different things and be shown the same thing. *I* saw parachutes dropping from the sky. They saw something quite different—or perhaps not so very different—different substance, same shape—the great inverted cone with the little morsel of Dignity at its nether tip. (56)

Jon identifies what he saw as "the beginning of the world" (56). Jon later calls this "inverted cone" a "little ghostly Cup" (57). From this Airborne Invasion, they gain insight into where humanity has come from, how it is now, and where it is going. They say it has come from "the gods" (56). Jon thinks of this "ghostly cup" that "it would need refilling from time to time; and that it was a vessel that could be brimmed with no other substance than its own magic Provenance awfully beheld" (64). Jon thinks of it as a "little Calyx of joy" (64).

It was this cup, this "grail" of joy, that frees Jon and his companions from the sewers of their biological reductionism. It takes them back to "the beginning of the world" (56). They see different things, but were shown the same thing. Here is an iconoclast that tears down the idols of life in the sewer,[9] and that iconoclast is the shape of the "grail."

In the consciousness of Jon and his Night Operation companions, the shape of the universe is in upheaval. All they had known was a sewer and a rare peek through a narrow pipe into the sky way up there somewhere. But when Jon boldly goes Aboveground:

> it is difficult to describe the general impression it was making; but whatever else it was, it was not Copernican. Vast empty spaces were no part of his experience and in no way structured his imagination. It was more as if the crown of his own head had been opened and expanded and he was looking into instead of out of it. (50–51)

The Copernican Universe was physically still there, but Jon is not attending to it. He is attending to meaning in the universe. He is no longer trapped and isolated in his inward, biologically reduced consciousness. He is beginning to look *outwardly*. This looking outwardly hearkens back to original participation, but it also differs from it. Jon is freed from an inward-*only* consciousness, but he still retains an inward, conscious awareness of self that was unknown in original participation. He can now look out into the cosmos as if he is looking inside himself. He has made the change in direction toward being both individually conscious

---

9   i.e., the three "E's." These are what the society in the sewer had been "attending to."

and aware of how he is connected to the external world. Jon is freed from his modern, reductionist idolatry by being shown "the beginning of the world." He is taken back into a pre-modern consciousness that is populated by gods. However, this vision comes to him in the form of a "cup," a "grail," that is an intimation of the move toward final participation in Christ.

I have shown how Barfield's views on language and consciousness influenced his grail story in *Night Operation*, and now I will show how his views influenced the other Inklings, including shape and direction in their Arthurian mythological geographies. Barfield's views on language and consciousness had a radical influence on Tolkien's view of philology. Tolkien invented his own languages and wrote his mythology to give them stories in which to live.

Several features of Tolkien's mythology speak to questions of human consciousness and ultimate reality. The first is the relationship of the Elves to the music of the Ainur. The Ainur, the "gods" of his mythology, are "of course meant to provide beings of the same order and beauty, power, majesty as the 'gods' of higher mythology, which can yet be accepted—well, shall we say baldly, by a mind that believes in the Blessed Trinity" (*Letters* 146). Similar to the medieval appropriation of classical gods and goddesses to describe planetary influence upon the sublunary realm, Tolkien baptizes another aspect of mythology. His Ainur are demiurges, but they are servants of Ilúvatar, the one true God and Father of All. Tolkien, in the first line of the "Ainulindalë" creation story in *The Silmarillion*, calls the Ainur the "offspring" of the thought of Ilúvatar. They have a role in shaping the creation of the world, Arda, first when it is propounded as a musical theme. The Ainur add their harmony (or discord, in the case of the rebel Melkor). Then some of them physically enter into the created world to live out the music and to physically shape the world according to their power and gifting.

Through the Elves, Tolkien explored aspects of human faculties and consciousness. Recalling Barfield's influence upon Tolkien's use of the term *light,* Tolkien's account in his letter to Milton Waldman follows:

> as far as all this has symbolical or allegorical significance, Light is such a primeval symbol in the nature of the Universe, that it can hardly be analysed. The Light of Valinor (derived from light before any fall) is the light of art undivorced from reason, that sees hings [sic] both scientifically (or philosophically) and imaginatively (or subcreatively) and says that they are good—as beautiful. (*Letters* 148n)

In Barfield's terms, the "art"[10] of the Elves would be made by acting in accordance with their understanding of how the "appearances" were saved. But they realized that these principles were not fundamental reality. They were, rather, incarnations of the Music of the Ainur. It would be this third degree of knowledge that could then be expressed in their art. Their art and their lore were not an irrational add-on from metaphors abstracted from a fundamental material or mathematical reality, but rather they flowed from their spiritual knowledge through the material. Much of their work may have been able to be measured and explained

---

10   "art" as encompassing their works: their kingdoms, architecture, weaponry, songs, and what is perceived as "magic" by other races.

scientifically. Perhaps it was in a very scientific way that the Elves worked their crafts, but this did not mean that this way of "saving the appearances" could discount the ultimate reality of the Music of Ilúvatar.

Contrast the Elves with technocratic utilitarians like Sauron and Saruman. For them, ethics are subordinate to usefulness, since reality, for them, is the quest for control. Control is, in their perception, ultimate reality. In this way they are like Melkor, who tried to cause discord in the Music in the creation myth and seize control of it for himself.

For Ogden and Richards, art is most definitely divorced from reason. For them, the ultimate way to see things is scientifically. Saving the appearances equals ultimate reality. Imaginative grasp is secondary at best, or at worst, misleading. In contrast, Tolkien, through the Elves and their "art undivorced from reason," was exploring Barfield's notions of participation. They are (to use Barfield's description of final participation) both individually conscious and aware of how they, as individuals, are interconnected to the external world of nature in a unified whole. In the Ainur, Tolkien baptized the role that gods in other mythologies played. In the Elves, Tolkien baptizes human consciousness. How? Though they were in a pre-Christian[11] mythical era, their knowledge of self and of the inherent meaning in the cosmos were intimations of final participation. Their art flowed from their reason in a conscious apprehension of not only individuality, but of unity in the cosmos.

Secondly, in Tolkien we can explore human consciousness and ultimate reality because in his mythology, the shape of the world undergoes a fundamental change. This is recounted in *The Silmarillion* in the *Akallabêth*, the story of the rise and fall of Númenor. Before the rebellion of the Númenorians against the Valar, when in their erroneous quest for immortality they sail to the west to the Undying Lands, the world is flat. One could sail west and reach the very edge of the world. After the Undying Lands are violated, the Valar appeal to Ilúvatar for judgment. Númenor drowns, and there is no longer a visible path (called "The Straight Road"; *LR 31*) for mortals to sail to what was once the Uttermost West. A mortal who sailed on would now eventually come back to where he started.[12]

I will show how this notion of sailing to the west, in a now round world, is intimately connected with Tolkien's Arthurian work. In Tolkien and Lewis' famous coin toss to decide which of them would write a book on space travel and which on time travel, it was Lewis who got space, Tolkien who got time. Lewis, in his usual fashion, completed his books speedily. Tolkien never finished what has now been published as *The Lost Road and Other Writings* (1987). In Christopher Tolkien's commentary on *The Fall of Arthur*, he quotes from the 1964 letter from his father that speaks of a thread in *The Lost Road* that "was to be the occurrence time and again in human families ... of a father that could be interpreted as Bliss-friend and Elf-friend

---

11   What would normally be thought of as original participatory or pagan.

12   It would be a mistake to think that the geography of Tolkien's mythology before the Fall of Númenor reflects a medieval view of the world. Lewis emphasizes in *The Discarded Image* that the Medievals understood the significance of a round planet (140). Rather, it was nineteenth-century followers of scientism who tried to project back upon the Medievals an erroneous view of a flat earth. There are important implications to this change of shape, however, that affect the geography of the Inklings' Arthurian works. These will be explored more fully later in the chapter.

.... It started with a father-son affinity between Edwin and Elwin of the present" (FoA 150). Christopher Tolkien also refers to what his father called "Atlantis Haunting" (LR 10), a feature of human consciousness that is the blurred memory of a distant, more beautiful past that is now unattainable. Christopher Tolkien concludes in his commentary in *The Lost Road* that the book was intended to conclude with the fall of Númenor (63). Fragments of poems related to Tolkien's unfinished epic poem *The Fall of Arthur* identify elements of Tolkien's mythology with features of the Arthurian legends. Among these is the identification of the island of Tol Eressëa, the island just to the east of Valinor, with Avalon. Later in this chapter, we will see the implications of Barfield's thinking on these connections.

Barfield's views on consciousness and participation can also illuminate the Arthurian works of Charles Williams. *Taliessin through Logres* and *The Region of the Summer Stars* are the two cycles of mostly lyric poetry that were intended to be parts of a complete work of Arthurian legends in poetry. However, Williams died before completing it. In Williams' Arthuriad, the Empire of Byzantium is an image of the rule of God over the world. The Emperor is identified closely with God, if not representing God himself.

In these works, the primary enemies of Byzantium are not modern reductionisms, but what might be seen as their predecessors; the "either/or-ness"[13] of a materialist reductionism manifest centuries before. Lewis explains in "Williams and the Arthuriad" that the primary enemy of Byzantium is Islam (308) and that the same "heresies which deny the co-inherence of Deity and flesh in Christ" (366) are found in other views such as Gnosticism and Manichaeism.

For the Manichean, either spirit or matter is good and the other evil—and it must be that spirit is good and matter evil. For Islam, God does not incarnate. There is God and there is Man, but no God-Man. It is as if these two beliefs have moved on from original participation, but refuse to continue on to final participation. Both are satisfied that their mystery-denying observations adequately save the appearances and reject that ultimate reality would be the Incarnation of God in a Man. The Grail then becomes an object to unify the empire against forces that would deny that God would incarnate. The Grail is connected with the preparation for the Second Coming of Christ. For the modernist, the doctrine of Christ's return is implausible. In Islam, however, there is indeed a Second Coming of Jesus in judgment.

In Williams' Arthuriad, Carbonek is the place of the Grail and other holy things. The ultimate destination, beyond Carbonek, is Sarras, the place of the Trinity. Only in this central doctrine is the mystery of the Incarnate God-Man, of spirit and flesh, held together. The prelude of *The Region of the Summer Stars* refers to the Empire awaiting "The Second Coming / of the Union, of the twy-natured single person" (ll. 50–51). Sarras is the place of ultimate reality that stands against the reductionisms of the day.

Among all the Inklings, Williams predominates in focusing his writings on legends concerning the Holy Grail. The Grail is central in one of his novels set in modern times, *War in Heaven*. In this story, people aligned with spiritually dark forces are hell-bent on harnessing the power of the Grail, or rather developing the technology of the Grail, for their own power-hungry ends.

---

13   For a helpful discussion of how Barfield avoided "either/or-ness," see his writing on the concept of "polarity" in the works of Samuel Taylor Coleridge in his essay "Either : Or: Coleridge, Lewis, and Romantic Theology."

C. S. Lewis' work provides the most robust material for exploring Barfield's views of language and consciousness and how they affected the Inklings' Arthurian material. Before the Inklings gatherings began to take shape, and even before Lewis' conversion to Christianity, Lewis and Barfield, in the context of a deep friendship, vigorously debated Lewis' agnostic materialism (which was much in line with the intellectual climate of his day). They also debated whether it was reason alone or reason and imagination together that gave humanity its faculty to arrive at discerning truth. Barfield believed it was both. In *Surprised by Joy*, Lewis refers to their debate as the "Great War" (207). Though Lewis was eventually dissuaded from his materialism, he never assented to Barfield in regard to imagination (see Barfield's essay "Lewis, Truth, and Imagination" in *Owen Barfield on C. S. Lewis* 90). But he often acted like it. Barfield wrote later that he deeply regretted that after his conversion, Lewis refused to engage in further debate about imagination and reason. Barfield writes of his experience of "Two Lewises," one the "combatively logical" Christian Apologist and the other the "gently imaginative" Lewis, author of poems and Narnia and the Space Trilogy and *Till We Have Faces* (94).

Lewis was highly skeptical of any confidence in knowing the direction in which human consciousness was headed. In his essay "Historicism," we see Lewis' great distrust of human attempts to impose an overarching narrative of "progress" or, for that matter, much of any discernible pattern upon human history. Barfield's notion of human consciousness evolving toward final participation would be met by Lewis with a resounding: "How could you be so sure?" In fact, Lewis had a great wariness about the anthroposophy that influenced Barfield's ideas. It had gnostic tendencies. It led to Barfield's unorthodox beliefs like reincarnation,[14] a belief that Lewis insisted no Christian can believe (*Barfield on Lewis* 133). Barfield himself grew up agnostic and was not baptized into the Church of England until middle age. Barfield told Flieger about an evening on which he tried to explain anthroposophy to a gathering of the Inklings and found it quite difficult indeed (Flieger 36). So, for Lewis, there is much tension with Barfield's expressed beliefs. Nevertheless, it is in the "second" of the "two Lewises" that we discern Lewis at least wrestling with them and even employing them in his imaginative works.

Lewis' first work of fiction after his Christian conversion was *The Pilgrim's Regress*. Its protagonist, John, is on an allegorical journey to fulfill his *Sehnsucht*, the transient, unfulfillable desire that comes to him from a vision of an island in the West. He travels in that direction, away from the Landlord in the East (symbolic of God and his Law). Along the way, he encounters characters who aid or hinder his quest. One of those who hinders him, and in fact imprisons him, is The Spirit of the Age, a giant monster made of rock (assisted by Mr. Enlightenment). The giant has the power to make whatever it looks upon become transparent. Thus, the inner organs of the bodies of other prisoners are visible. Even milk is shown just to be another bodily excretion like sweat or dung. The goal of the Spirit of the Age and his jailers is to teach the prisoners that the things they had once longed for are illusory. What the prisoners thought they had or sought for is debunked as wish fulfillment.

---

14   Tolkien's Elves reincarnated, but Tolkien defended this choice in a letter to a concerned priest that it was a literary device used in his secondary world and did not reflect his beliefs about the primary world (*Letters* 189).

However, the bright-shining, sword-bearing virgin Reason comes, and after she gives a series of riddles to the Spirit of the Age, she is able to slay him and set the prisoners free. The first riddle she asks him
is about the colors of objects in the darks (*PR* 52) The Giant is unable to answer. Reason explains to John
that the Giant was fooling him by revealing how human entrails *would* appear if they could be seen by the
human eye in a kind of x-ray vision—but that this is an unreality. In the way the world is designed, inner
organs cannot be seen. We experience them by our tactile sensations, not by our sense of sight. When they
are working properly, we experience our organs through movement, breathing, hunger and fullness, not
through looking at our guts as if they were sausages on a butcher's table. Vivisecting a person to make the
inner organs visible would kill the man, which would cause the organs to cease functioning, such that the
observer would still not see working entrails. Thus, the Giant's vision is a deception, designed to pretend
life is a hideous mass of entrails, when in reality it is rich and beautiful (see *PR* 61–62). It was the scientific,
anatomical knowledge of the human body and its systems that saved the appearances. But, for the Spirit of
the Age and Mr. Enlightenment, this was made to be ultimate. It was their idol. In their idolatry, they were
no longer able to see the ultimate reality of the sensations, longings, feelings, and knowledge produced
in them. And in their idolatry, they became iconoclasts of any that claim a knowledge beyond their idols.

In *Night Operation*, after his grail Encounter, Jon says that the "Real History" that people were taught in
the sewer "is based on the curious idea that what people are not attending to is not there; and they generally
go on from that to the even more curious idea (which they soon start calling the fact) that what people have
ceased attending to never was there" (55). The iconoclast for him, along with Jak and Peet, is the "grail"
shape and its contents of joy and dignity that frees their consciousness from the confines of the sewer. In
The Pilgrim's Regress, the sword of Reason and its knowledge of longing and emotion knocks down the idols of
the Spirit of the Age and frees his captives to know that they have been there all along. Both John and Jon
have an experience that hearkens back to original participation, in which they experience meaning that is
inherent to the cosmos. Since they also experience this consciously, it is a step toward final participation.

Other works by Lewis, namely *The Chronicles of Narnia* and the Ransom Trilogy, also show Barfield's
influence. Michael Ward in his recent work *Planet Narnia* has compellingly shown that the seven "personalities" of the medieval model of the universe have thematically influenced each of the seven books of Lewis'
Chronicles of Narnia series. It is the "personalities" of these planets that inform Lewis' treatment of Planetary
Intelligences, also known as Oyéresu (singular 'Oyarsa'), throughout his Ransom books. In the trilogy,
each planet of our solar system has an intelligence to govern it. These intelligences are encountered by the
protagonist, philologist Dr. Elwin Ransom, either on the world that they govern (as on Mars in *Out of the
Silent Planet* or on Venus in *Perelandra*) or when they come to Earth in *That Hideous Strength*. Ransom is opposed
in each novel by utilitarian technocrats, whether Weston in his attempts to exploit innocent, intelligent
creatures of the old world of Malacandra, or the diabolically possessed "un-Man" that Weston has become
in his attempt to induce a Fall in the first people of Perelandra. Systemic, technocratic, utilitarian evil
is embodied in the National Institute for Co-ordinated Experiments (N.I.C.E.) of *That Hideous Strength*.

The book describes the thought of Prof. Frost, the earthly mastermind of the N.I.C.E.:

For many years he theoretically believed that all which appears in the mind as motive or intention is merely a by-product of what the body is doing. But for the last year or so—since he had been initiated—he had begun to taste as fact what he had long held as theory. Increasingly, his actions had been without motive. He did this and that, he said thus and thus, and did not know why. His mind was a mere spectator. He could not understand why the spectator should exist at all. He resented its existence, even while assuring himself that resentment also was merely a chemical phenomenon. (*THS* 357)

Ransom and his cohort are in need of the aid of the Planetary Intelligences to intervene to stop the domination of the N.I.C.E. and their dehumanizing reign of terror. However, for the Intelligences to descend to our fallen, isolated, "silent" planet, a person is needed to act as "bridge." That bridge is none other than Merlin (291), and it is in his person that this paper will show the Barfield-influenced "change of shape" prevalent in the Inklings' Arthurian works in response to the intellectual issues of the day.

The Arthurian legends are curiously connected with the pagan (or "original participatory") past of the Celts and narrated in a Christian setting. Tolkien himself appears to have had trouble holding this tension and was much more comfortable with his mythology being in a pre-Christian setting. Lewis made much bolder attempts to hold this tension through his characterization of Ransom as Pendragon and of Merlin the Wizard.

In *That Hideous Strength*, Ransom is the Pendragon, one in a line of spiritual (or mythic?) kings of England, ruler of Logres, a sort of behind-the-scenes, parallel kingdom to Britain. Merlin the Wizard arises from his limbo-like state underground and aids in the battle against the scientistic technocrats who are attempting to dominate and destroy Logres and the world. But an important subplot in this narrative is that this is not only for the salvation of England, but also for the salvation of Merlin's soul.

To understand Lewis' portrayal of Merlin, it will help us first to understand Charles Williams' characterization of him. In Williams' *The Region of the Summer Stars*, in the poem "The Son of Lancelot," Merlin is called one of the "children of Nimue" (p. 7, l. 113) along with his sister, Brisen. In the poem "The Calling of Taliessin," they are pictured as performing incantations that are to bring about the kingdom of Logres. They "invoked the third heaven," (259) in which are the "living unriven truths, / climax tranquil in Venus" (lines 252–53). Who is Nimue? Lewis, in "Williams and the Arthuriad," identifies her as one whose archetype is Venus (285). Lewis also says that Williams may have been influenced by Renaissance Platonist thought, which saw Venus as "celestial love and beauty," the "pattern or model after which God created the material universe" (286).

We may connect Nimue with "Nature," but as Lewis writes:

To say Nimue is an image of Nature is true, but not very helpful since 'Nature' itself is a hard word. For Williams, as for Plato, the phenomenal world—the world studied by the sciences—is primarily a reflection or a copy or adaption of something else. Nimue, the 'mother of making' is that energy which reproduces on earth a pattern derived from 'the third heaven', i.e. from the sphere of Venus, the sphere of Divine Love. (WA 286)

Regarding Merlin and Brisen, Lewis sums up their work. These two were in the poem respectively called "time and space, duration and extension" (286). Lewis says, "all the works of Nimue, except where Grace intervene, are subject to these two" (286).

A wizard is one who is closely connected to nature and its inherent mythos. In *That Hideous Strength*, Ransom tells Merlin that in his early days, perhaps his craft and power as a wizard were somehow more "lawful" than they are now. But it was time for Merlin to be awakened, for Merlin to put an end to the modern idolatry and then to pass on. Merlin had heretofore only been acquainted with the "earthly wraiths" of the Planetary Intelligences whom Ransom knew "face to face," as it were (292).

If one is discussing "wraiths" in the work of the Inklings, Tolkien's use of the word may come to mind. Tom Shippey, in *J. R. R. Tolkien: Author of the Century*, explains that a wraith is defined by its shape rather than its substance (123). The Oxford English Dictionary gives two apparently contradictory senses of the word: 1. "An apparition or spectre of a dead person: a phantom or ghost"; 2. "An immaterial or spectral appearance of a living being" (qtd. in *Author* 123). Shippey explains that this word likely comes from the Old English verb *wridan*, 'writhe,' and that English has several words derived from 'writhe,' such as 'wreath,' a twisted form, and 'wrath.' Shippey highlights that Barfield suggested *wrath* is an internal 'twisting' of emotion (122). Shippey also points out that in *The Fellowship of the Ring*, the elf Legolas refers to a "wreath of snow," akin to a 'wisp,' something "barely substantial" (122), and that the Ringwraiths do not have physical bodies in the normal sense, yet they can wield weapons, ride horses, etc. (124). Therefore, wraiths are twisted into ghostly shapes in the semblance of something substantial. In *The Road to Middle-earth*, Shippey points out that (at least in one stage of the development of the legendarium), Orcs are twisted Elves, and that Satan is referred to in Lewis' Ransom Trilogy as the "Bent" Oyarsa (149). Shippey suggests that the Ringwraiths "are in origin, 'bent' people, and people who have been bent perhaps, into a perfect self-regarding 'wreath', 'wraith' or Ring" (149). To be ultimately self-regarding is to place what is supposed to be secondary as ultimate. Barfield's word for that is idolatry. As we have seen in Barfield, humankind's ultimate calling is to break away from this inward-focused self-regard.

The differences between the substantial Planetary Intelligences and their wraiths can be seen in the following portions of *That Hideous Strength*. When the utilitarian technocrats of the N.I.C.E. are defeated, there is in a sense a revival at St. Anne's, the house that serves as the headquarters of Logres. This revival is brought about by the presence of the Planetary Intelligence of Venus. Its ultimate fruition is the re-uniting of Mark and Jane Studdock in their marriage bed, as they turn away from their intentional childlessness and toward conceiving the next Pendragon to succeed Ransom.

Previously, Jane had encountered the earthly wraith of Venus in a vision, accompanied by mischievous male dwarfs. While beholding this vison, Jane's perception of this giantess is that it is mocking her. The presence of the wraith, who wears a flame-colored robe, brings intense heat to the room, and sets the room on fire, just before Jane is startled out of the vision by Mrs. Dimble. The wraith of Venus is described as "Mother Dimble's face with something left out" (304). The earthly Venus has a recognizable shape but is lacking something in substance. The "something left out" is the substance that is in Christ. She is the Venus of original participation, not final. In *Planet Narnia*, Ward shows how Lewis used the different traits of the medieval planets to color Aslan in Narnia, such as Aslan as Venus in *The Magician's Nephew*. Aslan the life-giver stands in contrast to the beautiful, yet cold and destroying Jadis. In Williams' Arthuriad, Nimue, Merlin's mother, is not Venus, but a copy of her. Nimue lives in the fallen sphere. We see in *That Hideous Strength* how what is good in the earthly wraiths (beauty, pleasure) is retained and yet completed and sanctified in the Planetary Intelligences. Where the original participatory wraith is untamed and destroys, the heavenly, final-participatory intelligence is ordered and gives life. Mother Dimble, a Christian, though on earth and subject to frustrations such as infertility, is complete in Christ and is a picture of the heavenly Venus.

What of shape and substance in Williams' Arthuriad? Among the reductionist enemies of Byzantium, the Manichaeans would deny substance to the shape that is the body. Why? Because they view matter as evil. Therefore, the body is evil. The Moslems would deny shape to the substance of God because they hold that God does not incarnate. They would deem such a notion of incarnation as idolatrous. The enemies of Byzantium are disconnected from God's fullness because of their "either/or" view and are left with a material world that is no more than a wraith.[15]

In Barfield's *Night Operation*, for those who had stayed Aboveground and whose consciousness had not been formed by the shape of the sewer: "A sort of cleansing had taken place, with the result that, for the few who had remained there, the divorce between seeing and feeling, and thus between outer and inner, instead of having to go on increasing, had been steadily diminishing" (46). Those Aboveground were free from the imprisonment of an inwardly turned consciousness that regarded metaphorical meaning or feeling-meaning as an abstraction from a more real, concrete scientific meaning: "They saw what they felt" (46). Freed from the shape of the sewer, they saw in nature the reflection of the substance of inherently meaningful realities of human experience.

The modern idolatry of technocrats like the N.I.C.E. was to reduce substance to shape. That is to say that the substance is merely the shape. In their view, the shape was biological impulses. To Frost, Venus would have been merely "a by-product of what the body is doing" (357), in this case the body exercising its sexual instincts. Just as the Spirit of the Age, by showing the inner organs of a person, tried to prove that human longing and noble sentiments are illusory, so also the technocrats tried to show that any notion of Venus was an illusory by-product of the reproductive system.

Looking at the encounters with Venus in *That Hideous Strength* in Barfieldian terms, ancient humanity participated in the earthly Venus. They saw lovers' embraces and fertility rituals in her. The modern idolatry, in the hands of iconoclasts like the frigid Jane Studdock, has been to try to banish her altogether. Yet ultimately, Venus' destiny is to be fulfilled in humanity's final participation in Christ, to whom belongs the substance, or "body" (σωμσ; see Colossians 2:17).

I wrote above that this paper will argue that Barfield's view of the direction of human consciousness fits on the Inklings' Arthurian works in two main ways. One of those is a change in shape from Wizard to Pendragon as the proper tension-holder between ancient and contemporary consciousness. Lewis' Merlin, perhaps even in his time in the days of Arthur, was an anachronism. His natural life was to be acquainted

---

15   As for "technocrats": in a Williams novel in a modern setting, such as *War in Heaven*, one might see the abuse of the Grail as *utilizing* shape and *ignoring* substance.

with powers that were of various shapes, whether powers to predict the future or to use force against ene-mies. But these powerful shapes were lacking in substance. The partaker of these powers was in danger of relying on them as ultimate. In many strands of Arthurian tradition, Merlin's father was not human, but a seducing incubus,[16] and thus Merlin was able to manipulate the material of nature with power. In a sense it was as if he manipulated it with hands that were in a spiritual realm.

Why is Merlin the one to bring down the N.I.C.E.? Ransom explains why the Lord did not choose Ransom himself for the task of bringing the powers of Deep Heaven (the Planetary Intelligences) down upon them:

> he will not suffer a mind that still has its virginity to be so violated. And through a black magician's mind their purity neither can nor will operate. One who has dabbled ... in the days when dabbling had not begun to be evil, or was only just beginning ... and also a Christian man and a penitent. A tool (I must speak plainly) good enough to be so used and not too good. (291)

It is striking to see, in Lewis, something that lines up quite similarly to Barfield's views of the evolution of human consciousness. In an age closer to original participation that was moving toward a Christian age, a "dabbling" with the earthly wraiths was perhaps not so evil as it would be now, or perhaps had not begun to be evil at all. When Merlin proposes going out and "renewing his acquaintance" with the surrounding countryside and its inherent mythos, in order to turn its power against the N.I.C.E, he is forbidden to do so by Ransom:

> If it were possible, it would be unlawful. Whatever of spirit may still linger on the earth has withdrawn fifteen hundred years further away from us since your time .... In this age it is utterly unlawful ... it never was very lawful, even in your day .... And because Our Lord does all things for each, one of the purposes of your reawakening was that your own soul should be saved. (288–89)

Just as Barfield repeatedly stresses that he does not advocate a return to original participation, it would be "unlawful" for Merlin to do so as well. He is to move ahead toward final participation, not go back. Perhaps it is no coincidence that the "resurrected" Merlin of *That Hideous Strength*, as he carries out his final mission, comes to the N.I.C.E. disguised as a priest, one who uses earthly hands to offer a heavenly substance that mediates between God and Man?

After Merlin fulfills his mission, he is nowhere to be found. Perhaps, after one last stand, having now encountered the fulfillment of the Powers he once only knew as earthly wraiths, his salvation is at hand. His original participation in the cosmos had come around to break down the modern idols and pass on into final participation. In his mission on earth, Merlin decreased so that the Pendragon might increase.

---

16 Or, may we say, a wraith? However, in *That Hideous Strength*, he says that the notion that he is "the son of a devil" is "a lie" (289).

In the popular contemporary imagination, Merlin is indeed a magician. However, even in early Arthurian works we see some shift to his characterization as a more ordinary human king. Take, for instance, Geoffrey of Monmouth's *Vita Merlini*. The poem's recent translator Mark Walker says that his Merlin:

> is not the staff-carrying, pointy-hat-wearing old man of later tradition. In fact, he doesn't seem much like a wizard at all. This Merlin is at once a king, a lawmaker, and a madman who shuns society; he is an unpredictable mischief-maker, an inspired prophet, and a repository of cutting-edge scientific knowledge. If this Merlin can be said to resemble any modern wizard at all, he is more like the benevolently tricksterish Wizard of Oz than any of his more obvious descendants—Gandalf or Dumbledore, to name but two.

Merlin indeed plays the role of prophet in much Arthurian material, most prominently as he prophesies about the rise and fall of Arthur, and we have seen how he is indeed a kind of nature priest, a handler of nature who offers it in service to a king. And it is toward this office of King that we find the Arthuriad, and particularly the Inklings' Arthuriana, moving. Of these three offices of Christ, as the New Testament looks at the present and toward the future, it says that prophecies will cease (1 Cor. 3:8), that Christ is the High Priest in the heavenlies (Hebrews 4), and that he had made his people to be a holy priesthood (1 Peter 2:5). But toward the end of the book of Revelation, the emphasis is on Christ the King, His reign, and His redeemed people's future reign with Him.

In II Samuel, the LORD promised David that his descendants would reign on the throne of Israel forever. His first descendant Solomon was invited by the LORD to ask for whatever he wished, and he chose wisdom. In the Inklings' literary works, there is a move from a magical, original-participatory handling of nature, to a King who rules with wisdom. King Aragorn returns, and the Elves fade with the dawn of the age of Men. In Narnia, some magicians were formerly stars; in *The Voyage of the "Dawn Treader,"* Coriakin is a former star who is under discipline and given the assignment of governing the foolish Dufflepuds. Coriakin uses spells to keep their foolish ways in check, but he looks forward to "the day when they can be governed by wisdom instead of this rough magic" (174). In the same book, Ramandu is a retired star who serves at Aslan's Table as a reward. Whereas the magician Coriakin governs by power, Ramandu serves a role that echoes the priestly service of the Eucharist, a role of final participation. Elwin (Elf-friend) Ransom also acts as prophet in his access to original (yet unfallen) participation in his mastery of the Old Solar language. Merlin is astonished that Ransom has communion with the gods in this tongue. Merlin's master, Blaise, knew only a few words of it. But Merlin had only participated with the wraiths, the skeletons. Ransom was acquainted with the substance, the body.

We can see this progression from Wizard to Pendragon in the dialogue between Ransom and Merlin at their meeting. Merlin asks Ransom three questions to verify that he is indeed the Pendragon. The second of these is "Where is the ring of Arthur the King?"

> "The ring of the King," said Ransom, "is on Arthur's finger where he sits in the House of Kings in the cup-shaped land of Abhalljin, beyond the seas of Lur in Perelandra. For Arthur did not

die; but Our Lord took him, to be in the body till the end of time and the shattering of Sulva, with Enoch and Elias and Moses and Melchisedec the King. Melchisedec is he in whose hall the steep-stoned ring sparkles on the forefinger of the Pendragon." (*THS* 274)

Here we are confronted with a list of biblical characters of either mysterious origin or end. And we are informed that Arthur is on Perelandra. Abhalljin is a variant on 'Avalon,' the mysterious isle in many versions of the Arthur legend. It is there where mortally wounded Arthur goes for healing and to prepare for his return. I have observed that Arthur, the Grail, and the return of Christ are connected. Notice that Abhalljin is "cup-shaped." It seems that even the geography here is a grail encounter. In the progression from Wizard to Pendragon, we encounter a progression from one who governs by interaction with the shapes of the wraiths to a cup of substance.

In Williams' poem "The Departure of Merlin," Merlin leaves on a ship, but not before a curious meeting with two others, "Joseph of Nazareth, Joseph of Arimathea ... /foster fathers of beatitude to the foster-father of Galahad; / twin suns of womb and tomb" (lines 17, 20–21). Joseph of Arimathea, the caretaker of Jesus' body after his death, is the caretaker of the Grail in many Arthurian legends. It is Galahad, Lancelot's son and Merlin's foster-son, who achieves the Grail. Merlin departs and arrives at Byzantium, the realm of the rule of God the King, and it is said of him: "Well has Merlin spoken the last spell, / worked the last image, gone to his own" (53–54). The Wizard has now decreased that the wise King (and his servants) might increase.

In Lewis' Arthuriana, we continue to see the change of shape, the progression from Wizard to Pendragon, with the third question Merlin asks Ransom: "Who shall be Pendragon in the time when Saturn descends from his sphere? In what world did he learn war?" (274). The answer is: "'In the sphere of Venus I learned war,' said Ransom. 'In this age Lurga shall descend. I am the Pendragon'" (274). The final-participatory Saturn (Lurga) comes down to make war against and to undo the bent works of the evil utilitarian technocrats. Saturn's frosty presence that brings decay is foretold in Ransom's declaration, an "I am" declaration that is an echo of Christ's "I am" declarations throughout the Gospel of John. Ransom, in his kingly role as Pendragon, also retains priestly qualities, or more accurately, properties of sacrifice. His heel is wounded on Perelandra as he defeats the Un-man, an echo of the Genesis 3 prophecy that the seed of Eve (Christ) would crush the head of the serpent and that the serpent would bruise His heel. In final participation, humanity participates in the substance, not just the wraith-shape. The world has been bent, but in Christ, in the cup of His suffering and sacrifice, it is being made to participate in His substance, and one day it shall no longer be bent, but be whole and be filled.

In the intellectual upheaval of the centuries preceding the Inklings, the shape of the universe had changed. Human consciousness experienced the shape of the universe in a different way than it used to in the way Lewis described in *The Discarded Image*. It was no longer experienced earth in the center of the revolutions of the spheres and their music, the planets and their intelligences with their influence on humanity.[17] It no longer viewed the permanence of translunary planets and the fixed stars. Earth became

---

17   Though in Medieval times it still experienced the earth as a tiny speck in a vast universe. It just wasn't meaningless.

a tiny speck in a vast, empty, meaningless universe. In modern consciousness, the spheres of heaven are opened to this very vastness. But for Barfield, and by extension for the other Inklings to varying degrees, this is a necessary intermediate stage toward final participation. The cosmos is bent (such as in the fall of Númenor) so that humanity can be unbent. In modern consciousness, the shapes changed, and in Ransom the Pendragon we see the time approach to raise up the wraiths of original participation, challenge the idolatry of the new shape, and perhaps set the old wraiths upon the straight path.

"How did Arthur get into space?" is a natural question to ask upon hearing Ransom say that Arthur is in Perelandra. This brings me to the second part of my argument. I showed above that there is a change in shape in the Inklings' Arthurian works. I will now show that Barfield's view of the direction of human consciousness leads to a change in direction in the Inklings' Arthuriana. It is an opposite direction, an outward course for the location of Avalon.

In Williams' Arthuriad, there is great importance attached to the direction of travel, and thus it is of great benefit to this study to consider the geography of his Byzantium and its surrounding areas. In Williams' unfinished work of poetry, there is no Avalon. But, the westward journey, as we have seen in other Inklings' works and shall see in more, is of great significance.[18] In the west part of Byzantium is Logres and to the west is Broceliande. Broceliande, this sea-forest, may be understood in terms of Lewis' idea of the numinous.[19] Broceliande is located to the west of Cornwall, the extreme southwest of Great Britain. But in the mythology, there is something beyond Britain and Ireland. Lewis called Nimue "the sovereign mistress of Broceliande" (WA 285). Lewis describes Broceliande as "what most romantics are enamoured of" (284), that it is "what you find when you step out of our ordinary mode of consciousness. You find it equally in whatever direction you step out" (285). Lewis says that it is easily mistaken for the Absolute, or fundamental reality. It does, however, come quite close. Lewis equates it with the Greek concept of the Apeiron, "the formless origin of forms" (285). Here we may be reminded of Plato's third level of knowledge, of gaining insight to the spiritual nature of the phenomena, or "the appearances." It seems then, that Broceliande takes us into original participation.

Lewis sees Logres (Arthur's kingdom) in Williams' work as the place where Byzantium (the ordered, rational, just, splendid rule of God) and Broceliande (the numinous, the visceral, the romantic) meet. It holds them in harmony and helps a person experience one through the other (288). And it is through a "certain part" of Broceliande (285) that one may pass on west to Carbonek (the place of holy things such as the Grail) and then onto Sarras (the Land of the Trinity). One can find Broceliande in whatever direction one goes. Not so for Carbonek and Sarras. Going the wrong way through Broceliande may lead one to P'o-lu, the domain of the headless emperor on the Antipodean Ocean, "the very fringe of Hell" (284). Going west may get one to places of immortality, but one must go through the right parts. One may go "through" original participation, but it is no place to stay, and it may lead one off the right path. Lewis says it is better to go to Broceliande after going to Byzantium (357). We saw in "The Departure of Merlin"

---

18   See chapter 4 by Charles A. Huttar. [Editor's note]

19   Lewis may have (mistakenly) understood the term "Númenor" to be connected with "numinous"—thus his spelling of it as *Numinor* when he connects Merlin with it (see *THS* 272).

that the very son of the mistress of Broceliande departs; his destination is none other than Byzantium, and for him it was a good end.

Go through the wrong part of Broceliande, and you will not be in the utter west, or in a higher spiritual realm, but cast into the void. The enemies of Byzantium wanted to establish their own Byzantium and banish Broceliande. If you sever Broceliande and keep only Byzantium, you have a God-fearing, but Incarnation-and-mystery-denying Islam. Islam is an iconoclast against this original participation, but it would never consent to move on to final participation. Lewis describes the anachronistic, symbolic use of Islam in Williams' Arthuriad, that it "stands for all religions that are afraid of matter and afraid of mystery, for all misplaced reverences and misplaced purities that repudiate the body and shrink back from the glowing materialism of the Grail" and that it "was for Williams the symbol (as it is certainly the greatest historical expression) of something which is eternally the opposite of Sarras and Carbonek" (308). The Grail affirms a kind of materialism but not a reductionist materialism of the modern, fragmented consciousness. It is material-affirming because of the Incarnation and the final participation that the Incarnation inaugurated.

In the mythology of Tolkien, one may go to the far West (the Utter West) for healing or to experience immortality. This was intended for immortals, the Elves. As mentioned previously, before the fall of Númenor it was possible to use physical (or technological) means to reach the Undying Lands. Mortal Men were forbidden to do so, but they were forbidden precisely because they were quite able. They merely had to sail west in ships. After Men do so and violate the Undying Lands, the "gods" appeal to God, who casts Númenor into the sea, but not only this; the shape of the world is changed. With this new shape of the world, mortals could still sail west, but the traveler would circle the world and come back to the starting point by going in one direction. The traveler would effectively never get anywhere.

There is still a way to restoration, but it cannot be reached technologically. "The Straight Path" is now "The Lost Road." In *The Lord of the Rings*, the Elves who are leaving Middle-earth never to return may make passage on ships from the Grey Havens. Occasional exceptions are made for non-immortals, such as Ringbearers, but they must take passage with the immortals. Even if they make the journey, it is to receive healing, not immortality. In any case, the place of healing and restoration is no longer "over there," but in a sense "up there," as it is in another, hidden realm.

I stated before that Tolkien's *Fall of Arthur* identifies elements of Tolkien's mythology with features of the Arthurian legends. Among these are the identification of Tol Eressëa, the island just to the east of Valinor, with Avalon (156). But Arthur could not have just sailed on any ship and reached Tol Eressëa. Just as Ransom was carried to Perelandra by an Oyarsa, Arthur must be granted passage in this spiritual way.

I have mentioned how the Elves were Tolkien's baptized look at participation. The Elves in their immortality were bound to the circles of the world while it lasted. Their consciousness was bound to it. This is in contrast to the exploiting technocrats who resisted such participation. The Elves were ontologically bound to the world as well. They did not die and thus never left it. Men, however, who experienced death (referred to by the Elves as "The Gift of Ilúvatar"; see the first chapter of the *Quenta Silmarillion*), left these circles. The Elves did not know where Men went after they died. Tolkien called death, for Men, "freedom from the circles of the world … it is a mystery of God of which no more is known than that 'what God has purposed for Men is hidden': a grief and an envy to the immortal Elves" (*Letters* 147).

Here is an intimation of a break from original participation. Even when Middle-earth was flat, this departure of Men from Middle-earth was not "over there" to a place still within the Circles of the World. After the world was made round, their departure was not like the Elves' "up-there-but-still-in-here" path to the Undying Lands. Because Tolkien was writing a pre-Christian myth, he was reticent about where departed Men go. They lived before the Incarnation of the Word that inaugurated final participation.[20] Arthur, however, lived after the Incarnation. Notice it is he only among those named by Ransom to dwell in Melchisedec's hall who was on earth after the coming of Christ, and it is he whose ring marks the order of the Pendragon. In Lewis' work, Arthur has left the circles of the world and entered Deep Heaven, though not yet the abode of God Himself.

In the Space Trilogy, we see Ransom undertake interplanetary travel in two ways. The first, in *Out of the Silent Planet*, is similar to convention in science fiction or space fantasy; he travels in a space ship to Malacandra (Mars). However, in *Perelandra*, he is taken there by the Oyarsa of Malacandra. Ransom's first trip is accomplished through technology. The second is through spiritual means, through his participation with a Planetary Intelligence.

The eldila governed the old world of Malacandra, under the Oyarsa as the highest ruler on the planet. When Ransom speaks with Tinidril, the first woman of Perelandra, he is surprised to find no eldila. Tinidril says: "in your own world also they ruled once but not since our Beloved became a Man. In your world they linger still. But in our world, which is the first of worlds to wake after the great change, they have no power. There is nothing now between us and Him" (*Per* 82). The embodied, intelligent beings of Malacandra live under the benevolent rule of the eldila and mythically participate (i.e. originally participate) in the nature of that world in an unfallen state. Ransom's enemy, Dr. Weston, however, makes both trips by means of technology. In *Out of the Silent Planet*, this technocrat goes to Mars (with the kidnapped Ransom) to exploit it. What drives him?

> He was a man obsessed with the idea ... that humanity, having now sufficiently corrupted the planet where it arose, must at all costs contrive to seed itself over a larger area: ... a dream begotten by the hatred of death upon the fear of true immortality .... The destruction or enslavement of other species in the universe, if such there are, is to these minds a welcome corollary. In Professor Weston, the power had at last met the dream. (81–82)

Weston is not only a technocrat; he is a reductionist. He believes that human life consists in "seeding ourselves" as a species and that biological propagation is pragmatically superior to any moral consideration or any spiritual reality, because both are illusory. For Weston's fragmented, modern consciousness, notions of morality, feeling intellect, or spirituality are merely metaphorical, drawn out of the only fundamental reality (the concreteness of physical reality). By attempting to exploit (or utilize) an original-participatory

---

20   However, Tolkien in some manuscripts portrays the Elves as having an intimation that one day Ilúvatar would Incarnate, "like an artist entering his creation." See *MR*, qtd. in Dickerson, p. 223–24.

world like Malacandra, he is bringing modern idolatry to a world in which there were no previous idols to tear down (unlike in the original participation in our world).

In *Perelandra,* when Weston flies in his spaceship to Venus, he then becomes possessed by spiritual evil and is driven to tempt Tinidril to turn away from being life-giving mother (in the image of unfallen Venus), obedient to Maleldil (God), toward taking an existential leap and becoming tragic hero. The temptation is to embrace courage as the ultimate virtue, the courage to express self-autonomy. In other words, the temptation was to make the planet Venus no longer Venus, but her wraith. And not her original-participatory wraith, but a modern one, one whose fundamental reality is self-referential and whose moral guidance would be that Maleldil wants her to disobey Him. We may see the Fixed Land, as it is easier for an embodied being to be in a measure of "control" on it, as representative of technology. After Tinidril resists the temptation to stay on the Fixed Land, the dwellers of Perelandra are then permitted to stay on it. Lewis may be indicating that technology is not intrinsically evil, but needs to be subject to moral considerations (Myers 65). Perelandra, a world made after the Incarnation of the Word, where there was "nothing between" its intelligent inhabitants and God, began in an infancy of final participation. Because of Tinidril's obedience, Venus remains Venus: a place of pleasure, refreshment, life, and healing, and not only that, but a place that is all these unfiltered, for it has begun in and will forever be in final participation.

Asking how Arthur got into "space" might not be the right question. For the medievals there was no "outer space." There were the orbs in which the Intelligences were set. But this image has been discarded. The Pendragon's (whether Arthur's or Ransom's) restoration in Deep Heaven awakens the modern, fragmented consciousness to the reality that "out there" in space is only "out there" if that is what one is attending to. There is a more fundamental reality of "up there" in the spiritual realm: one that also comes to visit us down here.

Barfield's editor says the Grail "heals the wounded king and restores the Wasteland to fruitfulness" (*Night Operation* xii). Part of humanity's healing from its current idolatry is a move outward from its isolated self-consciousness. Myths have looked for healing on far-off shores, from Lewis' apples in the far West in *The Magician's Nephew* to Tolkien's Undying Lands. King Arthur, in many forms of the legend, was sent to an isle for healing. In the Space Trilogy, Ransom is the wounded king in the line of Arthur, and he is sent "out there" in the other direction from our bent planet to Perelandra for his healing.

Over the course of centuries of intellectual upheaval in our cosmology, our epistemology, and our ontology, our consciousness has been wounded by viewing ourselves as existing on an isolated rock somewhere in a vast, meaningless nothingness. Our consciousness has turned inward as it finds no inherent meaning "out there." It requires a voyage out of our own idolatry and our own "chronological snobbery" to round the bend of the U-shape, to regain perspective and to be healed. In the works of Lewis, Tolkien, Williams, and Barfield, one may experience such a grail encounter.

Works Cited

Barfield, Owen. "Either : Or: Coleridge, Lewis, and Romantic Theology." *Imagination and the Spirit: Essays in Literature and the Christian Faith Presented to Clyde S. Kilby*. Ed. Charles A. Huttar. Grand Rapids, MI: Eerdmans, 1971. Rpt. *Owen Barfield on C. S. Lewis*. Ed. G. B. Tennyson. Middletown, CT: Wesleyan UP, 1989. 45–66. Print.

——. *History in English Words*. 1953. Grand Rapids, MI: Eerdmans, 1967. Kindle file.

——. *Owen Barfield on C. S. Lewis*. Ed. G. B. Tennyson. Middletown, CT: Wesleyan UP, 1989. Print.

——. *Night Operation*. Barfield Press UK, 2009. Print.

——. *Poetic Diction: A Study in Meaning*. 1928. 2nd ed. London: Faber & Faber Limited, 1962. Print.

——. *Saving the Appearances: A Study in Idolatry*. 1957. Middletown, CT: Wesleyan UP, 1988. Print.

Carpenter, Humphrey. *The Inklings: C. S. Lewis, J. R. R. Tolkien, Charles Williams and Their Friends*. Boston: Houghton Mifflin, 1979. Print.

Dickerson, Matthew T. *Following Gandalf: Epic Battles and Moral Victory in* The Lord of the Rings. Grand Rapids, MI: Brazos Press, 2003. Print.

Flieger, Verlyn. *Splintered Light: Logos and Language in Tolkien's World*. 1983. 2nd ed. Kent State UP, 2002. Print.

Gaertner, Christopher Bennett. *The Interplay of Logos and Tao in Tolkien's* The Lord of the Rings *and its Chinese Translations*. Master's thesis, Southwest Jiaotong University, 2007. Print.

Lewis, C. S. *The Abolition of Man*. 1947. NY: Macmillan, 1965. Print.

——. *The Allegory of Love: A Study in Medieval Tradition*. 1936. Oxford UP, 1976. Print.

——. *The Discarded Image: An Introduction to Medieval and Renaissance Literature*. 1964. Cambridge UP, 1979. Print.

——. "Historicism." *Christian Reflections*. Ed. Walter Hooper. Grand Rapids, MI: Eerdmans, 2003. 124–40. Print.

——. *Out of the Silent Planet*. 1938. NY: Scribner, 1996. Print.

——. *Perelandra*. 1943. NY: Scribner, 1996.

——. *The Pilgrim's Regress: An Allegorical Apology for Christianity, Reason and Romanticism*. 1933. Grand Rapids, MI: Eerdmans, 1992. Kindle file.

——. *That Hideous Strength: A Modern Fairy-Tale for Grown-Ups*. 1945. NY: Scribner, 1996. Print.

——. *Surprised by Joy: The Shape of My Early Life*. NY: Harcourt, Brace & World, 1955. Print.

——. *The Voyage of the "Dawn Treader."* 1952. NY: HarperCollins, 1996. Print.

——. "Williams and the Arthuriad." *Taliessin through Logres, The Region of the Summer Stars, Arthurian Torso*. 1948. Grand Rapids, MI: Eerdmans, 1974. 175–84. Print.

Myers, Doris T. *C. S. Lewis in Context*. Kent State UP, 1994. Print.

Shippey, Tom. *J. R. R. Tolkien: Author of the Century*. NY: Houghton Mifflin, 2002. Print.

——. *The Road to Middle-earth*. 1982. 3rd ed. NY: Houghton Mifflin, 2003.

Tolkien, J. R. R. *The Fall of Arthur*. Ed. Christopher Tolkien. London: HarperCollins, 2013. Print.

——. *The Letters of J. R. R. Tolkien*. Ed. Humphrey Carpenter. NY: Houghton Mifflin, 2000. Print.

——. *The Lost Road and Other Writings*. The History of Middle-earth 5. Ed. Christopher Tolkien. 1987. NY: Ballantine, 1996. Print.

——. *The Silmarillion.* 1977. London: HarperCollins, 1999. Print.

Walker, Mark. Introduction. *Geoffrey of Monmouth's* Life of Merlin. Stroud, Gloucestershire: Amberley, 2011. Kindle file.

Ward, Michael. *Planet Narnia: The Seven Heavens in the Imagination of C. S. Lewis.* Oxford UP, 2008. Kindle file.

Williams, Charles, and C. S. Lewis. *Taliessin through Logres, The Region of the Summer Stars, Arthurian Torso.* 1948. Grand Rapids, MI: Eerdmans, 1974. Print.

Williams, Charles. *War in Heaven.* 1930. Premium 7 Novel Collection. Business and Leadership Publishing, 2014. Kindle file.

Histories Past

From Myth to History and Back Again: Inklings Arthuriana in Historical Context

Yannick Imbert

Explicit liber regis quondam regisque futuri
The beginning
—T. H. White, *The Once and Future King*

Introduction

Laȝamon, a Worcestershire priest and author of the first Arthurian account written in English, wrote around 1200 that Arthur would be the subject of legend for centuries to come (Laȝamon lines 9406–12). His statement could not have been truer. Arthur has not only become the subject for legends but also the vehicle for social, philosophical, and cultural discourse, concentrating society's hopes, desires, and fears. This observation quickly becomes obvious to any student of Arthurian literature. It is even more important in the case of the Inklings' re-appropriation of the Arthurian material. Since most of them showed interest in the Arthurian legend, the question arises whether they shared common themes or interests in re-interpreting and re-imagining the figure of Arthur. Such might be the case for the three best-known authors: C. S. Lewis, J. R. R. Tolkien, and Charles Williams.

However, not only these three authors among the Inklings were interested in the Arthurian material. In fact, Nevill Coghill translated the *Canterbury Tales* (which includes Arthurian motifs), and Roger Lancelyn Green published an Arthurian retelling for children, *King Arthur and his Knights*. Owen Barfield, for his part, owned a copy of *Le Morte d'Arthur* and annotated it copiously.[1],[2] Lewis' successor at Cambridge, J. A. W. Bennett, edited *Essays on Malory*. Through their presentation of Arthur, the Inklings (in particular Lewis, Tolkien, and Williams) demonstrated a common vision: the essential relation between two worlds, two realities—the spiritual and material, the mythological and the historical—but in very different ways.

Considering this initial observation, we might be tempted to look for common themes in the Inklings' treatment of "Arthur." However, such a quest proves to be challenging, especially if the integrity and originality of each author be preserved. Probably one of the best places to start is to remember that authors are born out of a socio-historical age and that their writing most often reflects an interaction with the spirit of their society. Such is the case with the Inklings' "Arthur." Thus, to meaningfully interact with their reimagined Arthurian material, we will have to pay particular attention to their socio-historical context. First, we will have to put "Arthur" back into a late nineteenth- and early twentieth-century context. Second, the twentieth-century quest for a "historical Arthur" will also have to be considered. Finally, these contexts will illuminate how Lewis, Tolkien, and Williams used the figure of Arthur to answer various societal challenges.

Before moving to an exploration of the significance of Arthur for the Inklings, we must briefly mention one crucially relevant historical context: late-Victorian mythological study. During the nineteenth century, the newly formed discipline of comparative mythology attracted both admiration and fierce opposition. It had first been argued that mythology veiled truth. It had also been argued that myth must be removed from history in order to make it intelligible. This debate over the place of mythology further developed in the first half of the twentieth century, at the same time Tolkien and Lewis became well-known fantasy writers. In fact, there was a raging debate regarding the value of mythology from the mid-nineteenth century onward. This debate was in no small part due to the many complex dimensions of the end of the nineteenth century: a period of considerable social, theological, and scientific turmoil. The new scientific theories and the numerous theological controversies, both on the Continent and in Britain, provided fertile ground for a reevaluation of the meaning of history, the nature and origin of humankind, and the uniqueness and exclusivity of traditional Christianity. Furthermore, it was during this troubled period that scientific theories of language and literature flowered, especially in the new fields of mythology, folklore, and "fairy tales."

In particular, during the course of the nineteenth century, the new science of mythology became associated with the comparative method, making "comparative mythology" the main field of study. For twenty-first-century readers, an overview of comparative mythology can rapidly become confusing because diverse methods are named differently. Andrew Lang provides a helpful overview of this field, identifying three main schools of mythology. The first school is the one promoted by scholar Max Müller, which relied on a philological approach to the study of myths (subsequently labeled "the philological school of mythology"). Its main thesis is that myths are primarily the result of the savage man's contemplation

---

1   See Grimaldi 55–82 and also the epistolary exchange between Lewis and Barfield on the imaginary legal proceedings of King Mark against Tristram entitled *Mark vs. Tristram*.

2   See further chapter 1 by Sørina Higgins, which considers Barfield's *The Quest of the Sangreal*, and chapter 5 by Christopher Gaertner, which examines *Night Operation*. [Editor's note]

of nature (and so it has also been labeled the "naturist school" of comparative mythology). The second main school of mythology was the anthropological school, also known as the ritualist school, of which two of the main representatives were James Frazer and Andrew Lang. In addition to these two major schools of mythological study, Lang made reference to a third interpretation of mythology. This third school, Euhemerism (sometimes labelled manism) is probably the oldest. It goes back to the Greek philosopher Euhemerus and was revived by the nineteenth-century philosopher Herbert Spencer. Euhemerism is based on a historical and degenerative approach to the study of myth, mostly considering mythological motifs as vestiges of ancestor worship.[3] Even though there is no time here to look at these three main interpretative frameworks in depth, it should be noted that the Victorian interest in the nature and origin of legends and myths constitutes the historical background without which we cannot properly understand the importance of what Tolkien, Lewis, Williams, and the other Inklings accomplished.

The rise of comparative mythology as a field of study in turn nourished a renewed interest in legendary and mythological figures. Among such figures, Arthur stands out. If the historical and symbolic place and role of Arthur in nineteenth-century Britain were so important, it will be no surprise to see the persistence of interest in Arthuriana in the beginning of the twentieth century, though for different agendas. Here we come to our topic, for among the mythological interests shared by the Inklings, we find the Arthurian figure. In reviving Arthur, they also demonstrated their shared conviction that the symbolic/metaphorical is never easily opposed to the historical. If defending a historical Arthur has become quite a challenge, maybe one of the reasons is the simplistic choice often made between a symbolic or historical Arthur. In fact, this legendary figure is often relegated to the rank of a merely *symbolic*—that is, *non-historical*—figure. This chapter will present some characteristic features of the way Arthur serves as a paradigm for understanding the Inklings' view of "mythological history."

To understand the relevance of the Inklings' use of the Arthurian material, it is absolutely necessary to realize that theirs was essentially a post-Victorian Arthur. Therefore, we should begin our study with a consideration of the figure and nature of Arthur in the late nineteenth century. Interestingly, the nineteenth century saw a revival of interest in the Arthurian material. We can discern two explanations for the persistent presence of Arthur in the late Victorian and early Edwardian eras: the social challenges faced by late nineteenth- and early twentieth-century Britain and the reconsideration of the quest for a historical and imaginative Arthur.

Arthur: Herald of a Changing Society

The figure of Arthur (and the associated Arthurian materials) has always been the instrument of political discourse and social criticism, whether during the thirteenth and fourteenth centuries—when the Arthurian material served as political propaganda during the wars between England and Scotland—or during the sixteenth century—when James Henrisoun argued, in his *Exhortacion to the Scottes* (1547), against

---

3   See Spencer 280–300; Lang, *Custom and Myth* 199; Lang, *Magic and Religion* 90.

the Scottish claim that none of their rulers had acknowledged fealty before England.[4] The socio-political nature of "Arthur" was also present during the nineteenth century. For example, Edward Bulwer-Lytton published a three-volume epic *King Arthur*. He also published a successful series of historical tales, including *The Last of the Barons* (1843) on the Wars of the Roses and *Harold: The Last of the Saxon Kings* (1848). These two works, along with his *King Arthur*, shared "a central concern with the historical constitution—political and cultural—of England, with the construction and disintegration of the state, and with the cohesive role of the crown" (Brooks and Bryden 253). At the end of the nineteenth century, Victorian Arthur was not only an inspiration for the Romantic and Pre-Raphaelite imagination: he had also come to be the emblem of a vanishing world. In fact, "in contrast to the emphasis on the historical Arthur in the 1830s and 1840s, poets and critics such as Matthew Arnold … Morris, and Swinburne were interested in the domestic ideologies at work in Arthur's kingdom" (Brooks and Bryden 261).

This particularity of the nineteenth century is highlighted by Roger Simpson in his study of the Arthurian revival of the mid-nineteenth century. He remarks that for the Victorians, the Arthurian material came to have "a more tragic, doom-laden atmosphere" than for previous centuries (Simpson 225). Indeed, the mid- to late-nineteenth century in England was a period of intense and often traumatic changes. Only a handful of times every few centuries do societies go through the tremendous changes that transform the mindset, philosophy, education, and urban structure. Victorian England was such a time and place. One of the most visible witnesses to this radical transformation was the changing face of the cities. In fact, "the industrial city was bound to be a place of problems. Economic individualism and common civic purpose were difficult to reconcile. The priority of industrial discipline in shaping all human relations was bound to make other aspects of life seem secondary" (Briggs 18). Journalists of the epoch described this change as moving at an incredible pace, affecting the mindset and the daily practice of the people. The pace of change was, for many, so rapid that fields of grass could be seen in the spring and rows of houses in autumn: houses and factories would, quite literally, "spring up in a single night," as if Merlin himself, denying his attachment to the natural world, had become the wizard of industrialization. Carlyle noted that English society itself was moving so fast that Victorian England was disappearing under the mist of the industrial society (2),[5] and therefore Arthur's kingdom was vanishing into the mist of Avalon. As some reported, "the physical environment was transformed, most obviously in the great manufacturing districts and in ever-spreading London, but also in cathedral cities, market towns, and coastal resorts. Nostalgia for the rural past, frequently cast in medieval form, grew as the countryside was swallowed up or 'cockneyfied'" (Brooks and Bryden 252). The Victorian city, and for some the whole society of the late Victorian age, was founded upon change and movement.

---

4   And an answer came from the *Complaynt of Scotland* (1548), attributed to Robert Wedderburn, and the *Rerum Scoticarum Historia* (1582), by George Buchanan: the relationship between the two realms is mutual and equal. This allows the Scots to share in Arthur's glory without being subjected to a hierarchical rule. There is alliance but no subjugation.

5   See also Chapman 14.

These changes were expressed through various cultural and literary artifacts, including through the Arthurian material. For example, Matthew Arnold's three-part poem *Tristram and Iseult* (1852) can be read as a quest for a national epic. He famously created a "psychological" background to the Arthurian story using literary artifice that fragmented the story in very much the same way that English society was fragmenting itself. In fact, "in telescoping and revalidating the Arthurian legends for a modern readership, Arnold dealt with the difficult transition from a heroic past in which Arthur conquered Europe, to a fragmented, industrialized present" (Brooks and Bryden 261). Two connected but distinct cultural and aesthetic movements tried to answer this fragmentation of dramatic proportions. The first was the renewal of medievalism in the nineteenth century, of which Sir Walter Scott was a central figure. While much has been written on the subject, and even though the purpose here is not to explicate the nature and relevance of nineteenth-century medievalism, we certainly should take note of the profound influence it had on the development of Arthurian literature as a vehicle for social and cultural discourse. In fact, medievalism was not a purely aesthetic movement but an attempt to satisfy the needs of an "atomistic society" as well as to offer an alternative foundation for a "harmonious social order" (Chandler 12–13). This might also explain why the Arthurian material appeared so relevant to the Inklings, particularly to the two writers mostly concerned with the social and spiritual order needed in their society, namely Lewis and Williams.

However, Scott's medievalism, with which Tolkien was quite familiar,[6] was not the only answer to an increasingly industrialized and de-socialized society. Romanticism, a movement of its own, with a broad diversity of themes and expression, also stood as a philosophical and aesthetic answer to social challenges. This is the case of course for one of the main figures of Victorian romanticism: Alfred, Lord Tennyson. If his poetry was largely responsible for the great flowering of Arthurian poetry in the Victorian period, it should also be said that his was not, strictly speaking, a reaction against the mechanistic view of nature and against the ugliness of an ever more industrialized society. Rather, his concern, like that of Romanticism itself, was the condition of the Victorian society. Faced with a society in danger of losing itself, the necessity of Britain's being born anew was crucial. Arthurianism, Romanticism, and other medieval forms could then become sites of "cultural reassurance" (Brooks and Bryden 252).

Arthurian Consciousness

This Victorian atmosphere affected Arthurian literature well into the beginning of the twentieth century. This means, of course, that the Inklings were exposed to such a cultural mood early on in their education and careers. Therefore, late nineteenth-century Victorianism forms the essential background to their Arthuriana. Here, it is necessary to recall that the nineteenth century, with its political conflicts and turmoil, its social traumas and philosophical changes, made it so that many people tended to forget all that had come before them and were led to build their national identity anew (Barczewski 47). This entailed that the present and future, but also the British past, had to be re-constructed, and "as a result, the past became a blank slate that had to be filled in, and for this purpose both nations [England and France]

---

6   See Hunter 61–75.

turned to myth and legend" (Barczewski 47). Moreover, the exponentially changing pace of late Victorian England led to one other challenge to the Victorian "consensus." The fragile and even illusory unity of mind and people found during the Victorian age was shattered, and the social bond that some could claim had been forged in the nineteenth century was questioned.

One of these bonds was the way in which the eighteenth and nineteenth centuries had seemingly created an "English/British mind" of which, interestingly enough, Arthur had become one of the heroes. The distinction between "English" and "British" is an important one, especially for the Inklings. Famous among them is Tolkien's repeated vocal affirmation that he was "English" and not "British." For example, he was adamant that his family's ancestors had become "quickly and intensely English (not British)" (Tolkien, *Letters* 218). One also remembers Tolkien's statement to the effect that he would like to write a mythology he could dedicate simply "to England; to my country" (Tolkien, *Letters* 144). Thus, while "British" is a generic term describing the members of the broader society uniting the Scottish, the Welsh, and the English, it is not a proper "ethnic" qualifier but a socio-political one. Moreover, as a study of Arthurian literature makes abundantly clear, the people known as "Britons" are quite different in origin and ethnicity from nineteenth- and twentieth-century citizens of the "British Empire."

Furthermore, the rise of modern Anglo-Saxon studies led to an interesting social development, well explained by C. L. Wrenn, an occasional Inkling:

> Anglo-Saxon literature is in fact an all-important section of a continuing stream: and there is a sense in which the spirit which still animates English civilization has a derivative unity with Anglo-Saxon literature. Its study is part of that of the English developing *mind* in its wholeness. As R. W. Chambers put it, we may "dream of all our literature, whether in prose or verse, in modern English, in early English or in Latin, as the work of one spirit." (xii)[7]

It is quite easy to discern a connection in Wrenn's words among the development of Anglo-Saxon literature, the study of English literature, and the rise of a common consciousness—decidedly an important topic at the beginning of the twentieth century. Notice also that, in the words of R. W. Chambers, this "one spirit" transcended the different languages. Through the figure of Arthur, the Round Table, or Tristram, this collective consciousness had become cemented into a patriotic and social, if not political, belonging. However, the early twentieth century, still wrestling with the social implications of Darwin's anthropological revolution, clearly demonstrated that the issue of man's consciousness, especially "common consciousness," was still unresolved (Smith 15–44). This issue of "common consciousness" was most common in the late nineteenth to early twentieth centuries and affected a variety of disciplines. For example, the French sociologist Émile Durkheim was most interested in this subject. Arthur then became once more the center of the quest for a distinctively British consciousness. In 1849, *Sharpe's London Journal* described Arthur as "the beautiful incarnation of all the best characteristics of our nation" (374, qtd. in Barczewski 13). Through

---

7   Wrenn is here quoting R. W. Chambers, *Man's Unconquerable Mind* (London: J. Cape, 1939), 17. Tolkien was well acquainted with Chambers and probably had read this particular book.

the Matter of Britain, some writers were able to display their hopes for a common future based on essential features of humankind. Others were able to explain how the spiritual nature of any given society was the necessary foundation of such a "common consciousness." This is the case for Christopher Dawson, the famed Catholic historian, who deeply influenced the Arthurian poet David Jones (Staudt 124). Other scholars have noted Jones' connection to English Catholicism's "third spring." William Blisset, for example, has remarked that "Chesterton was a germinating presence for David Jones in the seedtime of his soul" (qtd. in D. Schwartz 303). It was also the case for Owen Barfield, one of the Inklings most interested in the "evolution of consciousness."[8] But it is in Williams that this issue becomes more and more present as one plunges into his mystical and occult ("veiled") Arthuriana.

Williams is probably the most obscure of the Inklings, despite the great influence he had on Lewis—and to Tolkien's bewilderment, the interest in alternative spiritualities that he shared with A. E. Waite. Yet he is a significant Arthurian writer, and to some he is the most important poetic interpreter of the Arthurian legend in the twentieth century (Lacy and Ashe 191). There are two main explanations for this observation. First, Williams clearly exposed a view in stark contrast to the suspicious scholarship of his days. Indeed, for him, the "mythological" dimension of the Arthurian stories was not a mere vestige of primitive and cultural thoughts. Instead, he brought the spiritual dimension of the Arthurian material back to the center of history—which explains why the center of Williams' Arthuriad is the Grail, not Arthur, Launcelot, or Guinevere. The "renaissance" of the Grail as the mystical center of the Arthurian story has in fact been called "the most exciting development of the legend in our day" (Starr 145).[9]

Further, beyond the centrality of the Grail and its importance for Williams' theological concept of the "hidden Church of Christ," the originality of Williams' Arthurian vision, while broad and complex, should be seen in the context of the quest for a common consciousness mentioned above. In fact, Williams, through his poetic interaction with archaeology and "occult" spirituality, sought to reunite humanity in the search for a communal meaning, a communal consciousness. In addition to this search for a common consciousness, another main trait of Williams' Arthuriad must be underlined.

This unity of consciousness is embodied in Williams' extensive use of Arthurian imagery; he demonstrates the essential unity of the spiritual and the natural, thus offering a transcendental solution to the problem of "common consciousness." In fact, Williams' poem "Mount Badon" distinguishes itself from others of the same vein by using Taliessin as the main character in the poem, not Arthur, Lancelot, or any other of his knights. While Arthurian scholars were mostly concerned about whether or not the figure of Arthur had actually won the battle of Badon, Williams concentrates his attention on Taliessin. It is only when the bard has completed his "spiritual vision" that the battle can be won by Arthur. History and legend have finally fused into one mythological history: the coming of the Grail and of the metaphysical

---

8   See chapter 5 by Christopher Gaertner. [Editor's note]

9   Lewis had an epistolary relationship with Starr, especially throughout the last decade of his life, including in 1954 when Starr published *King Arthur Today*. Lewis seems to have been quite sympathetic with the work. See Lewis, *CL* 3:499.

civilization. In poetically presenting such a metaphysical vision, Williams also provides the metaphysical grounds for the development of a "common consciousness."

While the fundamental unity of natural and spiritual is only hinted at in Lewis and Tolkien (at least in their Arthurian writing), it stands at the heart of Williams' fiction. In fact, we could even argue that the distinction between the "natural" and the "supernatural" becomes meaningless in describing Williams. These two categories are only useful to highlight Williams' uniting vision. The two worlds are no longer related by a temporal or symbolic distance. In fact, there is no more distance between them. "This" world and the "other" world become superposed, at least spiritually. Moreover, this was not for Williams a mere literary artifice, a fictional writing process, but a deep reflection on his conviction about the essential nature of reality itself. For Williams, the dual nature of reality (spiritual and natural) was a way of life. As A. N. Wilson notes: "Williams ... had an almost matter-of-fact awareness of the other world. Angels—or 'angelicals' as he would have preferred to call them in his strange idiolect—were as real to him as omnibuses or mortgage repayments" (149). This reality is expressed in Williams' Arthurian novel *War in Heaven* and in his poetry, especially the Arthurian volumes *Taliessin through Logres* and *The Region of the Summer Stars*.

Williams' spiritual awareness, along with his philosophical conviction that history and myth were not necessarily in opposition, made it possible for him to investigate the essential union of the natural and spiritual orders, as well as that of history and myth. In any case, Williams' use of "mythological history" is (without doubt) the most creative, as he conflated historical events to serve his own artistic and theological purposes, showing the co-inhering nature of the two worlds (Higgins 60–73). It is because of this co-inherence of the spiritual and the natural, or archnature and nature, that Williams was able to strengthen his view of mythological history. In fact:

> Williams often used the word "archnature," rather than "super-nature," and the point is that only when one sees life from the standpoint of archnature is nature truly seen and truly understood.... The archnatural is more "natural" than nature; it is nature as it ought to be, or "nature enveloped by grace." (Brown 220)[10]

Consequently, "mythological history" was for Williams nothing less than the natural world suffused with the essence of the spiritual, leading to an enlargement "of our understanding of the contemporary world" (Ashenden 177).

Coming to the question of the historical Arthur, things become even more complex in Williams. If Williams was not, properly speaking, an academic, he was nonetheless well aware of the academic debates surrounding the historical figure. He is indeed the one Inkling to explore in detail the significance both of the "historical quest for Arthur" and also of the Grail as a conduit of the divine. But to understand Williams' use of Arthurian symbolism, it is necessary to see what Williams' perspective on history was. In fact, in most of his novels, the reader cannot but be astounded by the relation between mystical symbolism and historical reality, the two often becoming one personal experience. The mystical/mythological

---

10   On this point, cf. Cavaliero 97–101.

symbolism and the historical reality are integrated into each other. Here one can discern Williams' doctrine of co-inherence, here a co-inherence of signification: myth is the key to history, but history, when considered for what it truly is, is the key to myth.

Co-inherence was, with the doctrine of substitution or "exchange," one of Williams' most original philosophical points. Simply stated, it is explained through the "'co-inherence' of the Divine Persons in each other, and it has been held that the unity of mankind consists in the analogical co-inherence of men with each other ..." (Williams, *Beatrice* 92). It is important to remember that Williams' concept of co-inherence is both universal and spiritual. Things in the world exist in an essential, universal, spiritual, mutual participation. Susan Wendling briefly presents Shideler's helpful summary of the three main elements of Williams' co-inherence: "First, there is the use of the body as an index of love. Then, there is the development of the feeling intellect and of faith. Finally, there are the primary acts of love, seen in the bearing of burdens, sacrifice, and forgiveness" (Wendling; cf. Shideler 141). At a basic level, the significance of Williams' co-inherence for our present topic is that through this notion Williams essentially presents a transmutation of myth and history, an almost mystical co-participation of myth and history in each other.

However, Williams' Grail is important not only to mythological reality but also to the nature of history itself. It has been noted that Williams' metaphysical perspective is monistic (Scheper 145). This monism is reflected in his view of history. History is one: material and spiritual.[11] Williams shares this conviction with the other Inklings. In Williams, this bears an important implication: the spiritual dimension of history is *common* to everyone. Those who know Williams will remember his fascination with the occult, that is, the hidden presence of the spiritual. This will seem in stark opposition to what was just affirmed. How can the spiritual nature of history be common if it is hidden at the same time?

Here, we should make a detour through G. K. Chesterton. Chesterton's influence on both Lewis and Tolkien has already been noted. However, this influence is often difficult to explain.[12] For example, Tolkien—who was always more than cautious in acknowledging possible influences on his own Faërie— referred to Chesterton's *Charles Dickens* (47–48) in "On Fairy-stories." Of course, there is much more to Chesterton's influence than Tolkien himself recognized. Chesterton was also quite influential on Lewis, because he "explained Christianity in a way that made sense to Lewis" (Dunckel and Rowe 270).[13] C. S. Lewis referred to Chesterton in several works, including *Surprised by Joy*, "Christian Apologetics," "Period Criticism," and "On Three Ways of Writing for Children."[14]

More surprising is the influence Chesterton might have had on Charles Williams. T. S. Eliot was most likely the first to notice this influence, pointing out that *All Hallows' Eve* descended from Chesterton's *The Man Who Was Thursday* (Eliot xiv). In Chesterton's , we find layers of meaning superposed in very much the same

---

11   Or temporal and metaphysical (Ashenden 165).

12   See chapter 7, "'All Men Live by Tales': Chesterton's Arthurian Poems" by J. Cameron Moore. [Editor's note]

13   See also McGrath 225, 279.

14   For a synthetic presentation of the influence Chesterton's *The Everlasting Man*, see Duriez 104–05. Chesterton was also positively referred to by Barfield in his *Poetic Diction* 174.

way Williams presents several layers of realities in *All Hallows' Eve*: two London(s), one a worldly city, the other a spiritual city. In addition, I believe Williams used another Chestertonian artifice: paradox. This is a literary device Williams uses to describe the importance of the Grail. Williams pays particular attention to the paradoxical tension between the "hidden" Grail and the fact that it is found in a common parish church. But in fact, this paradox is only apparent. Because the Grail is common, it is hidden. Because it is everywhere, it has to be searched for. Because Arthur, Logres, Avalon, and the Grail are everywhere, they are hidden, often in plain sight, in a common church. On this matter, it is significant that the novel *War in Heaven*, contrary to its title, is not concerned with what is happening in Heaven but what is happening in our world as the Grail manifests its power.

Williams makes clear, through his "Figure of Arthur," that the Grail is "universal," and as such it is in "plain sight." The Grail is not, "as in Tennyson, only for the elect; it is for all" (Starr 184). Because divine energy is immanent in history, it is hidden. Williams' use of the Arthurian symbolism is a Quest for real history. And if we often speak of Chesterton's use of a "common sense"[15] or what we might call "common reasonable sense," I think we could speak of Williams' use of "common spiritual sense." As Cavaliero points out, Williams'

> outward darkness masked an inward light: the poems of the 1920s reveal an awareness of a spiritual dimension ready to break through, a sense of momentousness in daily happenings, casual gestures, human organisations. In this it resembles the work of G. K. Chesterton, another writer whose entire output of novels, criticism, poems and journalism reflects a sacramental sense of physical reality. (Cavaliero 3)

Moreover, it is because of this "common spiritual sense" that Williams could write about a sacred history, a history that would serve as a meta-history, a global and holistic history. There may be some parallels to draw between Williams' sacred history and another writer who had an influence on Tolkien: the celebrated British historian Christopher Dawson, who argued for a "metahistorical" perspective.

This "common spiritual sense" is also revealed in history. It is crucial to see that in *Taliessin through Logres*, the importance of the mythical is embodied in the historical, and the two become one. When Logres becomes a part of the Byzantine Empire, Williams shows that the centrality of a historical Arthur lies in what he reveals about historical realities. Williams' Arthurian perspective is motivated by his deep conviction of the unity of the spiritual and the material in (and through) history. As T. S. Eliot further commented, to Williams "the supernatural was perfectly natural, and the natural was also supernatural" (xiv). For example, the historical dimension of the Grail serves to explain the monistic and sacred nature

---

15   For the importance of "common sense" in Chesterton's thought, see William Oddie, *Chesterton and the Romance of Orthodoxy: The Making of GKC, 1874–1908* [(Oxford: Oxford University Press, 2008), 350], and Dale Ahlquist, *G. K. Chesterton: The Apostle of Common Sense* (San Francisco: Ignatius Press, 2003). Of course, Chesterton's pivotal use of common sense is directly inspired by Thomas Aquinas. Cf. "The Ethics of Elfland."

of history. Charles Williams' Arthuriad, especially *Taliessin through Logres* and *The Region of the Summer Stars*, should be seen in the context of the need for a renewed communal human consciousness. This "consciousness," if never fully acknowledged by Williams, is nonetheless present, as when, referring to the gospel according to Mark (14:22–26), he remarks:

> The point at which the myth of the Grail begins holds in its first appearance the most important account of all. No invention can come near it; no fabulous imagination excel it. All the greatest mythical details are only there to hint at the thing which happens; that which in the knowledge of Christendom is the unifying act, perilous and perpetual, universal and individual. That origin took place in the Jerusalem to which (it was reported) the Captain-General Arthur had gone before his final victory. ("Figure" 197)

In Williams, Arthur becomes the center of a common consciousness not so much defined by a nationalistic and patriotic dimension but by a historical-spiritual one. Arthur is at the center of a spiritual civilization, a metaphysical civilization.

Arthur Became Fact: C. S. Lewis' Baptized History

C. S. Lewis shared some of the same misgivings as Williams against the wedge some Arthurian scholars were willing to drive between history and myth. His criticism is obvious in several places, including in a short article, published in C. L. Wrenn's *English and Medieval Studies*, entitled "The Anthropological Approach." Throughout this particular article, it becomes quite obvious that, for all the potentially interesting results of the anthropological approach, such a method could never provide true explanations concerning the value and meaning of myths and legends. Lewis notes that "to explain" can have two meanings: "to account for causally," or "to open out our eyes." For example, Gawain's peculiarity in Malory—he grows stronger as the sun ascends—is explained as a vestige of a myth about a sun god; this is a merely causal explanation that does not "open out our eyes" on anything else. Malory's Gawain would have been the same if this detail had been omitted (Lewis, "Anthropological Approach" 219). We should conclude with Lewis that, while the anthropological explanation might be true, it does not increase our understanding or enjoyment of mythological literature.

To Lewis, "the savage origins are the puzzle" and most likely would remain so; "the surviving work of art is the only clue by which we can hope to penetrate the inwardness of the origins. It is either in art, or nowhere, that the dry bones are made to live again" ("Anthropological Approach" 223). Here, Lewis' criticism is directed at a "materialization" of the Arthurian romances that would consider these accounts from a purely "material" perspective, completely obliterating their spiritual dimension. Williams shared the same suspicion against the "ritualistic school" and was opposed to its Arthurian interpretation. This is especially obvious in Williams in connection with the origin of the Grail. Regarding this issue, he argued against the explanation that made the Grail a Celtic vessel transferred into a Christian story (*contra* Nutt and Weston; cf. Goetinck 117–47). Of course, Williams voiced the strongest opposition to such a materialistic study of the Arthurian cycle, especially of the Grail.

The "stories" could not be regarded merely as vestiges of primitive thought. However, if this opposition to one of the prevalent schools of mythological interpretation is clear throughout Lewis' work, his Arthuriana is not merely a criticism of the devaluation of myth. While this was certainly of personal as well as of academic and aesthetic importance, the Arthurian material was for Lewis a vehicle for his social and philosophical criticism. It is well known that Lewis came to the Christian faith through the sudden awareness that myth and history were not necessarily opposed. In fact, Lewis later strongly defended this conclusion in both his apologetics and his fantasy works. But beyond the "myth became fact" tagline that has become the classic summary of "Lewis on myth," there is another important dimension to his exploration of myth, one that had an important apologetic value—in Lewis' case, the opposition to the scientism of his time ("Myth Became Fact" 63–67).[16]

Such a dimension is most clearly seen in his Ransom trilogy—*Perelandra*, *Out of the Silent Planet* and *That Hideous Strength*—in which "mythological history" becomes the point of reference from which Lewis can launch his criticism of scientism in the modern age. *That Hideous Strength* provides the most evident Arthurian comparison in Lewis' writings with the return, the re-awakening, of Merlin (Sammons 131–40; Edwards 53–70).[17] Further, Ransom receives two of the most significant Arthurian titles: "Pendragon" and "Fisher-king," the keeper of the Grail.[18] This already underlines the absolute necessity, for Lewis, of the union of the spiritual and the material. Furthermore, there is, in that same book, a parallel between Britain and Logres that directs us to the value of "mythological history." Toward the end of the book, Professor Dimble outlines English history, saying:

> Something we may call Britain is always haunted by something we may call Logres. Haven't you noticed that we are two countries? After every Arthur, a Mordred; behind every Milton, a Cromwell: a nation of poets, a nation of shopkeepers; the home of Sidney—and of Cecil Rhodes. Is it any wonder that they call us hypocrites? But what they mistake for hypocrisy is really the struggle between Logres and Britain. (Lewis, *Space Trilogy* 705)

Whether Professor Dimble represents Lewis' position is still in balance. However, one thing is probably correct: the two worlds, "ideal Logres" and "mere Britain," stand in stark opposition. In fact, Lewis had stressed this opposition between the spiritual nature of Logres and "mere Britain" in his "Williams and the Arthuriad" (364). However, at the same time, Logres and Britain belong to the same history, and maybe we could even say that they inhabit the same history. This is also exemplified in Lewis' clarification concerning the simultaneous Affirmation and Rejection of images (WA 365–67).

But what is also true is that within this dual-world description, the mythological world serves as the basis for the virtues found in the actual world of Britain, in figures such as Milton or Sidney. The parallel indeed implies a contrast between Arthur-Milton-Sidney and Mordred-Cromwell-Rhodes. We could

---

16   See chapter 9, "Spiritual Quest in a Scientific Age" by Jason Jewell and Chris Butynskyi. [Editor's note]
17   See chapter 3 on intertextuality in the Ransom cycle by Brenton D. G. Dickieson. [Editor's note]
18   See chapter 15 by Benjamin Shogren on Ransom's two names. [Editor's note]

think that the relation between Britain and Logres is merely a symbolic one: Logres is the symbol of virtues. But this is only partly the case. The relation between the two orders is not only symbolic; it is also
very real. The point is that along with, or within, the reality of Britain lies the reality of Logres, always.
Britain and Logres coexist, but they are never identical. Hence, Lewis is not merely concerned with a
contrast of virtues (the moral opposition good/bad, Logres/Britain). In fact, he is conscious of both the
spiritual opposition between the two orders and of their continuous coexistence. And since they coexist,
they do not stand on parallel levels of reality; rather, they intersect. Thus, Ransom, the Pendragon/Fisher-
King, hero of the story in Britain, is also the head of Logres, the spiritual dimension essential to Britain
in Charles Williams' novels (Downing 76). Here, the natural and the supernatural (or spiritual) stand in
essential unity. There are not two worlds, but one; not two realities, but one. This stands at the heart of
the struggle between the restored spiritual kingdom of Logres and the scientism of the N.I.C.E. (National
Institute for Co-ordinated Experiments). Indeed, the "hideous strength," the illusory absolute power of
man through "science deified,"[19] is the main threat throughout the work. This scientific reductionism was
regularly attacked by Lewis, who criticized its scientific naïveté and the threat it poses to the integrity and
freedom of humanity, but also to the integrity of science itself (see Larson 53–58, esp. 54–56).[20] Along
with these two criticisms, Lewis was wary of the pseudo-opposition between "science" and "religion."[21] The
main danger was the absolute separation of the spiritual and the natural—in many ways synonymous with the
absolute separation of myth and history. In Logres lies truth, mythological and historical, standing in an
almost mystical co-inherence with Britain. Only when the natural and supernatural, Logres and Britain,
actually come together, can the powers of the N.I.C.E. be vanquished. Mythological history, the union of
the two basic dimensions of creation, makes up the core of the struggle against the N.I.C.E.

In fact, it does not take long to see Lewis' strong opposition to the kind of naturalistic scientism proposed by two of his contemporaries, the great British biochemist J. B. S. Haldane and the writer H. G.
Wells. Their philosophy serves as the background to the introduction of the N.I.C.E. as "the first fruits
of that constructive fusion between the state and the laboratory on which so many people base their hopes
of a better world" (*THS* 359). He also questions the materialistic perspective characteristic of Haldane's or
Wells' atheism, especially when it becomes the center of humanity's hope. This excess is well expressed by
the character called Lord Feverstone in *That Hideous Strength* (he was called Richard Devine in *Out of the Silent
Planet*) when he says: "It does really look as if we now had the power to dig ourselves in as a species for a
pretty staggering period, to take control of our own destiny. If Science is really given a free hand it can now
take over the human race and re-condition it: make man a really efficient animal" (*THS* 379). A telling
example of Lewis' view of science is the following comment at the end of chapter 9:

---

19   From the title of Richard Olson's work *Science Deified and Science Defied*, qtd. in Aeschliman, *Restitution* 47.

20   This same criticism appears several places in Lewis, including in his comments on extreme forms of
      Behaviourism in *DI* 215; see also his essay "The Empty Universe" 83.

21   See the imaginary dialogue in Lewis, "Religion and Science" 72–75.

The physical sciences, good and innocent in themselves, had already, even in Ransom's own time, begun to be warped, had been subtly maneuvered in a certain direction. Despair of objective truth had been increasingly insinuated into the scientists; indifference to it, and a concentration upon mere power, had been the result. (Lewis, *THS* 539)

This, of course, is by no means a criticism of science as such, but of scientism.[22] Scientific progress deified through human hubris could never become the instrument through which humanity's hopes and desires could be achieved.[23]

But if the Arthurian motif is most clearly present in *That Hideous Strength*, it is not totally absent from other works. In particular, Lewis' apologetic Arthuriana directed against scientism is also present in *Out of the Silent Planet*. This earlier work is, in fact, in great part an answer to Haldane who, with his own brand of evolutionist utilitarianism, could well have been the model for the character of Weston. But, as Lewis indicates in other writings of the period:

> the "Westonism" that appears in the scientific speculations of J. B. S. Haldane or the novels of Olaf Stapledon should be conceived as the most recent fruit of a more fundamental change that has been taking place over the course of several centuries—the transposition of the principal locus of Being from a transcendent God to an immanent power that realizes itself in the dynamic development of Man. (S. Schwartz 29)

In fact, Lewis likely knew Haldane and owned his works, particularly his *Possible Worlds* (1927; Lewis, "A Reply to Professor Haldane" 74–85). In chapter 20 of *Out of the Silent Planet*, the last few words of Weston's speech—"It is enough for me that there is a Beyond"—are a direct reference to G. B. Shaw's *Back to Methuselah*, subtitled *A Metabiological Pentateuch* (1921), a work and author ironically heavily criticized by Haldane for not being evolutionist enough. For his part, Haldane held to a radical evolutionist conviction. In *The Causes of Evolution*, he comments:

> the hypothesis that mind has played very little part in evolution horrifies some people. Shaw's preface to "Back to Methuselah" is a good example of a strong emotional reaction. He admits that Darwinism cannot be disproved, but goes on to state that no decent-minded person can believe in it. This is the attitude of mind of the persecutor rather than the discoverer. (163–64)

Such a comment is precisely the kind of scientism that Lewis opposed in both his theological and his fictional works. In fact, if Lewis' apologetic against scientism's absolutist claims is clearly seen in theological form in *The Abolition of Man*, it is certainly as obvious in *That Hideous Strength*.[24] Moreover, because of Lewis'

---

22 See C. S. Lewis, *The Abolition of Man*.

23 According to Lewis, science, in and for itself, could not make human beings happier or better. See "Is Progress Possible?" 311–16.

24 In fact, Lewis refers to his *Abolition of Man* in the preface to *THS*, 345. Regarding the criticism of scientism in *Abolition*, see West, *The Magician's Twin*.

artistic vision, the criticism set forth in *That Hideous Strength* is more powerful than his theological commentary published earlier in 1943. All the fears and potential harm of scientism, including spiritual harm, are crystalized around the opposition of Logres to the N.I.C.E.[25] This opposition to a deviant form of scientism is also found elsewhere in Lewis' space trilogy. As David Downing perceptively remarks:

> There is indication of Lewis' opposition to materialism in the dedication of *Out of the Silent Planet*, that reads: "To my brother W.H.L. / a life-long critic of the space-and-time story." This life-long criticism was no doubt directed at a materialistic rejection of any non-material dimension within our created order. (Downing 34)

This attack on reductionism is, as Medcalf pointed out, "perhaps above all what united Lewis and Williams" (42). The Arthurian material was for Lewis, as for many other Arthurian writers of the past, the literary vehicle for philosophical debate.

The Historical Arthur in the Early Twentieth Century

It would be easy to disconnect issues about the relevance and role of the Arthurian material in the development of the Inklings' literary work from their contemporary academic debates. Lewis, among other Inklings, was well aware of the scholarly disputes surrounding the historicity of Arthur. Writing to Arthur Greeves, he could say: "After all your namesake king Arthur really lived once (if we are to believe the latest theories) but it doesn't follow that Malory's old book is history" (*CL* 1:234–35). While he was ready to entertain the idea of a historical figure behind "Arthur," Lewis was still not completely persuaded, as he wrote in a letter written in 1953: "I'm not committed to a real belief in Arthur, Merlin etc: all that comes in a *story*" (*CL* 3:349). Clearly then, if some of the major Inklings were that aware of the historical debates surrounding the Matter of Britain, to the student of literature, language, or mythology, a dis-incarnation of the Inklings' work would be a tragic mistake.[26] One of the most important questions raised by the renewed interest in Arthurian writing during the nineteenth century was that of the legendary king's historicity. While the question is complex, it is necessary to survey the state of the debate that influenced the Inklings' literary imagination. The historical quest for Arthur informed the writing of several Inklings, in particular Williams. But this historicity of "Arthur" was not the only fascinating development of Arthurian scholarship.

The reconsideration of the necessary distinction between literary device and historical factuality in Gildas, Nennius, and Geoffrey of Monmouth led Arthurian scholars to reflect on the serious differences between medieval and modern historical expectations. Gradually, they came to recognize that, as early as

---

25 This spiritual dimension of *THS* was, unsurprisingly, the heart of Orwell's complaint against this novel (Orwell 250–51).

26 Surprisingly enough, Christopher Tolkien's "The Poem in Arthurian Tradition" is merely concerned with the relationship *FoA* entertains with the works of Malory and Geoffrey of Monmouth. The place of Tolkien's poem within its historical setting is never considered, which is unfortunate. See Christopher Tolkien, "The Poem in Arthurian Tradition," in *FoA* 71–122.

the twelfth century, issues regarding the historicity of Arthur were debated. In fact, "the unresolved tension between the fabulous and the historical Arthur came into sharp focus in the twelfth century when we see a real disjunction between the Arthur of the vernacular romances and the Arthur of Geoffrey of Monmouth and his contemporaries" (Carley 47). The twelfth century was a particularly important era, and Charles Williams does not hesitate to build on this transitional historical period to affirm that it shaped "the new metaphysical civilization of Europe" (Williams, "Figure" 208).[27]

The question of historicity was complex, especially since "medieval ideas about authenticity were unlike our own" (Ashe, *Discovery* 14). Lewis writes extensively about this in *The Discarded Image*, arguing that medieval readers approached historical works not by asking whether they were true, but by suspending their judgement on whether they were false—or, more probably, by not asking questions about truth, falsehood, and historicity. They were interested in the story itself, and they left the problems of belief and factuality to critics (*DI* 181). Since writers as well as readers of the medieval era were focused more on the story than on the historicity, any historical assessment is difficult. Moreover, when they handled ancient history, writers like Geoffrey or Gildas "medievalized" ancient texts and characters and, in doing so, made their characters very much like their own contemporaries. This, in turn, made it very difficult for modern scholars to distinguish between literary function and historical realities. In fact, scholars began to realize that the questions that were asked were not so much complex as they were irrelevant. This probably serves to explain the rise of another quest, of imaginative nature.

From Mythological to Historical: The Fate of Arthur

The main Arthurian debate that forms the background to the Inklings' literary reinvention of Arthur is that of the historicity of King Arthur. That is not to say, of course, that the Inklings explicitly discussed Arthur's historicity. In fact, apart from Williams, they very rarely did. Arthur's historicity was crucial to Williams, because he "attaches considerable importance to the figure of the king in the actual history behind the legends, being eager to give his poetic treatment 'depth' and verisimilitude" (Scarf 24). While he relies on the evaluation of the sixth-century historian Gildas and the ninth-century monk Nennius, Williams also seriously considers the impact of Geoffrey of Monmouth's work, especially in the way Geoffrey's work goes beyond those who will follow in his footsteps, like Wace and Laȝamon (*contra* Scarf 24).

If most of the other Inklings did not explicitly interact with the academic issue of Arthur's historicity, the legendary king's place in history was nonetheless a familiar topic to them. This historicity was, at the time, an important subject open for debate. In fact, at the end of the nineteenth and beginning of the twentieth centuries, strong arguments were made against Arthur's historical existence. These arguments were based mainly on two different approaches born out of the new sciences of the nineteenth century. First, the comparative sciences, especially in the field of language and mythology, gave a new vitality to

---

27   Another writer who has stressed the centrality of the twelfth century is the Catholic "metahistorian" Christopher Dawson. See, for example, his comments regarding this transforming period in *The Crisis of Western Education* 12–13 and *Enquiries into Religion and Culture* 63–65.

the study of the historical dimension of European mythologies and legends. So everything came to be reinterpreted in light of proto-comparative literary studies. "King Arthur" did not escape this fate.

The second field opened during the first decades of the twentieth century is what has been called "source criticism." While the expression is a defining one in biblical studies, it can also be used to address questions regarding Arthur. The origins of this new approach are complex and took root in the late eighteenth century. However, the second and third decades of the nineteenth century came to define the use of source criticism, especially in view of its impact on historical issues. Under the influence of German scholar Leopold von Ranke (1795–1886), "source criticism" became one of the standard approaches to the scientific study of ancient texts. The specific objective of this scientific method was precisely to ascertain the historicity of these texts (Hardtwig 12739). One of the main objectives of this new science was to discover the diversity of materials that constitute a specific body of writing in order to reinterpret its intended meaning. This had strong appeal to the scholars of mythologies and legends. They believed that the association of source criticism with the comparative sciences could lead to the better understanding of the common origin of myths and, of course, to the hidden meaning lying beyond the apparently naïve mythological narrative. Hence the call for meticulous source-criticism analysis of the Arthurian material.

This new method of analyzing and reading mythological and legendary materials came into sharp focus in the case of Arthur. In fact, Arthur's historicity, while questioned by the mythological and anthropological schools, was never totally rejected. Here, we must consider what was, in the Inklings' historical context, the current state of the debate regarding the historicity of "Arthur." The issue at hand is complex. While Arthurian writers and scholars were by no means of one voice, a consensus emerged during the third and fourth decades of the twentieth century. The change was indeed significant. At the close of the nineteenth century, views regarding Arthur's historicity were largely informed and guided by the study of mythology and folktales. In fact, many options explaining the "rise" of the figure of Arthur were given. For example, Sir John Rhŷs (whose lectures on Welsh Tolkien most likely attended sometime between Hilary terms 1914 and 1915; Scull and Hammond 1:50, 59), recognized in 1891

> the problems of reconciling the widespread but generally localized Arthurian legends with the scanty pre-Galfridian texts ... suggested that we need to think in terms of two Arthurs. One was the by now commonplace Brittonic divinity who was a 'Culture Hero' or 'Celtic Zeus'. Rhys' was the academically respectable end of a growing literature on Arthur and many other Celtic herofigures .... (Higham 11)

This growing literature on Arthur tried to place the famous king squarely within the range of comparative mythology, seeing in him merely the vestige either of a sun-god legend or a "culture hero," as in the case of Rhŷs (Rhŷs 8). However, these explanations could not account for the rise of Arthur's fame (Ashe, *Discovery* 183–85). As Williams himself said: "it was, however, by no means certain that that name would last, still less that it would enter into a great literature" (Williams, "Figure" 194). The relation between the Arthur of literary history and the Arthur of medieval legends and romances is not explained away by the theories put forward by the different schools of comparative mythology.

In this context, E. K. Chamber's study *Arthur of Britain* (1927), "the first modern study of the place of Arthur in British history" (Higham, *King Arthur* 14), is of particular significance.[28] While he tended to acknowledge the presence of clear mythical elements in the traditional treatment of Arthur, he was nonetheless inclined to accept the historicity of an Arthurian figure,[29] thus taking issue with a purely mythological interpretation. As Chambers argued:

> The stories of Arthur, whether handed down in historical or literary form from Nennius onwards, or surviving in current folk-lore, contain obvious elements which do not properly belong to a Christian warrior and maintainer of the Roman tradition ... comparative mythology has not been slow to trace in them further examples of just that *detritus* of Celtic or other pre-Christian notions of the world and its governance which we found embedded in the *Mabinogi*. (Chambers 205)

Chambers could defend such a balanced view, because he argued for a certain degree of reliability for the sources dating from the ninth to eleventh centuries.[30] This enabled him to defend the existence of the historical figure behind the mythological Arthur. Many scholars followed in Chambers' footsteps, as did Jackson, Alcock, Morris, and Collingwood. They all argued that the historical realities actually lay in post-Roman Britain where Geoffrey had correctly put them.[31] Hence, while the literary account was not literally true, the historical setting was, by all accounts, correct. This seriously challenged the folkloric model for Arthur, so central to the late nineteenth century and the first decades of the twentieth century.

Another significant study that serves as transition between the mythological perspective of the nineteenth century[32] and the more nuanced view of the 1930–50 is the work of Kemp Malone, then professor of English literature at Johns Hopkins University. In his *The Historicity of Arthur* (1924), he argued for a "mythological Arthur" from the perspective of a philologist. In particular, philology led him to consider that Uther and Arthur were not only mythological culture heroes but also that they were identical figures. However, he was also quite ready to consider an early historical origin. Specifically, he could consider the historical figure of Lucius Artorius Castus as prototype for the mythological Arthur ("Artorius" 367–74). In doing so, Malone constructed a dual Arthur. On the one hand, there remained a popular Arthur, one that was a mere common and mythological device created for pseudo-historical purposes. On the other

---

28   It is also significant that he is, along with R. G. Collingwood and Eugène Vinaver, among the three main Arthurian scholars to whom Lewis makes explicit reference; see Lewis, *CL* 2:673.

29   Chambers writes that "Early in the ninth century ... Arthur was not merely a national British hero; he was also the centre of popular aetiological myths in South Wales and in Ercing, which is Herefordshire" (7).

30   Saklatvala recognizes that Geoffrey of Monmouth had access to "older records of some kind" (50).

31   Christopher Tolkien's comment that Geoffrey's account is "pseudo-historical," that is, in "the mode of history" most likely relates to this common view about the relevance of Geoffrey's literary work (*FoA* 73, 89–90).

32   If the mythological interpretation of "Arthur" is generally characteristic of the nineteenth century, it is by no means foreign to twentieth-century interpretations. For example, Richard Cavendish seems to take seriously, even though he does not make it his own, the option of Arthur being a vestige of sun-god adoration.

hand, there was (more likely) a second Arthur, the Roman-type commander familiar to Arthurian scholars. Malone's work is significant because it stands at the crossroad of divergent paths: the fascination with
comparative mythology and the quest for the historical Arthur. In fact, "the debate was to shift dramatically
in favour of a historical Arthur during the late inter-war years, with the publication of three seminal works
[by E. K. Chambers, John Edward Lloyd, and Kemp Malone] by distinguished scholars of the new, more
critical school of history and textual study" (Higham 16). Subsequently, when the Inklings were ready to
publish their own Arthuriads, the academic scholarship was more than ready to accept the existence of a
historical figure behind the literary Arthur.

This would indeed prove crucial to the monistic vision of Charles Williams. One can wonder what
Williams' work would have been if the academic consensus over the possibility of a historical Arthurian
figure had not been accepted. Williams' stress on the essential unity of spiritual and historical might well
have taken a very different turn. Of course, this observation might be mitigated by the observation that
Williams' own quest for "historicity" was guided more by a concern over the meaning and origin of the
Grail than of the king himself. On this matter, Williams' decision to insert a chapter on the Grail between
his "historical chapter" ("The beginning," 189–96) and his chapter "The Coming of the King" (208–28)
is highly significant. Despite the diversity of motivations in favor of a historical figure behind Arthur, a
rather rapid consensus—rapid considering the complexity of the issues at hand—was reached through the
reconsideration of the matter. The question was not whether the Arthur of literary works was historical or
not. In fact, many scholars agreed that if Geoffrey's Arthur did not exist as such, there nonetheless must
have been a historical figure behind the rise of the legend.[33]

In this way, a crucial distinction was made between historical realities and literary artifice. If Arthur,
with his court, his knights, his legendary sword, his enchanter, and his Round Table, could not have
existed, the monarch of literary invention must have had a real original. Of course, many scholars would
have agreed that, as Williams says, "[Geoffrey] first made Arthur a knight," and following that innovation
Arthur "grew into more than a fable; it became a fashion" ("Figure" 210).[34] The positive investigation into
the king's historicity took a new turn that was in part due to a more generous assessment of the histori-

33   Geoffrey Ashe's assessment on this matter is interesting:
      The legends never worked alone. What did finally begin to engage me was the attitude of one or two
      modern authors who took the legend seriously without taking them literally, and considered what
      lay behind them. Glastonbury was the first Arthurian theme to take hold. I am almost sure that it
      reached me through Chesterton's *Short History of England*, about 1945. As for the problem of the post-
      Roman dark age and the historical Arthur, it started to attract me about 1948 when I read *The Battle for
      Britain in the Fifth Century*. (Ashe, *Camelot and the Vision of Albion* 9)
      What is fascinating here is the underlying affirmation that the debate over the historicity and meaning
      of "Arthur" was not purely a matter of historical investigation but reached deeper. In fact, to Ashe, the
      objective of the historical quest for Arthur was not so much to reconstruct the historical figure but "a
      feeling," which at times sounds similar to the joyous melancholy of the young C. S. Lewis.
34   A few pages later, Williams adds: "Geoffrey had taken up a fable and so shaped and told it that it now had
      the potentiality of myth" ("Figure" 217).

cal value of Geoffrey's work. If the literary and fictional nature of Geoffrey's Arthur was not questioned, Arthurian scholars more readily accepted that "whatever Arthur may actually have been, he does belong where Geoffrey puts him" (Ashe, *Discovery* 15). The historical figure behind "Britain's last champion" truly belongs to the complex time that was the turn of the fifth and sixth centuries.[35]

In any case, by the 1920s and 1930s, a new picture of Arthur emerged: a historical figure behind the legend—whoever this historical figure might have been. As early as 1911, John Edward Lloyd, who took a highly scholarly approach to the study of Welsh texts,[36] had argued that there might have been a historical figure behind the literary Arthur.[37] While "he was highly dubious about the relevance of Arthur to Wales, [he] looked favourably on the suggestion that he might have been a successor to the late Roman Count of Britain" (Higham 13), thus maintaining the possibility of a historical Arthur in the south-east part of England. As for J. D. Bruce, author of one of the key studies of the early twentieth century (*The Evolution of Arthurian Romance*, 1923), while doubting the possibility of a "historical" Arthur having lived and fought during the Dark Age,[38] he suspended his disbelief to conclude that there might nonetheless have been some historical figure behind "Arthur." For him, as for other scholars, the central issue was not whether Arthur was historical but "what role was Arthur intended to perform" (Higham 8) and how he was used by author and audience, in time giving rise to the legends and romances.

This question somewhat influences work in the mid-twentieth century, allowing for Charles Williams' interaction with the study published by R. G. Collingwood on the historical Arthur in his prose "Figure of Arthur." In his 1936 book *Roman Britain and the English Settlements*, Collingwood argues that the name "Arthur," despite its unknown historical and philological origin and its appearance in Celtic legend, is best explained if such a figure really existed. As Williams concludes: "We have then, to put all together, at least a possibility, behind the chronicles and the hypotheses—and perhaps rather more than a possibility—of an historic figure" ("Figure" 194). Collingwood concluded that "through the mist of legend that has surrounded the name of Arthur, it is thus possible to descry something which at least may have happened" (Collingwood and Myers 324), and what happened was the identification of Arthur as commander of mobile troops (*comes Britanniarum*).[39] This argument, similar to that made by Zimmer in 1896, seems to have been the decisive "convincing suggestion" that led Williams to support this view ("Figure" 192–93). This, in turn, would form the historical background to Charles Williams' Arthuriad.

---

35   The expression "Britain's last champion" comes from the title of Beram Saklatvala's study.

36   It is interesting to notice that, toward the end of *THS*, Welsh is quite present and important. See Lewis, *THS* 609–11.

37   Already two decades earlier, John Rhŷs had argued that the Celtic influence on the Arthurian legends far outweighed the Saxon influence. See Rhŷs 390. While Tolkien and Gordon's introduction to *Sir Gawain and the Green Knight* does not refer directly to Rhŷs's study, but to Loomis's (Tolkien and Gordon xiv), Tolkien's acquaintance with Rhŷs's argument cannot be doubted.

38   Williams quotes Bruce's work twice from the 1928 edition republished by John Hopkins (original edition Göttingen: Vandenhoeck & Ruprecht, 1923) in "Figure" 206, 218.

39   *Comes Britanniarum*, that Williams translates as 'Captain-General.' See for example Williams, "Figure" 194, 197, 211.

Summarizing this "consensus" that emerged in the early twentieth century, Snyder concludes: "Although the legends of Arthur are fictitious, it is difficult to account for their existence unless there was originally a real man whose character and achievements formed the rock on which the towers and battlements of legend were raised" (qtd. in Cavendish 5). Many of the major studies between 1930 and 1960 argue in very much the same way. K. H. Jackson, one of the most brilliant Celticists of his generation, could say that the only possible honest answer to the question of Arthur's historicity was: "We do not know, but he may well have existed" (325). Proof was impossible, whether in favor of or against the historical Arthur.[40] If, for Jackson, the nature of evidence as to Arthur's historicity was, strictly speaking, inconclusive, "most scholars would agree that the Arthur of Geoffrey of Monmouth is not historical at all" (1). However, this did not weaken, but rather strengthened the argument in favor of a historical figure without whom the rise of the legendary Arthur was impossible to explain.[41]

The easiest and most obvious explanation was that it was "simplest to assume that behind the stories about King Arthur there must have been a real man" (Parry 331). Whether the name "Arthur" was the British form of a Roman "Artorius" or a Welsh "Artyr," his historical existence could be affirmed. This conclusion was so obvious that it has remained a major problem to Arthurian scholars, some uneasy with the inconclusive nature of the answer. However,

> faced with total frustration in trying to answer a question [about a historical Arthur], it is interesting to wonder if it was necessary to ask it in the first place. The desire to ask it, and the determination to arrive at a positive answer, has always been strong, as is evident in the account of the disinterment of the supposed Arthur's skeletal remains at Glastonbury in 1191 or in Caxton's determination to prove Arthur historical in his Preface to Malory's *Morte d'Arthur* (1485) by offering evidence on the present whereabouts of Lancelot's sword, Gawain's skull and the Round Table. (Pearsall 4)

Whether a historical figure stands behind "Arthur" will most likely remain an unanswered question. More interesting is the one about the rise of the "legend." In any case, the debate regarding the historicity of Arthur highlights a very interesting observation: scholars find an explanation to Arthur's origin through what is, to them, the most crucial social and philosophical need of their time.[42] In this respect, Williams is an interesting case study. Considering Williams' interest in the foundation of the "metaphysical civiliza-

---

40   Even "the absence of early written evidence for Arthur is ... startling, but it does not mean that Arthur did not exist" (Pearsall 2).

41   As Jackson reminds us: "Nothing is certain about the historical Arthur, not even his existence; however, there are certain possibilities, even probabilities. There may have been a supreme British commander of genius in late fifth-century who bore the Roman-derived name of Arthur, though I would be wrong to deduce anything about this background from the name" (Jackson, "The Arthur of History" 10).

42   No example is more telling than that of Churchill who, in his *History of the English-Speaking People*, famously said: "Let us then declare that King Arthur and his noble knights, guarding the Sacred Flame of Christianity and the theme of a world order, sustained by valour, physical strength, and good horses and armour, slaughtered innumerable hosts of foul barbarians and set decent folks an example for all time" (1:47).

tion," it is fascinating to see that the importance of the historical Arthur lies for Williams not so much in the figure of Arthur himself, or Guinevere, or the traditional romance of medieval Arthurian literature.[43] Rather, it lies in its spiritual dimension. In fact, Logres almost functions as an ideal spiritual location,[44] an ideal resting place for pilgrims, "analogous to St. Augustine's New Jerusalem and Tolkien's True West" (Göller 122n3). In fact, as Göller concludes, "[Logres] is a part or a province of the Byzantine Empire which for Williams represented the incarnation of Divine Order" (122).

The Mythopoeic Arthur: J. R. R. Tolkien's Mythological History

The quest for a historical Arthur had another, unexpected consequence: the rise of the "imaginative quest" for Arthur. In fact, the historical quest was sometimes met with relative skepticism or even suspicion by Arthurian writers. The reason was a literary objection. It was believed that such a quest was not only irrelevant but, more importantly, that the center and essence of the Arthurian material was the stories *in and for themselves*, and that the search for historicity might spoil the stories (Ashe, *Discovery* 185).

It has been remarked that some early twentieth-century Arthurian writers, while not opposed to the "historical quest," nonetheless took issue with the predominance of history over myth. For John Masefield, one of the most significant Arthurian writers of the first half of the twentieth century, the historical quest enriched the myth. He thought that history and myth should not be seen as opposing forces struggling for the heart of Arthur. It so happened, in the early twentieth century, that "alongside novels, plays, and films quarried from the old Matter of Britain, a new Matter of Britain has taken shape, which in no way detracts from it, and is a quest in its own right—a quest by way of imagination" (Ashe, *Discovery* 185).[45] Alongside John Masefield (*Midsummer Night*, 1928), the main figures of this imaginative Arthurian revival included Edwin Arlington Robinson (*Merlin*, 1917; *Lancelot*, 1920; and *Tristram*, 1927), T. S. Eliot (*The Waste Land*, 1922), the modernist poet David Jones (*In Parenthesis*, 1937; *The Anathemata*, 1952), R. C. Sheriff (*The Long Sunset*, 1955), and the Marxist playwright John Arden (the trilogy *The Island of the Mighty*, 1972).[46] Certainly when Charles Williams published his Arthuriad in 1938 and 1944, he was seen as being part of this imaginative quest for Arthur that had not only renewed the interest in the role and function of the Grail, but also built on the modern attempts to reconstruct history. Therefore, one of the issues raised by the "imaginative quest" was the relation between mythical and historical realities, a topic J. R. R. Tolkien knew very well indeed.

---

43   Even Williams' chapter "The Coming of the King" is only as much concerned with Arthur as it is, in this case, with Merlin. Almost half of the first part of this chapter ("Figure" 217–23) is devoted to the figure of Merlin.

44   The nature of the historicity of the Arthurian material in Williams also touches upon the symbolic absence of any opposition between Rome and Logres, underlining the essential spiritual unity of Byzantium-Rome-Logres.

45   See also Ashe et al. 35.

46   Cavaliero rightly associates David Jones with this "imaginative quest" without discussing their differences (173), though a comparison of Williams and Jones might lead to fascinating conclusions.

Until recently, most people would not have naturally associated the name of Tolkien with the Arthurian cycle, but instead would more easily associate him with Norse or Welsh material. Some would even argue for Tolkien's complete disinterest in the Arthurian matter because of his insistence that this material was British rather than distinctly English (Tolkien, *Letters* 144). However, this is a confusion between his motivation for writing a "new" mythology for England (his own mythological corpus) and the value of the Arthurian cycle in itself. If Tolkien could reject everything Arthur-related as unfit for a distinctive English mythology, he was clearly not ready to deny this cycle any significance, as the publication of his translation of *Sir Gawain and the Green Knight* and his original poem *The Fall of Arthur* clearly demonstrate.[47] Moreover, as David Doughan has pointed out, while Tolkien tried to avoid explicit use of Arthurian material, it keeps "breathing through" in his work (21–24).

Tolkien's interest in the Matter of Britain is evidenced in his lifelong project of writing a substantial Arthurian poem. Even though *The Fall of Arthur* is incomplete, it reveals Tolkien's interest in myth and history, particularly in history. In fact, the "mythological" material—if we can speak so—in *The Fall of Arthur* is in many ways much more historical than many other accounts of the Arthurian cycle. In particular, the figures of Lancelot and Guinevere are in Tolkien treated with a somewhat cold realism far removed from the moralized standard of Tennyson or other Victorian poets. Even if Tolkien's poem presents a diametrically opposed view to that of William Morris, one is left wondering if the latter's *Defence of Guenevere* (1858) might not be one of the inspirations behind Tolkien's Guinever.[48],[49] Not that Tolkien wanted, or claimed, to present a historical view of Arthur, but his retelling describes a much more believable setting, a much more coherent secondary world than most Arthurian novels of the nineteenth century. This would be consistent with both his view about the internal consistency of "secondary worlds" and with his "rejection" of Arthurian romance as "too lavish, and fantastical, incoherent and repetitive" (Tolkien, *Letters* 144).

Tolkien's historical treatment of Arthur can be seen notably in his treatment of Mordred's influence over Arthur—or in his relative silence over the relationship between Lancelot and Guinever (*FoA* 105–06). It can also be seen in several other passages in Tolkien's corpus, including in some of his minor works. Since Arthur is most connected to the notion of kingship, it is not surprising to find a reminiscence of Arthurian kingship in Tolkien's works. For example, French scholar Vincent Ferré has suggested that Tolkien's academic and fictional work presents a criticism of Arthur's kingship—associated with that of Beowulf and Beorhtnoth—and defends an alternative view of kingship embodied in Farmer Giles and Aragorn (Ferré 59–76). Here again, Arthur serves as a vehicle for socio-political discourse, as during the nineteenth century.

However, beyond the differences between *The Fall of Arthur* and, say, Malory's *Le Morte d'Arthur* or Geoffrey's *Historia Regum Britanniae*, Tolkien's poem is highly significant in the context of his mythological corpus. First,

---

47   For Verlyn Flieger, the Matter of Britain even forms the essential model for Tolkien's own legendarium ("Matter of Britain" 53).

48   Some have traced the influence on Tolkien's Guinever to Laʒamon's *Brut*. See Jensen.

49   See chapter 13 of the present volume, by Alyssa House-Thomas, for an extended discussion of inspirations for Tolkien's Guinever. [Editor's note]

Tolkien, while most interested in myth, was also concerned with the relation between myth and history or the way through which myth actually explained history. The poem displays this same concern, as pointed out by Christopher Tolkien (125–68). For example, when Tolkien talks about Arthur sailing West as the defining "Eärendel passage" (Tolkien, *FoA* 136), the relationship between the Arthurian cycle and his mythological corpus is obvious. This means that myth and history are deeply interwoven: the geography of Eärendel slowly evolves into the geography of England through the story of Eriol/Ælfwine, an Anglo-Saxon citizen of tenth-century England.[50] Maybe here lies the historical significance of Arthur for Tolkien: we move from a *first* parallel between the cycle of Eärendel and the cycle of Arthur, to a *second* parallel between the secondary geography of Middle-earth and the primary geography of England, and a *third* parallel between Arthur's Logres and medieval England. In each case, the meaning of the historical reality, England, is heightened through mythological writing.

But we can go further, for Tolkien provides a complex structure consisting of two related pairs of locations that serve to explain the nature of "mythological history." Tolkien reminds us that he

> began an abortive book of time-travel of which the end was to be the presence of my hero in the drowning of Atlantis. This was to be called *Númenor*, the Land in the West .... It started with a father-son affinity between Edwin and Elwin of the present, and was supposed to go back into legendary time by way of Eädwine and Ælfwine of circa A.D. 918, and Audoin and Alboin of Lombardic legend .... (*Letters* 347)

Already here a first "pair" appears: Númenor-Atlantis. This one is both the most obvious and the most well known. However, there is another connection that serves to illustrate Tolkien's relationship between history and mythology. This second "pair" unites Avallon and Tol Eressëa. If the Númenor "arch-story," alongside the Atlantis material, bridges history and mythology on a time-related scale, the Tol Eressëa story provides a space-related bridge with our world. This explains the topical importance of Tol Eressëa in Tolkien's mythological corpus, including the reason for the return of the Elves "into the West," where "such as obeyed dwelt again in Eressëa, the Lonely Island, which was renamed Avallon: for it is hard by Valinor" (Tolkien, *FoA* 151).

The two related pairs are necessary to each other. First, the Tol Eressëa/Avallon "arch-story" would be meaningless if not for the Númenor-Atlantis one. It is precisely because of the Fall of Númenor that the World was Bent and that the Straight Road was opened. Thus the Fall of Númenor is an unfortunate and dramatic precondition to the Tol Eressëa/Avallon development. Second, the "Tol Eressëa" (or Eärendel) account leads us directly to the legendary Avallon and to our actual history. A direct line can be traced, bringing together mythological history (Tol Eressëa), mythological-legendary accounts (Avallon), and our world. If that is the case, then we have Tolkien's idea of "mythological history" encapsulated here. When Arthurian material was integrated into this mythological history within the framework of a new distinctive English mythology, the "mythopoeic Arthur" was born.

---

50   See chapter 4 by Charles A. Huttar. [Editor's note]

If that is the case, then Tolkien's most relevant Arthurian material is not as much *The Fall of Arthur* as it is *The Notion Club Papers* (Flieger, *Question of Time* 61–88). Indeed, this work, however incomplete, provides the *necessary* explanation of how the mythology of Tol Eressëa (the Secondary World) became the history of the Primary World. The second part is especially relevant in several respects. We clearly see Tolkien's mythological history at work in the way one of the characters of *The Notion Club Papers* roots fiction and literary inventions, first in "Being," then in history (Tolkien, *SD* 227). Further, legends, while they may be "partly symbolical, [can be] arranged in designs that compress, expand, foreshorten, combine, and are not at all realistic or photographic, yet they may tell you something about the Past" (Tolkien, *SD* 227). This is quite revealing. We can discern here the same preoccupation Tolkien displays in his poem "Mythopoeia" with the relation between legend and history (the Past) or between mythology and "truth."

Legends and myths, according to Tolkien in "Mythopoeia," are the result of both "use and misuse" (l. 69) of man's "world-dominion by creative act" (59); they are both "light and dark" (lines 44 and 67).[51] In fact, Tolkien defends the dignity and legitimacy of the mythopoeic power in maintaining that the mythopoeic creation is a right. He claims that sowing the "seeds of dragons" (l. 68) is a worthy and glorious activity, a right that "has not decayed" (l. 69). Man's mythopoeic faculty witnesses to humankind's development and reflects the source of all creative power: God himself, the Divine Artist. Myths are the "heraldic emblems of a lord unseen" (l. 118), the flowing banner of God's artistic presence within man. This also means that myths and legends can convey metaphysical and historical truth. While Tolkien never commented on "mythological history" directly, it was an important subject for him. Because myths could convey truth, they could serve as reinterpretation of historical reality. History would then not be defined as much by events as by its relevance and philosophical significance. It follows that for Tolkien, myths and legends demonstrate the historical presence of an incontrovertible spiritual reality.

This explains one main difference between Tolkien and Williams. The former did not feel obligated to link Arthur to an explicitly Christian background, while in Williams the Christian myth is "undisguisedly the theme" (Cavaliero 173). The fact that the Matter of Britain was too obviously Christian was a problem for Tolkien: the Arthurian world "is involved in, and explicitly contains the Christian religion" (*Letters* 144). Tolkien preferred to rely not on symbolism, but on an implicit theological perspective, one that hallowed legends and tales (Tolkien, *OFS* 78). Hence, "myth" is for Tolkien a form of historical account of the unity between metaphorical, literal, and spiritual reality. Of course, not all myths reflect a true account of the historical past because of the blinding and corrupting power of sin upon the hearts of men. The conclusion is that, for Tolkien, the significance of the Arthurian cycle, as with most mythological motifs, is the way in which a spiritual truth could be manifested in history through myth and legends. History should then not stand opposed to myth but should be considered as a *literal* manifestation of things otherwise *literally* expressed in myths and legends.

---

51 See, for example, the importance of line 59, in which Tolkien refers to man's world-dominion, a dominion that is effected and actualized through man's creative activity.

Conclusion

A few final words are necessary. If we ask what are the common traits of Tolkien's, Lewis', and Williams' use of mythological history, we can identify two common elements. First, the Inklings, through their Arthuriad, present us with a "holistic" view of the world. To them, the natural and the supernatural are never completely separated. Therefore, the historical dimension(s) of the Arthurian material is a defense of the integrity of myth and history, but then again also of the integration of myth into history. The union of two worlds, of the natural and the supernatural, of history and myth, becomes the main focus of their Arthurian cycle. Consequently, they rejected a false dichotomy between symbolic and historical; between metaphorical and literal; or between mythological and historical. As far as history is concerned, the Inklings' Arthuriana should be seen as an exposition of the nature of history as well as an attack upon various brands of historical reductionism.

Beyond these two common traits, the Inklings shared a clear literary interest in the Arthurian material, but for various reasons. Some, like Bennett or Wrenn, had purely linguistic and literary interests. Others, including Owen Barfield, were mostly interested in the "Matter of Britain" for its imaginative and philosophical relevance. Others again used the Arthurian cycle to rise up to the challenges of their days, as we have seen with Tolkien, Lewis, and Williams. The power of "mythological history" can be seen in Lewis' use of it against the scientism of his time, in Tolkien's defense of the integrity of myth itself, or in Williams' stress on the essential unity of nature and archnature.

Despite these differences, one main topic emerges as the common thread, at least among these three writers: the historical-spiritual reality behind the rise of the Arthurian legends. A fascinating observation is the way in which, even when they obviously disagreed (see Tolkien and Williams), the Inklings were able to put forward a theory of myth that valued history and nature without disregarding the value and importance of both myth and the spiritual. In their fascination with the Arthurian cycle, most of the Inklings actually demonstrate their concerns about the nature of history. "Arthur" then appears as the paradigm through which we can approach the Inklings' view of mythological history. With this historical perspective, the Inklings were able to freely explore the roads leading from myth to history and back again. And now, they invite us to follow them on this road.

Works Cited

Aeschliman, Michael D. "C. S. Lewis on Mere Science." West 47–51.

——. *The Restitution of Man: C. S. Lewis and the Case Against Scientism*. Grand Rapids, MI: Eerdmans, 1998. Print.

Ashe, Geoffrey. *Camelot and the Vision of Albion*. NY: St. Martin's Press, 1971. Print.

——. *The Discovery of King Arthur*. Garden City, NY: Anchor Press, Doubleday, 1985. Print.

Ashe, Geoffrey, et al. *The Quest for Arthur's Britain*. NY: Praeger, 1968. Print.

Ashenden, Gavin. *Charles Williams: Alchemy and Integration*. Kent State UP, 2008. Print.

Barczewski, Stephanie. *Myth and National Identity in Nineteenth-Century Britain: The Legends of King Arthur and Robin Hood*.
      Oxford UP, 2005. Print.

Bennett, J. A. W., ed. *Essays on Malory*. Oxford: Clarendon Press, 1963. Print.

Blissett, William. "David Jones and the Chesterbelloc." *The Chesterton Review* 23.1–2 (1997): 27–55. Print.

Briggs, Asa. *Victorian Cities*. Berkeley: U of California Press, 1993. Print.

Brooks, Chris, and Inha Bryden. "The Arthurian legacy." *The Arthur of the English: Arthurian Literature in the Middle Ages*. Vol. 2. Ed. W. R. J. Barron. Cardiff: U of Wales Press, 1999. 247–64. Print.

Brown, Robert McAfee. "Charles Williams: Lay Theologian." *Theology Today* 10 (1953): 212–29. Print.

Carley, James P. "Arthur in English History." *The Arthur of the English, Arthurian Literature in the Middle Ages*. Vol. 2. Ed. W. R. J. Barron. Cardiff: U of Wales Press, 1999. 47–57. Print.

Carlyle, Thomas. *The Works of Thomas Carlyle: Critical and Miscellaneous Essays 5*. Vol 6. Cambridge UP, 2010. Print.

Cavaliero, Glen. *Charles Williams: Poet of Theology*. Eugene, OR: Wipf and Stock, 1983. Print.

Cavendish, Richard. *King Arthur and the Grail: The Arthurian Legends and their Meaning*. NY: Taplinger, 1978. Print.

Chambers, E. K. *Arthur of Britain*. London: Sidgwick & Jackson, 1927. Print.

Chandler, Alice. *A Dream of Order: The Medieval Ideal in Nineteenth-Century English Literature*. Lincoln: U of Nebraska P, 1970. Print.

Chapman, Raymond. *The Sense of the Past in Victorian Literature*. London, Sydney: Croom Helm, 1986. Print.

Churchill, Winston S. *A History of the English-speaking Peoples*. 4 vols. London: Cassell, 1956–58. Print.

Collingwood, R. G., and J. N. L. Myers. *Roman Britain and the English Settlements*. Oxford: Clarendon Press, 1936. Print.

Dawson, Christopher. *The Crisis of Western Education*. Washington, D.C.: Catholic U of America P, 2010. Print.

——. *Enquiries into Religion and Culture*. Washington, D.C.: Catholic U of America P, 2009. Print.

Doughan, David. "An Ethnically Cleansed Faery? Tolkien and the Matter of Britain." *Mallorn* 32 (1995): 21–24. Print.

Downing, David C. *Planets in Peril: A Critical Study of C. S. Lewis' Ransom Trilogy*. Amherst: U of Massachusetts P, 1992. Print.

Dunckel, Mona, and Karen Rowe. "Understanding C. S. Lewis' *Surprised by Joy*: 'A Most Reluctant' Autobiography." *C. S. Lewis: Life, Works, and Legacy*. Vol. 3: *Apologist, Philosopher, and Theologian*. Ed. Bruce L. Edwards. Westport: Praeger, 2007. 257–78. Print.

Duriez, Colin. *The A–Z of C. S. Lewis: An Encyclopedia of His Life, Thought, and Writings*. Oxford: Lion Books, 2013. Print.

Edwards, Bruce L., ed. *C. S. Lewis: Life, Works, and Legacy: Fantasist, Mythmaker, and Poet*. Westport, CT: Praeger, 2007. Print.

Eliot, T. S. Introduction. *All Hallows' Eve*. By Charles Williams. Vancouver: Regent College Publishing, 2003. Print. ix–xviii.

Ferré, Vincent. "The Rout of the King: Tolkien's Readings on Arthurian Kingship—*Farmer Giles of Ham* and *The Homecoming of Beorhtnoth*." *Tolkien's Shorter Works*. Eds. Margaret Hiley and Frank Weinreich. Zurich, Jena: Walking Tree, 2008. 59–76. Print.

Flieger, Verlyn. "J. R. R. Tolkien and the Matter of Britain." *Mythlore* 87 (2000): 47–59. Print.

——. *A Question of Time: J. R. R. Tolkien's Road to Faërie*. Kent State UP, 1997. Print.

Goetinck, Glenys Withcard. "The Quest for Origins." *The Grail Casebook*. Ed. Dhira B. Mahoney. New York, London: Garland, 2000. 117–47. Print.

Göller, Karl Heinz. "From Logres to Carbonek: The Arthuriad of Charles Williams." *Arthurian Literature* 1 (1981): 121–73. Print.

Green, Roger Lancelyn. *King Arthur and his Knights of the Round Table*. London: Puffin, 1953. Print.

Haldane, J. B. S. *The Causes of Evolution*. Ithaca: Cornell UP, 1932. Print.

Hardtwig, Wolfgang. "W. Ranke, Leopold von (1795–1886)." *International Encyclopedia of the Social and Behavioral Sciences*. Eds. Neil J. Smelser and Paul B. Baltes. Amsterdam, NY: Elsevier, 2001. 12738–41. Print.

Higgins, Sørina. "Double Affirmation: Medievalism as Christian Apologetic in the Arthurian Poetry of Charles Williams." *Journal of Inklings Studies* 3.2 (2013), 59–96. Print.

Higham, N. J. *King Arthur: Myth-Making and History*. London, New York: Routledge, 2002. Print.

Hunter, John. "The Reanimation of Antiquity and the Resistance to History: MacPherson-Scott-Tolkien." *Tolkien's Modern Middle Ages*. Eds. Jane Chance and Alfred K. Siewers. Basingstoke: Palgrave Macmillan, 2005. 61–75. Print.

Jackson, Kenneth Hurlstone. "The Arthur of History." *Arthurian Literature in the Middle Ages*. Ed. Roger Sherman Loomis. Oxford: Clarendon Press, 1959. 325–30. Print.

Jensen, Todd. "Tolkien and Arthurian Legend," *Beyond Bree* (1988): n.p. Print.

Lacy, Norris J., and Geoffrey Ashe. *The Arthurian Handbook*. New York, London: Garland, 1988. Print.

Lang, Andrew. *Custom and Myth*. London: Longmans, Green, 1893. Print.

——. *Magic and Religion*. London: Longman, Greens, 1901. Print.

Larson, Edward J. "C. S. Lewis on Science as a Threat to Freedom." West 53–58.

Laȝamon's Arthur: The Arthurian Section of Laȝamon's 'Brut.' Ed. W. R. Barron and S. C. Weinberg. Harlow: Longman, 1989. Print.

Lewis, C. S. *The Abolition of Man*. London: Geoffrey Bles, 1946.

——. "The Anthropological Approach." *English and Medieval Studies: Presented to J. R. R. Tolkien on the Occasion of his Seventieth Birthday*. Eds. Norman David and C. L. Wrenn. London: Allen & Unwin, 1962. 219–32. Print.

——. "Christian Apologetics." *Dock* 89–103.

——. *The Collected Letters of C. S. Lewis*. 3 Vols. Ed. Walter Hooper. NY: HarperSanFrancisco, 2004–07. Print.

——. *The Discarded Image: An Introduction to Medieval and Renaissance Literature*. Cambridge UP, 1964. Print.

——. "The Empty Universe." *Present Concerns*. Ed. Walter Hooper. San Diego: Harcourt, Brace, Jonavovich, 1986. 81–86. Print.

——. *God in the Dock: Essays on Theology and Ethics*. Ed. Walter Hooper. Grand Rapids, MI: Eerdmans, 1970. Print.

——. "Is Progress Possible?" *Dock* 311–16.

——. "Myth Became Fact." *Dock* 63–67.

——. "On Three Ways of Writing for Children." *On Stories: And Other Essays on Literature*. Ed. Walter Hooper. San Diego, New York, London: Harcourt, Brace, 1982. 31–44. Print.

——. "Period Criticism." *On Stories: And Other Essays on Literature*. Ed. Walter Hooper. San Diego, New York, London: Harcourt, Brace, 1982. 113–17. Print.

——. "Religion and Science." *Dock* 72–75.

——. "A Reply to Professor Haldane." *Of Other Worlds: Essays and Stories*. Ed. Walter Hooper. NY: Harcourt, Brace, and World, 1967. 74–85. Print.

——. *The Space Trilogy*. London: HarperCollins, 2013. Print.

——. *Surprised by Joy: The Shape of My Early Life*. NY: Harcourt, Brace, and World, 1955. Print.

——. *That Hideous Strength: A Modern Fairy-Tale for Grown-Ups*. 1945. NY: Scribner, 2003. Print.

——. "Williams and the Arthuriad." *Taliessin through Logres, The Region of the Summer Stars, Arthurian Torso*. 1948. Grand Rapids, MI: Eerdmans, 1974. 175–84. Print.

Malone, Kemp. "Artorius." *Modern Philology* 22 (1925): 367–74. Print.

——. *The Historicity of Arthur*. Urbana: U of Illinois, 1924. Print.

McGrath, Alister. *C. S. Lewis: A Life*. Carol Streams: Tyndale House, 2013. Print.

Medcalf, Stephen. "The Anathasian Principle in Williams' Use of Images." *The Rhetoric of Vision: Essays on Charles Williams*. Ed. Charles A. Huttar and Peter J. Schakel. London: Bucknell UP, 1996. 27–43. Print.

Nutt, Alfred. *Studies on the Legend of the Holy Grail*. London: D. Nutt, 1888. Print.

Olson, Richard. *Science Deified and Science Defied*. Los Angeles: U of California P, 1982. Print.

Orwell, George. "The Scientists Take Over." *Manchester Evening News* 16 August 1945. *The Complete Works of George Orwell*. Vol. 17. Ed. Peter Davison. Secker & Warburg, 1998. 250–51. Print.

Parry, John Jay. "The Historical Arthur." *Journal of English and Germanic Philology* 58 (1959): 331–35. Print.

Pearsall, Derek. *Arthurian Romance: A Short Introduction*. Oxford: Blackwell, 2003. Print.

Rhŷs, John. *Studies in the Arthurian Legend*. Oxford: Clarendon Press, 1891. Print.

Saklatvala, Beram. *Arthur: Roman Britain's Last Champion*. NY: Taplinger, 1967. Print.

Sammons, Martha C. *A Far-off Country: A Guide to C. S. Lewis' Fantasy Fiction*. Lanham, MD: UP of America, 2000. Print.

Scarf, Christopher. *The Ideal of Kingship in the Writings of Charles Williams, C. S. Lewis and J. R. R. Tolkien*. Cambridge: James Clark, 2013. Print.

Scheper, George L. "*All Hallows' Eve*: The Cessation of Rhetoric and the Redemption of Language." *The Rhetoric of Vision: Essays on Charles Williams*. Ed. Charles Huttar and Peter J. Schakel. Lewisburg: Bucknell UP, 1996. 132–61. Print.

Schwartz, David. *The Third Spring: G. K. Chesterton, Graham Greene, Christopher Dawson and David Jones*. Washington: Catholic U of America P, 2012. Print.

Schwartz, Stanford. *C. S. Lewis on the Final Frontier: Science and the Supernatural in the Space Trilogy*. Oxford UP, 2009. Print.

Scull, Christina, and Wayne G. Hammond. *The J. R. R. Tolkien Companion and Guide*. 2 vols. Boston, NY: Houghton Mifflin, 2006. Print.

Simpson, Roger. *Camelot Regained: The Arthurian Revival and Tennyson, 1800–1849*. Cambridge: D. S. Brewer, 1990. Print.

Shideler, Mary M. *The Theology of Romantic Love: A Study in the Writings of Charles Williams*. Grand Rapids, MI: Eerdmans, 1962. Print.

Smith, Kenneth. *Émile Durkheim and the Collective Consciousness of Society*. London, Anthem Press, 2014. Print.

Spencer, Herbert. *Principles of Sociology*. NY: Appleton, 1897. Print.

Starr, Nathan Comfort. *King Arthur Today: The Arthurian Legend in English and American Literature 1901–1953*. Gainesville: U of Florida P, 1954. Print.

Staudt, Kathleen Henderson. *At the Turn of a Civilization: David Jones and Modern Poetics*. Ann Arbor: U of Michigan P, 1994. Print.

Tolkien, J. R. R. *On Fairy-stories: Expanded Edition with Commentary and Notes*. Eds. Verlyn Flieger and Douglas Anderson. London: HarperCollins, 2008. Print.

——. *The Fall of Arthur*. Ed. Christopher Tolkien. London: HarperCollins, 2013. Print.

——. *The Letters of J. R. R. Tolkien*. Ed. Humphrey Carpenter. Boston; New York: Houghton Mifflin, 2000. Print.

——. "Mythopoeia." *Tree and Leaf*. 3rd ed. London: Unwin Hyman, 1988. 97–101. Print.

——. *Sauron Defeated*. The History of Middle-earth 9. Ed. Christopher Tolkien. Boston; New York: Houghton Mifflin, 1992. Print.

Tolkien, J. R. R., and E. V. Gordon, eds. *Sir Gawain and the Green Knight*. 1925. Oxford: Clarendon Press, 1967. Print.

Wendling, Susan. "Charles Williams: Priest of the Co-inherence." *Inklings Forever* 5 (2006). library.taylor.edu. Web. 13 November 2014.

West, John G, ed. *The Magician's Twin: C. S. Lewis on Science, Scientism, and Society*. Seattle: Discovery Institute Press, 2012. Print.

Weston, Jessie L. *From Ritual to Romance*. London: Cambridge UP, 1920. Print.

——. *King Arthur and his Knights: A Survey of Arthurian Romance*. London: David Nutt, 1899. Print.

Wilson, A. N. *C. S. Lewis: A Biography*. NY: Norton, 1990. Print.

Williams, Charles. *All Hallows' Eve*. London: Faber & Faber, 1945. Print.

——. *The Figure of Beatrice: A Study of Dante*. London: Faber & Faber, 1943. Print.

——. "The Figure of Arthur." *Taliessin through Logres; The Region of the Summer Stars; Arthurian Torso*. By Charles Williams and C. S. Lewis. Grand Rapids, MI: Eerdmans, 1974. 189–245. Print.

Williams, Charles, and C. S. Lewis. *Taliessin through Logres, The Region of the Summer Stars, Arthurian Torso*. Grand Rapids, MI: Eerdmans, 1974. Print.

Wrenn, Charles Leslie. *A Study of Old English Literature*. NY: Norton, 1967. Print.

7

"All Men Live by Tales": Chesterton's Arthurian Poems

J. Cameron Moore

Despite his many connections to the Inklings, Chesterton might appear at first as a strange inclusion in a collection on Arthur. Unlike in Lewis, Tolkien, and Williams, Arthurian myth does not figure largely in Chesterton's fiction. Likewise, Chesterton has no independent mythical geography that draws from Arthurian legend; there is no corresponding map of Narnia, Middle-earth, or the Byzantine Empire for Chesterton's fiction. While some of his novels have fantastical or mythical elements, they remain firmly grounded in England. They are tales closely linked to the political, social, and religious questions of Chesterton's day. Yet despite this, fairyland is nearly omnipresent in Chesterton's work. For Chesterton, Elfland is everywhere—even in the heart of industrial London—as demonstrated by both his poem "Modern Elfland" (late 1890s) and his novel *The Napoleon of Notting Hill* (1904).[1] If Chesterton had ever been asked to draw a map of Elfland, he would likely have drawn a map of England or of his neighborhood. Chesterton's mythical geography is a geography of England, and at the heart of this national fairy tale, Chesterton places King Arthur. For Chesterton, Arthur represents the defense of Christianity in England, and thus he bears witness to the real connection between Rome and Romance.

Chesterton's Arthurian poems demonstrate his understanding of Arthur's central place in the history of England. For Chesterton, Arthur is Mythic, Roman, and Christian. This paper will begin by examining

---

1   This poem was unpublished during Chesterton's lifetime, as were many of his poems; according to Aidan Mackay, editor of *Collected Poetry, Part 1: The Collected Works of G. K. Chesterton*, the poem can only be dated with regard to composition at the "late 1890s." The dating of all further poems follows the dates in *Collected Poetry*, which lists specific publication dates when they are available but otherwise provides a best guess at the date of composition.

the role of myth and history in the poem "The Myth of Arthur" (1923). Narrowing this examination of myth, I turn to the "Ballad of Arthur" (early 1920s), which deals particularly with England and Rome. Finally, relying on the context provided by the preceding two poems, I provide a reading of "The Grave of Arthur" (c. 1930), Chesterton's richest Arthurian poem. Undergirding this study is an understanding laid out by Stratford Caldecott, Lee Oser, Joseph McCleary, Joseph Schwartz, and others, including Chesterton himself, of the imagination as a necessary historical tool for discovering the truth of the past, a truth that cannot be divorced from being and thus from theology.[2]

Chesterton's poetry occupies the most neglected corner of Chesterton studies. Recent years have seen a number of monographs and articles on Chesterton's politics and nationalism, such as Julia Stapleton's *Christianity, Patriotism and Nationhood: The England of G. K. Chesterton* (Lexington, 2009) and Joseph McCleary's *The Historical Imagination of G. K. Chesterton: Locality, Patriotism, and Nationalism* (Routledge, 2009). The place of the city and Chesterton's celebration of the poetry of urban life and the city has garnered attention in the collection *G. K. Chesterton, London, and Modernity* (Bloomsbury, 2014). Likewise, studies of Chesterton's theology, philosophy, and engagement with modernism continue to be written; Ralph Wood's *G. K. Chesterton: The Nightmare Goodness of God* (Baylor UP, 2011) and Aidan Nichols' *G. K. Chesterton, Theologian* (Sophia Institute, 2009) are good examples. However, studies dealing primarily with Chesterton's creative work remain largely unattempted; Ian Boyd's *Art and Propaganda: The Novels of G. K. Chesterton* (HarperCollins, 1975) is the only full-length study to focus specifically on Chesterton's fiction.

Amid the relative dearth of criticism on Chesterton's creative literary work, his poetry has occasioned almost no comment. Michael Lichens has recently pointed out that although various aspects of Chesterton's poetry were praised by Christopher Hitchens, W. H. Auden, and Graham Greene, critical interest in his poetry has not materialized. While there are a few studies of Chesterton's two famous long poems, *The Ballad of the White Horse* (1911) and *Lepanto* (1911), the rest of his poetry, comprising three volumes in the Ignatius Collected Works series (1994–2010), has garnered only a handful of articles. The most notable is Harold Petitpas' 1971 *Renascence* piece, which addresses Chesterton's metapoetics. Petitpas concludes that Chesterton's understanding of poetry is grounded in his ontology: "the primal fact that things really are, that they really are there, that they are stubbornly other" (138).[3] Although Petitpas compares Chesterton's metapoetics with those of Wordsworth, Blake, and Maritain, contemporary criticism has bypassed most of his poetry.

---

2   At its core, this understanding of imagination and being is grounded in the theological tradition of the *analogia entis*. David Bentley Hart provides a useful short definition of this tradition:

I use the term "analogy of being" as a shorthand for the tradition of Christian metaphysics that, developing from the time of the New Testament through the patristic and medieval periods, succeeded in uniting a metaphysics of participation to the biblical doctrine of creation, within the framework of trinitarian dogma, and in so doing made it possible for the first time in Western thought to contemplate the utter difference of being from beings and the nature of true transcendence. (241)

3   Two principles follow from this for Chesterton, according to Petitpas; first, that poetry is Romantic in that it is concerned with the "elemental," the "mythic," the "subliminal stirrings within the psyche" in response to the real fact of the world (139, 144). Second, poetry is Christian because its goal is to "attune" people to the harmonies and mysteries of being (143).

The lack of attention paid to Chesterton's poetry may be because the quality of the work is uneven and much of it is occasional poetry or light nonsense verse; this problem is deepened by the sheer number of poems. The three volumes of poetry in Ignatius' *Collected Works* list over 1,000 titles. Moreover, Chesterton's poems in both their style—they rely heavily on rhyme and meter—and their content—nationalist, Catholic, distributist, pugilistic, and traditionalist—run counter to many modern sensibilities.[4] However, many of his poems deserve more notice, especially his Christmas poetry, which Ralph Wood identifies as his best, and his poetry of gratitude (Wood 36).

In addition to his Christmas poems and poetry of gratitude, much of Chesterton's poetry is concerned with battle, chivalry, and history and thus bears Arthurian overtones and nuances; in three poems, however, Chesterton deals with Arthur directly: "The Ballad of King Arthur," "The Grave of King Arthur," and "The Myth of Arthur." These poems fit thematically with his other poems of chivalry and battle; they are concerned with the value of myth in general and the Christian character of the myth of Arthur in particular. "The Myth of Arthur" responds to critics who doubt the historicity and therefore the reality of Arthur. "The Ballad of King Arthur" reflects on the importance of legend in order to highlight the participation of the Arthurian legend in the larger Christian story, that "endless tale / Whose old news never fails" (35–36).[5] The "Grave of Arthur" likewise links Arthur's death and foretold return with Christ's. Taken together, these three poems demonstrate Chesterton's understanding of the importance of Arthur, the meaning of myth, and the Christian provenance of the Arthurian saga.

"The Myth of Arthur"

Chesterton begins *A Short History of England* (1917) by defending his prerogative as a non-specialist to write a history. He claims that it is exactly his status as an amateur, as one of the common people, that guarantees his rights as an author since a popular history of England has not been properly accomplished. The so-called popular histories are "written against the people; and in them the populace is either ignored or elaborately proved to have been wrong," he argues (423). Chesterton specifically mentions John Green's *A Short History of the English People* (1874), but he has in mind all histories that claim to be popular and yet disregard the voice of the English people, especially of the medieval English population, as evidenced by their popular traditions.

King Arthur represents one of these popular traditions that are "trample[d]" on by historians, and "The Myth of Arthur" (1923) is directed against historians who practice the kind of anti-popular history that Chesterton bemoans in the introduction to *A Short History of England* (423). History, the kind of

---

4   In fact, the nuances of Chesterton's thought on many of these issues are beginning to be appreciated. The main opponent of Chesterton's fierce and fighting nationalism, for instance, is not other nations but imperialism generally and the British Empire particularly, as Anna Vaninskaya points out. Likewise, Chesterton's distributive economics are being rediscovered by groups like the Front Porch Republic who find in him a sympathetic voice for promotion of the local and the limited.

5   All citations of Chesterton's poetry are taken from *Collected Poetry Part I: The Collected Works of G. K. Chesterton* 10.

history that matters, the kind of history that is for everyone and not simply the specialist, for Chesterton, is personal and poetic. It is concerned with persons, persons who make history. Joseph McCleary begins his study of Chesterton's historical imagination with this point; according to McCleary, the importance of individuals formed by particular cultures is at the center of Chesterton's understanding of history (7). Since history is concerned with the human person, it is necessarily poetic, for poetry tells us how people have felt. The key passage for this theory, which critics widely acknowledge as the heart of Chesterton's historical method, comes from *The Everlasting Man*:

> We need a new thing; which may be called psychological history. I mean the consideration of what things meant in the mind of a man, especially an ordinary man; as distinct from what is defined or deduced merely from official forms or political pronouncements .... So long as we neglect this subjective side of history, which may more simply be called the inside of history, there will always be a certain limitation on that science which can be better transcended by art. So long as the historian cannot do that, fiction will be truer than fact. (139)

Standing on the outside of history in "The Myth of Arthur," the "learned man who never learned to learn" can only conclude from the evidence of smoke that fire doesn't burn and that tall tales must mean men are always short (1). The specialist critic, after examining the evidence, draws exactly the wrong conclusion: if there are many fabulous tales of Arthur, then he must indeed be a fable. The key fault of this kind of criticism, according to the poem, is that it ignores the enduring legacy of Arthur, the "one banner" which "all the background fills" (9). Whether he approaches Arthur through poetry or in his essays, Chesterton repeatedly argues that the thousand and one stories about Arthur testify to his historicity at least in the sense that those who came after him felt quite strongly about him. Rather than take account of the real and enduring feeling that Arthur has authored, modern historians ignore this legacy "lest human fable touch historic fact" (15). This is the anti-popular history that Chesterton so despises: a historical method that views human interpretation, development, and tradition as deceiving rather than disclosive. This historical approach views "myths as moths" and "fights them with a pin"; myth here is an object to be dispassionately dissected (16). Rest assured, Chesterton wryly comforts critics at the end of the poem, "You shall not be a myth, I promise you" (18).

For Chesterton, myths are not only positive but a constitutive element in history. History is a kind of poetry, or at least it needs poetry (Schwartz 59). After all, the human person is essentially poetic, according to Chesterton; thus, any study of the human person must address this dimension of the soul (*Orthodoxy* 32). Specialist histories, by virtue of their specialism, often miss these broad truths of the human person; this means that for Chesterton the best history is one that acknowledges the whole breadth of human existence; that is, a popular history.

In consequence, the best history of England is a popular history. This is what Chesterton thinks has not been done and what he sets out to do in *A Short History of England*. The link between the psychological history that he calls for in *The Everlasting Man* and the popular history of *A Short History of England* is clear. A popular history lays out that which really is popular in the two-fold sense of being possessed by everyone and of being imaginatively satisfying. This common pleasurable possession allows a glimpse into how persons of the past might actually have felt by examining those things about which they felt strongly enough to preserve; it highlights those things about which everybody felt passionately. The person of King Arthur is one of these popular things.

Arthur stands as a prime example of the kind of popular history that Chesterton calls for and practices because he really was popular; while this fact is held against him by the historians in "The Myth of Arthur," for Chesterton it demonstrates his real importance. After all, Chesterton points out in his Preface to *The Ballad of the White Horse*, it is popular legends that make the heroes interesting in the first place: "It is enough for me to maintain two things: that they [stories of Alfred] are popular traditions; and that without these popular traditions we should have bothered about Alfred about as much as we bother about Eadwig" (xxxv). The same argument applies to Arthur; it is the popular stories about him, such as his carrying an image of the Blessed Virgin on his shield, which are the most interesting. For Chesterton, Arthur stands as the representative of the old Roman order on the edge of the enchanted forest full of barbarians and elves, and because he is popular he tells us something about England as a whole with regard to Rome, order, and adventure.

First, Arthur demonstrates that England is Roman. The relevance of this thesis is demonstrated by Rémi Brague's 2002 book *Eccentric Culture*, whose thesis is that Europe ought to be understood as essentially Roman (22). Brague argues that the core of the Roman contribution is transmission: "This is precisely the content of the Roman contribution: the structure of the transmission of a content not properly its own. The Romans have done little more than transmit, but that is far from nothing" (32). In light of this, Brague argues that "to be Roman is to experience the ancient as new and as something renewed by its transplantation in a new soil, a transplantation that makes the old a principle of new developments" (34). It is this transmission, renewal, and dynamic continuity that Brague argues is at the heart of the European experience. Chesterton's Arthurian poems offer a confession of this transmission through their repeated references to Rome as a principle that lies at the foundation of the national consciousness and history. "The Ballad of King Arthur" references the time when "Britain trod the Roman way," and "The Grave of Arthur" describes the inscription on Arthur's tomb as the "Roman rhyme" (3, 26). Chesterton claims in *A Short History of England* that England and France do not merely have Roman remains; "They are Roman remains" (429).

Second, this land of Roman remains is a land where Roman Christian heroes go on adventures. This principle is at the heart of Chesterton's understanding of England and his tendency to regard all of England as fairyland. Fairyland might be wherever we happen to find ourselves, could we but see it; however, the English fairyland is particularly nuanced by the fact that beneath the English soil lie Rome and Romance. In *A Short History of England*, Chesterton imagines the Roman ruins buried like ancient bones beneath the English soil; all English adventures take place on top of this archaic foundation (429). Rome, the Church, rationality, and order precede fairyland, adventure, magic, and topsyturvydom. Thus, in Chesterton's poem "Modern Elfland," the speaker begins by gathering materials in a "churchyard copse" before he sets off to fairyland. Likewise, Arthur stands at the end of the Roman order in the midst of the chaos, and his appeal, his persuasive enduring legend, is based on this fact (*Short History* 437–38). In his 1922 article for the *Illustrated London News* "King Arthur: Myth and History," Chesterton argues that, regardless of his historical status, Arthur endures because he was one of the Christian heroes who defended Christian, Roman Britain against the heathens.

Benedict Anderson's *Imagined Communities* provides a helpful theoretical definition that enables us to better understand the place that Arthur holds for Chesterton. In an attempt to account for the startling rise of Nationalism since the late 1700s, Anderson argues that the nation is an "imagined political community—and imagined as both inherently limited and sovereign" (6). Fergal Casey has recently demonstrated the way in which Chesterton, particularly in *The Napoleon of Notting Hill*, anticipates Anderson's claims about the imagined limited community of the nation and the dangers of "official" nationalism (85). The importance of this definition for Chesterton's understanding of Arthur lies not in the particular qualities Anderson assigns to Nationalism, limited and sovereign, but in the idea that all communities are imagined; they are a creative construct that members hold in common. "Communities can thus be distinguished," Anderson claims, "by the style in which they are imagined" (6). This describes Chesterton's approach to history generally and Arthur's central place in English history particularly.

Although Anderson juxtaposes the "style in which [communities] are imagined" with an attempt to discover their "falsity/genuineness," Chesterton links the two; that is, imaginings can be richer or poorer, more or less conducive to human flourishing, closer to or further from rightly naming the kind of things that people are or that the world is. This point is made explicit in almost all of the battles that occur in Chesterton's work; the protagonists win first and foremost not because of their superior fighting ability but because of their imagined community, their imagined construction of themselves and their cause. Before the Battle of Ethandune, Alfred tells Guthrum, king of the Danes, after he has sung a song that confesses the ennui of nihilism, that "your end is on you" not because the Danes are pagan or the English heroic but because "it is only Christian men / Guard even heathen things" (3.371–72). Only the Christians can imagine the world as a thing worth saving, even the pagan parts of it; Guthrum can imagine no reason for saving anything. The difference between the two forces lies in their imagination of who they are and what they are doing. Likewise, Adam Wayne confesses at the end of *The Napoleon of Notting Hill* that he and his forces will be defeated in battle, and that they should be, that their defeat is right (119). Wayne and his Notting Hill forces ought to be defeated because their patriotism has become imperial and refuses the other boroughs of London their own honor and celebrations; flushed with the thrill of their original victory, the people of Notting Hill cannot conceive of the patriotism of those they have conquered. The imaginations of these communities demonstrate their essential characters; for this reason, Chesterton emphasizes the importance of Arthur.

"The Ballad of King Arthur"

Arthur, Chesterton claims, stands at the heart of the imagined community of England. He marks the presence of order and adventure, derived from Rome and Christianity, in the midst of the breakdown of the Roman Empire and the invasion of the Anglo-Saxon pagans. "The Ballad of King Arthur" presents the Roman, Christian Arthur as distinct from both his pagan foes and also the future monarchs of England.

"The Ballad of King Arthur" begins by recounting Arthur's victory at Mount Badon as a way to reflect on the particularly Christian provenance of Arthurian legend. As we have seen, for Chesterton, Arthur stood for the desperate defense of Christian Britain against the barbarians, and "The Ballad" celebrates that fact by recounting the battle at Badon. Badon is traditionally one of Arthur's great victories against the Saxons. Nennius lists it as the final battle in his litany of Arthur's twelve victories in *The History of the Britons*, and the *Welsh Annals* contain the following entry for the year 516: "The Battle of Badon, in which Arthur carried the cross of our Lord Jesus Christ on his shoulders for three days and three nights and the Britons were the victors" (qtd. in Halsall 20). Whether or not the battle actually happened, the tradition certainly holds that Badon represents one of Arthur's crucial victories against the pagans. Nennius' emphasis on Arthur's carrying the cross into battle reinforces the religious dimensions of the contest.

In Chesterton's poem, Arthur is particularly associated with Rome; this account of the battle occurs, after all, "When Britain trod the Roman way" and the sky above the battlefield is dim with the missiles "reared yet of Roman arts" (3, 12). Yet this is the Rome not merely of Caesar but also of Peter; the sun sets on the field and "hid[e]s the Roman wall / That hid[e]s the Christian town" (27–28). Indeed, it is Christianity, in the person of the Blessed Virgin, that Arthur is defending and that watches his triumph on Badon. Arthur carries an image of the Virgin Mary on the inside of his shield, and the field of battle is repeatedly described as an "altar" (19, 21).[6] The first part of the poem concludes with Mary's statue standing on Mount Badon, the witness to Arthur's victory and the defense of Roman Britain against the heathens.

However, after establishing Mary as the Queen behind Arthur's victory, the poem turns to questions of narrative and tale:

> Great tales are told of dead men gone
> And all men live by tales
> And glory be to the endless tale
> Whose old news never fails. (33–36)

This progress serves to link Arthur's tale to Christ's and to rescue myth from unbelief. These lines highlight the necessity of story. Chesterton claims in *The Defendant* that fiction (not literature) is necessary (17). Yet these tales we live by are not mere fabrications; after all, these tales concern "dead men gone," actual people of the past. Telling these stories of those who have died is an action that is natural to us. Nor is the action merely natural, but also a guide that structures our understanding of ourselves and our world; we all live by stories. Thus, this discussion of story leads directly to the Gospel; considering the tales of Arthur and his place in history makes sense within the "endless tale / Whose old news never fails." To

---

6   In "King Arthur: Myth and History," Chesterton cites the legend that Arthur carried some religious object into battle at Badon; although Nennius describes that item as a cross, earlier in the catalogue of Arthur's battles he describes the king as carrying an image of Mary into battle at Castell Guinnion (Halsall 19).

discuss story, myth, and legend is to discuss Christ, a point which my discussion of "The Grave of Arthur" will deal with at length.

After this account of narrative comes a list of the ways in which Arthur's story has been tampered with or added to, particularly by Tudor poets and monarchs. Fairies steal the "Roman" sword and cast over the tale an atmosphere of glamor and fiction (43). Yet far worse than the fairies are the Queens with whom Arthur's story has been mixed, the "dames of France / and witches out of Wales" (45–46). Then follows a litany of three Queens: Guinevere, Elizabeth I, and the Faerie Queene, who are praised by many yet distract us from the real importance of Arthur. Watching Guinevere walk with Lancelot and capture the attention of the world, Arthur "shrinks to a shadow" (61). This popularity of the Arthurian cycle and diminishment of Arthur himself continues into the next stanza: "The presses throbbed, the books piled high, / the chant grew rich and strong" (65–66). Yet this popularity of the "Virgin Queen" who has "much esteem for song" and of the "Faerie Queen" who has "Heard every fairy tale" is rooted in a misunderstanding of Arthur or at least a forgetfulness of who he was and what he meant (67, 69).

It is worthy of note that Chesterton links this fascination with Arthur to the Tudors, with the references to Elizabeth and Spenser. Indeed, John Burrow notes that the Tudors were obsessed with the Arthurian cycle; Henry VII named his first son Arthur (220). Arthur's allure for the Tudors came partly from Caxton's 1485 publication of Malory's *Morte d'Arthur*, according to Katie Stevenson, but also from a recognition that the legend of Arthur held serious political potential (608). Linking oneself and one's family to Arthur entailed inheriting both the glamour of Arthur and his rightful rule. As the famous King of Britain, Arthur stood as a symbol of political and dynastic legitimation for not only the Tudors but also the Stuarts of Scotland; James IV named his second son Arthur as well, for reasons quite similar to Henry VII's (Stevenson 608).

The role of the King's Champion at the coronation provides a good practical example of the enduring importance and presence of the Arthurian cycle for English monarchs. Aisling Byrne recounts the practice, beginning in 1377 and continuing until the 1800s, of the King's Champion who would enter the coronation feast on his horse and deliver a challenge to all present, daring anyone to dispute the right of the newly crowned monarch to rule (506–07). Byrne argues that this spectacle draws directly on Arthurian romance and demonstrates the importance of that romance to "English monarchical self-imaginings" (516). Likewise, the Kenilworth entertainments that lasted eighteen days in 1575 at Kenilworth Castle drew on Arthurian Legend—on her arrival, Elizabeth was met by the Lady of the Lake, who happened to live in the lake that surrounded the castle—to promote a Tudor "nationalist mythology" (Ellis 4). For the Tudors, Arthur was an important symbol who could substantiate their claims to rule.

This imagining of Arthur was not without its troubles for the Tudors, however. Andrew Escobedo details the way in which the Tudors, in the midst of their celebration of Arthur, were also concerned to disentangle the historical truth of Arthur from the fantastical tales told of him: a task that was simultaneously an attempt to establish a firmly non-Catholic, or at least non-Roman, national origin (128–29). For Henry VIII and his heirs—excluding Mary, obviously—Christianity in Britain needed a foundation other than Augustine of Canterbury's mission authorized by Gregory the Great. The Arthurian cycle provided a solution to this problem, however, in the person of Joseph of Arimathea, whose legendary arrival at Glastonbury provided "spiritual legitimacy" to early Reformation England (Stout 253).

This Tudor concern for Arthur as a foundation of historical, political, and spiritual legitimacy sets up the conclusion of Chesterton's poem, which argues against the Tudor interpretation of history through acknowledging the centrality of Mary to Arthur's rule. Having established all the ways in which Arthur's legend has been mixed with various women—Guinevere, Elizabeth, and the Faerie Queen—the poem ends by imagining all the Tudor celebrations of the Arthurian Romance crashing to a halt "if one such flash made plain / The Queen that stands at his right hand / If Arthur comes again" (78–80). Arthur does not underwrite Tudor historiography; quite the opposite: he demonstrates the real Catholic origin of English Christianity through his special devotion to the Blessed Virgin. "The Ballad of Arthur" argues for the special Christian provenance of Arthur; he stands as one of the great heroes who defended the faith of Rome against the Germanic invasion.

"The Grave of Arthur"

Chesterton concludes "The Ballad of King Arthur" with reference to the possibilities of Arthur's return, and this prophesied return is the central theme of "The Grave of Arthur," which considers how the mystery of both the history and the future of Arthur might be approached. "The Grave of Arthur" is the most complex of Chesterton's Arthurian poems. Taking up the central ideas about myth, history, and England that the other two poems present, "The Grave of Arthur" deals with the themes in a more nuanced way; the poem does not have a clear opponent at which Chesterton tilts, as his other two poems about Arthur do. Instead, the poem more directly addresses the mystery of Arthur as such; the answers that it provides are cryptic, and the images it offers more difficult to unravel than in the other two poems.

The epigraph of the poem gives the traditional formula for Arthur's grave: *Hic Jacet Arturus Rex Quondam Rexque Futurus*, and the poem itself begins at Glastonbury, the traditional home of Joseph of Arimathea and the Holy Grail. This location links Arthur with Christ—two kings who have died and yet live on and whose return is prophesied. Yet Glastonbury here is presented mythically or at least mysteriously; down beneath "the last long roots of the Glaston Thorn" lies Arthur: "Dead is the King that never was born / Dead is the King that never shall die" (2–4). The straightforward declaration of these lines highlights the paradox that each presents, the first a paradox of beginnings and the second a paradox of conclusions.

In the next stanza, however, the poem moves from this mythic register to the account of the discovery of Arthur's tomb at Glastonbury in 1191. Gerald of Wales provides a contemporary record of the unearthing of Arthur's tomb by monks from the abbey; they found the wooden casket buried deep in an oak between two stone pyramids. Gerald goes on to describe many wondrous facts of the exhumation: a lock of Guinevere's hair, the leaden cross on the inside of the sepulcher, the oral tradition given to Henry II by a British poet about the location of the tomb. Of importance to Chesterton's poem is Gerald's note that the bones of Arthur were of gigantic stature; the distance between the eye sockets and eyebrows of Arthur's skull measured more than the width of a palm. These details of the discovery of Arthur's tomb account for the second and third stanzas of Chesterton's poem, which recount the exhumation with reference to the "pyramids" and the "giant bones" (5, 9).

Scholars suspect the veracity of the 1191 discovery of Arthur's body. Adam Stout notes the great importance of Glastonbury Abbey in the Middle Ages; just behind Westminster in wealth and prestige, Glastonbury's own historians promoted an "elaborate mythology" regarding the origin and heritage of their monastery (250).[7] The poem acknowledges in the second stanza that the discovery is mediated by tradition: "They found him … men say" (5–6). The referent for "they" is nonspecific, pointing toward the "they" of history generally; this fact is reinforced by the observation that our knowledge of the event is based on what "men say."

Regardless of what body was exhumed in 1191, by turning to a historical account, the poem takes up the paradox offered in the first stanza by presenting the deceased body of the king "who was never born" and who "shall never die." Nor is the discovery of Arthur's body accompanied by resurrection; unlike Christ, Arthur does not arise to take up his mantle as the future king. There is no "rending nor rolling away / Of linen nor lifting of coffin-lids" (7–8). By first ascribing mythic qualities to Arthur and then describing his corpse and denying his body any death-defying properties, the first three stanzas set up the problem with which the rest of the poem grapples: how are we to understand the apparent contradictions of myth and history, between what is prophesied, "the king who shall never die" and what is, no "rolling away / Of linen"?

To pursue this mystery of identity, time, and myth, the poem turns to a description of the two objects with which Arthur's body is found: a horn on his left side and a sword on his right. The horn is described with circular and sinuous language; it is "coiled" and "curled," white as Jormungandr, the Mid-Gard serpent, and carved with sea snakes (13, 16). The sword, on the other hand, is "cross-hilted" and engraved with images of the Second Coming of Christ (18). This contrast between the pagan circle, represented by the encircling serpent, which stands for futility and recurring fate, and the Christian cross, which represents drama, action, and paradox, is a common Chestertonian trope.[8] He speaks at length on each symbol as demonstrative of pagan and Christian sensibilities in *Orthodoxy*, and the conflict between the circle and the cross is central to his novel *The Ball and the Cross*.

In the poem, Arthur lies between these pagan and Christian symbols, between "the first and the last he lies / And between the false and the true dreams he" (21–22). These lists of opposites—horn and cross, first and last, false and true dreams—all circle around the mystery of Arthur that is at its core a mystery of identity: he is both the once and future king. The end of the sixth stanza, the exact midpoint of the poem, reiterates this mystery: "Born without birth of a fabled sea / Armoured in death till the dead shall rise" (23–24). Arthur is born of fable, yet actually dead and ready to return with the Judgment.

---

7   Stout's premise assumes the historical outlook that Chesterton repeatedly bemoaned: because Glastonbury was important and powerful, therefore a suitably marvelous history must be invented for it. It is more sensible as a historical method, Chesterton argues in both *The Everlasting Man* and *A Short History of England*, to think that Glastonbury was the site of something marvelous and therefore was important and powerful.

8   Schwartz notes that for Chesterton, as for Augustine, history is linear rather than cyclical or circular (58).

The second half of the poem takes up this riddle of Time and Truth. "Forth and Backward the Roman rhyme," which is the Latin epigraph, "rolls in a ring that mocks at time / Tolling the truth that none can tell" (26–28). How is it that Arthur is actually the once and future king? No one can tell, at least on this side of Eternity. In Heaven, "the glass wherein God remembers tomorrow," the mystery of Arthur can finally be learned; it is there that the "riddle be learnt which is past all learning" (31, 38). This learning recalls Chesterton's castigation of academics who "never learned to learn" in "The Myth of Arthur." The riddle once finally learnt in Heaven is that Arthur is both Myth and Man who is "ever returning / And ever delaying" until the Second Coming (39–40).

The final two stanzas address what must happen until death finally reveals why truth "speaks double in dreams and day" and what must happen until the person of Arthur and the Myth of Arthur are finally conjoined (42). This culmination will occur at the return of Christ, where the whole eschatological sense of the poem will finally be resolved, and history, time, and myth will be joined and fulfilled. Yet until that final reconciliation occurs, we are left with the last stanza of the poem. The "dream shall wail through the worm-shaped horn / 'Dead is a King that was never born'" to which the "trumpet of truth" from the Cross replies, "Dead is the King who shall not die" (46–48).

The poem contrasts the actual Arthur with the mythic Arthur; he is both the body found and the man born of legend. Why both of these are permitted and how they are to be reconciled will only be answered at the Second Coming of Christ. Myth and History will only be fully joined at the Judgment. This is why the referent for the undying king becomes Christ at the end of the poem—the person in whom myth and History have been fully joined. All of the juxtapositions of the poem—between myth and truth, dream and day, pagan sorrow and Christian joy—are finally referred to the mystery of Christ.

This conclusion bears strong similarities to Tolkien's "On Fairy-stories." There Tolkien concludes that the fairy tale of the Gospel is a story that "embraces all the essence of fairy-stories" (78). The Gospel is the "specially beautiful fairy-story" that is "primarily true" without losing any of its "mythical or allegorical significance" (78). In the person of Christ, in Tolkien's famous phrase, "Legend and History have met and fused" (78). This meeting has implications for all other myths; the Incarnation has not done away with legends but has "hallowed them" (78).

"The Grave of Arthur" ends by pointing toward this truth. The final line of the poem substitutes Christ for Arthur. While the dream from the horn uses the indefinite article to describe the dead king, the trumpet from the Cross declares that this is "*the* king" who shall not die (emphasis added). The truth of the Incarnation and Resurrection of Christ becomes the final referent for understanding the meaning of Arthur, both the man and the myth. Arthur lies in the strange light of the Cross, and he must be read by that light. Arthur's return to which the poem looks forward is linked to Christ's own return. The truth of the Incarnation makes possible the truth of the once and future King. As Christ rose, so Arthur will rise.

In outlining Chesterton's theology of history, Schwartz argues that the historicist, while resembling the historian, the philosopher, and the scientist, is most of all like the poet in "realizing the mystery of being" through "using chiefly his imagination and his extraordinary sympathy for life" (58). It is in this sense that Chesterton approaches history as a riddle or a mystery: "To understand the whole, he seeks mytho-poetic truth, seeing patterns and then a design which brings the patterns into a whole—some overarching plot, as it were" (Schwartz 58). This method is clearly Chesterton's approach in "The Grave of Arthur"; he reads Arthur in the light and pattern of Christ. Arthur's prophesied resurrection makes sense within the Resurrection of Christ and His redemption of the whole of human existence.

Stratford Caldecott makes a similar point about the historical imagination with regard to England in particular. Because the whole cosmos is contingent, the "Great Might-Not-Have-Been" (*Orthodoxy* 64), not necessary but rather the act of a Creator, therefore imaginative creation that engages the mystery of being is a constitutive element of basic perception. England "cannot be perceived," Caldecott claims, unless we "view it as an imaginative construction, in other words as a story" (113). England can only be seen, Caldecott continues, "wrapped in the mists of imagination, in the myths and folklore that tell us what it feels like to belong to this landscape and this tradition" (113). Chesterton's Arthurian poems demonstrate the central importance of Arthur to this imagining of England—it is in this sense that Chesterton claims that Arthur is more real than Alfred (*Short History* 439).

Arthur stands at the heart of the English imagination or of the mythical geography of England; first he tells us what England "feels like," what England has meant to the English. Arthur gives us the history from the inside that Chesterton calls for. But even more than this, Arthur enchants the English landscape because he is a historical myth—an actual person and yet a fable—"born without birth of a fabled sea" (23). The full truth of what he means must await the return of Christ, Chesterton argues in "The Myth of Arthur," for Arthur's primacy of place in imagining England is established by the fact that he is not the past King of England only. Arthur's meaning, whatever it may finally be, is a meaning for the future. He tells us what it *has* felt like to belong to the English landscape and tradition, but the much more mysterious truth is that Arthur also tells us what it *will* feel like to belong to that place. He is *Rex Futurus*.

For Chesterton, poetry's end is to direct readers to the unfathomable wonder of the world. In summarizing Chesterton's understanding of poetry, Petitpas claims that "poetry also should mirror the radical mystery of the universe ... Poetry realises its end when it makes men wonder at the universe" (144). Chesterton's Arthurian poems point to the mysterious person who looms so large in the English imagination: the "one banner all the background fills" ("The Myth of Arthur" 9). Through his conjoining of fact and mystery, Arthur offers a framework from which we can begin to wonder not only at the English past but also at our own histories. Arthur's enchanting and mythologizing of the English landscape ought to provide us eyes with which to see anew both that landscape and also the spaces of our own lives. The mystery that even now enchants the ruined arches of Glastonbury also dwells in our own homes and lies waiting outside our windows.

Works Cited

Anderson, Benedict. *Imagined Communities: Reflections on the Origin and Spread of Nationalism*. NY: Verso, 2006. Print.

Brague, Rémi. *Eccentric Culture: A Theory of Western Civilization*. Trans. Samuel Lester. South Bend, IN: St. Augustine's Press, 2002. Print.

Burrow, John. *A History of Histories: Epics, Chronicles, Romances and Inquiries from Herodotus and Thucydides to the Twentieth Century*. NY: Alfred A. Knopf, 2008. Print.

Byrne, Aisling. "The King's Champion: Re-Enacting Arthurian Romance at the English Coronation Banquet." *English Studies* 94.5 (2013): 505–18. Print.

Caldecott, Stratford. "Tolkien's Elvish England." *The Chesterton Review* 31.3 (2005): 109–23. Print.

Casey, Fergal. "A Celtic Twilight in Little England: G. K. Chesterton and W. B. Yeats." *Irish Studies Review* 22.1 (2014): 80–90. Print.

Chesterton, G. K. "The Ballad of King Arthur." *Collected Poetry*, Part 1. *The Collected Works of G. K. Chesterton* 10. San Francisco: Ignatius, 1994. 531–533. Print.

——. *The Ballad of the White Horse.* 1911. San Francisco: Ignatius, 1993. Print.

——. *Charles Dickens.* NY: Dodd, Mead, 1911.

——. *Collected Poetry, Part 1. The Collected Works of G. K. Chesterton* 10. San Francisco: Ignatius, 1994. Print.

——. *The Defendant.* 1901. Rockville, MD: Wildside, 2005. Print.

——. *The Everlasting Man.* 1925. San Francisco: Ignatius, 2008. Print.

——. "The Grave of Arthur." *Collected Poetry*, Part 1. *The Collected Works of G. K. Chesterton* 10. San Francisco: Ignatius, 1994. 542–543. Print.

——. "King Arthur: Myth and History." *Illustrated London News 1920–22. The Collected Works of G. K. Chesterton* 32. San Francisco: Ignatius, 1989. 502–06. Print.

——. "Modern Elfland." *Collected Poetry*, Part 1. *The Collected Works of G. K. Chesterton* 10. San Francisco: Ignatius, 1994. 233–234. Print.

——. "The Myth of Arthur." *Collected Poetry*, Part 1. *The Collected Works of G. K. Chesterton* 10. San Francisco: Ignatius, 1994. 555–556. Print.

——. *The Napoleon of Notting Hill.* 1904. Ware, Hertfordshire, UK: Wordsworth, 1996. Print.

——. *Orthodoxy.* 1908. NY: Doubleday, 1990. Print.

——. *A Short History of England. The Collected Works of G. K. Chesterton* 20. San Francisco: Ignatius, 2001. Print.

Ellis, Jim. "Kenilworth, King Arthur, and the Memory of Empire." *English Literary Renaissance* 43.1 (2013): 3–29. Print.

Escobedo, Andrew. "The Tudor Search for Arthur and the Poetics of Historical Loss." *Exemplaria* 14.1 (2002): 127–65. Print.

Gerald of Wales. "The Tomb of King Arthur." Trans. John Sutton. *The Camelot Project: A Robbins Library Digital Project.* U of Rochester, 2001. Web. 1 March 2015.

Halsall, Guy. *Worlds of Arthur: Facts and Fictions of the Dark Ages.* Oxford UP, 2013. Print.

Hart, David Bentley. *The Beauty of the Infinite: The Aesthetics of Christian Truth.* Grand Rapids, MI: Eerdmans, 2003. Print.

Lichens, Michael. "Chesterton the Poet." *World Catholic Report.* 3 March 2015. Web. 8 March 2015.

McCleary, Joseph. *The Historical Imagination of G. K. Chesterton: Locality, Patriotism, and Nationalism.* NY: Routledge, 2009. Print.

Petitpas, Harold. "Chesterton's Metapoetics." *Renascence* 23.3 (1971): 137–44. Print.

Schwartz, Joseph. "The Theology of History in *The Everlasting Man.*" *Renascence* 49.1 (1996): 57–66. Print.

Stevenson, Katie. "Chivalry, British Sovereignty and Dynastic Politics: Undercurrents of Antagonism in Tudor-Stewart Relations, c. 1490–c.1513." *Historical Research* 86.234 (2013): 601–18. Print.

Stout, Adam. "Grounding Faith at Glastonbury: Episodes in the Early History of Alternative Archaeology." *Numen* 59 (2012): 249–69.

Tolkien, J. R. R. *Tolkien on Fairy-stories: Expanded Edition with Commentary and Notes.* Eds. Verlyn Flieger and Douglas A. Anderson. London: HarperCollins, 2008. Print.

Wood, Ralph. "The Lady with the Torn Hair Who Looks on Gladiators in Grapple: G. K. Chesterton's Marian Poems." *Christianity and Literature* 62.1 (2012): 29–55. Print.

Vaninskaya, Anna. "'My mother, drunk or sober': G. K. Chesterton and Patriotic Anti-imperialism." *History of European Ideas* 34 (2008): 535–47. Print.

The Elegiac Fantasy of Past Christendom in J. R. R. Tolkien's *The Fall of Arthur*

Cory Grewell

The imaginative relationship of the Inklings to Arthurian myth and literature represents, among other things, an instance of a set of phenomena that Umberto Eco noticed throughout the twentieth century in the West that he described as a tendency to "return to the Middle Ages." In an essay titled "Dreaming of the Middle Ages" (1986), Eco writes that we "are at present witnessing, both in Europe and America, a period of renewed interest in the Middle Ages, with a curious oscillation between fantastic neomedievalism and responsible philological examination" (63). Eco's essay is a somewhat casual, yet incisive, analysis of the phenomenon of cultural medievalism and the various forms it took in the latter half of the twentieth century. About halfway through his exploration, Eco reaches the following provisional conclusion: "Our return to the Middle Ages is a quest for our roots and, since we want to come back to the real roots, we are looking for 'reliable Middle Ages,' not for romance and fantasy, though frequently this wish is misunderstood and, moved by a vague impulse, we indulge in a sort of escapism á la Tolkien" (65).

Eco's tentative conclusion has some relevance to J. R. R. Tolkien's employment of Arthurian myth in his medievalist poem *The Fall of Arthur* (the poem that it will be the task of this essay to examine in some depth), for a few reasons. One is that the poem is to a large extent a nostalgic literary attempt to "come back" to England's mythic "real roots," and despite the poem's romantic flavor, it is also in its own way a reconstruction of a "reliable Middle Ages." I will say more on this below. The second point of interest in Eco's statement is its seeming dismissal of Tolkienian fantasy—surely a reference to Tolkien's better-known *Lord of the Rings*—as somehow not representing a serious reconstruction of the Middle Ages. The dismissive critique of the non-literary or non-serious quality of Tolkienian fantasy is common enough; it is something that Tolkien sought to counter in his own lifetime in the essay "On Fairy-stories." More recently, Tom Shippey has both surveyed and countered the criticisms of Tolkienian fantasy in his book *J. R. R. Tolkien: Author of the Century.*

The Fall of Arthur ostensibly does not leave itself open to the same criticism of being merely escapist fantasy as *The Lord of the Rings* does. It is, after all, an unfinished verse account of a well-established literary subject in an archaic and relatively difficult meter. I mention Eco's dismissive critique here, however, because I will attempt to show that the medievalist enterprise that Tolkien is about in *The Fall of Arthur* has much in common with the medievalist enterprise of *The Lord of the Rings*, particularly in terms of a response to the fragmentation and despair of twentieth-century modernism. It would appear that, in many ways, the medievalism of *The Fall of Arthur* serves the same literary ends, including the fairy-story aspects of "recovery" and "consolation," that the medievalism of *The Lord of the Rings* does (Tolkien, OFS 75ff). A final point to note in Eco's definition is that it clearly, if implicitly, establishes literary fantasy—what Tolkien prefers to call Faërie (38)—as a type of twentieth-century medievalism; this identification of the fairy-story as a type of medievalism will underlie the remainder of this analysis.

In what follows, then, I propose to examine certain strains of medievalism in the poem and, where appropriate, compare them to similar themes in *The Lord of the Rings*—themes (in the trilogy) that have been amply treated in current criticism. In doing so, I will attempt to show how Tolkien's medievalism responds to, or at least converses with, certain aspects of twentieth-century modernism.[1] I will then go on to engage in a bit of analysis of how the specifically Arthurian medievalism in the poem differs from the more idiosyncratically mythologized medievalism of the trilogy and suggest some possible imaginative benefits as well as some drawbacks of invoking Arthur in an imaginative response to the twentieth century. Finally, I will briefly comment on Tolkien's revisions to the story of Arthur's fall that he received from the medieval tradition and suggest that the project, had it been finished, may have imaginatively comprised a sort of cultural recovery and held out the hope of a eucatastrophe for humankind, both of these latter aspects deeply colored with tinges of medieval Western Christendom.

Arthurian Medievalism

In his essay "Medievalisms and Why They Matter," Tom Shippey draws attention to the burgeoning number of cultural medievalisms in the twentieth century and, like Eco, attempts to explore what the phenomenon means for modern culture. At the outset, he tries to draw a working definition of medievalism that would comprehensively describe how it works in our time, and he begins by citing the definition for medievalism

---

1   I use the lower case for "modernism," because in the essay, I use the term to denote more than a particular movement in literature in the arts in the early part of the century. Rather, I intend the term to more comprehensively encompass a number of cultural developments and traits in the twentieth century, including but not necessarily limited to increased industrialization and reliance on technology, reliance on the hard sciences rather than religion and philosophy as repositories of truth, globalization and its appertaining multi-culturalism, mechanized warfare, a movement away from tradition in politics and the arts, etc. I mean, I suppose, to invoke something along the lines of what Patrick Curry has called the "values of modernity—statism, scientism, economism, and secularism" (36).

in the *Oxford English Dictionary*, which reads: "The system of belief and practice characteristic of the Middle Ages … the adoption of or devotion to mediæval ideals or usages; *occas.* An instance of this" (qtd. in Shippey 45).

As Shippey points out, the *OED* definition accurately describes many instances of modern cultural medievalism. The most recent edition has this similar, but differently nuanced, definition: "Beliefs and practices (regarded as) characteristic of the Middle Ages … the adoption of, adherence to, or interest in medieval ideals, styles, or usages. Occasionally: an instance of this" ("Medievalism"). Interestingly enough, Shippey cites one of the Inklings as an example of the definition's twentieth-century currency: "The *OED* sense of the word … remains perfectly familiar: when a very recent book on C. S. Lewis refers to Lewis' 'medievalism' (modern spelling), his 'devotion to medieval ideals and usages' is exactly what is meant" (45). However, as Shippey goes on to show, the proliferation of medievalism*s*, plural, in the twentieth century has made the relatively limited nature of the *OED* definition inadequate to describe them all. Thus, he offers the following as a more comprehensive definition: "Any post-medieval attempt to re-imagine the Middle Ages, or some aspect of the Middle Ages, for the modern world, in any of many different media; especially in academic usage, the study of the development and significance of such attempts" (45). Shippey's more comprehensive definition might seem rather superfluous when dealing with the works of J. R. R. Tolkien, which, like the works of Lewis, could be readily categorized as medieval according to the *OED*'s definition. Certainly, both *The Lord of the Rings* and *The Fall of Arthur* are both readily identifiable as instances of "devotion to medieval ideals." There is something in Shippey's definition, however, that deserves mention in connection with *The Fall of Arthur*. Perhaps unlike *The Lord of the Rings*, *The Fall of Arthur* is in its very construction a particular re-imagining of the real Middle Ages: if not a reconstruction of the actual, historic Middle Ages—we have agreed for some time that the mythos of Arthurian Britain is more the subject of fiction than history—then certainly of the Middle Ages as they were conceived in the medieval imagination. To put it more accurately and succinctly, the poem is a re-imagining of a mythos that was extremely prevalent and culturally influential in the historic Middle Ages. This fact will be of some importance to the latter part of this paper, where I will examine Tolkien's employment of a specifically Arthurian mythos. At present, however, I would like to return to Shippey's discussion of twentieth-century medievalisms in general and further examine its relevance to Tolkien's work.

Shippey is not alone in identifying a plurality of medievalisms in the last century. Eco does the same,[2] and both of them note that each re-imagining of the medieval tends to work toward a contemporary cultural purpose. Shippey's essay, for instance, presents a warning about the possible dangers of "forging" nationalist ethoi out of the mythic medieval past—citing, for instance, the Nazi's use of "a fictional medieval [Germanic] world brought into being by scholars and by poets" to garner popular appeal in the years prior to World War II (51). It is probably not claiming too much to say that the medievalism in the work of Tolkien, or any of the Inklings for that matter, is nothing so pernicious, but it does remain to look more specifically at the nature of the medievalist imagery in *The Fall of Arthur* and to describe its function as a particular instance of twentieth-century medievalism.

---

2   The plurality of medievalisms has become commonplace in critical discourse. I refer readers to virtually any issue of the journal *Studies in Medievalism* for fuller discussion.

In the introductory essay to the October 2013 issue of the *Journal of Inklings Studies*,[3] I took a cursory look at the medievalist imagery in the poem and made a tentative argument that it served nostalgic purposes, invoking the romantic and idealist world of Arthurian Christendom as a desirable alternative to what I there called the "fragmented moral morass of 20th century [sic] modernism" (6). I did not invoke Umberto Eco's taxonomy of medievalisms in that essay, but I would like to do so here. The particular re-imagining of the medieval in *The Fall of Arthur*, I would suggest, produces something very close to the sixth of Eco's "Ten Little Middle Ages," which he describes as follows. The sixth little Middle Ages is, according to Eco, "The Middle Ages of *national identities*, so powerful again during the [nineteenth] century, when the medieval model was taken as a political utopia, a celebration of past grandeur, to be opposed to the miseries of national enslavement and foreign domination" (70). Of course, it might immediately be pointed out that this brand of medievalism lends itself exactly to the kind of nationalistic impulse that Shippey describes as dangerous, but where Tolkien's medievalist ethos importantly differs is that, at least in *The Fall of Arthur*, it looks primarily back rather than forward and, in doing so, serves mythic rather than politically ideological purposes. It undoubtedly invokes dreams of a sort of political utopia (Camelot) and days of bygone virtue and glory, but those days are located irrevocably in the past—arguably that is the case even in the beginning of the poem—and therefore, even though the nostalgic imagery comprises an implicit critique of the much fallen state of the modern West, it poses little to no danger of providing the ideological basis for an aggressive nationalism *a lá* nineteenth- and twentieth-century Germany. On the contrary, the elegiac tone that permeates *The Fall of Arthur* gives the sense that the "celebration of past grandeur" in the poem is more of a funereal celebration than anything of a rallying cry, and though the poem has a strong martial element, the "opposition to miseries" is more suggestive of spiritual warfare than it is of anything resembling a military industrial complex. Another way of putting it might be to say that Tolkien's medievalism is aesthetic rather than political. The medieval imagery in the poem associated with Arthur's kingdom invokes a utopian, romantic—if already fading—ideal and opposes it to a nascent materialist and pragmatic imagery that, I would argue, is in many ways indicative of the decidedly un-romantic tendency toward the loss of shared cultural ideals in the twentieth century.[4]

It remains then to turn to the text of the poem itself and look more closely at the medievalist imagery we find there and then to attempt to describe the imaginative purpose it serves *vis-à-vis* engaging the cultural conversation of the twentieth century. Given that the poem is fragmentary, there is relatively little imagery to draw from, especially in comparison with the intricately developed medievalist world of *The Lord of the Rings*. Thus, limiting myself to what is extant and published, I want to look particularly at the

---

3   Indeed, that entire issue of *JIS* was devoted to examining the Inklings' uses of medievalist imagery as an imaginative Christian apologetic.

4   I should perhaps acknowledge here that this phrasing betrays a bias, though I feel confident it is a bias that Tolkien would share, toward the ideals of pre-twentieth-century Western culture. A different way of saying "loss of ideals" might be the more positive "disillusionment" or the still more positive "demystification." I cannot, however, see either of those articulations as being consistent with Tolkien's imaginative or, for that matter, critical work.

imagery of nature, the imagery of valor and martial chivalry, and the imagery of Christendom as they are presented in *The Fall of Arthur*. All of these sets of images can usefully be described as instances of medievalist nostalgia, what Eco calls "celebration of past grandeur," and opposition to the miseries that accompany twentieth-century modernism.

Nature

I mentioned above that, arguably, the days of past grandeur—Camelot's glory, so to speak—are already gone at the opening of the poem's action. Appropriate to a poem titled *The Fall of Arthur*, Tolkien's work focuses on the last days of Arthur's kingdom and his battle with the usurping Mordred. The poem opens with Arthur in the midst of an expedition into the east to wage war on the heathen who have been harassing Britain. This is Tolkien's version of the continental quest, common to much of the medieval Arthurian tradition,[5] which absents Arthur from his kingdom and consequently provides the opportunity for Mordred to usurp the throne. It is not until the fragmentary fifth canto of the poem, therefore, that we get any vision of the idyllic nature of Camelot in the heyday of Arthur's reign, and when it is presented, it is a reminiscence. In Canto 5, lines 1–11, Arthur is returning to Britain in a ship to launch an assault on Mordred's forces. He looks out over his land and remembers the past. Gazing over his lands, he yearns to walk over its green grass once more, smelling the salt from the sea and the "wine-scented // waft of clover" (5.6). He longs to be at peace, see the sunlight on the lawns, listen to bells ringing in his kingdom, and know the proximity to heaven. In this opening of canto 5, the imagery may not be terribly ornate, nor is it necessarily specific to Camelot or even to Tolkienian medievalism. It is pastoral imagery that could be typical of any number of nostalgic literary paeans to the rustic days of virtue preceding the corruption of any relatively "modern" civilization. However, there are a few phrases in Arthur's reminiscence that point to a more particularly medievalist mythos, which, in turn, provides a desirable nostalgic alternative to the ethos of twentieth-century modernism.

It is interesting to note that the first thing to come into Arthur's mind as he looks over his kingdom is the desire to walk "on the grass again // there green swaying" (5.3). The image is almost Wordsworthian in its romantic valence. The greenness of the grass, the pleasant smell of the "wine-scented" clover, and the sunlight on the lawn seem to have a very romantic—if momentary—restorative quality to Arthur's soul (and by extension, to the modern reader's).[6] The romantically restorative power of the image is two-fold and is in both aspects dependent on the percipient (i.e. Arthur and by extension the reader) for its effectiveness.

One aspect of the restoration (or, to use Tolkien's term, Recovery) is the renewal of wonder in nature. Tolkien writes in "On Fairy-stories" that we "should look at green again, and be startled anew ... by blue

---

5   For a particularly useful survey of this tradition and its relevance as source material for Tolkien's poem, readers should examine Christopher Tolkien's chapter, "The Poem in the Arthurian Tradition," appended to *FoA* (73–122).

6   R. J. Reilly has commented extensively on the importance of Romanticism to the projects of Tolkien and fellow Inklings Lewis, Williams, and Barfield in *Romantic Religion*, cited below.

and yellow and red" (77). In the context, Tolkien is talking about overcoming our familiarity with created "things" in nature and seeing them for the dynamic, living entities that they are. R. J. Reilly, commenting on Tolkien's concept of Recovery as it is presented in "On Fairy-stories," writes:

> Recovery is a means of "seeing things as we are (or were) meant to see them ..." ([Tolkien] p. 74). All things become blurred by familiarity; we come to possess them, to use them, to see them only in relation to ourselves. In so doing we lose sight of what the things themselves really are *qua* things—and "things" here includes people, objects, ideas, moral codes, literally everything. (205)

One of the key problems with the blurred vision of familiarity is, as Reilly notes, the way in which it leads to possessiveness. Things, including the created things of Nature—and that includes other people—become dead objects to be possessed and put to pragmatic use. Incidentally, this is exactly the attitude taken toward both nature and the people in it by the villainous Mordred in *The Fall of Arthur*, as I will demonstrate below. The attitude is also characteristic, as Tolkien goes on to say in "On Fairy-stories," of "modern European life" with its "Morlockian horrors of factories" and its deluded view of the world as "one big glass-roofed railway station" (82).

It almost goes without saying that the recovery of the romantic, mythic, or medievalist—in this context all of the adjectives refer to the same thing—view of nature is a good thing because that perspective is more moral than the modern alternative. The medievalist perspective appreciates created things for what they are and enjoys them as they are rather than pragmatically evaluating them for what they can *do* for the observer. As Reilly says, the romantic view is substantially less egotistical and selfish, and one of the main goals of medievalist fantasy literature is to move the reader outside of the self. "Fantasy," Reilly argues, "provides the recovery necessary to those of us who do not have humility; the humble do not need Fantasy because they already see things as not necessarily related to themselves; their vision is not qualified by selfishness or egotism" (205–06).

The older view of nature is not only morally superior, however. According to Tolkien and the other Inklings, it is also a truer, more accurate view of nature, and in recovering this view, we thus recuperate a vision that has been blinded, blurred by familiarity, to the point that we no longer discern what is in fact real. Tolkien argues: "The notion that motor cars are more 'alive' than, say, centaurs or dragons is curious; that they are more 'real' than, say, horses is pathetically absurd. How real, how startlingly alive is a factory chimney compared with an elm-tree: poor obsolete thing, insubstantial dream of an escapist!" (OFS 81).[7] Reilly points us to C. S. Lewis' preface to the volume *Essays Presented to Charles Williams*, where Lewis asserts: "The value of myth is that it takes all the things we know and restores to them the rich significance which has been hidden by 'the veil of familiarity.' ... by putting bread, gold, horse, apple, or the very roads into myth, we do not retreat from reality: we discover it" (Lewis vi).

---

7   Hopefully the end exclamation point is not necessary to detect the tone of irony in Tolkien's last sentence here.

Recovering a true view of the dynamic reality of nature leads to the second aspect of recovery that is offered by the imagery in Arthur's reminiscence, and this is the idea of human participation in nature. Arthur's desire is to be actively present in the nature that was his kingdom. He longs to wander wherever his fancy takes him, communing with nature. Moreover, there is an implied synergy between the human aspects of his realm, what we might call the sub-created things of his kingdom, such as the sound of bells, and nature itself. Arthur's reign is retrospectively described as having been peaceful, "a holy realm // beside Heaven's gateway" (5.11). The image is one of a king who manages all aspects of his reign, including civil government, infrastructure, and the church in harmony with the created natural order. The picture is consistent with the world of Faërie that Tolkien describes in "On Fairy-stories" as the product of humanity's participatory sub-creative faculty (51). It is also consistent with what fellow Inkling Owen Barfield calls the "Medieval Environment," a worldview that sees the cosmos as a dynamic result of human participation with the divine.

To fully extrapolate Barfield's theory of participation would take significantly more space than I have here,[8] but the key relevance of Barfield's account of medieval participation to the medievalist imagery Tolkien employs in this poem is its emphasis on the synthetic unity between the king and his kingdom (i.e. nature). Barfield writes that, according to the medieval worldview, "Earth, Water, Air and Fire are part of ourselves, and we of them" (77). The things of creation in Barfield's account are far from dead, static objects to be possessed. Rather, the very cosmos itself is alive, participating in a dynamic synthesis with the humans that inhabit it. The medieval man, he argues, understood this. "If it is daytime," he writes, medievals "see the air filled with light proceeding from a living sun, rather as [their] own flesh is filled with blood proceeding from a living heart" (76). This medievalist sense of dynamic participation with the world is one of the things that can be recovered through the employment of the Faërie, medievalist imagery in Tolkien's poem.

Admittedly, this aspect of recovery that is provided by the imagery of symbiotic and synthetic participation with nature is inferred from rather sparse evidence in Tolkien's poem, but the symbiosis with nature of Arthur's reign in the poem is greatly highlighted when viewed in contrast to the sterile, possessive pragmatism of Mordred's usurped realm.

Throughout the poem, the imagery associated with Mordred is bleak, dark, and cold. The second canto of the poem, which focuses on Mordred's actions in usurped Britain, is littered with moribund, negative adjectives such as "drear and doubtful," "cold," "wan," and "grim." Some form of the word "dark" occurs no fewer than nine times in the space of the canto's two hundred and ten lines. The whole of the canto is profoundly unhappy. The imagery coalesces, however, in the fragmentary fifth canto in lines that follow Arthur's nostalgic reminiscence, referenced above. What Arthur actually sees on the shore of Britain from his ship deck as he waits at anchor is the polar opposite of the participatory symbiosis he remembers. Canto 5, lines 13–25, describes Mordred's Britain. In this description, there is a great deal of direct contrast with the Britain that Arthur nostalgically remembers. Under Mordred, the grass is "withered," and the wheat is

8   Christopher Gaertner explores Barfield's concept of "participation" at some length in chapter 5 of the present volume. [Editor's note]

"trampled." Rather than the "wine-scented // waft of clover," the poetry evokes the acrid scent of the burnt towers. The very ground groans under Mordred's treachery. Nor is nature the only element to suffer. The human additions to creation—Arthur's sub-creations, if you will—are also destroyed: the bells are silent and the towers are burned. Clearly, just as nature flourished in Arthur's realm, it suffers under Mordred's.

It would seem that nature in Britain suffers under Mordred because he is intent on sacrificing its well-being to his ends of military might and political power. To Mordred, Britain is something to be possessed. All of the things—including nature and people—in Britain are his to *use* toward the end of slaking his thirst for power. Interestingly enough, Mordred's possessiveness even extends to Britain's queen. Canto 2 records his overtures to Guinever in Arthur's absence, which are anything but romantic. He does not urge love or even desire on Guinever as a reason for their union; his argument is made from pragmatism. "The West is waning," he tells Guinever (2.147); neither Arthur nor Lancelot is returning. Guinever should accept his suit, he argues, because he is clearly in the ascendant. No higher reason is given, and on the basis of this pragmatic reasoning, he gives her the choice to lie at his side as either "slave or lady," "wife or captive" (2.154–55). As with the rest of Britain, Guinever is a thing to be possessed. Nor is she the only person who is something to be used in Mordred's economy. His army is composed almost entirely of mercenaries and those seeking to opportunistically climb the ladder of rank.

In his characterization as a pragmatic, time-marking grabber of power and destroyer of nature, Mordred is very similar to the character of Saruman in *The Lord of the Rings*. Tom Shippey has drawn attention to Saruman's "modernistic" pragmatism in *J. R. R. Tolkien: Author of the Century*, where he notes that the wizard's attempt to persuade Gandalf that they should side with Sauron is motivated by "no other reason than that it [Sauron's army] is going to win" (75). Like Mordred, Saruman is a time-marker and a power-grabber. Like Mordred, he tends to see Middle-earth and its denizens as things that can be used to his own ends, and like Mordred, he is perfectly willing to ruin nature to reach his military-industrial goals: witness the destruction of Fangorn forest and his depredation of the Shire. Interestingly, Shippey sees Saruman as symbolic of twentieth-century politics in his pragmatism, his philosophy of the political end justifying the means, and his twisting of rhetoric to serve his purposes. "Saruman," he argues, "is the most contemporary figure in Middle-earth, both politically and linguistically. He is on the road to 'doublethink' (which Orwell was to invent, or describe, at almost exactly the same time)" (76).

There is perhaps less to explicitly mark Mordred as a modern figure in the text of *The Fall of Arthur* than there is to mark Saruman in *The Lord of the Rings*. Mordred's military-industrial preparations and pragmatic politics are much less pronounced, though he does, like Saruman, lay a great deal of emphasis on the progress of time and the inevitability of change as a rationale for his ascendancy (2.132, 147–49). In any case, the similarity between the characters is telling, particularly their destructively utilitarian attitudes toward nature and community. Patrick Curry actually sees this latter set of attitudes in the villains as perhaps the essential component in Tolkien's implicit critique of modernism, though he finds them embodied most perniciously not in Saruman, but in Sauron. He writes:

> Tolkien's work that has had the greatest public impact is an account of resistance to the contemporary threat to three great goods, nested one inside another. First there is community: the hobbits,

social to the ends of their well-brushed toes, and firmly rooted in their place, the Shire. Next there is nature: Middle-earth itself in all its wonders.... Then there are spiritual values.... Where these dimensions overlap is the heart of Tolkien's tale. Finally, in stark contrast, the single-visioned, imperialist perfection of power that threatens the survival of these three ... [is] embodied in Sauron and Mordor. (Curry 35)

In *The Lord of the Rings*, the medievalist worlds of the Shire, Lothlórien, and Gondor (among others) stand as antitypes, one might say antidotes, to the militarism and utilitarianism that characterize both Mordor and the modern world. Arthur's kingdom in *The Fall of Arthur* stands in a similar relationship to Mordred's usurped kingdom and, again, by analogy, to modernism.

Martial Valor

The word "threat" in Curry's description of the "threat to [the] great goods" posed by the imperialism of Mordor is quite apt in regards to central conflict in *The Lord of the Rings*, where the danger that Sauron poses to Middle-earth is a literal one of military domination and conquest. Here again, something very similar might be said of the threat posed by Mordred in *The Fall of Arthur*. His grab for power is primarily martial. When Sir Cradoc arrives in the East to tell Arthur of his nephew's treachery, he tells him that Mordred's primary activity in his uncle's absence has been mustering forces against invasion. He warns Arthur that a hundred "dragon-prowed" ships have besieged his kingdom: "Wild blow the winds // of war in Britain!" (I.160). It is tempting to say that Mordred's military buildup is emblematic of the massive growth of the military-industrial complexes of the twentieth century, but that is an assertion that the text may not necessarily bear up and certainly does not demand. It is clear from the text, though, that there is little in the way of concern for any sort of righteous cause in Mordred's mustering of arms. As noted above, Mordred's concerns are entirely pragmatic in the service of getting and holding power. The makeup of his army is consistent with his aims. It is an army of mercenaries, both foreign and domestic. Canto 2, lines 101–08, describes the wickedness of his bought men. If it might be dubious to assert that Mordred's militarism is entirely modernist in its flavor, it is not at all dubious to say that the martial imagery Tolkien uses to describe Mordred's army shares the twentieth century's cynicism with regards to martial virtue and the justice of warfare. Militarism is for Mordred, as it is for Saruman and Sauron, and, for that matter, for the fascist regimes of the mid-twentieth century, the handmaiden to political power.

Mordred's army, however, is not the only picture of martial prowess we see in the poem. Opposed to the mercenary pragmatism of Mordred's forces is the medieval chivalry of Arthur's knights. Arthur's forces embody the flower of chivalry, the trope their literary forbears had carved out for them in the Middle Ages. Whereas Mordred's forces are held together by mercenary pay and the promise of preferment, Arthur's forces are held together by faithfulness to a common cause and loyalty to a virtuous liege-lord.

The ethos of Arthur's knights is most vividly embodied in the character of Sir Gawain, the greatest of the knights, who epitomizes chivalry in both word and deed. The text of the poem introduces Gawain in the list of the knights that journey east with Arthur and contrasts his characterization with Mordred's.

Gawain is remarkably un-pragmatic, particularly with regards to marking time. Mordred sees the changes in the air and capitalizes on them to his own advantage. Gawain pointedly stands against the tides of time, defending to his last breath an ideal that he half recognizes is fading. His idealism is that strong, as is evidenced by his defense of the efficacy of Arthurian knighthood. When Arthur receives news of Mordred's treachery, his first thought is worry over the knights who are not with him anymore, most notably Lancelot, who has been banished following his tryst with Guinever. Gawain challenges his king's worries with remembrance of the past glories of the Round Table. "Why more [knights] need we?" he asks (1.201). He reminds Arthur that the knights who fallow him are the flower of chivalry, the best men in the world. The epideictic language of Gawain's speech in 1.205–11 is in sharp contrast with the grim verses that describe Mordred's army. Of course, the martial power of the knights is part of Gawain's logic: both puissance and might are mentioned (though, it might be noted, in archaic rather than contemporary terms). However, the thrust of his rhetoric is the chivalric ideal that the knights represent. As if to drive the point home, he follows the lines above by noting that even if it were just himself and Arthur, they would still be enough, allied in hope and united in heart as they are (1.213).

This is not to say that Gawain's actual "puissance" is not an equally important part of his heroism. His martial actions in the fourth canto prove to a great extent the truth of the claims he makes to Arthur in the first. When Arthur's forces make their first encounter with Mordred's naval defenses, Gawain runs roughshod over Mordred's heathen mercenaries. Brandishing his sword Galuth, he smites the king of Gothland and destroys his ship (4.197ff). What makes Gawain heroic is the fact that his martial prowess is joined to a high-minded idealism. Martial valor is depicted as virtuous in Gawain because it is in the service of an ideal rather than a naked desire for getting and holding power. Gawain's heroism is not only marked as virtuous, however; it is decidedly medieval in its flavor.

Here again, Tolkien's medievalism comprises something of a recovery: in this case the recovery of an ideal of martial heroism that was badly damaged, if not altogether lost, in the West in the wake of World War I. Post-war poets and novelists like Wilfred Owen, Siegfried Sassoon, and Ford Madox Ford did much in the early twentieth century to demystify war in the imagination of the West, stressing the horrors of modern mechanized warfare and dispelling notions of martial sacrifice and valor. This trend toward disillusionment and cynicism with regards to all things military continued throughout the twentieth century, to the point that many in the West now find war to be entirely unpalatable under any circumstances. Certainly, the horrors of war have always counterbalanced the glory of martial valor, but the scales seemed to have been decidedly tipping in favor of a more cynical response to war in the West in the years following the devastation of World War I—so much so that much of Europe was overly reluctant to counter the Nazi threat militarily. The desire to avoid another "Great War" at all costs was doubtless behind Chamberlain's capitulation to Hitler at the Munich Conference in 1938.

Michael Ward discusses some of attitudes toward martial action that were held in the thirties in Britain in his chapter on Mars in *Planet Narnia*. There, he notes Lewis' defense of the necessity of martial valor and heroism, pointing out that Lewis was "unabashed in his belief that there was such a thing as a just war" (95). Importantly, as Ward notes, Lewis' defense of just war was not naïve. Lewis, as Tolkien, had seen first-hand the horrors of World War I, so his argument for martial virtue was not made out of an ignorant romanticism. Ward writes of Lewis' ideas concerning martial poetry:

> Lewis divided poets of war into the "Enchanted" (Sidney, Macaulay, Chesterton, Brooke), the "Disenchanted" (Sassoon),[9] and the "Re-enchanted" (Homer, the *Maldon* poet), and he obviously intends to include himself among the Re-enchanted: "One is not in the least deceived: we remember the trenches too well. We know how much of the reality the romantic view left out. But we also know that heroism is a real thing." (95)[10]

This cultural debate that was waged in the 1930s in Britain is the probable context for Tolkien's writing of *The Fall of Arthur*, according to Christopher Tolkien, who has edited the published text and tentatively places the range of the poem's composition between 1931 and 1934 (10–11).[11] Assuming this context is correct, then it seems safe to say that the medievalist heroic martial imagery in Tolkien's poem makes imaginatively the same argument for just martial valor that Lewis makes in prose. (Of course, Lewis makes the argument imaginatively as well in his own fiction.) The war against the aggressor Mordred is a just war, and it is in the service of this just war that Gawain's heroism is displayed.

The war against Mordred, of course, is not the only instance of martial valor in a just cause. Arthur's quest into the East, "the heathen to humble," is also arguably a virtuous martial enterprise (1.6). Even though Arthur has been duped into undertaking the quest by Mordred to get him out of the way, there is merit to the quest in the sense that it is an active defense of both his kingdom and western Christendom.

Christendom

I mentioned above that Arthur's quest into the East to subdue heathen invaders is Tolkien's own unique revision of the Arthur mythos he received from medieval tradition. In what Christopher Tolkien calls the "chronicle" tradition of the death of Arthur, deriving from Geoffrey of Monmouth, Arthur's continental quest is undertaken against Rome and the Emperor Lucius Hiberius (76). The quest is one of successful conquest and unification of Western Christendom, but it comes at the expense of a prior fracture within that very Christendom. In an alternate tradition, which derives from the French *Mort Artu* and culminates

---

9   It is probably foolhardy to attempt to correct by addition the scholarship of Lewis and Ward, but I would add Owen to this list.

10   The quoted material in this passage is from Lewis' essay "Talking about Bicycles."

11   Christopher Tolkien notes that the poem must have existed in some form by 1934, when it was apparently read by R. W. Chambers (10). As for the beginning date of composition, he says:
     I have suggested in *The Legend of Sigurd and Gudrún* (p. 5) "as a mere guess, since there is no evidence whatsoever to confirm it, that my father turned to Norse poems as a new poetic enterprise [and a return to alliterative verse] after he abandoned the Lay of Leithien near the end of 1931." If this were so, he must have begun work on *The Fall of Arthur*, which was still far from completion at the end of 1934, when the Norse poems had been brought to a conclusion. (10–11)

in Malory, the quest out of Britain that allows for Mordred's usurping of the throne is undertaken against Lancelot, as Arthur and his knights besiege the castle at Benwick. The quest itself is rather tragic in the latter tradition, and again, there is a fracturing of the unity of Christendom inherent in its very undertaking. Tolkien's revision of Arthur's continental quest into a quest against the heathen preserves the unity of Western Christendom. As Christopher Tolkien says, in revising the quest in this way, his father "preserved the 'chronicle' tradition of Arthur's eastern campaign overseas, but totally changed its nature and purpose. Arthur defends 'Rome', he does not assault it" (110).

Of course, Tolkien's revision is something of a fantasy, but it will be recalled that it is just this element of fantasy that Tolkien cites in "On Fairy-stories" that provides the recovery and consolation necessary to the human condition. In this case, the fantasy of a medieval Christendom that stands undivided against outside forces provides the restorative image of a unified West, a refreshing vision that is opposed to the fracturing of modernism, a fracturing illustrated by nothing so much as the two World Wars that tore Europe apart in the first half of the twentieth century.

In many ways, this fantasy of a united Christendom is the imagined context for the other two medievalist visions of nature and martial valor that I have discussed above. It is the mythic geo-political context for the synthesis with nature that is embodied in Arthur's kingdom, the "holy realm // beside Heaven's gateway" (*FoA* 5.11). It is also the bounded social entity of moral good that must be (martially) defended against the threat of evil from outside; this defense is ostensibly the reason for Arthur's quest into the East in Tolkien's poem. The importance of the boundary in this context deserves some comment, for the boundary between the "holy realm" and the threats from outside is essentially the boundary between good and evil.

Corinne Zemmour has noted the importance of the boundary in Tolkien's *Lord of the Rings* mythos. She describes the Hedge, which separates the Shire from the rest of Middle-earth to the east, as a type of boundary between the peaceful, restorative grounds of the hobbits and the dangerous world of adventure. Zemmour identifies this trope of adventuring beyond the boundary, moreover, as something that Tolkien borrowed from medieval Arthurian literature. She compares the Shire to "those meadows of Arthurian literature which soothe the knights as they return to their own world, after all their trials" (137). By contrast, the forest beyond the Hedge, like the wild lands of Arthurian literature, is described by Tolkien in words that have "sinister connotations" (146). It is an ambivalent place of danger and mystery where evil possibly lurks, but at the same time it provides a landscape of adventure where hobbits and knights can prove themselves (146). Inside the boundary is Christendom, the synthetic "holy realm" of peace and good where humanity can fully participate with nature; outside the boundary is wildness, danger, possibly evil, and the opportunity to exercise martial valor.

This, at least is the landscape as it is drawn in *The Fall of Arthur*. I have commented rather at length on the synthesized, participated nature of Arthur's kingdom (before it is usurped by Mordred) above, but I should here like to draw a bit more attention to the landscape of the forest. Arthur's campaign into the East takes him through heathen lands to—notice the name—Mirkwood (1.68). The land in which they are to battle the heathen is, like the wild lands in Middle-earth and medieval Arthurian romance, described in words with clearly sinister connotations. Rain and cold wind greet their arrival, and nature itself seems to rise up against them in this place: "The endless East // in anger awoke" (1.83). The usage of the name

"Mirkwood" to denote the marginal boundary separating the fringes of the West from "the endless East" is of particular interest, given that it is the same name given to the forest fraught with danger in *The Hobbit*. Shippey tells us that Tolkien derives the term from Norse Eddic poetry: "There seems to be a general agreement among Norse writers that Mirkwood is in the east, and forms a kind of boundary, perhaps between the mountains and the steppe" (*Author* 34). Like the Hedge and like its namesake in *The Fall of Arthur*, Mirkwood in Norse myth is a boundary that is crossed en route to doing battle with a nefarious enemy, as when medieval Burgundian heroes cross it on their way to confront Attila the Hun (33–34).

The importance of the borderline or the marginal forests that bound the idyllic nature of Christendom in Arthurian and medievalist literature is that it is a clear demarcation between good and evil.[12] Of course, it is not an impermeable boundary—as is evidenced by the impetus for Arthur's quest east, i.e. the antecedent raids of the heathen on his kingdom—both forces of good and of evil repeatedly cross over to, and even (e.g. Mordred) reside on the other side of the map. Still, the moral valences are physically marked on the medievalist landscape and clearly recognizable. Again, as with nature and martial valor, the medievalist mythos provides a clarity of vision as opposed to the muddiness of the twentieth century, with its entangling alliances, mixed political motives, and cultural moral relativism. *The Fall of Arthur*, what there is of it, is rooted in this medievalist mythos, and out of that mythos it offers a recovery of vision, which is in itself a form of consolation to the modern world of the twentieth century.

The Ambivalence of Arthur

It remains only to comment briefly on what Tolkien gains and perhaps loses in terms of composing a medievalist fairy-story by employing the mythos of King Arthur. One thing that Tolkien clearly gains by employing Arthur is the credibility of the long train of medieval tradition that the king brings with him. Undertaking something so long-established, literary, and deeply rooted in the imagination of the Middle Ages would seem to exempt Tolkien from the contempt that critics like Eco have cast upon the "fantasy" mythos of *The Lord of the Rings*. There is something closer to a "reliable Middle Ages," to use Eco's term, in *The Fall of Arthur* and therefore a greater chance that, among some audiences, the recovery of the medievalist ethos will be more likely to be well received.

On the other hand, the same thing that commends Arthur is that which might stand in the way of its restorative imaginative power. That thing is familiarity. We should recall Reilly's assertion that objects can become "blurred by familiarity" and turn into things to be possessed (205). Certainly, the myth of Arthur, particularly to a modern British audience, is very familiar. In another section of his study on the Inklings, Reilly argues that the familiarity of the Gospel is one factor that has contributed to its loss of effectiveness in the West and notes that one of the goals that C. S. Lewis was trying to accomplish in his imaginative works was to "re-mythologize" the Gospel, to render it less familiar by revealing it indirectly in narrative.

---

12   I have written at some greater length on the continuing tendency in popular culture to return to the medieval in order to mark a clear vision of good and evil in the essay "Neomedievalism: An Eleventh Middle Ages?" available in *Studies in Medievalism* 19.

Reilly writes that in Lewis' novels, "we see a professed Christian turning to romantic fantasy and myth with a serious purpose, uniting the religion with the myth so that the eternal good news of Christianity comes to the reader with an imaginative shock, comes to him, in fact, as romance" (116). In his later chapter on Tolkien, Reilly essentially argues that *The Lord of the Rings* serves much the same ends, mythopoeically embodying the eucatastrophic *evangelium* in an adult fairy-story (194). Perhaps it is to the extent that *The Lord of the Rings* is less familiar (or was upon its release) that it was more effective in the twentieth-century medievalist fairy-story genre than contemporary retellings of Arthur. I would stop well short of saying that this is *why* Tolkien spent his time in finishing the trilogy rather than the Arthurian poem. That would be horridly speculative guesswork. As Richard J. Finn points out, though, "Tolkien had a complex relationship with Arthur…. [He] did not feel that Arthur's story represented the natural mythology of England" (25). Perhaps in the end Tolkien would have felt that Middle-earth does, after all, provide a truer mythos for England than the mythos associated with Arthur.[13]

Finally, if *The Fall of Arthur* is a Tolkienian attempt at fairy-story, it is a curious choice for subject matter in that, at least on the surface of things, it seems to lack the *eucatastrophe* (the happy ending) that Tolkien sees as "the highest function" of fairy-stories (OFS 85). One can only speculate about the ending of *The Fall of Arthur* since it is unfinished, but the title seems to indicate that Tolkien intended to follow the medieval tradition, which would have the poem end with Arthur's fatal wounding and the end of Camelot. Internal evidence from the extant poem leans in that direction as well. The tone is gloomy and elegiac throughout, with numerous references to the turning of the tides of time (always for the worse). A refrain throughout the poem is "while the world lasted," wherein "the world" seems to allude to Arthur's kingdom. Both the subordinate clause itself and the contexts surrounding the occurrences of the phrase signal that the world will not last long, and, as if it needed more, the verb in the refrain is altered as the poem progresses: "lasted" is replaced with "darkened" (2.5), "faltered" (3.182), and finally "faded" (5.23). The sense of doom is pervasive.

Of course, the presence of a sense of doom does not entirely separate *The Fall of Arthur* from *The Lord of the Rings*. As Tom Shippey notes, in spite of the clear eucatastrophe of the destruction of the ring and the restorations of the kingdom of Gondor and the Shire, there is nonetheless a remaining undercurrent of doom at the end of the trilogy. Sauron has been defeated, but evil remains: "What Gandalf replies" to Sam Gamgee's question about whether everything sad was going to come untrue "is that 'A great Shadow has departed'—but it is not *the* great Shadow" (*Author* 207–08). Moreover, he says, "It should be added that most of the characters in *The Lord of the Rings* are staring 'universal final defeat' in the face" (211). The Ents are going extinct; the Hobbits exist, "but there is certainly no Shire anymore"; and, perhaps most tragically, the Elves are retreating from Middle-earth (211).

The departure of the Elves from the Grey Havens is similar to Arthur's departure for Avalon; both of them take with them magic that sustains the land. The vacuum of their absences, in each case, makes way for what Finn calls "the coming wasteland" (25). Oddly, though, if the eucatastrophe is only for the moment

---

13   Tom Shippey briefly discusses Tolkien's interest in Middle-earth as a mythology specifically for England in the Foreword to *J. R. R. Tolkien: Author of the Century*.

in the case of *The Lord of the Rings*, then perhaps the defeat is similarly for the moment in *The Fall of Arthur*, for there is in Arthur's story a strong note of hope, near the end, and in fact it is the same eucatastrophic note of hope that is present in the Gospels. For the Gospels themselves can be said to contain a strong note of the tragic in the death of Christ. It is the resurrection and, perhaps more pointedly, the promised return of Christ that provide eucatastrophic hope. Though Arthur is mortally wounded in his battle with Mordred at the end of his tale, tradition tells us that he is carried off to Avalon, where his wound will be healed and from whence he will return when Britain faces its greatest hour of need. It appears that Tolkien meant to keep this tradition in his retelling, as indicated by some penciled verses that appear to be a draft for an ending portion of the poem. These tell us that Arthur is "upon Earth's border in Avalon biding. / While the world w... .eth / till the world [??awaketh]" (139). The bracketed "awaketh" here is Christopher Tolkien's guess as to what the unreadable handwritten "w... .eth" in the manuscript might be, and the ultimate "till the world" seems obviously a variation on the "While the world"—the refrain oft repeated in the finished portion of the poem—in the line above. If in fact these lines would have read, "till the world waketh," then the poem would express a strong eucatastrophic hope for the return of Arthur and a renewal of "the world."

The hope of the resurrection contained in the *evangelium* is, of course, what Tolkien saw as the ultimate instance of eucatastrophe, the real eucatastrophe that fairy-stories only point at, which is perhaps why the eucatastrophe of *The Lord of the Rings* is only provisional (OFS 88). Reilly discusses this in a manner that perhaps resolves the apparent aesthetic contradiction in the tone of gloom that pervades the eucatastrophes of both *The Lord of the Rings* and *The Fall of Arthur*. He says:

> If the story of Christ is for Tolkien the archetypal fairy story, with the eucatastrophe consisting of the Resurrection, then it should be added that though Christ "defeated" death, even He did not return permanently to the land of the living, or at least not in His previous historical body. "To be a man," as Tolkien has said elsewhere, "is tragedy enough." Human life ends in human death, and fairy stories do not change this essential fact of the Primary World. What they do is hint at the *Gloria* that follows death. (210)

To some extent, this is what *The Fall of Arthur's* medievalist mythos does even in its extant form. The clear vision of an idealized nature, the boundary between good and evil, and the martial valor that can be used in the service of good point to a world beyond the Primary World where nature is used rather than idealized, where good and evil are hard to extricate from each other, and, consequently, where any martial exercise is dubious at best. Assuming Christopher Tolkien's reading of his father's notes is accurate and that a finished poem would have simply had Arthur retreating—*a lá* Christ—"until the world waketh," then the finished version would have held out an even greater hope of final eucatastrophe: the hope of a realized City of God, of which the Primary City of Man is only a type, a City where even the relatively clear vision of the medievalist mythos is still only, relatively speaking, seeing through a glass darkly.

Works Cited

Barfield, Owen. *Saving the Appearances: A Study in Idolatry*. 1957. 2nd ed. Middletown, CT: Wesleyan UP, 1988. Print.

Curry, Patrick. "Modernity in Middle-earth." *Tolkien: A Celebration*. Ed. Joseph Pearce. San Francisco: Ignatius Press, 2001. 34–39. Print.

Eco, Umberto. "Dreaming of the Middle Ages." *Travels in Hyperreality*. Trans. William Weaver. San Diego: Harcourt Brace Jovanovich, 1983. 61–72. Print.

Finn, Richard J. "Arthur and Aragorn: Arthurian Influence in *The Lord of the Rings*." *Mallorn: The Journal of the Tolkien Society* 43 (2005): 23–26. *EBSCO*. Web. 6 June 2015.

Grewell, Cory. "Medievalist Fantasies of Christendom." *Journal of Inklings Studies* 3.2 (2013): 3–10. Print.

——. "Neomedievalism: An Eleventh Little Middle Ages?" *Studies in Medievalism* 19 (2010): 34–43. Print.

Lewis, C. S. Preface. *Essays Presented to Charles Williams*. Ed. C. S. Lewis. London: Oxford UP, 1947. v–xiv. Print.

"Medievalism, N." OED Online. Oxford English Dictionary. Web.

Reilly, R. J. *Romantic Religion: A Study of Owen Barfield, C. S. Lewis, Charles Williams, J. R. R. Tolkien*. Great Barrington, MA: Lindisfarne Books, 2006. Print.

Shippey, Tom. *J. R. R. Tolkien: Author of the Century*. NY: Houghton Mifflin, 2000. Print.

——. "Medievalisms and Why They Matter." *Studies in Medievalism* I (2009): 46–54. Print.

Tolkien, J. R. R. "On Fairy-stories." *The Tolkien Reader*. NY: Del Rey, 1966. 33–99. Print.

——. *The Fall of Arthur*. Ed. Christopher Tolkien. NY: Houghton Mifflin, 2013. Print.

——. *The Lord of the Rings*. 1954–55. 2nd ed. 3 vols. Boston: Houghton Mifflin, 1967. Print.

Ward, Michael. *Planet Narnia: The Seven Heavens in the Imagination of C. S. Lewis*. Oxford UP, 2008. Print.

Zemmour, Corinne. "Tolkien in the Land of Arthur: The Old Forest Episode from *The Lord of the Rings*." *Mythlore* 24 (2006): 135–63. *EBSCO*. Web. 6 June 2015.

Histories Present

Spiritual Quest in a Scientific Age

Jason Jewell and Chris Butynskyi

Introduction

In November 1943, J. R. R. Tolkien wrote to his son Christopher, then serving in the Royal Air Force: "We were born in a dark age out of due time (for us). But there is this comfort: otherwise we should not *know*, or so much love, what we do love. I imagine the fish out of water is the only fish to have an inkling of water" (*Letters* 64). This sense of being a "fish out of water" in the mid-twentieth century was one, no doubt, that Tolkien's fellow Inklings shared. To be sure, they had found each other as well as like-minded thinkers, writers, and admirers in various parts of the world, but none of them could be said to be really in tune with the prevailing cultural or intellectual trends of their time.

Since at least the mid-nineteenth century, numerous thinkers have proposed variations on what has come to be known as the "secularization thesis," which predicts that as a society makes scientific and technological progress and modernizes in other ways, religiosity in that society will decline. Throughout much of the twentieth century, the secularization thesis was widely accepted among Western intellectuals, even among those who deplored declining religiosity, including some of the Inklings themselves. However, in recent years the secularization thesis has come under attack from various quarters. In 2003, syndicated columnist David Brooks, describing himself as a "recovering secularist," wrote in the *Atlantic*: "It's now clear that the secularization theory is untrue .... We are living through one of the great periods of scientific progress and the creation of wealth. At the same time, we are in the midst of a religious boom." Some scholars, such as Mark Morrisson and Robert Whalen, have begun the process of reexamining the nineteenth and twentieth centuries and have uncovered a religious energy not recognized by an earlier generation of scholars for whose research agenda secularization theory may have created blind spots.

Though they may not have recognized it at the time, the success of the Inklings' writings is itself further evidence against the facile picture of secularization that twentieth-century intellectuals often accepted.

Both popular and scholarly interest in their work, which is so laden with spiritual themes, has continued unabated and perhaps even increased in the twenty-first century. Nevertheless, even at the height of their literary careers in the middle decades of the twentieth century, they still justifiably considered themselves out of step with the *zeitgeist*, that of scientific secularism. Yet their responses to this outlook were actually part of a larger movement to find meaning in the spiritual, the occult, and the traditionally Christian, in which many other Arthurian works of the day participated.

This chapter explores in general terms the Inklings' relationship with the prevailing intellectual culture of their time. It begins with a brief historical survey of the rise of scientific secular thought from the seventeenth through the early twentieth centuries, a process that culminated in the widespread acceptance of *scientism*—the belief that the assumptions and methods of the natural sciences are appropriate and essential to all other disciplines, including the humanities, social sciences, and even religion—among Western intellectual elites in conjunction with a faith in progress (Curry 64). It continues with a discussion of the ways in which the best-known Inklings—C. S. Lewis, J. R. R. Tolkien, Charles Williams, and Owen Barfield—responded to this intellectual climate, both negatively through counterattacks against the far-reaching claims of scientism, and positively through the articulation of alternative moral visions. The attempt to articulate these visions can be seen as a "spiritual quest," and one can imagine the Inklings as modern Knights of the Round Table—not in the sense of a chivalric romance in the halls of Camelot, but as a group of men committed to a quest they believed would help to define their age. Our contention is that an understanding of this quest will help to provide an appropriate context for interpretation and appreciation of the Inklings' Arthurian works under consideration in this volume. The chapter concludes with a discussion of the ways in which the Inklings can be considered both pre-modern and postmodern, depending on which aspects of their visions are emphasized.

The Scientific Age

From at least the early seventeenth century, Western culture's intellectual and political elites had placed an ever-increasing trust in the natural sciences and the technologies their application produced. In *Novum Organum* (1620), Francis Bacon (1561–1626) articulated the tenets of empiricism (the "scientific method") and insisted that it was the only reliable method for acquiring progressive knowledge about the material world. Only through inductive reasoning grounded in controlled observation of nature could philosophers eliminate errors in thinking brought about by various "idols," such as the misuse of language, that have always plagued the human mind. Bacon also argued in *The New Atlantis* (1627) that scientific progress could improve both material and social conditions for a society's inhabitants.

The influence of Bacon's ideas grew steadily through the seventeenth and eighteenth centuries. Leading thinkers of the Enlightenment found empiricism congenial to their own emphasis on unassisted human reason as the means of addressing longstanding social, economic, and political problems. Thus, although Bacon himself was a Christian, his proposed method for investigating the natural world became a major element in the program of others, such as Voltaire, A. R. J. Turgot, and the Marquis de Condorcet, whose vision of human progress included the secularization of society.

One challenge for empiricists, of course, was the impossibility of direct observation of many phenomena, such as the origin of life or the choices made by the human mind, for which they desired an explanation. For Christians or others comfortable with acknowledging sources of knowledge beyond those provided by the natural sciences, this challenge was not insurmountable. However, philosophical materialists and agnostics continued to struggle well into the nineteenth century to find plausible natural explanations for many things they observed every day. This is not to say that many of them were not confident that such explanations would be forthcoming. Auguste Comte (1798–1857), acknowledged by many today as the father of sociology, theorized in works such as *A General View of Positivism* (1848) that as society progresses toward its highest stage of development—the "positive" stage—Enlightenment ideas about abstract laws of nature would be abandoned, replaced by a total reliance on empirical methods. A new "social science" would then uncover solutions to the problems of human society without reference to abstract notions such as "human rights," which in the minds of most ultimately relied on the existence of a creator deity.

Secular empiricists made occasional progress in the century's early decades, as when Charles Lyell's *Principles of Geology* (1830–33) popularized a uniformitarian theory of geological change, thus convincing many that the earth was older than the six thousand years suggested by a literal reading of the book of Genesis. Nevertheless, the biggest breakthroughs for the secular scientific interpretation of reality came between the mid-nineteenth and early twentieth centuries, when four major thinkers—Charles Darwin, Karl Marx, Sigmund Freud, and Friedrich Nietzsche—collectively erected a theoretical edifice allowing for a completely naturalistic and morally relativistic view of human life and society.

It is difficult to overestimate the impact of Charles Darwin's ideas on the modern world. He was not the first thinker to posit that the origin of human life came about through purely natural processes; some classical thinkers such as Lucretius had written as much. However, his theory of natural selection, outlined in *The Origin of Species* (1859) and *The Descent of Man* (1871), provided the modern mind with a plausible alternative to the traditional Christian account of creation found in the opening chapters of Genesis. His theory of biological evolution appeared to remove the need for an appeal to a divine creator to explain the panoply of life observable in the modern world, positing instead a process of "natural selection" in which accumulations of tiny variations in species over long periods of time would eventually lead to the development of entirely new species.

In *Origin of Species*, Darwin did not explicitly state his belief that humanity was also the result of this process, and some observers thought he had left room for special creation of the human species. However, in *The Descent of Man*, Darwin made very clear his conviction that similarities among the morphologies of humans and other mammals indicated human descent from a lower form of life. He went on to attack the conventional wisdom that human intelligence was of a different kind than those of other animals. Instead, he argued that a continuous spectrum of intelligence existed within the animal kingdom and that there was "no fundamental difference between man and the higher mammals in their mental faculties" (Adler 49:287). Many came to believe that this argument undermined the traditional claim that the rational nature of human beings was evidence of their being made in the image of God. Some Christian thinkers attempted to harmonize Darwinian thought with Christian orthodoxy by suggesting that no necessary contradiction existed between the two if God had guided the evolutionary process. However, Darwin himself always resisted the notion of purpose lying in back of natural selection; indeed, he wrote that "if God ordained that variations should be along beneficial lines, natural selection would be redundant" ("Darwinism").

Other than Darwin, the mid-nineteenth-century thinker who did more than anyone else to shape the intellectual assumptions of the modern era was Karl Marx, whose writings on social, economic, and political theory exercised extraordinary influence over many intellectuals by the early twentieth century. In the *Communist Manifesto* (coauthored with Friedrich Engels in 1848) and the three volumes of *Das Kapital* (1867–94), Marx proposed a comprehensive, materialistic theory of social development grounded in the notion of class struggle. On his reading, the "material substructure" of technology and economic relations are the foundation on which a ruling class builds an "ideological superstructure" of culture, religion, morality, and metaphysics to facilitate its control of the lower class. When economic developments change the material conditions of life, upper-class control is undermined. Eventually, the lower class revolts and establishes a new class structure more consistent with those conditions. Marx believed that Western civilization was ripe for just such a revolution, one that would usher in a system of socialism in which the state apparatus controlled and managed all property in the interests of everyone equally. Once the last vestiges of the upper class had been eliminated, there would be no further need for the state, which would wither away, leaving all property to be held in common. Then, for the first time in history, a classless society—communism—would exist. Marx was vague on the specifics of how this egalitarian, utopian society would look and function, but he insisted that it would be completely secular, religion having been a vehicle for class exploitation.

The Prussian philosopher Friedrich Nietzsche provided an idiosyncratic but highly significant contribution to Western thought. In works such as *The Gay Science* (1882), *Beyond Good and Evil* (1886), and *Thus Spoke Zarathustra* (1883–91), he argued that many of the traditional and foundational ideas of Western society were erroneous and that the West needed a new morality along with social and institutional arrangements that reflected it. In a way, his central idea echoes the evolutionary thought of G. W. F. Hegel (1770–1831), Darwin, and Marx. In other words, humanity in the modern age is in a state of flux; inevitably, ideas and values it once held sacred and immutable would become (or already had become) outmoded, and people would cease to believe them. Thus his often-quoted statement that "God is dead" was not an assertion that the Christian God had ever existed in reality, but that the changing conditions of European society and intellectual life in the modern age had eliminated God's role as the foundation of meaning and value, leaving humanity "straying through an infinite nothing" (*Gay Science* 203). Nietzsche welcomed this transition, arguing that the Christian ethic of pity "thwarts the law of evolution" by preserving "what is ripe for destruction" (*Antichrist* 130). He posited the need for an *Übermensch* to impose a superior will and perspective: "the superman is the meaning of earth" (*Zarathustra* 238). Nietzsche's maxim that "man is the *rule*, nature is *irregularity*" (*Human* 167; emphasis original) implies that man has the ability to redefine principles of truth and morality. In *Zarathustra*, Nietzsche confidently predicted the eventual rise of "those marvelously incomprehensible and unfathomable men, those enigmatic men predestined for victory and the seduction of others" (245).

The final architect of the modern secular scientific outlook is Sigmund Freud, the father of psychoanalysis, whose attempts to understand the functioning of the human mind in purely material terms paralleled Darwin's and Marx's respective efforts to explain features of the human body and socio-economic institutions. Freud believed that nervous disorders were the body's physical response to the mind's unresolved tensions at a subconscious level. He attempted to uncover these "repressed memories" in his patients with the technique of "free association," in which they were encouraged to say whatever came into their minds during their interviews with him. Freud theorized that repressed memories could also manifest in dreams; in *The Interpretation of Dreams* (1900), he famously asserted that dreams not only can, but *must* be "wish-fulfilments" the mind produces in order to preserve sleep when the subconscious manifests thoughts that would otherwise awaken the sleeper. In later works such as *The Ego and the Id* (1923), Freud elaborated on his ideas about the relationship between conscious and subconscious by positing the existence of three distinct parts of the psyche: the id, ego, and super-ego. The id is the unconscious and impulsive portion of the mind that operates on the pleasure principle, whereas the super-ego is the uncompromising moral center of the mind shaped in childhood primarily through parental guidance. The ego is the rational center that mediates the constant tension between the other two, seeking to satisfy the id in non-destructive ways while also placating the demands of the super-ego. Frequently this balancing act requires the ego to create rationalizations to cloak the naked demands of the id. By the end of his career, in contrast to those who held to some version of providence's direction of world affairs, Freud was proposing completely naturalistic ways of interpreting major social forces such as religion in works such as *Civilization and Its Discontents* (1929) and *Moses and Monotheism* (1939).

The Triumph of Scientism?

The cumulative influence of Darwin, Marx, Freud, and Nietzsche on Western intellectual life was immense. Thanks in large part to popularizers like T. H. Huxley (1825–95), who energetically argued for the mechanistic nature of biological evolution and who developed the theory of epiphenomenalism (itself a touchstone of twentieth-century scientism), Darwinian assumptions eventually permeated nearly every academic discipline, including those in the humanities and the new "social sciences."[1] Ernst Mayr, one of the leading Darwinist voices of recent years, claims that the modern mind, under Darwin's influence, came to reject teleology and all supernatural phenomena and causations and that it came to accept a scientific foundation for ethics. When Marx's projections of an imminent socialist revolution failed to bear fruit, "Marxist revisionists" in organizations such as the Fabian Society (which counted George Bernard Shaw [1856–1950] and H. G. Wells [1866–1946] among its members) argued that socialists could reach their

---

1   See, for example, Stoddart, D. R. "Darwin's Impact on Geography." *Annals of the Association of American Geographers* 56.4 (1966): 683–98; White, Paul. "Darwin's Emotions: The Scientific Self and the Sentiment of Objectivity." *Isis* 100.4 (2009): 811–26; Winter, Sarah. "Darwin's Saussure: Biosemiotics and Race in *Expression*." *Representations* 107.1 (2009): 128–61; Mayr, Ernst. "Darwin's Impact on Modern Thought." Proceedings of the *American Philosophical Society* 139.4 (1995): 317–25; Smith, Jonathan. "Domestic Hybrids: Ruskin, Victorian Fiction, and Darwin's Botany." *Studies in English Literature, 1500–1900* 48.4, The Nineteenth Century (2008): 861–70.

goals by working within established systems of government; there followed the formation of successful Marxist political parties throughout Europe, including the Labour Party, which became one of Britain's two largest parties by the 1920s. Early Zionists such as Theodor Herzl, German militarists, and Italian fascists alike drew inspiration from Nietzsche's ambiguous prose; later generations of scholars offered numerous reinterpretations and revisions of his central idea of the individual's creation of meaning and value. Most intellectuals dismissed Freud's theories at the beginning of the twentieth century, but by the time of his death in 1939 those theories occupied a major position in the social sciences; he had convinced many that the loftiest ambitions and creative impulses, far from reflecting some sort of divine stamp on the human mind, were in fact no more than the mark of the human mind's success in "sublimating" baser and more bestial urges.

Taken as a whole, the ideas of these four thinkers provided a comprehensive way to interpret human life and ethics without reference to religion or any non-material phenomena. In 1903, the philosopher Bertrand Russell (1872–1970) summarized the universe that scientific secularism claimed to have revealed:

> That man is the product of causes which had no prevision of the end they were achieving; that his origin, his growth, his hopes and fears, his loves and his beliefs, are but the outcome of accidental collocations of atoms; that no fire, no heroism, no intensity of thought and feeling, can preserve an individual life beyond the grave; that all the labours of the ages, all the devotion, all the inspiration, all the noonday brightness of human genius, are destined to extinction in the vast death of the solar system, and that the whole temple of Man's achievement must inevitably be buried beneath the debris of a universe in ruins—all these things, if not quite beyond dispute, are yet so nearly certain, that no philosophy which rejects them can hope to stand. Only within the scaffolding of these truths, only on the firm foundation of unyielding despair, can the soul's habitation henceforth be safely built.

Around the same time, sociologists such as Max Weber (1864–1920) and Emile Durkheim (1858–1917) proposed their theories of secularization, arguing that the modernizing of the world would inevitably lead to a decline in religiosity. Many followers of the great modernists confidently predicted that science would eventually explain the religious impulse itself. In lectures presented at Kings College, London, in 1902, Greville MacDonald declared: "Like all other human attributes, the religious sense is an inheritance from mighty small beginnings, else man is a special creation: a theory we cannot study biology and hold" (MacDonald ix). He claimed to find the roots of religious behavior in sponges and flowers and went on to call for increased study of the evolutionary progression of the religious sense (xvi).

Scientism's momentum continued to accelerate through the first half of the twentieth century with the development of schools of thought such as logical positivism. Thinkers associated with this movement insisted that only statements that could be verified through logic or empirical methods could be considered "cognitively meaningful." All other statements were relegated to the status of "pseudostatements," cognitively meaningless musings not fit for serious consideration by philosophers. Logical positivists thus attempted to banish discussion not only of metaphysics and the claims of religion, but also notions such as causality, on which scientists often relied.

Also under the influence of scientism, eugenics gained large numbers of adherents in the early twentieth century. This social philosophy aimed to encourage reproduction among members of society with "desirable" characteristics (e.g., good health, intelligence, ambition) and discourage reproduction among those with "undesirable" characteristics. Britain's two most influential eugenicists, Sir Francis Galton (1822–1911) and Karl Pearson (1857–1936), took Darwin's theories on environmental influence, extracted the "good and reliable facts," and applied them to their studies in heredity (Mosse 72). As early as 1869 in *Hereditary Genius*, Galton attempted to determine the civic worth of an individual on the basis of traits—"physique, ability, and character"—that could be passed on genetically (Blacker 108). A protégé of Galton's, Pearson also argued for the predominance of hereditary influence in *The Relative Strength of Nature and Nurture* (1915). For decades, he held an endowed chair in eugenics funded by Galton's estate at the University of London. Other British eugenicists such as Julian Huxley (1887–1975), the grandson of T. H. Huxley, believed that eugenics was necessary to prevent the genetic destruction of humanity (West 27). These ideas were not isolated to the United Kingdom, but spread to the continent and across the Atlantic through academic journals (e.g., *Journal for Racial and Social Biology*, 1904) and societies (e.g., Galton's Eugenics Education Society, 1907; National Academy of Sciences, 1863; Mosse 75; West 27).

Many of the most prominent socialists in Britain (including members of the Fabian Society) saw eugenics as a viable path toward the betterment of society. Literary elites—often the same as the socialists—also found much to admire in eugenics (West 27). H. G. Wells, George Bernard Shaw, D. H. Lawrence (1885–1930), and W. B. Yeats (1865–1939) were part of a sizeable contingent of authors who favored eugenics in the Western world. John Carey argues that the literary elite saw eugenics as a new humane ethics with the hope of creating a certain type of civilization and culture—one worthy of Western man's potential (Carey 63, 124–25). In works such as Wells' *Anticipations of the Reaction of Mechanical and Scientific Progress upon Human Life and Thought* (1901) and Yeats' *On the Boiler* (1938), one finds arguments for a scientifically driven "purification" of society *via* management of the masses' reproduction.

The impact of eugenics on the West in the early twentieth century is familiar to many. Britain and other Western nations openly considered legislation that would enforce the principles of the eugenics movement (e.g., the compulsory sterilization of the mentally and physically disabled). These discussions found their way into newspapers, journals, academic societies, and even royal commissions:

> A Royal Commission on the Blind, Deaf and Dumb concluded in 1889 that intermarriage between these groups was to be strongly discouraged. Its report was based upon advice from Alexander Graham Bell, the inventor of the telephone, who had warned in his 1883 work *Memoir upon the Formation of a Deaf Variety of the Human Race* that the "passions of the deaf and dumb are undoubtedly strong." In 1896 a pressure group entitled the National Association for the Care and Control of the Feeble Minded was set up in Britain to bring about the lifetime segregation of disabled people. (Brignell)

Although Parliament never passed legislation mandating compulsory practices, eugenics remained an eminently respectable field until it became tainted by association with the Nazis in the middle of the century.

Even after eugenics began to fall from favor, leading intellectuals of the mid-twentieth century often continued to combine the theories of the great modernists into an interlocking whole. J. B. S. Haldane (1892–1964), one of the greatest scientific popularizers of the time, was both a Darwinist and a thoroughgoing Marxist, helping to edit a Communist newspaper in London throughout the 1940s. C. H. Waddington (1905–75), an embryologist who also wrote for the general reader, called in 1941 for scientists to contribute to "the creative tasks of social reorganisation with which the world is faced" (Waddington 691). In later works such as *The Ethical Animal* (1960), he equated ethical behavior with what would promote human evolution.

It is not surprising that British society gradually followed its intellectual elites into a secular orientation in the twentieth century. Historian Peter Gay writes that even before 1900, "Western civilization seemed to be entering a post-Christian era" (28). Although not a perfect measure for various reasons, church attendance is the statistic most observers cite to measure this trend. Callum Brown has shown that although Britain retained some of its historic Christian character into the 1960s, already by 1930 declines in both church attendance and even more nominal "church adherence" were underway. Examining trends across all major churches in Britain, he concludes, "The first half of the century experienced a loss of something like a third of church attendances on a Sunday" (*Religion and Society* 27). C. S. Lewis offered anecdotal evidence of the rise of what might be called "vulgar scientism" when recounting his own experiences interacting with working-class Englishmen; they were skeptical of History in general but accepted what the T. H. Huxleys of the world told them about the supposed science about our ancestry. Modern people, then, according to Lewis, found it easier to believe in "scientific" facts about a prehistorical age then they did historical facts about more recent times that were yet far removed from their own experience (see "Christian Apologetics" 95).

In Response to Scientism

Leading voices of the modern scientific age had succeeded in raising a number of doubts about both the truth of specific religious doctrines and the need for spirituality more generally. However, many intellectuals found reasons to resist the calls to embrace science as the exclusive route to knowledge and social improvement. Scientific secularism received a mixed response because the Western world was not ready to abandon spirituality.

John West has noted that the goals of scientists and magicians overlap in that both hope to achieve power over nature in pursuit of human ends; thus in some respects they are "twins" (*The Magician's Twin* 29, 23). At certain historical junctures, such as the seventeenth century's Scientific Revolution, scientists frequently engaged in magical experiments and *vice versa*. The early twentieth century was another such era. According to Mark Morrisson, "during the period from the turn of the [twentieth] century to just before World War II, the trajectories of science and occultism briefly *merged*" (10). The increase in popularity of occult societies was evidence of a conscious spiritual grappling with the new scientific discoveries of the era, especially radioactivity; occultists "increasingly focused on alchemy as a material science validated by the new atomic chemistry and physics, even if it was a science with spiritual implications" (12). Peter Gay writes:

> To find a congenial doctrine among the varieties of spiritualism was a welcome move for thousands, educated and uneducated alike, who could no longer accept the Christian legend of a divine Saviour ... but found it repugnant to embrace what they thought the chilly, deadening materialism of natural science. (28)

Hermeticism, an esoteric school of thought attempting to blend the scientific and magical, had lain seemingly dormant since the seventeenth century, but it experienced a significant revival in the late nineteenth century with the formation of organizations such as the Hermetic Order of the Golden Dawn. The Theosophical Society, another such group, blended Western hermeticism with tenets of Hinduism and Buddhism; its co-founder, Helen Blavatsky, taught that adepts who learned to pierce the veil between man and astral bodies "would be capable of knowing all that had been known or could ever be known" (Mosse 95). Its members hoped to bridge religion and material science, effectively seeking to re-enchant scientific experiment (Morrisson 95). Anthroposophy, originally an offshoot of theosophy, attempted to encompass both natural science and Christianity within a spiritual vision that focused on the inner development of the individual.

These organizations and others like them questioned the certitude of the scientific community in regard to the material world. In the process, they attracted a number of prominent philosophers, literary figures, and even some scientists. Mystical societies fought a constant battle to resist scientism's attempts to reduce all knowledge to the material, and they had to justify their spiritual perspectives in the face of an "ever-growing public faith in the authority of science" (Morrisson 53). At the same time, they attempted to ride the coattails of science's prestige by incorporating as much of the scientific method as possible into their proceedings.

Resistance to scientific secularism did not come exclusively from adherents of the occult, of course. Even as theological modernists attempted to negotiate a partial surrender to the *zeitgeist* by revising several venerable doctrines in a more "rational" direction, other forces within Western Christianity renewed an emphasis on theological orthodoxy. In the English-speaking world, these forces were active on both sides of the Atlantic, but in Britain their most visible manifestation before World War II may have been the so-called Oxford Group, which emphasized prayer and other devotional activity and had the support of many Anglican clergy as well as high-profile figures in the media and sports (Graves 193–95). The controversy over proposed revisions to the Book of Common Prayer in 1927–28 showed that theological matters could still command the attention of Parliament and broad segments of the public (196). Christian orthodoxy resurfaced in other areas as well. For example, literary historians Harry Blamires and Amardeep Singh agree on the existence of a "minor" or "small" Christian literary renaissance that stretched throughout the 1930s and 1940s, including works by not only members of the Inklings, but also T. S. Eliot, Helen

Waddell, James Bridie, Christopher Fry, Dorothy L. Sayers, David Jones, Graham Greene, Evelyn Waugh, Rose Macaulay, Edwin Muir, Andrew Young, and Francis Berry (Blamires 15; Singh).

Scientism and the Inklings

The Inklings themselves offered a variety of responses to the climate of scientific secularism. At times they offered simple rebuttals to what they considered false claims of the secularists. At other times they argued from evidence that scientism necessarily presents an incomplete view of reality. Occasionally they fired salvos at scientism's foundational tenets in an effort to call into question its entire project. Several of these arguments resonated in academic and popular culture and continue to enjoy serious consideration today among philosophers and Christian apologists.

Of the four Inklings who are the focus of this chapter, C. S. Lewis in the course of his popular work in Christian apologetics dealt most frequently with popular misconceptions about religion or its adherents occasioned by vulgar scientism in British and American culture. One example of such a misconception is that ancient and medieval people thought that the earth was flat and the stars were quite close, and that this made the teachings of Christianity plausible to them, whereas modern science, having made known the true vastness of the universe, has rendered it ridiculous to think that an omnipotent God would pay any attention to miniscule people in a mediocre corner of the solar system (see "Religion and Science" 74). J. B. S. Haldane, who presumably should have known better, deployed this very argument in his hostile review of Lewis' Ransom trilogy, claiming that "five hundred years ago … it was not clear that celestial distances were so much greater than terrestrial" ("Auld Hornie").

Lewis replies to this particular argument by pointing out that Ptolemy's *Almagest*, the most influential text in ancient and medieval astronomy, displays a perfect awareness of the huge distance between the earth and the stars, although for some reason modern encyclopedias and histories of science fail to mention this fact. Humans have long known about the extent of the created order and the comparative smallness of the Earth. These were seen as scientific facts, not theological beliefs. Then, Lewis claims, in the middle of the nineteenth century the idea was dreamed up that the largeness of the universe and the smallness of the earth could somehow be used as proof against Christianity (see "Religion and Science" 75). The increase of human power, partly through the progressive acquisition of knowledge about the material world and partly through the devaluing of traditional, religious restraints on human behavior, may be the most enticing benefit of the scientific age for many. A culturally pervasive notion was the naïve belief in inevitable, science-led human progress that had somehow managed to survive in many quarters following the devastations of two world wars. Scientists and secularists create a narrative difficult to unseat as they claim to be concerned with the betterment of humanity. An understanding of the laws of nature could very well lead to a mastery of nature and a sort of secular salvation (P. Williams 49–50). According to its adherents, scientism should lead man to correct all that is wrong in nature, self, and society. As James Herrick writes, "Technology now advances at a rate more rapid than even the most dedicated observer is capable of tracking. Our contemporary moral guides offer us the astonishing speed of progress as assurance of the unquestionable correctness of progress; *rate* of change now equals *rightness* of change" (260).

Members of the Inklings saw this "progress" as tending toward "anti-nature," or "modern industrialism, scientism, totalitarian politics"; evidence of this can be seen in both their personal letters and the subjects of their fiction (*CL* 3:498). J. R. R. Tolkien's well-known technophobia led him to see despair, not hope, in the fast-paced age of technology:

> There is the tragedy and despair of all machinery laid bare. Unlike art which is content to create a new secondary world in the mind, it attempts to actualize desire, and so to create power in this World; and that cannot really be done with any real satisfaction ... And in addition to this fundamental disability of a creature, is added the Fall, which makes our devices not only fail of their desire but turn to a new and horrible evil. (*Letters* 88)

Tolkien did not see the effects of technology as harmless and material trifles, but thought that they would lead to paths of moral compromise. Toward the end of World War II he expressed his concerns, in a letter to his son Christopher, after hearing news of 'Atomic bombs': "The utter folly of these lunatic physicists to consent to do such work for war purposes: calmly plotting the destruction of the world! Such explosives in men's hands, while their moral and intellectual status is declining" (*Letters* 116).

Lewis himself had once held a naïve view of progress, snobbishly looking down on previous eras (*SbJ* 114). After his conversion, though, he vigorously attacked this popular view, in part by questioning the often-unstated goal toward which scientism's progress was tending. For example, in *Mere Christianity* he wrote that everyone wants to see the advancement of the human race. But he warns that rather than advancing toward a valuable goal, we could we on the wrong road, in which case, we need to go back to the point at which we went wrong and start again. Walking backwards is more progressive than continuing to walk forward in the wrong direction (see *MC* 25, 36). For Lewis, a corrupt and excessive use of technology develops a culture that erodes the complete nature of humanity, a culture in which science, rather than explaining things, increasingly explains them away (Reichenbach 17–19). For example, in a short poem titled "On the Atomic Bomb," Lewis challenges, in language similar to Tolkien's, the claim that all scientific advancement improves the quality of life:

> This marks no huge advance in
> the dance of Death. His pincers
> were grim before these chances
> of cold, fire, suffocation, Ogpu, cancer
> ...
> As if your puny gadget
> Could dodge the terrible logic
> Of history! No; the tragic
> Road will go on, new generations trudge it. (lines 13–16, 20–24)

Lewis provides his most thorough critique of the progress scientism promises in *The Abolition of Man* (1943). Although many of his contemporaries looked eagerly toward an age of limitless increase in scientific knowledge and power promised since the Enlightenment, Lewis warned that such a panacea was a logical impossibility:

> Each generation exercises power over its successors: and each, in so far as it modifies the environment bequeathed to it and rebels against tradition, resists and limits the power of its predecessors. This modifies the picture which is sometimes painted of a progressive emancipation from tradition and a progressive control of natural processes resulting in a continual increase of human power. (56–57)

Ultimately a generation would arise that had enough power to control the succeeding generation to the extent that the latter had actually less power than the former, and from that point human power would continue to decrease.

Lewis' critique of the naïve view of limitless progress thus meshes with the fear of political tyranny that had been manifest in his writing since the mid-1920s, before his conversion to Christianity. Lewis saw that those who desire power over others can manipulate the promises of scientism to gain control over their fellows and future generations. After reading *That Hideous Strength*, J. B. S. Haldane accused Lewis of believing that "the application of science to human affairs can only lead to hell" ("Auld Hornie"). Lewis denied the charge; rather, he expected that "any effective invitation to Hell will certainly appear in the guise of scientific planning" because every tyrant "must begin by claiming to have what his victims respect and to give what they want" ("Reply" 80). Scientific planning fits the bill for most modern Westerners; Lewis had envisioned such a dystopian world as early as 1926 in his narrative poem *Dymer*. The eponymous character is examined academically and medically, given vaccinations, given a number, surveilled, beaten, and generally controlled in every detail by totalitarian authorities (*Dymer* 1:6.4–6).

Several of the Inklings advanced the proposition that scientism necessarily communicated an incomplete view of reality. Without denying the value of empirical knowledge of the natural world, they attempted to point out blind spots from which scientism's adherents suffered. For example, in his landmark work *Poetic Diction* (1922), Owen Barfield showed the insufficiency of the modernist attempt to explain the poetic nature of ancient language; he labeled as pure fantasy the influential view of Max Müller that at some point in the distant past an age of poets infused names for brute objects with metaphor (84–85). Likewise, the ubiquity of myth in the ancient world exploded the "root" concept of language because it implies a parallel age of mighty philosophers that imbued names with abstractions (89–90). In reality, ancient language participated in "true metaphor," in which a given word could communicate several logically disconnected, but poetically connected ideas. In a key passage, Barfield criticizes moderns for failing to discern meaning originating from outside their disciplines: "The naturalist is right when he connects the myth [of Demeter] with the phenomena of nature, but wrong if he deduces it solely from these. The psycho-analyst is right when he connects the myth with 'inner' experiences, but wrong if he deduces it solely from these" (91–92).

J. R. R. Tolkien in *The Lord of the Rings* (1954–55) presents what can be interpreted as a subtle critique of scientism's claim that inductive reasoning is the only way to gain reliable knowledge. As Peter Kreeft points out, Tolkien often places characters, especially Frodo, in situations where reliance on pure reason or experience is more likely to lead them astray than when they follow their intuition. When the hobbits must decide whether to trust Strider upon meeting him for the first time, Frodo goes against the advice of both the innkeeper and Sam and confides in him, stating: "You have frightened me several times tonight, but never in the way servants of the Enemy would, or so I imagine. I think one of his spies would—well, seem fairer and feel fouler, if you understand" (*LotR* 187). Both Bilbo and Frodo take pity on Gollum when a reliance on calculating reason probably would have resulted in their killing him; Gollum, of course, later plays a critical role in the destruction of the One Ring (*LotR* 73, 643). Kreeft notes that a crucial element in the success of Frodo's frequent reliance on his intuition is his moral goodness; intuition "is only trustworthy in the virtuous." Tolkien can thus be interpreted to say that "epistemology depends on ethics; knowledge (of the highest and most important things) depends on goodness" (Kreeft 123). This view appears consistent with that of J. S. Ryan, who writes: "It is a commonplace of Tolkien criticism that it should be observed of the hobbits that they possess 'a Parzival-like innocence'" (Ryan 25). Ryan argues that Frodo, like Parzival, seeks "only to serve, from which acts come all true strength" (37). One can hardly imagine a view further from that of scientism's.

Two of the Inklings devoted considerable energy to their involvement with the esoteric or occult societies mentioned above as a means of overcoming the limitations of scientism. For about a decade, Charles Williams participated in the activities of an offshoot of the Hermetic Order of the Golden Dawn called the Fellowship of the Rosy Cross, organized by the poet A. E. Waite in 1915. Members of the Fellowship attempted to revive an alleged centuries-old secret tradition whose practices led to an empirical union between the supernatural and natural (*The Hidden Church* 523). According to Mark Morrisson, in Williams' novels the Holy Grail becomes "essentially a radioactive atom, a 'storehouse of power' 'encompassed' by 'radiations,' a 'material centre' that could be 'dissipated'" (28). Likewise, Gavin Ashenden writes that Williams' treatment of the Grail echoes the Order's belief in the possibility of unity rather than dichotomy between the two realms. For example, the nature of Christ exemplifies the idea that the body does not bow to the whim of the soul: "the body is unique and divine" (134). In the face of contemporary prejudices (e.g., a devaluing of the non-scientific), Williams promotes the use of myth to "supercede the limitations of a metaphysic truncated by a materialistic culture" (158).

Owen Barfield had similar concerns about scientism's attempt to discard the spiritual component to the existence of man. He was a lifelong devotee of Rudolf Steiner (1861–1917), the founder of anthroposophy, who in *Philosophy of Freedom* (1894) attempted to articulate a philosophical understanding of the relationship between man and nature. Where Williams was drawn to the mystical union of the material and immaterial, Barfield was drawn to Steiner's belief that the gaps between modern science and humanity's religious strivings could be bridged through a refocusing of scientific study on the evolution of the human soul. Barfield wrote: "We are sometimes asked to say 'in a few words' what Anthroposophy is. It is of course impossible. But let us in this context say that the kernel of Anthroposophy is *the concept of man's self-consciousness as a process in time*" (*Romanticism* 189).

According to Steiner, modern science increasingly defines nature separately from man and focuses all its energy on observing the former. In the modern era, the evolutionary theory of Darwin, the materialism of Marx, and the psychoanalysis of Freud have slowly pushed out the spiritual component (188–90). Steiner made the argument that these modern systems were evidence of a spreading scientism that would eventually redefine the relationship between man and nature. As Barfield puts it elsewhere: "It wasn't a new idea about the relation between man and nature; it was an idea of the new relation between them" (*Speaker's Meaning* 138). The response of philosophic anthroposophy was one that links the present with the consciousness of the past and its belief in classical "spiritual hierarchies" (*Romanticism* 199). Without Steiner's system, Barfield believed that the scientific outlook would move into a floundering existentialism. Anthroposophy would provide an objective method of inquiry that enables a recovery of the spiritual. If man is more than matter, then man has a "divine relation to the Cosmos" (201).

Another way the Inklings suggested that scientism offers an incomplete view of reality is by contrasting its outlook with that of the Middle Ages, not to argue that the achievements of medieval science were greater than those of modern science, but to demonstrate that scientism's adherents had lost sight of some important truths. Before the modern scientific age, thinkers accepted that an adequate knowledge of the world required engagement of both the material and the immaterial. In his fiction, Williams sought to convey the distinction that the modern world reduces the mystical and imaginative to certain forms of the occult, whereas the pre-modern world was in tune with it: "ancient desire; he longed to be married to the whole universe for a bride" (*WiH* Loc. 758). Principles relating to the immaterial were usually held *a priori*, but scientism's insistence on empiricism results in a modern acceptance of the material alone. Thinkers such as the logical positivists, whom C. S. Lewis dubbed "plaguey Philosophers" (*CL* 3.540), threatened to drain of meaning and render absurd humanity's free will and purpose (P. Williams 12). The Inklings feared that the radical epistemological move to deny the immaterial would result in modern society's dehumanization.

The modern mind prizes utility to a much greater extent than did the medieval mind. Taking a cue from the Enlightenment, it also views knowledge as something attained rather than something received, another departure from the classical and medieval mindset. Lewis argues that if this new knowledge is merely empirical, it will create a society of people who have an incomplete knowledge of themselves: "They are not men at all, they are artefacts" (*Abolition* 64). The understanding of man without the transcendent reduces him to a material object. Unlike the pre-moderns, the scientific age will have abolished man and replaced him with sterile empirical data. He will be nothing more than an object functioning within the laws of nature. No longer will the posterity of man be a concern because the end of the story is known and there is nothing else to look forward to or meaning and purpose to fulfill. Any duty to posterity will be filed under superstition (*Abolition* 44).

For the Inklings, the reinvention of humanity would lead to inevitable difficulties due to the denial of any possibility of metaphysical reality. Scientism attempts to claim an omnicompetence for the natural sciences, but the Inklings argued that science oversteps its bounds when it begins to address the question of "why"—a question it is not equipped to answer. Many medieval thinkers were committed to scientific knowledge and discovery as well. The difference between the two eras is that the medieval mind was comfortable with conscious limitations regarding the answers it might discover. Medieval scientists were not necessarily concerned with more than the empirical, but they recognized the metaphysical and did not attempt to manipulate it into their paradigm. They perceived the workings of natural laws and the submission of all occurrences to those laws. Created objects and beings, they believed, were animated by desires or longings that drove them to seek their proper level, place, or purpose. The very material of creation strove toward its Creator in a yearning to fulfill its teleology (*DI* 92). In *Saving the Appearances* (1957), Barfield draws attention to the problematic nature of scientific inquiry. He takes issue with the claims that scientific inquiry produces a more accurate and objective knowledge of all subjects, pointing to the problem of reconciling differing sets of scientists' conclusions. The process of empirical research assumes that a consistent approach to any subject should result in repeatable conclusions. When scientists reach divergent conclusions, especially in instances where for Barfield the sciences do not provide the appropriate methodology, one must resort to unscientific criteria for favoring one set conclusions over another (38).

The Inklings called for scientism's adherents to recognize that science can respect, even if it cannot explain, the mythic or metaphysical. They sought to recover a view more representative of the medieval mindset toward humanity and nature. The modern age created a popular science that did not recognize the need for self-reflective exercises (see Lewis, *DI* 17). The Inklings hoped for a recovery of that self-reflection in the natural sciences and an admission that its scope is limited, that it can explain the order, but not what or who does the ordering.

The final way in which the Inklings responded to the expansive claims of scientism is by challenging its first principles. Owen Barfield's *Worlds Apart* (1963) is perhaps the most elaborate example of this kind in their writings. The work is arranged as a fictional dialogue among eight intellectuals in various fields: law, historical theology, rocketry, physics, biology, linguistics, psychiatry, and Waldorf-Steiner (anthroposophical) education. The participants' attempts to penetrate the "watertight compartments" of their respective disciplines lead them to reexamine their underlying assumptions. Barfield refrains from presenting any one perspective as definitively correct, but as the dialogue proceeds, the emphasis shifts from the three physical scientists, who begin the process by confidently proclaiming the perspective of scientism, to the other characters, who point out the insufficiency of its foundational assumptions that are usually asserted but not argued:

> There are many different kinds of knowledge, and one kind is the kind which we require to enable us to control our material environment and make it serve our purposes ... But there is also another kind of knowledge—knowledge about *man* and about the values which make him man and the best way of preserving them; knowledge about his relation to God and God's creatures. The mistake you make—the mistake nearly everyone makes—is to assume that the first kind necessarily includes the second. (*Worlds Apart* 20–21)

Barfield's characters fail to reach consensus on the various problems they discuss, but the direction of the dialogue indicates which perspectives Barfield favors. Not surprisingly, the anthroposophist speaks more than any other character in the final section.

One of C. S. Lewis' most discussed attacks on scientism is his challenge to the validity of reason given scientism's own assumptions. This argument appears in its fullest form in the third chapter of *Miracles*: "The Cardinal Difficulty of Naturalism." In abbreviated form, the argument begins by noting that the possibility of human knowledge depends on the validity of reasoning. Theism has grounds for asserting this validity because it holds that reason—divine reason—precedes Nature, causes Nature's orderliness, and illuminates the human mind in its act of knowing.

Naturalism's grounds for making the same assertion are much more doubtful. It holds that reason is itself the product of nature; that it evolved through the Darwinian process of natural selection out of organisms' non-rational responses to their environment. The problem, as Lewis states, is that "it is not conceivable that any improvement of responses could ever turn them into acts of insight, or even remotely tend to do so. The relation between response and stimulus is utterly different from that between knowledge and the truth known" (*Miracles* 19). Likewise, experience can produce the mental behavior of expectation but not of reason, which infers connections between conjoined things or events and then attempts to discover those connections. Inferring that a useful reason must have developed from the sub-rational by appealing to the tendency of natural selection to favor the useful is simply begging the question because the validity (usefulness) of inference is precisely what is at issue: "Reason is our starting point. There can be no question of attacking or defending it. If by treating it as a mere phenomenon you put yourself outside it, there is then no way, except by begging the question, of getting inside again" (21).

This argument against naturalism, now commonly known as the "argument from reason," occasioned debate when Lewis first proposed it, and it continues to do so in the twenty-first century, having influenced a number of other thinkers. Lewis himself revised the argument after Oxford philosopher Elizabeth Anscombe criticized it at length in a 1948 paper. In recent years, Peter van Inwagen has judged the argument from reason a failure because it does not prove that naturalism is inconsistent with the thesis that our beliefs are grounded in reasoning, whereas Marcel Sarot has maintained the argument's validity: "All Lewis needs in order to show that naturalism undermines rationalism is the claim that if a thought is caused, it is *not likely* to be grounded. As soon as we accept this claim, naturalism through its claim that *all* our thoughts are caused will lead to a distrust of our own thoughts" (Sarot 49).

The Spiritual Quest

At the outset, we employed the image of the Inklings as Arthurian knights embarked on a quest. That quest was the reaffirmation of defining traditions of Western civilization and the defense of the doctrines of Christianity, especially the belief that human beings are comprised of both the material and immaterial, and thus occupy a status distinct from other living things on earth. The Inklings highlighted in this chapter—Lewis, Tolkien, Williams, and Barfield—sensed a deep responsibility to communicate what they considered timeless ideas during an age facing rapid "progress" at every level.

Rapid change can have a seductive quality; the exciting promise of new discoveries and advances can make the traditional seem hopelessly outmoded. For many educated people, the modern scientific age literally changed the definition of a human being. Scientism's promise to explain human life and human nature entirely through reference to the physical, as we have already seen, was at the same time a promise to destroy the uniqueness of humanity. Confronted with what G. K. Chesterton (1874–1936) called "the huge modern heresy of altering the human soul to fit its conditions, instead of altering human conditions to fit the human soul," the Inklings articulated competing visions, ones that not only defended the faith they held dear, but also gave positive alternatives to replace scientism (*What's Wrong* 109). As Lewis once said: "Christianity is a fighting religion .... I don't want to retreat; I want to attack .... We shall probably fail, but let us go down fighting for the right side" (Carpenter 217–18). We have already seen how this quest led Williams and Barfield into paths associated with the occult. The remainder of this chapter surveys other ways in which the Inklings went beyond negative critiques of scientism and positively articulated alternative moral and spiritual visions.

One obvious theme affirming the existence—in fact, the primacy—of the immaterial was the Christian dualism, at times extending into Platonism, evident in the writings of Williams and Lewis. Williams' Arthurian works, both novels and poetry, display this philosophical tendency. In "Williams and the Arthuriad," a lengthy critical essay on Williams' two cycles of Arthurian poetry, *Taliessin through Logres* and *The Region of the Summer Stars*, Lewis provides several examples of Williams' use of celestial and biological phenomena to reflect spiritual truths. For instance, both the Eye of Jupiter (which is read as a wound in the side of the king of gods) and the menstrual flow in women are for Williams a participation in the sacrifice of Christ (WA 334). Elsewhere in the essay, Lewis writes: "For Williams, as for Plato, the phenomenal world—the world studied by the sciences—is primarily a reflection or copy or adaptation of something else" (285). In contrast to scientism's insistence that an ultimately meaningless phenomenal world is all that exists, Williams takes the position that phenomena do have meaning, but that their meaning can only be fully understood by one who first acknowledges their connection to an immaterial reality.

Another area in which Williams displays this sensibility is in his theology of romantic love, which he explains most directly in two books published roughly twenty years apart: *Outlines of Romantic Theology* (1924) and *The Figure of Beatrice* (1943). Williams contends that romantic love is an avenue for experiencing the love of God. Alice Mary Hadfield summarizes Williams' thesis: "In experiencing romantic love, we experience God: He has been in the experience from the beginning, and the more we learn about it, the more we learn also about Him" (*ORT* xi). Romantic love carries with it, not only a natural experience of humanity, but the spiritual significance (9). Being struck by romantic love is equated to experiencing the glory of God—a coalescence of "spiritual emotions, intellectual perceptions, and organic sensations" (*Beatrice* 20). To Williams, love is a "noble virtue" led by proper reason—romantic adoration as proper intellectual investigation—one worthy of Christ (15, 21). Christ, the Word made flesh, is the link between the material and immaterial world. Scripture presents the marriage covenant as an earthly picture of the relationship between Christ and the Church. Williams' view is distinct from popular notions of romantic love focusing exclusively on sexual desire and emotional experience, what for Freud could be interpreted as merely the working out of base, subconscious urges. Williams saw a much deeper potential for the meaning behind romantic love: mystical union.

For Williams, God extends romantic love, available to every human being, as an opportunity to experience the mystical union between creation and Creator. In every aspect, from the vows through consummation and until death, marriage embodies the epitome of communion with the Divine (*ORT* 45). Williams appears to view marriage as a form of sacramentalism: The Lover *becomes* Christ to the Beloved, and vice versa. It is even more than enactment: it is reality. It works to repair the relationship between man and God: "it is because marriage is a means of the work of redemption that two lovers in whom it has been begun are required by the Church to submit themselves to that work to the end" (47). If Christ represents God's act of reparation with man, and romantic love is representative of Christ, then romantic love expressed through marriage points upward to a mystical union between God and man. This idea is the core principle of his romantic theology: "The principles of Romantic Theology can be reduced to a single formula: which is, the identification of love with Jesus Christ, and of marriage with His life" (14). Once again, Williams interprets the material as a reflection of the immaterial.

Lewis sprinkles his writings with insights born out of an understanding of the world best described as Christian Platonism. Both *The Pilgrim's Regress* and *Surprised by Joy*, his two spiritual autobiographies, explore the significance of "joy," which Lewis defines as an intense desire for something indefinable beyond one's grasp. In his own life, beginning in childhood, Lewis experienced this feeling several times and believed that it was the most important element of his autobiography (see *SbJ* 11). Joy could result on a first encounter with certain works of literature, art, or music; however, the thing that occasioned the joy was not its object. Lewis ultimately concluded that the joy he experienced was a sort of momentary Platonic participation in the spiritual, a brief glimpse of and connection to a higher form. He believed it was "valuable as a pointer to something other and outer," namely the Christian God (130).

Platonic language occurs in several places in *The Chronicles of Narnia*. In both *The Lion, the Witch and the Wardrobe* and *The Last Battle*, Digory Kirke expresses the view that other characters would understand Narnia and Aslan's country if only they had read Plato. In the former volume, Digory brings Peter and Susan to recognize the possibility that Lucy could be telling the truth about her visit to Narnia through Socratic questioning. In *The Silver Chair*, the heroes find themselves in an underground kingdom bearing more than a passing resemblance to Plato's "Allegory of the Cave." There an enchantress attempts to convince them in Freudian fashion that their memories of life above ground are figments of their imagination, wish-fulfilments arising from their childlike desire to see things "bigger and better" than what exist in reality. In *The Magician's Nephew*, Uncle Andrew falls into the Platonic sin of self-deception, persuading himself that Aslan is a simple brute and that none of the Narnian beasts can speak. The common thread running through these passages is the theme of a spiritual awareness that ought to enlighten characters' interpretation of the world of the senses.

In addition to a Christian dualism, another of the foundational spiritual beliefs that finds expression in many of the writings of the Inklings is the Christian insistence on the existence of a personal deity Who confers an ultimate purpose (*telos*) on the creation. According to Colin Duriez, Lewis for some time held onto the cosmic impersonalism shared in common by materialism and idealism even after he had been persuaded of theism. A "treaty with reality" was his attempted means of maintaining personal autonomy and control of his own life (McGrath 40). Only when he embraced Christianity did he also assent to the concreteness of a personal God, expressed most clearly in the Incarnation of Christ. Duriez writes: "A God who is fully personal, Lewis discovered, is also more interesting. The deity is involved in the contingency of the world, including the stuff of history; he is not an unchanging, abstract entity (even though his character is unchanging), as Lewis was to argue powerfully in his book *Miracles*" (Duriez 57).

The personal nature of God, of course, is a major feature of Lewis' imaginative literature as well. Although Maleldil, the name used for God in the Ransom trilogy, never appears directly in the narrative, references to him as a personal, causal agent abound in all three volumes; for example, the angelic Oyarsa states that Maleldil "has taken strange counsel and dared terrible things, wrestling with the Bent One [Satan] in Thulcandra," a reference to the Incarnation (*OSP* 120). The Aslan of *The Chronicles of Narnia* (1950–56), as the Trinity's second person, performs an even more visible role in bringing about the creation of Narnia, the defeat of the White Witch and the Telmarines, and the prompting of other characters' actions through appearances in dreams and visions. Ultimately, Aslan brings about the destruction of Narnia, too.

The Hobbit (1937) and *The Lord of the Rings* provide only suggestions and hints of the presence of a personal deity ruling over Tolkien's Middle-earth, although several of these hints are none too subtle. For example, in *The Hobbit*'s final chapter, when Bilbo appears dismissive of ancient prophecy, Gandalf asks whether fulfilling a prophecy oneself invalidates the predictive nature of the original oracular statement. He implies that something (or Someone) other than luck arranged all of the details of Bilbo's story (*Hobbit* 244). It is difficult to avoid the implication that Gandalf's declaration should affect our interpretation of the numerous occurrences of "luck" and "chance" throughout the narrative, and that Bilbo all along has been an instrument of divine providence in some form (Olsen 304).

The role of a personal deity in the various parts of *The Silmarillion* (1977) is even less ambiguous. The "Ainulindalë" describes the creation of the world by Eru/Ilúvatar. The angelic beings who descend to Arda and become known as the Valar and Maiar are also his creations. The conflict among these beings drives much of the history of Middle-earth, but Tolkien makes clear that the purposes of Ilúvatar cannot be thwarted. Whoever tries to frustrate the plans of the One will find that he has become a tool in Ilúvatar's hand for making wonders beyond what he could envision (*Silm* 16). Throughout most of the rest of *The Silmarillion*, Ilúvatar remains off stage, but his presence is still felt in, for example, his invocation in the terrible oath sworn by Fëanor and his sons to retrieve the Silmarils (95). The most dramatic reminder of his role and power occurs in the *Akallabêth*, when he responds in cataclysmic fashion to the Númenórean invasion of Aman, where the Valar dwell. Manwë temporarily gives up his authority, invoking Ilúvatar's assistance. The terrifying power of Ilúvatar reshapes the planet, destroying the kingdom of Númenor and removing Aman eternally away from mortals' reach (326).

The function of the "Flame Imperishable" or "Secret Fire" in *The Silmarillion* and *The Lord of the Rings* provides us with a further example of cosmic personalism and even Christian orthodoxy in Tolkien's fiction. In the "Ainulindalë," Melkor desires take the Flame from its place with Ilúvatar and to use it to create things of his own. Ilúvatar's subsequent sending of the Flame into the Void results in the creation of Arda. The Flame rests in the World's heart; the context of the passage seems to imply its functioning as a force that sustains the world. Thus far we could interpret it simply as an object of great power. However, in *The Lord of the Rings,* Gandalf declares to the Balrog in Moria that he is a "servant of the Secret Fire," a statement that sounds more like a confession of faith. During the arduous editing process for *The Silmarillion*, Tolkien revealed "very specifically" to a colleague that "the Secret Fire sent to burn at the heart of the World in the beginning was the Holy Spirit" (Kilby 59).

Some advocates of scientism, even those who otherwise viewed Tolkien's writings favorably, saw this cosmic personalism ultimately as a limitation or shortcoming of his fiction. For example, in the *Quenta Silmarillion*, Tolkien explains the creation of the sun and the moon as the last fruit and flower produced by the Two Trees of Valinor after they had been poisoned by Melkor. The Valar made containers to hold the light of the trees and entrusted these vessels to two Maiar who guided them through the sky. For a time both remained continuously in the sky, a situation which hindered Melkor but also gave rise to the complaint that no one could sleep due to the continual light. Thus the Valar established regular patterns for the sun and moon, giving the world periods of rest (*Silm* 114–16). Charles Kocher, a historian of science and English literature and author of two books on Tolkien, paused in his summary of Tolkien's account to editorialize:

> Tolkien's handling of the whole matter of the making of the Moon and the Sun is of particular interest because it illustrates one of the central distinctions between myth and physical science. In science events are caused by the interaction of inanimate forces …. In myth, however, everything is done at every level by living beings …. Tolkien well knows these scientific explanations [of gravity and the chemical composition of stars], of course, but finds no juice in them. The universe of myth runs on the doing of beings who have powers and sorrows and wisdom and folly like our own, but magnified. And none is more aware than he that the two kinds of worlds must never mix, or both will explode. (Kocher 80–81)

Kocher could not be clearer; in his opinion, a scientific view of the world is fundamentally at odds with a view of the world that ascribes purpose or personal agency to "events." On this interpretation, Tolkien's real-world Roman Catholicism would make it impossible for him to think scientifically. Tolkien and the other Inklings no doubt would see such assertions as evidence of scientism's impoverished view of reality as discussed in the previous section.

Another of the Inklings' core principles for understanding human life in both its material and immaterial aspects was upholding and advancing the unique power of the imagination. They believed that the imagination, in the face of the modern "isms," preserves a connection to something bigger than the self. Along with writing, reading, and the pursuit of truth in spirituality, the exercise of the imagination aids in the preservation of the humane and helps prevent people from becoming merely bestial. Others noted this emphasis in the Inklings' writing and conversation. David Cecil, who occasionally attended the group's meetings, observed:

> The qualities, then, that gave the Inklings their distinctive personality were not primarily their opinions; rather it was a feel for literature, which united, in an unusual way, scholarship and imagination. Their standard of learning was very high. To study a book in translation or without a proper knowledge of its historic background would have been to them unthinkable: they were academic in the best sense of the word. But—and this is what made them different from most academics—they also read imaginatively. The great books of the past were to them living in the same way as the work of a contemporary …. Yet they did not try to bring them up-to-date. Simply they read their books in the spirit in which they were written. And they could communicate their sense of this spirit to their hearers so that, for these also, these great books sprang to fresh, full life. This was a unique achievement in the Oxford of their time. (10–12)

Imaginative literature often involves a journey into the unknown. The best works use reality to inform their creations while looking beyond it to possibilities from which scientism shrinks: "We can suspend our disbelief in an occasional giant or enchantress. They have friends in our subconscious and in our earliest memories; imagination can easily suppose that the real world has room for them" (*FoA* 75). The reading of such legends and epics does not improve the material conditions of society, but it does affect the spirit. For the Inklings, the spirit is more important than automation, luxury, and convenience: "A real transfusion of spirit involves intangibles: to study it is to study things that can only be known by long and sympathetic reading of originals" (Lewis, "Idea" 14). Part of the Inklings' quest was to preserve a generous space for the spirit within an increasingly secular world. As much as the scientific age attempts to exclude the human spirit, humanity could not flourish without it.

Honest scientists acknowledge the importance of imagination in the formulation of scientific theory (Adler 56:697–702). However, the modern scientific outlook sometimes fails to appreciate the role of imagination in other areas. R. S. Loomis (1887–1966), an American literary critic known for theorizing that Celtic myth is the source of the Grail legends, wrote of "absurdities" and "irrationalities" occurring in the plots of Chrétien de Troyes' Arthurian romances, concluding they must have been the result of medieval misunderstandings of language and myth. In a review of Loomis' *Arthurian Literature in the Middle Ages* (1959), Lewis argues that this reaction is typical of the modern age; it treats medieval romancers as scribes making errors of transcription rather than imaginative and creative forces in their own right ("Arthuriana" 219). For Lewis, the medieval imagination deserves engagement on its own terms, not merely the demythologized rendering most twentieth-century critics wanted to provide (Moynihan).

Of course a very prominent exercise of the imagination for the Inklings was an immersion in myth. Through it they perhaps could maintain most easily certain metaphysical possibilities in the face of scientism's attempted redefinition of reality and knowledge (Miller 330). Many of the Inklings' fictional works are often classified as *mythopoeia*, a genre in which the author creates a mythology and integrates it into the narrative. The frequently dense, self-referential nature of mythopoeia arguably demands a deep level of imagination on the reader's part (Lewis, "On Science Fiction" 72). For the Inklings, myth resonates with the core of what it means to be human. It converses with the transcendent nature of God and the Incarnation. Myth is at the heart of reality and truth because it surpasses rational thought and because Christ's Incarnation surpasses myth. Christianity itself is both a myth and an historical reality" (see Lewis, "Myth Became Fact" 66). Lewis actually sees the act of myth's becoming merely a fact as humiliating, as if to say it lowers itself for the sake of man's inability to elevate himself to belief (*WG* 130). Imaginative literature possesses the ability to converse with such deep themes in part because it avoids the analytic mode usual in scientific works.

Thus one could argue that mythopoeic literature provides the best platform for treating certain mysteries of theism, especially if one's intended audience is likely to resist other genres even more. For example, J. G. Bradbury has argued that the themes Williams treats in his cycles of Arthurian poetry may be more suited to devotional poetry. However, the latter genre had declined significantly by the late 1930s in part because of increased hostility to assertions of religious faith in the intellectual milieu. This fact provided Williams with an incentive to turn to myth, which was experiencing a revival in the twentieth century, a point also noted by Cornelius Crowley (3). "Williams' use of this mode allowed him the possibility of expressing a singularly Christian vision to a world in which such vision was in danger of becoming anathema" (Bradbury 33).

One of the reasons why imagination is so integral to accepting the possibility of myth is that thought and imagination are distinct from one another; imagination allows for description to exist beyond literal explanation (see "'Horrid Red Things'" 70–71). Crucially, imagination allows for the participation of the reader, allowing him to experience the events on the pages he reads. In the eyes of the Inklings, places like Narnia and Middle-earth are not so far away. If the reader's imagination allows him to participate, the objective account becomes a subjective experience. *Contra* the claims of scientism, to the Inklings subjectivity does not necessarily lead to the lack of truth or value: Lewis thinks that *not* believing in the historical truth of a story often leads to its having great imaginative, emotional, or spiritual power (see "Myth Became Fact" 67). Myth causes an involvement that cannot be avoided or maintained by simple observation; it creates a reality based on the participant's desire to be invested in the subject matter. The Inklings consciously constructed stories that involved the natural relationship between the material and immaterial.

The Arthurian cycle is one example of a link between the historical (material) and the imaginative (immaterial) ideas of the Inklings. The Arthurian legends add depth and character to Britain's historical record while also providing moral exemplars for the reader's contemplation. They engage the imagination, potentially transporting the reader into another time and place more effectively than a mere reliance on history would. The ideas of the quest, the Grail, fairy stories, etc., possess a dynamic of myth and history that can be unsettling to moderns. The tension between myth and reason/history/knowledge has existed since ancient times. Only in the modern world has this tension been seen as a crisis in knowledge; before then the tension created great literature (Duriez 59). The ancient and medieval worlds were more comfortable with this dynamic and negotiated it more successfully.

Rather than dismissing myth as the pre-scientific groping of people who were attempting to explain natural phenomena, the Inklings saw it as a valuable way to gain insights about the nature of things at the intuitive and imaginative level. In this they were not alone, particularly with respect to Grail quest literature; contemporary authors such as Arthur Machen in *The Great Return* (1915) and T. S. Eliot in *The Waste Land* (1922) utilized the Grail to represent the need for spiritual enlightenment or fulfillment in the modern world.

One example of this high view of myth is found in *The Lord of the Rings*' Galadriel, who represents the wisdom gained from long experience participating in a fight against evil with no promise of victory:

> For the Lord of the Galadhrim is accounted the wisest of the Elves of Middle-earth, and a giver of gifts beyond the power of kings. He has dwelt in the West since the days of dawn, and I have dwelt with him in years uncounted; for ere the fall of Nargothrond or Gondolin I passed over the mountains, and together through ages of the world we have fought the long defeat. (*LotR* 376)

In one of his letters, Tolkien used the same language to describe his own view of history and the value of communicating that view through myth: "Actually I am a Christian, and indeed a Roman Catholic, so that I do not expect 'history' to be anything but a 'long defeat'—though it contains (and in a legend may contain more clearly and movingly) some samples or glimpses of final victory" (*Letters* 255). Thus, Galadriel participates in what for Tolkien is a Christian archetype. As Stratford Caldecott writes, "For Romantics such as ... Tolkien, imagination is an organ of perception, not merely of fantasy. Mythology may be the only way that certain truths can find expression" (Caldecott 129).

We have defined the Inklings' spiritual quest as the attempt to articulate a positive alternative to scientism. That alternative was a cosmic personalism and Christian dualism communicated largely through the medium of imaginative literature, especially myth. As the quotes from Tolkien and Lewis above show, they did not assume that their efforts would stem, much less reverse, the secular tide in mid-twentieth-century Britain. Nevertheless, the vision their writings communicated succeeded in capturing the imaginations of many millions of readers, and it would be reasonable to judge their quest a success.

Conclusion

It might have been a simple matter for Cold War era believers in the secularization thesis to dismiss the Inklings as reactionaries participating in the Western world's last gasps of spirituality. However, events of recent decades, such as the gradual falling from favor of Freudian theory in academic circles and the fall of Marxist governments in Eastern Europe, have severely shaken the modernist paradigm that was dominant when the Inklings published their most important works. At the same time, the return to prominence of religion in public life and in international affairs, with the rise of Islamic fundamentalism as the most obvious example, demonstrates that scientific secularism is not as inevitable as it may once have seemed.

The Inklings occupy an intriguing place in the dialogue with and response to the scientism of the mid-twentieth century. On the one hand, it is clear that their reaffirmation of important traditions of Western civilization such as Platonism and Christianity, along with their love of classical and medieval literature and their embrace of myth, make it reasonable to describe their outlook as pre-modern. Lewis stated it best when he declared to his colleagues at his inaugural lecture as a professor of literature at Cambridge in 1954:

> I read as a native, texts that you must read as foreigners .... It is my settled conviction that in order to read Old Western literature aright you must suspend most of the responses and unlearn most of the habits you have acquired in reading modern literature. ("De Descriptione")

On the other hand, it seems entirely plausible to describe certain aspects of the Inklings' outlook as postmodern. Most obviously, much of their body of work constitutes a response to the failure of modernity's promise to facilitate never-ending progress for humanity. Postmodern thinkers, too, take modernity to task for this failure. The Inklings, like many postmodernists, attacked the cultural privilege of rationalism and scientism (Clay Brown 59).

Also coinciding with the postmodern sensibility is the Inklings' focus on narrative as a valid way to communicate important ideas, perhaps a way superior even to expository writing. It would be an error to overlook obvious divergences between the Inklings and postmodernism, such as the Inklings' acceptance of the Christian meta-narrative as normative—Barfield went so far as to write that it might be considered absurd, if not blasphemous, to speculate "for the sake of doing so" how the world would be different without the Fall—whereas postmodernism tends to reject meta-narrative of any sort (*Saving the Appearances* 171). Nevertheless, so much of what the Inklings wrote can be seen as a direct response to modernity that "postmodern" often seems an appropriate adjective to use when describing it. Perhaps this is one reason why poets such as Malcolm Guite have argued that the Inklings' works remain particularly relevant in our own historical moment.[2]

The Inklings are likely to continue to figure significantly in scholars' ongoing reinterpretations of twentieth-century religion and spirituality. Their quest to reaffirm the things of the spirit in a scientific age has already helped to inspire a worldwide following of extremely diverse people. In time, perhaps, mainstream scholarship will view the enduring popularity of works like *The Lord of the Rings*—"the UK's Best-Loved Book"—as part of the fruit of that spiritual quest.[3]

Works Cited

Adler, Mortimer, ed. *Darwin*. Great Books of the Western World 49. Encyclopedia Britannica, 1990. Print.

——. *Natural Science: Selections from the Twentieth Century*. Great Books of the Western World 56. Encyclopedia Britannica, 1990. Print.

Ashenden, Gavin. *Charles Williams: Alchemy and Integration*. Kent State UP, 2008. Print.

Barfield, Owen. *Poetic Diction: A Study in Meaning*. 1928. Middletown, CT: Wesleyan UP, 1973. Print.

——. *Romanticism Comes of Age*. 1944. Middletown, CT: Wesleyan UP, 1966. Print.

——. *Saving the Appearances: A Study in Idolatry*. 1957. Middletown, CT: Wesleyan UP, 1988. Print.

——. *Speaker's Meaning*. London: Rudolf Steiner Press, 1967. Print.

——. *Worlds Apart: A Dialogue of the 1960's*. Middletown, CT: Wesleyan University Press, 1963. Print.

"The Big Read." www.bbc.co.uk. 2 September 2014. Web. 15 October 2014.

Blacker, C. P. *Eugenics, Galton, and After*. London: Duckworth Overlook, 1952. Print.

Blamires, Harry. "Against the Stream: C. S. Lewis and the Literary Scene." *Journal of the Irish Christian Study Centre* 1 (1983): 15. Print.

Bradbury, J. G. "Charles Williams' Arthuriad: Mythic Vision and the Possibilities of Belief." *Journal of Inklings Studies* 1.1 (2011). 33–46. Print.

Brignell, Victoria. "The Eugenics Movement Britain Wants to Forget." *The New Statesman* 9 Dec 2010. newstatesman.com. Web. 25 November 2014.

Brooks, David. "Kicking the Secularist Habit: A Six-step Program." *The Atlantic*. 3 March 2003. www.theatlantic.com. Web. 21 October 2014.

Brown, Callum. *Religion and Society in Twentieth-Century Britain*. NY: Routledge, 2006. Print.

---

2   See also Malcolm Guite's conclusion to this volume. [Editor's note]

3   The BBC's "Big Read" survey in 2003 determined that "*The Lord Of The Rings* is officially the UK's Best-Loved Book."

Brown, Clay. *C. S. Lewis and Postmodernism: Areas of Convergence and Divergence*. Ph.D. Diss. Trinity Theological Seminary, 2005. Print.

Caldecott, Stratford. *Secret Fire: The Spiritual Vision of J. R. R. Tolkien*. London: Darton, Longman, and Todd, 2003. Print.

Carpenter, Humphrey. *The Inklings: C. S. Lewis, J. R. R. Tolkien, Charles Williams, and their Friends*. Boston: Houghton Mifflin Company, 1978. Print.

Carey, John. *The Intellectuals and the Masses: Pride and Prejudice among the Literary Intelligentsia, 1880–1939*. London: Faber & Faber, 1992. Print.

Cecil, David. "Oxford's Magic Circle." *Books and Bookmen* 24.4. (1979): 10–12. Print.

Chesterton, G. K. *What's Wrong with the World*. Hollywood, FL: Simon and Brown Amazon Digital Services, 2012. Kindle file.

Crowley, Cornelius P. *A Study of the Meaning and Symbolism of the Arthurian Poetry of Charles Williams*. Ph.D. Diss. U of Michigan, 1952. Print.

Curry, Patrick. *Defending Middle-earth: Tolkien: Myth and Modernity*. NY: Houghton Mifflin, 2004. Print.

Darwin, Charles. *The Descent of Man*. Great Books of the Western World 49. Ed. Mortimer Adler. Chicago, IL: Encyclopedia Britannica, 1990. Print.

Darwin, Charles. *The Origin of Species*. New York, NY: Bantam Dell, 2008. Print.

"Darwinism: Selection, Adaptation, Teleology." *Stanford Encyclopedia of Philosophy*. plato.standford.edu. 19 January 2010. Web. 1 November 2014.

Duriez, Colin. *Tolkien and C. S. Lewis: The Gift of Friendship*. Mahwah, NJ: Paulist Press, 2003. Print.

Freud, Sigmund. *The Interpretation of Dreams*. New York, NY: Basic Books, 2010. Print.

——. *The Ego and the Id*. New York, NY: W.W. Norton & Company Inc., 1960. Print.

Gay, Peter. *Modernism: The Lure of Heresy*. NY: Random House, 2007. Print.

Graves, Robert, and Alan Hodge. *The Long Week-End: A Social History of Great Britain 1918–1939*. 1941. NY: Norton, 1994. Print.

Guite, Malcolm. "The Inklings: Fantasists or Prophets?" St. Edward King and Martyr, Cambridge, UK. November 2011. Lecture Series. malcolmguite.wordpress.com. Web. 15 November 2014.

Haldane, J. B. S. "Auld Hornie, F. R. S." *Modern Quarterly* 1 (1946): 32–40. Web. 28 August 2014.

Herrick, James. "C. S. Lewis and the Advent of the Posthuman." West 235–64.

Hollingdale, R. J., ed. *A Nietzsche Reader*. London: Penguin Books, 1977. Print.

Kilby, Clyde. *Tolkien and the Silmarillion*. Chicago: Harold Shaw Publishers, 1976. Print.

Kocher, Paul H. *Reader's Guide to the Silmarillion*. NY: Houghton Mifflin, 1980. Print.

Kreeft, Peter. *The Philosophy of Tolkien*. San Francisco: Ignatius Press, 2005. Print.

Lewis, C. S. *The Abolition of Man*. NY: HarperCollins, 2001. Print.

——. "*Arthuriana: Arthurian Literature in the Middle Ages: A Collaborative Study*, ed. R. S. Loomis." *Image and Imagination* 217–22.

——. "Christian Apologetics." *God in the Dock* 89–103.

——. *The Collected Letters of C. S. Lewis*. Ed. Walter Hooper. 3 Vols. Harper One, 2004–07. Print.

——. *The Collected Poems of C. S. Lewis*. Ed. Walter Hooper. London: HarperCollins, 1994. Print.

——. "De Descriptione Temporum." Inaugural Lecture from the Chair of Mediaeval and Renaissance Literature at Cambridge University. Cambridge UP, 1954. *Internet Archive*. archive.org. Web. 12 July 2014.

——. *The Discarded Image: An Introduction to Medieval and Renaissance Literature*. Cambridge UP, 1964. Print.

——. *Dymer: A Poem*. 1926. London: J. M. Dent and Sons, 1950. Print.

——. "'Horrid Red Things'." *God in the Dock* 68–71.

——. "The Idea of an English School." *Image and Imagination* 3–20.

——. *God in the Dock: Essays on Theology and Ethics*. Ed. Walter Hooper. Grand Rapids, MI: Eerdmans, 1970. Print.

——. *Image and Imagination*. Ed. Walter Hooper. Cambridge UP, 2103. Print.

——. *Mere Christianity*. 1952. NY: Simon & Schuster, 1996. Print.

——. *Miracles: A Preliminary Study*. 1947. Harper One, 2009. Print.

——. "Myth Became Fact." *God in the Dock* 63–67.

——. *Of Other Worlds: Essays and Stories*. Ed. Walter Hooper. NY: Harcourt, 1994. Print.

——. "On Science Fiction." *Of Other Worlds* 59–73.

——. *Out of the Silent Planet*. 1938. NY: Scribner, 2003. Print.

——. *The Pilgrim's Regress: An Allegorical Apology for Christianity Reason and Romanticism*. 1933. London: Geoffrey Bles, 1945. Print.

——. "Religion and Science." *God in the Dock* 72–75.

——. "A Reply to Professor Haldane." *Of Other Worlds* 74–85.

——. *Surprised by Joy: The Shape of My Early Life*. 1955. *The Inspirational Writings of C. S. Lewis*. NY: Inspirational Press, 1994. 1–130. Print.

——. *The Weight of Glory*. NY: HarperCollins, 1980. Print.

——. "Williams and the Arthuriad." *Arthurian Torso*. Ed. C. S. Lewis. London: Oxford UP, 1948. 91–200. Print.

Loomis, Roger Sherman. *Celtic Myth and Arthurian Romance*. NY: Haskell House, 1967. Print.

MacDonald, Greville. *The Religious Sense in its Scientific Aspect*. London: Hodder and Stoughton, 1904. Print.

Marx, Karl and Friedrich Engels. *The Communist Manifesto*. 1848. *Marxists Internet Archive Library*. marxists.org. Web. 1 October 2014.

Marx, Karl. *Das Kapital*. 1867–94. *Marxists Internet Archive Library*. marxists.org. Web. 1 October 2014.

Mayr, Ernst. "Darwin's Influence on Modern Thought." *Scientific American*. www.scientificamerican.com. 24 November 2009. Web. 10 January 2015.

McGrath, Alister. *The Intellectual World of C. S. Lewis*. Oxford: Wiley & Sons, 2014. Print.

Miller, Michael Matheson. "C. S. Lewis, Scientism, and the Moral Imagination." *West* 309–38.

Morrisson, Mark S. *Modern Alchemy: Occultism and the Emergence of Atomic Theory*. Oxford UP, 2007. Print.

Mosse, George L. *Toward the Final Solution: A History of European Racism*. NY: Howard Fertig, 1985. Print.

Moynihan, Martin. "C. S. Lewis and the Arthurian Tradition." *Inklings Jahrbuch fuer Literatur und Aesthetik* 1 (1983). 21–41. Print.

Nietzsche, Friedrich. *Beyond Good and Evil*. 1886. Hollingdale 179–82. Print.

——. *Human, All Too Human*. 1878. Hollingdale 167–8.

——. *The Gay Science*. 1882. Hollingdale 202–03.

——. *The Antichrist.* 1895. London: Penguin Books, 1990. Print.

——. *Thus Spoke Zarathustra.* 1883–91. Hollingdale 237–40.

Olsen, Corey. *Exploring J. R. R. Tolkien's* The Hobbit. NY: Houghton Mifflin, 2012. Print.

Pearson, Karl. *The Relative Strength of Nurture and Nature.* Cambridge UP, 1915. Print.

Reichenbach, Bruce. "C. S. Lewis and the Desolation of Devalued Science." *VII: An Anglo-American Literary Review* 4 (1983): 14–26. Print.

Russell, Bertrand. "A Free Man's Worship." 1903. *Philosophical Society.* philosphicalsociety.com. Web. 1 November 2014.

Ryan, J. S. "Uncouth Innocence: Some Links between Chrétien de Troyes, Wolfram von Eschenbach and J. R. R. Tolkien." *Inklings Jahrbuch fuer Literatur und Aesthetik* 2 (1984): 25–41. Print.

Sarot, Marcel. "The Cardinal Difficulty for Naturalism: C. S. Lewis' Argument Reconsidered in Light of Peter van Inwagen's Critique." *Journal of Inklings Studies* 1.2 (2011): 41–53. Print.

Singh, Amardeep. *Literary Secularism: Religion and Modernity in Twentieth-Century Fiction.* Newcastle: Cambridge Scholars, 2006. www.lehigh.edu. Web. 20 January 2015.

Tolkien, J. R. R. *The Fall of Arthur.* Ed. Christopher Tolkien. NY: Mariner Books, 2014. Print.

——. *The Hobbit.* 1937. London: Folio Society, 1979. Print.

——. *The Letters of J. R. R. Tolkien.* Ed. Humphrey Carpenter. NY: Houghton Mifflin, 2000. Print.

——. *The Lord of the Rings.* 1954–55. Boston: Houghton Mifflin, 1993. Print.

——. *The Silmarillion.* 1977. London: Folio Society, 2004. Print.

Waddington, C. H. *The Nature of Life.* 1961. Great Books of the Western World 56. Chicago, IL: Encyclopedia Britannica, 1990. Print.

Waite, A. E. *The Hidden Church of the Holy Graal: Its Legends and Symbolism Considered in Their Affinity with Certain Mysteries of Initiation and Other Traces of a Secret Tradition in Christian Times.* London: Rebman, 1909. Print.

West, John G., ed. *The Magician's Twin: C. S. Lewis on Science, Scientism, and Society.* Seattle: Discovery Institute Press, 2012. Print.

Whalen, Robert W. *Sacred Spring: God and the Birth of Modernism in Fin de Siècle Vienna.* Grand Rapids, MI: Eerdmans, 2007. Print.

Williams, Charles. *The Figure of Beatrice: A Study in Dante.* 1943. NY: Octagon Books, 1980. Print.

——. *Outlines of Romantic Theology.* Ed. Alice M. Hadfield. Berkeley: Apocryphile Press, 2005. Print.

——. *War in Heaven.* 1930. Grand Rapids, MI: Eerdmans, 1947. Kindle file.

Williams, Charles, and C. S. Lewis. *Taliessin through Logres; The Region of the Summer Stars; Arthurian Torso.* Grand Rapids, MI: Eerdmans, 1974. Print.

Williams, Peter. *C. S. Lewis vs the New Atheists.* Milton Keynes: Paternoster, 2013. Print.

10

The Stripped Banner: Reading
The Fall of Arthur as a Post-World War I Text. [1]

Taylor Driggers

In his famous 1939 essay "On Fairy-stories," J. R. R. Tolkien outlined three principles that characterized the role of myth in culture: Recovery, Escape, and Consolation (OFS 52). Myths and fairy-stories help us to regain "a clear view," escape the "prison" of our own time, and receive "a fleeting glimpse of joy" (OFS 53–62), Tolkien claimed, because they "open a door on Other Time, and if we pass through, though only for a moment, we stand outside our own time, outside Time itself, maybe" (OFS 32). Viewing these comments in historical context, it is not at all difficult to understand Tolkien's desire to disappear into other worlds and other times. At the time of Tolkien's writing, Britain was on the cusp of the second "War of the Machines" (as Tolkien termed the World Wars; *Letters* 111) and still attempting to recover from the previous one. With the First World War having destroyed not only many lives, but also older ways of living and thinking about the world, the apparent inaccessibility of Other Time was lamented by many. Yet to Tolkien, "fairy-stories were plainly not primarily concerned with possibility, but with desirability" (OFS 39). It was in the textual spaces of myth—"secondary worlds," as Tolkien called them (OFS 46)—that consolation from the senseless violence characterizing modernity and the two World Wars could be found; escape into Other Time, however temporary, could be achieved; and a sense of meaning could be recovered.

And yet, for a post-World War I audience, the escape into mythic worlds presents its own set of pitfalls; as Margaret Hiley notes: "the archaic worlds of fantasy seem to call for ancient heroes that are … no longer credible to a modern readership" (Hiley 85). Verlyn Flieger has similarly observed that the First World War deeply problematized the archetypes of heroic, ostensibly nationalistic, and usually militaristic ideas

---

1   This chapter is a heavily edited expansion of a portion of his M.Sc. dissertation for the University of Edinburgh.

of superiority that were often used to justify it (Flieger 220). From a modern perspective, the world of Western mythology is defined by violent forms of heroism largely discredited by the brutality and destruction of World War I. Stefan Goebel has gone so far as to suggest that the mythic or medievalist imagery commonly seen in "rehearsals of Victorian sentiments" (Goebel 194) was partially responsible for Britain's eagerness to join the conflict in the first place, reconfiguring "the act of killing as a bloody yet noble deed" (Goebel 200). What resulted was a "clash of 'big words' like honour and glory with the terrors of combat," in which "those who experienced the ugliness of war identified the 'big words' with the elder generation who had sent them into battle" (Goebel 11). Therefore, as Tom Shippey notes, post-war expressions of myth "needed a new image for ultimate bravery, one which would have some meaning and some hope of emulation for the modern and un- or anti-heroic world" (Shippey, *Author* 149).

The chief question, then, facing any post-World War I mythmaker is *how* myth can even hope to offer recovery, escape, and consolation amid such disillusionment with the very idea of heroism. When violence is built into the very nature of myth, what sort of secondary world can offer suitable escape from a violent modern society? What archaic values and ideas are worthy of being recovered, and how can they console the reader, preparing him or her to face modernity anew? This study will analyze these questions as addressed by Tolkien's own mythic works, with particular attention to his unfinished epic poem *The Fall of Arthur*. While some scholars have read Tolkien's use of violence as escapist and uncritical at best, I will argue that *The Fall of Arthur* presents a mythic narrative that actively engages with modern views of violence *through* its escape into an archaic world. Additionally, *The Fall of Arthur* shares narrative and thematic parallels with *The Lord of the Rings* that shed new light on the grand battles for which Tolkien's magnum opus has become notorious to readers and thoroughly confusing to scholars.

An Escape into Violence?

Despite Tolkien's personal experience of World War I and his extensive commentary on World War II in letters to his son, a satisfying critical analysis of the role of violence within Tolkien's stories themselves is strangely lacking. Much has been made of the former from a biographical standpoint; John Garth's *Tolkien and the Great War* thoroughly documents Tolkien's war experience as the beginning of his mythmaking. Similarly, Verlyn Flieger has drawn attention to the many perverse parallels between the war experience and Tolkien's thematic treatment of the experience of Faërie, noting that "both war and Faërie can change out of all recognition the wanderer's perception of the world to which he returns, so that never again can it be what it once was" (Flieger 224). While Tolkien famously dismissed claims that his work was a direct, conscious reflection of the British cultural landscape during and after the two World Wars, he also acknowledged "its varied applicability to the thought and experience of readers"; neither the reader nor the author can "remain wholly unaffected by his experience" (*LotR* xxii). Only Shippey has examined such "applicability" regarding war, reading Tolkien as "one of a group of ... 'traumatised authors'" of modern fantasy (Shippey, *Road* xvii). Even then, however, his studies mainly focus on Saruman, Denethor, and the nature of evil, rarely commenting on the implications of fantastical violence itself.[2]

This is not to say that there is any shortage of warfare and violence in Tolkien's works; in fact, Hiley notes that Tolkien goes so far as to structure "Middle-earth's history entirely around great wars and battles" (Hiley 43). Hiley reads Tolkien's entire approach to mythmaking as an attempt "to utilise [war's] unreality and reconstruct the war as a fantastic and supernatural experience" (Hiley 40). In her view, "fantasy texts fear (war's) fragmentation and the modern acceleration of reality … but they obviously also fear stagnation, and thus resort to the dynamics unleashed by war" (43). Violence is therefore necessary to the very structure of mythic narratives, even while, in Hiley's view, such narratives are born out of a reluctance to engage with the violence of the primary world.

Along similar lines, Andrew Lynch posits that "Tolkien, as a learned medievalist, dealt with the memory of 'hideous' modern war by transforming it into a superior version directly along medieval lines" (Lynch 79). Lynch likens Tolkien's descriptions of battles and heroism in *The Lord of the Rings* to those of Tennyson in the *Idylls of the King*, who "seeing his own era as morally superior to Geoffrey of Monmouth's or Malory's … committed himself to capturing the true 'spirit' or 'ideal' of Arthurian chivalry without much of its troubling military substance" (Lynch 77). For Lynch, Tolkien's mythic heroism is not simply the denial of modernity that Hiley's reading suggests, but an attempt to mask the so-called "empirical history" (Lynch 83) of the war experience behind "the idea of war as an ennobling cultural and moral struggle" which "is allowed precedence over the unpleasant history of war itself" (Lynch 90). Lynch thus positions Tolkien's act of mythmaking along the same lines as the commemorative expressions of chivalry that Goebel documents, with medievalist fantasy in both cases superseding the real horrors of the primary world.

The problem with both of these readings, of course, is that they engage in the same patronizing view of Faërie that Tolkien discourages in "On Fairy-stories." Shippey astutely observes that "when people start appealing to 'truth', 'experience' and 'reality,'" as Lynch does in his language of "empirical history," "they imply very strongly that they know what these things *are*" (Shippey, *Road* 136). To Tolkien, the very act of participating in myth, whether as author or as reader, challenges and upends such assertions. He does not, as Hiley does, view fantasy as an unstable construction designed to preserve a familiar sense of stability; in fact, the process of recovery offered by fantasy is one of *de*-familiarization. Tolkien writes that "we need … to clean our windows; so that the things seen clearly may be freed from the drab blur of triteness or familiarity" (OFS 53). Recovery, for Tolkien, means that fantasy—or good fantasy, at least—*reveals* the otherwise unspeakable beauty and horror underlying familiar words, images, and experiences, rather than obscuring them as Lynch and Goebel suggest.

As for the consolatory escape Tolkien seeks in myth, "it does not deny the existence of dyscatastrophe, of sorrow and failure: the possibility of these is necessary to the joy of deliverance" (OFS 62). The modern mythmaker, for Tolkien, is like a man "who, finding himself in prison … thinks and talks about other topics than jailers and prison-walls[.] The world outside has not become less real because the prisoner cannot see it" (OFS 55–56). The purpose of Faërie is not to attempt to transform the author or

2

reader's own imprisonment within modernity into a more pleasant or morally justifiable experience, as Lynch argues. Instead, Tolkien aims to bring the reader's perspective *outside* of that prison in order to face the primary world with renewed clarity, "satisfying [desire] while often whetting it unbearably" (OFS 39). And yet, Tolkien is not myopic where fantasy is concerned; he is keenly aware of its ability to "delude the minds out of which it came" (OFS 52), which will be very important to understanding *The Fall of Arthur*.

Tolkien and Tennyson

Since Lynch links the kind of modern medievalism embodied in Tolkien with Victorian expressions of myth, a brief note on Tennyson's contributions to the Arthurian tradition is in order. The significance of Tennyson's odd fusion of medieval and Victorian sensibilities for the generation that fought in World War I has not escaped the notice of historian Paul Fussell, who comments that the "experiences of a man going up the line to his destiny cannot help seeming to him like those of a hero of medieval romance." For most well-read young men at the time, the main frame of reference for such tales would have been "Victorian pseudo-medieval romance, like the versified redactions of Malory by Tennyson" (Fussell 135). While Fussell's comments risk over-generalizing the individual soldier's experience, they also echo Goebel's analysis of the "big words" and chivalrous re-framing of warfare that became deeply troubling in the traumatic wake of the conflict itself. Given this, we may conclude that *Idylls of the King* was a massively influential text for the appropriation of mythic heroism in modern war propaganda.

Idylls of the King appropriates the familiar Arthurian narratives in order to romanticize Victorian sensibilities of autonomy and progress, many of which carried over into early twentieth-century cultural discourse. Fussell has called World War I "a war representing a triumph of modern industrialism, materialism, and mechanism" (Fussell 115). Similarly, Crystal L. Downing has noted how the Victorian rise of industrial capitalism, social Darwinism, and secular humanism gave rise to the early twentieth-century celebration of "persons of genius who advanced the evolution of society by rising above it" (Downing 79). Tennyson establishes his Arthur as one such genius, a god among men who has achieved perfect autonomy. The first idyll begins with Arthur gloriously conquering a savage Britain "wherein the beast was ever more and more, / But man was less and less" (1.11–12). He drives "The heathen; after, [slays] the beast" (1.59), this violent act paradoxically symbolizing his triumph over wild, animalistic nature and the less evolved, "heathen" other. This cycle is repeated throughout the *Idylls*, as Arthur strikes down his morally inferior opponents, and the natural order is re-imagined as a hierarchy with Arthur, the figurehead of British superiority, at its pinnacle (8.232–40).

Tennyson, however, recognizing the ethical questionability of real warfare even pre–World War I, largely withholds the details of such campaigns. In fact, Arthur himself is strangely absent from the *Idylls* as a character in his own right, functioning instead as "a symbolic presence [that] hovers over all the idylls" (Lupack 147).[3] What results is a text that establishes "war [as] a school of moral order, a preparation for

---

3   Cf. chapter fifteen in the present volume, "Those Kings of Lewis's Logres: Arthurian Figures as Lewisian Genders in *That Hideous Strength*" by Benjamin Shogren, for a study of the evolving role of Arthur in (and out of) literary texts as the tradition developed.

future rule," but also refuses to engage with warfare itself in any meaningful way, with "the description of war often [tending] more toward ideological symbol than toward direct description of military action" (Lynch 86). Paradoxically, this meant that "in the later Victorian period war became the main selling-point of medievalism as symbolic heroism and chivalry" (Lynch 77), leading Tennyson's highly allegorical secondary world to impact the conflicts in the primary world in devastating ways, by which its ideas of noble, chivalrous war in the name of progress were appropriated.

As a result, it comes as no surprise that Tolkien's *Fall of Arthur* represents an attempt to resurrect the Arthurian tradition's medieval origins (and by extension, its connection to Tolkien's own Roman Catholic beliefs and practices) rather than its Victorian adaptations. This is not to suggest that Tolkien denies the cultural fluidity of myth; after all, fairy-stories "are by no means rocky matrices out of which the fossils cannot be prised except by an expert geologist. The ancient elements can be knocked out, or forgotten and dropped out, or replaced by other ingredients with the greatest ease" (OFS 33). As I will demonstrate, Tolkien himself takes part in this practice, significantly altering the narrative details and thematic subtext of the legend to reflect more modern concerns.

Yet his aesthetic choices in crafting his own version of the Arthurian narrative still suggest a desire to resurrect something closer to the legend's origins than Tennyson's hyper-idealized appropriation of the tale. To Tolkien, the values that Tennyson expressed in his *Idylls* are diametrically opposed to the very ethos of mythmaking and true medievalism. Here, Tolkien adopts the Germanic tradition of alliterative verse, favoring gritty, textured syntax over Tennyson's more elevated, Romantic verse. Additionally, while many narrative details of the poem are unique to Tolkien, it draws inspiration primarily from Geoffrey of Monmouth, Sir Thomas Malory, and the alliterative *Morte Arthure*,[4] with virtually no acknowledgement of any post-fifteenth-century Arthurian literature. Even these surface-level aspects of the poem point toward an attempt at a more thoroughly medieval Arthurian text, even if "by looking backwards [Tolkien's] fantasy reflected the present, and the temporal dislocation of his 'escape' mirrored the psychological disjunction and displacement of his century" (Flieger 11). If Tolkien's work makes a case for medievalism as a solution to modernity's problems and anxieties, then his mythmaking can hardly take cues from texts whose philosophies are partially responsible for the predicaments of his own era.

> While Tennyson's text equated moral uprightness with autonomy and the suppression of nature, Tolkien suggests that the heroism of the Round Table comes from neither strength in arms nor the authority of a more "evolved" ruler, but from loyalty and comradeship. When Arthur longs for the help of the banished Lancelot in the war against Arthur's treacherous bastard son Mordred, Gawain reminds him that the solidarity of Arthur's few remaining faithful knights is preferable than the "doubtful swords" of those who have deserted him (1.198–208)

---

4   See Tolkien, Christopher, "The Poem in Arthurian Tradition," *The Fall of Arthur* (London: HarperCollins, 2013)

Tolkien desires an escape into a secondary world where love and mutual brotherhood govern people's actions above all else; his Camelot represents neither an ideal social order nor a hierarchy ruled by a divinely perfect Arthur, but rather a community whose virtue stems from its members' fierce loyalty to one another. Tolkien felt that this familial bond was at the core of myth, arguing that the purpose of storytelling is "to hold communion with other living things" (OFS 17). In this passage, then, the Round Table comes close to representing fantasy itself, already threatened even in the poem's medieval setting.

By contrast, Mordred and his mercenaries are repeatedly described with language and imagery associated with opportunism and betrayal for the sake of individual gain—attributes which Downing aligns with "the 'survival ethic' of social Darwinism" (Downing 68). Mordred's assumption of the throne of Camelot in Arthur's absence is accompanied by the sound of cocks crowing (2.46), and his followers are described as "lovers of treason, // lightly purchased" (2.104–06). Such radical self-interest represents a particularly extreme embodiment of modern autonomy and individual progress; indeed, Mordred's words to Guinever in the second canto reinforce this, heralding the rise of the triumphant individual unbound by allegiances (2.147–53). The chief conflict in *The Fall of Arthur*, therefore, is one between medieval community and the modern individual's will to dominate, which Tolkien would later symbolize through the insidious power of the Ring in *The Lord of the Rings*. in *The Lord of the Rings*.

A (self-)destructive Arthur

The first canto of *The Fall of Arthur* uses this temporal conflict as a subtle subversion of heroic violence as Arthur journeys to the continent on a military campaign , albeit without disclosing much detail of the campaign itself. Christopher Tolkien himself notes the strangeness of the fact that "in the hundred lines of the first canto of the poem from the beginning of Arthur's expedition at line 39 to the coming of Sir Cradoc with his evil tidings there is ... only one reference to the destruction of heathen habitations by the invading host" (C. Tolkien 87), and this lack of narrative description would at first seem to indicate a discomfort with the details of battle in a Lynchian sense. Yet gone from this portrayal are all hints even of the archetypal imagery of black-and-white morality that Lynch reads into *The Lord of the Rings*' battles.[5] Tolkien might not describe specific feats of battle as medieval authors do, but neither does his recourse to environmental imagery portray the campaign in a flattering light.

Arthur's soul may yearn for one last demonstration of glorious might (1.14–16), but what follows strongly suggests that his efforts are vain and foolish. Instead of the victorious tone and triumphant imagery traditionally associated with such a conquest in medieval narrative, Tolkien's language focuses on the barren wasteland Arthur and his knights make of the landscape, as they pillage and plunder "till earth was empty, // and no eyes saw them" (1.64). Here again we have a subtle subversion of Victorian versions of the tale; whereas in Tennyson's version Arthur subdues an untamed landscape to establish his control over humanity's animalistic nature, here the effect is much more bleak and foreboding. The drive to dominate

---

5   See Lynch's interpretation of color-coded morality in *The Lord of the Rings* on p. 80 of *Tolkien's Modern Middle Ages*.

and "tame" the wilderness is not, to Tolkien, an admirable one. On the contrary, Matthew Dickerson and Jonathan Evans argue that "throughout Tolkien's oeuvre, woods and forests—often wild, untamed, and trackless—serve as a potent image for the primordial value of the natural order" (Dickerson and Evans 124). Nature does not need to be artificially assembled or cultivated, as Tennyson's text implies; its wild, untamed state is good in itself, "irrespective of and sometimes inimical to the self-centered concerns of Elves, Men, and other beings" (Dickerson and Evans 124). In this canto, Tolkien reveals the destructive implications of Tennyson's heroic paradigm, and in doing so, renders it darkly ironic.

The bleak imagery becomes more surreal in the lines that follow, blurring distinctions between the metaphorical and literal. A powerful tempest becomes almost indistinguishable from a battalion of horsemen (1.87–89), calling to mind, among other possible allusions, the Biblical apocalypse, and thus foreshadowing the inevitable downfall of Camelot prophesied by the poem's title. Coupled with the war-like imagery accompanying it, the scene indicates that the true enemy of Arthur and his knights is time itself, and the ruination it can bring. Further signifying the impossibility of glorious war in this new world, the knights' "fair banners / from their staves [are] stripped" (1.91–92) by the howling winds. The archetypal imagery often associated with medieval warfare—the streaming standards, the shimmering of swords and armor—loses its heroic luster (1.91–93), and the knights are left to face this new, hostile environment they have created without access to the triumphant symbols or sentiments of the past.

Nevertheless, Gawain loudly defies the stormy blast by invoking Arthur's strength in arms (1.104). Miraculously, the storm subsides, but no sooner do the winds and rain die down than a chilly fog sets in as "[t]ime [wears] onward" (1.119). Soon after, Sir Cradoc arrives to warn Arthur of Mordred's treachery, and the canto ends with Arthur journeying back to Britain to meet Mordred in battle. Gawain's defiance of the storm and the coming of the mist represent a microcosm of the thematic and narrative structure of the first canto, a repeated cycle in which Arthur and his knights continually attempt to subdue time and the forces of nature, only for the destruction they leave in their wake to fall back upon themselves. This, too, dramatizes a key principle Dickerson and Evans highlight for Tolkien's environmental vision: "mistreatment of the natural world results in an environment that is less hospitable to its inhabitants" (Dickerson and Evans 140). To assert dominance over the landscape and to blindly conquer simply because one is able to do so are not acts of progress to Tolkien, but of self-destruction.

The poem's fourth canto, in which Arthur and his knights return to Britain to fight Mordred, demonstrates a slight variation on this bleak outlook. While the battles in the remainder of the poem do indeed contain striking instances of morbid and apocalyptic imagery in accordance with the first canto's gloomy outlook on warfare, instances in which Tolkien revels in at least the aesthetics of battle and heroism are just as common. The return of Arthur's warships to meet Mordred's army in battle is heralded by a change in weather, from the gloomy tempests of the first three cantos to a clear sky streaming with sunlight. The battle that ensues begins with sharp bursts of archetypal imagery and striking, almost onomatopoeic, diction to thrilling effect (4.168–70). For a moment, all specificity of character or location disappears beneath the very *idea* of medieval warfare itself, so effectively rendered in Tolkien's description. Taken on its own, this passage would seem to support Lynch's claims that Tolkien's "war may be 'grim' and 'terrible,' but it is often valorous and lofty in style" (Lynch 79).

Yet this imagery, too, is just as soon subverted as the battle spirals into a disturbing bloodbath, symbolically staining red the white shores of Arthur's Britain. (1.217). Tolkien continues to withhold specific details of the carnage, but his tone suddenly shifts from triumphant to morbid as he describes the battle's aftermath. Tolkien's description of Arthur's victory in the battle and return to his kingdom may read like a fanfare, but instead of ending with Arthur re-assuming his throne, the canto lingers on the shore among "dead men and drowned, // a dark jetsam" (1.228). Once again, a sinister, destructive undertone has crept into Arthur's misguided longing for noble, chivalrous warfare, and Tolkien allows these conflicting ideas to inhabit the same space.

Temporality and exile from Faërie

What is to account for such striking dissonances in the narrative? Why is it impossible for Arthur, with all his virtues and idealism, to overcome Mordred? Part of the answer to this lies in the temporal setting of the poem itself. Tolkien's Camelot is one in which the Round Table has already been irrevocably ruptured, and the entire poem is tinged with the impending fall of the kingdom. Tolkien describes Gawain, for instance, as "defence and fortress // of a falling world" (1.55), and Mordred's betrayal of Arthur is described as though time itself is Arthur's enemy (1.178–79). Even key plot points are framed in terms of the past; Guinever's escape from Camelot, for instance, alludes to the mythic history of the setting (2.201–03). The third canto of the poem, focusing on the exiled Lancelot, contains similarly complex temporality, with the entire story of his affair with Guinever and subsequent banishment from Camelot told in flashback as Lancelot looks out on the desolate landscape.

By setting his poem at the tail end of Arthur's reign, Tolkien not only creates a secondary world in Camelot, but also creates a tertiary world of Camelot's history buried deep within the narrative, resurfacing in incomplete fragments through the telling of the story, but unable to be fully resurrected. This suggestion of discontinuity with a glorious, mythic past even within the text's secondary world parallels Tolkien's own imprisonment within modernity and sharply contrasts with Lynch's theory about attempts to establish clear continuity with the past.

Christopher Tolkien has noted that "from the first lines of *The Fall of Arthur* it is seen that [J. R. R. Tolkien] was departing radically from the story of Arthur's last campaign overseas as told by Geoffrey of Monmouth and his successors" (C. Tolkien 75). Instead of "a very mighty monarch, unbeaten in battle, his knights and his household the model and pattern of chivalry and courtly life" (C. Tolkien 76–77), we are presented with an Arthur toward the end of his reign, hoping "the tides of time // to turn backward" (1.5) with his continued conquest of foreign realms. In a Camelot from which Lancelot has already been banished, where the ties of love and brotherhood responsible for Camelot's greatness have begun to be severed, Arthur hopes to revive Camelot's previous glories by venturing out on the warpath. By temporally dislocating this episode in the narrative (which in other versions is one of the establishing moments at the start of Arthur's rule), Tolkien also ironically subverts it, suggesting that Arthur fights to uphold virtues that have already eluded his grasp.

To Tolkien, Arthur's vastly misguided attempt to resurrect past glories that belong to Other Time within his own present represents a gross perversion of the desire that Faërie awakens in author and reader. Christine Chism has keenly noted Tolkien's awareness of mythic appropriation in not only his post-World War I writings, but also his work during World War II, including *The Lord of the Rings*. She observes in Tolkien "the realization that mythmaking is not innocent, that it can become a killing tool" through its appropriation by violent or oppressive causes (Chism 63–64). Such an observation is vital to understanding Tolkien as a wartime writer, and helps us make sense of *The Fall of Arthur* as a post-War text without resorting to mere allegory (a mode of storytelling that Tolkien famously disliked). Yet Chism mistakenly interprets this awareness as a final, wholesale rejection of mythmaking on Tolkien's part. Misinterpreting the Ring in *The Lord of the Rings* as a symbol for mythmaking, Chism chronicles its power as a slow, natural process in which "imagination degenerates to appetite; powerful speculation, to malignant dominion" (80). She thus concludes that *The Lord of the Rings* is "a tale of the renunciation of mythology and the willed return to history" (64).

The Ring, however, is neither a latent power of the earth like Faërie nor a natural human impulse like "sub-creation" (Tolkien's term for the artistic impulse; OFS 71), but rather an artificial construction that has only the power to manipulate, corrupt, and re-appropriate power. In a similar way, Arthur's desire for conquest is not entirely of his own making, but instead spurred on by Mordred, who, jumping at the opportunity to seize the throne in Arthur's absence, "with malice ... [Arthur's] mind hardened" (I.19) for war. Mordred, representing the modern autonomy and will to dominate that contrasts the community of the Round Table, nonetheless invokes the broad concepts and signifiers associated with Arthur's glorious reign and (similarly to Tennyson and others) aligns Arthur's nobility with his strength in arms. Mordred's urging of Arthur into battle, entirely unique to Tolkien's account, acts as the catalyst for the fall of Camelot and the death of Arthur. By appropriating the language of a medievalist discourse ultimately incompatible with his own motives, Mordred, as Tolkien's proto-modernist, has ensured the destruction of that medieval sensibility. Such a conscious departure from the Arthurian tradition, especially by such a staunch literary traditionalist as Tolkien, reads as a metatextual critique of the use of chivalric diction in war propaganda, rather than an earnest invocation of it. Tolkien himself demonstrates an awareness and distaste for this phenomenon as it related to both British and German public discourse in his letters, calling it "war hypnotism" (*Letters* 89).

In light of Goebel's analysis of the latter phenomenon in wartime British culture, the narrative parallels are indeed hard to deny: Mordred invokes a discourse of past glories so as to thrust Britain into a conflict on the continent. Just as the war signified for Britain a destruction of older values and ideals in favor of an impersonal, destructive, and mechanistic society, Tolkien suggests that the "long glory" (I.15) Arthur experienced during his reign and the ideals he established have now been destroyed. This is given even greater significance by the fact that Arthur's reckless war leaves Mordred, the embodiment of modern cynicism, free to assume the throne in Arthur's absence. While it would be rash to assume that this situation is a direct allegory or "veiled rewrite" of World War I—which Shippey calls "an exercise with almost no point" (*Author* 167)—it is nonetheless applicable to the cultural landscape Tolkien inhabited.

By intentionally twisting the longing for Faërie into bloodlust, Mordred has transformed the myth of Arthur's glory into a gross parody bearing little resemblance to the original. Even the dissolution of the brotherhood characterizing the Round Table at its peak is not entirely a natural process, but brought about by Lancelot and Guinever's infidelity and Mordred's own ulterior motives for exposing the same. Tolkien recognizes full well the limitations of myth; indeed, all of his stories contain some element to remind us that all journeys into a secondary world must end somewhere and that the revelatory and consolatory magic of Faërie is temporary for us in the secondary world. And so, as Flieger notes, Tolkien's mythmaking is not an attempt to establish continuity with the past but a reminder of its inaccessibility: "it shows what seems to be the futility of trying to go back, to have any real connection with the past, or to hold onto beauty and enchantment" (Flieger 218). As we see with Arthur, this often has very real and destructive consequences.

Yet despite all of this, Tolkien still places a fundamental value on fantasy as narrative. Using his childhood experience of fairy-stories as an illustration, he recalls his "profound desire" for dragons, while acknowledging that he "did not wish to have them in the neighbourhood" (OFS 40). Fantasy can still have power and applicability for those of us in the primary world without becoming harmful delusion. In *The Fall of Arthur*, however, we see not the eucatastrophic power and desire created by fantasy at its best, but instead the tragic manner in which oppressive ideologies—both familiar and foreign—destroy Faërie through their blind appropriation of mythic symbols.

Fatal distractions: *The Fall of Arthur* and *The Lord of the Rings*

If a careful reading of the Ring's destructive influence can help us interpret Mordred's agency in the downfall of Camelot, then we may also better understand the War of the Ring by observing Mordred's warmongering influence on Arthur. Particularly in a post-Peter Jackson cultural landscape, *The Lord of the Rings* is as often remembered for its grandiose battle scenes as it is for its exhaustively detailed world-building. And yet, in Tolkien's text, the role of these battles in the struggle against Sauron is often downplayed, with no one character fulfilling the traditionally Arthurian role of "hero." Even Aragorn, whom Lynch interprets as "a symbolic return of Arthur, completing the cycle of Tennyson" (Lynch 82), is decentered in the narrative in favor of small, humble, and peaceful hobbits—hardly the sort of people Tennyson would choose as his heroic figures.

Chief among these is Frodo, whom Shippey rightly identifies as "a peacemaker, indeed in the end a pacifist ... [who] will not kill Saruman even after his mithril coat has turned a treacherous stab" (Shippey, *Road* 207). However much Lynch may claim that Tolkien "[ennobles] battles and military symbols" (Lynch 82), it is the merciful Frodo, and not the warrior-king Aragorn, who serves as the hero of *The Lord of the Rings*. Moreover, as Flieger notes, Frodo "fails in his quest" to destroy the Ring, a narrative detail that "many readers (to Tolkien's great concern) ... miss" (Flieger 6). Sauron is not defeated by any means of force or destruction, nor can the magic of the Ring be used against him; instead, it is Frodo's act of mercy in sparing Gollum's life that eventually leads to Sauron's destruction.

Why, then, all the violence and bloodshed at Helm's Deep and Pelennor Fields before that moment? The reason is, simply, because Sauron himself operates according to a violent and oppressive ideology, and as such expects others to do the same. As Gandalf puts it, "imagining war he has let loose war, believing that he has no time to waste" (*LotR* 497). Sauron fears "what mighty one may suddenly appear, wielding the Ring, and assailing him with war, seeking to cast him down and take his place" (*LotR* 496–97); his obsession with autonomy and power—the chief quality that characterizes him as modern—renders him incapable of imagining that anyone "should wish to cast him down and have *no* one in his place" (*LotR* 497). Seeking to overthrow Sauron by force and take his place, as Tolkien felt the Allied forces did in World War II, would only "breed new Saurons, and slowly turn Men and Elves into Orcs" (*Letters* 78). Arthur cannot preserve his kingdom's ideals of love and community through vicious conquests that devastate the landscape, and neither can the Fellowship hope to destroy Sauron through the kind of violent, oppressive force the Ring constantly tempts them to use. In *The Lord of the Rings*, violent force is only ever used to keep Sauron's armies at bay and protect the defenseless and marginalized (in this case meaning women, children, and the poor).

And yet, careful readers will note that Tolkien problematizes even these arguably justifiable displays of military force. The tone of the battles is, as in *The Fall of Arthur*, decidedly apocalyptic, with thrill and horror comingled, the fields perpetually haunted by carrion fowl. Nor is the characterization of war as "just" or "necessary" without its pitfalls; it can easily mutate into a celebration of violence as heroic. Shippey points to a scene at the end of *The Return of the King* in which Ioreth tells her cousin the more traditionally "heroic" version of Frodo's quest, in which he "went with only his esquire in to the Black Country and fought with the Dark Lord all by himself, and set fire to his Tower." Moreover, we learn that this version of the story "is the tale in the City," that is, in Minas Tirith (*LotR* 966). In both Middle-earth and Camelot, as in our world, "one sees how all achievement is assimilated to essentially active, violent, military patterns" (Shippey, *Road* 208). With this brief scene, Tolkien has already anticipated the reactions of less astute readers who, whether for purposes of wish-fulfilment or critical dismissal, read *The Lord of the Rings* as a straightforward, symbolic battle between good and evil.

If *The Fall of Arthur* ironized Tennysonian ideals by linking them with events like those of World War I, then *The Lord of the Rings* signifies a direct subversion of those same ideals. While *The Fall of Arthur*'s first canto offers a bleak perspective on Tennyson's hegemonic man/nature binary, for example, *The Lord of the Rings* completely upends it with the tree-like Ents' reclamation of the industrialized Isengard. Ents, according to Dickerson and Evans, embody what eco-critics call feraculture, "a perspective that highlights the value of unordered nature—Middle-earth in its original form" (Dickerson and Evans 123), the antithesis of a Tennysonian view of the natural order.

Arthur, then, in both Tennyson's and Tolkien's accounts, finds his analogue in *The Lord of the Rings* not in the selfless Aragorn or peaceful Frodo, but in domineering figures like Denethor and especially Saruman. Like Tolkien's Arthur, who is easily seduced by the rhetoric of glorious warfare, Shippey reads the latter two as applicably modern figures, "both of them originally on the right side but seduced or corroded by evil" (*Road* 170). Just as *The Fall of Arthur* foregrounds the environmental destruction brought on by Arthur's pointless war abroad, Saruman "considers the trees and their guardians his enemies," and "his war on Rohan is also a war against the land itself" (Dickerson and Evans 196). Not only is Isengard under Saruman's rule an industrial wasteland, but it is also a military state, "a war-camp where soldiers are being mustered for battle" (Dickerson and Evans 202). At the head of this hierarchy is Saruman himself, presiding over the masses in his monolithic tower, much like the statue of Arthur described in Tennyson's Grail narrative.

The most significant thematic parallel *The Lord of the Rings* shares with *The Fall of Arthur*, however, is that of violence deployed primarily as a distraction. In the climactic battle at the Black Gates of Mordor, Tolkien reverses the dynamic he sets up at the opening of *The Fall of Arthur*. While Mordred manipulates Arthur's human desire for glorious conquest as a distraction from his own insidious intentions, the armies of Gondor and Rohan engage Sauron in battle, securing (relatively) safe passage through Mordor for Frodo and Sam on their mission to destroy the Ring. This manipulation of Sauron's violent nature differs from Mordred's actions, however, in one very important manner: the armies of the West fight knowing that they likely "shall perish utterly in a black battle far from the living lands" (*LotR* 880). In this way, we may see *The Lord of the Rings* as a response to the bleak devastation of *The Fall of Arthur*; while Arthur seeks to establish himself as a hero in his campaign abroad, Aragorn understands that he is *not* to be the savior of Middle-earth, and so his leadership in battle is transformed from a violent act into a profoundly sacrificial (and therefore truly heroic) one.

Conclusion

While *The Fall of Arthur*, as an unfinished poem, lacks a proper conclusion, we must not forget that in the Arthurian tradition, Mordred and Arthur destroy each other, just as evil effectively destroys itself in *The Lord of the Rings*. Mordred, Arthur, and Sauron all seek domination and power through immortality—whether in the flesh or in myth—and so are destroyed. Aragorn and Frodo, however, willingly risk their lives with no hope of personal gain, and so, in accordance with Tolkien's Catholic beliefs, preserve them, living on through the telling of their story. Taking *The Fall of Arthur* on its own terms, we may well see it as a grim statement on the role of myth in a violent modern world; through the destructive actions of Mordred and Arthur we see the tragic results of myth appropriated to harmful ends.

Yet while its message might be more disturbing than consolatory, it is useful to read *The Fall of Arthur* primarily as an act of recovery. Viewing the poem in the context of Tolkien's later mythmaking, we can see it as a painful but necessary freeing of a culturally established myth from its confused state after World War I, preparing the mythic landscape for Tolkien's more consolatory acts of sub-creation with *The Lord of the Rings* and other works. By deconstructing the ideas of violent heroism resulting from appropriations of myth, Tolkien allows himself to more freely address a selfless, less violent mythic heroism as a response to the anxieties of late modernity. It is for this reason that *The Fall of Arthur* is not only a crucial work in the oeuvre of J. R. R. Tolkien himself, but a vitally important text in the canon of post-Great War fantasy as a whole.

Works Cited

Chism, Christine. "Middle-earth, the Middle Ages, and the Aryan Nation: Myth and History in World War II." *Tolkien the Medievalist*. Ed. Jane Chance. London: Routledge, 2003. 63–92. Print.

Dickerson, Matthew T., and Jonathan D. Evans. *Ents, Elves, and Eriador: The Environmental Vision of J. R. R. Tolkien*. U of Kentucky, 2006. Print.

Downing, Crystal L. *How Postmodernism Serves (my) Faith: Questioning Truth in Language, Philosophy and Art*. Downers Grove, IL: IVP Academic, 2006. Print.

Flieger, Verlyn. *A Question of Time: J. R. R. Tolkien's Road to Faërie*. Kent State UP, 1997. Print.

Fussell, Paul. *The Great War and Modern Memory*. NY: Oxford UP, 1975. Print.

Garth, John. *Tolkien and the Great War: The Threshold of Middle-earth*. Boston: Houghton Mifflin, 2003. Print.

Goebel, Stefan. *The Great War and Medieval Memory: War, Remembrance and Medievalism in Britain and Germany, 1914–1940*. Cambridge UP, 2007. Print.

Hiley, Margaret. *The Loss and the Silence: Aspects of Modernism in the Works of C. S. Lewis, J. R. R. Tolkien and Charles Williams*. Zurich: Walking Tree Publishers, 2011. Print.

Lupack, Alan. *The Oxford Guide to Arthurian Literature and Legend*. Oxford UP, 2005. Print.

Lynch, Andrew. "Archaism, Nostalgia, and Tennysonian War in *The Lord of the Rings*." *Tolkien's Modern Middle Ages*. Ed. Jane Chance and Alfred K. Siewers. NY: Palgrave Macmillan, 2005. 77–92. Print.

Shippey, Tom. *J. R. R. Tolkien: Author of the Century*. Boston: Houghton Mifflin, 2001. Print.

——. *The Road to Middle-earth*. Boston: Houghton Mifflin, 1983. Print.

Tolkien, J. R. R. *The Fall of Arthur*. Ed. Christopher Tolkien. London: HarperCollins, 2013. Print.

——. "On Fairy-stories." *Tree and Leaf*. Boston: Houghton Mifflin, 1965. Print.

——. *The Letters of J. R. R. Tolkien*. Ed. Humphrey Carpenter. Boston: Houghton Mifflin, 1981. Print.

11

"Lilacs Out of the Dead Land":
Narnia, *The Waste Land*, and the World Wars

Jon Hooper

T. S. Eliot's *The Waste Land* is a defining text of modernism and undoubtedly one of the most influential poems of the twentieth century. It was published in Eliot's own *Criterion* magazine in October 1922 and appeared in America shortly thereafter in *The Dial*. It emerged, therefore, in the aftermath of the First World War. According to Harold Bloom, its "spirit is one familiar in the period between the two world wars: the disgust and despair with everything that haunted the survivors of what Gertrude Stein called 'the lost generation'" (20). Those who survived were left to try to make sense of the "heap of broken images" (22) left behind after the collapse of the old European order.

C. S. Lewis' *The Lion, the Witch and the Wardrobe* appeared nearly thirty years later, in October 1950. Like Eliot's poem, Lewis' novel was published within a few years of the ending of a world war—though an aborted attempt at the story, consisting of a single paragraph, seems to have been made in 1939, presumably inspired by the children who were evacuated to the Kilns shortly before Britain declared war on Germany (Hooper 401–02). Further volumes of *The Chronicles of Narnia* appeared throughout the 1950s, ending with *The Last Battle* in September 1956. The *Chronicles* are concerned with healing the disenchantment and despair that the Great War and *The Waste Land* had left upon the modern mindset, which not even the revived sense of chivalry that arose in the atmosphere of the Second World War could lift. To do this, Lewis frequently uses the Arthurian symbol of the blighted land and the theme of the Grail quest.

According to Eliot himself, *The Waste Land* took its underlying structure and some of its symbolism from Jessie L. Weston's anthropological interpretation of the Arthurian Grail literature in *From Ritual to Romance* (1920; Eliot *Selected Poems* 68n). What fascinated Weston was the waste land motif and the ritual that was meant to restore the land: the waste land is the Arthurian kingdom under a curse, where crops do not grow, cattle do not breed, and women do not bear children. The land's plight is mysteriously bound up with the condition of its ailing and impotent ruler, the Fisher King.[1] The ultimate fate of the land resides with the questing knight, who, when given a vision of a Grail cup and a bleeding lance, must then enact the proper response by asking ritual questions. Only if the Knight asks the right questions can the king be healed and health return to the land.

Weston saw the Fisher King as deriving from an ancient vegetable deity, whose Mystery cult symbolized the death and rebirth of the seasons, like the rituals enacted for the gods Attis and Adonis (41, 107). This was a dying god story that Weston believed provided the ancient source of Christianity and the Grail literature. According to Weston, the symbols of the lance and the Grail were "sex symbols of immemorial antiquity and world-wide diffusion, the Lance, or Spear, representing the Male, the Cup, or Vase, the Female, reproductive energy" (71). Here indeed was a once and future king, upon whom the health of the land depended: in the ancient ritual, the god-king would be put to death while still in his prime so that a new king could succeed him (33, 38–39). The story was thus a narrative of renewal for both king and land.

In the poem, Eliot uses the waste land for its cultural and spiritual symbolism. It is a barren desert, and the lives lived within it are blighted with sterility and with isolation from the lives of others, from the past, from any sort of higher purpose. Eliot offers a hellish picture of crowds flowing over London Bridge, undone by death; of the decay and collapse of great cultures; and of legendary figures of history and literature whose glory is diminished by the modern context, such as the seer Tiresias, who is made to witness the illicit and loveless couplings between a typist and a "young man carbuncular":

> (And I Tiresias have foresuffered all
> Enacted on this same divan or bed;
> I who have sat by Thebes below the wall
> And walked among the lowest of the dead.) (lines 231, 243–46)

Eliot's point is not that the past was as lacking in passion as the present (which "foresuffered all" suggests); it is that the modern waste land consciousness has infected the way the past is perceived.

The blight extends to the poem's form and language: *The Waste Land*'s fragmentary structure fits the dislocation of sensibility the war had brought about, while its language eschews the elevated speech of Victorianism and Romanticism, the chivalric high diction that, as we shall see, has been held responsible for duping a generation into sacrificing itself. Eliot does not just strip away ornament; he strips away sense and the familiar from language, rejecting the stock responses Lewis so valued.

It is a poem haunted by absence: the absence of the Grail. Richard Barber has pointed out that "it would seem apt that a poem about the sterile secularity of the post-war world should have at its heart an empty space where the expected and ultimate religious symbol should be" (328). Eliot's waste land is the barren postwar world, where civilization has severed itself from its own roots, where lilacs (paschal flowers) grow ironically out of blood-stained soil, and where the survivors can "connect / Nothing with nothing" (lines 301–02) because all that are left are the fragments of a once holistic culture.

---

1   See chapter 15 by Benjamin Shogren for an extended discussion of the Fisher King. [Editor's note]

Early critics of *The Waste Land* tended to see it in one of two ways. It was seen by some as an expression of modern chaos, a disturbingly accurate "vision of modern life" (Gossedge 127) in which the social collapse following the Great War is perfectly expressed through the fragmented and chaotic surfaces of the poem. For example, the anonymous reviewer in the *Times Literary Supplement* thought that there was "no effect of heterogeneity, since all these flashes are relevant to the same thing and together give what seems to be a complete expression of this poet's vision of modern life" (qtd. in Grant 127). Gilbert Seldes, for the *Nation*, is typical of early reviewers who saw no higher meaning, writing that "the poem is not an argument" (Grant 142), whilst Louis Untekmeyer opined that Eliot had given "form to formlessness" and called the poem "an echo of contemporary despair ... a picture of dissolution, of the breaking-down of the very structures on which life has modelled itself" (qtd. in Grant 144).

Others tended to make more of the Arthurian materials, and detected, in the structure Eliot had derived from Weston's reading of the Grail myths, a puzzle to be solved (Gossedge 123–24). For those who saw *The Waste Land* as a solvable puzzle, the desolate landscape was often taken as a symbol of the lack of religious values in the modern world, contrasting a spiritually healthy past with a spiritually impoverished present through symbols of fertility and sterility. F. L. Lucas, for instance, speculated whether the poem was a "theosophical tract" and took the gist of the poem to be the belief in salvation vs. the "desolation which is human life," even while finding it an unsatisfying parody (qtd. in Grant 192–94); Gorham B. Munson viewed it as an esoteric text which could be grasped only if one knew Eliot's sources and worked through his notes (Grant 202). What these have in common is that the critics were unable to offer any satisfying solution to the puzzle.

Many of the critics who followed Edmund Wilson, one of the pioneers in the Weston-centric school of *Waste Land* criticism, argued that the poem focused on the need for spiritual regeneration; Wilson himself had called the waste land "the concrete image of a spiritual drouth" (Wilson 134). In fact, the two schools of criticism need not be classed as so distinct from one another. It is possible to see even the religious interpretation as being relevant to the ruined world left behind by war, where faith in institutionalized religion had been irrevocably lost. Though the roots of the collapse might have been earlier—as we shall see in a moment when we turn to Lewis—faith in all kinds of authority was demolished on the Western Front. The Great War witnessed the end of the old European Order, with three million men killed in the service of Britain and Germany (Gossedge 83). Disenchantment characterized the inter-war years, and although some kind of nationalist spirit revived during World War II, cynicism and distrust of authority, coupled with a sense of collective guilt, became permanent parts of the national character in the postcolonial years.

It is perhaps no accident that an Arthurian structuring device was adopted by one of the foremost poets of the age, for so much that was Arthurian had also been employed in the war machine that led to the carnage. One of the great propagandist strategies of the War was an appeal to chivalric ideals, often couched in language that elevated battle to a more noble plane, and Arthurian role models were at the forefront.

The times witnessed a cult of Galahad, the young unblemished knight who achieves the Grail, and fighting for one's country was made into a sort of Grail quest (Gossedge 88). Galahad had already been in place as an ideal hero before the War. Preaching at Saint Paul's, the Bishop of London, Arthur Winnington-Ingram, had remarked about the Joy that the world "could neither give nor take away"; explicating the phrase "whom the gods love die young," he said of the Christian, "like the young knight, Sir Galahad, when he had clad himself in shining armour, he must look up through prayer and sacrament for Divine help and he would never look in vain" ("The Bishop of London").[2] Even with the war well underway, Galahad was invoked: the Reverend J. D. Jones likened the Christian soldier to Galahad engaged in a spiritual struggle, writing "courage and purity—these are the conditions of spiritual victory."[3]

Propagandists used the ideal of the maiden knight to inspire young soldiers, virgin warriors in their own right. The Galahad we find in, for example, *The Quest of the Holy Grail*, is from the first a perfect knight, born of the chivalric and spiritual through the line of Galahad and also descended from King David and Joseph of Arimathæa; in a world in which comeliness is equated with virtue, he is "marvelously endowed with every beauty" (8); he alone can occupy the Perilous Seat (13) and draw the sword from the stone (16).

The eventual fate of this generation of young Galahads changed the consciousness of the age. In the aftermath of the War, the use of chivalric language and Arthurian role models was seen as part of the great betrayal. Chivalry was discredited and mocked by the realists and modernists who took the place of the Georgians. Paul Fussell, in *The Great War and Modern Memory*, has detailed how the high ideals of Victorian medievalism and literary language led men to their deaths. In the postwar atmosphere, there was a feeling of having been betrayed by illusory ideals couched in high diction, as witnessed in Wilfred Owen's "Dulce et Decorum Est," with its satirical quotation from Horace, "*Dulce et decorum est pro patria mori*"[4] (Myers 3).

What it left behind was widespread disenchantment. Disenchantment did not spell the end of the fascination with Arthurian matters, however. It turned out that one particular aspect of the Arthurian myth could still speak to the age: The Grail. The so-called Celtic school—Alfred Nutt, mentor to Jessie Weston, and all those who followed him—was obsessed with digging to find the roots of the Grail story, which were invariably located in the remote past and thus not tainted by association with Christendom and its ultimately imperialistic aspirations. It is appropriate that a culture that had been torn up by the roots would seek to ground itself in something far older than Christendom itself. In Celtic myth they found cauldrons of plenty and rebirth, prized symbols in an age of absence and sterility, and these were taken as Celtic antecedents of the Christianized Grail symbols. Weston went back even beyond the Celtic school, into primitive cults from prehistory (Gossedge 118).

That Eliot, the poet of a disenchanted age, was influenced by Weston, an advocate of primitive sources, is significant. In the postwar atmosphere, it would have been difficult for a modernist poet to utilize Christian symbolism. Christianity was the foundation upon which the old European order had been built, and now that order lay in ruins. Those who sought the meaning of the Grail motif in prehistory found something that spoke more powerfully about the generation that had been sacrificed (Gossedge 113–15). Celtic antiquity, and, better, primitive history, were more attractive than Christian medieval Europe to those who had lost faith. One could even go so far as to suggest that these ritualistic roots were more appropriate to a world accustomed to mass slaughter.

---

2   Winnington-Ingram meant for Galahad to represent the young in spirit, rather than the young in years.

3   Jones, J. D. "Sir Galahad." *Quiver* 51 (1916): 661–63. Qtd. in Bontrager.

4   "It is sweet and fitting to die for the fatherland."

One writer who survived the war, Robert Graves, tended to write fiction that elevated primitive goddess-worship over the later, usurping Olympians, and featured ritualized slayings. His reworking of *The Golden Fleece* (1944) features a goddess of the orange groves who can turn people to stone, the ritualized slaying of worshippers, and the withering of crops when the mystical source of fertility—this time a Fleece rather than the Grail cup—is removed from its homeland. The ritual slaying of god-kings also made more sense in the postwar atmosphere; Paul Fussell notes that David Jones equated men "disemboweled or torn apart by machine guns with dismembered antique gods in sacred groves" (152). The likes of these primitive cults served the modernist cause well.

Eliot had tried unsuccessfully to enlist in the First World War. Lewis, on the other hand, was a veteran of the trenches. His description of dismembered bodies in *Surprised by Joy* is a picture of a waste land. Lewis, however, was reluctant to speak or write about the War. In *Surprised by Joy*, he wrote that he could barely remember the terror, cold, stench, horribly wounded men, corpses, and the blasted landscape. They were long ago, far away, and impersonal (*SbJ* 227). In the War's immediate aftermath, he joined in the atmosphere of cynicism in *Spirits in Bondage*, but in the twenties and thirties that changed as he turned to theism and eventually Christianity. Lewis himself experienced renewal. He was not quite a man standing alone—there were the other Inklings—but his taste for pre-modernist literature and ideals went against contemporary trends.

It was a time when renewal was needed. As the world entered a second global war, nations that had lost their faith in chivalric ideals and had even begun to question traditional morality found it difficult to respond to Hitler's aggressive territorial expansion. The fact is, Britain, once mighty Logres, was still a waste land, its knights haunted by the memory of betrayal.

Paul McKusker, examining the context that gave rise to *Mere Christianity*, points to Neville Chamberlain's deal brokered with Hitler, and points out that the "more aggressive Hitler became, the more passively the leaders in the surrounding countries seemed to respond to him" (1). Chamberlain was very much a person of the waste land consciousness, jaded with national heroics and reluctant to enter into supposedly morally justified wars. Intellectuals, meanwhile, were distrustful of morality itself, for it had been used to justify slaughter. As McKusker points out, Chamberlain believed that Hitler wanted peace and "pursued a policy of appeasement" (2). It took Churchill to come along and wake people up to the existence of evil, as Churchill had a firm grasp of the threat Hitler posed.

When war eventually broke out, Lewis was persuaded to make broadcasts for the BBC that centered on the question of faith in God; his scripts later formed the basis of *Mere Christianity*. The point of his wartime broadcasts was to persuade those fighting to return to the Christian faith. Only then could the land be healed. In his apologetics, Lewis makes the point of stressing that the pattern of rebirth rising from death is the great narrative in so many pagan stories.[5] In broadcasting for the BBC, even though he did not seek out the public platform, Lewis began a project that would bear fruit not just in *Mere Christianity* but also in

---

5   See, for example, "Is Theology Poetry?" 16 and "Religion without Dogma" 165. Though he drew different conclusions, Lewis was as aware as Weston or Eliot of the connection between the health of the land and spiritual health.

Narnia. His themes were right and wrong, the belief in ultimate authority, and the revival of the Christian faith. Bound up with this was culture itself—although Lewis believed that the roots of the modern paradigm were older, he acknowledged that the interwar years were a time of unprecedented disbelief. In "The Decline of Religion" (1946), he notes that church attendance and other external markers of Christian commitment have dropped sharply since 1900 (179).[6]

Lewis became a defender of the very values and ideals that had been rejected by many because they had supposedly resulted in the death of innocence in the Great War. The modernist movement had asserted that because such values had been appropriated to justify war, the values themselves must be corrupt: a lapse of logic that was fatal in the view of a stern logician like Lewis. Doris T. Myers has recognized that Lewis was a champion of traditional values at this time, noting that "Lewis lived through the anxieties of the Battle of Britain, when England stood alone against Nazi Germany and it seemed that civilization would be destroyed.... Lewis hoped to preserve the ancient verities of classicism and traditional Christianity" (126). In "The Necessity of Chivalry" (1940), he praises the chivalry of the RAF pilots then fighting in the skies above Britain for combining "sternness" and "meekness" in a way that is proper to a chivalric knight and reckons them superior to the "1915 model" (719).

During the interwar years, Lewis set himself against the seemingly implacable tide of modernism. He frequently wrote on the subject, co-writing a pseudonymous parody of Eliot's style for *The Criterion* (which was rejected),[7] alluding to the incomprehensibility of Eliot's "A Cooking Egg,"[8] and spending thousands of words (though he framed it in the much wider context of his concept of the "Great Divide") on the break with tradition brought about by the modernists. Lewis saw Eliot as one of the enemy. In a letter to Paul Elmer More, dated 23 May 1935, Lewis made his position toward *The Waste Land*, and to Eliot himself, clear. By that time, both men had converted (to Anglicanism), but this did not seem to make a difference. He regards Eliot's work as "a very great evil" and his poems works of "disintegration." *The Waste Land* itself is an "infernal poem" and Eliot himself is described as a "literary traitor to humanity." Although Derek Brewer claims that Lewis grew to admire Eliot's poetry (Brewer 50), at this stage he was adamant that "no man is fortified against chaos by reading the *Waste Land*" and that "most men are by it infected with chaos" (*CL* 2:163). He mounted a defense of one of the literary heroes of the old order, under attack by Eliot, in his book *A Preface to* Paradise Lost (1942). But perhaps more than anything, Lewis' fiction (especially the books that emerged after the end of the World War II) reveals the extent of his project of renewal.

---

6   However, he also argued, in the same essay, that the decline was in some way positive, for it had meant the decline of a fuzzy kind of Theism (180), leaving Christianity itself as an intellectual option. Lewis saw Christian renewal on the rise and declared that neither a simplistic unbelief nor a simplistic belief could now survive (181). He compared his times to the moment when the fellowship of Round Table was shattered and each knight had to make a clear choice to go with Galahad or Mordred. There could be no more vague hovering in a middle space (181). But ultimately, he strikes a note of caution, for he feels that an intellectual climate conducive to Christianity will not last.

7   The Eliot parody is mentioned in Lewis' diary, *All My Road Before Me*, on page 413.

8   The symposium on "A Cooking Egg" is mentioned in *"De Descriptione Temporum"* in *Selected Literary Essays*, page 9.

If his wartime broadcasts can be seen as an attempt to restore faith in Christianity in a country that was losing its center of faith, *The Chronicles of Narnia* can be seen as his response to the waste land consciousness that the Great War had left behind and that infected the morale of those who were called to fight against the new manifestation of evil.

The *Chronicles* are concerned with land, with the fate of England itself, for they grew out of a wartime atmosphere. This is true even though certain symbols, such as the faun carrying parcels in a snowy wood, had their origins much earlier. Lewis believed that faith and traditional values were at stake: the foundational values of England. The fate of the land in the Grail story is tied up with its king, and because Lewis worried about declining faith in God, he makes a point of bringing the king to the land. The relative health of the land in each of the *Chronicles* depends on the absence or presence of its rulers, be they the kings and queens or Aslan himself. In *The Voyage of the "Dawn Treader,"* he writes: "when the Pevensie children had returned to Narnia last time for their second visit, it was (for the Narnians) as if King Arthur came back to Britain, as some people say he will. And I say the sooner the better" (429).

Narnia is a land blessed and preserved by kingship, by strong rulers in the tradition of Arthur. It is also a land of questing knights, its own versions of Galahad. In several of the books, we are concerned with the fate of children who must acquire the valor and virtues of knights, their chivalry inseparable from their faith in Aslan. Richard Barber says of the Grail hero that the "dual legacy of spiritual and knightly perfection means that the Grail hero has to represent the ideal of both earthly and heavenly chivalry" (159). Just as the Siege Perilous has been awaiting the pure Galahad, so the seats in Cair Paravel have been awaiting the four children in *The Lion, the Witch and the Wardrobe*. They are the young, the generation who will inherit the kingdom now that the rightful king has returned. Whereas the realm Eliot depicts in *The Waste Land* was laid waste, the sacrifice of its young leading to distrust, despair, and a lack of faith in any kind of rhetoric, Lewis' project is to restore faith in culture and in spiritual matters.

As well as presenting models of kingship and chivalry, upon which a healthy land depends, the *Chronicles* also address the waste land paradigm that dominated after the First World War, and each book deals with banishing certain aspects of this waste land. The role of Lewis' fiction is to offer a way out of the waste land condition.

The Lion, the Witch and the Wardrobe is in a sense the overture, the book in which the themes of the banishment of the waste land, the return of chivalry, and the restoration of traditional virtues are brought to the fore. It is also the Chronicle that deals most directly with renewal of the land and the restoration of its rightful king. In this first book, Narnia is gripped by an endless winter where new growth and the appearance of Spring have been forestalled, a natural analogue of the cultural and spiritual. The dying god ritual, according to Weston, was meant to avert the "dreaded calamity": "the temporary suspension of all the reproductive energies of Nature" (49).

The winter has been caused by the magic of a witch, a usurper, associated with legendary figures like Lilith and the giants; she has diverted the seasons from their proper purpose, her motive being the impulse to rule and to subvert the works of the true King. A reference to the origins of the waste land in Chrétien is illuminating: the kingdom of Logres was once the land of the ogres (457). That the kingdom of Logres might once have been a kingdom of giants is thus echoed in Narnia, since the witch (at this stage in the

Narnian mythology) is said to have come from their race. In *The Silver Chair*, the ruined city of the giants points to a much older civilization that has declined, again suggesting a more barbarous age.

This snowbound Narnia is a fictional analogue of the modern world, which has lost its faith in its glorious past (this explains the wistful longing behind Mr. Tumnus's description of the midnight dances with the Nymphs and Dryads). This does not, however, mean that Lewis agrees with Weston and the Celtic or primitive school. The pagan tradition that interests Lewis has its origins in ancient Greece and forms the foundation of western values, extending through the medieval period right through the so-called Renaissance, until the period in which he located the "Great Divide." What Lewis called the "Great Divide" was the years between the era of Scott and Austen and our own, when the paradigm shift occurred that gave us the modern world.[9] Although Lewis insisted that the roots of the schism were earlier, his opposition to modernism obviously makes it clear that he recognized the importance of the First World War in dealing the decisive blow to people's faith. In rejecting the values of virtue and chivalry, the modern waste land consciousness had cut people off from the entire western tradition. It is no coincidence that the Narnia Lucy first ventures into is akin to a police state, where the classical tradition has been neglected, and anyone answering to the description of Sons of Adam and Daughters of Eve (a view of human beings not as mere animals but as immortal souls) are to be reported to the authorities.

In the faun's first meeting with Lucy, Lewis makes Tumnus speak in the very high diction that had been rejected by the modernists and realists, elevating Lucy's mundane and disenchanted England to a mythic level (Tumnus refers to the land of "Spare Oom" and "War Drobe"). Interestingly, in the list of high diction examples given by Paul Fussell in *The Great War and Modern Memory*, we find Lewis' particular favorite: "the heavens" (22). Part of Lewis' project is to reclaim high diction for the young. At the very end of the book, the children themselves have learned to speak in this form of high diction, a courtly language befitting kings and queens:

> Then said King Peter (for they talked in quite a different style now, having been Kings and Queens of Narnia for so long), "Fair Consorts, let us now alight from our horses and follow this beast into the thicket; for in all my days I never hunted a nobler quarry."
> "Sir," said the others, "even so let us do."
> So they alighted and tied their horses to trees and went on into the thick wood on foot. And as soon as they had entered it Queen Susan said,
> "Fair friends, here is a great marvel, for I seem to see a tree of iron." (195)

Lewis, like Tolkien, obviously realized that the manipulation of such language by propagandists did not mean the language itself was inherently deceitful—the problem was the uses to which it was put.

---

9   Lewis explains the replacement of the medieval world model in *The Discarded Image* (1964) and in essays like "De Descriptione Temporum" (1954). Instead of the medieval model of the universe, the modern paradigm is based on the machine or on popular evolutionism.

With the return of Aslan to Narnia comes the thawing of winter and the return of Spring, which Michael Ward has persuasively argued represents the conquest of the Saturnine by the kingly spirit of Jupiter (57–60). Nature, even before Aslan's sacrifice, becomes sacramental nature. It is arguable that Aslan is close to the notion of Christ as victor, as we find in medieval texts like the dream-vision Anglo-Saxon *The Dream of the Rood*, because the snow begins to melt and the first flowers appear as soon as he enters Narnia, even before the Stone Table episode. Nevertheless, Aslan, without any diminishing of his might, goes willingly toward sacrifice at the hands of the witch so that Edmund can be saved. His sacrifice is of course still connected with the fate of the land, for it will bring about the events that will defeat the witch for good and put the kings and queens in their rightful place as rulers of a just kingdom. The difference between the dying god rituals in Frazer and Weston and Aslan's death is that Aslan, as a type of Christ, is the original foreshadowed by all the dying god figures throughout pagan myth, and unlike them the effects of his sacrifice will be permanent, lifting the long-term winter forever.

Aslan takes the place of Edmund because Edmund's blood is demanded by the witch according to the ancient law written on the Stone Table. Despite the fact that he is a child, his is not innocent blood: he is a traitor to the land. This is, of course, Lewis insisting on original sin and subtly decrying the postwar myth of innocence betrayed. The Lewis who experienced the horrors of the Western Front is well aware that futile sacrifices are often called upon because the need for sacrifice is written into Creation itself.

As in our own world, the paradigm of sacrifice is prevalent in Narnia. In *The Horse and His Boy*, Aravis is to be an autumn sacrifice through marriage to a much older man, the wealthy Ahoshta, and in order to escape, she makes a fiction that she will go out to make secret sacrifices to Zardeenah, the Narnian equivalent of the moon goddess Artemis. The marriage of the girl is a passing from night to day, or from winter to spring, for here the sun is associated with the husband. However, the land in which this occurs is not a green and verdant place like Narnia (reference to which, in *The Horse and His Boy*, invariably places emphasis on its fertile qualities) but a hostile desert, a place where water, symbolic of spiritual refreshment as well as bodily, is scarce and the sun an enemy. Ahoshta, like the Tisroc, is a false deity and Aravis must escape being sacrificed to him.

Lewis also echoes vegetation myths in *The Silver Chair* in the encounter with the giants. The children are sent to Harfang as a gift to the giants for their Autumn feast. Frazer and Weston both recount how the sacrifice of the god took place in Autumn, with the intention of appeasing the winter and bringing about the earth's rebirth in the Spring. The rocky and snowbound lands around Harfang are a waste land, a great contrast to the fertile valley land of Narnia. There is also a ruined city, emblematic of the fate of civilizations that do not have a healthy culture. The sacrifice of children, of course, does not lead to renewal but to destruction.

Lewis does not simply content himself with the ending of the waste land in *The Lion, the Witch and the Wardrobe*. He understood what had been lost in the interwar years, and wanted to restore a sense of virtues and chivalric values to Britain. Throughout the *Chronicles*, he returns to the modern waste land in order to draw attention to those aspects of the modern world he finds most harmful. Importantly, he shows us how various aspects of the waste land can be banished or overcome.

In *Prince Caspian*, Narnia is a diminished kingdom: a land in which Cair Paravel has been overgrown and abandoned, for it has no need of the true heirs of the throne, the chivalric knights-turned-kings who inherited the thrones in the first book, much as Arthur had done in the legends. At the same time, the older Narnian culture, with its talking animals and mythical creatures, has been suppressed by the invading Telmarines, who function as the Narnian equivalent of modern realists. The wilderness here is hostile and disorienting, and the children have great difficulty making their way to Aslan's How, once the spiritual center of the kingdom, a Narnian Jerusalem now overgrown and neglected.

Lewis deplored the fact that the modern world had abandoned its faith in chivalric and spiritual matters (represented here by the ruined castle and neglected holy site). He also knew it had turned once-enchanted nature into disenchanted wilderness because of its cynical and reductive way of perceiving reality. This is true of the modernism of Eliot. Modernism is frequently urban, but when it does turn its gaze to Nature, it invariably invests the natural world with the consciousness of humanity. The roots of this, as Lewis well knew, were in Romanticism. What happens, however, when the consciousness of man becomes traumatized and disturbed, as it had done in the Great War, is that the nature he perceives becomes distorted and diseased. The spiritual aspect is no longer perceived. In the last section of *The Waste Land*, the grail chapel has become an image of absence:

> There is the empty chapel, only the wind's home.
> It has no windows, and the door swings,
> Dry bones can harm no one. (388–90)

The ability to perceive the sacred quality of nature was threatened on the Western Front. It was difficult to even think about the beauties of nature as the land was being churned up and turned into a literal waste land. However, with a certain irony, soldiers raised on classical motifs tended to notice the singing of larks and nightingales during moments of peace (Fussell 241–42). For example, Sergeant Ernest Boughton Nottingham wrote of "the lark's rapture at fresh May dawnings" (qtd. in Housman 198), but later admitted that he had come to associate the sound with "stand to" in the trenches (202),[10],[11] whereas Lieutenant Robert W. Sterling wrote that their "sightless song" seemed to "repeat in some degree the very essence of the Normal and Unchangeable universe carrying on unhindered and careless amid the corpses and the bullets and the madness" (qtd. in Housman 263). Second Lieutenant Alexander Douglas Gillespie, hearing a nightingale sing in a cherry orchard, observed that "the song seemed to come all the more sweetly and clearly in the quiet intervals between the bursts of firing." He concluded that "the nightingale's song was the only real thing which would remain when all the rest was long past and forgotten" (111).

---

10   This second reference to the lark is from a letter to Charles Williams. Writing of things that bring intimations of "another world," Nottingham mentions the "ecstasy of a lark" as an example of the "hardening of experience" because he now associates the sound with the reality of the trenches.

11   The "Charles Williams" to whom the above letter is addressed must be Charles Walter Stansby Williams, the Inkling studied in this volume: his two best friends were Harold Eyers and Ernest Nottingham, both killed in World War I (see Hadfield, *Exploration* 23, 25; Lindop, *Third Inkling* 46–47). [Editor's note]

In *Prince Caspian*, Lucy hears the "twitter of a nightingale" close by her as the children are struggling through the wilderness (369). Following it to a lighter place, she hears the nightingale burst into full song. At this point, she looks at the trees and imagines them coming alive, as they did in the old Narnia. The scene is reminiscent of the sensitivity to nature displayed by soldiers during lulls in the fighting, particularly at dawn and twilight; although Nature itself had been largely silenced by the guns, the birds brought a miraculous reminder of natural beauties.

Lucy is not finally able to achieve the state of enchantment she experienced in the "golden age" of Narnia. It is only later, with the lion's roar, that the trees will finally come alive and dance. But for now this is a diminished Narnia where everything spiritual is remote. When Edmund finally sees Aslan and tries to run to him, the lion leads off the other way, more remote than before. The source of all joy and comfort has become elusive, like the Grail. Aslan is sought, much like the Grail is sought, and like the Grail he has the tendency to appear and reappear at will, as it does in *The Quest of the Holy Grail* (19); when he does reappear in earnest at the end of this Chronicle, he is the bringer of fecundity, returning the classical gods to their rightful place.

One of Lewis' most memorable waste land settings is found in *The Silver Chair*, and it is telling that Lewis thought about calling *The Silver Chair* "The Wild Waste Lands" (*CL* 3:229–30). Jill and Eustace, accompanied by the marsh-wiggle Puddleglum, must follow the signs Aslan has left for them. The signs are vital because their journey is through a waste land of rocks, among which they find the ruins of an older city and civilization. The letters that spell "Under Me" are described in terms of trenches cut into the landscape. From the low perspective of the trenches, the travelers cannot see the proper state of things and begin to despair. Higher places in *The Silver Chair* afford more truthful perspectives. On the Mountain, Aslan had told Jill that he could speak to her clearly because "the air is clear and your mind is clear" but that down in Narnia "the air will thicken" and confuse her mind. Aslan warns her to follow the signs and to "pay no attention to appearances" (560). Lewis' point is that in a land (and indeed in a culture) wholly unfamiliar and hostile, where no real path can be found and no reliable maps read, navigation is still possible if one holds to basic Christian principles.

The trenches of World War I presented a similar narrowing of perspective. Paul Fussell tells us that to "be in the trenches was to experience an unreal, unforgettable enclosure and constraint, as well as a sense of being unoriented and lost" (51). One soldier described the experience thus: "'The trenches are a labyrinth, I have already lost myself repeatedly.... you can't get out of them and walk about the country or see anything at all but two muddy walls on each side of you'" (qtd. in Fussell 51). *The Silver Chair* thus resonates with wartime accounts of trench warfare. The giants of Harfang, after all, feast upon children given to them as sacrifices by elusive and unseen rulers.

The ultimate expression of this confusion of perspective is Underland itself, whose depth and darkness really do obscure sight. The underlying myths that inform *The Waste Land* are also, of course, myths that feature the descent of a god into an underworld or Hades. Here, it is also a descent into a more reductive vision of the cosmos. It is under the ruined city of the giants that the travelers seek Prince Rilian, who has been kidnapped by the Lady of the Green Kirtle, another witch figure. Rilian's disappearance into the underworld echoes that of Adonis as detailed in Frazer's *The Golden Bough*, and the Lady of the Green

Kirtle resembles Persephone, with whom Aphrodite vied for the affection of Adonis (Frazer 7). This is a seasonal underworld with a descent in the Autumn, though the ascent, miraculously, comes not in Spring but in the heart of Winter.

The fact that, led away by the enchantments of a witch, the prince is preparing to launch an attack on his own kingdom reminds us of the bewitchments of Morgan le Fay from the late romances and the treacherous Mordred, Arthur's illegitimate son. Should the witch succeed, the fate of the kingdom will be much the same as at the end of Tennyson's *Idylls of the King*, in which Mordred "usurp'd the realm / And leagued himself with the heathen" (233), bringing a foreign army to conquer Arthur's kingdom. That Rilian is under an enchantment does not make the outcome any less destructive—indoctrination is exactly the point when we come to discover traitors in our midst, says the Lewis of *The Abolition of Man*.

The waste land of *The Silver Chair* is the disenchanted and reductive cosmos, where everything is explained and reduced to bare facts; inferior things are taken to be the originals of greater. The witch, who has styled herself the Queen of Underland, weaves an enchantment to try to convince the children and Puddleglum that the sun and Aslan himself are no more than wish-fulfillment fantasies. The witch challenges them thus: "What is this *sun* that you all speak of? Do you mean anything by the word?" (631). Her challenge goes right to the heart of modern semantics and the breakdown of signifier and signified that characterizes the postmodern world. Doris T. Myers sees one of the consequences of the First World War as a low and distrustful view of language. She writes: "In postwar society at large this need was reflected in a widespread conviction that people had been duped by language into sacrificing themselves and their well-being in the war. There is no doubt that World War I caused people to look at language in a new way" (2). Myers notes the influence of C. K. Ogden and I. A. Richards, who had attempted, in *The Meaning of Meaning* (1923), to promote a more scientific and neutral language, freed from emotion, rhetoric, and metaphor: "Ogden and Richards see World War I as an extreme example of the tyranny of language and concern themselves with building a theory of language that will get rid of traditional philosophic and religious assumptions about it" (Myers 4). As Ogden and Richards put it, "in war-time words become a normal part of the mechanism of deceit" (qtd. in Myers 17).

The modern world has cut the connection between word and external world, between signifier and signified. A world of meaning has become a world of arbitrary signs. The witch's argument is the bottom-up model—that because the sun they claim to exist resembles the lamp, it must be a sort of wish-fulfillment of the lamp writ large. Lewis believes that modern thinkers make themselves the inhabitants of an underland, a world turned upside down, stripping all higher things—once enchanted things—of their beauty and quiddity. It is one of the legacies of the War and one of the most disturbing ways in which the land has become a waste land. In such an atmosphere, where the young believe in no higher virtues, we should expect nothing less than treachery.

Despair must be countered by remembering the signs. Puddleglum calls the witch's world a "black pit of a kingdom," and the Deep Lands eventually crumble at the death of the witch, her claimed reality becoming illusion, and their name turning out to have been ironic after all. Again we can see that the waste land, Lewis insists, must be held in check, and Logres saved, by faith in higher things, both virtues and the Creator himself. The lost prince rises up again out of the earth, reborn and ready to take control of the kingdom, while the old king—Caspian, aged and close to death—departs for Aslan's Country.

The desert of Calormen in *The Horse and His Boy* is a symbolic as well as a literal desert, for it represents a kingdom ruled by a people who practice slavery and oppose justice. Calormen, with its insufficient water, is contrasted to the fertility of the valley land of Narnia. When Shasta comes to the desert "it was like coming to the end of the world" (244). The sand is "endless," and the stretch of desert makes the mountains (which lead to Archenland and Narnia) look farther away than ever; in other words, it changes perspective and works against objective judgment of distance. The desert is a deceptive place: it is "blindingly white," and at night, the sand "gleamed as if it were smooth water" (264), as if to mockingly draw attention to the absence of true refreshment. This is indeed a waste land place, "a dead world," stripped of the harbingers of natural joy that usually inhabit his landscapes. Lewis usually makes a point of mentioning the birds that herald the arrival of morning or of the new season, or are present in a pleasant place. It is significant, then, that he mentions that when morning comes, it is "without a single bird to sing about it" (265).

When Shasta reaches Archenland and ascends the high ground, he encounters darkness and loneliness as he tries to reach King Lune. His encounter with Aslan is evocative of Grail literature. In the sense of being followed by an invisible companion, there are shades of the road to Emmaus (Luke 24:13–35). Eliot also alludes to this in "What the Thunder Said":

> Who is the third who walks always beside you?
> When I count, there are only you and I together
> But when I look ahead up the white road
> There is always another one walking beside you. (359–62)

In the notes to the poem, Eliot points to the Road to Emmaus as one of the themes (72n) but also indicates that the lines were inspired by reports of Antarctic expeditions, in which the explorers were conscious of there being one extra member they could not account for. Like the experience of invisible companions in the Great War, this would appear to be associated with great stress.

The sensation of being "secretly observed" was also reported by some World War I soldiers (Fussell 137). Shasta encounters an invisible companion when it is pitch dark and he is most alone and nearest despair. The creature, which seems very large, breathes on him. The companion, of course, is Aslan, who breathes on Shasta to prove he is not a ghost.

Shasta's journey—through the desert into higher elevations, and finally an encounter with the divine within a cloud of darkness—has parallels with the experiences of knights in search of the Grail, who also ride out from a blighted and thirsting kingdom into a fertile place. The vision of the lion is described by Lewis thus:

> The High King above all kings stooped toward him. Its mane, and some strange and solemn perfume that hung about the mane, was all round him. It touched his forehead with its tongue. He lifted his face and their eyes met. Then instantly the pale brightness of the mist and the fiery brightness

of the Lion rolled themselves together into a swirling glory and gathered themselves up and disappeared. He was alone with the horse on a grassy hillside under a blue sky. (*HHB* 282)

There are echoes here of scenes in the Grail romances where the Grail appears and shines with brilliant light. In fact, the Grail is often depicted as a vessel of light rather than a vessel bearing spiritually refreshing water. In Wauchier's *Second Continuation*, Perceval encounters the Grail when he sees what appear to be candles in the forest late at night, "'so bright and clear that it seemed that the great, dense forest was lit up and blazing with their light on every side'" (qtd. in Barber 32). It is a light that cures despair. In the *Lancelot-Grail*, it appears to Perceval and Ector thus: "At the point when they were in such danger and anguish that they truly thought they would die, they saw a great brightness coming toward them, as if the sun were descending upon them, and they were mystified as to what this might be" (328). Like Shasta's experience of Aslan, the Grail also appears, in Tennyson's *Idylls of the King*, "cover'd with a luminous cloud" (Tennyson 177). In *The Voyage of the "Dawn Treader,"* the quest will take them to the land of the sun, the source of drinkable light, the country of Lewis' own version of the Grail.

When the mist and the darkness that have surrounded Shasta are gone, he wonders if it was all a dream; but then he sees the lion's paw print, which fills up with water and makes a stream flowing down the hillside, symbolizing the spiritual refreshment he has sought and which drove him from the hostile lands of Calormen. This is spiritual refreshment standing in for the Grail cup's healing draught, and it is a suitably symbolic climax to a Chronicle that has been concerned with escaping from a waste land.

In *The Magician's Nephew*, the deplorable word, which lays waste to civilizations and worlds, which brings lifelessness and desolation, is a kind of dolorous stroke resulting in a waste land. In Gerbert's continuation of the *Perceval*, it is Perceval's own word that restores the land:

> All this was done by what he said,
> This land whose streams no water fed,
> Its fountains dry, its fields unplowed,
> His word once more with health endowed. (qtd. in Weston 14)

Just as a single word can restore health to the land, Lewis shows that it can also take it away. Deserts are made, in Lewis' eyes, by denying the meaning inherent in language and the value of stock responses, as we find in twentieth-century semiotics and post-Saussurean linguistics.

There are obvious parallels between the city of Charn and the cities of *The Waste Land*, particularly the most ancient cities like Jerusalem, Athens, and Alexandria. Charn, we are told, was once a mighty civilization. In the fight at the lamp-post, the Witch curses thus: "You shall pay dearly for this when I have conquered your world. Not one stone of your city will be left. I will make it as Charn, as Felinda, as Sorlois, as Bramandin" (59). "Jerusalem Athens Alexandria / Vienna London / Unreal" (374–76): the list of worlds—presumably ancient and magnificent civilizations—that have suffered the fate of Charn echoes Eliot's own list of diminished cities. With the deplorable word, spoken out of spite and jealousy by Jadis, their culture and existence are blown away as if by wind.

When Digory and Polly arrive, Charn is a silent, infertile, dead city. It has the properties of a maze with no way outside. Significantly, there is both a dried-up river and bone-dry fountain—fountains, like pools and waterfalls, are Lewisian symbols of natural fertility and spiritual refreshment. Pillars have been toppled, and in the stony places of the broken flagstones no grass or moss can take root. Lewis' description matches Eliot's description of the agony in stony places, where new life cannot grow. Not even death seems to exist in Charn: the figures they meet in the Hall of Images are like waxworks.

In *The Last Battle*, the beauty of Narnia is stripped away and the green land made into desert as the kingdom falls for the last time. In the other *Chronicles*, the only way to escape the waste land has been Aslan. Even in *The Horse and His Boy*, it is thanks to Aslan (in disguise) that Shasta meets Aravis and ultimately crosses the desert and reaches the fertile North. In *The Last Battle,* all the world is laid waste, and Aslan brings about a cleansing flood so that the characters can be sent on to their permanent home. Lewis clearly chooses purgation by water because it is appropriate to the waste land theme and to the role the Grail plays in the myth.

The climactic battle is as doomed as the pagan and Anglo-Saxon battles that fired Tolkien's imagination, or the battles of the Western Front. In the sermon that became "Learning in War-time," Lewis clarified his feelings toward conflict and both World Wars:

> What does war do to death? It certainly does not make it more frequent; 100 per cent of us die, and the percentage cannot be increased. It puts several deaths earlier; but I hardly suppose that that is what we fear. Certainly when the moment comes, it will make little difference how many years we have behind us. Does it increase our chance of a painful death? I doubt it. As far as I can find out, what we call natural death is usually preceded by suffering; and a battlefield is one of the very few places where one has a reasonable prospect of dying with no pain at all. Does it decrease our chances of dying at peace with God? I cannot believe it. If active service does not persuade a man to prepare for death, what conceivable concatenation of circumstance would? Yet war does do something to death. It forces us to remember it. (Lewis, "Learning" 61–62)

Here, Lewis turns against the despair that haunted the generations after the Great War. As we have seen, he downplayed his war experience, which obviously did haunt him. In all of his writings, there is little reference to the horrors of the Great War, and critics have sometimes remarked that it is surprising that he did not write more about it. But perhaps had he expended more words on the war, on the betrayal that his fellows felt, on the devastation, on the sacrifice, he would have turned our attention, much like Eliot did, toward human misery and away from our own accountability; in other words, away from God. His *Last Battle* is a rewrite of Camlaan. It is like Maldon, or like Tolkien's long defeat. Hope is lost, yet they fight on nonetheless, because the fate of the soldier is ultimately that of every mortal. "Learning in War-time" reminds us that "Human life has always been lived on the edge of a precipice" (49). The fact that carnage awaited the generation of the Great War was no excuse to question civilization itself, to bewail lost innocence or to lose faith in noble values.

Thus are the waste lands of the seven *Chronicles*. Throughout the books, there are nevertheless places that offer respite from the waste land, versions of the *locus amoenus*. The *locus amoenus* or pleasance is a staple of classical rhetorical landscape writing (Curtius 193). Found in Greco-Roman texts, it is traditionally a garden or pastoral landscape. Jeffrey Burton Russell has written of how, since Homer's day, "poets [have] described a land of music, dancing, sunny meadows, flowers, fountains, and sweet refreshment and repose in shady groves, a land in which death and disease have no dominion and no one lacks anything" (Russell 21). Petronius's *Satyricon* features one of the earliest such descriptions in literature:

> The lofty plane-tree spreads its summer shade,
> Metamorphosed Daphne near by, crowned with berries.
> Cypresses tremulous, clipped pines around
> Shuddering at their tops.
>   Playing among them
> A stream with wandering waters,
> Spume-flecked, worrying the stones
>   with a querulous spray.
>   A place right for love.
> Witness the woodland nightingale,
>   and Procne turned urban swallow—
> Everywhere amidst the grass and soft violets,
> Their woodland homes a temple of song. (*Satyricon* 147)

It will be noted that one effect of such rhetoric is that nature becomes animated, particularly landscape features like trees and streams. One might say that while Petronius's rhetoric makes the trees appear to dance and the stream come alive, the Lewis of *Prince Caspian* was to make it do so in a more literal sense.

In the Great War, soldiers raised on classical education would have thought of such *loci amoeni* as they heard the lark at stand-to in the morning or the nightingale in the evening. Lewis, in fact, makes the nightingale a feature of *loci amoeni* in both *Prince Caspian* and *The Horse and His Boy* to herald a pleasant reversal of fortune, whilst a lark appears on the verdant island of Felimath in *The Voyage of the "Dawn Treader."* In Tolkien, too, we find it performing a similar function, as John Garth reminds us: "Tinúviel's attendant bird, the nightingale, is a fitting emblem of eucatastrophe, pouring out its fluting song when all is dark" (265). In *The Waste Land*, Eliot, aware of the relevance of the nightingale not just in classical tradition but to the soldiers of the Great War, wrote that "the nightingale / Filled all the desert with inviolable voice" (100–01).

What all of these places offer is the same as one of the Grail's main aspects—healing. In the Great War, the fact that nature carried on despite the horror that was happening in the human world was sometimes taken as a great irony, and Eliot, the arch-modernist, draws out this sense of irony in his image of cruel April in *The Waste Land*. However, Nature's indifference to man could also serve as encouragement, and we can see how ancient cults placing meaning on the implacability of the seasons would appeal.

In *The Voyage of the "Dawn Treader,"* the ostensible aim is finding out the fate of the lost lords of Narnia, but as much as this it is a journey into the beyond, to the Grail country at the eastern edge of the world and beyond. The numinous space of Aslan's country, the source of all light and healing, lies beyond the last sea. It is also the place where food is offered in abundance. At Ramandu's island, the Questers reach Aslan's table, which is magically filled with bounteous food every sunset, and cleared away by the birds of morning if there is any left at dawn. In the *Elucidation Prologue*, too, the Grail magically appears and serves everyone in the Grail Castle even though there is no serving-man or seneschal in sight (303–14). In Wolfram's *Parzival*, the Grail has become a magical stone; on Good Friday a dove flies down from heaven bearing a small white wafer and places it on the stone, so that "the Stone receives all that is good on earth of food and drink, of paradisal excellence" (240).

In the Grail romances, the Grail is ultimately an object too holy for this world. At the end of *The High History of the Holy Grail*, Perceval is told that the Grail must depart from the world. After being told this, Perceval embarks on a holy ship of "worshipful men" and is never seen again by earthly man (362). This departure resembles Reepicheep's, whose great desire is to sail beyond the limits of the world, in search of his own Grail. In certain Grail adventures, the ship of Solomon carries knights to Sarras: in Malory's *Tale of the Sangreal*, based on *The Quest of the Holy Grail*, Galahad is borne by ship to Sarras, bearing the Holy Vessel, which must "depart from the realm of Logris, that it shall never be seen more [there]" (66–67). In Albrecht's *Later Titurel*, Parzival and Titurel set out with the Grail to take it beyond the evils of the west, into eastern lands, eventually coming to the land of the mythical Prester John, whose palace lies in the Earthly Paradise (Barber 196). According to Barber, "Albrecht retells this story, but, more important, he develops the idea of the Grail kingdom as a Utopia; its mission is to protect the Grail company from sin, and to assure their salvation" (Barber 196).

The eastern edge of the world is Reepicheep's goal. Although Lewis lifts the waste land and provides places of healing, the *loci amoeni* are only temporary places of rest. Reepicheep, the ideal of knighthood, knows that the end of the quest lies in Aslan's Country. Reepicheep is the *Chronicles'* maiden knight, its Galahad, and when he reaches the lilied sea at the edge of the world, he throws his sword into the water, an action symbolic of his recognition of the limits of chivalry and earthly struggle. The scene is evocative of Excalibur being returned to the lake. Beyond this point, the healing of harms will take place in Aslan's own country.

Aslan's mountain, lying in the east, is the equivalent of the Grail castle in some romances, which is set on a mountain. In Wolfram's *Parzival*, Wolfram names the Grail castle as Munsalvaesche, which could mean either "the savage mountain" or "the mountain of salvation" (Barber 76). In Albrecht's *Titurel*, Titurel establishes the Grail kingdom at:

> Munt Salvatsch in the land called Salvaterre: these are the Munsalcaesche and Terre de Salvaesche of *Parzival*. Albrecht describes Munt Salvatsch as surrounded by impenetrable forest, the Foreist Salvasch, and ringed by thirty miles of mountains: no one could find their way there, unless the angels so wished, and the castle itself was fortified against all comers. (Barber 193)

Aslan's country is also a form of the Earthly Paradise, which was traditionally located in the East. Umberto Eco roots the legend in the Eden of Genesis and in classical tradition, a place of "bliss and innocence" that is "often represented as a kind of anteroom of the Celestial Paradise" (Eco 145), which is essentially what we have in Narnia. Some features of the Earthly Paradise from various traditions include: it is the source of rivers; it contains a fountain of eternal youth or a spring that can cure all ills; there is no pain or winter there; and there is a great abundance of food, including fruit that can heal every human ailment (Eco 148).

In the Arthurian tradition, the Earthly Paradise has its analogue in the Isle of Avalon. Gerald of Wales wrote that what

> is now called Glastonbury was, in antiquity, called the Isle of Avalon …. In Welsh it is called Inis Avallon, that is, insula pomifera, "The Island of Apples", because the apple, which is called aval in the Welsh tongue, was once abundant in that place. After the Battle of Camlann, Morgan, a noble matron, mistress and patroness of those regions, and also King Arthur's kinswoman by blood, brought Arthur to the island now called Glastonbury for the healing of his wounds." (Ashley 314)

Though Lewis places his Avalon at the end of the *Dawn Treader*'s journey east, it can also be reached via the west, as we see in *The Magician's Nephew* and *The Last Battle*. In the Great War, upper-class soldiers had referred to dying as "Going West" (Fussell 177).[12] The image of a ship delivering the Grail or Grail Knights, or indeed the wounded Arthur, was also seized upon in the Great War, and Paul Fussell reminds us that the "Big Ship" became "the troops' mythological, pseudo-Arthurian term for the once only imaginable boat plying between France and Demobilization" (142).

Throughout the *Chronicles*, the mountain is where characters like Arthur are taken to be healed. When Aslan leads the dragoned Eustace up into the mountains to cure him, it is presumably again to the Earthly Paradise that lies on Aslan's mountain. In the end, Eustace is stripped of his several skins and thrown into the well ("like a very big, round bath"; 474) by Aslan—and the water is of course "perfectly delicious" and heals the pain in his arm. The scene looks ahead to when the characters bathe in Caldron Pool, a place that obviously contains echoes of the Weston reading of the Grail myth, in the paradise at the end of *The Last Battle*. Lewis, of course, was not in any way satisfied with anthropological approaches to literature, and this included Weston's theory about the origin of the Grail cup as a fertility symbol. However, he is drawing from the same myth pool as the Arthurian writers Weston examines, and so there is a definite movement in the *Chronicles* toward healing of the spirit and refreshment given by water.

In *The Last Battle*, Farsight the Eagle reminds us that "all worlds draw to an end, except Aslan's own country" (717). Ultimately Narnia itself has to pass away before the waste land can be escaped for good. All of the places the children have known in Narnia are perfected and made anew. In the paradise of the remade Narnia, the journey "further up and further in" is a journey westward, as are so many Arthurian journeys. This is indeed paradise, a land of inexpressible meaning, and the source of the healing and the fecundity that surrounds the children and Narnians is the great water source, the aptly named Caldron Pool. They all plunge into the pool and are cleansed, but the final lap is a journey, following the water courses toward Aslan's Country. The Grail has been found at last.

---

12   See chapter 4 by Charles A. Huttar for an extended discussion of Avalon and Western longing. [Editor's note]

Works Cited

Ashley, Mike. *The Mammoth Book of King Arthur*. London: Robinson, 2005. Print.

Barber, Richard. *The Holy Grail: Imagination and Belief*. London: Penguin, 2004. Print.

"The Bishop of London at St. Paul's." *The Times*, 17 April 1911: 5. www.newspapers.com. Web. 14 August 2015.

Bloom, Harold, ed. and intro. *The Waste Land*. Bloom's Guides. NY: Bloom's Literary Criticism, 2007. Print.

Bontrager, Shannon Ty. "The Imagined Crusade: The Church of England and the Mythology of Nationalism and Christianity during the Great War." 2002 American Society of Church History. *The Free Library*. Web. 12 March 2015.

Brewer, Derek. "The Tutor: A Portrait." *C. S. Lewis at the Breakfast Table*. Ed. James T. Como. NY: Harvest, 1992. 41–67. Print.

Chrétien de Troyes. *Arthurian Romances*. Trans. William W. Kibler and Carleton W. Carroll. London: Penguin Books, 2004. Print.

Curtius, Ernst Robert. *European Literature and the Latin Middle Ages*. Princeton UP, 1990. Print.

Eco, Umberto. *The Book of Legendary Lands*. NY: Rizzoli, 2013. Print.

Eliot, T. S. *Selected Poems*. London: Faber & Faber, 1976. Print.

The Elucidation Prologue. Trans. William W. Kibler. *The Camelot Project*. U of Rochester. 2007. Web. 13 March 2015.

Frazer, James. *The Golden Bough: A Study of Magic and Religion*. Ware, Hertfordshire: Wordsworth, 1993.

Fussell, Paul. *The Great War and Modern Memory*. NY: Oxford UP, 2000. Print.

Garth, John. *Tolkien and the Great War: The Threshold of Middle-earth*. NY: HarperCollins, 2003. Print.

Gossedge, Rob. "'The Old Order Changeth': Arthurian Literary Production from Tennyson to White." Ph.D. Diss. Cardiff U. 2007.

Grant, Michael, ed. *T. S. Eliot: The Critical Heritage*. Vol. 1. Taylor and Francis e-library, 2005. www.tandfe-books.com. Web. 13 March 2015.

The High History of the Holy Grail. Trans. Sebastian Evans. *Camelot On-line*. heroofcamelot.com. PDF file. 13 March 2015.

Hooper, Walter. *C. S. Lewis. A Companion and Guide*. London: Fount, 1997. Print.

Housman, Laurence, ed. *War Letters of Fallen Englishmen*. NY: E. P. Dutton, 1930. Print.

Lewis, C. S. *The Abolition of Man*. London: Geoffrey Bles, 1946.

——. *All My Road Before Me: The Diary of C. S. Lewis 1922–1927*. Ed. Walter Hooper. London: Harvest, 1991. Print.

——. *The Chronicles of Narnia*. 1950–56. London: HarperCollins, 2001. Print.

——. *The Collected Letters of C. S. Lewis*. 3 vols. Ed. Walter Hooper. NY: HarperSanFrancisco, 2004–07. Print.

——. "The Decline of Religion." *Essay Collection* 179–83.

——. *Essay Collection and Other Short Pieces*. Ed. Lesley Walmsley. London: HarperCollins, 2000.

——. "The Necessity of Chivalry." *Essay Collection* 717–20.

——. "Learning in War-time." *The Weight of Glory*. NY: HarperCollins, 2001. Print. 47–63.

——. "Religion without Dogma." *Essay Collection* 163–78.

——. *Surprised by Joy: The Shape of My Early Life*. 1955. London: HarperCollins, 2002. Print.

——. "Is Theology Poetry?" *Essay Collection* 10–21.

Malory, Sir Thomas. "The Noble Tale of the Sangreal." *Le Morte d'Arthur*. Carleton U. Web. 13 March 2015.

McKusker, Paul. *C. S. Lewis and Mere Christianity: The Crisis That Created a Classic*. Carol Stream: Tyndale, 2014. Print.

Myers, Doris T. *C. S. Lewis in Context*. Kent State UP, 1994. Print.

Lancelot-Grail: The Old French Arthurian Vulgate and Post-Vulgate in Translation. Lacy, Norris J. Lacy. Vol. 3. NY: Garland, 1993–96. Print.

Ogden, C. K., and I. A. Richards. *The Meaning of Meaning*. NY: Harcourt, 1989.

Petronius. *The Satyricon* (with Seneca, *The Apocolocyntosis*). Trans. J. Sullivan. London: Penguin, 1986. Print.

The Quest of the Holy Grail. Trans. W. W. Comfort. Old French Series. Cambridge, Ontario: In parenthesis Publications, 2000. York U. www.yorku.ca. PDF file. 12 March 2015.

Russell, Jeffrey Burton. *A History of Heaven: The Singing Silence*. Princeton UP, 1997. Print.

Tennyson, Alfred. *Idylls of the King*. NY: Dover, 2004. Print.

Ward, Michael. *Planet Narnia: The Seven Heavens in the Imagination of C. S. Lewis*. Oxford UP, 2008. Print.

Weston, Jessie L. *From Ritual to Romance*. NY: Cosimo, 2005. Print.

Wilson, Edmund. "The Poetry of Drouth." *T. S. Eliot: The Critical Heritage*. Vol. 1. Ed. Michael Grant. Taylor and Francis e-library, 2005. www.tandfebooks.com. Web. 13 March 2015.

Wolfram Von Eschenbach. *Parzival*. Trans. A. T. Hatto. London: Penguin, 1980. Print.

12

"What Does the Line along the Rivers Define?": Charles Williams' Arthuriad and the Rhetoric of Empire.[1]

Benjamin D. Utter

> ... the glory of the Emperor stretched to the ends of the world ...
> "Prelude" to Taliessin through Logres

No poet taking up the "Matter of Britain" can remain for long the subject of purely literary analysis. Laurie Finke and Martin Shichtman have argued that Arthurian narrative is hard to separate from its latent potential for use and abuse in the cause of racial and nationalist politics, for, as they demonstrate, "King Arthur has been used by historians—medieval and modern—as a potent, but empty, social signifier to which meaning could be attached that served to legitimate particular forms of political authority and cultural imperialism" (2). A typical instance of such discourse opens their study: a passage from *The Birth of Britain,* the first volume of Winston Churchill's *History of the English-Speaking Peoples*:

> Let us then declare that King Arthur and his noble knights, guarding the Sacred Flame of Christianity and the theme of a world order, sustained by valour, physical strength, and good horses and armour,

---

1   Portions of this article represent heavily revised elements of my M.A. Thesis, *"A dark rose of sunset between tree and tree": Landscape Imagery in The Arthuriad of Charles Williams,* Wake Forest University, 2008 (unpublished). Special thanks to David Lenander and members of the Minneapolis Rivendell Discussion Group of the Mythopoeic Society for their helpful comments on an early draft.

slaughtered innumerable hosts of foul barbarians and set decent folk an example for all time.
(Churchill 60)

In holding up Camelot as an example of a "decent" world order enduring against a "barbarian" threat,
Churchill clearly had in mind the Axis powers only recently defeated at the time of his writing.[2] Ironically,
Germany had also seen itself as heir to the glory of the mythic king. "There can be little doubt," assert Finke
and Shichtman, "that Arthurian histories played some part in the Third Reich's efforts to romanticize—
perhaps even mythologize—itself" (191–92). Twentieth-century writers were only the latest to find Arthur
useful for nationalist purposes; he has found a place in histories, pseudo-histories, and nationalist poems
from at least as far back as Geoffrey of Monmouth's *Historia Regum Britanniae* (History of the Kings of Britain)
in the twelfth century. These myths of origin, in their varying expressions, employ two often mutually
reinforcing elements: the romanticizing of self in order to justify *translatio imperii*, that is, the "translation"
or transfer of imperial legitimacy; and national or ethnic self-differentiation achieved through the dehumanizing, if not demonizing, of an encroaching "Other."

To what extent, then, is Charles Williams' contribution to the canon of Arthurian poetry, in his
two published cycles of verse, *Taliessin through Logres* and *The Region of the Summer Stars*, a perpetuation of this
tradition, in which Camelot's splendor serves as a powerful symbol for national self-mythologizing, the
legitimation of empire, and religious triumphalism? His poems' vision of English national unity might
indeed be a uniquely spiritual one, but if, as W. H. Auden wrote admiringly, Williams was "the only one
since Dante who has found out how to make poetry of theology and history,"[3] nonetheless readers attuned
to the politically freighted history of the Arthur myth cannot help but take note of the fact that Williams
sketches this poetry across a landscape of empire, one representing an idealized Christendom, threatened
both politically and spiritually by a rapacious Islamic Caliphate crouched on its eastern doorstep. Indeed,
from one point of view, Williams' Arthuriad represents nearly everything that recent postcolonial criticism has undertaken to redress. I suggest that it is important to acknowledge the ways in which even so
highly metaphysical and symbolic a vision of the Arthurian myth as this relies on themes of Western order
and imperial authority under threat from a doctrinally disordered foreign enemy, for by doing so we gain
a greater appreciation for the effort of Williams' sympathetic imagination, or what he calls "the feeling
intellect," to identify with the Other.[4]

---

2   Anti-fascist themes are important as well in the construction of Arthur's distinctly British heroism in
    the novel of English poet laureate John Masefield, *Badon Parchments*, written shortly after the Second World
    War. See Peter Noble, "Arthur, Anti-Fascist or Pirate King?"

3   From a letter to Williams, dated 11 January 1945, acknowledging the receipt of a gift copy of *RSS*. The letter
    is in the Marion E. Wade Center, Wheaton College, Wheaton, IL. Letters of Charles Williams, folder 163.

4   Williams uses the phrase "the feeling intellect" once in *TtL* ("The Son of Lancelot," line 56) and twice in
    RSS ("The Calling of Taliessin" 255; "The Departure of Dindrane" 127). Drawing on Wordsworth before
    him (*Prelude* 14.226), he employs it to describe the creative state of the emotive and reasoning faculties in
    cooperative action at their highest pitch (Lewis, WA 285–86).

Distinguishing Williams from many other heirs to the Arthurian material, including Tolkien, is that the "difference" of the enemies of Logres is not a pretext for domination, eradication, or conversion by force, but rather for reflection on one's own sins. As I will show, if his reductive use of Islam as a symbol of schism is in some ways troubling, it is also in the service of a searching critique of the individual Christian self and of the larger church body. If reading Williams' Arthur poems through the lens of postcolonial criticism serves to underscore both some of the darker elements at the heart of the Arthur myth ("the violence inherent in the system," to borrow a phrase from *Monty Python and the Holy Grail*) and Williams' own approving attitude toward hierarchical authority, an accompanying attention to the temper of his spiritual themes, expressed elsewhere in his theological writing, reveals a deep awareness of his *own* capacity for wrongdoing. Williams' imagination, I argue, is not captive to an "imperialist nostalgia" that mourns what it has destroyed (Rosaldo 68–70) or to a resentful anxiety over what may soon be lost, but instead strains forward, toward a spiritual "Vision of the Empire" in which, as the poem of that name opens near the beginning of *Taliessin through Logres*, "The organic body [sings] together" (1).

The Postcolonial Critique

For admirers of Charles Williams (and I should say at the outset that I number myself among them), it might very well seem that his poems are in another category altogether from what could be called "imperialist writing," their symbolic complexity and breathtaking imaginative reach offering a cheering reassurance that (*pace* Finke and Shichtman) Arthur is not inescapably ensnared in discourses of ethnic and national power. The poems are, after all, an intentional expression of Williams' spiritual vision, a further working-out of his complex symbolic system comprising what he calls the themes of Exchange, Co-Inherence, and the Affirmation of Images.[5] In the preface to his 1939 prose work *The Descent of the Dove: A Short History of the Holy Spirit in the Church,* Williams invites readers to consider *Taliessin through Logres,* in which "the themes of this book are also discussed, from different points of view ..." (viii). Those who have taken Williams at his word have tended to regard his Arthur poems as apolitical, their incarnationalism excluding nationalism, so to speak. But the publication in 2002 of Williams' letters to his wife during the years of the second World War have revealed a side of the man quite at odds with the almost beatific persona he maintained among admiring friends and (it is not too much to say) disciples: one far darker and more anxious about the state of the war and the future of Europe. The revelation that an Englishman, even one given to a deeply spiritual turn of mind, should struggle deeply during that period with depression and with emotions of violent hatred for Germany should not, perhaps, surprise us, but it has nevertheless exposed new terrain for scholarly reevaluation of his wartime fiction.[6] I suggest that it calls into question as well the largely unchallenged assumption that Williams' Arthur poems, composed during the build-up to and height of

---

5   For Williams' most succinct explanation of these themes, see his pair of essays, "The Way of Exchange" and "The Way of Affirmation," collected in Ridler (147–58).

6   See Ashley Marshall, "Reframing Charles Williams: Modernist Doubt and the Crisis of World War in *All Hallows' Eve.*"

the second World War, can be regarded merely as what Jan Curtis calls "a theology of physical beatitude in the language of dogma and myth" (Curtis, "Byzantium" 28). They are certainly that, but they are also, as Bernard Hamilton recently pointed out, "a meditation about the place of Christianity in a world at war" (6), and although Williams' Christian ideas drew on esoteric occult symbolism for their expression, they were also rooted in lived and historical experience, including the institutions, geographies, and nationalities in which that Christianity developed and lived.

Thus, in *Taliessin through Logres* and *The Region of the Summer Stars*, the Arthurian pageant plays out over what Williams envisions as a vastly expanded Byzantine empire, set in conflict with both an encroaching nation of Islam and an imagined region called P'o-L'u, all overlaid—on the map Williams commissioned Lynton Lamb to draw for the flyleaf of the original edition of *Taliessin through Logres*—by a spiritually allegorical anatomy of a nude, reclining female body.[7,8] Just as film theorists have described how map shots in cinematic representations of the Middle Ages can connote a sense of Western imperial surveillance and mastery over the non-Western world (Shohat 27), so feminist and eco-feminist critics have long recognized that the exploitation of nature shares a common "logic of domination" with the exploitation of human bodies, particularly women's bodies (K. Warren 124, qtd. in Garrard 26), a perspective from which some troubling implications quickly emerge about the imagistic association of the imperial territories with the body of a nude and supine woman.[9] While a critique of Williams' poetics from the vantage of gender politics must remain the subject of another study, and is indeed the topic of chapter 14 of this present volume, I want to anticipate a critique of the way in which his poems celebrate imperial authority and represent the enemies of Logres.[10]

The field of postcolonial literary criticism, which developed originally to address writings by and about non-Western eighteenth- and nineteenth-century colonial subjects and the representation of "orientalism" and "exotic" difference more broadly,[11] has expanded only in the past decade and a half to address how the roots of those formations extend well past the Early Modern period and back into the Middle Ages.[12] Arthurian history and romance too played a role in the self-legitimizing rhetoric of imperial authority and

---

7   For a useful guide to the geographical-narrative structure of the poems, see Jan Curtis, "Byzantium and the Matter of Britain: The Narrative Framework of Charles Williams's Later Arthurian Poems."

8   Andrew Rasmussen deals with the gendered nature of this map in chapter 14. [Editor's note]

9   Anne McClintock, for example, writes: "If, at first glance, the feminizing of the land appears to be no more than a familiar symptom of male megalomania, it also betrays acute paranoia and a profound, if not pathological, sense of male anxiety and boundary loss" (24). She identifies several themes of western imperial dominance in an "explicitly sexualized" map in the opening pages of Henry Rider Haggard's novel *King Solomon's Mines* (4).

10   For more on his treatment of female characters, see Judith Kollman, "Charles Williams's *Taliessin through Logres* and *The Region of the Summer Stars*," 194–200.

11   Edward Said locates the formation of Orientalism in the eighteenth century, arising in tandem with western colonialism and imperialism at that time (123).

12   For a detailed discussion of what some have called the "postcolonial turn" in medieval studies, see Bruce Holsinger, "Medieval Studies, Postcolonial Studies, and the Genealogies of Critique."

dominance, and critics have shown how twentieth-century historians were hardly the first to find Arthur usefully malleable to their own political ends.[13] Imperialistic use of the Arthurian myth goes back at least as far as Geoffrey of Monmouth's twelfth-century *Historia Regum Britanniae,* likely written with an eye toward stabilizing the uneasy cohabitation then existing between the occupying Normans and their recently conquered neighbors (Finke and Shichtman 2).[14] To create a unified and unifying past, Geoffrey describes the ancient founding of Britain by Brutus, grandson of Aeneas, the legendary founder of Rome. Later in the work, Geoffrey mentions a certain general named "Arthur" whose accomplishments included conquering Rome. Subsequent writers embellished Geoffrey's pseudo-history, including the Anglo-Norman poet Wace, in his *Roman de Brut,* and the English poet Laʒamon in his early thirteenth-century *Brut,* the latter narrating Arthur's conquest of Rome in an archaically stylized English that hearkened back to an Anglo-Saxon past in order to create what some consider the first national epic of England.[15] At the heart of Geoffrey's account of Arthur is, according to one critic, an "insatiable desire for possession,"[16] and if this desire ebbs and flows in the retellings of Arthur in the centuries that followed, as pseudo-history blurred into romance, the potency of the myth did not diminish and proved no less useful to the powerful. The pageantry described in the Arthurian romances furnished an appealing pattern for ceremonies of knighthood, coronation, patronage, and war. In England, Edward III did more than any of the Plantagenet rulers to revive and nourish the cult of chivalry, styling Windsor as the "New Camelot" and founding the Order of the Garter around 1348 to help motivate and reward the nobles who aided him in the costly wars to maintain England's foreign territories.[17] The same elegant propaganda helped to bind the loyalties of warrior aristocrats in France, Germany, and Castile as well, ideals of knightly valor, gentleness, and courtesy helping to shape the rules of military conduct and recruit the sacrifice of men's wealth and bodies in the service of royal ambition.[18]

---

13 See, for example, Stephanie Barczewski, *Myth and National Identity in Nineteenth-Century Britain: The Legends of King Arthur and Robin Hood,* and Patricia Clare Ingham, *Sovereign Fantasies: Arthurian Romance and the Making of Britain.*

14 See also Michelle R. Warren, "Making Contact: Postcolonial Perspectives through Geoffrey of Monmouth's *Historia Regum Britannie.*"

15 John Brennan writes: "Laʒamon reconstructed a lost English language and revised an alien myth to create a past that would be usable in the present, enabling his contemporaries to re-imagine the future" (29).

16 Monmouth's Arthur, argues Felicity Riddy, resembles the nineteenth-century heroes described by Peter Brooks, in whom ambition "is inherently totalizing, figuring the self's tendency to appropriation and aggrandizement, moving forward through the accomplishment of more, striving to have, to do, and to be more ... The ambitious heroes of the nineteenth-century novel ... may regularly be conceived as desiring machines whose presence in the text creates and sustains narrative movement through scenarios of desire imagined and then acted upon" (Brooks 107, qtd. in Riddy 61–62).

17 See Juliet Vale, *Edward III and Chivalry: Chivalric Society and its Context, 1270–350.* And for an excellent discussion of Plantagenet politics and Arthurian poetry, see Francis Ingledew, *Sir Gawain and the Green Knight and the Order of the Garter.*

18 The essays in D. J. B. Trim, ed., *The Chivalric Ethos and the Development of Military Professionalism,* give a sense of how far-reaching and enduring the influence of the knightly ideal was.

Despite greatly diminished interest in medieval romance during the Renaissance, the Arthur myth continued to play a part in helping to sustain the British dynastic project. It was not by chance that Henry VII gave the name Arthur to his son and heir, and after young Arthur's untimely death, his brother, the ascendant Henry VIII, had himself painted as King Arthur in the Round Table portrait at Winchester.[19] Edmund Spenser, who bore approving witness to England's brutally maintained colonization of Ireland, includes Arthur in *The Faerie Queene,* his hymn to the unification of the British Isles. Tennyson, writing at the climax of British imperial breadth and power, dedicated his *Idylls of the King* to the memory of Prince Albert, and repeatedly identifies the expanse of Arthur's realm with Queen Victoria's own "ocean-empire with her boundless homes / For ever-broadening England" ("To the Queen" 29–30).[20] For Tennyson, Arthur served as a symbol of "the faith / That made us rulers" (18–19), much as Churchill would later describe Arthur as a guardian "of the Sacred Flame of Christianity."

One would be mistaken, of course, in thinking that literary theorists of the late twentieth century were the first to notice and question the nationalist impulses underlying Arthur's conquest. Williams himself certainly recognized the excesses of the early Arthur historians and distances his own project from theirs. A full half century before literary critics subjected Geoffrey of Monmouth's *Historia Regum Britanniae* to a postcolonial critique,[21] Williams, in an unfinished prose work on the history of Arthur, cited Geoffrey's account of Arthur's campaign against the Roman emperor as evidence that "Nationalism (too often attributed only to the Renascence) is already there getting slightly out of hand" ("Figure" 267). Leaving aside the implications of his understatement, Williams' parenthetical remark shows a historical awareness in step with recent scholarship, at least as it concerns the early date at which Arthur commenced his career as an instrument of political rhetoric.

Perhaps because of this awareness, Williams repeatedly tries to distance his own poems from easy association with the international politics of his day. Where his contemporary Arthurian writers such as T. H. White and, to a lesser extent, E. A. Robinson, wove thinly concealed allegories of Europe's struggle against fascism into their fiction and verse,[22] Williams' imaginative vision always resists the present moment, instead seeking a height from which to view all things as connected across temporal boundaries. In a brief preface to *The Region of the Summer Stars,* he explains, "the time historically is after the conversion of the Empire to Christianity but during the expectation of the Return of Our Lord" (117). And though Logres, which he defines as "Britain regarded as a province of the Empire with its centre at Byzantium," occupies a real political and geographical space in his complex and mystical imaginative vision, it is *sub specie aeternitatis,* the consequences of spiritual, geographical, and political disunity imagined, as he admits in his

---

19   For an entertaining account of this exceptional story, see Martin Biddle, "The Painting of the Table."

20   Elleke Boehmer includes "the later poetry of Tennyson" among the body of Victorian writings in which "the view of the world as directed from the colonial metropolis was consolidated and confirmed" (15). See also Ian McGuire, "Epistemology and Empire in 'Idylls of the King.'"

21   See, for example, M. R. Warren, "Making Contact: Postcolonial Perspectives through Geoffrey of Monmouth's *Historia Regum Britannie.*"

22   See Hagedorn Hermann, "Edwin Arlington Robinson: Arthurian Pacifist."

notes, with "any real objection to time and distance being ignored" (qtd. in Ridler 171).[23] The Emperor of the poem (though he seems to owe a great deal to Charlemagne) should be regarded, writes Williams, "as operative Providence." And several years after the completion of the poems, he wrote of the imagined "infernal" region of P'o-L'u, "I should regret now an identification with any particular nation or land. It is rather a spiritual threat than a mortal dominion" (Preface to *House of the Octopus*, 246).[24]

Such disavowals seem rather unpersuasive, however, in the face of his explicit comparison elsewhere of eighth-century Islam with the Axis powers. In his mythopoetic history of the Holy Spirit, *Descent of the Dove*, published in 1939, he likens the situation of Byzantium, threatened on its borders by an aggressive Islamic power, with that of "London to-day" (92). And wary though he claimed to be of the excesses of Geoffrey of Monmouth's nationalism, there is no getting around his poems' pervasive use of the image of empire and the theme of unification beneath Eurocentric, albeit Eastern, Christian imperial rule. Like Spenser's nationalistic epithalamion celebrating the union of the Thames and the Medway in *The Faerie Queene* (4.11), Williams' fanciful vision of the Byzantine Empire is an "imaginative reshaping of landscape which subordinates geographical reality to an ideological ideal" (Fitzpatrick 82).

Furthermore, in selecting as his protagonist the king's poet, Taliessin—a character with whom Williams seems to have identified personally to a degree that Glen Cavaliero speculates was "more total than he himself was perhaps aware" (Cavaliero, *Lalage* 4)—Williams places himself in the Virgilian tradition of the national poet, the literal voice of a nation, whose poetry defines a national identity by bearing imaginative witness to its origins. Myth-making and the violence of state-building collide in the poem "Mount Badon," in which Taliessin, serving as "captain of horse in the wars," experiences a moment of mystical communication across time with Virgil himself (*TtL*, "Mount Badon" 1). The Roman poet's labor of composing a founding epic, as "he sought for the invention of the City by the phrase" (36), blurs with field strategy in a battle that will be decisive for Arthur to fulfill his own Aeneas-like mandate, issued by Merlin: "I am Camelot; Arthur, raise me" (*TtL*, "The Calling of Arthur" 36). In a sudden visionary glimpse, Virgil's lines reveal to Taliessin the opportune moment for attacking the line of the enemy:

> Civilized centuries away, the Roman moved.
> Taliessin saw the flash of his style
> dash at the wax; he saw the hexameter spring
> and the king's sword swing; he saw, in the long field,
> the point where the pirate chaos might suddenly yield. (41–45)

---

23   For a discussion of Williams' narrative strategy of deliberate anachronism, see Sørina Higgins, "Double Affirmation: Medievalism as Christian Apologetic in the Arthurian Poetry of Charles Williams," esp. 60–73 on "Historical Conflation as Theological Communication."

24   C. S. Lewis, writing in about 1947, hastens to disabuse readers of another conceivable explanation, and insists that the tentacles of P'o-L'u are "not a 'poetic' description of the Japanese advance on India and its failure. The whole of Williams' P'o-Lu was conceived, and (I think) this poem ['The Prayers of the Pope'] written before the Japanese entered the war: his 'gift of prophecy' therein was a common topic of raillery among us" (Lewis, WA 369).

At the precise moment, Taliessin "fetche[s] the pen of his spear from its bearer" (72), and directs the cavalry under his command to take devastating action against the Saxon enemy. Michel de Certeau's observation that systems of law or socio-economic order are "inscribed" on the bodies of their subjects takes on new meaning in this poem, in which pen and spear are conflated, the instruments of writing and of war shown to be co-participants in the work of establishing and legitimizing rule (Certeau 148). The poem's final line shows the completion of that work, as, the battle won, "the candles of new Camelot shone through the fought field" (l. 69).

Authority, Order, and Discipline in the "crown'd Republic"

Arthur's taming of "the pirate chaos" reminds us that, although wreathed in an aura of ancient magic and the sometimes absurd generic tropes of romance, Arthur is a national hero-king, and to the extent that he is champion of fading Roman order against "barbaric" invasion, he is a part of "The rational discourse of Western knowledge," which "opposes reason to madness and truth to falsehood, placing its enterprise on one side of each such antithesis" (Spurr 63). That dichotomy is a strong thematic presence in the twenty-four poems of *Taliessin through Logres* and the eight poems of *The Region of the Summer Stars,* which chronicle the establishment, rise, and fall of Arthur's kingdom, and the subsiding of the spiritual Logres into "mere" Britain, from the vantage of Taliessin. In the poem "The Calling of Taliessin," the eponymous poet encounters anarchy:

> As he came on the third day down the way to the coast
> he saw on his left a wilderness; Logres lay
> without the form of a Republic, without letters or law,
> a storm of violent kings at war—smoke
> poured from a burning village in the mid-east;
> transport had ceased, and all exchange stilled. (103–08)

To this disordered landscape, Arthur will bring justice, which was, Williams writes in *Descent of the Dove*, "in everything, the pattern-word of the Middle Ages" (130). By "justice" he means not only fairness, but order, mathematically precise beauty, "the balance and poise needful to all joys / and all peace," and, by extension, the ceremonies and mechanisms of authority by which these are imposed, maintained, and enforced (*RSS*, "Taliessin in the Rose-Garden," 124–25). It is no accident that the most persistent natural image in the poems is the cut hazel branch, the traditional material of divining rods and of Merlin's wand, which Williams recruits as a neo-classical "instrument of order and measurement," symbolically corresponding "to the arm and to prosody, to anatomy and to law, to all roads and rules" ("The Making of *Taliessin*" 182).

　　Concerning both art and religion, Williams insisted that "Accuracy, accuracy, and again accuracy!" is essential, "accuracy of mind and accuracy of emotion" ("The Making of *Taliessin*" 157). But such accuracy comes with a price, as many poets writing about poetry have acknowledged; in "Adam's Curse," Yeats admits, "a line will take us hours maybe" (4). For every scene in which Taliessin's verse seems to pour forth *ex nihilo*, there is another showing him laboring at composition, "cutting and trimming verse as the gardeners the roses" (*RSS*, "Taliessin in the Rose Garden," 4). Accordingly, just as Merlin ordains with his hazel wand the calling of Arthur in order to bring political discipline to "unformed Logres," so the poet Taliessin invokes and envisions hazel as a symbol of the artistic control necessary to the creation of verse. It appears in "The Last Voyage" as a baton of the poetic genius and labor to which Taliessin is heir:

> ... in a laureate ceremony
> Virgil to Taliessin stretched a shoot
> of hazel—the hexameter, the decasyllabic line—
> fetched from Homer beyond him. (15–18)

Taliessin, Byzantium-bred, follows the poetic line of succession descending from Greece to Rome to the eastern Empire of Byzantium. There are few straight lines in nature, but once disciplined to straightness, the hazel stands in clear symbolic contrast to the Islamic crescent moon and scimitar, "the sharp *curved* line of the Prophet's blade / that cuts the Obedience from the Obeyed" (*TtL*, "The Coming of Palomides" 7–8, emphasis mine).

One additional form of discipline and control that the "implacable hazel" takes in the poems is alarmingly non-figurative (*TtL*, "The Son of Lancelot" 49). It is with a hazel rod that barbarian slave-girls, now captive in Logres, are disciplined to satisfy the "needful law" (*TtL*, "The Ascent of the Spear" 27). "'I have known,'" one slave girl recalls to Taliessin:

> with the scintillation of a grave smile,
> "the hazel's stripes on my shoulders; the blessed luck
> of Logres has a sharp style, since I was caught free
> from the pirate chaos ...." (*TtL*, "The Coming of Galahad" 109–13)

It was this in particular that prompted a very hostile early review by Robert Conquest, who denounced as "totalitarian" not only Williams' apparent preoccupation with whipping, but also with patterned order and the discipline required to maintain it. Writing under the shadow of Stalinism in 1957, Conquest argued that Williams' "admirable talent" had been subverted by the "ideological straightjacket" of religion—and religion without even the redeeming virtues of charity, pity, or humility—and condemned the Arthur poems as an example of the ruinous effect of totalitarian thought on art (43). Though acknowledging their flashes of brilliance, Conquest found Williams' verses burdened by a "dull and heavy 'Imperialist' vocabulary"—he gives as examples "porphyry," "largesse," "glory," "propolitan," and "ban" (51)—which is but symptomatic of the ideological corruption at their heart. Conquest concludes his damning critique by roundly condemning Williams' entire symbolic schema: "the psychology of totalitarianism—of hierarchy and of sadism—is the essential of his work and ruins it irretrievably" (55).

Subsequent defenders of Williams have shown how at least one element of this criticism was owing to misrepresentation by C. S. Lewis in his admiring explanatory essay "Williams and the Arthuriad." As Jan Curtis argues, Lewis gravely misrepresents the scar symbol [in *TtL*'s "The Sister of Percival"] when he says, "the scar symbolizes all the violence and suffering by which alone barbarian souls can be brought, against their will, into the confines of the City in order that, at a later stage they may, by their will, remain there" (WA 323). Nowhere does Williams suggest, with the arrogance of Lewis' totalitarianism, that the slave is a barbarian who must first be whipped into the Holy City. (Curtis, "Sister" n14)

Be that as it may, hierarchical order and authority are so thematically essential to the poems that even one of Williams' more appreciative critics has been led to ask outright, "Is Williams really totalitarian?" (Scarf 34).[25] Williams' theological writing, too, describes human relationships as a microcosm of graded heavenly order:

> By an act of substitution [Christ] reconciled the natural world with the world of the kingdom of heaven, sensuality with substance .... [U]p and down the ladder of that great substitution all our lesser substitutions run .... It is supernatural, but it is also natural. The dreams of nationality and communism use no other language. The denunciation of individualism means this or it means nothing. The praise of individualism must allow for this or it is mere impossible anarchy." (*Dove* 235)[26]

This sounds very much like an Aristotelian-Thomistic cosmology, Williams' use of "ladder" recalling the so-called "great chain of being," the *scala naturae* (literally "ladder" or "stair of nature"), in which each link must know and keep its obedient place. It is interesting to note that another of Williams' favorite images of order is the Porphyry Stair, borrowed from occult symbolism.[27] A closer analysis of this image, however, reveals a crucial additional element in Williams' ideas about authority and obedience: their relationality.

In a 1943 essay, "A Dialogue on Hierarchy," Williams attempted a reconciliation of the tension between the "Hierarchy" and the "Republic," describing the two as an interrelated system in which "equality" and "degree" are not at odds, but instead arranged in a "great exchange of duty" (127). Although proposing that there is in everything "always a kind of hierarchy present," Williams envisions it as a sort of dance of mutual-deference, in which every creature "owes discreet obedience to all others and all others to him ... each is in the base and at the apex, zenith and nadir at once .... The classless Republic is a republic of hierarchies, and each hierarchy is the fleshing out of ranked equalities" (129).

---

25 Scarf concludes that, "while we should not see Williams as actually totalitarian, we must concede there is a decidedly violent atmosphere in 'Mount Badon,' Arthur's battle for the taking of Camelot" (37).

26 Some implied sympathy with Communism can be found in Williams' poems, as well. See, for example, his allusion to the hammer and sickle to image revolt against the tyranny of King Cradlemas in *TtL*, "The Calling of Arthur" (27; 30).

27 For an explanation of Williams' use of the combined images of the porphyry stair and Sephirotic Tree, see Roma King, "The Occult as Rhetoric in the Poetry of Charles Williams," 176–78. An extended analysis of occult symbolism in Williams' prose fiction may be found in Aren Roukema, "A Veil that Reveals: Charles Williams and the Fellowship of the Rosy Cross."

Williams expresses these same ideas in *Taliessin through Logres* in "Taliessin in the School of the Poets," wherein Taliessin considers the Emperor's throne room in Byzantium. There, in the "macrocosm" of the stair's "huge and heavy" head,

> all measures, to infinite strength,
> from sapphire-laced distances drawn,
> fill the jewel-joint-justiced throne;
> adored be the God and the Emperor ... (43–47)

Once again, the imperial order embodied here is not only hierarchical but relational, and the complexity Williams develops in the image of the throne and "the magnanimous path of the stair" (51) is not vertical but diagrammatic, not only a ladder but also a web:

> to a tangle of compensations,
> every joint a centre,
>   and every centre a jewel.
> Each moment there is the midmost
>   of the whole massive load ... (52–56)

Williams denies neither greatness nor authority, and enjoins obedience (at the center of Dante's hell, he reminds us elsewhere, are "traitors to 'lords and benefactors'" [*Dove* 136]), but it is a mutual obedience. Each and all, he suggests, exist under God, yes, but also in and with God who became man, and—crucially—in and with one another, "dying each other's life; living each other's death."[28] This mutuality of being, beginning in the "exchange" of human conception, extends even to participating in one another's redemption and salvation, as the poem "Taliessin on the Death of Virgil" suggests, when the as yet "unborn pieties" of his future disciples cast with their goodwill a "net of obedient loves" to catch and lift the pagan poet from perdition (19, 30).

Political and ethnic nationalism can be an emancipatory as well as pernicious force,[29] and several of the poems of *The Region of the Summer Stars* serve to remind us that Arthur did not begin as a conqueror of worlds, but as leader of a rebellion in the overthrow of a tyrant. "The Calling of Arthur" describes young Arthur's response to Merlin's charge that he build Camelot. Arthur rallies the people, deposes the last remaining Roman suzerain, King Cradlemas (a consolidation of the eleven kings Arthur must battle to establish his rule in Malory's *Morte Darthur*), and builds Camelot on what was Roman Caerleon. The poem's terse final stanza is one of Williams' most evocative:

---

28 This line occurs in *TtL*'s "Bors to Elayne: on the King's Coins (188) and *RSS*'s "The Founding of the Company" (63). It is a loose translation from Heraclitus, as discussed below.

29 Elleke Boehmer describes how an emergent national identity, separate from the colonizing state, served the causes of liberation for colonized people in the twentieth century. Boehmer, *Colonial and Postcolonial Literature: Migrant Metaphors*, chap. 3.

Arthur ran; the people marched; in the snow
King Cradlemas died in his litter; a screaming few
fled; Merlin came; Camelot grew. (38–40)

If modern, post-Foucauldian criticism is reflexively (and not unjustly) suspicious of all political and institutional authority, Williams asks only that those in authority be good. The problem with Cradlemas is not that he is a ruler, but that he is a bad ruler. Lear-like, he has taken too little care of his kingdom. "On the waste of hovels snow falls from a dreary sky," at the sight of which the king had only mused abstractedly "that the winter is hard for the poor" ("The Calling of Arthur" 22, 24). Arthur is a far better ruler by contrast, one whose reign, at its best moments, exemplifies one of Williams' favorite mottos, from Dante's *De Monarchia*: "Unde est, quod non operatio propria propter essentiam, sed haec propter illam habet ut sit," which Williams translates in *The Figure of Beatrice* as "The proper operation (working or function) is not in existence for the sake of the being, but the being for the sake of the operation" (40).[30]

Unfortunately, this is also precisely where Arthur's reign goes wrong at its worst moments. In what David Llewellyn Dodds calls "a radical act of improper self-exaltation" (9), Arthur incorrectly answers the question, "the king made for the kingdom, or the kingdom made for the king?" and in so doing, upsets the patterned order between hierarchy and republic whose co-inherence is "the glory of Logres" (*TtL,* "The Crowning of Arthur" 63, 44).

Despite these failures, the high king remains the high king, and for all Williams' professed admiration for a "republic of hierarchies," in which "each hierarchy is the fleshing out of ranked equalities" ("A Dialogue on Hierarchy" 129), there is no getting around the fact that he appears to have held very seriously to a belief in what can only be called the divine right of kings. In the aforementioned essay, he writes that the "anointed figure of the King does not 'deserve' to be royal, and this is so clear that it saves us from the claims of merit which oligarchies and aristocracies are apt to set up. It is of a different order" ("A Dialogue on Hierarchy" 128). Such a romantic vision of what Tennyson called the "crown'd Republic" ("To the Queen" 59–60) is perhaps understandable in someone so steeped in Arthurian romance, but as anything like a theory of governance, it is at best platitudinous and naïve, and at worst, a legitimization of authoritarianism.

Williams sounds very like Spinoza when he writes, in *Descent of the Dove*, "The very nature of the Church involves the view that, apart from human sin, what happened was right" (30). Though he acknowledges that such a statement "certainly gives a great advantage in argument to any hostile, intelligent, and skeptical mind ... the belief can hardly be abandoned because of that intellectual inconvenience" (30). The years immediately after he wrote these lines would test that attitude, even as he tried to remain consistent. At the declaration of World War Two, Williams urged a number of his friends "to know co-inherence, including the enemy, including Hitler and he with us, and all in Christ" (qtd. in Hadfield 176). To Williams' admirers, this is the attitude of a saint—albeit, perhaps a somewhat naïve one; to others, who have noted

---

30   For an argument that this dictum is key to the whole of Williams' Arthur cycle, see Jan Curtis, "Charles Williams's 'The Sister of Percivale': Toward a Theology of 'Theotokos.'"

the absence of the Jews from this prayer, the whole attitude suggests an irresponsible and possibly willful blindness, even to the point of anti-Semitism (Loewenstein 206).[31]

Sympathetic Imagination and the Fearsome Self

Williams' fiercest critic in recent decades, Freud Loewenstein, who includes Williams among a group of writers she pathologizes as anti-Semitic and gynophobic, insists that critics must "look within [them] selves for 'that terrible other' rather than to complacently assume that we ourselves exist outside the ideology of power" (73). But this, I argue, Williams does, and it shows in his representation of the enemies of Logres. If some of his ideas about power are outmoded even by the standards of his day, he could not be called naïve about the tendency toward abuse of those who wielded it; if anything, his Augustinian view of the soul, of the "ancestral and contemporary guilt" lodged in each being, made him more skeptical about human nature than most of his modern critics (*Dove* 234). Rather than making him acerbic, these dour assumptions lead to some of the most humane and amusing passages in his prose account of church history, in which he describes the all-but-inevitable corruption of authority succeeding flawed authority in both ecclesiastical and political institutions. And beyond that, one can see glimpses suggesting that the heart of darkness that he sensed most intimately, and that weighed on him most heavily, was his own.

That his heart was not innocent of some very dark shadows indeed, there can be no question. Fans too much in his thrall may find their ardor unsettled by reading the collected letters from the nearly sixty-year-old Williams to the twenty-six-year-old Lois Lang-Sims, one of his numerous female disciples.[32] What they reveal of Williams' fascination with bondage and whipping complicates any attempts to explain the "cry of joy and pain," and the "suddenly now / new-treasured servitude" of Taliessin's slave-girl as merely a metaphor for the paradox of the free will yielding to divine love, along the lines of Donne's fourteenth holy sonnet (*RSS,* "The Departure of Dindrane" 56–57).[33] Even his close friend Anne Ridler acknowledged that he had "an impulse toward violence" and that there is "a certain sadism in a few of the Taliessin poems," in tension with an opposing "loving-kindness so remarkable that it caused T. S. Eliot to inquire of him whether he was to be called the Blessed Charles in his lifetime" (Ridler xxxii).[34] Ridler was not alone in this realization. Saints, as Williams acknowledged, "are few in any age" (*Dove* 117), and if he enjoyed playing the master to his disciples and made W. H. Auden feel sanctified in his presence, "transformed into a person who was incapable of doing or thinking anything base or unloving" (qtd. in Cavaliero, *Poet* 4), Williams' letters and essays give ample evidence that he was clear-eyed about his own capacity for cruelty. David Dodds

---

31   Though Ashley Marshall, in her response to Williams' critics, reminds us that public understanding of the horrific situation of Europe's Jews was far from fully developed at this point (73).

32   *Letters to Lalage: The Letters of Charles Williams to Lois Lang-Sims.*

33   For a helpful discussion of Williams' use of slavery as a metaphor of personality and spiritual exchange, see Brenda Boughton, "The Role of the Slave in Charles Williams' Poetry."

34   I note that although Loewenstein includes Ridler's remark about sadism in her scathing criticism of Williams, she omits the corresponding remarks about his much-remarked-on aura of sanctity (Loewenstein 208).

comments that Williams' "desire for everything to be reconciled and unified can appear too strong, with Williams in danger of confounding good and evil, or seeming to say, evil is good" (13), but Williams also stresses the reverse in his writing, professing a wariness about the perversion of pure—or what only seem to be pure—motives: "Deep, deeper than we believe, lie the roots of sin; it is in the good that they exist; it is in the good that they thrive and send up sap and produce the black fruit of hell" (*Dove* 108). The hero of one of Williams' novels declares, "I dislike tyranny, treachery, and cruelty" (*Many Dimensions* 134), and this statement is not a bad summary of the temper of much of his fiction and poetry, in which villainy often takes the form of bullying, and heroism means bringing action into alignment with the spirit of fair play. And yet Williams knew those unsavory qualities to be far from alien to his own nature. "There are wells of hate in one which are terrifying," he confessed in a letter to his wife, "wells of suspicion and even malice" (*To Michal* 149, 17 February 43).

I do not wish to venture too far into the details of Williams' personal life or toward either an indictment or an exoneration of his character, though I wonder whether he would object to the exercise. In a letter to Anne Ridler, he wrote, "We must not make poetry serve our morals, yet we must not consider it independent of our morals. It is not a spiritual guide, yet it possesses a reality which continually persuades us to repose upon it even in practical things of every day" (qtd. in Ridler liv). I suggest that understanding his profound awareness of his own inner night is important for a fair assessment of his depiction of the enemies of Logres. Like St. Paul, whom Williams calls the "thorned-in-the-flesh" apostle (*RSS*, "Prelude" 13), and who wrote, "for not what I would, that do I practice; but what I hate, that I do" (Rom. 7:15), Williams appears all too aware of his own capacity for sin. This awareness, I argue, is reflected in his presentation of foreign threats, particularly Islam, which he uses as an outward expression of tendencies toward error that he believed lay also within the Church itself. As a character in Williams' Grail novel, *War in Heaven*, remarks, "One's foes are always in one's own household" (249).

"Recalcitrant Tribes": The Barbaric and Islamic Other

In the same way that Arthur could function as a "potent but empty signifier" for the putatively righteous cause *du jour* (Finke and Shichtman 2), the enemies of the Round Table served as a handy cipher for barbarity in any form. Having wrested Camelot from the last of the pagan Roman kings and brought order to the "pirate chaos," the foremost threat that Arthur and the Empire face in Williams' poems is from Islam.

As Donald Hoffman puts it with admirable succinctness, "Whoever the 'Saracens' were, they were always someone else .... quintessentially Other even if that otherness is not always determinate" (43).[35] It is that convenient indeterminacy, the product of pervasive (if not necessarily willful) western ignorance

---

35   Bonnie Wheeler writes with similar economy, "If Camelot is home, Sarras is away" (Wheeler 13). Arthurian scholars have recognized the inadequacy of the term "Saracen" since at least 1940, when W. W. Comfort described its function for writers of medieval romance as little more than shorthand for a civilized, monolithic enemy of Western Christendom, though a tendency "to expand the definition of Saracen to encompass all pagans" has persisted even among recent Malory critics (Goodrich 10).

about the Arab, Turkish, and Persian worlds, that made Islam a useful cipher for medieval writers, for whom Saracens could be made to stand for a spiritual as well as political threat; what better way to show Arthur as a champion of Christianity than by having him lead a charge on Christ's foes?[36] In the *Alliterative Morte Arthure*, written around 1400, Arthur exhorts his men to kill Saracens as an act of piety, and promises heavenly reward for the slaughter:

> Sett one theme sadlye, for sake of oure Lorde!
> Зif vs be destaynede to dy to-daye one this erthe,
> We sale be hewede vn-to heuene, or we be halfe colde!
>
> ----------
>
> Set on them grimly for the sake of our Lord!
> If we be destined to die today on this earth
> We shall be gathered to heaven before we are half cold![37]

Malory's *Morte Darthur*, too, as Hoffman explains, "implies a complicated pattern of understanding and misunderstanding of the Saracen" (43), and on first appraisal, Williams' use of Islam in the poems does not seem much more enlightened. It occupies on the poems' frontispiece map the same "undifferentiated, marginal site" to which, as film critics have noted, the Arab world is predominately relegated in western film (Shutters 80). And used as they are in his poems, Saracens begin to bear more than a passing resemblance to "colonized people," who, in Anne McClintock's definition, "do not inhabit history proper but exist in a permanently anterior time within the geographic space of the modern empire as anachronistic humans ... the living embodiment of the archaic 'primitive'" (40). Williams' convenient transplantation of the nation of Islam across several centuries in order that it might serve as a foil to the ideals of Logres and the Empire renders Muslims "anachronistic humans" indeed. Williams kept a mythological scrapbook (c.1912–16) in which he wrote notes related to the legends of King Arthur, including one in which he proposes to

> ? Bring [A̶r̶] Arthur and his surroundings in England [Britain], about A.D. 500, forward + parallel to Charlemagne + his surroundings in France, A.D. 800: so as to obtain the full effect of Islam, in Africa, in Spain. (*Arthurian Commonplace Book* 12)

---

36   It seems unlikely that Malory, for example, could distinguish between the Ottoman Turks of his own century and the Seljuk, Khwarezm, and Mamluk Turks described in the thirteenth-century sources on which he drew for the creation of the *Morte Darthur*. For the probable limits of Malory's knowledge and its influence on his depictions of Saracens, see Peter H. Goodrich, "Saracens and Islamic Alterity in Malory's 'Le Morte Darthur,'" 10–28.

37   Middle English text of the *Alliterative Morte* from Larry D. Benson and Edward E. Foster, eds, "Stanzaic Morte Arthur," in *King Arthur's Death: The Middle English* Stanzaic Morte Arthur *and* Alliterative Morte Arthure, TEAMS Texts (Kalamazoo, Michigan: Medieval Institute Publications, Western Michigan University, 1994), ll. 4089–91. Translation mine.

Thus it is that the map in the poems' frontispiece shows the Empire's European holdings much as they were at the end of Justinian's reign in 565 (in fact, since its borders extend to include Spain and the British Isles, the map better resembles the unification achieved under Constantine in the fourth century), but anachronistically shows a southern frontier under pressure from Arabian incursion that would not occur until the eighth century.[38]

This oppositional arrangement of Christian empire and a historically vague but monolithic Islamic threat appears to participate in maintaining the facile boundary between "foul barbarians" and "decent folk" to which Churchill appeals. The Emperor, after all, is a Christian emperor, and Christian faith is the measuring rod—the "straight hazel"—separating good subjects of the realm from the barbarians who threaten it. The final poem in *The Region of the Summer Stars*, "The Prayers of the Pope," narrates how "Against the rule of the Emperor the indivisible / Empire was divided" as war between Mordred and Arthur spreads outward from Logres throughout the Empire, and describes Mordred as an "infidel," placing him alongside "unstable pagan chiefs" such as "the Khan of the Huns or the Khalif of Asia" (145, 156, 159).

This vision of disunion is the opening to the first poetic cycle in the "Prelude" to *Taliessin through Logres*, which narrates three phases of the Empire and its quarrel with Islam. The first section announces the hegemony of the Emperor's rule, recalling something of the role of the *logos* in the opening of the Gospel of John, in which "The word became flesh and dwelt among us" (John 1:2): "The word of the Emperor established a kingdom in Britain" ("Prelude" to *TtL* 5). But this *pax* is only temporary, for in the second section we find that "the Moslem stormed Byzantium; / lost was the glory, lost the power and kingdom" (14–15). The third section leaves off chronicling the political history of the Empire, and instead describes the philosophical and metaphysical consequences of Islamic monotheism, which "destroyed the dualism of Persia" where:

> Evil and good were twins
> once in the alleys of Ispahan; the Moslem
> crying *Alla il Alla* destroyed the dualism of Persia.
> Caucasia fell to the Moslem;
> the mamelukes seized the ancient cornland of Empire.
> Union is breached; the imams stand in Sophia. (21–26)

Despite the reconciliation, "Union is breached" as a new theological division opens between spirit and flesh: "*Good is God*, the muezzin / calls, but lost is the light on the hills of Caucasia, / glory of the Emperor, glory of substantial being" (25–27). The descriptive "substantial" is the key word here. The peril Williams imagines in the "Moslem" incursion is its Manichean rejection of substance, of the bodily and the material, and this rejection interrupts the interpenetrating balance between the spiritual and material, the apophatic "way of negation" and the cataphatic "way of affirmation."

---

38   See n23, above.

The poem "Bors to Elayne: on the King's Coins" is a convenient point of entry into Williams' pet theme of Exchange, which, along with Co-Inherence and the Affirmation of Images, is crucial for an understanding of his overall vision. Only by understanding these doctrines can we recognize what he feels is at stake in his use of Islam as a proxy for Manichaeism in all its forms.[39],[40]

In the poem, Bors, always one of the more thoughtful members of the Round Table, returns to his farm from a visit to London and reports that Arthur "has set up his mint by Thames. / He has struck coins" (33–34). Since the withdrawal of Rome, we are to imagine, Britain has been existing on a system of barter rather than coinage (Lewis, WA 316). The poem's argument implies that the value carried by currency (engraved with Arthur's head on one side and a heraldic dragon crest on the other: "little loosed dragons"; l. 68) displaces not only the value of actual material goods, but also the spirit in which they are exchanged. The poem's opening image, and the first thing Bors sees as he enters, is "the bread of love" in the hand of his wife, Elayne (lines 2, 23). She has been about the business of preparing food for their household, and Bors speaks with pleasure of how

> corn comes to the mill and the flour to the house,
> bread of love for your women and my men;
> at the turn of the day, and none only to earn;
> in the day of the turn, and none only to pay;
> for the hall is raised to the power of exchange of all ... (22–26)

But now the king's new economic system will decree that everyone must know the price of everything and upsets the communal model by making money, rather than goods and goodwill, the medium of exchange. In the second half of the poem, the matter comes before the council of lords, where the ever-churlish Kay, "wise in economics," approves the convenience of the system, for "Gold dances deftly across frontiers" (55, 60). He fails or does not choose to realize, as Bors and Taliessin do, that the new law will "germinate a crowded creaturely brood / to scuttle and scurry between towns and towns, / to furnish dishes and flagons with change of food" (35–37). The "brood" described in these lines suggests at once an invasion of the coins themselves, and also the creation of a miserable new service class, a distortion of creaturely regard between fellow subjects of the realm.

Taliessin's response to Kay is the kind of anti-capitalist critique that only a semiotician or a poet could utter:

----

39   Williams' use of the term "Manichaean" is somewhat confusing in that he uses it to denote both the dualism preached by the third-century Mani— "a supposed primeval conflict between light and darkness" (Cross and Livingstone 1027)—and a more generalized Cartesian dualism that regards mind and body as discreet, if not necessarily oppositional, entities. The distinction is essential to understanding the doctrinal progression narrated in the "Prelude" to TtL, in which Islam first displaces the dualism of Mani with monotheistic unity in which a gnostic wariness of materiality, and the body in particular, persists.

40   In the notes he wrote to Lewis about these poems, Williams wrote: "Islam is (a) Deism (b) Manichaenism (c) heavy morality (d) Islam" (Rateliff, "Lost Letter" 4). [Editor's note]

Sir, if you made verse you would doubt symbols.
I am afraid of the little loosed dragons.
When the means are autonomous, they are deadly; when words
escape from verse they hurry to rape souls;
when sensation slips from intellect, expect the tyrant;
the brood of carriers levels the good they carry.
We have taught our images to be free; are we glad?
are we glad to have brought convenient heresy to Logres? (67–74)

Reducing one another to means, in other words, risks cutting off sources of spiritual nourishment both interpersonal and divine, for "greed bid[s] God, who hides himself for man's pleasure / by occasion, hide himself essentially" (78–79). So warns the archbishop, who follows Taliessin in addressing the council. He gets the last word, countering Kay's satisfied "Money is the medium of exchange" by asking: "What saith Heracleitus? —and what is the City's breath? — / *dying each other's life, living each other's death.* / Money is a medium of exchange" (87–88, emphasis original). This reprimand is a tidy summary of Williams' doctrine of "exchange," which imagines each individual participating in a system of interdependence with all others. It is a vision mystical as well as ethical, resembling in some ways Kant's Categorical Imperative, which forbids any use of human beings as means rather than ends.[41] Williams' theme of Exchange qualifies the rule only slightly, lest individuals conclude that they are therefore ends unto themselves. Thus the archbishop expounds, "we must lose our own ends; / we must always live in the habitation of our lovers, / my friend's shelter for me, mine for him" (82–84).

As an indictment of money as "the" rather than "a" medium of exchange, this is all clear enough. But Taliessin's remarks direct attention to a broader implication of the breach between signifier and signified. Heraclitus's dictum as the archbishop quotes it is taken from Yeats's *A Vision*, the reference vastly broadening the scope of Williams' doctrine by implying that exchange operates in a broader context than individual transactions, since Yeats' fascination was with the interconnectedness of empires, the cyclical influence upon and borrowing from and between one civilization and the next:

Each age unwinds the thread another has wound, and it amuses one to remember that before Phidias, and his westward moving art, Persia fell, and that when full moon came round again, amid eastward moving thought, and brought Byzantine glory, Rome fell; and that at the outset of our westward moving Renaissance Byzantium fell; all things dying each other's life, living each other's death. (Yeats 152)

---

41   In his *Groundwork for the Metaphysics of Morals*, Kant offers one practical formulation of this imperative: "So act as to treat humanity, whether in your own person or in that of any other, in every case at the same time as an end, never as a means only" (88).

Williams' doctrine of "exchange" extends beyond even this to include the relationship between humanity and the divine, of which atonement enacted in the crucifixion is the apex, the "exchange of the knowledge of good as evil for Christ's knowledge of evil as an occasion of good" (Cavaliero, *Poet* 149). C. S. Lewis' summary of co-inherence adds that "All salvation, everywhere and at all times, in great things or in little, is vicarious" (WA 307). When the Fisher King is healed at one of the climaxes of the cycle, it is by way of substitution that the cure is enacted, Arthur having just died: "At the hour of the healing of Pelles / the two kings were one, by exchange of death and healing" (*TtL*, "The Last Voyage," 123–24). Similarly, Williams treats Lancelot's siring of Galahad with Helayne not as a case of womanly cunning or tragic mistaken identity so much as an instance of "heavenly substitution," Merlin deliberately arranging that the princess Helayne occupy the place (and bed) of Guinevere ("Preface" to *RSS*, 118).

This, then, is the nature of Islam in the poems: the threat it poses is not primarily military; its civilization neither obstructs further expansion nor competes for resources. Rather, it is the embodiment of doctrinal error.[42] Much as Dante places Mohammad among the schismatics in the eighth circle of the *Inferno*, Williams uses Islam to figure one side of the two competing impulses either to honor or reject images, including their living human form. This is the tension between worshipful recognition of God in all that is, and the rejection of all that is not God as idolatry. The reconciliation of these two paths is the theme of Williams' theological writing, fiction, and poetry, for although he insists that both paths are beneficial and each necessary to the other, they are out of balance in all of the monotheistic traditions, Christianity as well as Islam.

In his Arthurian vision, the two paths converge in the figure of Galahad. "The High Prince has remained as an intense symbol of the two Ways; he is not on them, but they are both in him. He is the flesh and blood in the union with the Flesh and Blood" (*Dove* 117). But what co-inheres so mystically and wonderfully in Galahad, he suggests, grew out of balance as the "gathering strength of the church suppressed itself as dominion," and in the "imposition of belief, the practice of the Co-inherence seems driven back more and more ..." (*Dove* 117). In an essay on "Sensuality and Substance," Williams warns of a pernicious "unofficial Manicheism" in the Christian church, where above all other places the "soul ought not to be allowed to reduce the body to its own shadow": "the great world and energy of the body have been either deprecated or devotionalized ... turned into a pale imitation of 'substance' ... thus losing their own powers and privileges without, in general, gaining any others" (69).

---

42   C. S. Lewis explains:

The anachronism whereby Islam is made contemporary with Arthur is deliberate: Islam was for Williams the symbol (as it is certainly the greatest historical expression) of something which is eternally the opposite of Sarras and Carbonek. Islam denies the Incarnation. It will not allow that God has descended into flesh or that Manhood has been exalted into Deity .... It stands for all religions that are afraid of matter and afraid of mystery, for all misplaced reverences and misplaced purities that repudiate the body and shrink back from the glowing materialism of the Grail. It stands for what Williams called 'heavy morality'—the ethics of sheer duty and obedience as against the shy yet (in the long run) shameless acceptance of heaven's courtesies flowing from the 'homely and courteous lord.' (WA 308)

While the opening poem in *Taliessin through Logres* describes how "Union is breached" by the Muslim capture of Constantinople, the first poem in *The Region of the Summer Stars* shows how the foreign heresy has roots much closer to home. The "Prelude" stresses the Hellenic influence behind what came to be known as the "Nestorian heresy," the doctrine that two separate persons inhered in the incarnate Christ, one human, the other divine (Cross and Livingstone 1138–39). This is contrary to what Williams calls in the "Prelude" the "twyfold Nature [of] the golden Ambiguity," the orthodox *magnum mysterium* of the single person, simultaneously God and man, first articulated by St. Paul to the early Christian church in Rome. The poem describes how, even after Paul "defined in speech the physiological glory," Hellenic strains of Gnosticism endured:

> ... the ancient intellect
> heard, delaying and playing with its archives, and demurred
> that pain was easy, and completeness of belief costly,
> and flesh too queasy to bear the main of spirit.
> The converted doctors turned to their former confessions,
> the limitary heresiarchs feared the indiscretions of matter ....
> Professing only a moral union they fled
> From the new-spread bounty. (20–25, 33–34)

The fear of "indiscreet" matter did not end there, of course, but persisted, as Williams was only too aware, among even early twentieth-century Christians. Mordred might as well be describing the modern church when he considers how Camelot is "apt to maintain a double poise / of Catholic morals and another kind of catholic mockery" (*RSS,* "The Meditations of Mordred" 17–18). It is interesting to consider a bit of light verse in which Tolkien mixes baffled admiration and good-natured derision of the geographical schema of his fellow Inkling's Arthurian landscape:

> Geography indeed! here he again
> exerts a subtle mind and labouring pen.
> Geodesy say rather; for many a 'fen'
> he wrote, and chapters bogged in tangled rhymes,
> and has surveyed Europa's lands and climes,
> dividing her from P'o-L'u's crawling slimes,
> in her diving buttocks, breast and head
> (to say no fouler thing), where I instead,
> dull-eyed, can only see a watershed,
> a plain, an island, or a mountain-chain.
> In that gynecomorphical terrain

       History and Myth are ravelled in a skein

       of endless interchange .... (qtd. in Carpenter 124)[43]

Admiring but bewildered readers of Williams' poems might be inclined to sympathize with some of Tolkien's friendly heckling at what he perceived as their overwrought symbolic associations, but that aside, his unfortunate choice of words provides a convenient case in point. The disdainful words "fouler thing," presumably as a euphemistic reference to the genitals of the nude illustration on the map, is the sort of statement that Williams likely would have deplored. We as modern readers might object to Tolkien's remark on the grounds that it is unbecomingly fastidious, but for Williams it bordered on heresy, an example of what he feared was the Christian church's inclination toward an "unofficial Manicheism," described above ("Sensuality and Substance" 69).

    But if Islam is to some extent a proxy for division internal to Christendom, the fact remains that it is Islam that Williams uses to assume the primary identification with Manichaeism in the poems. Of course, the threat of an alien Other has frequently been figured as an error in thought—whether ideological or religious. The key difference lies in both the tone and substance of Williams' response to that error. Nowhere does it constitute a *causus belli*, a pretext for eradication.

    Tolkien too, in his *Fall of Arthur* fragment, had imagined a political conflict that is, at its heart, a clash of religions, as Arthur and Gawain lead a counter-assault against a threat that is marked first and foremost by its paganism. For Tolkien, as for Churchill, this threat was Teutonic, and the violence of the enterprise makes an interesting point of comparison to Williams' handling of the Arthur myth (see 1.1–6). This is not to suggest that Tolkien's attitude toward war is uncomplicated: he gives it to Mordred to council Arthur that "war was wisdom and waiting folly" (1.20), which ought to put us on guard against assuming that Tolkien is altogether approving of Arthur's acting as a self-appointed sword of divine judgment, when they fought eagerly in spite of foes all around (1.63). And yet, there is little ambiguity about Tolkien's presentation of the enemy's barbarousness; he calls them "wan horsemen wild ... grey and monstrous ... shapes disastrous" (1.83–89). From this, it is clear that the Saxon foe is unequivocally wicked, so that when Gawain finally bellows his challenge, Tolkien does not seem to have given his readers much reason to resist thrilling to its stirring poetry (1.96–108). The next canto will find Arthur racing back westward to Camelot, after news reaches him of Mordred's betrayal at home. But although the campaign against Saxon foes will turn out to have terrible consequences, the existing fragments of *The Fall of Arthur* offer no clues that Tolkien questions Arthur's driving motivation: "the heathen to humble."

---

43   Raymond Edwards writes: "In November 1943, or thereabouts, Tolkien wrote a poem on Williams, titled 'A Closed Letter to Andrea Charicoryides Surnamed Polygrapheus, Logothete of the Theme of Geodesia in the Empire, Bard of the Court of Camelot, Malleus Malitiarium, Inclinga Sum Sometimes Known as Charles Williams'. Though it is an affectionate treatment, Tolkien's exasperation with Williams' writing (particularly his occasionally ludicrous mock-cabbalistic identification of his idiosyncratic geography with human anatomy—'buttocks to Caucasia!') is obvious" (Edwards 188).

Of course, Tolkien was if anything *more* Augustinian than Williams in his assumptions about the innate corruption of human nature, and many of his stories show how evil can spring from the recesses of one's own inner Gollum. That ambivalence does not find a prominent place in his version of the Arthurian myth, however, at least in its existing form, which follows his many predecessors in counterpoising Camelot against a wholly undifferentiated and menacingly barbaric horde. Here, as in *The Lord of the Rings,* evil lies in the East, and must be subdued.[44]

For Williams, by contrast, difference does not seem to warrant conquest, eradication, or dominance, either through proselytization or forced assimilation. The object, rather, is restoration and reconciliation. One senses this in Williams' tone; he is unable or unwilling to create a sense of menace. True, his Arthur confronts a Saxon foe that is bestial in its cry and undifferentiated in its barbarism: "the sea's indiscriminate host" who "roared at the City's wall" (*TtL*, "Mount Badon" 7). But elsewhere his lexical approach borders on the whimsical; these Saxon invaders are not, like Tolkien's, nightmare shapes in the mist, "grey and monstrous grimly riding." Rather, Williams refers to them repeatedly as "pirates"—a threat, certainly, but decidedly human. Likewise, Islam's encroachment is more than anything an index of the Empire's attention to heavenly over earthly concerns, "the nearness or distance of hostile armies" is important for whether or not it gave space for "the organization of the speculative intellect" (*Dove* 101).

These choices are at times a poetic liability. Certainly when compared to Tolkien's mastery of steadily mounting dread, the arcane symbolism of Williams' verses seems intellectual to the point of being remote and cold. But it is important to remember that the reconciliation of sense and intellect, as well as of form and matter, authority and obedience, is one of the poems' chief themes, and Williams is less interested in evoking a sense of Logres's enemies as physically threatening than he is in mourning for what is lost in the Manichean sundering of spirit from flesh, which he shows to be as lamentable as the dissolution of Arthur's company.

Loathing, Loss, and the "Imposition of belief"

What further distinguishes Williams' mythopoetic vision from nationalist myth-making is the absence of what has been called "imperialist nostalgia" (Rosaldo 68–70). If, as we have seen, Arthurian poetry has indulged in fantasies of conquest, expansion, and imperial grandeur, the very title of the *Morte Darthur* serves as a reminder that its dominant theme is defeat, and this, too, the opposite of triumphalism, can provide the impetus for nationalist myth-telling "as a means to rekindle memory. For a people shipwrecked by history, a story of the past, even if wholly or in part a fiction, again offers a kind of restitution" (Boehmer 189). Stories or poems of ancient glory can console as well as inspire, offering readers and listeners "the potential to forge imaginary connections between the reduced present and the legendary past" (Boehmer 189). Rather than celebrating the glories of an imagined national past or summoning readers to imagine a renewal of that grandeur despite

---

44 While being mindful of the biographical fallacy, it does not seem altogether facile to speculate that the roots of Tolkien's repeated identification of the East with a growing menace lie in the trauma of his own experiences during World War I. See John Garth, *Tolkien and the Great War: The Threshold of Middle-earth.*

the present threat of neighboring enemies, Williams (who died only months too soon to witness the Allied victory) yearns expectantly toward a state of cosmic Union, describing a pattern of order that is interpersonal as well as international, and concerned with twentieth-century European turmoil as only the latest skirmish in a spiritual "war of the frontiers," to borrow a phrase from *The Descent of the Dove* (73).

His aim, though, prefigured in the ecstatic vision of "The Prayers of the Pope," is not to push the limits of that frontier, but to dissolve it. Rather than conquering, dehumanizing, or excluding the Other, Williams is preoccupied with bringing it *into* the companionship of Christian co-inherence. As Roma King points out, the site of Lancelot's altar "rests on the spot where the Lupercalia was celebrated, where 'rods of divination between Lupercal and Lateran' (*TtL*, "The Son of Lancelot" 8) link the old with the new, Christian with Pagan Rome" (King "The Occult as Rhetoric" 173). Williams' note on "The Departure of Merlin" reads: "the distance from the Antipodes is no greater, in Grace, than from, say, Camelot" (qtd. in Lewis, WA 357).

Ultimately, Williams refuses the demonization or dehumanization on which the discourses of empire so often rest; instead, his doctrine of co-inherence requires an imaginative identification with the Other, even to the point of losing oneself. "'Oneself' and 'others,'" he writes, "are only the specialized terms" of the technique of "substitutions [and] exchanges in love" (*Dove* 236). Despite their heavy use of the rhetoric of empire, the poems envision the enemies of Christendom as integral to it, nonetheless, and imagine the processes by which such exchanges, and thus reconciliation and re-integration, may occur. The concluding poem of *The Region of the Summer Stars,* "The Prayers of the Pope," asks:

> Where is difference between us?
> What does the line along the rivers define?
> Causes and catapults they have and we have,
> and the death of a brave beauty is mutual everywhere. (80–83)

To write lines such as these during a time of increasing pressure from the Luftwaffe, one would need to be either politically childlike, a holy fool, or a poet possessed of an abundance of sympathetic imagination. I do not think Williams was either of the first two; he may, though, have been an example of the third. "Not one mind in a thousand," he writes, "can be trusted to state accurately what its opponent says, much less what he thinks," but it is precisely this difficult task, he suggests, that is the fitting work of the Christian apologist, historian, and poet (*Dove* 112). In a 1940 lecture, he stated that his

> chief objection to the champions of Christianity is that the objections to Christianity do not come from them. You may really sympathize with the other fellow, but you never *sound* as if you really felt the force of his argument .... Let us see them, see where they are, feel them, almost create them .... (qtd. in Ridler xxi)

Here again, Williams emphasizes "the feeling intellect," and reading his theological writing, poetry, and fiction, one senses that he took his own advice, for all of them show a great willingness not only to attempt to see through the eyes of others—as when, in *Descent of the Dove,* he describes vividly the "abomination" that iconography and the growing devotion to Mary were to Jewish and Muslim belief "and to the awful Otherness of Deity in which they both believed" (93)—but also to create a sense of that depth of feeling. In the novel *Many Dimensions,* for example, Williams paints a quite poignant picture of the bewildered sadness of an elderly Persian Hajji at the failure of Christians to reverence the unity figured in Islam (229).

But even these laudable expressions of sympathy and admiration may alert us to another side of imperialist nostalgia, which, in Renato Rosaldo's description, can use "a pose of 'innocent yearning' both to capture people's imaginations and to conceal its complicity with often brutal domination" (70). It "occurs alongside a peculiar sense of mission, the white man's burden, where civilized nations stand duty-bound to uplift so-called savage ones." Describing the missionaries' "reverential mood, not of nostalgia for the old form of life, but of a similar tenderness toward the transformed precious lives of new converts," Rosaldo asks, "Can one speak of nostalgia for the new?" (80). Concerning Williams' ideas, I do not think one can.

I cannot attempt here an explication of Williams' soteriology, but it may be worth noting that at the conclusion of the aforementioned novel, *Many Dimensions,* it is not the venerable Hajji but a British Lord High Justice who makes a profession of Christian faith. He reaches this decision through no external compulsion, and indeed, the only proselytization or indoctrination in the novel is in the form of a deliberate campaign of public *disbelief* in the actual metaphysical properties of a sacred relic, engineered by a cynical bureaucrat and a union leader for the purpose of exerting political and economic control (239). That it should be the villains of his story who engage in indoctrination helps to underscore the point that Williams' thought allows no room for what he called "the imposition of belief" (*Dove* 117).

Williams' handling of the conversion of the knight Palomides, who leaves his Saracen heritage to join the Christian world of the Round Table, is a case study that deserves at least a few observations, for it suggests that although Williams held Christian conversion as the desirable and perhaps natural end of individual being, he also saw it as one which—save for the aid of mystical experience or insight—cannot occur at the cost of one's free will or intelligence. Palomides is the subject of two poems in Williams' early verse collection, *Heroes and Kings*: "Palomides' Song of Iseult" and "A Song of Palomides,"[45] and of three poems in *Taliessin through Logres*: "The Coming of Palomides," "Palomides Before his Christening," and "The Death of Palomides." The latter three, which rank among the most challenging in the published cycles, depart significantly from the earlier poems,[46] but consistent throughout those revisions is a portrait of Palomides that is notably more admiring than in any of Williams' sources. I want to point out that this admiration seems independent of Palomides' eventual conversion, which Williams depicts as the completion, rather than the wholesale rejection and replacement, of his Islamic worldview.

---

45 A revised version of "A Song of Palomides" is included in the collection of unpublished poems *The Advent of Galahad* as "Colophon made by the Copyist in a Monastery of Benwick on the Day of the Epiphany, in the year one thousand of the Fructiferous Incarnation of the son of God" (q.v. in Dodds 250–15).

46 For a brief explanation of several of the revisions, see Dodds 154–55. For a concise discussion of Williams' use of Islam, as well as C. S. Lewis' most extensive remarks on Islam that I am aware of, see WA 308–11; Roma King's explication of the three Palomides poems in *TtL* is very helpful: King, *Pattern* 64–69; 91–97; 108–11.

Sir Palomides's restless and futile desire for the love of Iseult, his violent yet admiring rivalry with Tristram, and his "frustrated desire to succeed according to the codes of an alien society" of the Round Table (Rovang 119) make him one of the most fascinating of Arthur's knights, particularly in Malory's *Morte Darthur*. Whereas in Malory's sources, the *Prose Tristan* and *Queste del Saint Graal*, Palomides was essentially compelled to convert at the point of the peerless Galahad's sword, in the *Morte* he evinces a desire for conversion and integration that is at once more genuine and more ambiguous. Seeming both to desire and resist assimilation, Palomides claims to be a Christian in his heart and vows to fight seven battles before he will consent to being christened, and only his failure at the seventh of these forces him to yield at last to baptism.[47] And yet, Palomides' frustration at his unconquerable Otherness always risks slipping from his careful control, erupting in unchivalric attempts to get the upper hand on his rivals at tournaments and in fits of hysteria when those disgraceful actions fail. After one such misadventure, he sits on the ground, "romynge and cryynge as a man oute of his mynde" (Malory 1.423.3). Later, he is so overcome by his frustrated love for Iseult and envy of Tristram that he is reduced to a frenzy of gesticulation, making "many straunge sygnes and tokyns" before a mystified Tristram (2.528.30). For some critics, these episodes attest Palomides' subaltern status in the *Morte Darthur*,[48] where his

> distance and difference from Arthurian chivalric identity renders his actions ... unintelligible to the knight who encounters him—and indeed to the narrator who describes this moment—and thus, locates him in a space very like to the subaltern .... The pagan outsider tentatively invited in, who identifies his heritage as inferior and longs to replace it with that of the dominant culture, Palomides is a colonized subject, though not, in the geographical sense, a subject of colonialism. (Armstrong 177, 180)

Not even baptism can make anyone forget his alien status. In the *Morte*, Palomides's christening marks his formal Christianization and the fullest extent of his potential assimilation into his adopted society, but thereafter he faces the dilemma of being both a member of the Christian fellowship and yet more than ever a restless outsider. He spends the rest of his days chasing the Questing Beast through the outer reaches of Arthur's kingdom, "drifting in and out of the narrative space that should now ... be Home, but instead remains ever and always Away" (Armstrong 198).

Palomides fares better in Williams' hands, at least in some respects, for Williams does not equate Christianization with civilization. If Palomides is for Malory an anomaly, a lone "good Saracen" set starkly against a monolithic backdrop of alien strangeness (Goodrich 10), for Williams he is a microcosm of Islamic thought—or at least Williams' interpretation of it—and embodies its fastidious, uncompromisingly reasoned doctrines. Whereas in the *Morte Darthur*, Palomides is "only intelligible ... as a colonized Other," forced to do his best imitation of the dominant discourse within a narrative space in which "[t]he Saracen

---

47   Peter Goodrich describes these and other ways in which "Malory deemphasizes the fullness of Palomides's conversion and assimilation to the Round Table" (Goodrich 17).

48   See Gayatri Spivak, "Can the Subaltern Speak?" 90–104.

qua Saracen cannot speak" (Armstrong 177), this is far from the case in *Taliessin through Logres,* in which the three Palomides poems are gorgeous, difficult soliloquies, uttered by a knight who proudly and carefully resists fully submitting to the scandalous doctrines of the Trinity and Incarnation.

To be clear, Williams does not whitewash Palomides or neglect to mention his shameful failure of character at the tournament. Here as in the *Morte,* his desire for Iseult has driven him to what Lancelot reprovingly calls "unknyghtly delynge" (2.422.21–22). Moreover, Williams uses the Questing Beast to signify a dangerous concupiscence infecting his love for Iseult in what C. S. Lewis calls "a Beatrician experience gone wrong" (WA 308). But though he "loved, feared, fought, was angry" ("The Death of Palomides" 34), the poems do not corroborate Malory's portrait of a man whose ferocious emotions reveal an almost primitive savagery. In *Taliessin through Logres,* Palomides' chief problem is intellectual, a subtle but massive barrier of hard convictions.

Co-inherence finds its highest exemplification in the paradoxical relationship between the Incarnation (God made man in the figure of Christ) and the presence of "God-in-man," of which Palomides seeks to learn. Having learned from classical and Arabian scholars all that can be known of "the measurement of man," he leaves home for "the cross-littered land of Gaul," where "Gospels trigonometrical / measure the height of God-in-man" (*TtL,* "The Coming of Palomides" 9–11). Williams' point here is that Islam deemphasizes the image of the divine in the human body, and by denying the doctrine of the Incarnation destroys the doctrines of "exchange" and "co-inherence" in which flesh and spirit are mutually glorified. For this reason, Palomides remains a man divided within himself, unable to embody the Unity he espouses. This debate takes the form of a carefully reasoned and profoundly felt internal dialogue in the poems. His acceptance of Christian materialism joins with rather than supplants his reverence for essence above image, in a process that Williams finds flowing naturally—if not easily—from hard-won individual experience. Williams does not so demean Palomides as to have him, in Jan Curtis' phrase, "whipped into the holy city," his conversion exacted by external force or the threat of violence, as in some of Williams' sources ("Sister" n14). Rather, his way is hard along a purgatorial path of his own choosing. Fragmented but resolute, he describes how "I followed my self [sic] away from the city / up a steep trail" (*TtL,* "Palomides Before his Christening" 34–35). Only with his last breath does he grant that "The Lord created *all things* by means of his blessing": The Way of Affirmation joins at last with his severe and exclusive reverence of the Creator (*TtL,* "The Death of Palomides" 52, emphasis mine).

Crucially, there is nothing here of the well-meaning but dominating "tenderness toward the transformed precious lives of new converts" (Rosaldo 80). Palomides's conversion is hard, bruising, and isolated, and it coincides with his death. There is no tender "nostalgia for the new" life of Palomides here. His is a joyless yielding, exquisitely conscious "of the extreme surrender and the sadness which must accompany it" (HCD 95). Right up until the final moment of his death, Palomides laments all that he has lost: "I left the Prophet; I lost Iseult; I failed / to catch the beast out of Broceliande" ("The Death of Palomides" 45–46).

Williams insists upon the error of Palomides's pride while also respecting it and the venerability of the traditions in which it is founded. "Hell," he wrote in an introduction to Milton, "is always inaccurate" (qtd. in Ridler 30), while "heaven is always exact" (*Collected Plays* 298), but one may be inaccurate while still commanding respect: in *Many Dimensions,* a Persian says of his fallen countryman: "Outcast and accursed as that man now is, he comes of a great and royal family. He shall writhe in hell for ever, but even there you shall not be worthy to see his torment" (10). For all that, though, Williams seems reluctant that any should perish. Just as the pagan Virgil is retrieved from perdition by the prayers of his poetic disciples (*TtL*, "Death of Virgil" 19, 30) no less a voice than that of "the Prophet" himself is among those Palomides hears calling out to him as he dies ("The Death of Palomides" 54). Yet again, the poems insist on reconciliation, the enemies of Christendom literally joining in chorus to affirm their mutual blessedness: "The Lord created all things by means of his blessing" ("The Death of Palomides" 52).

Conclusion

Williams' ideas did not always sit easily even among his friends. C. S. Lewis recalled that at one meeting, a minor Inkling, Charles Wrenn, "almost seriously expressed a strong wish to burn Williams, or at least maintained that conversation with Williams enabled him to understand how inquisitors had felt it right to burn people .... Williams is eminently combustible" (*CL* 2:283). There are those who would burn him still.[49] Readers of Lewis and Tolkien may find Williams' brand of Christian mysticism uncomfortably distant from a recognizable orthodoxy, even as secular readers are alienated by his metaphysics. His political ideas, such as they are, are no more likely than his theology to provoke unified acclaim, but I hope that I have shown that for all his audacious symbolic use of the "theme of the design of the Empire," those sublunary zones themselves and the often-regrettable history of their governing were largely incidental to his fascination with the myth (*TtL*, "The Vision of the Empire" 49).

In his discussion of the Reformation, Williams writes, "Luther at Worms said 'I can no other'; it was magnificent, but it was not politics" (*Dove* 171). The same, I think, could be said of Williams' poems. As policy, they are not useful—but then, I know few poems that are. However, as an expression of the "feeling intellect" attempting to reconcile weighty contradictions within a not-quite-orthodox Christian worldview and to overcome instinctive and inherited fear and loathing of the Other, there is much to recommend them to any era that can identify with what Williams described as "our present distresses, of international and social schism" (*Dove* 236).

Works Cited

Armstrong, Dorsey. "Postcolonial Palomides: Malory's Saracen Knight and the Unmaking of Arthurian Community." *Exemplaria* 18.1 (2006): 175–203. *JSTOR*. Web. 10 February 2015.

Auden, W. H. Letter to Charles Williams. 11 January 1945. MS. Folder 163. Marion E. Wade Center, Wheaton College. Wheaton, IL.

Barczewski, Stephanie. *Myth and National Identity in Nineteenth-Century Britain: The Legends of King Arthur and Robin Hood*. Oxford UP, 2000. Print.

---

49 See Sturch, Richard. "Charles Williams as Heretic?" *Charles Williams Quarterly* 136 (2010): 7–19. Print. [Editor's note]

Biddle, Martin. "The Painting of the Table." *King Arthur's Round Table: An Archaeological Investigation*. Ed. Martin Biddle and Sally Badham. Woodbridge: The Boydell Press, 2000. 425–74. Print.

Boehmer, Elleke. *Colonial and Postcolonial Literature: Migrant Metaphors*. 2nd ed. Oxford UP, 2005. Print.

Boughton, Brenda. "The Role of the Slave in Charles Williams' Poetry: A Talk Presented to the Charles Williams Society's Annual General Meeting on 11 May 1991." *The Charles Williams Society Newsletter* 61 (1991): 7–20. charleswilliamssociety.org.uk. Web. 17 November 2015

Brennan, John P. "Rebirth of a Nation? Historical Mythmaking in Laʒamon's Brut." *Uses of the Past*. Essays in Medieval Studies 17. Ed. Allen J. Frantzen. Chicago: Illinois Medieval Association, 2001. 19–29. www.illinoismedieval.org. Web. 15 October 2014.

Brooks, Peter. *Reading for the Plot: Design and Intention in Narrative*. NY: Alfred A. Knopf, 1984. Print.

Carpenter, Humphrey. *The Inklings: C. S. Lewis, J. R. R. Tolkien, Charles Williams, and Their Friends*. London: HarperCollins, 1978. Print.

Cavaliero, Glen. Introduction. *Letters to Lalage: The Letters of Charles Williams to Lois Lang-Sims*. Kent State UP, 1989. 1–14. Print.

——. *Charles Williams: Poet of Theology*. Grand Rapids, MI: Eerdmans, 1983. Print.

Certeau, Michel de. *The Practice of Everyday Life*. Berkeley and Los Angeles: U of California P, 1984. Print.

Churchill, Winston S. *A History of the English-Speaking Peoples. Volume I: The Birth of Britain*. NY: Mead, 1956. Print.

Comfort, W. W. "The Literary Role of the Saracens in the French Epic." *PMLA* 55 (1940): 628–59. *JSTOR*. Web. 16 February 2015.

Conquest, Robert. "The Art of the Enemy." *Essays in Criticism* 7.1 (1957): 42–55. Print.

Cross, F. L., and E. A. Livingstone, eds. *The Oxford Dictionary of the Christian Church*. 3rd ed. Oxford UP, 1997. Print.

Curtis, Jan. "Byzantium and the Matter of Britain: The Narrative Framework of Charles Williams' Later Arthurian Poems." *Quondam et Futurus: A Journal of Arthurian Interpretations* 2.1 (1992): 28–54. *JSTOR*. Web. 10 September 2014.

——. "Charles Williams' 'The Sister of Percivale': Toward a Theology of 'Theotokos.'" *Quondam et Futurus: A Journal of Arthurian Interpretations* 2.4 (1992): 56–72. *JSTOR*. Web. 3 November 2014.

Dodds, David Llewellyn, ed. *Arthurian Poets: Charles Williams*. Arthurian Studies 24. Woodbridge, Suffolk: Boydell Press, 1991. Print.

Edwards, Raymond. *Tolkien*. Robert Hale, 2015. Print.

Finke, Laurie A., and Martin B. Shichtman. *King Arthur and the Myth of History*. Gainesville: UP Florida, 2004. Print.

Fitzpatrick, Joan. "Marrying Waterways: Politicizing and Gendering the Landscape in Spenser's *Faerie Queene* River-Marriage Canto." *Archipelagic Identities: Literature and Identity in the Atlantic Archipelago, 1550–1800*. Ed. Simon Mealor and Philip Schwyzer. Aldershot, UK: Ashgate, 2004. 81–91. Print.

Garrard, Greg. *Ecocriticism*. 2nd ed. The New Critical Idiom. NY: Routledge, 2012. Print.

Garth, John. *Tolkien and the Great War: The Threshold of Middle-earth*. NY: HarperCollins, 2003. Print.

Goodrich, Peter H. "Saracens and Islamic Alterity in Malory's 'Le Morte Darthur.'" *Arthuriana* 16.4 (2006): 10–28. *JSTOR*. Web. 10 February 2015.

Hadfield, Alice Mary. *Charles Williams: An Exploration of His Life and Work*. Oxford UP, 1983. Print.

Hamilton, Bernard. "Some Popes in English Literature, c.1850–1950." *The Church and Literature*. Studies in Church History 48. Eds. Peter Clarke and Charlotte Methuen. Woodbridge, Suffolk: The Ecclesiastical History Society, 2012. 374–84. Print.

Hermann, Hagedorn. "Edwin Arlington Robinson: Arthurian Pacifist." *King Arthur through the Ages*. Ed. Valerie M. Lagorio and Mildred Leake Day. Vol. 1. NY: Garland, 1990. 165–79. Print.

Higgins, Sørina. "Double Affirmation: Medievalism as Christian Apologetic in the Arthurian Poetry of Charles Williams." *Journal of Inklings Studies* 3.2 (2013): 59–96. Print.

Hoffman, Donald L. "Assimilating Saracens: The Aliens in Malory's 'Morte Darthur.'" *Arthuriana* 16.4 (2006): 43–64. *JSTOR*. Web. 10 September 2014.

Holsinger, Bruce. "Medieval Studies, Postcolonial Studies, and the Genealogies of Critique." *Speculum* 77 (2002): 1195–227. *JSTOR*. Web. 26 October 2014.

Ingham, Patricia Clare. *Sovereign Fantasies: Arthurian Romance and the Making of Britain*. Philadelphia: U of Pennsylvania P, 2001. Print.

Ingledew, Francis. *Sir Gawain and the Green Knight and the Order of the Garter*. U of Notre Dame P, 2006. Print.

Kant, Immanuel. *Groundwork for the Metaphysics of Morals*. Trans. Thomas K. Abbott and Lara Denis. Ed. Lara Denis. Ontario: Broadview Press, 2005. Print.

King Arthur's Death: The Middle English Stanzaic Morte Arthur *and* Alliterative Morte Arthure. Eds. Larry D. Benson and Edward E. Foster. TEAMS Middle English Text Series. Kalamazoo: Medieval Institute Publications, 1994. Print.

King, Roma A. "The Occult as Rhetoric in the Poetry of Charles Williams." *The Rhetoric of Vision: Essays on Charles Williams*. Ed. Charles Adolph Huttar and Peter J. Schakel. Lewisville: Bucknell UP, 1996. 165–78. Print.

——. *The Pattern in the Web: The Mythical Poetry of Charles Williams*. Kent State UP, 1990. Print.

Kollman, Judith. "Charles Williams' *Taliessin through Logres* and *The Region of the Summer Stars*." *King Arthur through the Ages*. Vol. 1. Ed. Valerie M. Lagorio and Mildred Leake Day. NY: Garland, 1990. 180–203. Print.

Lang-Sims, Lois. *Letters to Lalage: The Letters of Charles Williams to Lois Lang-Sims*. Kent State UP, 1989. Print.

Lewis, C. S. *The Collected Letters of C. S. Lewis*. 3 vols. Ed. Walter Hooper. NY: HarperCollins, 2004–07. Print.

——. *God in the Dock: Essays on Theology and Ethics*. Grand Rapids, MI: Eerdmans, 1970. Print.

——. "Williams and the Arthuriad." *Taliessin through Logres; The Region of the Summer Stars; Arthurian Torso*. By Charles Williams and C. S. Lewis. Grand Rapids, MI: Eerdmans, 1974. 275–384. Print.

Loewenstein, Andrea Freud. *Loathsome Jews and Engulfing Women: Metaphors of Projection in the Works of Wyndham Lewis, Charles Williams, and Graham Greene*. NYU Press, 1993. Print.

Malory, Sir Thomas, *Le Morte Darthur*. Ed. P. J. C. Field. Cambridge: D. S. Brewer, 2013. Print.

Marshall, Ashley. "Reframing Charles Williams: Modernist Doubt and the Crisis of World War in *All Hallows' Eve*." *Journal of Modern Literature* 30.2 (2007): 64–85. *JSTOR*. Web. 17 October 2014.

McClintock, Anne. *Imperial Leather: Race, Gender, and Sexuality in the Colonial Contest*. NY: Routledge, 1995. Print.

McGuire, Ian. "Epistemology and Empire in 'Idylls of the King.'" *Victorian Poetry* 30.3/4, (1992): 387–400. *JSTOR*. Web. 15 October 2014.

Noble, Peter. "Arthur, Anti-Fascist or Pirate King?" *Quondam et Futurus* 3.3 (1993): 46–54. *JSTOR*. Web. 13 November. 2014.

Riddy, Felicity. "Contextualizing Le Morte Darthur: Empire and Civil War." *A Companion to Malory*. Eds. Elizabeth Archibald and A. S. G. Edwards. Cambridge: Boydell & Brewer, 1996. 55–73. Print.

Ridler, Anne, ed. *The Image of the City and Other Essays*. By Charles Williams. Berkeley, CA: Apocryphile Press, 2007. Print.

Rosaldo, Renato. *Culture and Truth: The Remaking of Social Analysis*. Boston: Beacon Press, 1993. Print.

Roukema, Aren. "A Veil that Reveals: Charles Williams and the Fellowship of the Rosy Cross." *Journal of Inklings Studies* 3.2 (2015): 22–71. inklings-studies.com. Web. 30 May 2015.

Rovang, Paul. *Malory's Anatomy of Chivalry: Characterization in the Morte Darthur*. Lanham, MD: Fairleigh Dickinson UP, 2015. Print.

Said, Edward. *Orientalism*. NY: Vintage, 1979. Print.

Scarf, Christopher. *The Ideal of Kingship in the Writings of Charles Williams, C. S. Lewis and J. R. R. Tolkien: Divine Kingship Is Reflected in Middle-earth*. Cambridge, UK: James Clarke, 2013. Print.

Shohat, Ella. "Gender and Culture of Empire: Toward a Feminist Ethnography of the Cinema." *Visions of the East: Orientalism in Film*. Ed. Matthew Bernstein and Gaylyn Studlar. New Brunswick, NJ: Rutgers UP, 1997. Print.

Shutters, Lynn. "Vikings through the Eyes of an Arab Ethnographer: Constructions of the Other in *The 13th Warrior*." *Race, Class, and Gender in "Medieval" Cinema*. Ed. Lynn T. Ramey and Tison Pugh. NY: Palgrave Macmillan, 2007. 75–90. Print.

Spivak, Gayatri. "Can the Subaltern Speak?" *Colonial Discourse and Post-Colonial Theory: A Reader*. Eds. Patrick Williams and Laura Chrisman. NY: Columbia UP, 1994. 90–104. Print.

Spurr, David. *The Rhetoric of Empire: Colonial Discourse in Journalism, Travel Writing, and Imperial Administration*. Durham: Duke UP, 1993. Print.

Starr, Nathan Comfort. *King Arthur Today: The Arthurian Legend in English and American Literature, 1901–1953*. Gainesville: U of Florida P, 1954. Print.

Tennyson, Alfred. *Idylls of the King*. London: Penguin Classics, 2004. Print.

Tolkien, J. R. R. *The Fall of Arthur*. Ed. Christopher Tolkien. Boston: Houghton Mifflin, 2013. Print.

Trim, D. J. B., ed. *The Chivalric Ethos and the Development of Military Professionalism*. History of Warfare 2. Leiden; Boston; Koln: Brill, 2003. Print.

Vale, Juliet. *Edward III and Chivalry: Chivalric Society and Its Context, 1270–1350*. Woodbridge, Suffolk: Boydell Press, 1982. Print.

Warren, K., ed. *Ecological Feminism*. London: Routledge, 1994. Print.

Warren, Michelle R. "Making Contact: Postcolonial Perspectives through Geoffrey of Monmouth's *Historia Regum Britannie*." *Arthuriana* 8.4 (1998): 115–34. *JSTOR*. Web. 14 October 2014.

Wheeler, Bonnie. "Grief in Avalon: Sir Palomydes' Psychic Pain." *Grief and Gender: 700–1700*. Ed. Jennifer C. Vaught. NY: Palgrave Macmillan, 2003. 65–80. Print.

Williams, Charles. *Arthurian Commonplace Book* (as "Notes on the Holy Grail"). MS. Eng. e. 2012. Bodleian Library, Oxford University. Oxford, UK.

——. "A Dialogue on Hierarchy." *Image* 127–30.

——. *Collected Plays.* London: Oxford UP, 1963. Print.

——. *Descent of the Dove: A Short History of the Holy Spirit in the Church.* Grand Rapids, MI: Eerdmans, 1939. Print.

——. *He Came Down from Heaven* and *The Forgiveness of Sins.* Berkeley: Apocryphile Press, 2005. Print.

——. "The Figure of Arthur." *Taliessin through Logres; The Region of the Summer Stars; Arthurian Torso.* By Charles Williams and C. S. Lewis. Grand Rapids, MI: Eerdmans, 1974. 189–245. Print.

——. *The Figure of Beatrice: A Study in Dante.* London: Faber & Faber, 1943. Print.

——. *Heroes and Kings.* 1930. Berkeley, CA: Apocryphile Press, 2013. Print.

——. *The Image of the City and Other Essays.* Ed. Anne Ridler. Berkeley, CA: Apocryphile Press, 2007. Print.

——. "The Making of *Taliessin.*" *Image* 179–83.

——. *Many Dimensions.* 1931. Grand Rapids, MI: Eerdmans, 1993. Print.

——. *To Michal from Serge: Letters from Charles Williams to His Wife, Florence, 1939–1945.* Ed. Roma A. King. Kent State UP, 2002. Print.

——. *The House of the Octopus. The Collected Plays of Charles Williams.* Ed. John Heath-Stubbs. Oxford: Oxford University. Press, 1963. 245–324. Print.

——. "Sensuality and Substance." *Image* 68–75.

——. *War in Heaven.* 1930. Grand Rapids, MI: Eerdmans, 1980. Print.

——. "The Way of Affirmation." *Image* 154–159.

——. "The Way of Exchange." *Image* 147–154.

Williams, Charles, and C. S. Lewis. *Taliessin through Logres, The Region of the Summer Stars, and Arthurian Torso.* Grand Rapids, MI: Eerdmans, 1974. Print.

Yeats, W. B. *A Vision: The Original 1925 Version. The Collected Works of W. B. Yeats* 13. Eds. Catherine E. Paul and Margaret Mills Harper. NY: Scribner, 1925. Print.

Geographies of Gender

13

"Fair as Fay-woman and Fell-minded": Tolkien's Guinever. [1]

Alyssa House-Thomas

Guinevere: the most notorious of faithless Welsh wives; Guinevere: Chrétien and Wolfram's mistress of taste and arbiter of the court of love; Guinevere: Laȝamon's political traitor fit only to be torn apart by wild horses; Guinevere: Malory's repentant canoness, an object lesson in seemly contrition—King Arthur's queen has fulfilled all these descriptions and more. She is a figure of persistent interest because her role in the drama of the splendid Arthur's downfall may be envisioned in many different ways. Like her spouse, Guinevere assumes varying guises for varying ages, drawn not so much from life as from the need for her myth to respond to timeless human concerns such as the relation of the sexes, destiny and choice, and impermanence. Her tale, as related by manifold tellers, also comes to address narrower preoccupations determined at the level of cultural or individual authorship.

J. R. R. Tolkien's uncompleted work *The Fall of Arthur* is a modern Arthurian retelling cast in an ancient mode. Within it, the queen's treatment may be seen as a microcosm of "Tolkien's Arthur," a singular blend of inherited materials inflected by Tolkien the writer's own scholarly and creative tendencies. *The Fall of Arthur*'s depiction of Guinever's[2] personal characteristics reaches for an aesthetic balance of themes drawn not only from specifically Arthurian works, but more broadly from two premodern legendary traditions intimately known to Tolkien: Celtic and Germanic. In addition, intense narrative focus on Guinever's culpability in the titular conflict engages a theme that pervades much of Tolkien's other fiction: the inter-

---

1   This article represents a working version of my M.A. thesis for Signum University. It is published here for the first time. I am grateful to Dr. Verlyn Flieger, my Signum advisor, for much aid in its development.

2   Throughout I have preferred the spelling "Guinever" to designate Tolkien's character, since that is the usage that predominates in *The Fall of Arthur* (See "Notes on the Text," *FoA* 64n2.27).

333

relationship between fate and free will. Tolkien's Guinever, strong-willed yet vulnerable, both proceeds from and transcends her earlier literary models, providing a unique contribution to Arthurian tradition. Her complex presentation also evidences the high degree to which Tolkien's processes of textual development can explore a female character and her role in her narrative world, a quality that has been disputed in earlier criticism considering primarily his legendarium of Middle-earth.

Who is Guinevere?

Tolkien's Guinever emerges from a conglomeration of folklore, chronicle, and romance traditions almost as complex as that of Arthur himself. Throughout changes of age and genre, the character of Guinevere has waxed and waned in agency, as she has changed also in her relative narrative and thematic importance to individual Arthurian works.

The earliest British folkloric materials show us a queen defined both as Arthur's possession and as an instigator of disruption in his realm. The Welsh tale "Culhwch and Olwen" was probably first written down in the twelfth century, but it incorporates elements four hundred years older (Davies xxii–iii) and so is considered one of the oldest Arthurian works. In it the queen is prized, but as chattel. Her character and activities are not elaborated. Arthur lists among his dearest treasures his ship, his mantle, "Rhongomyniad my spear, and Wynebgwrthucher my shield, and Carnwennan my dagger, and Gwenhwyfar my wife" (*Mabinogion* 183). Other than as a nominal embellishment to Arthur's wealth, Gwenhwyfar plays no significant role in the story.

As does the *Mabinogion*, the *Triads of the Island of Britain* survive in manuscripts copied from the late medieval period, but preserve oral and folk material centuries older (Bromwich, Introduction lxiii ff.). The *Triads*, too, establish the queen as a commodity in the hands of powerful male figures around her. Yet they also enhance the picture given in "Culhwch and Olwen" by hinting at fragmentary stories in which Gwenhwyfar is responsible for a break in relations between Arthur and other chieftains. In Triad 54, Gwenhwyfar is the recipient of an insulting blow by Medrawd, which Arthur must avenge by ravaging Medrawd's court (*Trioedd* 147–49). Triads 53 and 84, meanwhile, agree that Gwenhwyfar receives a blow not from Medrawd but from another woman, which becomes the precipitating factor for the Battle of Camlan (*Trioedd* 144). Yet it is the "Faithless Wives" triad, Triad 80, which most directly bears on later stories of Guinevere's abandonment of Arthur for the sake of love with a paramour:

> 80. Three Faithless Wives of the Island of Britain.
> Three daughters of Culfanawyd of Britain:
> Essyllt Fair-Hair (Trystan's mistress),
> and Penarwan (wife of Owain son of Urien),
> and Bun, wife of Fflamddwyn.
> And one was more faithless than those three: Gwenhwyfar, Arthur's wife, since she shamed a better man than any. (*Trioedd* 200)

Guinevere did not, however, remain solely the possession of legendary Welsh folklore, even within the premodern period. Differing high medieval iterations of the character may each be taken as representative of a particular approach to Guinevere's characteristics and role. In Geoffrey of Monmouth's fictitious chronicle, *The History of the Kings of Britain*, Guinevere is an aristocratic lady of good breeding, "descended from a noble Roman family" (221). She is "the most beautiful woman in the entire island" (221), but otherwise a flat character. Her main contribution to *The History of the Kings of Britain* is her treacherous alliance and romantic partnership with Mordred, a treason that is "simultaneously marital and political" (Samples 225). This union allows Mordred to symbolically establish a wrongful sovereignty in Arthur's domestic space, just as in his territorial holdings. Later Arthurian works, including Wace's *Roman de Brut* and Laȝamon's *Brut*, follow Geoffrey's pseudohistorical "chronicle" approach in characterizing Guinevere's threat to Arthur in terms of her relationship with Mordred, a defection that destabilizes Arthur's role as conqueror and political leader. The Middle English *Alliterative Morte Arthure* is also among the works in this style, and Tolkien adopts most directly from the *Alliterative Morte* the martial themes and the sense of Arthur's political and philosophical destiny that pervade his own retelling (*FoA* 116ff).

The romances of Chrétien de Troyes introduce another Guinevere altogether to the Arthurian corpus. Chrétien's queen is a psychologically developed character, "intelligent, level-headed, and determined" (Samples 227), who is nonetheless guided by her passion. Far from being a politically motivated actor, Chrétien's Guinevere reaches for the fulfillment of her desires in love. She commits adultery not with the conniving Mordred, but with the noble Lancelot. She first pretends to reject Lancelot as a joke (Chrétien 218–19), but believing him dead, bitterly repents of her action (221). "Alas, wretch that I am, how much better should I have felt, what comfort should I have known, had I but once held him in my arms," she cries. "How? Yes, naked body against naked body, of course, so I might know greater pleasure"—a fantasy that is later fulfilled, but on which Chrétien's narrator is decorously silent (227). Such plots provide the basis for the "courtly love" strain of Arthurian legend. In these tales, the adulterous relationship between Lancelot and Guinevere creates strife between Arthur and Lancelot, leading to the king's downfall. The Middle English *Stanzaic Morte Arthur* is one of the texts following Chrétien's courtly love model and is Tolkien's most immediate source for the Guinever-Lancelot romance in his own story (*FoA* 94ff).

It may now be seen how Tolkien attempts to combine variant medieval Arthurian motifs in his own version. One strand is Arthur's rise and fall as a potent political figure, the other the human tragedy of crossed lovers. In Tolkien's narrative, they are blended into one great catastrophe, at once social and personal.[3] Malory was the first major Arthurian compiler who attempted such a project, and while Tolkien chose to derive many details of his story directly from Middle English materials rather than Malory, doubt-

---

3   For more extensive comparative study of the shifting image of Guinevere in the medieval English, French, and German traditions, see Samples, and for the romance tradition especially, the monographs of Bethlehem, Cross and Nitze, and Rich. Korrel's tripartite characterization study treats the historical development of Arthur, Mordred, and Guinevere together, while Tolhurst provides an in-depth feminist reading of the chronicle tradition. Additional scholarship on medieval versions of Guinevere may be found in collections by Fenster and Wheeler/Tolhurst, as well as in articles by Kaufman and Holbrook.

less he owes something of his integrative technique to Malory's example. More contemporary versions of Guinevere that may also have had an effect on Tolkien's treatment include those of Alfred, Lord Tennyson, and William Morris.

Tennyson's *Idylls* were not fully published until 1885 (Gray 9), but an early quartet plotted a moral context for Guinever, contrasting her against other female lovers both admirable and base. The grouping "Enid," "Vivien," "Elaine," and "Guinevere" was published together in 1859 (Gray 7), doubling the size but maintaining exactly the contrastive theme of the privately printed dyad *Enid and Nimuë: The True and the False* from two years earlier (Eggers 45). Like its predecessor, the four-poem collection has the explicit principle of pointing up the opposition between the Arthurian legend's admirable women and its disgraces. Enid and Elaine are plainly the virtuous pair, placing Guinevere alongside the seducer and sorceress Vivien and leaving readers in no doubt about the intended judgment of her character. The complete *Idylls* cycle maintains much of this structure, despite individual alterations to the earlier poems. As Mordred espies Guinevere's meetings with Lancelot in the garden, Guinevere is literally and metaphorically seated "betwixt her best / Enid, and lissome Vivien, of her court / The wiliest and the worst" (Tennyson 269, "Guinevere" lines 27–29). Repentant in the end, Tennyson's Guinevere is nonetheless assigned primary responsibility in the dissolution of the Round Table. The condemnatory attitude of Tolkien's text may take something from the Tennysonian exclamation, "'Yea ... this is all woman's grief, / That *she* is woman'" (274, lines 216–17, emphasis original). Apparently, Guinevere's crimes are so arrant that even difference in rank is no object; in Tennyson's Camelot, a lowly maid has the narrative authority to pass judgment on a queen. A similarly negative opinion of Guinever is attributed to the populace generally in *The Fall of Arthur*, where Mordred's retainer Ivor reveals that "few love her" (48, 4.70).

As for Morris, Tolkien was a known devotee of his work, purchasing several of his romances as an undergraduate (Carpenter 77–78). It might be surprising, then, to see that Morris' poem "The Defence of Guenevere," which Gordon-Wise terms "one of the most sympathetic portrayals of the queen in Arthurian literature" (20), appears to run counter to Tolkien's practice. Tolkien's Guinever has been called "what ... must be his least sympathetic female character" (Rateliff). If Tolkien was familiar with "The Defence of Guenevere," he nonetheless chose to take his own Guinever in a direction that contrasted strongly with Morris'. Rather than taking the radical view of defending the queen, as Morris did, Tolkien instead continued in Tennyson's vein of harsh criticism. Still, perhaps he found in Morris, as also in Tennyson, a model for examining at length the queen's own interior viewpoint. Guinevere's interiority is a notable feature in both these predecessors, just as it is in *The Fall of Arthur* itself.[4]

---

4   Nineteenth- and twentieth-century versions of Guinevere are most thoroughly covered by Gordon-Wise, who also provides a comprehensive and useful history of Guinevere down the ages before turning in her concluding chapters to her subject proper. I recommend this source for more information on the Guinevere character in Tennyson, Morris, and many other modern Arthurian works.

More Traditions Assimilated

In a letter to Milton Waldman, Tolkien stated that it was his original intention to dedicate his personal legendarium "to England" (*Letters* 144). This resolve came about through his perception of a lack of native myth and folklore in English tradition and his desire to fill the gap with new legendary works (*Letters* 144). Why, one might fairly ask, would Tolkien attempt to treat the legend of Arthur, given the character's roots in British, but not English, tradition? For all Arthur's iterations in English productions of the Anglo-Norman period and after, the legend's first sources are indisputably Celtic, oral tales reflected in the later medieval Welsh of the *Mabinogion* and *Triads*. Arthur's story began among a people whose dwelling in the Island of Britain far predated the fifth- and sixth-century migrations of Germanic tribes to it and after those migrations remained a society apart. True, the Celts were pushed to the west and north margins of what came to be called England, after one of the constituent Germanic tribes, the Angles; but the Celts remained unassimilated into Englishness, politically and culturally, during the authoring of the most important medieval Arthurian works.

In addition to recognizing this problem of being "associated with the soil of Britain but not with English," Tolkien also disqualified the Arthurian complex as a suitable mythology for England on the grounds of its artistic principles. These he found problematic. He wrote of the Arthurian tradition that "its 'faerie' is too lavish, and fantastical, incoherent and repetitive" (*Letters* 144). The criticism is common to Celtic fantasy in general, and it did not originate with Tolkien. In fact, a publisher's reader in 1937 assessed the perceived Celtic qualities of Tolkien's own tale of Beren and Lúthien in similar terms, writing that "it has something of that mad, bright-eyed beauty that perplexes all Anglo-Saxons in the face of Celtic art" (Carpenter 207). Expectations for story and stylistic execution that are "mad" and "bright-eyed," "lavish ... and fantastical," characterized by passion and irrationality, are English stereotypes of Celtic literature (Fimi, "Mad Elves" 166). They are stereotypes that Tolkien by turns enters into, as in the apparatus to his edition of *Sir Gawain and the Green Knight* with E. V. Gordon, and passionately deconstructs, as in his later 1955 lecture "English and Welsh." In "English and Welsh," Tolkien goes so far as to insist that *Beowulf*, the quintessential English epic, is far more "Celtic" in literary effect than many actual Celtic texts (*Monsters* 172–73).

Phelpstead, Fimi, Burns, and Flieger have previously explored the issue of Tolkien's simultaneous antagonism and indebtedness to things that are "Celtic" either in historical origin, perceived aesthetic, or both. Such scholarship advances the conclusion that Tolkien was imaginatively invested in the Matter of Britain on a consistent basis, whatever his own claims at various times. Criticism by these authors and others has enumerated and analyzed the "Celtic" influence in Tolkien's creative output, ranging from Celtic-inspired grammar and phonology in Tolkien's invented languages to his use of narrative motifs as compared to Celtic models. Tolkien's Guinever is true to the established type: she is a figure come down to him from British legends, and in his hands, she remains "Celtic" in presentation, as will be examined shortly.

Yet Guinever is not merely or solely Celtic. In examining evidence for the presence of Celtic components in Tolkien's work throughout his career, Fimi ultimately asserts Tolkien's chronological tendency toward increasing incorporation of fusion among differing ethnic or national traditions, although such an impulse was always present in his legendarium to some extent.[5] Fimi states that

> by the end of his life Tolkien explicitly acknowledged what is true for many nation-states and their history: that purity of tradition is not a realistic part of the process of nation-building, and that significant merging of peoples, languages, and cultural elements occurs. Especially in the case of the British Isles, a long troubled history of invasions, conquests, and linguistic amalgamations created the modern state of the United Kingdom, and the mythology of Middle-earth, either consciously or not, reflects this process right from its original conception. ("Tolkien's 'Celtic'" 66)

When it comes to *The Fall of Arthur*, a work mostly though not wholly unconcerned with Middle-earth, it too seems to reflect Tolkien's impulse toward assimilation from different cultural sources.[6],[7] In this period, "the Silmarillion" existed in outline based on earlier prose tales and poems, and hobbits had just appeared on the creative horizon.[8] Tolkien was neither a new writer, nor as experienced as he later became. In regarding *The Fall of Arthur*, it is interesting to see that already, by the early 1930s, Tolkien had reached quite an extensive sociocultural admixture, rendering Arthur's queen using elements both Celtic and otherwise.

Not only does Tolkien's image of Guinever incorporate "a fusion of Celtic origins [with] its French reworking, and its Middle English context" (Fimi, "Tolkien's 'Celtic'" 62), it additionally—and so far as I know alone within Arthurian tradition—hearkens back to a Germanic strain of theme and aesthetic that is older and less stately than that available in the chronologically nearer Middle English works. Nor does this element come from late medieval German Arthuriana, which Tolkien seems not to have used as a source.

---

5   Burns, too, argues for fusion throughout her monograph, but without the emphasis on diachronically tracing its degree.

6   It is beyond the scope of this paper to address the implications of the fascinating "Eärendel passage" which unexpectedly shows Tolkien's story of Lancelot and Guinever to be, while continued from a base of inherited material, proceeding also from Tolkien's own idiosyncratic legendarium. See Tolkien, *FoA* 136ff.

7   Several other chapters in this volume deal with the possible connections between *The Fall of Arthur* and the rest of Tolkien's legendarium. See Higgins, Huttar, and Gaertner. [Editor's note]

8   While Tolkien would speak of returning to work on *The Fall of Arthur* as late as 1955 (*FoA* 9), by Christopher Tolkien's best guess, the poem had its beginnings between late 1931 and late 1934. The range is bounded at each terminus by Tolkien's probable availability and the time at which R. W. Chambers commented favorably on the piece in progress (*FoA* 10–11). This dating would place the poem in the middle of Fimi's schema of heightening tendency to fusion. Tolkien's two substantial verse projects immediately previous to it would then be the long poem of Beren and Lúthien, with its mingled French-Celtic air of *chanson de geste* that the publisher's reader mistook as genuine "Celtic" (see above), and the retellings of the Norse matter of the Völsungs which have since been published as *The Legend of Sigurd and Gudrún* (*FoA* 10–11). With such inspiration at hand, is it any wonder that Tolkien should then turn his attention to a poem that mingles the virtues of the two preceding pieces to make a piece doubly of Celtic Faerie and Germanic starkness?

The literary traditions of earlier Heroic Age Northern and Western Germanic cultures were near and dear to Tolkien's heart as both reader and scholar, and in *The Fall of Arthur* he makes frequent reference to them. It is not particularly surprising that he should do so when portraying Arthur's Germanic enemies, Mordred's allies; it is more surprising that he should do so particularly while delineating the character of Guinever.

As I shall argue, Tolkien ascribes to his Guinever both a Celtic fay quality, mysterious and perilously alluring, and a Germanic fell temper of spirit, grim, greedy, and determined. The larger narrative effect is to bring the heritage of ancient "English" and its cultural sibling "Norse" to stand beside the ancient "Celtic" and its later elaborations in a mirror of the historical disposition of peoples within the Island of Britain. *The Fall of Arthur* may not be a legend suitable to be dedicated "to England," but it is certainly worthy of being dedicated "to Britain." Meanwhile, for Guinever considered alone, the synthesis makes for a character of extraordinary narrative richness, one who both honors and surpasses her origins in multiple traditions.

Celtic Faerie

The side of Tolkien's Guinever that represents a continuation of the character's Celtic roots centers on the motif of the fairy woman who takes a mortal lover. This is an exceptionally popular element in old Celtic tales, as Fimi notes ("Tolkien's 'Celtic'" 63). It also attains prominence in later French and English literature, likely through Celtic influence. Shippey and Lakowski each examine the medieval tradition of the powerful female fay through comparison of a complex of texts that Tolkien would have encountered in his scholarly work. These include *Sir Orfeo, Sir Thomas of Ercledoune,* "Lanval" and its Middle English analogues, *Thomas the Rhymer,* and Chaucer's "The Wife of Bath's Tale." Their common theme is the dual nature of the fairy bride or fairy queen, which Shippey describes as producing a mixed response in mortal men, "an apparent discrepancy of fear and attraction" (59). As for attraction, the fay lady is a peerless benefactress. Some tales highlight her benevolence along with her beauty, showing her in the positive role of a donor as she bestows supernatural gifts or grants access to the delights of Faerie (Lakowski 64). Yet the fay also possesses a much more sinister side, a representation of elemental fear. This is manifested in "hideous hag" plots in which the fairy transforms into a literal hag (Lakowski 68–69) or ones in which she abducts her mortal lover so that his escape from the fairy world is blocked or delayed (Lakowski 64; Shippey 59–60). In some variations, the fay-woman simply abandons her human paramour, leaving him to the horror of loneliness, "not seduced but deserted" (Shippey 59).

Inspired by such Celtic-derived or Celtic-styled tales, Tolkien wrote a modern Celtic fay romance of his own. Like the Breton ballad on which it is based, "The Lay of Aotrou and Itroun" is set in Brittany and features a fay called the Corrigan who dwells within the magic realm of Broceliande (Tolkien, "The Lay of Aotrou" 260). "Corrigan" is the traditional Breton word for a "wanton, sprightly female fairy … who desires sexual union with humans" (Phelpstead 93). As Phelpstead remarks, Tolkien takes this Corrigan's nature and actions directly from his Breton folklore sources (99ff). The Corrigan is at first

helpful, granting a childless aristocratic couple the promise of children by her magic ("Aotrou" 260).[9]
But when she is denied the payment she desires, congress with the husband Aotrou, she exacts a terrible
vengeance, causing the deaths of both lord and lady with a curse. The Corrigan, naturally a hideous hag,
changes her shape to that of a fair maiden while unsuccessfully attempting to seduce Aotrou. She appears
with pale hair, a slow smile, and a white hand, and she beckons to him "in Broceliande" ("Aotrou" 261).
Her transformation from loathly but sponsoring lady to provocative, perilous beauty exemplifies in every
way the standard figure. In the Celtic fay, "the allure and the danger are mixed" (Shippey 59).

One of the most striking properties of *The Fall of Arthur* is its overt slotting of Guinever into this tradition,
aligning her with the trope of the fairy lover who is both extremely desirable and extremely dangerous.[10]
The text first introduces us to Guinever in Canto 2, through Mordred's fevered musings on

Guinever the golden	with gleaming limbs,
as fair and fell	as fay-woman
in the world walking	for the woe of men
no tear shedding.	(27, 2.27–30)

Tolkien's Guinever possesses the "gleaming limbs" that are a standard medieval trope of feminine beauty,
and she is noted for her fine golden hair. Tolkien takes over the latter detail from his medieval Arthurian
sources, along with its moral implications in those works. Gerald of Wales recounts that a monk finding
Guinevere's grave in Glastonbury made so bold as to touch a tress, "blond and lovely to look at … a fair
indication of his wanton thoughts, for female hair is a snare for the feeble-minded" (284–85). Living up
to Gerald's depiction of a woman whose sheer beauty is a hazard, Tolkien's Guinever plays up to the trope

---

9   Tolkien's poem withholds the name of the area in which the Corrigan's cave and fountain are located until
     the scene of Aotrou's temptation in the middle of the piece. Although "The Lay of Aotrou and Itroun"
     never mentions Arthur by name, Tolkien nonetheless chose to situate the drama of the Breton lord
     and the Corrigan within the traditionally Arthurian legendary forest of Broceliande. While Phelpstead
     argues that the "corrigan" creature is in Breton folklore specially associated with Broceliande (93), in fact
     the ballad that was Tolkien's primary source never mentions Broceliande at all ("Aotrou Nann Hag Ar
     Gorrigan" 40–45). Broceliande had been a place name connected to Arthuriana since at least Chrétien's
     Yvain (Chrétien 259), and in Tennyson's *Idylls* is the place of Merlin's defeat by the sorceress and seductress
     Vivien (142, "Merlin and Vivien" l.2). In the context of Aotrou's temptation, the sudden invocation of
     Broceliande, where even the great Merlin was overcome by the seduction of a beautiful woman of magic,
     emphasizes the incredible transformation of the Corrigan's character in Aotrou's beholding. Aotrou's
     Corrigan moves from one guise of the fay-woman, a hag who despite her ugliness grants great gifts, to
     another, the beautiful but perilous enchantress and seductress.
10   *Thomas of Ercledoune*, intriguingly, treats an instance of fay-mortal adultery in which the fairy queen is afraid of
     the consequences that would follow should her affair be discovered by her husband the fairy king (Lakowski
     67–68). The unorthodox twist of danger being located not only in the capriciousness of the fairy herself,
     but also in the reaction of her cuckolded lord, invites comparison with Tolkien's scenario. Tolkien's "fair as
     fay" queen is sentenced to death (*FoA* 38, 3.75–76) by an Arthur who, while not quite a fairy king, apparently
     also has connections to the fay and is able to call up fairy or human soldiers (25, 1.202–04).

of the *belle dame sans merci*. She is described as performing a role similar to that of the baneful fairies like the Corrigan, who also "in the world wal[k] // for the woe of men." In line 30, she is characterized as pitiless like them, too: indifferent in her lack of tears for the woe she brings.

These lines represent Mordred's point of view; he is held in "thraldom" (2.26) by his lust for Guinever, symbolically reminiscent of the tendency of fairy brides to imprison mortal partners (Lakowski 64), but it may be that his very desire makes a warped image of Guinever with no objective validity. Yet it soon becomes evident that the fay-woman formulation exceeds the interior perspective of Mordred alone, as Christopher Tolkien records in "Notes on the Text" (*FoA* 66). A closely analogous passage, "fair as fay-woman // and fell-minded / in the world walking // for the woe of men" is instead transmitted through the omniscient narrator at 3.55–56. In Tolkien's earlier drafting for the poem, the admirable Sir Lionel speaks identical remarks. Their ultimate origin is in Tolkien's third synopsis, identical but for lack of punctuation and one difference of conjunction (179). The narrator is again the source of the partial formula "fair as fay-woman," which occurs at 3.75 in combination with a reference to burning Guinever at the stake: anti-witchcraft measures against a fay-woman's enchantment, perhaps?[11] Then, Ivor's curse at 4.71–76 once more names Guinever "the fay-woman." While Ivor as Mordred's servant may be expected to be as partisan as his master, the evidence in aggregate shows that the characterization of Guinever as qualitatively like a fairy is both widely distributed and applied evenly among interested and disinterested parties. This suggests that it should be taken more or less as narrative truth.

Fairy images and their associated ideological valences are clearly significant to the person of Guinever in *The Fall of Arthur*, both in terms of Tolkien's own composition process of character sketch, and in the insistent, building concept that results from stylized repetition within the published text. The recurring phrases evoke the motif of the Celtic fairy woman in her perilous aspect, along with the oft-associated theme that "beauty is itself dangerous" since it confers on men a potentially destructive desire (Shippey 59). "Fell-minded" is in this context the expression of Guinever's pitiless nature that pairs, fay-like, with her beauty, which is so exceptional as to be almost unworldly. Just like the fays in many Celtic fairy tales, Guinever is a classic beautiful, ruthless, perilous woman (*FoA* 3.54; 194, 194n).

Additionally, Tolkien's Guinever has a supernatural inheritance that could be read as not merely fay-like, but fay in fact. When Guinever flees from Mordred, she seeks refuge in the land of her father Leodegrance. He is called a "lord enchanted" and his land is "the hidden kingdom" (4.67–70). The poem does not reveal how Leodegrance was enchanted, but the phrase "the hidden kingdom" smacks of the Welsh Otherworld.[12] The ancient Britons imagined the Otherworld to occupy the same landscape and time as

---

11   Guinever's intended fate of judicial burning as punishment for her adultery is traditional, occurring in the *Stanzaic Morte* (*King Arthur's Death*, *Stanzaic Morte* 1.1925ff) and in Malory (682). Still, it is difficult for the modern reader of *FoA* not to create associations with the burning of suspected witches, however much that practice properly belongs to the early modern period, not the medieval.

12   "The hidden kingdom" is also a styling of Gondolin within Tolkien's legendarium, as was pointed out to me by Kris Swank and Verlyn Flieger (private communication). Tolkien's elves owe much to Celtic myths of the hidden Otherworld, from the hidden kingdoms of "the Silmarillion" to the disappearing woodland revelers and unseen hunters of *The Hobbit*. See Burns 44–74 and Shippey 63–64.

the dwellings of ordinary mortals, but on a different plane of being. They were regarded as "simultaneous realities" with "relatively easy interchange" (Burns 52).

Guinever's ability to elude Mordred's men and the qualities of the enchanted landscape through which she flees are further nods to Celtic mysticism. The second element of the Welsh name *Gwenhwyfar* is cognate with the Irish *síabáir*, meaning "phantom, spirit, fairy" (Bromwich, "Notes to Personal Names" 380; "Additional Notes" 553). Melville Richards, making an argument on the relevant semantic field, contends that "perhaps we should not dwell too much on equivalents like phantom, wraith, apparition, [but] should think rather of fairy, enchantress"—as Tolkien evidently did (qtd. in Bromwich, "Additional Notes" 553). Nevertheless, Tolkien's Guinever possesses a ghostly or phantom nature in her evasion of Mordred's pursuing riders (*FoA* 4.65). In the letter to Waldman, while distinguishing between things of historic Celtic origin and those possessing a "Celtic" aesthetic, Tolkien describes one feature of the "Celtic" as that which cannot be apprehended or grasped. His Guinever in flight embodies this quality: "fair [yet] elusive beauty" (*Letters* 144).

Fairies are not unique to the Celtic tradition. However, among those traditions that became naturalized to the British Isles through successive waves of invasion and settlement, fays are far more characteristic of Celtic lore than of Germanic, whether Anglo-Saxon or Scandinavian. "There are no songs or stories preserved about Elves ... in ancient English, and little enough in any other German language. Words, a few names, that is about all," Tolkien wrote with regret (*Letters* 314). Tolkien's "fay" Guinever owes her elvish qualities to the well-attested Celtic strain of fairy-lore, not to one of the Germanic remnants that Tolkien was elsewhere interested to reconstruct or adapt.[13] This is most evident when Guinever is compared to a prominent Arthurian character conspicuously absent, in any manifestation, from Tolkien's retelling in *The Fall of Arthur*: Morgan le Fay.

Missing Morgan

Morgan is a solid representative of the "fairy queen" tradition. Geoffrey of Monmouth makes her a sorceress, a healer, and a denizen of a mystical, paradisiacal Otherworld isle west over sea. In later Arthurian literature, she acquires the explicit label *Fée*, in the French *Lancelot-Grail* Vulgate Cycle and beyond into Malory. Scholars have linked her to the Celtic war goddess the Morrígan (Burns 111–12), "sometimes alluring, sometimes hideous ... referred to as the Queen of Demons (in her more vicious and vindictive modes)" (Burns 108). Morgan's repute in Arthurian materials is mixed, just as might be expected from the descendant of a Celtic goddess with contradictory fertility and death aspects, and just as might be expected of a capricious fay in any case. In some texts, Morgan is Arthur's benefactress, and in others, an agent of disruption to his court's activities and moral standing. Loomis writes of her dualities: "Morgain may be

---

13   Shippey's classic *The Road to Middle-earth* still provides the clearest account of the phenomenon by which the tangles and gaps Tolkien found in the literatures he studied professionally served as an inspiration for his creative work.

the most beautiful of nine sister fays, or an ugly crone. She may be Arthur's tender nurse in the island valley of Avilion, or his treacherous foe … a virgin, or a Venus of lust" (105).

An example from the antagonistic category is the Morgan who haunts the edges of the Middle English *Sir Gawain and the Green Knight*. Near the end of that poem, it is suddenly revealed that Morgan has been the chief architect of all the plot's mischiefs. These devilments begin with an astonishing game at Arthur's Christmastide court and culminate in the moral faulting of Arthur's virtuous knight Gawain (*Sir Gawain* 141, l.2498–512).[14] Morgan's presence in the text is otherwise minimal; she might or might not be identical with an ugly crone accompanying the lovely lady who tests Gawain's courtesy and resolve (55–57, l.947–69; 139, l.2463) and otherwise does not appear. Carter has found in the work a "productive textual absence" (73) through which "Morgan remains a stranger: as such, she can be blamed as agent so that the males can bond more effectively" (71). Building on the work of gender theorists such as Eve Sedgwick, Dinshaw similarly offers a reading of *Sir Gawain* in which homosocial bonds among the male heroes are foregrounded by the feminine presence that first disrupts and then inadvertently repairs them (205ff).[15] In this gendered power structure, Morgan the Fay's power is demonstrated not by overt works of direct enchantment, but by indirect influence on men's relationships.

Tolkien had deep familiarity with *Sir Gawain and the Green Knight*, as both editor and translator. Thus far we have examined Tolkien's Guinever in her Celtic fairy aspect as bringing woe to particular men: to Mordred, who broods on her with lustful desire and furious anger (*FoA* 28, 2.40), as also to Lancelot, whom she turns from stern nobility, softening his steely nature (37, 3.60–62). But consideration of *Sir Gawain* and of Morgan's disruption of Arthur's court through the means of challenge to male homosocial bonds leads us to a further understanding of Guinever's part in Tolkien's story. The line "In the world walking // for the woe of men" does not merely mean that Guinever is a burden on certain men who love or lust after her. The phrase also ascribes to her a wider culpability in the destruction of Arthur's realm, through her effect on the relationships of men. Tolkien's Guinever serves as a thematic substitute for Morgan, who does not appear in *The Fall of Arthur*. Just as the queen's beautiful and merciless qualities represent the capricious fay side of the absent Morgan, she is in Morgan's terms the enemy of Arthur's fellowship of knights. Gawain's initial doubts of her wholesomeness (36, 3.36–38) are ultimately ratified by what follows.

Not wholly restricted by the archetype of the pitiless fay, Tolkien treats the aftermath of Guinever and Lancelot's adultery, their flight and repentance, with psychological depth and sensitivity. *The Fall of Arthur* explores the lovers' personal pain and yearning, their contradictory desires that cause each to see the other as a changed being (39, 3.95–96, 106–107). The Guinever who leaves Lancelot in cold wrath (42, 3.166–67) yet suffers pains of the heart, albeit they are only on her own account. *The Fall of Arthur* takes her passion as seriously as Lancelot's, pairing their emotions in a parallel language of partners who suddenly find that they are strangers to each other. Yet Tolkien's poem also emphasizes the enduring harm

---

14   The virtues of Gawain, who is described as "voided of every villainy," are discussed at the outset of his journey, as he arms himself with his equally faultless pentangle shield (*Sir Gawain* 39–41, l.631–69).

15   For another gendered reading of *Sir Gawain and the Green Knight* that examines Morgan's liminality, see Fisher.

done to the bonds among Britain's (male) knights and lords in the wake of Lancelot and Guinever's affair. According to Tolkien, the tragedy of the love triangle extends far beyond the principals' feelings. Though Arthur and Guinever are reconciled, Lancelot is banished over the sea to Benwick, and with him go many of the Round Table's best. Arthur loses this important fighting force as well as his noble knight and friend (40, 3.128–35). The loss of Lancelot and his companions has martial implications for the coming contest against Mordred and his Saxon mercenaries. In this way, Arthur's entire establishment suffers from an estrangement that was personal in origin.

Guinever is not only complicit in this schism at its beginning, but also bears a shared responsibility for its continuation. In the climax of the unfinished poem, Lancelot in exile waits upon either of two possible warrants to rejoin the battle for Britain: Arthur's call, or Guinever's. Arthur trusts in Gawain's advice that Lancelot must prove his renewed faith by coming unasked (*FoA* 24–25, 1.180–220). The king fails to issue a summons; for the sake of this roundabout test of loyalty, he loses Lancelot whom he sorely needs (40, 3.127). Yet neither does Guinever, hiding from Mordred beneath the walls of Wales, summon her once-lover to Britain, which would rectify Arthur's mistake. Guinever could choose to summon Lancelot: either explicitly for the purposes of furthering Arthur's battle, or more directly for her own aid, where her personal freedom from being hunted and lusted after must still necessarily involve the defeat of Mordred, Arthur's chief enemy. Instead, she watches and waits while the kingdom falls apart (42, 3.182). Arthur and Guinever's forbearance is syntactically connected at 3.174–75, suggesting that the king and queen bear equal responsibility for Lancelot's absence from the crucial conflict (42). Even under the gathering threat, a renewed alliance between Lancelot and Arthur (with their followers) could still maintain the kingship and defend Camelot (41, 3.151–53). Guinever's and Arthur's combined folly, however, prevents this healing fellowship.

The scenario differs from *Sir Gawain and the Green Knight* in ascribing responsibility for the status of homosocial bonds as much to a man's actions as to a woman's. By contrast with *The Fall of Arthur*, *Sir Gawain* lays blame for breaches in the male-dominated social order on the fay-woman character alone. Gawain excuses himself to Bercilak by referencing various Biblical men who, like himself, were brought low by female antagonists, as Bercilak's wife and the old dame prove to be in the matter of his honor (*Sir Gawain* 137, 1.2411–28). Bercilak's answer finally implicates Morgan herself as the force behind all his and Gawain's opposition to each other (137–39, 1.2445–66), including not only the challenge of the beheadings, but also the trial of Gawain's virtue that Bercilak directed his wife to make (133, 1.2360–63). While Lady Bercilak is cleared of malicious motive, the responsibility for the temptation is transferred onto Morgan, so that Bercilak's response indicates essential agreement with the spirit of Gawain's complaint. Woman are the ruin of many a great man; if men falter in their exercise of manliness, such as maintaining friendly comradeship, it is due to women's wickedness. Dissipating the tension brought by Lady Bercilak's temptation and the two men's beheading blows against one another, this discourse between male interlocutors actually serves to strengthen their damaged masculine bond, as they commiserate with each other and with fellow unfortunates who were "through the wiles of women bewitched into woe" (137, 1.2415).

Unlike Morgan, who comes between Bercilak and Gawain by obliging each to test the other, Tolkien's Guinever is never regarded as a lone actor in the fatal distance that develops between Arthur and Lancelot.

Nonetheless, the narrative structure of *The Fall of Arthur* accentuates Guinever's blameworthiness, in a sense beyond even the overt condemnation of Morgan in *Sir Gawain*. Where *Sir Gawain* comedically circumvents Morgan's meddling by showing her intentions ironically turned upside down, leaving not only the estranged male pair but also the entire court of Arthur united in loving laughter and sympathy (141, l.2513–21), *The Fall of Arthur* instead doubles down on Guinever's trespass by teasing a mitigating effect and then removing it.

After the first disruption of the mutually loving relation of king and knight, Lancelot's return to Arthur becomes predicated on a remedial role that the fair-as-fay queen is placed to perform. Yet, in the pivotal moment (*FoA* 44, 3.221–23), Guinever fails to act in the way that would restore the homosocial bond that was first broken on her account. Lacking Morgan's single blame when Arthur's idleness is as great, Tolkien's Guinever still receives a double burden of guilt in the fall of Arthur's kingdom: she commits sins of both commission and omission. Guinever's characterization as "in the world walking // for the woe of men" thus goes beyond seduction into unwilled nation-breaking.

Or is it unwilled? For another outstanding attribute of Tolkien's Guinever is her prominent will. No less than Arthur, Guinever is caught up in a process of "will unyielding / in war with fate" (*FoA* 17, 1.17). Tolkien's poem highlights Guinever's individual autonomy as her will emerges from within a complex framework of fate. Her stubborn attempts at self-determination seem admirable, even heroic. Yet the narrative explores how she may use that formidable will for evil. Guinever demonstrates her capacity for selfishness and pride by pursuing her corrupt desires with a tragic single-mindedness. Among her most notorious behaviors are her acquisition and jealous guard of treasured things and her ruthless promotion of her own favored causes to the exclusion of good results for anyone, herself or others. Supplementing the image of the Celtic "fay-woman" substitute Morgan-figure, these grim and tragic traits richly develop the other half of Guinever's signature descriptor, "fell-minded." In the process, they link her to another national tradition entirely. Tolkien's Guinever holds her fell-mindedness in common with several literary Germanic queens. The text's interest in her precarious position at the intersection of fate and free will is also a feature shared with the Germanic legendary world. Through adoption of such motifs, Tolkien adds to the Celtic side of his "fair as fay-woman" Guinever a distinctly Norse or Anglo-Saxon tempering. It is a novel take on the character of the queen and one of Tolkien's most decisive contributions to Arthurian tradition.

Germanic Maleficence

As we have seen, *The Fall of Arthur* takes inspiration from both the "courtly love" and the "chronicle" Arthurian conventions. Tolkien's tale includes both the love of Guinever and Lancelot and the quasi-historical story of Arthur's temporal power in flux and even promotes the love plot to a chief motive in the political. As such, the Lancelot-Guinever relationship is critical to the narrative of *The Fall of Arthur*. Yet Tolkien's poem is not courtly romance in the sense of Chrétien and all the courtly strain, which are centered on the amusements of love and high chivalry. Instead, it is romance of another sort: revivalist medievalism. This is true not merely of its Celtic elements, which replicate fairy enchantment from medieval lore and folktale, but of its Germanic components as well.

Although *The Fall of Arthur* is written in modern English for a modern English audience, Tolkien's mimesis of Heroic Age Germanic style[16] recreates a semi-historical atmosphere of conflict between Romano-Britons and Saxons. The poem is presented completely in the alliterative Germanic meter. Its text includes many Germanic themes and images: Mirkwood (19, 1.68)[17] and the beasts of battle (20, 1.76–78)[18]; dragon-prowed ships like an anticipation of Viking vessels (26, 2.8; 89–90); and even a surprisingly Germanic smith-enchanted and rune-marked sword for Gawain (53, 4.197–200).[19] Collectively, these invest the normally "Celtic" Arthurian world with a tonal sense of the "Germanic." The technique is, so far as I know, unique to Tolkien within Arthurian literature. Its effect is to foreshadow the eventual failure of Arthur's kingdom, that final transference of primary dominion from Celtic to Germanic peoples that occurs both within the fictional Arthurian frame and in Britain's recorded history.

Amid such appropriations of Germanic features, Tolkien's delineation of Guinever's character partly through Germanic images and thematic references must be regarded as deliberate. The Guinever of *The Fall of Arthur*, as much Germanic in presentation as Celtic, is at the very heart of the poem's representation of a historical transition between the supremacy of these two cultures in the Island of Britain and of the meeting of their differing moral and aesthetic values. While Tolkien's Guinever partakes in the trope of the Celtic fay by her role as the lust-inducing temptress who breaks men's happiness, she also has specific models in the Germanic tradition, including the motifs of the grasping, avaricious queen who functions as a cautionary tale and of the hell-bent, destructive queen who is the mistress of tragic havoc.

First, there is Guinever's lust for treasures, which relates her to the figure of the avaricious Germanic queen. The Guinever who sleeps soundly in luxury (*FoA* 27, 2.32–33) seems as if she could still belong to the trope of the Celtic fay. In Marie de France's Breton-style *lai*, the knight Lanval's fairy benefactress couches on a similarly fantastic bed, whose linens are "worth a castle" ("Lanval" 107). However, the Guinever whose adulterous desire for Lancelot is figured in the language of treasure demonstrates not merely a taste for fine fabrics, but a Germanic hoard-oriented greed. She compares Lancelot to precious metals and finds him more fair than any other wealth at her command: "Fair she deemed him / beyond gold or silver // to her grasp lying" (*FoA* 37, 3.57–58). Yet it is not enough for her to think Lancelot handsome or to enjoy the benefits of interacting with him in the setting of the court; she must *possess* him, as one amasses coins or jewelry. She desires to grasp precious metals in her hands, rather than admiring treasure from afar (37, 3.49–51). Guinever is not content to have Lancelot serve her in a purely courtly relationship, as a knight openly doing deeds for the sake of his queen. Instead, she covets a secret, intimate relationship, valuing

---

16   Here I am concerned to distinguish Germanic literature looking backward to the Heroic Age, such as the Norse sagas and the Anglo-Saxon epic *Beowulf*, from a category of courtly medieval German works on Arthur such as *Parzival* by Wolfram von Eschenbach and *Erec* by Hartmann von Aue. For more on the medieval German "courtly Arthur," see Samples.

17   Compare Tolkien's interpolation of the common Norse poetic concept of "Mirkwood" into his own *Sigurd and Gudrún* (227–28n14).

18   For the "beasts of battle" motif in Anglo-Saxon poetry, see Chickering 14–15.

19   Compare Tolkien, *Sigurd and Gudrún* 102, 5.9: "There wrought Regin / by the red embers / rough iron hewing / and runes marking."

most highly something that only she possessed "darkly hoarded" (37, 3.52–53). Such an avaricious attitude toward desirable objects, more than the mere fact of being rich, is a characteristic of great lords and ladies in the Germanic legendary tradition. Many noteworthy personages in Norse and Old English works, both male and female, are portrayed as having a particular lust for gold and silver. As is the case with Tolkien's Guinever, their cupidity is typically cast in a disapproving light by explicit authorial censure, narrative trajectory toward an unhappy outcome, or both.

One such character is the greedy Queen Olof of Saxony, who in *The Saga of Hrolf Kraki* is kidnapped and raped by King Helgi of Denmark. Helgi induces the queen to go out unprotected from her stronghold by sending her word that he has found two chests of gold and silver in the woods, which should belong to Olof since the forest is her property (*Saga of Hrolf Kraki* 35–36). Olof takes none of her warriors with her to retrieve the treasure, only the thrall who carried Helgi's message, and is subsequently overpowered by Helgi lying in wait. Helgi's trap depends on his knowledge of Olof's greed, which he first obtains by interviewing the thrall while himself disguised as a beggar. "'Is the queen at all avaricious?' said the beggar. The thrall said she was the most covetous of women" (*Kraki* 35–36). Armed with this intelligence, Helgi is able to predict that his lure of treasure will be enough to bring Olof to the place of his choosing, and also that because of her covetousness she will come there without guards, unwilling to suffer any challenge to her claim or to share the spoils with anyone else. Olof's greed is her undoing. Both duped and ravished, this queen is finally a figure of scorn.

Another Germanic queen for whom greed goes amiss and who is duly punished is Queen Modthryth in *Beowulf*. Modthryth is renowned for her wickedness in dealing with retainers. Later she is reformed from her evil ways, perhaps forcibly reformed, in her marriage to Offa (*Beowulf: A Dual-Language* 160–63, l.1925–62). Modthryth's correction under her new husband's oversight appears to strip her of a regard that previously set her on a footing with great warriors, so that while she was reviled for her malice she was respected as a formidable foe: "None of the boldest // among the retainers / dared to approach her, // unless a great lord" (161, l.1933–34). However much it improves her life's virtue, the relegation of such an intimidating woman to a bride given away at her father's behest, "adorned in gold, // to the young champion" (163, l.1948), is a diminishment of person. Modthryth may have come to enjoy her lot, eventually holding "noble love // toward the leader of heroes" and keeping his high seat in goodness, but the poet's understated description of her recovery from depravity holds a note of knowing mockery: "The kinsman of Hemming // put a stop to all that" (163, l.1953–54; l.1944). One can deduce that Modthryth herself might not have relished the means by which she was subdued. Yet her behavior as an independent agent poses a dangerous problem to the community, one that virtually requires intervention. The subordination of Modthryth under Offa reads within the Germanic legendary convention as both a satisfying punishment for her nefariousness, and, importantly for the understanding of Tolkien's Guinever, as a judicious means of social damage-containment.

Modthryth is most infamous for violence against her retainers in the form of harsh or unwarranted punishments (*Beowulf: A Dual-Language* 161, l.1935–43). Yet immediate juxtaposition between Modthryth and her foil the good Queen Hygd shows how important generosity is in the Germanic court and how Modthryth betrays the royal ideal in part by being excessively stingy.[20] Hygd is young, yet

	nor was she thereby
The more close-fisted,	a niggard in gifts
to the men of the Geats.	Modthrytho, however,
that mighty queen,	did terrible crimes (161, l.1929–32).

In Northern societies both historical and legendary, wealth was customarily hoarded only to be shared out again as gifts in order to strengthen oath-bonds between leaders and the retainers who were sworn to fight for them (Tolkien, *Beowulf* 149). Modthryth, who is guilty of dealing violently with individual men, is also terribly grasping with treasure, acquiring a gift-hoard and sitting on it. This is described as criminal behavior because it is violence against the social order, interfering with the oath-loyalty system that is the foundation of the heroic Germanic court.

Tolkien's Guinever correspondingly, if more symbolically, practices treasure-acquisition that proves highly destructive to the warrior fellowship of Arthur's court. Although Camelot and the Round Table are nominally Celtic and the Saxons are their enemies, even outside of Tolkien's text Arthur's retinue is depicted as operating on principles that are somewhat similar to those of a Germanic warband: sworn affiliation and mutual love and reward between a king and his fighters. These are the common inheritance of the early medieval Heroic Age in Europe, irrespective of nation, and in later peoples' imaginations of those times, though differing from the very earliest texts, the tellers are influenced also by ideas of later feudal knighthood. Yet *The Fall of Arthur*, quite unusually among Arthurian works, relates Guinever's affair through the exact vocabulary of treasure-hoarding and oaths that Germanic cultures, particularly, used to talk about treasure's central role in maintaining their societies. This provides a distinctively un-British, Northern view of the consequences of Guinever and Lancelot's infidelity for Arthur's kingdom.

In the act of Guinever's acquiring and hoarding Lancelot to herself, "strong oaths they broke" (*FoA* 37, 3.62). On a surface level, these are her marriage vows; on a deeper one, they are Camelot's principle of fealty between vassal and king. As discussed above, the text stresses that Guinever is at fault for causing and furthering damage to the bonds among lords who should be fighting together as one band of warriors, defending Britain against its enemies. The estrangement applies first to the broken relationship of Arthur with Lancelot, who violated his vows of love and loyalty to his lord (40, 3.141). This estrangement extends beyond those individuals to encompass fractures in the loyalties of other members of Arthur's retinue. Guinever's characterization of Lancelot as a treasure like gold or silver points not only to her

---

20   For an example of greed as it applies to the failure of a male ruler, see also the story of the grasping and ungenerous king Heremod in *Beowulf* (*Beowulf: A Dual-Language* 147–49, l.1709–24). While I focus on greedy queens, the importance of the issue for Germanic cultures was such that their cautionary tales address the issue in both male and female leaders.

own greed, but to Lancelot's linchpin role in Arthur's maintenance of stable relationships with his other knights, Lancelot's powerful kindred.

In Guinever, as in Modthryth, a queen's selfish greed has adverse repercussions for an entire social system that is mediated by fealty and by glorious treasures as guarantors of strong loyalty. When the metaphorically gold-and-silver Lancelot has once been taken into Guinever's possession, he becomes a treasure removed from circulation for the long term. Vacillating from loyalty to his lady back to his king (*FoA* 40, 3.140–41), Lancelot's heart in theory belongs once more to Arthur at the time Guinever is restored as queen. Yet in being hoarded, this treasure has acquired a tarnish. The disgraced Lancelot may no longer fulfill Arthur's need, not just for his particular service, but for him to act as a bridge to other knights' loyalties. A glorious treasure is supposed to be a means for a king to secure the loyalty of his knights. Instead, where Lancelot goes into exile in France, there too go the rest of the Benwick knights, their pledges to Arthur lapsing even as his own (*FoA* 40, 3.129–30). Refusing Lancelot's suit for pardon, Arthur is left with his war-band much reduced, lacking not just Lancelot, but also Blamore, Bors, Lionel, Lavain, and Ector. No longer is it wholly the case for Arthur, as it is for a proper heroic king according to the Germanic understanding, that "there cleave to him loyal knights of his table, and the people stand by him when war comes" (Tolkien, *Beowulf* 13). Guinever's building of her hoard impoverishes Arthur's, reducing his ability to fulfill the functions of a ruler with respect to keeping retainers' loyalty, just as Modthryth's hoarding problems contribute to her infamous reputation and necessary eclipse. Because of the dire threat that Modthryth and Guinever pose to the concept of heroic lordship itself, they surpass the greedy figure of ridicule represented by Queen Olof and are brought additionally into the circle of the tragically destructive Germanic queen who produces widespread mayhem in pursuit of a self-interested goal or desire.

Not all examples of this traditional figure are motivated by greed, as Modthryth and Guinever are; in fact, the most common motivation seems to be revenge for wrongs, which is highly valued in the Northern ethic. *The Legend of Sigurd and Gudrún* is Tolkien's rendition of the ancient Germanic story of the intertwined legendary families the Völsungs and the Niflungs.[21] The Völsung-Niflung complex includes a series of destructive queens, the majority of whom seek revenge in one terrible form or another. Signý commits incest with her brother Sigmund in order to create a twice-blooded child who will avenge the deaths of their father and other brothers upon her husband, their murderer (*Sigurd* 82–83, 2.30–32). An unnamed queen of Sigmund serves her stepson poisoned drink in order to avenge her father, whom the stepson had killed (89, 3.6). A third avenging queen is Gudrún, who brings home the deaths of her brothers upon

---

21   To create the two long poems in alliterative "Eddaic" meter that were published together under the editorial title of *The Legend of Sigurd and Gudrún*, Tolkien used multiple medieval sources of Scandinavian or German origin including *Völsunga Saga,* the *Poetic Edda* and the *Prose Edda*, and the *Nibelungenlied*. While some features are inventions by Tolkien, the basic plots and many of the details come from one ancient Germanic source or another. Christopher Tolkien's editorial apparatus analyzes the author's choices in weighing, reconciling, and occasionally departing from the individual works that constitute the convoluted and conflicting heritage of his topic.

her husband Atli, first by tricking Atli into consuming the remains of their own sons whom she slaughters (301–02, st.146–47), then by stabbing Atli to death in his bed (303, st.150).

Brynhild, a Valkyrie and "Odin's chosen" (*Sigurd* 117, 5.54; 121, 6.8), may be the most efficient destructive queen of them all. Unlike the preceding three queens, who seek and find retribution for the deaths of their male kin, Brynhild avenges only her own wrongs, compounding ferocity with a selfishness more like Guinever's. Brynhild is deprived by sorcery of the chance to marry Sigurd, whom she loves, and to fulfill her prideful oath of wedding only the man who surpasses all others (158–59, 9.17–19). Grieving, she takes sweeping revenge on every one of those who were party to her defeat. Brynhild's single smear against Sigurd's conduct at once results in Sigurd's murder (163–64, 9.32–33; 174, 9.63–64); turns Sigurd's brothers-in-law and sworn companions Gunnar and Högni into oath-breakers like Brynhild herself (175–76, 9.67–69); makes a grieving widow of Sigurd's wife Gudrún, who first taunted Brynhild about the magical deception perpetrated against her (162, 9.28; 174, 9.65); and deprives the queen mother Grímhild (as "woe's contriver," the mastermind and ultimate worker of the magic in her ambition to see her children well wed) of the champion son-in-law who would help her sons hold their lands against their enemies (158, 9.16; 138, 7.33).

Discussing the Valkyrie character, who is a type of the Germanic destructive queen, Donovan emphasizes among other qualities that such women both "choose actions based on the operation of their own strong wills" and "undergo the loss of something central and precious to their lives" (111). Brynhild loses something precious to her—Sigurd—and in revenging that wrong is a prime example of the principle that "the [V]alkyrie's will often results in tragedy, death, and destruction" (Donovan 123). Like Guinever, Tolkien's Brynhild is named "fell-hearted" (*Sigurd* 175, 9.66) and like her is vilified in gendered terms for spreading woe among a circle primarily of men: "Woe worth the words / by women spoken!" (168–69, 9.50).[22] Högni grumbles that Brynhild was born "'from curséd womb / to man's evil / and our mighty woe'" (176–77, 9.71). The complaint is a near-match to Guinever's byline "in the world walking for the woe of men" (*FoA* 27, 2.29). It is not a mere misogynistic comment; as with the men observing the strife sown by Guinever, Högni has ample grounds for asserting Brynhild's fault.

Yet Brynhild's own misery even in her victory is unmistakable: while she laughs at hearing Gudrún's wails over the dead Sigurd, Gunnar observes "little thou laughest / for delight of soul ... Thy colour blancheth, / cold thy cheeks are" (*Sigurd* 175, 9.66). Brynhild soon after takes her own life, "longing only / for her last journey" (176, 9.70). Signý and Gudrún, too, take their own lives as well as the lives of others. In Tolkien's text, Signý's reference to being called into death by the spirit of her husband Siggeir (86, 2.41), Gudrún's invocation of the spirit of Sigurd to fetch her into the afterlife (307, st.163–64), and Brynhild's request that her remains be burnt on one pyre with Sigurd's (177–78, 9.73–75) collectively gesture toward a Germanic convention whereby heroic noblewomen may accompany their husbands or lovers in death. The motif is possibly a reflection of one of the Valkyrie's traditional functions, ceremonially attending slain heroes to Valhalla (Donovan 115). Meanwhile, Tom Shippey points to a "combination of pride, ferocity and

---

22   The same lines are also used by Sigurd, lamenting Gudrún's unwise decision to pick a fight with Brynhild by enlightening the latter to the fact of her deception (162, 9.29).

sadness" as a defining feature of Germanic heroism that Tolkien emulated in his own *legendarium* as well as in his retelling of the Sigurd legend (qtd. in Donovan 108). In both Tolkien and his sources, a self-willed death at the height of a triumph that nevertheless is twined with sorrow is culturally a fitting end for these tragic queens, who, like their male counterparts in the Northern heroic tradition, are each "caught in the chains of circumstance or of their own character" (Tolkien, *Monsters* 17).

Departing somewhat from the tendency of the destructive Germanic queen, Tolkien's Guinever does not take the course of ending her own life. Nonetheless, the bleakness of her end is commensurate with the proud and tragic lots that Brynhild, Signý, and Gudrún establish for themselves, whilst also containing the more wholly shameful valences of the unhappy but contemptible fates suffered by Olof and Modthryth. The theme of Guinever's wretchedness is developed in the author's notes for the continuation of the poem beyond the point actually reached in composition (*FoA* 136; 167–68). Christopher Tolkien concludes his essay on "The Unwritten Poem" with some remarks on Guinever's future. Unable to hold Lancelot to her as he seeks for Arthur, Guinever is left to watch her treasure slip away from her grasp. She sees Lancelot's "silver banner vanish[ing] under the moon," by which she is brought "utterly to grief" (136). "From my father's few pencilled sentences," Christopher Tolkien writes, "it seems that her life henceforward held nothing but grievous loneliness and self-pity; 'but though grief was her lot it is not said that she mourned for others more than for herself'" (167–68). Even in such straits, she conforms to the archetype of the miserly, grasping queen; she is unwilling to spare pity or mourning for others, grieving most for her own singular woes. This is in sharp contrast to Lancelot, whose more selfless grief for his departed lord puts the final end to her desire, her "greed thwart[ing]" (39, 3.104). Yet the completeness of the devastation Guinever has wrought, extending even to herself, is also in line with the literal self-ruination common in the catastrophically destructive queens.

As Christopher Tolkien comments (*FoA* 168), there is an epitaph-like quality to a short passage of verse on Guinever's ultimate destiny:

> Guinevere grew grey in the grey shadow
> all things losing who at all things grasped.
> .... gold .... and was laid in dust
> as profitless to men as it proved of old. (137)

There is a striking evocativeness in Guinever's aging, or fading to grey in some more spiritual sense, in a world that is dimmed partly as the result of her action. The second line of the fragment only strengthens the impression of Guinever's Germanic-queenly acquisitiveness that is given in the finished parts of the narrative. She not only covets Lancelot, nor even that other reflected glory and splendor of a queen's position, twice mentioned as something she would not want to do without (31, 2.130ff.; 39, 3.100–01). She is grasping, greedy, and possessive.

The third line of the fragment, meanwhile, is tantalizingly obscured by lacunae: what is gold? This may be a recollection of Gerald of Wales's story of Guinevere's bright hair found in her tomb (284–85). Yet gold, as either a precious metal or a worked material such as coins or jewelry, has been the constant symbol in the poem for Guinever's inappropriate romantic desire. With the verse in its corrupted state, there are insufficient cues for a reader to determine the subject of the concluding lines. Is it Guinever's divisive but storied beauty that is commemorated, as it is physically laid to rest at her life's end? Or do the lines comment on a more metaphorical conclusion? Deceased, Guinever can no longer exercise her propensity for insisting on the satisfaction of her desire for the treasure of Lancelot, which has the cost of her own and others' undoing. Her death puts a terminus on her capacity for causing harm, which, like that of the destructive Germanic queens, proves both other- and self-ruinous. The locus of Guinever's baleful influence, her conquest of the true-hearted Lancelot's loyalties, is left finally incomplete after Lancelot's latest repentance, and in that Guinever is less than the Norse queens who each achieved their ends. Yet the consequences of her pursuit are unfavorable for all, including the tragic queen herself. After all the tragic failure of fellowship in the battle against Mordred, Arthur's following departure West over sea, and Lancelot's ensuing chase after him in the fervor of his regret—these leave no one fulfilled, least of all Guinever.

Guinever's closest Germanic inspirations are surely the malign legendary queens, but by her hoarding impulse and the contribution that makes to the waste of Arthur's Britain and her own life, she is also connected to a more surprising model in the Germanic tradition: the dragon. If the greedy royal is the Germanic tradition's humanized image of greed, exalted but still within the scope of ordinary experience, the dragon who sits on hoarded gold is its fantastical epitome, a more-than-human expression of the idea of greed. Dragons are also monstrous, inimical to human life in their destructive habits both direct and indirect: neither the solitary dragon's fiery force in advancing and protecting a selfish claim to its hoard, nor the hoarded gold itself, contribute to the good of individuals or their larger society; they only harm.

A notable feature of *The Fall of Arthur*'s Guinever fragment, not commented on by Christopher Tolkien, is that its final two lines paraphrase material from the concluding scene of *Beowulf*. The setting is the burial of the titular hero-king along with the cursed dragon-hoard he won in his last battle:

They gave to the earth	for its final keeping
the treasure of princes,	gold in the ground,
where it lies even now,	as useless to men
as it was before.	(*Beowulf: Dual-Language* 243, l.3166–68)[23]

While in *The Fall of Arthur*, Guinever's greed is given the generally dragonish metaphor of hoards or treasure, the lines borrowed from *Beowulf* parallel her greed much more precisely to that of the *Beowulf* dragon and express the price and futility of her efforts in terms of the spoils of a successful but vain treasure hunt. A Germanic dragon's gold gives no profit to men: with characteristic dramatic understatement (Chickering

---

23   With the recent publication of Tolkien's *Beowulf: A Translation and Commentary*, it is now possible to compare Tolkien's own rendering of the Old English: "… abandoning the treasure of mighty men to earth to keep, gold to the ground where yet it dwells as profitless to men as it proved of old" (105). The final phrase is, in fact, identical to the last line of the Guinever fragment.

9–10), the *Beowulf*-poet remarks on the terrible result of transferring the gold from the dragon's clutches into the possession of Beowulf's folk. The price of the enterprise is the king and champion Beowulf's life, which leaves his people vulnerable to attack by their enemies (*Beowulf: A Dual-Language* 240–41, l.3150–55). The bespelled gold thus brings only woe to the nation of the Geats, just as Guinever's love brings only woe to the men of Britain. One might also remark that the gold is equally "useless" to the dragon. Guinever attempts to seize and guard her happiness as a Germanic dragon might, taking what is not rightfully hers simply because she wants it, all for an ultimate futility and to greater damage, since she keeps neither Lancelot nor any other joy, as the dragon in the end can keep neither its hoard or its life.

All the while that she engages in her own kind of hoarding, "Guinever the golden // with gleaming limbs" (*FoA* 27, 2.27) is, moreover, like a type of the dragon's gold herself, a curse to the wider society: the source not of fellowship but of strife, when men so disparate as Mordred and Lancelot think to steal the hoard from Arthur, the lawful possessor. At the same time as the dragon is a mythicized image of greed, it is also an image of calamity, giving imaginative shape to the power of wealth and the power of desire to make or break whole societies by means of systemic effects. On the individual level, the dragon speaks to the destructive force of a single human will which, whether recruited to greed, vengeance, or lust, can scorch and burn all around. It is a dragon's nature to be self-serving and malevolent, just as it is for it to be greedy for gold; it is not expected of dragons that they repent, since what they represent in Northern literature is ineffable and unalterable wickedness. In the context of the role Guinever occupies in *The Fall of Arthur*, acting as the center for meditations on these old Germanic themes, her persistence in selfishness and lonely, wasting grief is not out of place, although it is unusual for Arthurian tradition as a whole.

This unredeemed Guinever is a far cry from her precursors in either the *Alliterative* or the *Stanzaic Morte*. In both the Middle English poems, as also in Malory's cycle, the repentant queen retires to a nunnery. The texts differ about the cause of her shame, which is her alliance and adultery with Mordred in the politically oriented *Alliterative Morte*, and adultery with Lancelot in the *Stanzaic Morte* and Malory, which have the romance element. But Guinever's penitence at the nunnery, "ask[ing] there the habit // in honour of Crist / And all for falshed and fraud // and fere of her lord" (*King Arthur's Death*, *Alliterative* l.3917–18), is a consistent thread through them all, crossing the divisions of chronicle and romance. For Tolkien's Guinever, by contrast, there can be no "mark of reparation" (Holbrook 43), such as occurs in a key scene in Malory where her sudden reunion with Lancelot elicits only a chaste, pious reaction. Faced with temptation, Malory's reformed queen bids Lancelot go on his way, never to see her again but instead to marry another. She asks him to "pray for me to the Everlastynge Lorde that I may amende my mysselyvyng" (Malory 720). Tolkien's Guinever, however, embodies a spirit that is not Christian, but older, grimmer, pagan. Greedy and destructive as the queens and dragons who inhabit Germanic legends, Guinever's is indeed a spirit shared with those Germanic foes whom Arthur pursues abroad and at home, while she and they both threaten his peaceful, godly rule (*FoA* 55, 5.10–11).

Northern Doom

The influence of Germanic tradition on the styling of Tolkien's Guinever is especially evident in the poem's emphasis on her self-will and independence as she attempts to defy fate for the satisfaction of her desires. As we have established, these desires are wicked and ruinous. But Guinever's tenacity in following them is not wholly negative, and may indeed be positive, following the standards of Northern myth. While the paradox of destiny and free will is a timeless concern in literature, tragic heroes and heroines of a particularly defiant cast are especially well represented in the Germanic tradition. At once enmeshed in fate's workings and fiercely independent, the proud figures of Northern legend always seek to make their own way. They span from martial heroes such as Sigurd and Beowulf, bearing arms in physical struggles, to the queens like Modthryth or Brynhild who, we have seen, typically gain or lose power through social cachet. For Northern heroines, power is treasure-wealth, or beauty, or elvish magic, and most especially the right to demand championing by kin or lover: all of them tools they may use to influence and manipulate the behavior of men, who hold the overt strength to achieve their desired outcomes. The heroic action of women in a Northern tale is more artful than physically impressive, but it is action all the same and speaks toward a broad Germanic tradition of self-sufficiency and striving, even when it is recognized that defeat is possible or inevitable.

Whether for men or for women, St. Clair identifies "the concept of fate ... the need for courage, a conception of evil, the tragedy of mortality ... and the paradox of defeat" as key elements of the Norse literary and cultural imagination (66). Burns explains that the stereotypical "Northman was a realist ... ruthless but pragmatic," plying these traits by necessity while negotiating an essentially hostile world, one where human settlement takes place in a small protected circle surrounded by the deadly elements and where even the gods will one day die (14–15). Guinever's own world is charged with a sense of doom and is hostile to her wishes and at times to her safety. Her stubborn and cunning reaction to it places her once again firmly in the company of Germanic queens.

The Fall of Arthur does not directly partake of Norse cosmology, having no mention of Midgard or Asgard, frost-giants or fire-giants. Nonetheless, its characters, Guinever and others, are depicted within a similarly stark and uncompromising setting. Storm and the turning tides of the untamable cold sea are the poem's dominant visual images, as for instance in the "ogre anger" of the storm Lancelot views from Benwick (35, 3.9), a rather Northern personification of natural force as monster. Even in the poem's woodland scenes, there is a pervasive sense of loneliness and smallness, of human beings beset in a fearful world of unknown dangers (22, 1.133–34). *The Fall of Arthur* features several characters who, just as in Germanic stories, attempt to master the hostile world and its unknown but probably unfavorable destiny by their own active undertakings. Concurrently, as Arthur hopes to turn back the clock (17, 1.5) in his Eastern campaign, Mordred at home tries to exploit uncertain fate to his own advantage. Half propositioning, half threatening Guinever, he speaks to her about his purposed rebellion (in which he intends her to take part). He claims that the West is waning and only the bold will prosper (32, 2.147–53). The winners will be the ones who, pragmatic and ruthless, will "snatch" their aspirations from a chaotic environment where fickle doom is in the process of altering the existing order. Such an approach might be expected to appeal to the greedy Guinever. Yet she rejects his offer of alliance and declines willing complicity in his treason. It is an important change from the "chronicle" tradition, one that does not reflect Guinever's increased faithfulness to Arthur, but rather her increased independence in the effort to be mistress of her fate.

While Guinever in distaste seeks to avoid Mordred's vision of romantic union and their rule together, ironically her character is drawn nearer to his in intrepidity and initiative. There is Northern heroic pragmatism on display in her stalling, as she consults with herself about staging an equivocation that will grant her space (32, 2.159–60). There is also a forlorn Germanic courage in her following flight by night, undertaken in the immensity of her fear (34, 2.190–91). Like the Norse and Anglo-Saxon heroes in their hopeless battles, and like the Norse and Anglo-Saxon women who play the game of power in a world where men physically dominate, she is overmatched by her opponent but nonetheless takes action on her own behalf. The motif of Arthur's queen laying a gambit to escape from Mordred is a traditional one, present in the *Stanzaic Morte* and Malory. In those texts, Guinevere arranges a trip to London, supposedly to prepare for the bridal, and takes advantage of the city's fortifications to ensure that she is beyond Mordred's reach. Yet Tolkien in his retelling develops Guinever's agency far beyond the sources, fleshing out her motives for running from Mordred and her hopes in her time of hiding, just as he depicts her emotions and underlying aspirations in a flashback to her interactions with Lancelot while they are together in exile.[24] Such psychologically realistic characterization for Guinever is one of the most remarkable properties of Tolkien's Arthurian work. The technique consistently enhances the reader's picture of Guinever as a proud, shrewd, and striving woman in the Germanic model.

In Canto 2, strong language outlines Guinever's ambition to use what the time has given to her advantage, drawing attention to both her insecurity and her manipulative mood. While in hiding (*FoA* 34, 2.205, 204), waiting for either Arthur or Mordred to destroy the other, she wonders what Lancelot will do when he hears of her plight. Would he come rescue her? Would she be joyful again? And, more interestingly, would she "master chance / and the tides of time // turn to her purpose" (34, 2.204–13)? What exactly Guinever's strategy is requires some parsing. How, a fugitive awaiting rescue, should Guinever have such a great measure of active control as she thinks to find?   In consideration of this paradox, canto 3, lines 181–86 is also worth examining. Here, "in her dark counsel," she hopes "men's fate to mould // to her mind's purpose" (42).

While the earlier quotation shows Guinever contemplating calling Lancelot to her aid, she does not follow through on that impulse (42, 3.174–75); yet the second passage also shows her thinking to arrange events to her purpose. Why? In the first consideration, it is an issue of timing. We can imagine the chances that Guinever weighs when she decides that a summons to Lancelot would be premature. If Arthur were to win his day against Mordred only to find Lancelot and Guinever already reunited, the same strife would be

---

24   In Canto 3, it is recalled how Lancelot first suggested returning Guinever to Arthur. Her mixed desires are reported directly, on the one hand to persist in her course and on the other to avoid exile and the loss of love (*FoA* 39, 3.98, 100–01). This closely echoes her position later, when she waits under the walls of Wales; there, attention is called to her resolve, her masterful attitude, and her desire to conquer and wield others (39, 3.97–101).

renewed as during her previous exile. Arthur might pursue them; and if he did not, Lancelot might return her to his lord, as he did once before. If, however, she were only to call Lancelot to her side after it was seen how the battle would turn, summoning him solely in the event of Arthur's loss, she would altogether avoid the fraught prospect of once again being caught between Arthur and Lancelot.

It should be noticed that, while unpleasant, the possibility of renewed romantic contest between the king and his knight has some small possibility of benefit for Guinever either way. As the restored Arthur's queen, she still would be secure in a splendid position according to her liking (39, 3.101). But her personal preference is to be secure in love with Lancelot. Mordred she seems hardly to count as an obstacle to that scenario, believing implicitly that Lancelot could defend her from Mordred's unwanted attention. However, by laying plans for a summons to Lancelot but holding off until the appropriate time, Guinever maximizes her chances of finding gladness somewhere. Either she will be Arthur's glorious queen in state without the tarnish of having run off once again, or she will revert to being Lancelot's ignoble but happy lover, who with the death of her husband in battle against Mordred is in no danger of being returned to him against her will.

"Men's fate to mould // to her mind's purpose," however, adds another complication to the situation. Guinever hopes to manipulate not just her own gladness, as was said in the first extract, but also "men's fate." The fate of which men? Of Lancelot and Mordred, certainly, but it may be that we are supposed to understand that she thinks of influencing the fate of Arthur also, rather than simply waiting for a natural outcome in his strife with Mordred.

Guinever, in evident urgency for freedom from her marriage, might knowingly be hastening Arthur's fall by purposely depriving the king of his best knight. If she were to call Lancelot to Britain for her own sake, there is a chance that, seeing Arthur's need and being already so close, Lancelot would join forces with his king in opposing Mordred. Benwick's presence in Arthur's cause would not only strengthen the king's army in the usual sense of increased military might. Lancelot is Arthur's best chance to defeat Mordred in a less concrete way.

On the eve of battle, Mordred is left in doubt, because he knows of a prophecy that Lancelot and the men of Benwick will certainly vanquish him if they come into conflict. A witch once spoke words to him that he has never forgotten (49, 4.104): that Lancelot would return to fight alongside Arthur (49, 4.102–03, 99–100). There is no direct evidence in the text that Guinever is familiar with this same foretelling, but the great emphasis that is placed on it from Mordred's perspective illustrates its importance to the doom that unfolds. The poem's register is raised to suspense as the ships slowly enter Mordred's sight, and he waits to see whether Lancelot's banner is among them (50, 4.132–33). The tension finally breaks in Mordred's laughter, when he realizes that the pale lily of Lancelot is missing (51, 4.159). In the absence of textual proof that Guinever considers or works from this prophecy, the interpretation that she does so must remain tentative. Yet such a reading makes sense of the otherwise vexing question of how Guinever's forbearance can be framed with such active verbs as "master" and "mould," when her position otherwise seems not only one of extreme vulnerability to Mordred's sexual threat, but also defined by passivity as she waits in hiding.[25]

Tolkien's Guinever is indeed more passive than the male Germanic heroes who endure doom no matter their heroic challenge upon it, but die "with their backs to the wall" (Tolkien, *Monsters* 17). Be that as it may, her relative weakness is balanced by Northern fortitude and by a typically Northern grim but clear-eyed assessment of her predicament and how she may contest it from within the male-dominated power structure. We have looked extensively at greedy queens and destructive queens. Another staple of the Germanic story-hoard is the inciting heroine.

Germanic heroines may burn down halls with their enemies in them, as Gudrún does (*Sigurd* 304, st.153). They may perform other physical assertions of their will, such as Signý's rescue of her brother and son by smuggling them tools with which to escape their execution-chamber (198); Brynhild's setting obstacles for her suitors (143, 8.6); or Gudrún's assassinating a despised husband in his bed (303, st.150–52). But action by non-physical influence is even more common for a Germanic woman. Scholars of Norse literature have documented the motif of women playing an "inciting" or "egging" role in heroic plots. Powerful women in this model influence events not by acting themselves, but by setting up male heroes to act (Donovan 110; 131n10).[26] Usually the men are their husbands and lovers, or their male kin. Brynhild falls into this category when, by asserting the lie that Sigurd slept with her, she convinces her husband Gunnar to kill his oath-brother Sigurd (*Sigurd* 167–69, 9.43–50). Signý is also an inciter figure, secretly conceiving and birthing in grim silence a child doubly of Völsung heritage (82–83, 2.30–32), and, while this son is still a child, sending him to his sire, armed with his grandfather's sword, in order to learn the arts of plunder and murder so that he may use them to avenge Völsung (83–84, 2.33–36).[27]

Queen Skuld from *The Saga of Hrolf Kraki* is an even closer parallel to Guinever. Incidentally "the greatest sorceress and ... come of elfin stock," the elf-associated Skuld prods and whets her far less fell-minded husband Hjörvarth into starting a conflict with his liege lord, the mighty king Hrolf (*Saga of Hrolf Kraki* 89). The resulting war breaks up the greatest court in the whole of Scandinavia, all for the sake of Skuld's avarice in the matter of tribute payments (89). King Hrolf Kraki and his retainers, as famous in Scandinavian literature as King Arthur and the Knights of the Round Table are in British and Continental European

---

25 One index to the queen's vulnerability is the metaphor of hunter and quarry, which encodes her interactions with Mordred. See *FoA* 31, 2.120–23; 33–34, 2.188–95; 46, 4.26–33. A much earlier use of a similar theme is "Whoso list to hunt" from the period of the English Renaissance, interpreted by critics as referring to Henry VIII's pursuit of Anne Boleyn (Wyatt 595). A fruitful area for further study is the parallel that Tolkien's Guinever, running scared as the deer, finds within Tolkien's own *legendarium*. While similarly including a gendered dimension, Tolkien's *The Children of Húrin* additionally uses the imagery of the deer hunt to figure the discrepancy between human vulnerability to fate and the human struggle to master it, in a tragic fashion more comparable to *FoA* than to Wyatt's romantic sonnet.

26 See also Jochens, Jenny. *Old Norse Images of Women*. Philadelphia: U of Pennsylvania Press, 1996. Print.

27 In Tolkien's medieval sources, but not appearing in his own version, additional tales tell of Signý that she had more than one son who might have been Völsung's avenger, but that she participated in the testing and killing of those who were not hard-minded enough for the task (*Sigurd and Gudrún* 196).

literatures, are in the end brought utterly to nothing (97): this because Queen Skuld covets a prize for herself and does not care who should be hurt in the process, very like another greedy and calamitous queen.

Guinever's role in profoundly influencing Arthur's war is all the more conspicuous because her participation does not take the expected egging format, as Skuld's does. In fact, it assumes the very opposite. Rather than cajoling her lover Lancelot into action, Guinever attempts to accomplish her end by *withholding* her inciting from him. Donovan observes that Tolkien does not make much use of the inciter function for the Germanic-inspired female characters in his own legendarium (131n10). This fact is congruent with Tolkien's statements in *Sigurd and Gudrún* that he found Gudrún, whom he called "a sensitive but weak character" (52), more interesting than Brynhild the dangerous Valkyrie (55). Gudrún is no supernatural maiden nor ordinarily a very effective personality, as indicated by her being twice married off by her mother and brothers against her foreboding (127, 7.1–5; 259–62, st. 18–28) and failing either to convince her brothers against her husband's trap with a secret warning (267–71, st. 44–56) or to move her husband to mercy when they are in his power (291–93, st. 116–20). Yet she proves surprisingly strong-willed when finally driven to extremities by grief and desperation. Nearing her final crisis of character, she successfully performs the classic inciting function of calling to arms in advance of taking up retributive violence herself (280, st. 81–82).

Tolkien's choice with Guinever to reverse the controlling behavior from warmongering to the absence of warmongering, speech to the absence of speech, as like any inciter she attempts to control her man and her world, has not only the artistic effect of bringing the egging theme into sharper relief within the Northern-biased *Fall of Arthur*, based on upset expectations; it also follows Tolkien's expressed interest in the potential diversity within the tradition of effectual Germanic women, represented by such liminal inciters as Gudrún. Like his mild Gudrún, who is easily disregarded until she hits a breaking point, Tolkien's fell-minded but hounded and wilderness-torn Guinever respects and even furthers the conventional Germanic distinction between the plain strength of heroes and the more complex strength of heroines, which may coexist with significant weakness.

Just as the inciting queens and all other Northern heroes do, so also Guinever acts with no guarantee of actually changing "the tides of time" whose doom she recognizes. She can have no certainty of achieving her primary desire, when so much depends on the outcome of uncertain battle. As Guinever cunningly designs her fate from a position that, on the surface, is not strong, her characteristics accord closely once again with those of legendary Germanic ladies from Brynhild and Signý to Skuld and Gudrún. Surpassing their cultural and physical limitations, such heroines exemplify the Northern value of dogged and intelligent courage when ranged against greater opposing forces. From notice of this combination of potent will and delicacy, we may turn to examining Tolkien's Guinever, not just as a medievalist reiteration of Celtic and Anglo-Saxon or Norse themes, but as a modern literary creation situated within Tolkien's canon. There she rests in continuum with one feature of his legendarium: the portrayal of powerful yet limited female characters.

Guinever as a Tolkienian Woman

The depiction of women in Tolkien's fiction is a topic with a thorny critical history.[28] Readers' reaction to Tolkien's female characters, whether these are taken on their own or considered in combination with female characters belonging to other members of the Inklings, has covered the entire spectrum from denouncement to praise. The arguments range from claims of frank misogyny in Tolkien's depiction of the feminine to opposing assertions of his texts' fundamental compatibility with a feminist understanding of power and gender dynamics.

As Crowe explains, a common complaint is the "disappointingly low percentage of females that appear in [Tolkien's] best-known and best-loved works, *The Hobbit* and *The Lord of the Rings*" (272). Other unfavorable analyses, focusing on quality rather than quantity, find faults of conventionality and idealistic portrayal among those female characters Tolkien does include. Stimpson calls Tolkien's women "the most hackneyed of stereotypes" (18), while Battis writes that "women are not given easy identities to inhabit within *The Lord of the Rings,* and many are stereotyped to the point of excess" (913). In Fredrick and McBride's understanding of Tolkien's gender aesthetic, "Men are the doers, workers, thinkers, and leaders. Women are homemakers, nurses, and distant love interests" (109). In the words of Enright, Fredrick and McBride further convict the (all-male) intellectual community of the Inklings of being "blatantly sexist" (Enright 94), and regard the gendered features of Tolkien's works as symptomatic of a shared dysfunction. Myers disagrees with Fredrick and McBride's characterization as it applies to the fiction of Charles Williams, but concurs that "the worlds created by Tolkien and Lewis are indisputably 'man's worlds' based on the traditional masculine-feminine stereotypes" (14).

Dissenting critics, however, assert that there is indeed a depiction of women's power within Inklings texts, and they search for a framework with which to define this element. Hopkins differentiates Lewis and Williams from Tolkien in their respective treatments of the feminine. She finds a tendency in Williams and Lewis to depict colorful, powerful women, and yet to show them as "at best a contradiction in terms, at worst a fear of nightmare proportions" (Hopkins 364). She distinguishes this tainted portrayal from the more wholly favorable qualities of Tolkien's women. For Tolkien's female characters, Hopkins finds that their "very scarcity seems to invest them with an air of uniqueness and of almost talismanic status, and in some cases their very femininity, seen as such a disadvantage in Lewis, is in Tolkien the very source of their strength" (365). Other commentators share and further Hopkins' conception of a Tolkienian strength sourced particularly in femininity. Enright posits that "Tolkien's female characters epitomize his critique of traditional, masculine and worldly power, offering an alternative that can be summed up as the choice of love over pride" (93). Making advances to an earlier argument that complementarity among gendered principles is a primary virtue in Tolkien (Rawls 5), Crowe concludes that "Arda is a world in which females share power in spiritual and temporal realms ... more importantly, it is a world in which attitudes and values associated in the Primary World with the feminine are highly valued" (277).

---

28   For this section, I am much indebted to literature reviews by Donovan (106–07) and Enright (94–95) and to Robin Anne Reid for assistance in locating sources.

Where does Tolkien's Guinever fit within these debates about Tolkien's women? Where within his literary creations in general? She is, as I have argued, a woman of great power. She merges the seductive and enchanting power of the Celtic fay with the temporal and emotive power of the corrupt and driven Germanic queen who, though "Fate sen[ds] her forth" as an agent of destruction (*FoA* 3.57), and corrupted by selfish desire, nevertheless attempts by her choices to conquer Fate itself. Somewhat surprisingly, given the differences between male and female heroes and the overall disapproving eye *Fall of Arthur* casts on her, Guinever in her attitude toward fate bears a distinct resemblance to the greatest tragic hero of Tolkien's legendarium: the dragon-slaying warrior Túrin Turambar. Readers of Túrin's tale are left to judge for themselves the appropriateness of Túrin's proud self-naming as "Master of Doom" (*Children of Húrin* 196). *The Fall of Arthur*, while incomplete, has enough of a resolution in its backmatter for a similar calculation to be made about Guinever and weighted to the side of failure. Failed mistress of doom or not, Guinever compares favorably with Túrin in tragic effect. We may not care for her, as we do for Turambar, but the downfall of great realms and lordly lineages in either case possesses intrinsic narrative interest, and tragedy in both tales comes from effects on innocents as well as the instigators. As a Tolkien *character* regardless of her sex, Guinever is a compelling figure for her role in a venerable tragedy that, in Tolkien's handling, becomes largely about the interplay of destiny and willed action. The machinations that Tolkien assigns to Guinever partake deeply of this favorite Tolkien theme, which otherwise in the author's canon is brought to its fullest fruition in the male hero Túrin.

Yet Guinever's womanhood is also important. Tolkien's Guinever is an archetypally powerful woman navigating and advancing the conflicts within a mythic story; matching this gravity, she is drawn partly from inspirations in deep-rooted world legend and epic, just as are Tolkien's other heroines.[29] Still, she does not have the role-model appeal of the idealized women of the Middle-earth legendarium. Rather than Arwen, Éowyn, and Galadriel from Tolkien's *The Lord of the Rings*, each a locus of female goodness, Guinever resembles most their inverse: the monstrous female quantity whom select scholars have found represented in Shelob and her forbear Ungoliant (Donovan 118–21; Fenwick 20–23; Rawls 6). While Shelob is not a woman *per se*, but a female spirit incarnated "in spider-form" (*LotR* 707, 4.9), by her very name she is characterized as an explicitly female monster (Fenwick 20). She is presented as an entity of "ultimate selfishness, consuming lust," a being who "only desire[s] ... for herself a glut of life" according to her own happiness (*LotR* 707, 4.9). Rawls interprets Shelob's egocentrism and greed as "the feminine concern with the individual and with the inner life ... taken to the extreme" (6). Parallels with Guinever's epic selfishness are immediately apparent. There is also a Northern strain in Shelob, just as in Guinever. Shelob's unusual strength and destructive effect and her associations with fettering, binding, and weaving, which are symbolic of her snaring of heroes and her sealing of fate, have been identified by Donovan as aligning with the dark aspect of the Germanic Valkyrie (118–21). Tolkien's Guinever is admittedly far more woman and far less monster than Shelob, dragon-likeness aside. But the queen's negative traits acquire a

---

29 See Donovan and Fenwick. Donovan focuses on the typing of female characters from *LotR* in relation to Germanic mythology, specifically the image of the Valkyrie, while Fenwick explores their debt to powerful female figures in classical Greek epic.

mythically sinister note when one sees how closely they compare with those of that typological destructive force Shelob, the antithesis of the female generative energy (Fenwick 20).

In addition to her monstrous qualities, Tolkien's Guinever is, one may say, conventionally feminine in her terror of Mordred. She is stereotypically restricted even in her great ambition, accomplishing her ends mainly through the process of waiting passively, refraining from action rather than acting. Even so, Guinever is a high-water mark for demonstrating Tolkien's capacity in the enterprise of three-dimensional development of a complex female character, however extrinsically limited or unlovely in heart. *The Fall of Arthur*'s elaboration of Guinever's motives and desires surpasses comparable development for any other female character in Tolkien's canon except perhaps Galadriel or Erendis.[30] From Guinever's confusion and hurt at Lancelot's love withdrawn (*FoA* 39, 3.95–107), to her hatred of Gawain for his betraying the secret of her infidelity (195), as well as the many glimpses of covetousness, fear, ambition, and final grief already considered above, the poem and its drafts are consistently concerned with detailed depiction of Guinever's interior perspective. This psychological realism is valuable in its own right as a foundation of the artistic value of *The Fall of Arthur*. It is also a new datum for the continuing critical conversation about women's status for Tolkien and within his literary circle. My scope to discuss it here is limited, but I hope that others will further examine Guinever in light of her implications for the study of Tolkien and gender.

Conclusions

In "On Fairy-stories," Tolkien writes that although Arthur, Guinevere, and Lancelot are not diminutive sprites like those recognizable to Victorian and Edwardian tastes, yet "the good and evil story of Arthur's court is a 'fairy-story'" (*Monsters* 112). While there he means "fairy-story" in a generic sense, not as a story *of* the fay, Tolkien's "fair as fay-woman" Guinever possesses qualities that, striking back to the British origins of the Arthur legend, embody Celtic magic and mystery. Tolkien's use of Guinever as a thematic substitute for the fay witch Morgan is an inventive yet fitting twist. This bit of narrative torsion provides Tolkien's

---

30   Galadriel, who makes her first appearance in *LotR* rather than in Tolkien's earlier "Silmarillion" work, continued to be developed well past the publication of the book, with Tolkien making substantial revisions to her history and character. See "The History of Galadriel and Celeborn" in *UT* 239–280 and, e.g., *Letters* 431. Erendis, from Tolkien's short story "Aldarion and Erendis: The Mariner's Wife" (*UT* 181–227), is another exceptionally well-rounded female character and rivals the better-known Galadriel in emotional depth. Also, as Christopher Tolkien recounts, there is a chronological spread to be found in the elder Tolkien's materials relating the Númenórean story of Erendis and her daughter Ancalimë. The "notes and jottings" that Christopher arranges at the end of the unfinished sequential text "do not constitute the fragments of a wholly consistent story, being composed at different times and often at odds with themselves" (*UT* 215). Just as is the case for Guinever and Galadriel, Erendis is a figure whose development Tolkien considered diachronically. For all three of these outstanding fictional Tolkien women, complexity consists not just in dimensional presentation within the main text, but also in multiple overlapping writings that originated in the composition and revision process and that, surviving still today, stand witness to intricate authorial engagement.

Arthur tale with the mixed appeal and peril of the Otherworld that is a characteristic of its Celtic heritage, and does so with an unparalleled economy of dramatic cast.

Just as truly, Tolkien's Guinever is heir to the Germanic traditions of gold and greed, ferocity and fame, and tough-minded, pragmatic struggle for self-determination in a doomed world. She is not out of place among the company of shrewd and self-serving Germanic queens and heroines, fell-minded to the (often bitter) end. Through her as through them, we see reflections of the old Northern meditation on the problem of unchecked desire and its destructive force upon both individuals and social or civil structures. Lacon, writing before the publication of *The Fall of Arthur*, surmises that Tolkien would have extensively mixed Arthur's story with Germanic elements. "Tolkien's poem will almost certainly interlace with *Beowulf*, featuring many of the same places, characters, and peoples, and having some of the same events mentioned," she predicts. Notwithstanding that there is little *direct* connection beyond the adaptation of a single *Beowulf* line, certainly not interlace of the kind Lacon envisions, overlap of characters and events, she correctly anticipates that *The Fall of Arthur* would possess significant alignment with Germanic traditions as well as with Celtic. The poem received is close to the poem that would be expected, given previous knowledge about Tolkien's scholarly interests and the integrative impulses he demonstrated throughout his writing career. To this extent, *The Fall of Arthur* confirms standing theories, such as Fimi's, about the overall character of Tolkien's interaction with various mythical traditions throughout his career.

Tolkien's approach to Guinever, as to the Arthur legend more broadly, is one of syncretistic, mimetic medievalism. As in other projects, he assimilates traditions with a sensitivity to the simulation of the properties and artistic effect of his materials, even as he adds to them. In this, he is set apart from his fellow Inklings. Williams' Arthurian poetry collections *Taliessin through Logres* and *The Region of the Summer Stars* are also medievalist and syncretic in technique, yet to a much higher degree than Tolkien, they demonstrate a source-independent approach, rather than concern for imitation. Their handling of mystical and occult themes owes as much to Williams himself as to the old authorities. Meanwhile, Lewis' creative response to Arthur is represented in a different genre altogether from the pseudomedieval: the science fiction of *That Hideous Strength*. The Inklings, clearly, did not respond to Arthur with one voice. The contrast among them serves to call attention to Tolkien's poem as a product of his own style, as he worked at making a modern myth simultaneously new and foreknown.

Certain feminist criticism suggests that Tolkien differs from his Inklings compatriots also in the general patterning of his female characters. Tolkien's Guinever is impassioned and decisive, a powerful and powerfully imagined figure who never quite leaves behind the challenges of womanhood in a heroic world. Throughout *The Fall of Arthur*, she remains thoroughly unlikable as a villain of the piece, despite the room that Celtic beauty, Northern strength, or rich psychological detail might otherwise leave the reader for admiration and identification. In this mixture of traits, she supports the nuanced picture that emerges from critical debates about Tolkien's women, while providing a new point for analysis in those debates. Fair and fell with Tolkien's own stamp, Guinever in *The Fall of Arthur* is a memorable and thought-provoking expansion of Arthur's ever-renewing legend.

Works Cited

"Aotrou Nann Hag Ar Gorrigan." *Barzaz-Breiz: Chants Populaires de La Bretagne*. Ed. Théodore Hersart de la Villemarqué. Vol. 1. 2ⁿᵈ ed. Paris: A. Franck, 1846. 40–45. GoogleBooks. Web. 8 September 2015.

Battis, Jes. "Gazing Upon Sauron: Hobbits, Elves, and the Queering of Post-Colonial Optic." *Modern Fiction Studies* 50.4 (2004): 908–26. *Project MUSE*. PDF file. 1 November 2014.

Beowulf: A Dual-Language Edition. Trans. Howell D. Chickering. 1983. NY: Anchor, 2006. Print.

Bethlehem, Ulrike. *Guinevere, a Medieval Puzzle: Images of Arthur's Queen in the Medieval Literature of England and France*. Diss. Universität Bochum, 2001. Heidelberg: Winter, 2005. Print.

Bromwich, Rachel. "Additional Notes to the Second Edition." *Trioedd Ynys Prydein: The Welsh Triads*. 524–66.

——. Introduction. *Trioedd Ynys Prydein: The Welsh Triads* xi–cxliv.

——. "Notes to Personal Names." *Trioedd Ynys Prydein: The Welsh Triads* 263–523.

Burns, Marjorie. *Perilous Realms: Celtic and Norse in Tolkien's Middle-earth*. 2005. 2ⁿᵈ ed. Toronto: U of Toronto Press, 2008. Print.

Carpenter, Humphrey. *Tolkien: A Biography*. NY: Ballantine, 1978. Print.

Carter, Susan. "Galadriel and Morgan le Fey: Tolkien's Redemption of the Lady of the Lacuna." *Mythlore* 25.3/4 (2007): 71–89. Print.

Chickering, Howell D. Introduction. *Beowulf: A Dual-Language Edition* 1–28.

Chrétien de Troyes. *The Complete Romances of Chrétien de Troyes*. Trans. David Staines. 1990. Bloomington and Indianapolis, IN: Indiana UP, 1993. Print.

Cross, Tom Peete, and William Albert Nitze. *Lancelot and Guenevere: A Study on the Origins of Courtly Love*. 1930. NY: Phaeton, 1970. Print.

Crowe, Edith. "Power in Arda: Sources, Uses and Misuses." Reynolds and GoodKnight 272–77.

Davies, Sioned. Introduction. *The Mabinogion* ix–xxx.

Dinshaw, Carolyn. "A Kiss is Just a Kiss: Heterosexuality and Its Consolations in *Sir Gawain and the Green Knight*." *Diacritics* 24 (1994): 205–26. Print.

Donovan, Leslie A. "The Valkyrie Reflex in J.R.R. Tolkien's *The Lord of the Rings*." *Tolkien the Medievalist*. Ed. Jane Chance. Routledge Studies in Medieval Religion and Culture. NY: Routledge, 2003. 106–32. Print.

Eggers, John Philip. "The Weeding of the Garden: Tennyson's Geraint Idylls and *The Mabinogion*." *Victorian Poetry* 4.1 (1966): 45–51. *JSTOR*. PDF file. 8 September 2015.

Enright, Nancy. "Tolkien's Females and the Defining of Power." *Renascence: Essays on Values in Literature* 50.2 (2007): 93–108. Print.

Fenster, Thelma S., ed. *Arthurian Women: A Casebook*. Garland Reference Library of the Humanities. Vol. 1499. NY: Garland Publishing, 1996. Print.

Fenwick, Mac. "Breastplates of Silk: Homeric Women in *The Lord of the Rings*." *Mythlore* 21.3 (1996): 17–23, 50. Print.

Fimi, Dimitra. "'Mad Elves' and 'Elusive Beauty': Some Celtic Strands of Tolkien's Mythology." *Folklore* 117.2 (2006): 156–70. Print.

——. "Tolkien's '"Celtic" Type of Legends': Merging Traditions." *Tolkien Studies 4* (2007): 51–71. *Project MUSE*. PDF file. 1 November 2014.

Fisher, Sheila. "Leaving Morgan Aside: Women, History, and Revisionism in *Sir Gawain and the Green Knight.*" *The Passing of Arthur: New Essays in Arthurian Tradition.* Ed. Christopher Baswell and William Sharpe. NY: Garland, 1988. 129–51. Print.

Flieger, Verlyn. "Tolkien and the Matter of Britain." *Green Suns and Faërie: Essays on J.R.R. Tolkien* Kent State UP, 2012. 127–40. Print.

Fredrick, Candice, and Sam McBride. *Women Among the Inklings: Gender, C.S. Lewis, J.R.R. Tolkien, and Charles Williams.* Contributions in Women's Studies 191. Westport, CT: Greenwood Press, 2001. Print.

Geoffrey of Monmouth. *The History of the Kings of Britain.* Trans. Lewis Thorpe. 1966. NY: Penguin, 1987. Print.

Gerald of Wales. *The Journey Through Wales and The Description of Wales.* Ed. and trans. Lewis Thorpe. 1978. NY: Penguin, 2004. Print.

Gordon-Wise, Barbara Ann. *The Reclamation of a Queen: Guinevere in Modern Fantasy.* Westport, CT: Greenwood Press, 1991. Print.

Gray, J.M. Table of Dates, Introduction. Tennyson 6–10.

Holbrook, Sue Ellen. "Guenevere: the Abbess of Amesbury and the Mark of Reparation." *Arthuriana* 20.1 (2010): 25–51. *Project Muse*. PDF file. 1 November 2014.

Hopkins, Lisa. "Female Authority Figures in the Works of Tolkien, C.S. Lewis, and Charles Williams." *Mythlore* 21.2 (1996): 364–66. Print.

Jochens, Jenny. *Old Norse Images of Women.* Philadelphia: U of Pennsylvania Press, 1996. Print.

Kaufman, Amy S. "Guenevere Burning." *Arthuriana* 20.1 (2010): 76–94. *Project MUSE*. PDF file. 1 November 2014.

King Arthur's Death: The Middle English Stanzaic Morte Arthur *and* Alliterative Morte Arthure. Ed. Larry D. Benson. Rev. Edward E. Foster. TEAMS Middle English Text Series. Kalamazoo: Medieval Institute Publications, 1994. Robbins Library Digital Projects. University of Rochester. Web. 21 August 2013.

Korrel, Peter. *An Arthurian Triangle: A Study of the Origin, Development and Characterization of Arthur, Guinevere and Modred.* Leiden: E. J. Brill, 1984. Print.

Lacon, Ruth. "On *The Fall of Arthur*: Pre-Publication Speculation by a Longtime Student." *Tolkien Library.* 20 March 2013. Web. 21 August 2013.

Lakowski, Romuald Ian. "'Perilously Fair': Titania, Galadriel, and the Fairy Queen of Medieval Romance." *Tolkien and Shakespeare: Essays on Shared Themes and Language.* Ed. Janet Brennan Croft. Jefferson, NC: Walking Tree, 2007. 60–78. Print.

Lancelot-Grail: The Old French Arthurian Vulgate and Post-Vulgate in Translation. Ed. and trans. Norris J. Lacy. 5 vols. NY: Garland, 1992–96. Print.

Laʒamon. *Laʒamons Brut, or Chronicle of Britain.* Ed. and trans. Sir Frederic Madden. Vols. 2. and 3. London: The Society of Antiquaries of London, 1847. *GoogleBooks.* Web. 21 August 2013.

Lewis, C. S. *That Hideous Strength: A Modern Fairy-Tale for Grown-Ups.* 1945. NY: Scribner, 2003. Print.

Loomis, Roger Sherman. *Wales and the Arthurian Legend.* Cardiff: U of Wales Press, 1956. Print.

The Mabinogion. Trans. Sioned Davies. Oxford World's Classics. NY: OUP, 2007. Print.

Malory, Sir Thomas. *Malory: Complete Works*. Ed. Eugène Vinaver. 1977. 2nd ed. Oxford UP, 2006. Print.

Marie de France. "Lanval." *The Lais of Marie de France*. Ed. and trans. Robert Hanning and Joan Ferrante. Grand Rapids, MI: Baker Academic, 2008. 105–25. Print.

Myers, Doris T. "Brave New World: The Status of Women According to Tolkien, Lewis, and Charles Williams." *Cimarron Review* 17 (1971): 13–19. Print.

Phelpstead, Carl. *Tolkien and Wales: Language, Literature, and Identity*. Cardiff: U of Wales Press, 2011. Print.

Rateliff, John D. "The Fall of Arthur." *Sacnoth's Scriptorium*. *Blogspot*. 23 May 2013. Web. 21 August 2013.

Rawls, Melanie. "The Feminine Principle in Tolkien." *Mythlore* 10.4 (1984): 5–13. Print.

Reynolds, Patricia and Glen H. GoodKnight, eds. *Proceedings of the J.R.R. Tolkien Centenary Conference, Keble College, Oxford, 1992*. *Mythlore* 21.2; *Mallorn* 30. Milton Keynes, U.K.: Tolkien Society; Altadena, CA: Mythopoeic Press, 1995. Print.

Rich, Janet Bubar. *Exploring Guinevere's Search for Authenticity in the Arthurian Romances*. Lewiston, NY: Edwin Mellen, 2012. Print.

The Saga of Hrolf Kraki. Trans. Stella M. Mills and E. V. Gordon. 1933. Marcellus, MI: Nodens Books, 2012. Print.

Samples, Susann. "Guinevere: A Re-Appraisal." *Lancelot and Guinevere: A Casebook*. Ed. Lori J. Walters. Garland Reference Library of the Humanities. Vol. 1513. NY: Garland, 1996. 219–28. Print.

Shippey, Tom. *The Road to Middle-earth*. 1982. Rev. ed. Boston: Houghton Mifflin, 2003. Print.

Sir Gawain and the Green Knight. Ed. and trans. William Vantuono. 1990. Rev. ed. U of Notre Dame Press, 1999. Print.

St. Clair, Gloriana. "An Overview of the Northern Influence in Tolkien's Works." Reynolds and GoodKnight 63–67.

Stimpson, Catherine R. *J.R.R. Tolkien*. Columbia Essays on Modern Writers. Vol. 41. NY: Columbia UP, 1969. Print.

Tennyson, Alfred. *Idylls of the King*. Ed. J. M. Gray. 1983. NY: Penguin, 1996. Print.

Tolhurst, Fiona. *Geoffrey of Monmouth and the Feminist Origins of the Arthurian Legend*. NY: Palgrave Macmillan, 2012. Print.

Tolkien, J. R. R. *Beowulf: A Translation and Commentary together with Sellic Spell*. Ed. Christopher Tolkien. Boston and NY: Houghton Mifflin Harcourt, 2014. Print.

——. *The Children of Húrin*. Ed. Christopher Tolkien. Boston and New York: Houghton Mifflin, 2007. Print.

——. "English and Welsh." *Monsters* 162–97.

——. *The Fall of Arthur*. Ed. Christopher Tolkien. Boston and New York: Houghton Mifflin Harcourt, 2013. Print.

——. "The Lay of Aotrou and Itroun." *The Welsh Review* 4.4 (1945): 254–66. Print.

——. *The Legend of Sigurd and Gudrún*. Ed. Christopher Tolkien. Boston and New York: Houghton Mifflin Harcourt, 2009. Print.

——. *The Letters of J.R.R. Tolkien*. Ed. Humphrey Carpenter. 1981. Boston and New York: Houghton Mifflin, 2000. Print.

——. *The Lord of the Rings*. 1954–55. Boston and New York: Houghton Mifflin, 2003. Print.

——. *The Monsters and the Critics and Other Essays*. Ed. Christopher Tolkien. 1983. London: HarperCollins, 2006. Print.

——. "On Fairy-Stories." *"The Monsters and the Critics" and Other Essays*. Ed. Christopher Tolkien. 1983. London: HarperCollins, 2006. 109–161. Print.

——. *Unfinished Tales of Númenor and Middle-earth*. Ed. Christopher Tolkien. 1980. NY: Del Rey, 1988. Print.

Trioedd Ynys Prydein: The Welsh Triads. Ed. and trans. Rachel Bromwich. 1961. 2nd ed. Cardiff: U of Wales Press, 1978. Print.

Wace. *Arthurian Chronicles: Roman de Brut*. Trans. Eugene Mason. *The Internet Archive*. Project Gutenberg. 16 December 2003. Web. 1 November 2014.

Wheeler, Bonnie, and Fiona Tolhurst, eds. *On Arthurian Women: Essays in Memory of Maureen Fries*. Dallas, TX: Scriptorium Press, 2001. Print.

Williams, Charles, and C. S. Lewis. *Taliessin through Logres; The Region of the Summer Stars; Arthurian Torso*. 1938. Grand Rapids, MI: Eerdmans, 1980. Print.

Wyatt, Sir Thomas the Elder. "Whoso list to hunt." *The Norton Anthology of English Literature*. Ed. Stephen Greenblatt. Vol. 1. 8th ed. NY: W. W. Norton, 2006. 595. Print.

14

Beatrice and Byzantium: Sex and the City in the Arthurian Works of Charles Williams

Andrew Rasmussen

After the unexpected death of Charles Williams in 1945, C. S. Lewis rushed to publish *Arthurian Torso,* a collection of Williams' notes on the Arthurian myth and Lewis' own commentary on Williams' Arthurian poetry. He published this book as a tribute to his dear friend and out of concern that the lyrical cycle "if left without a commentary, might soon become another such battlefield for competing interpretations as Blake's *Prophetic Books*" (1). His concern was well founded. Like Blake, Williams was a startlingly original thinker whose dense poetry relies upon layers of his own iconography that resist even the most dedicated readers. Indeed, even T. S. Eliot warns potential readers that the poems will "expect a good deal" of them, though he offers the encouraging note that the poems are "absorbing after we have got the hang of what [Williams] is after." *Arthurian Torso* is designed to help readers get the hang of the lyrical cycles, but this interpretive schema has not entirely prevented clashes over *Taliessin through Logres* and *The Region of the Summer Stars.* A number of scholarly skirmishes have sprung up over the years as critics have grappled with Williams' complicated works. Many of these discussions center on Williams' controversial portrayals of women, particularly when read in light of his romantic theology. For Williams, romantic theology is the study of romantic love as a pattern of, and stepping stone toward, divine love. The most vivid example, for Williams, is Dante's love of Beatrice, where the poet learns that experiencing earthly love is also literally experiencing heavenly love (*ORT* 56). While the role of sanctified lover is theoretically gender-neutral, Williams' work generally casts men in this role while women serve as the beloved who bestows sanctification. In this, Williams seems to echo the worst habits of his nineteenth-century predecessors; however, this reading is complicated by Williams' doctrine of the City—presented in his Arthurian poetry through the figure of Byzantium. By reading Williams through this civic lens, this essay complicates existing readings of Williams by specifically engaging with his concepts of individuality, submission, and hierarchy.

Such a reading is essential for understanding Williams, because women lie at the heart of his imagination. It is not coincidental that his novels regularly star female heroines or that his Camelot is populated with more ladies than knights. Yet their centrality is rarely independent. Men and women exist as men and women in relation; their gendered distinctions are defined by the nature of their unity: The City, an image that Lewis says "had always haunted Williams" and that is linked inextricably with marriage (WA 104).[1] Although the term is clearly drawn from St. Augustine, Williams redefines the City through his works into a blend of religious unification and erotic fixation. Like Augustine, Williams envisions the City as both Being and Becoming. When he defines the City as "the sense of many relationships between men and women woven into a unity," Williams is imagining these relationships as both participating in the present City and pointing toward the City that is to come ("Image of the City" 92). Because of this, men and women in Williams' poetry need to be understood in terms of their present relationships and the relationships that they are developing.[2] A discussion of gender in Williams is necessarily a discussion of the City.

Williams is certainly not alone in his equation of marriage and civic life, drawing extensively upon the works of nineteenth-century poets and thinkers. Coventry Patmore, whose poem "The Angel in the House" is widely viewed as the premier illustration of Victorian marriage ideals, was a particular favorite of Williams', but it is the works of G. W. F. Hegel that most directly anticipate his own. While it is not clear whether Williams read Hegel, his intense interest in Søren Kierkegaard suggests the possibility. In any case, it is Hegel who most clearly articulates the nineteenth-century doctrine of civic marriage that would serve as a crucial foundation for Williams' myths.

For Hegel, marriage is understood as the "consent" of the concerned parties "to *constitute a single person* and to give up their natural and individual personalities within this union. In this respect, their union is a self-limitation, but since they attain their substantial self-consciousness within it, it is in fact their liberation" (Hegel 201; emphasis original). By framing marriage in this way, he hopes to resist attempts to categorize marriage as either sexual intercourse, as in primitive societies; arbitrary social contract, as in Kant; or "the transient, capricious, and purely subjective aspects of love" as seen in particularly bad love poetry (201). Instead, marriage combines all three components into a single objective reality with its own union as a substantial end. In this way, marriage becomes the model for Hegel's *sittlichkeit,* the ethical life, or what Williams would later call the City.

The state, or the highest form of *sittlichkeit,* consists of a complicated relationship between individuals and the state. In this system, individuals submit their wills to the state in order to achieve their highest sense of individuality: "Since the state is objective spirit, it is only through being a member of the state that the individual himself has objectivity, truth, and ethical life. *Union* as such is itself the true content and end, and the destiny of individuals is to lead a universal life" (276; emphasis original). The key to *sittlichkeit* is aligning the individual will with the will of the state, just as the key to marriage is the unification of personalities within a single person. Williams describes it this way: "It is hierarchic and republican at

---

1   For Williams, marriage is the proper end of romantic relationships and is discussed in both its romantic and sexual functions. In this paper, I follow his use of the term.

2   This is most clear in his novel *The Place of the Lion* (1931).

once … where everything and everyone is unique and is the subject of due adoration so, and yet, all being unique, 'none is afore or after other, none is greater or less than another'" (*HCD* 98).

Like Hegel, the mutual submission of wills necessary for Williams' City is modeled in, and created by, marriage and romantic love. It is difficult not to hear an echo of Hegel when Williams writes: "The name of the City is Union … the process of that union is by the method of free exchange. The methods of that exchange range from childbirth to the Eucharist—the two primal activities of the earth and the Church" ("Redeemed City" 103). But Williams does not merely restate Hegel. Instead, he begins to mythologize his thinking. It is highly significant that in "The Image of the City in English Verse," a 1940 essay for the *Dublin Review,* he claims that "The best single image of the heavenly City is perhaps in the prose sentence from the Apocalypse: 'I saw the Holy City, the New Jerusalem, descending out of heaven from God'" (*Image* 92). We must remember, however, that the "prose sentence from the Apocalypse" that Williams quotes is not the complete sentence. St. John does not see merely a city descending from God, but rather one "descending out of heaven from God, prepared as a bride adorned for her husband" (Rev. 21:2). Marriage is no longer a stepping-stone toward the City, but now an act of the City itself. The New Jerusalem is both a City and a Bride; it is both Beatrice and Byzantium.

The most explicitly developed version of this myth can be seen, as Lewis has suggested, in Williams' Arthurian poetry. While it is extremely important throughout the cycle, the link between Beatrice and Byzantium is particularly important to *Taliessin through Logres,* the first Arthurian cycle, which centers on the relationship between the Empire[3]—imagined as a woman—and the Emperor, a masculine God-figure. Indeed, Williams quite literally begins and ends his first volume with the image of Empire-as-woman. This occurs first in the glorious poem "The Vision of the Empire," when Taliessin returns to Logres. He imagines the Empire-as-woman luxuriating in the harmony of her body, witnessing as "the stripped maids laughed for the joy of the province, / bearing in themselves the shape of the province" ("The Vision of the Empire," lines 36–37).[4] Maidens bear the image of the Empire, as men bear the image of the Emperor, and the entirety of Creation is briefly imagined as Edenically joined in civic and erotic unity. The poem continues in this way, defining the geography of the myth, wandering lovingly over the body of Byzantium. Then, in the end, as readers are left with the last hopeful lines of "Taliessin at Lancelot's Mass," they are again confronted with the image of Byzantium. Here, at least in the 1938 edition of *Taliessin through Logres,* is a rather startling end-piece of a nude woman lounging over and as Europe: Byzantium. Her anatomy is mapped out precisely, each part of the body reflecting its corresponding geography as described in "The Vision of the Empire." This extended conceit that quite literally begins and ends the cycle undergirds all that happens within.

And yet, despite the many illustrations of gendered relationships, the "many relationships between men and women" remain clouded behind Williams' rich poetic pageantry. Even in the partial explanation that "the process of [the City] is by the method of free exchange. The methods of that exchange range from childbirth

---

3   Lewis identifies this Empire as the final, most mature, image of Williams' City (WA 104–05).

4   References to poems from *TtL* and *RSS* are from David Dodds's *Arthurian Poets* volume unless otherwise noted. [Editor's note]

to the Eucharist—the two primal activities of the earth and the Church," he does not offer clear definitions for the range of activities between these two "primal activities" ("Redeemed City" 103). This ambiguity is where scholars have fought their skirmishes, attempting to define the roles left to women in Williams' poetic vision. One of the first areas that needs to be addressed is Williams' tendency, particularly in his poetry, to submerge characters' personalities within their symbolic roles. This neo-platonic tendency can be difficult to follow, particularly if one is not familiar with Williams' views. A clear example of this technique occurs in "Taliessin in the Rose Garden," where Taliessin, the king's poet, encounters three women:

> the feminine headship of Logres, the queen Guinevere,
> talking to Dindrane, Percival's sister; beyond,
> as the ground-work she was and tended, a single maid
> hardened with toil on the well-gardened roses:
> what was even Dindrane but an eidolon of the slaves?
> ("Taliessin in the Rose-Garden" lines 14–18).

Each woman is introduced by Williams as a symbolic figure whose present Being points inexorably to her future Becoming. Guinevere, Taliessin observes, is "the feminine headship of Logres," and this title contains all the symbolic possibilities available to her. C. S. Lewis argues that this poem shows Guinevere "as she truly is; sees both what she was intended to be and what she has become; sees in the fall of Guinevere the Fall of Man and sees also the cosmic significance of Woman" (WA 146). Guinevere, as the head of Logres, comes to stand in for her kingdom metonymically. Her relationship with Arthur stands for the Emperor's relationship with Byzantium, and her fall from that union due to the affair with Lancelot parallels Byzantium's own fall from Imperial union. As Lewis observes:

> The whole City, the Divine Order, is a marriage between the will of the Emperor and the response to that will in His creatures. Caucasia itself, the body, the world of the senses, is feminine in relation to Carbonek, the Spirit; for sanctity orders and uses all the body's energies. (WA 148)

The cosmic significance of Woman is its physicality; the body that it provides for the masculine thought of the Emperor. However, a distinction must be made here between "cosmic" Woman and women such as Guinevere, Dindrane, and the "single maid / hardened with toil." Cosmic Woman exists as a response to the will of God, the Emperor; but for Williams, Cosmic Woman is also the Church. When the City descends as a Bride in the Book of Revelation, it is not only the female saints who wed Christ.

Thus when Guinevere symbolically serves as Byzantium, she is representing all of Creation. Her fall to temptation does not occur because she is a woman, but because she is human. Guinevere's appearance in the rose-garden evokes Eden; she herself is a rose: thin, dressed in green, with only the rose-red-royal ring of Logres as decoration. She is the rose of Logres, the consort of the king. The ring serves as both her pride and her fall, her genitalia and sexuality.

Taliessin observes that the rose-garden is "a verse into the wound" of the Dolorous Blow, the point of rupture in union between Emperor and Empire. In Byzantium, this rupture occurs at Jerusalem—the genitalia of the Empire. The garden, the wound, and the queen's ring blur together in a blend of reds, and the king's poet "heard himself say: / 'The Wounded Rose runs with blood at Carbonek'" ("Taliessin in the Rose Garden" 50–51). Taliessin combines the Dolorous Blow with the menstrual cycle, arguing that women's bodies bear the mark of the Fall. He claims that women "sob with the curse" and are "warned from serving the altar," because they already "share with the Sacrifice the victimization of blood" (158, 160, 162). Williams is particularly unpersuasive here, but he seems to be arguing that the location of the wound symbolically bars women from offering sexual and spiritual union. In this, Williams again recalls the distinction between matter and form, emphasizing the feminine nature of matter:

> Flesh knows what spirit knows,
> but spirit knows it knows—categories of identity:
> women's flesh lives the quest of the Grail
> in the change from Camelot to Carbonek and from Carbonek to Sarras,
> puberty to Carbonek, and the stanching, and Carbonek to death.
> Blessed is she who gives herself to the journey.
> ("Taliessin in the Rose-Garden" 163–69).

Elisabeth Brewer writes that this passage "may offend those who argue for the ordination of women," but prefers to note the way that Williams "never underestimates [women's] spiritual potential" (100–01). Guinevere herself is a failure because she "prevents the sensuous from achieving the integration with the intellectual and spiritual which is to be desired," but the poem is ultimately successful because it "give[s] rise to the formulation of a series of insights into the nature of women. They enable men better to know and understand themselves" (Brewer 101).

Although it is tempting to read this tendency of Williams' allegorically and to then say that his treatment of Guinevere is a condemnation of all women, it may be more helpful to recall Hegel's claim that "the destiny of individuals is to lead a universal life" (276). Guinevere is not an allegory of the Fall, but rather an individual whose fallen nature inevitably comes to imitate the Fall. Here again is the pattern of Being and Becoming. Guinevere is fallen, but she also falls as she commits adultery.

Dindrane, in contrast, is recognized as the completed woman who remains chaste and holy. Williams does not immediately make it clear why Dindrane is allowed to escape the fall and make the "correct" choice (we must assume the Anglican doctrine of prevenient grace), but it is her contemplative and intellectual purity that leads Dindrane to reject earthly pleasures. She ultimately seeks out a convent, becoming a symbol of intellectual virtue removed literally and figuratively from the world. Her holiness, as much as Guinevere's carnality, is again viewed symbolically: "what was even Dindrane but an eidolon of the slaves?" ("Taliessin in the Rose-Garden" 18). In a sense, the Queen and Dindrane, adulterous and chaste women, are presented as the options for the slave tending "roses"—themselves a metaphor for women. The slave girl is drawn to the sort of universal life that Dindrane and Guinevere have already achieved.

While Guinevere stands symbolically for the Fall of all creation, a number of critics have noticed that Williams consistently shows women falling and bearing the marks of the Fall. Even "good" women who resist temptation, such as Dindrane, are banished "off-screen" to convents or similar locales. The most significant work of criticism on this subject is likely Andrea Freud Loewenstein's *Loathsome Jews and Engulfing Women*. The study, which emerged from her doctoral dissertation, offers an exploration of what might be called the Native Other: English Jews and Women who, despite their Anglo heritage, are nonetheless often treated as outgroups. Loewenstein offers a psychoanalytic reading that draws upon novels and biographical information as equally essential texts for understanding the authors. She is careful to clarify that she is not simply equating the opinions of a character with those of the author, but rather that she is referring "to an attitude which seems to me pervasive, basic to the works in question, and clearly indicative of the author's own conscious or unconscious attitude or feelings" (9).

In her chapter on Williams, she argues that he is a textbook obsessive-compulsive who "suffers from the need to control the universe and the grandiose fear that he might do so" (189). This world-conquering desire, she observes, always motivates at least one of his characters who must be stopped by the intervention of various manifestations of Williams' City—resubmitting the individual ego to the corporate. Loewenstein describes this process as an "extrusion machine" founded upon the double nature of man that takes sins and through "various mechanistic operations, including role-playing, arrangement into rigid hierarchies, exchange, co-inherence, and substitution, convert[s] these raw materials and extrude[s] them out in the form of Christian goodness" (189). This is a system that, she believes, Williams applied to both himself and others and that manifests itself in his works. In this reading, Williams' symbolic writing is not so much neo-platonic as it is misogynist. Women are forced to submit to masculine desires or are banished from the City.

In "The Departure of Dindrane," it is possible to see a clear example of this extrusion machine. Taliessin and Dindrane are in love. Yet rather than consummate their love through the sacrament of marriage, Dindrane is escorted by Taliessin to the convent at Almesbury. And yet for Williams, this is a celebration and not a rejection of their love. A slave girl from Athens notes that

> the hands of the great personalities linked as they rode,
> as they rode fast, close-handed, oath-bonded,
> word-in-the-flesh-branded, each seconded
> to the other, each in the crowd of Camelot vowed
> to the other .... ("The Departure of Dindrane" 106–10)

They are not married, and yet their union is higher than a physical marriage. Dindrane has rejected the "gay hunter and his spear flesh-hued" in favor of the "intellectual nuptials" demanded by great poets and poetry ("Taliessin's Song of the Unicorn" 17, 36). The two have become, intellectually, as one person. In the terms of Loewenstein's extrusion machine, Taliessin and Dindrane have transformed their sinful, earthly lust into a spiritual love and adoration. They do this by precisely the means that Loewenstein has identified: their burdens are exchanged with each other and with the households that they embody.

Yet although both are able to achieve this holiness, it must be noted that they achieve it in very different ways. Taliessin is allowed to return to Camelot and the court after escorting Dindrane to Almesbury, but she must remain cloistered away from the world. Williams is careful to frame this scene as a balance "between city and convent, the two great vocations, / the Rejection of all images before the unimaged, / the Affirmation of all images before the all-imaged," but it is only in Dindrane's heart that "servitude and freedom were one and interchangeable" ("The Departure of Dindrane" 86–88, 77). Taliessin is not required to offer the same self-denying submission, and even Dindrane's household is only Taliessin's on temporary loan. After she, a jewel of the court, is deposited safely at Almesbury, they are to return to Camelot.

For Loewenstein, this division of roles is not accidental:

> Through his system, Williams manages to distance or disarm women as needed. It classifies them into two categories: evil, grasping bitches who are instruments of the devil and Slave-Goddesses. The evil women must be hunted down and destroyed before they can achieve their aim of destroying men, while the Slave-Goddesses must be worshiped at a safe distance and punished for their own good. (190)

In this reading, Dindrane becomes a Slave-Goddess imprisoned at Almesbury. She is able to bless Taliessin, and thus the realm, by inspiring his poetry, but she must be kept away from him lest her tempting beauty ruin his spiritual inspiration.

This certainly is the lesson taken by the Athenian slave girl. Contemplating her own upcoming freedom, she considers returning home to Athens or marrying a friend and having her own house. Instead, drawing from Dindrane's example, she decides to swear herself to Taliessin's service for life ("The Departure of Dindrane" 167–73). Bondage to such a lord is preferable to her own, potentially dangerous, freedom. Her service is presented by Williams as admirable, of the individual aligning her desires with the household, but in Loewenstein's reading it is telling that it is the woman who must submit her desires. Indeed, the admiration that Williams offers to Dindrane and the Athenian slave makes his apparent misogyny "especially disturbing" to her "because it is hidden under the saccharine religiosity and gentle loving-kindness which are so central to his self-image" (240). She fears that he lays a trap for his female readers by offering women "obeisance, gentle attention, and the appealing doctrines of co-inherence and exchange. Only later does one realize that in his system, the Goddess is a slave" (240).

While this criticism of Williams is certainly valid, it seems that Loewenstein, ironically, goes too far by denying the agency of many women in the poems. As Elisabeth Brewer argues:

> Of course women in the "Taliessin" poems are important for him as symbols rather than as individuals, and for their spiritual potential rather than as sexual objects, but such recognition as this implies is surely to be welcomed. Women are presented as symbols, without condescension, enabling Williams to make profound observations about the nature of women's experience: "dying each other's life, living each other's death." (114)

Dindrane's choice is her own, not Taliessin's: "the shell of her body / yearned along the road to the cell of vocation" ("The Departure of Dindrane" 161–62). She is, in fact, so focused on her vocation that she does not turn back. Taliessin and his horse are the only participants in this poem who seem to regret Dindrane's monastic aspirations, but he submits to her will out of love.

While it could be argued that this portrayal of a woman whose own desires conveniently enslave her at Almesbury is wish-fulfillment of the worst sort, it must be noted that Dindrane's self-denial is echoed most directly by Galahad. He, raised amongst nuns, begs forgiveness for his birth before achieving the Grail and reuniting Logres and the Empire ("Percivale at Carbonek" 38–40). This is a complete denial of self that is portrayed as the ultimate act of the City. Williams is not an egalitarian, but his belief in the importance of submission and self-denial in order to participate in the union of the City should not be confused with misogyny. Indeed, Lewis suggests that Arthur's own sin of incest with Morgause, accidental as it may have been, is precisely the same lack of self-denial practiced by Guinevere: "Arthur, had he been chaste, would not have begotten Mordred" (WA 130).

Yet although Loewenstein goes too far in her broad condemnation of submission, which at least theoretically for Williams is grounded in Christian self-denial, she is right to observe that Williams is more likely to require women to submit than men. Because of this, Loewenstein's next criticism is more complicated. She notes that the submissive role of women in Williams' poetry often extends to literal slavery and that such slavery is often erotic in Williams' poetry and life.

In "The Queen's Servant," he presents another of Taliessin's female slaves being sent from his service to the queen's. Because the royals of Logres cannot be served by slaves, the servant is granted freedom, which she prefers to view as "the final task of servitude" (17). She is released from service through a ritual in which she is stripped of her old garments and old life in order to stand "shining naked / and rose-flushed" before Taliessin (42–43). As she stands nude before him, she casts rose petals at his feet while he in turn magically transforms those petals into a gown and cloak for her. Throughout the poem, Taliessin's magic, though intellectual, remains strongly focused on her body. The rose buds, Williams tells us repeatedly, "clung to her" and as her clothes are fashioned "the roses climbed round her; shoulder to knee, / they clung and twined" (60, 84). The fantasy is completed when she begs him for a final gift that he grants:

> Lightly he struck her face; at once the blast
> of union struck her heart, the art-magic
> blended fast with herself, while all she
> burned before him, colour of cloak and kirtle
> surpassed by colour of flesh. (115–19)

Her freedom, like that of the Athenian slave girl and Dindrane, is best realized in submission. But here the submission is reinforced by a ritual blow. She submits and is struck. The striking brings her into "union"—another word for the City—and her body flushes rose, the color Williams associates with idealized femininity. By freely choosing this submission, the queen's new servant is able to rise above the limitations of herself.

The "ritualized bondage and flagellation" that Williams describes in this poem, and others, reflects the interactions that he appears to have had with at least one of his disciples, the much younger Lois Lang-Sims, as he wrote *The Region of the Summer Stars*. In *Letters to Lalage*, she tells us how he renamed her (Lang-Sims

52—although she chose the name), commanded her to do him service (33, 37), struck her with a ruler—for which she thanked him (47), spanked her (68), and reimagined their interactions through poetic role-play (41, 67–70). He, of course, was Taliessin, while she was cast as Lalage, Taliessin's neglectful slave girl who frequently needed to be punished (Lang-Sims 38, 47; cf. Loewenstein 210–15).

For Loewenstein, the sadomasochistic tendencies of Williams' life and poetry reflect his obsessive need to control the world.[5] Women, she argues, exist for him as an Other that is frightening in its autonomy. By engaging in hierarchical eroticism and role-play, Williams is able to extend his control even to something as intrinsically chaotic and uncontrollable as sexuality and romance. She grounds this theory in Freud and Shapiro, arguing that Williams' preference for ritualized eroticism reflects his obsessive-compulsive need to control the world:

> The rigid boundaries of these relationships helped him to confine his own unacceptable libidinal impulses and assert his fragile boundaries while functioning within the safe confines of his private myth. He was able to chastise and beat down invasive and evil women as well as the evil and invasive female inside himself, while simultaneously gaining access to the female energy or force which he so badly needed. (Loewenstein 213)

By conflating Williams' doctrine of submission and self-denial with the ritual bondage of his personal life and poetry, Loewenstein badly misrepresents Williams. Considering only Dindrane and Guinevere, it is clear that Williams is not as interested in "chastis[ing] and beat[ing] down invasive and evil women" as Loewenstein asserts. It is Dindrane, the model woman, who is confined to a convent and not the wicked Guinevere.

As has already been discussed, Loewenstein interprets the convent at Almesbury as a prison in which Dindrane remains kept as a Slave-Goddess to bless Taliessin at a distance. This reading denies Dindrane her own agency, instead insisting that her desire to join a convent is no more than the representation of Williams' fantasies about a woman who imprisons herself. That Dindrane herself seems to view the move as a representation of her preference for intellectual, rather than physical, love—a step toward her own universal life—is ignored. Further, it equates Dindrane's preference for life in a convent with the slave's desire to be physically struck and beaten. For Loewenstein, feminine self-denial is always a tool of oppression, but for Williams, self-denial is an essential part of participating in the kingdom of God. Dindrane and Galahad are lauded for their self-denial, just as Arthur and Guinevere are punished for their lack of self-denial.

Recognizing the distinction between submission and bondage, however, does not address the troubling scene that Williams paints of a slave girl asking to be struck in the face by her master. Loewenstein's portrayal of this scene as the result of Taliessin's masculine, abusive power is compelling, but it relies on

---

5   Grevel Lindop, in the newly released biography *Charles Williams: The Third Inkling*, claims that Williams' sexual behavior with his disciples was an "addiction," a "compulsive pattern of dependency" (340), and provides many more instances, not all of which were consensual. [Editor's note]

a stigmatizing view of bondage that has little support in the literature on the subject or amongst participants in the lifestyle.

Despite Loewenstein's claim that this scene draws on Williams' own obsessive-compulsive desire for control, "Consensual Sadomasochistic Sex (BDSM): The Roots, The Risks, and the Distinctions Between BDSM and Violence," a 2013 study by Eva Jozifkova of over two hundred participants in the lifestyle, argues that "practitioners of consensual sadomasochistic sex (BDSMers) do not suffer from psychological disorders, nor were [they] victims of child sex abuse" (1). Taliessin is not acting out of a deep-seated need to control and oppress women when he strikes the slave girl, nor is the slave responding to forgotten abuses. Indeed, their activities seem to echo Jozifkova's description of "healthy BDSM," as opposed to violent or abusive. Healthy sadomasochism relies on good communication, an agreement on theatrical "scenes," and the submissive's power to call off the scene and/or relationship with a "safeword" or other gestures (3–4). In this poem, the action is driven by the submissive slave—she requests the ritual, she requests the blow, and ultimately it is she who leaves and walks free.

A similar argument is made by Beverly L. Stiles and Robert E. Clark. In "BDSM: A Subcultural Analysis of Sacrifices and Delights," they quote an anonymous twenty-four-year-old female submissive who argues directly against the various stigmas attached to BDSM: "A misconception is that BDSM (S&M) is abuse. It is portrayed that way on many shows (*CSI*, *NYPD Blue*, *The Inside*). What is being portrayed is abuse and criminal and wrongly mislabeled as BDSM" (174). For her and other participants in the study, there is a sharp distinction between criminal abuse and "real" BDSM. Like Jozifkova, she insists that BDSM behavior is not a mental illness or aberration resulting from abuse as a child, but rather a natural sexual preference. Others in this study note the increased sense of intimacy experienced in a BDSM relationship, observing the extreme levels of trust needed to perform some of these scenes.

Now, I want to be careful to not overstate this point. These studies show that the BDSM scenes portrayed and hinted at in Williams' life and poetry are neither necessarily abusive nor the result of psychological trauma. Yet at the same time, Williams does have a troubling tendency to portray men as dominant and women as submissive. Williams' sadomasochistic tendencies may not be abusive, but they are also certainly *not* egalitarian. For the sake of his poetry, however, it may be more fruitful to explore these tendencies through Foucault rather than Freud. The most striking thing about Williams' sadomasochism is his consistent portrayal of these rituals as possessing spiritual and artistic value. When the slave in "The Queen's Servant" is struck in the face, she is brought into the holy union of the City of God, and Williams insists that he himself is only able to write poetry by drawing energy from his disciples in these rituals (qtd. in Loewenstein 212; cf. Lang-Sims 69, Hadfield 106).

Williams' insistence on talking about sex and sexuality is not a revelation of his progressive nature. His frankness does not anticipate the sexual revolution of the 1960's, but rather points back to the rationality of the eighteenth and nineteenth centuries. Foucault observes that the sexual repression of the Victorians led unexpectedly to a proliferation of sexual discourse:

> One had to speak of sex; one had to speak publicly and in a manner that was not determined by the division of between licit and illicit ... one had to speak of it as of a thing to be not simply condemned

or tolerated but managed, inserted into systems of utility, regulated for the greater good of all, made to function according to an optimum. (24)

For Foucault, this public discourse becomes necessary as the state begins to note the economic power of populations as opposed to individuals. They become invested in recording sexuality and quantifying it, and this act of recording leads to an ever-increasing variety of sexual categories. Sex then becomes a double thing: the dominant discourse and ineffable secret. Foucault could almost be speaking of Williams when he writes that these societies "dedicated themselves to speaking of [sex] *ad infinitum*, while exploiting it as *the secret*" (35; emphasis original).

In Williams, sexuality is justified precisely through Foucault's formula; it is discussed as marriage, the foundation of union and the City. Viewed in this way, the various romantic pairings of his poems—Bors and Elayne, Arthur and Guinevere, Lancelot and Guinevere, Taliessin and Dindrane, and so forth—are his explorations of the various possible relations between men and women. The relationships that function intellectually, such as Taliessin and Dindrane's, are held up as models for the City. Those that are based on a more physical romance, such as Guinevere and Lancelot's, are discouraged. Understood this way, it is possible to see the BDSM episode appealing to Williams as a way to transform the physical sexual act into an intellectual, poetic scene.

These explorations on romance and sexuality are the most mature form of a process that had begun for Williams over a decade earlier in *Outlines of Romantic Theology* (unpublished until after his death). In this pamphlet, which he had worked on in 1924–25 while composing many of the early drafts for *Taliessin through Logres*, Williams articulates in prose some of his early thoughts on the subject. Although it is not as thoughtful or well-researched as his later works of theology, witnessing the development of his thought will help clarify the later Arthurian works.

In *Outlines of Romantic Theology*, he presents his view that those in love quite literally experience a piece of heaven, and he is concerned that these experiences be taken seriously. He argues that

> This term [Romantic Theology] does not imply, as will inevitably at first be thought, a theology based merely on fantasy and dream, and concerning itself only with illogical sentimentalities. It is a theology as exact as any other kind, but having for cause and subject those experiences of man which, anyhow in discussions of art, are generally termed "Romantic." (7)

For Williams, this area of theology is just as important as Christology or soteriology, but it has been neglected by the church, since most theologians are priests, and priests who, historically, are celibate. Due to celibacy, they cannot fully write on romance—which to Williams is physical, spiritual, and intellectual—and so Williams instead turns to a sort of surrogate, secular priesthood: poets. He is particularly interested in Dante, Wordsworth, and Malory. Dante is especially important because he understands the relation between romantic love—in Beatrice—and divine love. Williams argues that Beatrice is at once both a woman *and* theology; that love for the one naturally points to the other. If earthly cities are patterned on and point to heavenly cities, then likewise earthly love is patterned on and points to heavenly love. Indeed, when fully realized, the love does more than merely hint at divinity:

> By the writings of Dante and of minds like his the rest of us have been made aware of the profundities which are concealed in this fastidious and passionate devotion … we become aware that we do not excusably exaggerate in saying, for example, "It's heaven to be with her", but on the contrary express without perhaps realizing it an eternal and immortal truth. (*ORT* 56)

Building from this understanding, Williams argues that romantic theology is primarily worked out through the sacrament of marriage. Again, Williams is very deliberate in his choice of words. Marriage is important precisely because of its sacramental nature; like Communion, marriage functions as an expression of free and holy grace. Because of this, Williams writes, "In marriage, as everywhere else, the Church is concerned with the regeneration of man" (10). This is to say that, for Williams, marriage is not an end in and of itself. Instead, marriage is meant as a step toward the end; the end is to be assumed into Divinity (59), to be made one with the Body and Blood of Love (60).

Even in these early stages, it becomes clear that Williams is confused when it comes to the practical, physical aspects of marriage. Sex, the literal union between a man and a woman, is in many ways the ultimate realization of his ideas. Despite this, his discussion over marriage remains centered on the spiritual and intellectual components. He acknowledges the importance of sex, particularly in his criticism of priestly celibacy, but primarily discusses it poetically. Indeed, "Taliessin's Song of the Unicorn" actively rewrites a woman's orgasm into poetry:

> ... O she
> translucent, planted with virtue, lit by throes,
> should be called the Mother of the Unicorn's Voice, men see
> her with awe, her son the new sound that goes
> surrounding the City's reach. (29–33)

It is significant that Williams views the importance of this woman's orgasm through a male, potentially voyeuristic, gaze. Her pleasure in the moment is immediately subordinated to the needs of men and then to the needs of the City. Her sexual experience is not valued for the act of union between her and her lover, but rather because of the union provided by male poetry—imagined here as her son—that was produced by her experience. In this passage, Williams almost echoes one popular misinterpretation of St. Paul's declaration that women "will be saved through childbearing" (1 Tim. 2:15). Union is a product of her child's work rather than her own agency.

This method of discourse is not only his latent Victorian modesty, but also a result of his inability to escape his male subjectivity. Female sexuality is acknowledged, but only insofar as it serves a male end. While union is theoretically available to both men and women, Williams is only able to imagine it as a masculine reunification of the Self with the Other. Thus, male subjectivity is served by female objectivity, and the old forms of romance—in which the male achieves the woman/grail at the end of the quest—re-emerge in

Williams' poetry. Williams' ambiguity about sex then is really his ambiguity about the relationship between the old doctrines of romance and the union offered by the City to all.

This dialectic can be seen by observing the development of Williams' Arthurian vision. Even in his earliest poetry, Williams is attempting, unsuccessfully, to resolve this tension. This can be most clearly seen in "Percivale's Song to Blanchfleur," a predecessor of "The Vision of the Empire," which was composed only two or three years after *Outlines of Romantic Theology*. In this poem, written for his platonic mistress Phyllis Jones, Williams takes up the role of Sir Percivale, answering questions from his "sister in sanctity"[6] concerning Arthur's court. Williams' guilt over his adultery and his belief in the genuinely revelatory power of romantic attraction plays itself out through a virginal eroticism. The open discussion of this romance again seems to work as Foucault suggests that it might: the transgressive power of sexuality, here adultery, is transformed into civic virtue and holiness.

In order to accomplish this transformation, Williams turns to the traditional Arthurian quest for the Holy Grail. He notes that the grail quest is "the supreme invention of Christendom of a story concerned with the adventures and ineffable destiny of romantic love" (*ORT* 60). The quest succeeds, in Malory, for three knights: Galahad, Percivale, and Bors. In Williams' reading, each knight comes to express one of "the three degrees of love—love in marriage, love between two persons who are in contemplation of, but without desire for, each other, their desire being only toward God, and love whose contemplation and desire alike is toward nothing but God" (59). Galahad's virginal focus on the grail allows his mystical union and communion, but this same unity is not denied to Percivale and his intellectual nuptials nor to the wedded Bors. Instead, it is implied that each degree of love offers the same concluding unity. Just as Hegel's *sittlichkeit* is achieved by means of marriage or the Holy Spirit, Williams' City is achieved by marriage or the Grail. Unlike Hegel, however, Williams' schematic does not offer the same opportunity to both men and women. In his Romantic theology, women become equated with the grail—they are objects for which one quests. The grail quest successfully solves the tension between eroticism and chastity, but only for the male subject.

In a sense, the grail functions in these earlier poems as Louwenstein's extrusion machine. The quest for the grail is a quest for freedom from and transformation of sin. Adultery and lust are transformed by a sort of mystical alchemy into Christian virtue, and the land is saved from the Dolorous Blow. Yet the price for this salvation is the extrusion of not only adultery and lust, but also the physical fact of women's bodies. They instead exist as symbols of the City, incarnate Ideas that men are able to partake in.

This is why "Percivale's Song to Blanchefleur," which is modelled on a traditional blazon, seems to hesitate in its descriptions of Blanchefleur's body. For Percivale, the intellectual lover that Williams so admired, Blanchefleur's body is important only in so far as it points to the poet's ideas. In this case, she comes to incarnate the myth of Britain. C. S. Lewis suggests that "consciously or not Williams is here

---

6   For Williams, it never made sense that Percivale had an actual sister with him when he achieved the Grail. In his own poetry, he assumed that the "sister" was platonic love in which physicality did not intervene. David Llewellyn Dodds points out that this understanding of Percivale and his "sister" is a selective synthesis of "Malory, where Percivale has an actual, and unnamed, sister, with Gerbert's continuation of Chretien's *Perceval*, where Perceval and Blanchefleur are virginal *lovers*" (158).

recalling the Greek doctrine that Form is masculine and Matter feminine" (WA 147); but I suspect that Williams is actually recalling another Greek doctrine: Gnosticism, that rejects the world of the flesh for the world of the mind. It is a curious thing to accuse Williams of Gnosticism, but his physical descriptions at this early stage are surprisingly not physical: "Are not those deep eyes / Merlin," he wonders without telling us their color or effect. Blanchefleur's breasts are awkwardly described as "the queen Morgause of Orkney, on the right / Guinevere: O living breasts of love and light" (lines 73–74, 49–50). Here the breasts have been related to the court, but the relation is forced and unpersuasive. In what ways are breasts like queens, save only that knights and kings admire them? Fortunately, Williams realized the inadequacy of these metaphors and few made it into later drafts. One particularly interesting connection remains, as Dodd observes, between the hands and palms of women and the clergy.[7]

Williams is most reticent, of course, when describing Blanchefleur's genitalia. They, as the instruments of unity, are the center of the poem, but they are never explicitly named or described. Instead, Percivale drops the metaphor of the body and deals with the signified Idea directly:

> This is the destined and thrice holy place
> where is the Action and the last embrace,
> this is the Mother of the Achievement, here
> the Symbol that is fashioned everywhere. (61–64)

Percivale does not mention the vulva, the clitoris, or the vagina. Instead, Blanchefleur's genitalia are combined into a single "Action and the last embrace." This is not a surprising move, of course. An Englishman writing to a lady in 1927 could not possibly make such distinctions. He would need to overcome both his own masculine ignorance and a general societal stigma against such conversations. And yet, by equating the grail with women's genitals, Williams demands such precision. The achievement of the Grail is the moment when two are made one; it is both the physical sex act and the holy act of Communion. If romantic theology is to remain as "exact" as any other theology, then it must be particularly precise in its consummation—yet Williams limits himself to metaphor. "What then is the Achievement of the Grail?" he writes, "to be conscious of [God's presence in the Sacrament] as one is conscious of oneself, Christ-conscious instead of self-conscious. The achievement of the Grail is the perfect fulfillment of this, the thing happening" (ORT 78–79).

In this metaphor, Williams begins to introduce some of the precision that he requires. In the first place, as has already been discussed, by identifying the grail—and thus women—as something to be "achieved," he limits it—and them—to a role as object. This status as object is reinforced by its role as the location of

---

7   Williams has long associated hands with salvation and the act of the sacraments. Hands are the tools by which humans make their will known; clasping hands is an image that Williams equates particularly strongly with unity. Dodd notes that this can be traced back to the previous decade in "Ecclesia Docens," published in *Poems of Conformity*, where the hands of Florence Conway (his then fiancée) and of the Apostles are compared. The image is even stronger in "Churches," of the same volume, where Williams writes that "our linked fingers teach direct / our spiritual intellect" (68).

"the Action and the last embrace." In his metaphor, the grail exists to receive the quester's actions in a loving, enfolding embrace. For Williams, channeling Freud and anticipating Lacan, female sexuality is valued "for the 'lodging' it offers the male organ when the forbidden hand has to find a replacement for pleasure giving" (Irigaray 23). Feminine pleasure is not hinted at because the grail does not enjoy itself. It is enjoyed by those who achieve it and offers them blessings, but is not in turn blessed.

In this particular poem, sexual pleasure is replaced by blessings in the form of children. Blanchefleur's sexuality is removed and replaced with motherhood, recalling Williams' caution against physical lust in *Outlines of Romantic Theology*. He warns that "Herod is desire establishing himself in the holy city," ready to kill the infant Love (19). True lovers must ensure that their romance is intellectual, else the promised heaven will be a hidden hell. The anatomical connection between male and female is useful only as long as it remains a pattern that points to the spiritual connection between Christ and the Church. Although this connection is only hinted at in this early poem, it illustrates the lifelong fascination that would be most explicitly elaborated on in *Taliessin through Logres*. In this later work, however, he inverts the imagery of Percivale's song. It is no longer a woman's body that points to empire, but rather an empire that points toward a woman's body.

Curiously, Williams tries to downplay the significance of this symbolism. He writes that, "The Empire then is (a) all Creation—with logothetes and what not as angels and such (b) Unfallen (c) a proper social order (d) the true physical body. I left it female in appearance because the Emperor must be masculine, but this is accidental" ("Notes" 178). The use of the word "accidental" is a curious one, as he could not have meant accidental in the common sense of an unplanned coincidence. As the poet, he could have made the Empire male, but did not "because the Emperor *must* be masculine" (emphasis mine). That is an interesting enough statement on its own, but it is most peculiar as an explanation for the Empire's feminine appearance. Since Williams says that he chose the gender of the Empire in relation to the gender of the Emperor, the feminine appearance could not be considered an "accident."

Further, it is unlikely that Williams, a man who believed, literally, that "Hell is always inaccurate" ("John Milton" 30) chose a sloppy or inaccurate word and thus meant "accident" in the sense of unimportant. Instead, it seems likely that Williams was using the philosophical sense of essence and accident. The Empire is not *essentially* feminine, as the Host is the body and blood of Christ, but merely accidentally, as the Host is bread and wine. The essence of the Empire is, instead, complementary; it is not a thing for itself, but for the Emperor. The feminine appearance allows for union with Emperor, but it does not in and of itself explain anything of the quality of Empire. We may again think of the Host; the form of bread and wine allows Christians to partake of the spiritual feast without necessarily saying anything about the quality of the spiritual essence. The form of the Empire exists for precisely the same sort of union. Again, we see Williams' tension between a belief that women are equal partners of union and his romantic portrayal of them as objects that exist in response to male subjects.

Williams further complicates matters by rewriting the myth of the Motherland. By using what Annette Kolodny has elsewhere called "the land-as-woman" metaphor, Williams is invoking a set of stock experiences that guides his reader's understanding of Byzantium, "each one of which details one of the many elements of that experience, including eroticism, penetration, raping, embrace, enclosure, and nurture"

(150). By embodying his concept of the City in the woman Byzantium, Williams invites readers to understand her through the powerful mythic archetypes of Mother, Mistress, and Virgin. As we have already seen, Williams is comfortable with the Mother and the Virgin, but will grow uncertain about the role of Mistress.

The metaphor is most fully developed in "The Vision of the Empire." In this poem, Taliessin describes the anatomical geography that is presented in the end piece of *Taliessin through Logres* that we have already discussed. The poem paints Byzantium as a vibrant, thrilling woman in touch with the beauty of her flesh: "The organic body sang together" (lines 1, 45, 164). Yet she is not alone. Instead, she is in communion with the god-like Emperor; the songs of her joy are carried to and from the Emperor by logothetes who fly up and down "the porphyry stair" (lines 10, 42).

These logothetes are the masculine, phallic logos penetrating and impregnating Byzantium with the meaning of the Imperial words that they carry. Lewis' comment on masculine will and feminine form comes to mind as the words of these logothetes delineate and define the body of Byzantium. In the battle of "Mount Badon," when Arthur's forces of order triumph over barbarians and chaos, the victory is one of verbal definition as well as martial prowess. Taliessin surveys the battlefield and strikes with the doubly phallic "pen of his spear" against the brigands (l. 48). While the knights achieve martial victory, Taliessin's poetry achieves a civic victory as he establishes the legend of Arthur. Byzantium's body is at once conquered, or perhaps rescued, by male force and given shape by male words.

Yet while Byzantium's body is certainly dependent upon her lords, it is not deprived of its own dignity and glory. In the nude girls dancing innocently in Caucasia, Williams offers the image of the smiling Virgin. "The Princess of Byzantium," he writes, "recurs constantly throughout as the image of all that a mistress is to her love, and the Blessed Virgin is to the Church, and every elect soul is to the world" ("Notes" 178) They show the joys of true spiritual union and invite readers to participate. Similarly, in Logres "the theme of the design of the Empire" can be found ("The Vision of the Empire" l. 49) and "milk rises in the breasts of Gaul, / trigonometrical milk of doctrine" (lines 66–67). Byzantium as Mother is not only nurturing, but intelligent and learned. She instructs her children in right living. Indeed, in this line we can almost see an echo of the old belief that the act of nursing instills the mother's virtues in the child. Byzantium is a grand and powerful lady, at least until we encounter her sexuality in Jerusalem: "Conception without control" (125).

Jerusalem is associated with Byzantium's genitals and, perhaps unsurprisingly, it is thus the site of the Fall. The Adam—Williams' conception of Adam and Eve before the Fall—lusts for knowledge and climbs the tree of good and evil, saying, *"Let us grow to the height of God and the Emperor"* ("The Vision of the Empire" 107; emphasis original). The sin of the Adam in Jerusalem is a lustful pride that desires to know as God knows. It is a sinful desire for self-sufficiency, for union with self. This radically isolating act, that Williams elsewhere calls the sin of Gomorrah,[8] dramatically mars Jerusalem. The Adam achieve their fulfillment without union; they receive the Knowledge of God without God.

---

8   On Gomorrah: "there's no distinction between lover and beloved; they beget themselves on their adoration of themselves, and they live and feed and starve on themselves, and by themselves too, for creation ... is the mercy of God, and they won't have the facts of creation" (*DiH* 174).

The success, however, is not triumphant. Instead of portraying the Adam as promethean heroes striving after forbidden knowledge, Williams portrays their fall as pitiful masturbation. They see the rejected offerings of the Emperor as "a white pulsing shape ... the ejection to the creature of the creature's rejection of salvation" ("The Vision of the Empire" 123–24). Turning this intellectual sin into a sexual sin is curious, but Williams claims to be merely following the story of Genesis: "The tale presents the Adam as naked, and in a state of enjoyment of being naked. It was part of their good; they had delight in their physical natures ... They then insisted on knowing good as evil; and they did .... Sex had been good, it became evil" (*HCD* 21). This is why, Williams claims, the Adam first cover themselves: the intellectual fall is necessarily a sexual fall. The Adam's rejection of the Emperor's gift then leads to self-rupture; the Adam becomes Adam and Eve. Union with others in the body is dependent upon union with the Emperor, and that union has been broken. This is the Dolorous Blow, the misuse of sacred things for one's own desires. As a result of this act, the genitals of Byzantium are wounded and cannot achieve union until they are healed by the Grail.

In this metaphor, Williams' confusion is clearest. On the one hand, the logic of the City is upheld: the means of union, Byzantium's genitalia, deny union and instead participate in masturbatory self-fantasy. As a result, the ejaculation that should have led to generation and creation is wasted and spent. This is consistent with Williams' doctrines, but it is not consistent within the poetic imagery. Despite Byzantium's feminine nature, the language of the Adam is undeniably masculine: it grows high until it releases a white pulsing shape. Byzantium is a hermaphrodite.

This understanding of only masculine eroticism is the center of Williams' confusion. For him, union is only understandable as two becoming one. Thus, in his prelapsarian account of the embodied world, he is forced to imagine prelapsarian genitals as one: The Adam, the phallus. Eve is not present, subsumed entirely into the masculine unity of the Adam. But as Luce Irigaray observes:

> Woman's autoeroticism is very different then man's. In order to touch himself, man needs an instrument: his hand, a woman's body, language .... And this self-caressing requires at least a minimum of activity. As for woman, she touches herself in and of herself without any need for mediation, and before there is any way to distinguish activity from passivity. Woman touches herself all the time, and moreover no one can forbid her to do so, for her genitals are formed of two lips in continuous contact. Thus, within herself, she is already two—but not divisible into one(s)—that caress each other. (24)

Williams cannot imagine a unity with the self that is not self. For him, the Adam exists as a single self, even when split. Thus even male and female union is not union with the Other, but a reclamation of original union. The Adam is punished by being split into two, man and woman. In a sense then, the metaphor almost seems to imply that femininity is a result of the original fall. Read this way, it must be noted that the punishment for the sin of self-love—rejecting union—is castration of a sort, a wounding of both the land and its inhabitants. The Adam is cut down, replaced with a hole. Byzantium becomes truly feminine, able to participate in union, only when presented with the masculine logos.

Williams, of course, does not think that women are a result of the Fall. His original image of creation implies a relationship between the masculine Emperor and a feminine Empire. Instead, this confusion again points to Williams' difficulty in reconciling the romantic tales of wounding and restoration with his vision of the City. Using the language of romance, he cannot imagine Byzantium having her own desires or an alternative sexuality to the phallic oneness suggested by the Adam. Thus, when the great lady Byzantium bleeds, she is not the cause of her wound. Instead, she—matter—embodies the masculine form of rupture. She cannot heal herself, but must wait, docile, for the Grail knights to complete their quest and to erect the great logocentric phallus of the porphyry stair. Yet once the stair is erected, women such as Dindrane and Elayne are imagined as participating fully in the City. They are no longer passive, dependent upon the penetrating will of the male.

Ultimately, Williams' poetry reveals a man at war against himself. Lewis wrote and compiled *Arthurian Torso* to avoid scholarly battlefields, but he was unable to shield Williams' poetry from the author's own uncertainty. On the one hand, Williams presents his startling doctrine of the City. It is egalitarian in principle, encourages charity, and points toward heaven. On the other, he remains mired in the old doctrine of the romance in which women wait in towers to reward men for rescuing them. The mutual submission of co-inherence should not be sloppily equated with feminine submission, but rather both should be read for their own merits. When reading Williams' poetry, it is necessary to recognize that his own thoughts continued to develop and that he does not present a unified worldview. Instead, one should join the discussion and enjoy the journey of Taliessin.

Works Cited

Brewer, Elisabeth. "Women in the Arthurian Poems of Charles Williams." *Charles Williams: A Celebration*. Ed. Brian Horne. Leominster, UK: Gracewing, 1995. 98–115. Print.

Eliot, T. S. "The Significance of Charles Williams." *The Listener* 19 December 1946. Print.

Foucault, Michel. *History of Sexuality: An Introduction*. Trans. Robert Hurley. London: Allen Lane, 1979. Print.

Hadfield, Alice Mary. *Charles Williams: An Exploration of His Life and Work*. Oxford UP, 1983. Print.

Hegel, G. W. F. *Elements of the Philosophy of Right*. Ed. Allen W. Wood. Trans. H. B. Nisbet. Cambridge UP, 1991. Print.

Irigaray, Luce. *The Sex Which Is Not One*. Trans. Catherine Porter and Carolyn Burke. Ithaca, NY: Cornell UP, 1985. Print.

Jozifkova, Eva. "Consensual Sadomasochistic Sex (BDSM): The Roots, the Risks, and the Distinctions between BDSM and Violence." *Current Psychiatry Reports* 15.9 (2013). *Academic Search Complete*. Web. 30 March 2015.

Kolodny, Annette. *The Lay of the Land: Metaphor as Experience and History in American Life and Letters*. Chapel Hill: U of North Carolina, 1975. Print.

Lang-Sims, Lois. *Letters to Lalage: The Letters of Charles Williams to Lois Lang-Sims*. Kent State UP, 1989. Print.

Lewis, C. S. *A Preface to* Paradise Lost. 1942. NY: Oxford UP, 1961. Print.

—. "Williams and the Arthuriad." *Arthurian Torso*. Ed. C. S. Lewis. London: Oxford UP, 1948. 91–200. Print.

Loewenstein, Andrea Freud. *Loathsome Jews and Engulfing Women: Metaphors of Projection in the Works of Wyndham Lewis, Charles Williams, and Graham Greene*. NYUP, 1993. Print.

Stiles, Beverly L., and Robert E. Clark. "BDSM: A Subcultural Analysis of Sacrifices and Delights." *Deviant Behavior* 32.2 (2011): 158–89. *Academic Search Complete*. Web. 2 March 2015.

Williams, Charles, and C. S. Lewis. *Arthurian Torso*. Oxford UP, 1948. Print.

Williams, Charles. *Arthurian Poets: Charles Williams*. Arthurian Studies 24. Ed. David Llewellyn Dodds. Woodbridge, Suffolk: Boydell, 1991. Print. Arthurian Studies.

—. *He Came down from Heaven: With Which Is Reprinted The Forgiveness of Sins*. 1938. Berkeley, CA: Apocryphile, 2005. Print.

—. "The Image of the City in English Verse." 1940. *Image* 92–102.

—. *The Image of the City and Other Essays*. Berkeley, CA: Apocryphile, 2007. Print.

—. "John Milton." 1940. *Image* 26–36.

—. "Notes on the Arthurian Myth." *Image* 175–79.

—. *Outlines of Romantic Theology; with Which Is Reprinted, Religion and Love in Dante: The Theology of Romantic Love*. Ed. Alice Mary. Hadfield. Grand Rapids, MI: Eerdmans, 1990. Print.

—. *Poems of Conformity*. London: Oxford UP, 1917. Print.

—. "The Redeemed City." 1941. *Image* 102–110.

15

Those Kings of Lewis' Logres: Arthurian Figures as Lewisian Genders in *That Hideous Strength*

Benjamin Shogren

Even long-time readers of C. S. Lewis' *That Hideous Strength* may be puzzled over why Ransom is unexpectedly given the two new names 'Pendragon' and 'Fisher-king.' While there is a specific explanation in the narrative for Pendragon (it is a title passed down from the historical King Arthur), Ransom's acquisition of the name Fisher-king in the narrative is seemingly incidental and unimportant. Readers of Arthuriana will recognize the name as a reference to the Fisher King character of the Arthuriad, just as Pendragon is a reference to King Arthur himself, but this does not clarify things much; that these two Arthurian names are shared by the same person is itself curious. There certainly are some similarities between Arthur and the Fisher King in Arthuriana, but in general the two kings are very different in kind and are usually on opposite ends of a given Arthurian narrative with no direct relationship to each other whatsoever. What is the meaning of Ransom's sudden acquisition of these two titles that are at once related in their common Arthurian origin and disparate in their respective references to two very different characters? Why are these two related yet different crowns placed on one head? The answer is that the unity-in-difference of the two Arthurian figures in the person of Ransom is emblematic of the entire imaginative bent of the Ransom Trilogy toward the genders: Ransom's dual roles as King Arthur and the Fisher King are being used respectively as icons of the Masculine and the Feminine.

Though we may rightly note, along with Michael Ward, that *That Hideous Strength* is an "overstuffed book" (67), the novel's parallel elements of medieval cosmology, gender, marriage, Naturalism vs. Supernaturalism, Arthurian imagery, and Christian edification are often woven together to form complex relationships among mutually informative images. This kind of imaginative relationship is most apparent in the character of Ransom. When we encounter Ransom for the first time in *That Hideous Strength*, he is being used to remind us all at once of King Arthur himself, the "bright solar blend of king and lover and magician" of Solomon, and "the word *King* itself, with all linked associations of battle, marriage, priesthood, mercy, and power" (140). Such use of double meaning and multifaceted imagery in a single character or image is rampant in Lewis' fiction and is an example of a medievalist usage of symbolism, in which "a single emblem may have many meanings" (*Spenser's Images* 99). We can be assured, therefore, that it is totally in keeping with the imaginative complexity already plainly operative in *That Hideous Strength* that Ransom's dual Arthurian roles could be used simultaneously as faithful Arthurian images and as images of the Masculine and the Feminine.

Which Arthur? Which Fisher King?

In showing that Ransom's Arthurian roles are reflections of the Masculine and Feminine, I will have a recurring difficulty in defining our key terms, several of which are either notoriously nebulous or just plain controversial. Before moving on to the much more difficult task of defining the genders of the Ransom Trilogy, I will first briefly clarify what is meant by the Arthurian names themselves.

When *That Hideous Strength* uses the Pendragon and Fisher King titles, what is actually being referenced from the Arthuriad? The difficulty of this question lies in the fact that the Arthuriad as a whole does not present King Arthur and the Fisher King to us as clear and consistent characters. Arthur himself is present in every Arthurian work, but in some major works he exhibits serious inconsistencies as a character. The Fisher King appears in far fewer works, but in almost every appearance is presented as multiple characters or multiple versions of the same character, leaving the question "Who, here, is the Fisher King?" virtually impossible to answer.

The inconsistency of Arthur in some stories is a frustration to anyone attempting to come up with a definitive Arthur. But in these curious cases of literary schizophrenia, a quite clear contrast is revealed between two main versions of the renowned king. Chrétien often seasons his romances with glowing praises of King Arthur's virtues that are absent in his own Arthur character, who is commonly known by such terms as "ineffectual" (Loomis 49) or "passive" (Archibald 140): Arthur's valor "teaches us to be brave and courteous" in the introduction to Chrétien's *Yvain* (295), but we see him act with despondency and cowardice in the face of Meleagant in *Lancelot* (208) and the Red Knight in *Perceval* (393). Likewise, Malory makes Arthur both a great warrior and a great pushover, at once God's righteous elect and a man fornicating with his sister.

One can see in these works a recurring pattern: once the setting for the story is established as the famous court of King Arthur, Arthur himself is sent to the margins and degraded to the level of the bumbling, incompetent, and imbecilic master. As Rosemary Morris points out, "the name 'Arthur' comports a world, and any author who uses it means to evoke something of that world" (2). The inconsistencies of the Arthurs of Chrétien and Malory are the result of an invocation of the Arthurian world shared by all works of the Arthuriad, followed by a rejection of what we might call the shared Arthur—the Arthur whose name acts as a key to the shared Arthurian world. The authors of these inconsistent Arthurs intend to set their stories in the world of Excalibur and Merlin and the Round Table, but they do not welcome the King who is the heart of that world, the star around which all of those elements orbit.

This move to summon the Arthurian world by invoking the name of the shared Arthur while simultaneously rejecting the shared Arthur as a character amounts, ultimately, to a grudging agreement with the mainstream of Arthurian contributors over what kind of Arthur belongs in and is truly native to the Arthurian world. The shared Arthur is the Arthur that Chrétien and Malory can never fully get away from, the Arthur characterized, in Morris' words, by aspects that "defy all conscious attempts at modification" and that have passed into "a peculiarly literary, and popular, subconscious" (6). It is this Arthur who is represented by Ransom Pendragon in *That Hideous Strength*: the famous figure of legend, the mighty warrior, the magnificent king victorious over invaders and giants and dragons.

We will have an easier time defining the shared Fisher King. The ambiguities of the Fisher King lie in the fact that in every appearance the role is seemingly inhabited by multiple characters who all share very similar characteristics, such as an unhealable wound, the stewardship of the Grail, and an involvement with the Grail quest. But these ambiguities are ambiguities of narrative, not of the primary defining characteristics or qualities of the Fisher King role itself within the Arthuriad. Since it is these shared characteristics that we are looking for in order to talk about a shared Fisher King, the work of drawing out the essence of what makes the Fisher King the Fisher King is already done for us, and we can therefore avoid such problems as the presence of multiple Fisher King-like characters in a given narrative and the equivocal relationship between the Fisher King and the Wounded King. We can confidently define the shared Fisher King as the Arthurian character who is the keeper of the Holy Grail and who waits in his hidden castle for the healing of his unhealable wound by the Grail Knight through the conclusion of the Grail Quest. This is the Fisher King represented in Ransom.

For the rest of this work, the names 'Arthur' and 'Fisher King' will be used to mean the shared Arthur and the shared Fisher King specifically. In order to accurately identify the shared Arthur and the shared Fisher King, I will be drawing on a number of original Arthurian texts, but will by no means exhaust all possible sources. The Arthuriad is a vast literary tradition and not all permutations can be accounted for here. Rather, our focus will be on the mainstream of medieval Arthurian literature along the lines of the "dominant traditions" of Latin, French, and English (Putter and Archibald 3) and also along the development of the Grail story. My aim here is to draw on those works that have been the most read and the most influential within the Arthuriad over time and so could be considered representative of the developing tradition and among the greatest contributors to the continued lives of the shared Arthur and the shared Fisher King in popular imagination.[1]

The remaining terms in need of clear definition are 'masculine' and 'feminine.' Unfortunately, the meanings of 'masculine' and 'feminine' in the Ransom Trilogy are very often seriously misunderstood by readers and critics alike, for a number of reasons: they have complex definitions on both the imaginative and technical levels, they do not mean what the words 'masculine' and

---

[1] The only two sources that may not fit this criterion are the works of Laȝamon and Charles Williams, which will be used here partly because of Lewis' own particular esteem of both works ("Genesis" 18–33, WA 375–84), but especially because they are, along with Malory, the only works of Arthuriana mentioned by name in *THS* (29, 191).

'feminine' mean in contemporary usage, and discussion of gender in general involves serious political implications that tend to draw focus away from Lewis' actual vision. Before we can compare Ransom with the Arthurian figures and all three with the genders, I will first have to take a somewhat lengthy detour to establish what the genders *are*, on both the imaginative and technical levels, as they are actually found in the Ransom Trilogy. In this, the longer way round will end up the shorter way home. But in identifying the genders, it will be crucial to intentionally limit our scope to only those of Lewis' texts that are immediately relevant to our understanding of gender in the Ransom Trilogy. Gender and sex in the whole corpus of C. S. Lewis, or in his personal biography, is a topic too large for a single chapter, and most of the content of that broad discussion would not help us in better seeing the Pendragon and Fisher King roles as Masculine and Feminine images, which is the primary interest of this essay. In order to maintain our focus and prevent any distraction by Lewisiana in general, the name 'Lewis' will be used for the rest of this chapter to refer primarily to the author of the Ransom Trilogy.[2]

The Genders

Gender in the Ransom Trilogy is not easily defined, particularly because it contradicts the assumptions of most contemporary readers. But if we have any interest in the Ransom Trilogy, we must do our best to enter into the world that is being presented to us while we are reading the stories—to set aside for a while our own imaginative difficulties in order to make room for this other image. Whether the cosmos of the Ransom Trilogy ends up looking to us either beautiful or repugnant, we of course cannot take it to be either before we have given it a good look.

Before all else, it must be understood that in the Ransom Trilogy gender and sex are not at all the same thing. While a rough technical definition of the word 'gender' as it is currently used would be something like "roles, norms, and expectations associated with the sexes," the word 'gender' is often used interchangeably with the word 'sex.' Diana Pavlac Glyer rightly points out that when discussing Lewis and gender, the conflation of gender terminology with sex terminology quickly leads to confusion (477). Gender in the Ransom Trilogy is emphatically *not* the same thing as sex. When Lewis talks of "masculine" and "feminine," he is not talking about male and female or men and women, nor does he necessarily intend any direct implication for the sexes; "Gender is a … more fundamental reality than sex" (*Per* 200). What does Lewis mean, then, by gender?

The complex nature of the genders of the Ransom Trilogy is difficult to put into a few succinct words and is best communicated through multiple images and allusions. Glyer points out that the genders are expressed this way because

---

2   Intentional, strict focus on a single work, or a single set of works, is not a usual approach in much of contemporary Lewis scholarship, which has the tendency (whether consciously or otherwise) to tackle Lewis' work as a whole in the interest of making biographical conclusions about the author. The focus of this essay is not biographical, but literary.

abstract terms are (for Lewis) too *thin* .... Following Owen Barfield, Lewis believed that old words (and old languages) tend to "bundle" meanings together, combining a wealth of denotations within a single term. Contemporary words and languages, in contrast, tend to splinter meaning into terms that are more precise but also less rich and rounded. Lewis' impulse, then, is to bundle these meanings back again .... "Lion" is more than majesty and leadership. "Dryad" is more than delicacy and sensitivity. (478)

By showing the nature of the genders in these "bundles" of images, Lewis is attempting to communicate to the reader something more robust and rich than can be expressed in a flat definition or in a list of traits. We will deal with some of these bundled images in greater detail later when we look at the Pendragon and the Fisher King of *That Hideous Strength*. For now, let us briefly consider some of the more obvious images.

The "real meaning of gender" is most clearly revealed in the later chapters of *Perelandra* (200), when Ransom meets the primary groupings of Masculine and Feminine images in the eldila Malacandra and Perelandra, the angel- or god-like ruling planetary archons of Mars and Venus:

The Oyarsa of Mars shone with cold and morning colours, a little metallic—pure, hard, and bracing. The Oyarsa of Venus glowed with a warm splendour, full of the suggestion of teeming vegetable life .... Malacandra was like rhythm and Perelandra like melody .... The first held in his hand something like a spear, but the hands of the other were open, with the palms toward him. (199–200)

The difference between the Masculine and the Feminine is like the difference between cold and warm, metal and vegetable, shining and glowing, rhythm and melody, vertical and horizontal, convex and concave. From these contrasts, we see first of all the fundamentally relational and interdependent nature of the genders: the image of *rhythm* is an inadequate expression of the Masculine unless accompanied by *melody* as a contrasting expression of the Feminine. To see one gender means to also see it in relation to the other. The description continues:

Malacandra seemed to him to have the look of one standing armed, at the ramparts of his own remote archaic world, in ceaseless vigilance, his eyes ever roaming the earth-ward horizon whence his danger came long ago. "A sailor's look ... eyes that are impregnated with distance." But the eyes of Perelandra opened ... inward, as if they were the curtained gateway to a world of waves and murmurings and wandering airs, of life that rocked in winds and splashed on mossy stones and descended as the dew and arose sunward in thin-spun delicacy of mist. On Mars the very forests are of stone; in Venus the lands swim. (201)

The Masculine and Feminine are like warrior and hostess, distance and nearness, outward-facing and inward-facing, still and wandering, stone forest and floating island. These are our primary impressions of the genders.

In the eldila, gender itself is revealed to be not an "imaginative extension of [biological] sex" (200), but rather a kind of elemental pattern, expressed, by analogy, in pairs of relationally opposite and contrasting archetypal images. These images exhibited in Malacandra and Perelandra are not arbitrary: in them we are meant to see the Masculine and the Feminine as "a fundamental polarity which divides all created beings" (200), the opposites that in relation to each other are the transcendental modes of being in the pattern of the cosmic order that in the Ransom Trilogy is called the Great Dance.

In a vision brought on by the eldila, Ransom sees that the Great Dance is a hierarchical order descending from the "simplicity beyond all comprehension" (219)—God—down through every level of his creation, linked together by "unions of a kneeling with a sceptered love," wherein every participant is "equally at the centre," not by being equals, "but some by giving place and some by receiving it" (217). The Great Dance is a comprehensive pattern of the whole order of beings in fluid and multidimensional hierarchical relation to each other and to God, in which any two members relate to each other in the respective roles of Masculine and Feminine—the interdependent polarities of "rule and obedience, begetting and bearing, heat glancing down, life growing up" (214). The Masculine is imaged in Malacandra, the cold, hard, distant warrior, and is characterized as the initiating, giving, transcendent, and ruling "sceptered love"; the Feminine is imaged in Perelandra, the warm, soft, inviting hostess, and is characterized as the responsive, receptive, immanent, and obedient "kneeling love." Together, the Masculine and the Feminine are the dancing union of unlikes that make up the ordered pattern of beings in relationship.

The pattern of the Great Dance between the Masculine and the Feminine transcends the created order by having its ultimate origin in God, who in *Perelandra* is known as the "simplicity beyond all comprehension, ancient and young as spring" (219), and also by the explicitly Trinitarian language of "Maleldil," "His Father," and "the Third One" (210). Lewis provides an explanation for how gender and hierarchy originate in the traditional Christian understanding of the life of the Trinity in his essay "Christianity and Literature," in which he explains that in I Cor. II he finds an analogical pattern in which the First Person of the Trinity is to the Second Person of the Trinity as God is to mankind and as man is to woman. He pictures an original divine virtue being passed down a hierarchical ladder through the Great Chain of Being, every rung of which is gifted the divine virtue, the image, and the glory of the rung above, and every rung of which gives of its own divine virtue, image, and glory to the rung below. Particularly striking to Lewis is the apparent equivalence between the woman-man and mankind-God relationships and the relationship between the First and Second Persons of the Trinity ("Christianity and Literature" 4–5): the gendered relationship between the sexes is ultimately a reflection of the dynamic life of the Trinity, of God the Father who begets and God the Son who is begotten.

In response to Lewis' use of hierarchical language to describe the dynamic of the Trinity, some bring against him the charge of Arian heresy (the belief that God the Son is not truly divine; Van Leeuwen 71–74). But Lewis was certainly aware of this possible objection, as in the same essay he goes on to argue that this image is not a criticism or contradiction of the Nicene or Athanasian creeds, which he himself wholly accepts (5). In fact, Lewis considers this analogical, proportional relationship between the Father and Son to be a biblical principle, and finds it operative in several other passages, such as I Cor. 3:23, John 10:15, and John 15:9 ("Christianity and Literature" 5). Ward backs up Lewis: "Obviously, Christ was subject to the Father as man; but Lewis also thought he was subject to the Father as God. This position is distinguishable from the heresy of subordinationism; its *locus classicus* is I Cor. 15:27–28" (135). By Lewis' description, the hierarchical order between God the Father and God the Son is of such a kind that it does not violate or contradict the strict equality between the two that is stressed in the creeds and of such a kind that the Son is not of lesser glory or less deserving of worship *than* the Father for being begotten *of* the Father. Rather than submitting to an "either-or" definition in which equality and order are assumed to be mutually exclusive, Lewis sticks with the "both-and" of traditional Trinitarian theology by emphasizing both equality and order in the dynamic life the Trinity.

Perhaps the confusion over Lewis' Trinitarian hierarchy results from a misunderstanding of what Lewis actually has in mind when it comes to hierarchy. In the Ransom Trilogy, as in "Christianity and Literature," the *ladder* is a crucial image for understanding the nature of hierarchy. But the hierarchy of the Ransom Trilogy is just as significantly characterized by the image of the *dance*. As Monika Hilder notes, "Unlike the typical understanding of hierarchy as consisting of rigid, discrete parts, Lewis, like Milton ... emphasizes its fluidity" (80). Hilder sees this fluidity in the eldilas' abdicating power and bowing down to the new King and Queen at the end of *Perelandra* (75). The same fluidity is also found in the mutual bowing between Ransom and the new King and Queen: Ransom bows to Tor and Tinidril (204), and Tor tells him that though it is proper for him to bow and call them Lord and Lady, "in another fashion we call you Lord and Father" for his work in Maleldil's plan (208). Tor will then later kneel to wash Ransom's wounded foot (220). The dynamic of the Great Dance is exhibited in these interactions as an interplay of mutual bowing and receiving bow, giving place and receiving place.

The Great Dance is also characterized as having place for all diverse kinds of being. We have seen this already in the above "dancing" between the unlikes of the planetary angels, the new sinless human King and Queen, and Ransom the "middle-aged scholar" (*Per* 155). Hilder notes that "Lewis consistently celebrates unity-in-difference as the sacred cosmic order: there is a holiness in the communion of 'wedded *unlikes*'" (74). In the vision of the Great Dance, we are told that "Each thing, from the single grain of Dust to the strongest eldil, is the end and final cause of all creation and the mirror in which the beam of His brightness comes to rest and so returns to Him" (*Per* 217). This high affirmation of differing kinds of glory is essential to the character of the Great Dance between the Masculine and Feminine; "each is equally at the centre and none are there by being equals, but some by giving place and some by receiving it, the small things by their smallness and the great by their greatness" (*Per* 217). In this dance, the greater glory of the greater participants is no threat to the glory or place of the smaller participants. As Hilder says, "To ask the question, 'who wields the most power?' is like a blunder that interrupts the dance" (72). The Great Dance is a wedding of unlikes in which all have a place: a dance in which no two participants are the same, but all are welcome.

In the Great Dance, every position is at once Feminine in relation to all higher positions and Masculine in relation to all lower positions. This is because gender is not primarily a set of traits that either are or are not appropriate to a given participant in the Great Dance. For every member of the dance, it is at some times or in some relationships appropriate to be Masculine and at other times or in other relationships appropriate to be Feminine. Hilder points out an example of this from *Perelandra*: "Together Tor and Tinidril represent ... the feminine response of obedience to the divine voice; and together they also represent the masculine authority over the planet [Venus]" (72). Their royal office makes Tor and Tinidril at once

Feminine to God and Masculine to their kingdom. The "great" participants of the dance mentioned earlier are not exempt from practicing Feminine submission to their own rulers. Every participant in the dance will play the Masculine part in some relationships and the Feminine part in others—and the roles in even a single relationship may at times change, as we witnessed earlier between Perelandra and Tor and Tinidril.

The Sexes

In the Great Dance, there are some creatures that of their nature specially image either the Masculine or the Feminine. Though there are a number of such creatures (*Per* 200), the most apparent to us are the sexes. As we look at the sexes and consider what they communicate about the Masculine and the Feminine, we must continue to keep in mind that the topic of gender and sex in Lewis' work as a whole is very broad, and that we here as everywhere must limit our scope to the fraction of that broader topic that will help us better understand gender in the Ransom Trilogy. The work of exploring (or objecting to) possible political implications, or of reconciling Lewis' words here with his comments on the sexes in other works, I will mostly leave to the side in order to maintain our course of seeing the Arthurian roles of Ransom as Masculine and Feminine representations.

The pattern of the Great Dance is so embedded in creation that particular creatures embody its movements. The sexes, then, are "the adaptation to organic life" of the Masculine and the Feminine (*Per* 200). This means that while male and female are not the same as Masculine and Feminine, the sexes by their very nature truly image the genders in small scale as faithful, though not exact, representations: "The male and female … are rather faint and blurred reflections of masculine and feminine. Their reproductive functions, their differences in strength and size, partly exhibit, but partly also confuse and misrepresent, the real polarity" (*Per* 200). Lewis elsewhere calls this real, but limited, representation of the genders in the sexes the gender "uniform" ("Priestesses" 92–93).

The gender uniforms do not exempt any creature from participating in the normal ebb and flow of the Masculine and Feminine modes in the Great Dance. All creatures are sometimes in one role and sometimes in the other. As we saw earlier in the "dancing" between the eldila and the new King and Queen, Tor (who specially images the Masculine in his sex) was at one time Feminine in relation to the eldila, just as the eldil Perelandra (who specially images the Feminine) was Masculine in relation to him. A man, even though he wears the "uniform" of Masculinity in his sex, might in a given relationship have the Feminine role—just as Ransom in *That Hideous Strength* has to God (despite his having, according to Jane, a masculinity "more emphatic than that of common men"; 312). In a given instance, such might even be the case between a husband and wife, as we see between Tor and Tinidril: of architecture, Tor says to his wife, "It may be that in this matter our natures are reversed and it is you who beget and I who bear" (*Per* 211). As Ransom tells Jane in *That Hideous Strength*, "obedience and rule are more like a dance than a drill—specially between man and woman where the roles are always changing" (147).

Ann Loades' critique, that Lewis creates "severe difficulties for men" by requiring them to be assertively Masculine as men while also being receptively Feminine in relation to God (169–70), is therefore not applicable in light of the Great Dance—it points out neither a hole in Lewis' system nor a difficulty peculiar to men. Rather, in the Great Dance it is a requirement shared by every creature to possess all virtues necessary to stand in appropriate relation to God and to all other creatures—virtues that in some relationships are of the Masculine aspect and in others of the Feminine aspect. It is not only *allowed* for a creature who wears a gender uniform to play the role of the opposite gender in a given relationship; it is in fact *required* by the nature of the pattern of the Great Dance. Every creature is suited for both modes, gender uniform notwithstanding. Glyer points out that in Lewis' view,

> we are called on a daily basis to behave in masculine ways or feminine ways based not on [sex] but on context .… healthy individuals should exhibit traits that are commonly associated with both genders, and each individual should see life as a series of shifting hierarchies that depend not on one's [sex] but rather on the social standing and the relationship of the individuals involved. (479–80)[3]

A person's sex does not determine whether he or she is expected to pursue Masculine or Feminine virtue; Masculine and Feminine virtue are both to be pursued by all members of both sexes. Masculine assertiveness is not exclusive to men; neither is the receptiveness of the Feminine appropriate only for women. Every human creature must hold in itself and exercise in its behavior all the enthroned kingliness, bracing assertiveness, and bold strength of the Masculine side by side with the humble obedience, warm openness, and glad self-giving of the Feminine.

Marriage

It may well be asked whether in the Great Dance there are any relationships or roles in which it is required that the uniformed gender and the gender of the role must match—in which the Feminine role must be played by a woman or the Masculine role by a man. In the Ransom Trilogy, Lewis points out only one such relation, and it is that particular relation in which the differences between the sexes, rather than the similarities, are emphasized: the procreative marriage bed. As Ward points out, "The very first word of *That Hideous Strength* is 'matrimony,' which denotes not just marriage … but, literally, 'mother making.' Mark and Jane must come together so as to make of her the mother of the new Pendragon" (171). The story opens by presenting to us the broken marriage between Jane and Mark and concludes with the two heading toward procreative sex as the beginning of the healing of their marriage.

Marriage and the marriage bed are, in the cosmos of the Ransom Trilogy, a special image of the correct relationship between the Masculine and Feminine, similar to (or harkening to) the Christian doctrine that marriage is a sacrament specially representing the relationship between Christ and his Church. In a conversation with Ransom, Jane comes to realize that marriage is a basic participation in and conformity to the pattern of the Great Dance between the genders:

---

3   Glyer twice uses the word "gender" here where she technically means "sex."

she had been conceiving this world as "spiritual" in the negative sense—as some neutral, or demo-cratic, vacuum where differences disappeared, where sex and sense were not transcended but simply taken away. Now the suspicion dawned upon her that there might be differences and contrasts all the way up, richer, sharper, even fiercer, at every rung of the ascent. How if this invasion of her own being in marriage from which she had recoiled ... were not, as she had supposed, merely a relic of animal life or patriarchal barbarism, but rather the lowest, the first, and the easiest form of some shocking contact with reality which would have to be repeated—but in ever larger and more disturbing modes—on the highest levels of all? (312)

In the act of sex, the participants enact in small scale the larger transcendental pattern of the Great Dance between the Masculine and the Feminine. Jane's rejection of the genders reinforces and is reinforced by her neutering approach to her marriage with Mark: in her rejection of the image of the Masculine in Mark, she rejects the Masculine itself—in her rejection of the Masculine in general, she rejects Mark in particular in the marriage bed. Spiritual healing and reintroduction to the Great Dance will, for Jane and Mark, require the healing of their marriage bed as well. Ransom tells Jane that God would have allowed "a virginal rejection of the male," which could still leave room for an even deeper surrender to "something far more masculine, higher up" (312); "The male you could have escaped, for it exists only on the biological level. But the masculine none of us can escape. What is above and beyond all things is so masculine that we are all feminine in relation to it" (313). A Feminine response to the ultimate Masculinity of God is a basic requirement of all created beings and so can be achieved without the special habilitation to the pat-tern of the genders that is available in marital sex. But because she is already married, Jane cannot repair her relationship with God without also repairing her relationship with the Masculinity of her husband in her marriage.

It is significant in the story that it is to the *procreative* marriage bed that Jane and Mark are sent for the healing of their marriage and of their relationship to the Masculine and Feminine. The Masculine and the Feminine are imaged not just in sex in general but particularly in fully functional sex—sex that is not closed to its full reproductive potential. It is noted early in the story that though Jane and Mark are having sex (12), they are avoiding having children (12, 71), and it is implied that they use contraception (276). In Ransom's encouragement to Jane to have children with Mark (378), it is implied that the contracepted nature of Jane's marriage bed con-tributed to, or was a means of, her overall attempt to neuter herself and Mark. While we cannot here fully explore the anti-contraceptive undercurrents in *That Hideous Strength*, it suffices to note that the repair of Jane and Mark's relationships to the Masculine and the Feminine and to each other apparently requires that they stop "protecting" themselves from each other in their mar-riage.[4] Once they have done so, they will be able to join the Great Dance and take their places as the parents of the new Pendragon.

---

4   Much more remains to be said of the negative presence of contraception in the general course of Jane and
    Mark as protagonists, in the statements made by Merlin and Ransom on the subject, and especially in the

Readers might point out that in his telling Jane to be "obedient" to Mark, Ransom indicates that in the marriage relationship the wife inhabits the Feminine role not only in the sex act but in general—that the role of the wife entails a generalized obedience to her husband in everything. This is not what is being communicated by Ransom in his words to Jane. It might be claimed that Ransom makes Jane practice wifely submission when he refuses to let Jane join the company of St. Anne's without talking to her husband about it first (142–44). But Ransom's reason for requiring this is that he does not want to separate wife and husband. He tells Jane that "it would be hard for the same person to be the wife of an official in the N.I.C.E. and also a member of my company .... You and I and your husband could not all be trusting one another" (142). He then tells Jane that "things might come to such a point that you would be justified in coming here, even wholly against his will, even secretly." But he considers this willing separation between wife and husband a desperate remedy and wants Jane to try to convince Mark to leave the N.I.C.E. first (142–43). Ransom's clear purpose here is not to impress on Jane that she needs to practice wifely submission, but rather to preserve the unity between Jane and Mark as wife and husband as much as possible.

By a certain point, outright disobedience by Jane is even acceptable to Ransom in her refusal to join Mark at the N.I.C.E.—eventually, Jane's location *is* kept secret from Mark, against his will, when he goes to get her location from Dimble (214–19). In this desperate situation, though the separation between wife and husband is (from the perspective of the Great Dance) a true dissonance, it is unfortunately the necessary course for Jane, who must weigh the claims of God (through Ransom) against the claims of her husband.[5]

In fact, all of Ransom's explicit exhortations to Jane about "obedience" to her husband are in the context of her and Mark's marriage bed. He uses the word with reference to Jane and Mark's relationship three times. The first is when he tells Jane that she has fallen out of love with Mark because she never attempted obedience (*THS* 145). The second is when he tells Jane that "obedience—humility—is an erotic necessity" (146). The third is when he sends her to bed with Mark; Ransom tells Jane: "Go in obedience and you will find love. You will have no more dreams. Have children instead" (378).[6] All of these statements, made in Ransom's guidance of Jane to participation in the Great Dance between the Masculine and Feminine, point, again, to the fruitful marriage bed as the primary image of the genders in the sexes, rather than to general leadership in the husband or general submission in the wife. The humility and obedience Ransom encourages Jane to practice toward her husband is the normal female participation in the consummation of a living and fruitful marriage—the wife's loving and willing reception of her husband in sex.

It should be mentioned that, though Jane's humble reception of Mark in the sex act is a special enactment of Femininity, to which Mark is in the role of the Masculine, we are shown that Mark also needs to

---

strong contraceptive imagery associated with the moon in both *THS* and *Per*. A thorough exploration of this theme reveals a firm anti-contraceptive attitude in the Great Dance, despite there being no explicit rejection of contraception in the Ransom Trilogy.

5   This whole situation harkens back to Tor's anguished realization in *Perelandra* that if Tinidril were to give in to the Satanic temptation, it would still be his duty to serve God and so refuse to join her: "Though a man were to be torn in two halves ... The living half must still follow Maleldil" (210).

6   The "dreams" referenced here are her psychic visions.

approach the marriage bed with humility, albeit of another kind that is appropriate to his role. This distinction between the humility of the wife and the humility of the husband is found in Mark's own thought as he approaches his reunion with Jane: Mark realizes that "That same laboratory outlook upon love which had forestalled in Jane the humility of a wife, had equally forestalled in him ... the humility of a lover" (378). In order to fully accept his place as the Masculine in his marriage bed, Mark must humbly acknowledge that the failure of their marriage bed was his failure, the result of his own neutered "laboratory" approach; "how had he dared? And dared too with no sense of daring, nonchalantly, in careless stupidity!" (379).

Though the marriage bed is clearly emphasized in the Ransom Trilogy as the place that the sexes especially represent or reflect the genders, *Perelandra* makes clear that the sexes reflect the genders in other characteristics as well, such as in bodily size and strength (200). But in what other particular ways the man exhibits the Masculine or the woman the Feminine, the Ransom Trilogy is not much concerned to say—it leaves the door open for further expressions of the genders in the sexes, but in its pages it does not clearly endorse any. And it is crucial to keep in mind, when discussing how the sexes reflect the genders in particular sex-specific characteristics, that all such images of the genders are at most *limited* images. In the sexes we see the genders in small scale; the sexes "partly exhibit, but partly also confuse and misrepresent" the Masculine and the Feminine (*Per* 200). Because the reflections of the genders are limited in this way, we should expect it to be difficult (though not necessarily impossible) to point to one or another characteristic of a given sex as a reflection of the corresponding Ransom Trilogy gender, so long as we do so with appropriate caution and care and with the awareness that to do so would be to step beyond the bounds of the Ransom Trilogy's scope and attention.

Some critics have posited that *That Hideous Strength does* imply that women are required to play a more generalized Feminine role outside of the marriage bed. One position in particular, articulated by Mary Stewart Van Leeuwen, I will now address as a significant misunderstanding of both the sexes in particular and the Great Dance in general. Van Leeuwen writes that in *That Hideous Strength*

> Lewis paints a rather limited picture of what Christian females should aspire to. As chaste single women, they can become learned professionals like Grace Ironwood ... who interacts on a somewhat collegial level with director Ransom. As married women, they can become like Mrs. Dimble ... who, though childless herself, channels her maternal instincts into taking care of her husband's students. But they should not, like Jane, try to combine both in pursuit of a third possibility. (44)

Van Leeuwen adds that her point is "emphatically *not* that, for women, the intellectual life is preferable to nurturing children, or vice versa. It is that Lewis, in his uncritical embrace of archetypal thinking, tries to force readers into choosing between the two" (163). Van Leeuwen contends that the universe of the Ransom Trilogy has little room for women—that Jane is forced into one of two vocations for no reason other than that she is a woman.

This claim is not based on evidence. As we have seen, Ransom surely does tell Jane, who is already married, to have children. But nowhere in *That Hideous Strength* does he or any of the company of St. Anne's tell her to leave her career or imply that married women should not have a career. In fact, the only one in the story who draws a dichotomy between having children and pursuing a career is Jane herself prior to her conversion (12)! In the company of St. Anne's, one sees instead an openness to different vocations for both men and women in a manifestation of the fluidity of the Great Dance; as Hilder notes, St. Anne's welcomes diversity (114). Grace Ironwood is an unmarried doctor, Mother Dimble is a married woman with no children, Ivy Maggs is a married woman who works outside the home (46), and the married Camilla Denniston—in her familiarity with the difficult Arthuriana of Charles Williams and her overall interest in the Arthuriad—shows that she has some kind of significant involvement with literature (191, 365–67). The characteristic fluidity and affirmation of difference in the Great Dance can be most vividly seen applied to women in one scene in which some of the ladies of St. Anne's are getting dressed for a banquet. One by one, each lady is presented to us in her gown as having a beauty that is both appropriate to herself in particular and wholly distinct from the beauties of the other ladies (359–62). In the women of St. Anne's, we see that in the Great Dance difference and variety are by no means discouraged among members of the same sex. Here, as everywhere else, the cosmos of the Great Dance revels in diversity of beauty through an embrace of defined and identified particular beauties.

In the Great Dance between the Masculine and the Feminine, Lewis is trying to communicate to us the complex image of a cosmos that is at once ordered by hierarchy and enacted in fluidity—an image of a unity in which difference is glorified and every creature has its own place to exercise the freedom to be itself. Masculinity and Femininity, originating in the dancing life of the Trinity, is the pattern by which there could be anything like a true unity of unlikes—a marriage. Now that we see what the Masculine and the Feminine are in the Ransom Trilogy, we are in a position to see them manifested in the images of the shared Arthur and shared Fisher King of the popular Arthurian imagination as they are exhibited in Ransom's dual Arthurian roles in *That Hideous Strength*.

Ransom Pendragon

In *That Hideous Strength*, Ransom as Pendragon is an image of King Arthur. But the image is not manifested primarily through what we would call "character traits"—it is not as though Ransom and Arthur just have similar personalities. Rather, Ransom represents Arthur by exhibiting or evoking the primary imagery associated with the role of Arthur that makes up the lion's share of what I have called the shared Arthur, the Arthur that transcends particular works and lives on most vibrantly in a shared imagination. In order to highlight the imaginative associations between Ransom and Arthur and the Masculine in *That Hideous Strength*, our pattern will be to note an image or aspect of King Arthur of the Arthuriad, track how that particular image is represented in Ransom, and then show how the image is also an image of the Masculine as we find it in the Ransom Trilogy.

An Ancient Figure

In the shared Arthurian imagination, it is central to King Arthur as we know him that he is a figure of the past, one in a long line of Kings of Logres; we see even as early as Geoffrey of Monmouth that Arthur is the latest of an ancient order that stretches all the way back to Aeneas of Troy (6). This imaginative aspect of Arthur is reinforced in that most of even the oldest books we have about Arthur are themselves looking back to a king believed to have lived hundreds and hundreds of years in the past. The backward-looking perspective of the Arthuriad automatically puts Arthur, already the last in a long line of kings, in the place of an ancient figure.

Arthur's association with Merlin and other supernatural peoples also underlines his place as an ancient figure by giving him direct relationships with ancient and preternatural forces of the past. Frequently, Merlin is credited with aiding Arthur's rise to power, either by occasioning his conception (Geoffrey 186; Laȝamon 13–21; *Vulgate Merlin* 75; Malory 1–5), prophesying his reign (Laȝamon 11), choosing him as the next ruler on behalf of the British barons (Malory 6–8; Tennyson 13), prophesying his repose in Avalon and return to reign (Laȝamon 255), or by a combination of these acts.

The "other supernatural peoples" I mentioned can be called 'elves' as a shorthand, and some of our Arthurian sources use that language. What I mean by elves is that somewhat indefinable class of human-like supernatural peoples populating medieval literature that Lewis himself named the "High Fairies" in his chapter on the *longaevi* in *The Discarded Image* (130). The elfish peoples of Avalon, the fairies who bless the newborn Arthur in Laȝamon, the Lady of the Lake, and the women who carry Arthur away to Avalon all belong to this group. These elves support Arthur by imparting on him magical blessings and arms (Geoffrey 198; Laȝamon 21, 69; Malory 38–39; Tennyson 15) and, more famously, by taking Arthur away to Avalon to heal and to await his return to rule (Laȝamon 255; Malory 792; Tennyson 251–53).

In *That Hideous Strength*, Ransom is the Pendragon, and so is the latest of the same long line of Kings of Logres as King Arthur. "Pendragon" is not always a title used for Arthur in Arthuriana, but here it is used as a title that has been handed down not only to Arthur from his royal ancestry, but also from Arthur all the way to Ransom as well. In this cunning use of the Pendragon title, Lewis has made the crown of Arthur cover yet more vast amounts of time, descending not only from Troy to Arthur, but from Troy to the present day.

Merlin is represented in *That Hideous Strength* by himself, as he upholds and serves Ransom as agent and counselor just as he had served King Arthur. Merlin is here also used as a symbol of time past: Dimble says of Merlin, "we've all been imagining that because he came back in the Twentieth Century he'd be a Twentieth Century man. Time is more important than we thought, that's all" (279). But Merlin is even older than his own time, as it turns out that Merlin's art was the "last survival of something older and different—something brought to Western Europe after the fall of Numinor" (*THS* 198).

The eldila similarly (though less obviously) play the part of the Arthurian elves to Ransom's Arthur. Malacandra tells Perelandra that Ransom's "very name in his own tongue is Elwin, the friend of the eldila" (*Per* 195)—though in fact the name "Elwin" actually means "elf-friend" (Tolkien 150). Dimble also draws a clear association between the eldila and the elves in his discussion of the *longaevi* (*THS* 281–82). It is the eldila who take Ransom to Avalon on Venus (*THS* 374), and though the eldila do not bless him with special gifts like the elves in Laȝamon, it is certainly through his relationship with the eldila and the qualities he has as a result of his encounters with them that Ransom is equipped to be Pendragon by the time of *That Hideous Strength*.

As the Pendragon crown draws the eye to kings of the past, so Arthur's associations with magical peoples draw the eye to the old preternatural inhabitants of Arthur's kingdom while also occasioning a look, both through the far-seeing prophecies of Merlin and the direct agency of the elves, into the distant future with Arthur's return as future king. In this way, Arthur's reign transcends very great distances in time imaginatively and narratively. By using the title "Pendragon" as a double reference to ancient Arthur himself and to his place in the long line of successive ancient kings, and by retaining the Pendragon's associations with ancient magical peoples that occasion his own undying life and reign in the distant future, Lewis is capitalizing on age and on age's analogous counterpart, distance, as Masculine aspects in the person of Ransom.

Ward notes age as an especially important image of Malacandra in *Out of the Silent Planet* (Ward 82), and *Perelandra* similarly employs age-distance imagery in its description of Malacandra: his world is "remote" and "archaic"; his eyes are "impregnated with distance," and they face the earth "whence his danger came long ago" (201). Age and distance as Masculine aspects have their roots in Trinitarian theology, where greater age on the part of the Masculine half is imaginatively evoked (not technically implied) in the language of "Father and Son," and priority is implied by the language of "First and Second." As Ransom sees in the vision of the Great Dance, the "final cause" for which God "spreads out Time so long and Heaven so deep," is that they are in likeness to the "Abyss of the Father, into which if a creature drop down his thoughts for ever he shall hear no echo return to him" (*Per* 218). Explicitly Trinitarian language is rare in the Ransom Trilogy, and in this case is used to point to age and distance as Masculine images tasked with communicating the reality of divine mystery and transcendence. As the representative of King Arthur, the once and future king of distant past, Ransom is an image of this Masculine age and distance.

An Assailant Warrior

Another essential quality of Arthur is that he is a warrior—the "best of all knights" (Laʒamon 21), "from spur to plume a star of tournament" (Tennyson 252). Certainly his heading the Knights of the Round Table has a very strong place in the popular subconscious of Arthurian imagery. Since his very earliest appearances in literature, Arthur has been known for his power on the battlefield, both in personal prowess and in his skill as a commander. In Nennius he is said to have fought and killed nine-hundred and sixty men by himself in a single day at the battle of Badon Hill (the last of his twelve major victories as a commander; 35), in many stories he fights and kills a giant (Geoffrey 226; Laʒamon 191; *Vulgate Merlin* 459–60; Malory 135–36), and not infrequently he resolves military or political conflicts through personal combat (Geoffrey 206–08; Laʒamon 137–39). In some stories, he is practically credited with inventing chivalry with his company of knights (Laʒamon 113). Frequently he goes to war, often invading other countries all over Europe (Geoffrey 192, 206, 220; Laʒamon 39, 81, 97–125), and in one common story he boldly attempts to conquer the Roman Empire (Geoffrey 204; Laʒamon 167–69). Though it is not at all uncommon for Arthur to be fighting on his own lands, one gets the impression from many stories that even in those fights he is on the offensive rather than the defensive. His rise to power often involves him taking his own land back from Saxons, unlawful British tyrants, beasts, and beast-like men (Geoffrey 192; Laʒamon 39; *Vulgate Merlin* 101, 254; Malory 19–28; Tennyson 8–9).

As the Pendragon, Ransom in *That Hideous Strength* leads Logres to war in his struggle with the N.I.C.E. Being chronically injured keeps Ransom from much physical activity in this book, but we still see the knightly aspect in his character, which we first sensed all the way back in *Out of the Silent Planet* when Malacandra commanded him to "be courageous" and to fight Devine and Weston back on earth (142). When Jane meets Ransom for the first time in *That Hideous Strength*, she marvels at his strength: "Now it was manifest that the grip of those hands would be inescapable, and imagination suggested that those arms and shoulders could support the whole house" (139). Not too long previously on Perelandra, that grip had been put to good use in Ransom's very physical and bloody duel with the Un-man, during which he received the wound in his heel (*Per* 187); indeed, it is hard not to think of Ransom as knightly when he is fighting in defense of a Lady and shouting lines from the *Battle of Maldon* at the same time (*Per* 155).

We also see Ransom in *That Hideous Strength* in the role of military commander, most significantly in two places. The first is when he sends Dimble and Denniston out with pistols to find Merlin (225). Here the two men are Christians who have taken up arms to serve a just cause, as Lewis defines the knight in *Mere Christianity* (107). Ransom is in the role of military commander a second time when he orders Merlin (filled with the powers of the eldila) to make war on the N.I.C.E. (291), which results in much bloodshed and the destruction of both the N.I.C.E. and Edgestow (344–47, 369). In fact, the very language used to describe the eldilas' possession of Merlin is that of invasion (288). In this instance, we can imagine a hierarchy descending from Maleldil to the eldila to Ransom to Merlin. In his stern command to Merlin to receive the eldila, Ransom is representing the eldila to Merlin—he is the spearhead, the point of the eldilic invasion.

Aggression, invasion, and bellicosity are all Masculine aspects, as can be seen in Malacandra's holding in his hands "something like a spear" (*Per* 200) and having the look of one "standing armed ... in ceaseless vigilance" (201). When he sees Malacandra, he receives confirmation that he is "man of war" (201). Tor foresees that he and Malacandra will go to war against the corrupted eldila of Earth and will break the Moon, which is "as the shield of the Dark Lord of Thulcandra" (212). In *The Four Loves*, Lewis describes the Masculine as "assailant" and "conqueror" (145); Tor, Malacandra, King Arthur, and Ransom Pendragon can all be described this way.

While it is easily understood why aggression and warlike strength are good virtues to have when one is dealing with an enemy, it may seem more difficult to explain the place that such virtue could have in the relationship between Masculinity and Femininity, where the object is not to produce destruction but rather to image the loving life of God. The place of aggression and invasion in the Masculine-Feminine relationship can be seen in a few scenes from *That Hideous Strength*, to which I now turn.

When Jane meets the Director for the first time, it is also in many ways her first encounter with the Masculine (or at least her first receptive encounter with it), and the result is that "her world was unmade" (*THS* 140). The Director's "voice also seemed to be like sunlight and gold. Like gold not only as gold is beautiful but as it is heavy: like sunlight not only as it falls gently on English walls in autumn but as it beats down on the jungle or the desert to engender life or destroy it" (140). We are told that she is so taken by what she encounters at that meeting that before him she is left without any power of resistance and "without protection" (141). After some time with Ransom and the company of St. Anne's, Jane, now more receptive of the Masculine, is considering the company's approach to their faith. They do not think of "religion" drifting up to God, but rather of "strong, skillful hands thrust down to make, and mend, perhaps even to destroy" (*THS* 315). As she ponders this, she has something like a vision of God or a sense of the presence of God, a presence that meets her with "no veil or protection between" (315); in that experience "her defenses had been captured" (316).

In light of these encounters, we can define the warlike nature of the Masculine as the positive quality of being that which cannot be defended against—of having power of such vitality that it cannot be resisted. Where there is attempted resistance, it is in Masculinity to break defenses, to shatter shields as Tor and Malacandra will shatter the Moon. But we can imagine non-destructive applications of this quality when no defense is attempted: God acts with irresistible power and might when he creates, and a baby cannot resist being conceived.

The King

The last and most important characteristic of Arthur is that he is King. Unlike the Fisher King, whose reign is mostly defective, Arthur is the kingly ideal. This characteristic is the hallmark of Arthur's place in the popular subconscious and is frequently referenced even in those stories where the given Arthur character does not live up to the Arthur of legend. As a king, it is Arthur's job both to provide the means for his subjects to live well and to expect them to do so. In doing so he protects his people from strife (Geoffrey 204; Laȝamon 87–89), generously provides for them (Geoffrey 192; Laȝamon 39; Malory 10–11), and upholds the good laws of the country and God's laws (Geoffrey 204; Laȝamon 37). As Tor said of his own place, so it is with Arthur's subjects: "All is gift" (*Per* 209).

As all readers know, Ransom is kingly in *That Hideous Strength*. When Jane first meets him, "she tasted the word *King* itself with all linked associations of battle, marriage, priesthood, mercy, and power" (140), and she is reminded of the "imagined Arthur of her childhood" (140). Ransom protects and provides for his company in his own property, St. Anne's: they are all his "charities" (165). Like their king, he gives commands: earlier we saw him command Dimble and Denniston to look for Merlin, and he commands Merlin to receive the power of the eldila, saying to him: "You will not disobey me" (291). He is authoritative in his refusal to allow Jane to join St. Anne's without Mark (146). In his book-long rehabilitation of Jane's relationship with the Masculine, it is by his "sovereign power" as king that Ransom brings Mark and Jane together (Ward 49). Ransom enforces the laws of the land, both the proper relationship between husbands and wives and the policy of the chore rotation between the men and the women of the house (*THS* 164). Ransom, through his generous provision and righteous rule as king, raises his subjects to higher life. He takes citizens of mere Britain and makes them citizens of the holy kingdom of Logres; he takes wild animals and makes them real members of his house (162); and he takes the dead, futile marriage of Jane and Mark and breathes into it the pattern of the Masculine and the Feminine, bringing from it new and bountiful unity.

In the Ransom Trilogy, kingliness is Masculine. When the dark eldilic master of Earth blights Mars with deadly cold and infects its inhabitants with his corrupting influence, Malacandra, like a king, provides for his subjects by unleashing the planet's hot springs and exercises his rule over his subjects to root out the demonic corruption from them: "Some I cured, some I unbodied" (*OSP* 120, 138). The image of the king who gives life and imposes laws on that life sounds very much like the "hands thrust down to make, and mend, perhaps even to destroy" and the sun that beats down to "engender life or destroy it" that we saw in our discussion of the assailant warrior. There certainly is much overlap in the qualities captured by the images of the knight and the king, and it is no accident that the two roles are always blending into one another—there does not seem to be a problem in the minds of those authors closest to the shared Arthur of making the best king also the best knight. This is because a kindred ethos drives both roles.

But for our purposes there is an important difference between the knight and the king as distinct images of the Masculine: the knight especially images the *ability* to dominate, and the king especially images the *authority* to dominate. In one is emphasized the armor and spear, in the other the crown and scepter. The knight is the mighty assailant and cannot be resisted; the king is the rightful sovereign and should not be. This distinction between the king and the knight is traceable over what Malacandra holds in his hand in *Perelandra*: it is "something like a spear"—not a spear necessarily, because it is being used to represent both the spear and the scepter at once. In the "unions of a kneeling with a sceptered love" the Masculine is the sceptered, the sovereign.

The order of Maleldil is characterized by the relationship between the opposites of the sceptered and the kneeling, between "rule and obedience, begetting and bearing, heat glancing down, life growing up" (*Per* 214). And in this dance between unlikes, the Masculine is the sceptered, the ruling, the begetting, the heat glancing down, the one "giving place" as opposed to receiving it (*Per* 217). The Masculine lives in the Great Dance where the only rule is righteous rule, and where rule itself is not vilified but celebrated—where between good kings and dutiful subjects there is no shadow of abusiveness in the former or resentment in the latter. The Masculine rules not only with the strength of the knight, but with the ordained authority of the king who judges with righteousness and makes of his people a kingdom of heavenly order.

Ransom the Fisher King

So much for Ransom Pendragon—we now turn to Ransom as the Fisher King. My approach in illustrating the Fisher King in Ransom and the Feminine in both will be to follow the same pattern used above to associate Arthur, Ransom, and the Masculine. As with Arthur, I am not merely trying to show that Ransom and the Fisher King have similar personalities; what we are after are those images that are most central to the role of the Fisher King in the shared Arthurian imagination. But unlike with the shared Arthur, the images of the shared Fisher King are less centralized in the Fisher King character proper and are also at times difficult to neatly distinguish from one another. In noting that this relative ambiguity in the primary informing imagery is itself a Feminine quality, we can begin perceiving the association of the Fisher King with the Feminine already.

The Wounded

The primary informing image of the Fisher King is his suffering a wound that cannot be healed other than by the fulfillment of some version of the Grail quest (Chrétien 425; Wolfram 106–08; Malory 61).

Though the nature of the Fisher King wound varies, it is often the work of a spear, and often in the thigh or groin area (Chrétien 424; Wolfram 202; *Post-Vulgate Merlin* 93; Malory 60). In Chrétien we are told that because of the pain of his wound, the Fisher King is unable to ride a horse or hunt; the only diversion he can tolerate is to sit in his boat and fish (hence his name; 424); the Post-Vulgate Merlin tells a similar story (440). The Fisher King is often crippled by his wound and forced to be at rest: in early versions the image is of the king reclining on a couch by a fire surrounded by his people (Chrétien 419; Wolfram 97)—later versions will have him bedridden (*Vulgate Quest* 166; Malory 669). The cause of the wound also varies. The most remembered version is the infamous Dolorous Stroke, when the Fisher King is stabbed with the hallowed spear used to pierce the side of Christ (*Post-Vulgate Merlin* 93; Malory 60). There is no usual reason for why the wound will not heal without the achievement of the Grail quest, but from the first the Wounded King is kept alive by the power of the Grail (Chrétien 460).

In *That Hideous Strength*, Ransom also suffers from an unhealable wound—indeed it is the fact that Ransom shares this chief characteristic of the Arthurian Fisher King that assures the reader of a serious imaginative association between the two in the first place. Ransom's unhealable wound is on his heel, and, as with the Fisher King, both the cause of the wound and the reason it cannot be healed are relatively insignificant to the story. While the Fisher King is kept alive by the power of the Grail, Ransom lives on in spite of his wound as a result of his time on Perelandra, and it is back on Perelandra in the "cup-shaped land of Abhalljin" (*THS* 271, 366) that the wound will finally be healed (*THS* 366).

Like the Fisher King, Ransom is crippled by his wound and is almost always either resting (*THS* 139, 283, 365) or walking with a crutch (260). There is one notable instance of Ransom's setting aside his crutch: the scene in which Merlin joins St. Anne's and the company finds him and Ransom standing together looking down from the balustrade. The two are robed, and Ransom is wearing a crown. Ransom has laid aside his crutch, and "Jane had hardly seen him standing so straight and still before" (275). The Pendragon imagery used here—the kingly glory and verticality of the Masculine aspect—is in sharp contrast to the primary imagery of a scene soon after: Merlin and Ransom are talking alone together in the Blue Room, and Ransom has put aside his crown and robe and is lying on the sofa, his face "full of torment" (283–84). As the Pendragon standing crowned on the balcony is an image of the Masculine, so the Fisher King reclining in agony is an image of the Feminine.

There are of course some obvious imaginative parallels between the woundedness of the Fisher King and female sexuality: before *That Hideous Strength* was published, Charles Williams had already associated the Fisher King's perpetual wound with menstruation in his own Arthuriana ("The Son of Lancelot" 71–74), and "reclining in pain" is often appropriate descriptive language both for the loss of female virginity and for childbirth. The rampant use of both erotic and maternal imagery for the Feminine we will explore more as we go—for now we are more interested in how suffering in particular is Feminine.

Suffering is Feminine in mainly two ways. The first is found in the primary definition of the word "suffer"—to be subjected to something. The sufferer is the patient to an outside agent, the responsive to a foreign active. This sense of the word "suffer" is enshrined as a central virtue in the motto of Perelandra: "No fixed land. Always one must throw oneself into the wave" (210). Those who live on the floating islands of the ocean planet Perelandra are in a constant state of patience to the waves, and are called by Feminine virtue to surrender control and receive the world as it comes to them. The Feminine is the responsive, the obedient, the bearing, and the kneeling love, like Christ who humbles himself in obedience to the will of his Father. As the eldil Perelandra herself appears standing with hands open and palms outward, so are receptivity, patience, and suffering shown to be essential qualities of the Feminine.

Suffering is Feminine, secondly, when it is suffering for others. This form of suffering—reflected in the female bearing and birthing of children—we see primarily in the persons of Tinidril, Perelandra, and Ransom in *Perelandra*. Much of the book is taken up with Tinidril's constant and laborious temptation to disobedience by the diabolical Un-man, a trial and suffering from which her husband Tor is absent. Because Tinidril ultimately endures her suffering and obediently resists temptation, she has kept her husband and future children from corruption and far worse suffering (133). It is revealed toward the end of the book that the eldil Perelandra herself has also long been laboring, in patience and silence, to ready the world for the sake of the new King and Queen who are ultimately to take her place (196). And lastly, we see Feminine suffering for others accompanied by real pain in the wound Ransom receives when he battles the Un-man to spare Tor and Tinidril corruption and death. In the giving of his own health and safety for the sake of the new King and Queen, Ransom becomes a Feminine patient—a representation of Christ, the wounded and suffering servant.

The Grail Castle

Our next informing image of the Fisher King is the Grail Castle, which has been an important symbol of the Fisher King's place in Arthuriana since the beginnings of the Grail legend. It is in the Grail Castle that the Fisher King resides, waiting for the achievement of the Grail quest and tending to the Grail while it sustains his life. The Grail Castle represents the Fisher King on the imaginative level in three main qualities: hiddenness, hospitality, and mysterious ceremony.

Hiddenness in the Grail Castle is common in the early Grail romances. In Chrétien, Perceval has a hard time finding the Grail Castle, even though the Fisher King had given him clear directions (418–19). Wolfram's Fisher King warns Parzival about getting lost on his way to the Grail Castle (96), since it usually cannot be found by anyone looking for it (106). The hiddenness of the Grail Castle is essential again in the mayhem of the Grail quests in Malory, which has the Knights of the Round Table scouring the countryside for the Grail and almost none of them finding anything (Malory 615)—only a few find the Grail Castle and with it the Grail (666). In Tennyson, Arthur is afraid that all those who set out on the Grail quest will end up only chasing "wandering fires" (177).

Inside the Grail Castle, the wanderer is usually met with great welcome and treated to lavish hospitality. In Chrétien and Wolfram, the interior hall is lit by an enormous fire and the guest is treated to a very costly and elaborate feast (Chrétien 419–22; Wolfram 97–102). In the *Vulgate Lancelot*, guests are met with good smells and fine food (4.376–77; 5.101–02; 6.301). Likewise, in Malory Lancelot is treated with "savour as all the spicery of the world had been there" and "all manner of meats and drinks that they could think upon" (Malory 524); Bors later gets the same treatment when he himself is a guest (527–28).

Lastly, the Grail Castle is characterized by ceremony and mystery, as it is where the Grail is kept and seen in procession along with the Sacred Spear (Chrétien 420–21; Wolfram 98–102) and where the Grail bestows mystical visions when it is eventually achieved (*Vulgate Quest* 162–66; *Post-Vulgate Quest* 355–58; Malory 666–69). The sense of mystery and wonderment at the Grail procession is a recurring experience among guests of the Grail house: Perceval continually wants to ask about the Grail (Chrétien 421), and Lancelot responds to the procession by asking: "O Jesu … what may this mean?" (Malory 524). The presence of mystical artifacts in dimly lit chambers imparts on the Grail Castle an atmosphere not only of wonderment but also of haunting—a haunting by strange, inexplicable entities driven by their own independent purposes and unknown powers.

Ransom's own mansion, St. Anne's, also embodies the Grail Castle's peculiar combination of hiddenness, hospitality, and mystery. St. Anne's is hidden and private from the chief areas of action in the narrative; much of Ransom's company are staying there to avoid the N.I.C.E. invasion of Edgestow, and Jane also hides there from Mark and the N.I.C.E. (*THS* 214–16). We learn from Frost and Wither that Ransom himself is also being looked for by the N.I.C.E. and cannot be found (272)—the reader knows he is at St. Anne's.

The hospitality of the Grail Castle is found in what Hilder calls St. Anne's "informal symbols, including an inviting meal in a tidy kitchen with a hearth ablaze with warmth (163), a well-tended vegetable garden, congenial conversation, and a festive banquet," all of which she interprets as underscoring the "feminine" in St. Anne's (Hilder 114). Indeed, the presence of food, fire, and gardens at St. Anne's is pervasive.

Mystery is also present in St. Anne's from the first. Jane witnesses the mysterious in her first encounter with Ransom, which is terminated by the uncanny intrusion of mystical eldilic presence (*THS* 147). Ivy Maggs once says to Ransom: "They're so eerie, these ones that come to visit you. I wouldn't go near that part of the house if I thought there was anything there, not if you paid me a hundred pounds" (*THS* 259). The reader may also be unnerved by the presence of the eldila in *That Hideous Strength*. Unlike in the first two books of the Ransom Trilogy, here the eldila are never heard speaking, and their mystical haunting of Ransom's house is hinted at and suggested long before they appear in bodily form and by their names (318–24). This drawn-out, subtle introduction succeeds in turning up the mystical nature of the eldila to Grail-like levels. In the previous books, the eldila were explained using primarily scientific language that suited the science fiction medium. In *That Hideous Strength*—the "fairy-tale for grown-ups"—the scientific explanations of the eldila have been replaced with the images, suggestions, and questions of living mystery: an atmosphere better suited to the presence of the Grail.

In the qualities of hiddenness, hospitality, and mystery, the Grail Castle is an image of the Feminine. Hiddenness and privacy are seen in Perelandra's hiding her face from Tor and Tinidril until they were grown (*Per* 195–96) and in her eyes that are opened inward "as if they were the curtained gateway to a world of waves and murmurings and wandering airs" (201). The place where Ransom finds the eldila and the coronation ceremony, the valley of the Holy Mountain, is a "secret place," something "soft and flushed" (193), and is found (like the Grail mansion in Chrétien; 418) in a cleft between two mountain peaks (*Per* 193, 204). The imagery used here is certainly evocative of the form of the female body.

Warm and nurturing hospitality is frequently seen in Perelandra. Her halo glows with "a warm splendour, full of the suggestion of teeming vegetable life" (*Per* 199); she is the "life growing up" to the Masculine "heat glancing down" (214). She holds her hands open in sign of receptiveness (200). When Ransom is recovering from his fight with the Un-man, he is "breast-fed by the planet Venus herself" in the form of "grape-like fruit" from which he sucks "delicious life" (185). The very planet itself, with its rocking islands (40), dim lighting (36), warmth (36), and abundant food (49–50, 199), is an environment that embodies nurturing hospitality.

Strange ceremony and mystery are also apparent in Perelandra's sphere. Ransom's journey through the tunnels of Perelandra after he has killed the Un-man is full of mystery and the uncanny, as Ransom finds himself wandering through a world not made for humans, but assuredly made for *something* (183). Mystery is also seen in his journey from the caves of Perelandra to the Holy Mountain: we are told that had Ransom died and been travelling through the "trans-mortal mountains," his journey "could hardly have been more great and strange" (192).

Twice now, I have drawn some imaginative association between the eldila and the Grail: first in the similarity between the valley of the Holy Mountain and the valley of the Grail Castle, and then again in the similarity between the mystical presence of the eldila in St. Anne's and the presence of the Grail in the Grail Castle. Another connection between the eldila and the Grail is in their enacting something like the Grail procession in Ransom's presence at the end of *Perelandra*. Like the wanderer who enters the Grail Castle in its valley and is shown the procession of the Sacred Spear and the Holy Grail, Ransom enters the valley of the Holy Mountain and is shown "something like a spear" in Malacandra's hands and something like a grail in the openness and concavity suggested by Perelandra's hands, which are held open with palms outward. And like the one who completes the Grail quest and is shown its mysteries, Ransom is shown by Malacandra and Perelandra a mystical vision of the Great Dance of the Masculine and the Feminine.[7]

Hiddenness, nurturing hospitality, and mystery are all necessary conditions of the engendering and bearing of "life growing up"—of both the maternal and the erotic Feminine qualities especially symbolized in Ransom's emergence from the Perelandrian caves and his entering the valley of the Holy Mountain. In these episodes, it is primarily in the environment that Ransom sees the Feminine, and so what is being imaged is what we might call the Feminine environment: the hidden place of nurturing in which the mystery of new life begins.

The Grail Knight

Lastly, the Fisher King is informed by his relationship to the Grail Knight, who is to finally complete the Grail quest and heal the unhealable wound. The Fisher King's relation to the Grail Knight is manifested

---

7   Though the eldila do seem to be performing some Grail-like functions in the Ransom Trilogy, they are not the Grail proper. In Merlin's reference to the Dolorous Stroke—"the stroke that Balinus struck" (*THS* 275)—and in the revelation that in the world of *THS* "the Arthurian story is mostly true history" (367), we have good reason to assume that the traditional Holy Grail did (or does) exist in the Ransom Trilogy universe.

primarily in his waiting for the Grail Knight to complete the Grail quest and in his occasioning the Grail Knight's conception and birth.

In the Arthur stories, the Fisher King waits for the Grail knight to complete the Grail quest, as he knows that the arrival and success of the Grail Knight will mean both healing of his wound (Wolfram 333; *Vulgate Quest* 166; *Post-Vulgate Quest* 355; Malory 669) and the passing of his office to the Grail Knight (Wolfram 333; *Vulgate Quest* 169; *Post-Vulgate Quest* 372; Malory 672). In the earlier Grail romances, the Grail Knight finds his way into the hidden Grail Castle without any idea that the hope of the healing of the Fisher King and the achievement of the Grail are laid on him. The Grail Knight needs to ask concerning the wound and the Grail to complete the quest and heal the king (Chrétien 425; Wolfram 106–08), but the Fisher King cannot tell the Grail Knight what is going on. The image is of the rich Fisher King doing honor and great hospitality to the Grail Knight, presenting him with the mysterious procession of the Spear and the Grail and being unable to ask for his help or advise him on how to conclude the quest, hoping only that the piteousness of the unhealable wound and the strangeness of the Grail will incite the knight to question. The Fisher King's pastime of fishing takes on new meaning as his role in the Grail quest turns out to be mostly sitting, waiting, and hoping that the Grail Knight will take the bait and achieve the Grail.

In later works, when the Grail Knight is no longer Percival but Galahad, the Fisher King has another part to play in his adventure. While Lancelot is staying in the Grail Castle (not on the Grail quest), the Fisher King tricks him into lying with his daughter, thinking, correctly, that the resulting child, Galahad, would be the next Grail King (*Vulgate Lancelot* 5.101–14; Malory 524). Though we sense in this act of trickery and complicit fornication some of the usual moral confusion of the late Arthurian romances (in Malory, the Fisher King will explain in a few pages that none can win worship in the Grail country but by "clean living" and the love and dread of God; 528), this function of the Fisher King is essential to his place in the late Grail legends.

We have already seen that Ransom in *That Hideous Strength* is also awaiting the healing of his own wound, which will come only after he has finished his work on earth and returned to Perelandra. We have also already seen that he is, like the Fisher King, a matchmaker, awaiting the arrival of his heir. By his continual mentorship, Ransom plays a crucial role in rehabilitating Jane's relationship with Mark and encouraging her toward a fruitful marriage bed, which she achieves in the book's last passage. Mark and Jane's child is to be Ransom's heir as the next Pendragon.

But though the succession of his office depends on it, Ransom cannot directly cause a fruitful union between Jane and Mark. Though he is able to mentor Jane in the right direction, Ransom has no influence whatsoever over Mark. Ransom can only wait to see if Mark will come back to Jane and whether he will be spiritually ready for the fruitful marriage bed when he does. Ransom can only occasion, make room, and hope to be provided with a successor. He is the patient to the agency of Jane and Mark, who must achieve the Masculine and the Feminine of their own will.

The waiting and matchmaking of Ransom and the Fisher King are both Feminine. The receptiveness and patience exhibited in the Fisher King's waiting for the Grail Knight and Ransom's waiting for the next Pendragon we have already seen as Feminine qualities in our discussion of Feminine woundedness. It again appears as appropriate for both the erotic and maternal images frequently used for the Feminine in the Ransom Trilogy: it can be seen in the bride waiting for her bridegroom, or, combined with Fisher King-like pain, the woman in labor waiting to give birth to her child. The Grail Knight's dual imaginative roles as one being born and as bridegroom we saw above being reflected by Ransom in his journey out of the Perelandrian caves and into the valley of the Holy Mountain in *Perelandra*.

Birth imagery certainly has precedence in the Feminine definition given in *Perelandra*, some of which we looked at already. On Perelandra, the Feminine world, a new life is born—a new kind of life, even—in the successful ascension of Tor and Tinidril, the first fruits of a humanity that never sinned. "The world is born to-day," says Malacandra on that day (197). Likewise, bringing together the Masculine and the Feminine in unity to cause new life is also Feminine. Since Perelandra is Venus, the goddess of Love, it is in her sphere, the Third Heaven, that we see the Masculine and the Feminine standing together in clear relation to each other in the presence of Malacandra and Perelandra for the first time. And it is as the goddess of love that Perelandra presides over all the male-female pairings of the ceremony at the end of *Perelandra* (203–04), as well as over the many male-female pairings (the healed marriage bed of Jane and Mark in particular) at the end of *That Hideous Strength* (373–78, 380). As the Grail Castle is an image of the Feminine environment from which comes new life, so are the patience and unitive influence of Ransom and the Fisher King images of the Feminine participation in the engendering and bearing of new life.

The Union of the Genders

We now see that the particular purpose of putting Ransom in the roles of the two very different Arthurian kings, King Arthur and the Fisher King, was to use him as an icon of both the Masculine and the Feminine and therefore an iconographic representation of all who inhabit the genders relationally as joyful citizens of the Great Dance.

The present scope has been limited, and from where we must leave the discussion there remains much more to be said about the application of the Masculine and Feminine to Ransom in his roles as Pendragon and Fisher King. But there are also a few other directions the discussion could be taken. Firstly, we, who have been focusing so far only on the way that the Arthuriad sheds light on the Ransom Trilogy genders, might ask whether the Ransom Trilogy genders have something to say about the Arthuriad. Does the Masculine help us to know Arthur, and the Feminine the Fisher King? This is a natural question from where we now stand in the history of the Arthuriad, after Williams and Lewis have both made serious Arthurian contributions heading in this direction.

Secondly, we might further inquire what place the Masculine and Feminine images could have—or already do have—in Christian theology. What is the extent to which Masculine and Feminine imagery is operative in our knowledge of God, the Ancient of Days, the Almighty, the King of Kings, who is also the God of all Comfort, the Bread of Life, our Dwelling Place? Or in Jesus Christ in particular, who is both the triumphant Lion of Judah and the crucified Lamb of God—the wearer of both the crown of gold and the crown of thorns?

In giving Ransom both Arthurian crowns, Lewis has used Ransom as a multifaceted symbol communicating all at once the images of the Masculine and Feminine, the pattern of the Great Dance, and even the life of the Godhead—an icon of joyful order and Trinitarian giving and receiving. Having achieved the Masculine and the Feminine in *Perelandra*, Ransom is able to inhabit his proper place in the Great Dance between the eldilic powers of the heavens and his company of St. Anne's. As a properly ordered creature, he is able to suffer the orders of his eldilic masters in obedience on the one hand and order his kingdom in the fight against the N.I.C.E. on the other. Ransom is a representative of both the ideal king and the ideal subject. The eldila, looking down on Ransom, see in him the humility, the obedience, and the wounded sacrifice of the Suffering Servant just as they are portrayed in the keeper of the Grail, who waits patiently for the Grail quest to be achieved and for his suffering to find healing. Looking up, the company of St. Anne's sees the royalty, majesty, and ancient power of the King of Kings, who judges the world and prepares a place for those who love him, just as it can be seen in faithful portraiture in King Arthur, who frees his people and makes of them the most magnificent kingdom in the world. As Pendragon and Fisher King, Ransom has achieved in the measure due him the opposite virtues of the fundamental polarity of the universe, the ruling iron scepter and the welcoming open hand of Malacandra and Perelandra, of the Father and the Son, of the Masculine and the Feminine.

Works Cited

Archibald, Elizabeth. "Questioning Arthurian Ideals." *The Cambridge Companion to the Arthurian Legend.* Ed. Elizabeth Archibald and Ad Putter. Cambridge UP, 2009. 139–53. Print.

Chrétien de Troyes. *Arthurian Romances.* Trans. William W. Kibler and Carleton W. Carroll. London: Penguin, 1991. Print.

Geoffrey de Monmouth. *The History of the Kings of Britain.* Ed. Michael D. Reeve. Trans. Neil Wright. Woodbridge: Boydell, 2007. Print.

Glyer, Diana Pavlac. "'We are *All* Fallen Creatures and *All* Very Hard to Live With': Some Thoughts on Lewis and Gender." *Christian Scholar's Review* 36.4 (2007): 477–83. Print.

Hilder, Monika B. *The Gender Dance: Ironic Subversion in C. S. Lewis' Cosmic Trilogy.* NY: Peter Lang, 2013. Print.

Lancelot-Grail: The Old French Arthurian Vulgate and Post-Vulgate in Translation. Ed. Norris J. Lacy. 9 vols. Cambridge: D. S. Brewer, 2010. Print.

Laȝamon. *Laȝamon's "Arthur": The Arthurian Section of Laȝamon's "Brut" (lines 9229–14297).* Ed. and trans. W. R. J. Barron and S. C. Weinberg. U of Exeter, 2001. Print.

Lewis, C. S. "Christianity and Literature." *Christian Reflections.* Ed. Walter Hooper. Grand Rapids, MI: Eerdmans, 2003. 1–11. Print.

——. *The Discarded Image: An Introduction to Medieval and Renaissance Literature.* 1964. Cambridge UP, 1994. Print.

——. *The Four Loves.* NY: Harcourt Brace Jovanovich, 1960. Print.

——. "The Genesis of a Medieval Book." *Studies in Medieval and Renaissance Literature.* Ed. Walter Hooper. Cambridge UP, 1998. 18–40. Print.

——. *Mere Christianity.* 1943. NY: Macmillan, 1952. Print.

——. *Out of the Silent Planet.* 1938. NY: Scribner, 2003. Print.

——. *Perelandra.* 1943. NY: Macmillan, 1970. Print.

——. "Priestesses in the Church?" *God in the Dock: Essays on Theology and Ethics*. Ed. Walter Hooper. Glasgow: Collins, 1979. 87–94. Print.

——. *Spenser's Images of Life*. Ed. Alastair Fowler. Cambridge UP, 1967. Print.

——. *That Hideous Strength: A Modern Fairy-Tale for Grown-Ups*. 1945. NY: Scribner, 2003. Print.

——. "Williams and the Arthuriad." *Taliessin through Logres; The Region of the Summer Stars; Arthurian Torso*. By Charles Williams and C. S. Lewis. 1948. Grand Rapids, MI: Eerdmans, 1974.

Loades, Ann. "On Gender." *The Cambridge Companion to C. S. Lewis*. Ed. Robert MacSwain and Michael Ward. Cambridge UP, 2010. 160–73. Print.

Loomis, Roger Sherman. *The Development of Arthurian Romance*. Mineola, NY: Dover Publications, 2000. Print.

Malory, Thomas. *Le Morte Darthur*. Ware, Hertfordshire: Wordsworth Classics, 1996. Print.

Morris, Rosemary. *The Character of King Arthur in Medieval Literature*. Bury St Edmunds: St. Edumundsbury Press, 1982. Print.

Nennius. *Nennius: British History and the Welsh Annals*. Arthurian Sources 8. Ed. and trans. John Morris. London and Chichester: Phillimore, 1980. Print.

Putter, Ad and Elizabeth Archibald. Introduction. *The Cambridge Companion to the Arthurian Legend*. Ed. Elizabeth Archibald and Ad Putter. Cambridge UP, 2009. 1–17. Print.

Tennyson, Alfred. *Idylls of the King*. Radford, VA: Wilder Publications, 2007. Print.

Tolkien, J. R. R. *The Fall of Arthur*. Ed. Christopher Tolkien. London: HarperCollins, 2013. Print.

Van Leeuwen, Mary Stewart. *A Sword between the Sexes?: C. S. Lewis and the Gender Debates*. Grand Rapids, MI: Brazos, 2010. Print.

Ward, Michael. *Planet Narnia: The Seven Heavens in the Imagination of C. S. Lewis*. NY: Oxford UP, 2008. Print.

Williams, Charles, and C. S. Lewis. *Taliessin through Logres, The Region of the Summer Stars, Arthurian Torso*. Grand Rapids, MI: Eerdmans, 1974. Print.

Wolfram von Eschenbach. *Parzival; And, Titurel*. Trans. Cyril W. Edwards. Oxford UP, 2006. Print.

Cartographies of the Spirit

16

"Servant of All": Arthurian Peregrinations in George MacDonald

Kirstin Jeffrey Johnson

> *... as into the solid land run the creeks and gulfs from the unresting sea; as the lights and influences of the upper worlds sink silently through the earth's atmosphere; so doth Faerie invade the world of men.*
>
> *—Phantastes, 146*

The Arthurian element in George MacDonald's writing has been largely overlooked in both MacDonald scholarship and Inklings scholarship. This is surprising, given the pervasiveness of medieval revivalism throughout the writings of MacDonald and the fact that this was in part what drew both C. S. Lewis and J. R. R. Tolkien to his work.[1] This chapter considers MacDonald's engagement with medieval revivalism in his two most explicitly Arthurian novels, the first of which is best known to Inklings scholarship for its profound effect upon Lewis. Correlations and responses within the works of the Inklings to MacDonald will be set aside for future studies (such as the kinds of intertextual examinations initiated by Brenton D. G. Dickieson in chapter 3 of the present volume); the intent of this chapter is to further inform such work.

To begin with, MacDonald is situated within the medieval revivalism movement. Personally acquainted with many of its most successful evangelists, he was at the vanguard of its literary and social reforms. This

---

[1] Lewis' delighted description of Tolkien to his friend Arthur Greeves was: "The one man absolutely fitted, if fate had allowed, to be a third in our friendship in the old days, for he also grew up on William Morris and George MacDonald. Reading his fairy tale has been uncanny—it is so exactly like what we both have longed to write (or read) ... describing the same world into which all three of us have the entry" (*CL* 2:103).

framed his response as the fashion for things medieval and Arthurian gradually seeped into all facets of Victorian society. In particular, MacDonald challenged the Romantic notion of chivalry manifested as the "Victorian gentleman": a *noblesse oblige* that reinforced an attitude of national and nationalistic feudalism. MacDonald recalls his readers to what he believes to be a more truly English rendering of the concept, rooting it in medieval English vocabulary. Deeply committed to social reform, MacDonald was not—like some medieval revivalists—suggesting that a reversion to England's past would solve social ills incurred by the Industrial Revolution; rather, he was arguing that new perceptions informed by attention to that past might do so. Thus, in attending to both etymology and myth, MacDonald provokes a re-examination of contemporary attitudes toward gender, class, and spiritual identity. In *Phantastes: A Faerie Romance for Men and Women*, he portrays the fantastical adventures of a young Englishman who has to relinquish his romanticized notions of chivalric adventure in order to discover how to be a true knight. In *The Seaboard Parish*, a switch in genre allows MacDonald to shift his angle, yet his broad challenge to a readership obsessed by Arthurian faerie remains the same: a truly English chivalry quests for neither acquisition nor status, but rather to become a "servant of all" (*Seaboard* 94). In consequence, to act as a truly English knight cannot but effect social change.

The Victorian medieval revivalism of which MacDonald was a part began gradually. During the eighteenth century, matters medieval had been largely the preserve of antiquarians, and the new age Arthurian legend remained a minority interest primarily of social historians (Jenkins 182–84). In 1817, when Poet Laureate Robert Southey wrote an introduction to the new edition of Malory's *Morte D'Arthur*—previously out of print since 1634—the text was little known.[2] By the end of the century, however, references to Malory were ubiquitous from political cartoons to mundane advertising. Although today this Arthurian revival is commonly attributed to iconic names such as Alfred, Lord Tennyson (Southey's successor, often cited as the official instigator of Arthur's return), F. J. Furnivall, William Morris, and the Pre-Raphaelites, in reality these famed writers and artists were but few amongst many, and their enduring work emerged from a burgeoning company of fellow enthusiasts (Bryden *passim*).[3] Scholars such as the education and social reformers A. J. Scott and F. D. Maurice—two of the very first English Literature professors—generated early enthusiasm with their impassioned arguments that England was insufficiently familiar with her own literature and myths.[4] Scott, championed by the likes of Southey and his dialogue partner Thomas Carlyle,

2   1816 was the first run; Southey wrote the introduction for the second run in 1817. By 1853, it was still plausible that a well-educated Archdeacon's son (as in Yonge's very popular novel *The Heir of Redclyffe*) was ignorant of Malory's *Morte d'Arthur*; but by the 1870s such ignorance would have been impossible (Jenkins 211).

3   William Morris's Arts & Crafts movement was inspired by the medievalism and social critiques of John Ruskin and Augustus Pugin. The aesthetic and social vision was first developed in the 1850s and had cohered by the 1860s. MacDonald, like Morris, was a careful student of Ruskin's *Modern Painters* during this period. An acquaintance between Ruskin and MacDonald in 1863 quickly turned to deep friendship and enabled for the latter an even greater familiarity with the Pre-Raphaelite and Arts & Crafts circles.

4   Scott and Maurice were highly successful campaigners, founders, and teachers of institutionalized secondary and tertiary education in England for persons regardless of class, gender, or religious affiliation:

spent hours translating forgotten texts in the British Museum, and then regaling his students and public audiences with their contents. John Ruskin later joined these men not only in literary discussions but also in their social reform efforts—a surprisingly consistent fusion amongst the instigators of the medieval revival. Despite the diversity of social backgrounds, educational experiences, and theological, philosophical, and political perspectives, there grew a social network of reformers and writers keen on England's early texts and myths. In this company, Arthurian legend loomed large.

Sharing more than ideologies, many of these reformers and writers worked and socialized together. Tennyson met Maurice at university when he joined the Cambridge Apostles, and, although less involved in the educational reform than many other early Arthur-enthusiasts, he did write a poem to celebrate Maurice's endeavors for female education.[5] Furnivall (after studying under Maurice) took up both social and educational causes and responded to the call for better awareness of England's own literature by facilitating the publication of many medieval texts, beginning with Arthuriana. Reformers Ruskin and Carlyle—who both claimed A. J. Scott to be one of the best medieval literature scholars they knew—had, like Tennyson, profound literary and philosophical influence upon the Pre-Raphaelites and their associates.[6] These Pre-Raphaelite men and women produced a vast array of Arthurian-inspired paintings, writing, and literary reproductions. A number of them joined A. J. Scott and Maurice in their social and educational programs, and their associate William Morris became renowned for his own social reform initiatives.

Situated right in the midst of this collective enthusiasm for both literary and social reform was George MacDonald: Ruskin was an intimate friend, Maurice was his minister, Tennyson borrowed books from his library. When Furnivall founded a Shakespeare society, MacDonald was made vice president. Members of the Pre-Raphaelite circle were guests of MacDonald in England and in Italy; his children were occasionally models for them; and as a magazine editor, he produced some of their work.[7] One Pre-Raphaelite

---

these were all privileges contended in Parliamentary debate throughout the century. (Until the founding of such institutions as Kings and University College, only members of the Church of England could earn a degree. In 1871, the "University Test Act" finally opened the privilege to persons regardless of religious faith at both Cambridge and Oxford.) Scott had spent the early decades of the nineteenth century arguing for his English audience to better value (and thus read and study) these rich stories of their own heritage, and he (along with F. D. Maurice) chartered the profession of teaching English Literature. Scott, a gifted medievalist and linguist, admonished his audiences for considering classical and foreign literature better than their own, and opined, for example, that whilst there was a trending interest in the *Nibelungenlied*, scarcely anyone had yet read *Beowulf*. MacDonald followed in Scott's footsteps, both in the classroom and on the page. For more detailed discussion on A. J. Scott and his work, see Kirstin Jeffrey Johnson's *Rooted In All Its Story: More Is Meant Than Meets the Ear* (2010).

5   Maurice founded Queen's College in 1848 for women and girls—it was the first institution in the world to award academic qualifications to women. Tennyson (godfather to one of Maurice's sons) wrote "The Princess" while living with Maurice one winter.

6   See "The Late Professor A. J. Scott"; *The Carlyle Letters Online* 20, 72–74; and Ruskin, *The Winnington Letters* 109–10.

7   See the Beinecke Archives for further details. Morris, though hardly impressed with the homespun décor, even purchased Kelmscott House from MacDonald in 1875.

associate, Arthur Hughes, became MacDonald's primary illustrator. Most importantly, A. J. Scott—the scholar who argued so vociferously for a rediscovery of England's literary past—was MacDonald's principal mentor, educationally and spiritually. He invested deeply in MacDonald's literary training, recruited him for reform efforts, and encouraged his writing and teaching.

The spheres of engagement of these "medievalist" writers, teachers, and artists widened and diverged over the decades, as did the advancements in technology and industry that vastly increased the audiences that read, listened to, and viewed their work. England was expanding and changing at a speed not experienced since the Renaissance, and unease with some of the negative consequences heightened the popular appeal of what appeared to many to be a simpler, cleaner, more heroic past (Jenkins 182). Early in the century, the primary emphasis evoked by Arthurian legend had been its model of British Christian heroism, but as the legends entered the vernacular, the emphasis shifted to "'knight' heroes of contemporary society" (Bryden 2–3). The general population was more interested in medieval literature and Arthurian legend as mythic inspiration than as history or even as literary text (Matthews 359). By the 1850s, the popular concept of Arthurian England was that of an idealized realm "where the borders of national, cultural, and mythological identities overlap" (Bryden 1).[8] Its allure was widespread: Arthurian images adorned the Queen's Robing Room at Parliament, the Oxford Students Union, and many a village memorial to fallen soldiers (Landlow 72). Gothic architecture pervaded public spaces in both the North and the South; societies for social reform bore names such as "The Guild of St George"; and the Arts and Craft movement brought regal medieval design into middle-class homes. The notion that "Arthurian chivalry should inform modern behavior," that one might imitate imagined Arthurian heroes, became "an important Victorian phenomenon" in general culture—yet, to whom that expectation applied remained fairly gender- and class-specific (Matthews 359). A popular text describing how to manifest chivalry in modern life, *The Broad Stone of Honour: Or, Rules for the Gentlemen of England* (later subtitled *The True Sense and Practice of Chivalry*), defined chivalry as "only a name for that general spirit or state of mind which disposes men to heroic actions, and keeps them conversant with all that is beautiful and sublime in the intellectual and moral world" (Matthews 359, Digby 109).

It was before this great popularization occurred that MacDonald began engaging with those who taught and facilitated explorations of medieval texts and represented them in art, literature, and design, while simultaneously facilitating social and education reform. Since 1845, those people had been his intellectual, social, and spiritual community. After seminary and a very short spell as a minister, he joined the newly developed profession of teaching English Literature. Privately, in colleges, and through public lectures, MacDonald taught medieval tales and the literature that engaged with them—from Sidney, Spenser, and Shakespeare, right up to contemporaries such as Tennyson—to classrooms of women, working-class men, and dissenters. Strikingly, MacDonald was also amongst the earliest of these Victorian scholars to compose his own fiction based on Arthurian topics such as the Grail, Galahad, and Percival. His first such piece, the novel *Phantastes: A Faerie Romance for Men and Women*, was published in 1858—a year before the first of

---

8   Edward Bulwer-Lytton's *King Arthur* (1849) was a key text in the appropriation of Arthur as part of emerging racial and ethnographical discourses of national identity.

Tennyson's *Idylls*.[9] And although, according to Tennyson critic David Staines, the specific "revival of interest" in the Grail element of the legends only began in the early 1860s (probably provoked by Furnivall's 1861 reprint of the fifteenth-century epic *Seynt Graal*), MacDonald had begun work on that aspect as early as 1859 (Staines 65). His poem "The Sangreal: A Part of the Story Omitted in the Old Romances" was one of the first Victorian poems to specifically focus on the Holy Grail, published in June 1863 (six years before Tennyson's).[10] Nor were such Arthurian references a passing phase for MacDonald: they figure throughout his entire corpus, frequently significant to the plot; even his essays and sermons draw upon Arthurian imagery.

MacDonald was not simply taking advantage of a promising trend. From *Phantastes* onwards, he was carefully manifesting his mythopoeic approach to literature: engaging in new ways with old myths; crafting new stories exploring old truths. The general popularization of Arthurian legend had been causing a decrease in the interest in authenticity and accuracy, thus increasing the propensity to use its images to promote agendas—in particular those connecting Arthurian legend to national identity and an idea of English gallantry. Aware of this, MacDonald intentionally meets his audience "where the borders of national, cultural, and mythological identities overlap" (Bryden 1). He sets Lancelot and Guinevere aside and relegates Arthur to his role as Spenserian knight more than as king.[11] Using his knowledge of the medieval Arthurian texts and the engagements with them that follow, MacDonald the literature scholar reminds his readers—re-images for them—what the Old English word *knight* (or *cniht*) technically means: "one who serves."

MacDonald seeks to redefine the concept for his generation by showing how one can be such an authentically *English* knight-hero. He initially does so implicitly in *Phantastes,* a fantasy novel about a young man eager to take on his role as family patriarch and filled with romantic notions of his own gallantry. The tale is guided throughout by MacDonald's readings of authors for whom the chivalric vision was not make-believe, even if the settings in which they explored it might be. A decade later, however, in *The*

---

9   William Morris's "Sir Galahad: A Christmas Mystery" was also published in the same year. The period widely recognized as prime artistic output on Arthurian and medieval themes, the 1850's to 80's, are MacDonald's prime writing years (Landlow 71–76).

10 In a letter to Lady Byron on 2 Nov 1859, MacDonald discusses the Grail poem that he has completed. The later publication was accompanied by an engraving by Horatio Joseph Lucas (*Good Words* 4 [1863]: 454–55). The next year, Robert Hawker published "The Quest of Sangraal," which was followed by Thomas Westwood's "The Quest of Sancgreall" in 1868. Although Tennyson had mentioned the Grail in his idyll of "Sir Galahad," it is but a light treatment. His poem on the Grail (also on Percival and "the failed quest") was published in 1869.

11 This would have pleased Furnivall. The year after MacDonald published "The Sangreal," Furnivall—whilst declaring his highest esteem for Tennyson—expressed his revulsion at the combination of Arthur's nobleness from early legend and the appearance of Guinevere in the later versions, stressing that in the early legends nothing is said of the sin of Arthur, nor of Guinevere with Lancelot (Staines 66). For MacDonald, Spenser's *Faerie Queene*—full of Arthurian reference—is "the great poem of the period" (*Antiphon* 63). He writes in *England's Antiphon* of "the profound religious truth contained in this poem," quoting as example a passage that declares the Redcross Knight's survival due to the care of his female companion, Una (63).

Seaboard Parish, MacDonald is much more explicit about what knighthood actually is and the social reform it might—perhaps uncomfortably—evoke. In this later novel, set on England's very concrete west coast, he spells it out in careful detail (communicating the concept is clearly important, for he repeats this explanation elsewhere in his work):[12]

> No man could rise to the honour of knighthood without service. A nobleman's son even had to wait on his father, or to go into the family of another nobleman, and wait upon him as a page, standing behind his chair at dinner. This was an honour. No notion of degradation was in it. It was a necessary step to higher honour. And what was the next higher honour? To be set free from service? No. To serve in the harder service of the field; to be a squire to some noble knight; to tend his horse, to clean his armour, to see that every rivet was sound, every buckle true, every strap strong; to ride behind him, and carry his spear, and if more than one attacked him, to rush to his aid. This service was the more honourable because it was harder, and was the next step to higher honour yet. And what was this higher honour? That of knighthood. Wherein did this knighthood consist? The very word means simply *service*. And for what was the knight thus waited upon by his squire? That he might be free to do as he pleased? No, but that he might be free to be the servant of all. By being a squire first, the servant of one, he learned to rise to the higher rank, that of servant of all. (*Seaboard* 94)

For MacDonald, an *English* "chivalry," including one's sense of identity and understanding of gallantry, must be that of an etymologically true English *cniht*: a servant of all.

As MacDonald explores and models an etymologically true knight in *Phantastes* and *Seaboard Parish*, he also sets aside specific discussion of the Holy Grail. In the traditional tales, the Grail first appears before Arthur and his knights during the Feast of Pentecost, and—as shown in MacDonald's poem "Sangreal"—it is because Galahad is a pursuant of holiness rather than of gallant deeds that he is successful in his Grail quest. Thus the theme of *peregrinatio* is as important as the Grail itself. Adventures of the "solitary knight-errant" serve as progressive self-revelation, and in the motif as borrowed by Malory from the Arthurian legends of Chrétien de Troyes, epiphanic confrontations typically arise in consequence of the traveler's own sin, "as much from sin within as without" (Jeffrey 256).[13] The motif continues in English chivalric tales from Spenser right up to Bunyan and beyond, serving all the time that English word *cniht* (Jeffrey 256). MacDonald participates in this tradition, referencing with particular frequency the peregrinations of Sir Percival and of Spenser's Redcross Knight—perhaps most explicitly in *Phantastes* (in which the references and pilgrimage structure are sufficiently dominant as to impede some readers unfamiliar with the genre). Percival's journey is central to *Phantastes* and is evoked again by his namesake in *Seaboard Parish*. But just as both tales merge the medieval Percival with Spenser's Renaissance knight, both tales also detail the

---

12   Reiterated almost verbatim in his "True Christian Ministering" (1882).

13   The specific term *knygt erraunt*, meaning wandering or roving knight, first appears in the fourteenth-century *Sir Gawain and the Green Knight*.

peregrinations of more than one adventurer. In *Phantastes*, the *peregrinatio* of the modern "gentleman" receiving education in the land of faerie is repeatedly held in contrast to that of a "Repentant Knight" who more successfully emulates the noble acts of Sir Percival. In *Seaboard Parish,* a journey to the West Country and the actual English landscape of Tintagel (location of Arthur's birth and Merlin's cave) requires a Londoner named Percivale and his senior, Reverend Walton—contemporary versions of the newly questing and the well-travelled knight—to negotiate their chivalric relationship not only with each other, but with the various "damsels-in-distress."

In these challenges to popular Victorian medievalism, MacDonald's literary commitment is evident: Arthurian history, literature, and myth all meet and intertwine. In both *Phantastes* and *Seaboard Parish*, he explicitly and implicitly alludes to an abundant number of external texts, through titles named, quotations acknowledged and unacknowledged, and symbols borrowed; from biblical and classical sources through to contemporary. Out of careful attention to the ongoing engagement of these tales, MacDonald's new tales emerge: the mythopoeia of which Tolkien and Lewis named him a master (Lewis, *Anthology* xviii; Tolkien 26; Warren Lewis, *Letters* 271). These two Arthurian novels are densely infused with acknowledgements of dramas and poems, scripture and exposition, ballads and folklore, romances (both British and French) and Romanticism (both British and German). *Phantastes* weighs more heavily with Jacobean and Elizabethan references (including some that deal with the darker side of sexuality), and *Seaboard Parish* more heavily with the Metaphysical poets. While MacDonald's audience would recognize, in name at least, Dante, Chaucer, Shakespeare, Milton, and Bunyan, and perhaps even all the classical mythologies referenced, a vast number of his literary references would have been as novel to most readers in 1858 and 1868 as they are today. For MacDonald, these are not simply displays of synergistic intertextuality: they are also introductions and invitations to other makers and engagers of myth. From his first novel, he calls Arthurian fans to delve deeper and discover the riches that gave rise to the pop culture.

Thenceforth in his writing, both realistic as well as fantastic, MacDonald's central characters are typically readers of fairy tales. Rather than simply being caught up in a new trend (as were so many mid-Victorians), his characters are familiar with multiple engagements with Arthurian legend and consider this akin to spiritual nourishment—sometimes the familiarity even directly aids their survival. MacDonald's "educated" protagonists—male or female—read Sidney's *Arcadia* and Spenser's *Faerie Queene* and have "read a good deal of the history of Prince Arthur" (*Cumbermede* 104). It is as a result of such reading that his characters become "conscious of a desire after honour" (50) as expressed by the protagonist of *Cumbermede*: "their spirit had wrought upon my spirit, and armour and war-horses and mighty swords were only the instruments with which faithful knights wrought honourable deeds" (72).[14] Such tales give a hue of faerie to everyday engagement with the world, all the more so for being the "genetic literary history" of the readers. MacDonald specifically encourages his readers to make connections between the swords and grails within his tales and those of myth. The hearts of his protagonists glow at such legends; their daydreams are fed

---

14   This is strikingly akin to Lewis' reflection on the effect of reading *Phantastes* upon his own young self; it is reminiscent, too, of Tolkien's careful representation of Faramir, with repeated emphasis on that character's preparation for "knighthood" through literary study.

by the visions; they retell them to their peers. The more mature characters "read rejoicingly" when they page through England's poets, engaging so deeply that they share a sort of "song-worship with ... all who have thus at any time shared in his feelings, even if he has passed centuries ago into the 'high countries' of song" (*Antiphon* 2). In doing so, MacDonald's characters recognize that these writings of the past equip them to better assess and engage with the present. As the narrator of *Seaboard Parish* explains:

> A true knowledge of the present, in literature, as in everything else, could only be founded upon a knowledge of what had gone before; therefore, that any judgment, in regard to the literature of the present day, was of no value which was not guided and influenced by a real acquaintance with the best of what had gone before, being liable to be dazzled and misled by novelty of form and other qualities which, whatever might be the real worth of the substance, were, in themselves, purely ephemeral. (204)

Thus when a reader of MacDonald returns to *Phantastes* and discovers that in this tale the protagonist has no knowledge of what has gone before—is relatively unstoried, and even unaware of his actual genetic fairy heritage—it is clear that he is therefore an Englishman little aware of what it truly means to be a knight. He must endure a long peregrination of *aventures* before he wins his spurs.

As the fantastical novel *Phantastes* begins, the protagonist Anodos has just celebrated his twenty-first birthday.[15] A young "Victorian gentleman," he has reached the age of legal responsibility and must now take charge of his family's British castle estate, be guardian of his sisters, and execute new duties such as overseeing the farm-laborers. But though he is apparently of noble blood and has grand ideas of gallantry, Anodos is barely practiced (as the character Sir Percivale later explains) in nobility of thought, let alone of deed. His is little more than a Victorian pop-culture concept of chivalry: he knows the trends, but not the texts. Mere hours before Anodos is to assume his role as lord of the manor, he is accosted by a faerie ancestress who chides him for knowing so little of his genetic inheritance.[16] As she further chastises him for his general atheism regarding faerie, her star-gaze fills him with "an unknown longing" (*Phantastes* 8) for a celestial sea. She tells him he will find it "in Fairy Land" (8). The next morning, Anodos awakens

---

15   His name in Greek has the potential of a curious *double-entendre*: it can be construed as indicating "without a way," even though the accurate translation is "progress upward." As a careful reader of Plato, and of *The Republic* in particular, MacDonald would also know of Plato's use of the word *anodos* to indicate enlightenment. In his last fantastical novel, *Lilith* (1895), MacDonald hints that the protagonist Mr. Vane is a descendant of *Phantastes*'s Anodos—for Vane's ancestor is referred to as "Sir Upward" (reiterated eight times). Vane later recognizes a song, as will the reader of *Phantastes*: "Many a wrong, and its curing song; / ... / Room to roam, but only one home ..." (325–26).

16   In subtle contest to Spenser's hint of nationalism in *The Faerie Queene*, Anodos is shown to be the inverse of the Redcross Knight: while Spenser's knight is purportedly of English blood yet raised in Faery Land, Anodos has fairy blood and yet has lived thus far only in Britain. It is in coming to know this foreign land of his ancestry—and the stories that inhabit it—that Anodos will be better enabled to venture well in his *terram patrum*.

as his bedchamber transforms from a room with Arts and Craft décor into an actual sylvan bower, and he follows a path leading out of his room, in search of Fairy Land and the sea. His awakened interest in his inheritance of faerie is but the beginning of a long peregrination of self-revelation in which he will have to gradually set self aside and learn to serve others. Although he is certainly *disposed* to heroic actions and believes himself conversant with the "beautiful and sublime" (Digby 109)—thus, culturally a "Gentleman of England"—Anodos is quickly forced to accept that this does not make him a knight, English or otherwise.

It is Anodos's fairy blood that enables him to wander through these stories, and although Arthurian legends are dominant, they are not the only ones evident: Faerie is not confined by nationality. *Contes de fées* flow into *märchen* that flow into Celtic myth. Anodos discovers early on, from another person of similarly mixed genes, that those who have ancestry such as theirs must live by faerie borders and eat at least occasionally of its food, or else they become ill. This woman infers that Anodos is less aware of the want than she, due to his "education and the activity of [his] mind" (17); it is dubious whether this is a compliment. Identifying her as of "the lower orders" (a mere cottager), Anodos is astonished at the woman's facility with language: "It seemed that intercourse with the fairies was no bad education in itself" (26). Anodos' surprise at the intellectual abilities of a woman of this class is representative of many of his contemporary countrymen—and likely some of the first readers of *Phantastes* too. The concurrent Parliamentary arguments in London against education reform efforts were often based on the supposed inability of lower classes and women to healthily sustain such intellectual strain.[17] Although Anodos is forced to acknowledge this cottager's abilities (despite her class) and accept her hospitality, he yet remains "disinclined to talk" (20) with her and, as a result, misses the opportunity to learn important information. Nonetheless, it is under the auspices of her hospitality that he begins to supplement the education that he does have, taking up to read her "great old volume" that contains "many wondrous tales of Fairy Land, and olden times, and the Knights of King Arthur's table" (20). Thus, one of Anodos' first positive acts in Fairy Land is not a physical engagement in adventure, but rather a reading of adventure. He reads for hours, following the exploits of Sir Galahad and Sir Percival. Just as he is about to discover why Sir Percival appears in such dishonored state beside the shining Sir Galahad—and how this relates to the wiles of the evil Alder-maid—he is interrupted and reads no more (22). The consequences of leaving the tale unfinished prove dire.

As the novel *Phantastes* unfolds, it becomes evident that in not having conquered that trial of the Alder-maid alongside Sir Percival on the page, Anodos is ill-equipped to avoid her wiles in person. Nor does he heed the warnings of the one he dubs "the repentant knight" (79); for despite the fact that this knight has rescued him (let alone the man's resemblance to Sir Percival), the knight's attitude of repentance over past chivalric failure does not match Anodos' image of a "knight hero" (Bryden 3). Yet Anodos' own attempts to prove a knight errant only sink him deeper into errancy. As he increasingly recognizes the selfish motivations behind even his seemingly good deeds, he starts to see the actions of the Repentant Knight in a new light. When he has, finally, sufficiently matured to feel honored to travel with the knight and learn from him, it is but a short passage. A shadow acquired through an encounter of willful disobedience impedes

---

17   For further discussion on this topic, see Joan N. Burstyn, "Education and Sex."

this and every one of Anodos' relationships. It besmirches good will and frequently causes him to distrust or dislike others:

> In a land like this, with so many illusions everywhere, I need [the Shadow] to disenchant the things around me. He does away with all appearances, and shows me things in their true colour and form. And I am not one to be fooled with the vanities of the common crowd. I will not see beauty where there is none. I will dare to behold things as they are. And if I live in a waste instead of a paradise, I will live knowing where I live. (*Phantastes* 104)

Self-satisfied with his own realism, Anodos becomes determined not to be taken in. He chooses cunning over companionship.

But when Anodos's self-oriented errors eventually lead to his abusing the trust of a young maid, the resultant self-loathing in this would-be knight can be healed only by the food, drink, and ritual washing proffered at the Fairy Palace. A greater maturity comes to him in this period of repose, during which day upon day of reading finally improves his fashion-fed knowledge of "Victorian chivalry" with the literary education he has lacked. Anodos becomes an itinerant traveler by paging through the books of a most astounding library—recognizing as he does so that this is also a form of peregrination, through which he is vicariously living many lives. The experiences are fortifying: in a narrative aside, he informs the reader that once back in England, "portions of what [he] read there have often come to [him] again, with an unexpected comforting" (183). However, Anodos still does not understand that the new life he has found within these books is but cerebral; that he must put it into practice or it will become null and void, or worse. This is evidenced when, attempting to free an imprisoned "White Lady," he himself is too free, assuming a champion's right to the damsel. His vision of chivalric glory, even for all the tales he has read, is still self-oriented: to conquer evil, earn the maiden, gain the glory. In consequence, the Lady flees, and Anodos is banished from the Palace.

Anodos has much to learn in his relationships with women before he earns the adage of a knight, rather than being a mere gallant. He must eschew his chauvinist attitude that a woman is either something to be rescued and claimed if beautiful and noble, bested if a temptress, or ignored if common. This progress takes him time, even though right from the beginning of his adventures he was both rescued and instructed by a matron cottager, her daughter, and a female tree.[18] After his banishment, when he is in the depths of despair, a character identified as the Wise Woman takes Anodos into her humble dwelling. By now he is sufficiently chivalric to give her the respect he did not have for his earlier lowly hostess. The experiences this old woman guides him through force him to reconsider his relationships back home in England—it is an emotionally difficult advancement in his peregrination of self-knowledge. Despite his learning, Anodos still endangers himself and his hostess in an impetuous moment of willful disobedience,

---

18   The Beech-maid who saves Anodos early in his journey, whilst yet remaining in arboreal confinement herself, gives him a leafy girdle of protection—one of a myriad of such references to Arthurian legend that occur in *Phantastes*.

and the Wise Woman makes an immense sacrifice in order to save him. Her actions model the enormity of forgiveness—a lesson reinforced some time later by that young maid whose trust Anodos had abused near the novel's beginning. Precipitating the tale's end, it is this maid's forgiveness that sets Anodos free from physical and emotional entrapment.

Thus it is quite late in the tale that Anodos is finally able to recognize true knights when he sees them, and even then he remains for some time yet unable to truthfully assess his own proximity to this state. Through the example and model of character in a pair of brothers, he finally understands that a knight does not rush headlong from one glorious rescue to another, but must labor: mental, emotional, and physical rigor are required in order to serve well. He also learns the importance of preparation for future endeavors and of seeking advice: these knights have spent years readying themselves, requesting guidance from the old Wise Woman. Yet though he delights in the experience of being part of their team, Anodos still believes he can be a knight on his own. He becomes cavalier about the shadow that continues to haunt him and numbers himself "amongst the glorious knights of old," even "an equal to Sir Galahad" (272). His self-delusion eventually results in solitary confinement, and it is from this that the absolving maiden frees him, her forgiveness all the more powerful for her honesty at the hurt that he had caused. Finally, Anodos is able to recognize that the truly valiant individual is not him, who would be champion, but rather the lowly young female who has rescued him. He strips himself of his armor, declaring: "I might do for a squire; but I honoured knighthood too highly, to call myself any longer one of the noble brotherhood" (287). In this act of self-abasement, he finally loses his evil shadow.

No longer self-aggrandizing, Anodos's comprehension of what it means to be a knight is radically improved, but it is not until he willingly puts himself in service to one who intentionally seeks to be a servant that he really understands. In his first "adventure" as squire, Anodos discovers that the Repentant Knight makes no distinction between low- and high-born for his chivalric missions: he risks his life to rescue a mere peasant child. Although this knight has already "won" his damsel (over whom he does not rule, but rather with whom he confers) and has achieved the valiant shine of Galahad, he yet continues to face deep peril regardless of reward. Anodos marvels as his knight treats the petrified parents of the peasant child with the same dignity as he does his own lady, accepting their hospitality and sitting with them in their lowly cottage. The knight honestly enjoys their lowborn company, "talking most familiarly with the simple host" and tending to the child "if possible even more gently than the mother" (221).[19] This scene is a striking contrast to Anodos' own treatment of his peasant hostess earlier in the tale. Anodos now understands that the knight's countenance is noble not because he is high-born, but because "loving-kindness beamed from every line of his face" (294).[20] The knight builds upon this experience for Anodos in a later conversation with him, challenging the romantic notion of questing for fame and fortune:

---

19 It is difficult to appreciate today just how shocking such an act would be not just to Anodos, but also to MacDonald's readers. Years later, reviewers would balk at his even making mention in novels of such vulgarities as dirt floors in cottages ("New Books" 25).

20 The partnership of the Repentant Knight and his White Lady, in addition to her name, repeatedly recalls Spenser's *Faerie Queene* and the Percivalian knight who only succeeds through his partnership with Truth.

"All a man has to do, is to better what he can. And if he will settle it with himself, that even renown and success are in themselves of no great value, and be content to be defeated, if so be that the fault is not his; and so go to his work with a cool brain and a strong will, he will get it done; and fare none the worse in the end, that he was not burdened with provision and precaution."

"But he will not always come off well," I ventured to say.

"Perhaps not," rejoined the knight, "in the individual act; but the result of his lifetime will content him." (296)

Anodos finally recognizes that *this* is noble service. This is true knighthood.

Once Anodos understands what being a knight actually means, his time in Fairy Land is complete. Proving that he is finally able to put into deed a nobleness that is true, he commits a sacrificial act that he knows will cost his life and thus fully dies to self. He is allowed to taste the "clear mountain-air of the land of Death" (200) and to reflect on his journeying in Fairy Land; but as soon as he vows a future of selfless service, he is abruptly returned alive to his childhood home.[21]

While his sisters receive the returned Anodos with profound joy, they also observe that he is changed. He, too, is aware that he is now equipped with "a power of calm endurance to which [he] had hitherto been a stranger" (318). The reader is reminded that before the adventures in Fairy Land Anodos was about to take up a new mantle of responsibility: "I began the duties of my new position, somewhat instructed, I hoped, by the adventures that had befallen me in Fairy Land. Could I translate the experience of my travels there, into common life? This was the question" (320). Anodos knows that he will continue to face trials and even failures. He must stay on guard, laboring in mental, emotional, and physical preparation, so that he "might be free, strong, unwearied, to shoot like an arrow to the rescue of *any and every* one who needed his ready aid" (*Seaboard* 83; italics mine). He is now a true knight, rather than an aspiring hero; knowing that at times he will be defeated, he yet will continue to serve. Anodos' memories of his faerie adventures—those read, observed, and partaken—will fortify him as he puts into practice the actions required of an English *cniht*.

Phantastes: A Faerie Romance for Men and Women was well received by the reading public, unique as it was in its melding of Arthurian legend into a fantastical novel.[22] This tale—of a man who, on his quest for knighthood, is rescued repeatedly by women, hosted and educated by peasants, and finally realizes his goal once he learns to serve others regardless of status or potential reward—has remained one of MacDonald's best-known stories. It is credited for being at the beginning of a whole new genre of English literature. But despite its reception, as Victorian passion for Arthurian chivalry reached new heights mid-nineteenth century, MacDonald chose to change his tack.

---

21   Parts of this passage bear comparison to the passage concerning Caspian's death in *The Silver Chair*.

22   Unfortunately, because MacDonald quotes an unflattering review in a now-published letter, this has led to the mistaken assumption in some critical studies that this review was representative (cf. *Golden Thread* 6; *Anthology* 108; Triggs 73; Bloom 138). M. A. Gillies is amongst those who have clarified from broad primary research that, in actuality, the reviews of *Phantastes* were quite positive, as indicated in an 1861 article: "'Phantastes' has proved a success even as regards its circulation, and a very decided success as concerns the influence it has exerted on minds of the highest order" (Gillies 186).

Ten years after the publication of Anodos's adventure in *Phantastes,* and now a popular author of realistic novels as well as fantasies, MacDonald wrote *The Seaboard Parish,* the novel in which the previously discussed definition of knighthood is found. Significant advancements had been made in education reform (although it would still be decades before Parliament approved public education),[23] but MacDonald the Scottish suffragist, now a father of several teenage girls, was well aware of remaining cultural repressions. That he was ten years further into his career as an English Literature professor and lecturer, and not least that he was engaged with Ruskin's *Modern Painters,* Dante's *Commedia,* and the Greek myth of Psyche, is evidenced in the complex discourse of literary criticism that lies beneath the surface of *Seaboard Parish.* Conversation of texts within texts remains a delight for MacDonald, and this composition is another rich dialogue of multiple literatures (and real history) on a number of interrelated themes. But the Arthurian overtones are the most explicit, and MacDonald's continued evangelism of an etymologically consistent concept of knighthood remains an important element of the textual conversation. However, this novel is not a stylistically ancient, episodic fantasy, as was *Phantastes.* In *Seaboard Parish,* MacDonald addresses the same themes in the modern "realistic" medium and roots them in an identifiably contemporary English time and place.

G. K. Chesterton writes that in MacDonald's non-fantasy, "the fairytale was the inside of the ordinary story and not the outside," yet in *The Seaboard Parish,* faery is both inside and out (Chesterton 303). In response to the new stage of Arthurian hype in English culture, MacDonald makes the very contemporary move of having his characters become Victorian tourists (tourism itself was a swelling trend), occasioning their explorations of true knighthood whilst journeying in the region that claims to be Arthur's own historical setting. That MacDonald has the Walton family travel to this specific location is all the more remarkable for the novel's being written before the transformation of nineteenth-century Tintagel into a shrine of Victorian tourism (Hale 2). Awareness of the anticipatory nature of this setting gives today's reader a context for just how contemporary MacDonald's novel is.

Not only did he still have his finger on the pulse of popular culture, but his family also conducted first-hand research for this novel. Just three years before *Seaboard Parish* was published, the MacDonalds had travelled to Cornwall and Devon, and visited the not-yet famous Tintagel.[24] In general, it was a trip of recovery and convalescence, as it is in the novel, only MacDonald was the convalescent, recovering from one of his bad bouts of tubercular hemorrhaging (Greville MacDonald 262). The location, adventures, and persons with which MacDonald engaged on that visit shaped the framework for *Seaboard Parish.* During this time, F. D. Maurice came down to visit and read to him from Ruskin's *Modern Painters III;* his wife Louisa

---

23 England as a nation did not have general free primary education until the establishment of the National Board of Education in 1899. Secondary education was not publicly available until 1902.

24 Tennyson had been here years before, guided by the poet-priest Robert Hawker whose "Quest of Sangraal" had been published a year after MacDonald's Sangreal poem. Charles Kingsley, author and reformer in the same circles as MacDonald, had also visited Hawker, and it is possible that some of MacDonald's inspiration for *Seaboard* comes from tales of this coastal vicar who helped with shipwrecks and shared poetry with his parishioners (Gould 69, 70). F. H. Broome claims that Hawker and MacDonald were acquainted, which would be an obvious and very interesting link, but Broome gives no source for this information (Broome 69).

spent the time landscape painting; his family visited Tintagel (Raeper 135; Greville MacDonald 262–63).[25] MacDonald discusses a Pre-Raphaelitesque Arthurian painting in the novel; this work, *Knight of the Sun*, actually exists. It is by Arthur Hughes, and it was new to England's actual public at the time MacDonald was writing: one rendition paired with a poem by MacDonald (c. 1862) sold at Christie's only months before *Seaboard Parish* began appearing in installments in *The Sunday Magazine*.[26]

This realistic Arthurian novel of MacDonald's begins in considerable contrast to *Phantastes*. Rather than the speculations of a pathless protagonist on his twenty-first birthday, the reader of *The Seaboard Parish* is presented with the ruminations of an aging minister upon the complexities of audience and Story and with his warning to older readers not to become complacent and stagnant. This narrator of *Seaboard* explains that *peregrinatio* is life-long: The adventure of living never ceases; it is an on-going pilgrimage in which none is too elderly to participate nor, indeed, to serve. Reverend Henry Walton is familiar to readers of *Seaboard*, as the book is the second in a trilogy. In the first, *Annals of a Quiet Neighbourhood*, a much younger Walton discovered sacred vocation in his ecclesial occupation (as well as in introducing his rural congregation to the "heroes" of English literature through a public lecture series). Walton had also proved rather chivalric in dashing fashion: he triumphed over the vile machinations of a local evil matriarch, rescuing—and marrying—her daughter, a veritable damsel-in-distress once imprisoned in a real (former) castle. Now, in *Seaboard*, Walton is "settled into [being] a gray-haired, quite elderly, yet active man" (*Seaboard* 6). He is also a contemplative, and (in a popular genre of the time) the novel is filled with his ruminations and sermons. While the story weaves in and out of these, it is a mistake to think that either tale or exposition stands alone; each serves to exegete the other, and both serve to explore an etymologically accurate understanding of English knighthood.

When a dramatic horse-riding accident in the first few pages renders Walton's vivacious daughter Constance a physical prisoner of paralysis, it is quickly evident that she refuses to be confined in spirit. This is set in contrast to her elder sister Winnie, who is physically fit but entrapped by spiritual malaise. Once so successful in rescuing his wife, Walton now struggles with impotence at the travails of these two daughters. When an invitation offers him an opportunity to take the entire family on a visit to the Devonshire and Cornish coast, "a vision of the sea … rush[es] in upon [him]" (111) and soon the household is a cavalcade, invalid and all, traveling to the West Country, the primary setting of the novel. Whilst there, they visit Tintagel, the birthplace of England's greatest crowned knight and thus of its greatest myth. They also find a wandering young Percivale, painting visions on the shore. This ever-present sea, the whole family learns, is a place of mystery and myth; of new beginnings (the reader is reminded that nothing lies between the Coast and "New-found-land," a land of promise toward which emigrants journey); and of death (drownings and storms are a constant theme, even for the emigrants).

---

25 Five years later, one of MacDonald's daughters—Mary Josephine—became engaged to a tall, handsome, bearded Pre-Raphaelite follower, strikingly similar to the character Charles Percivale. He was a nephew of Arthur Hughes, the real-life artist of the *Knight of the Sun*. Sadly, she died of the family haunt of TB before she and E. R. (Ted) Hughes were married.

26 Hughes worked on various versions of this painting throughout the decade. See Roberts's *Arthur Hughes* for further detail.

Ruminating upon this variously beautiful and foreboding entity, life-giving and life-claiming, Walton details the immaterial seas of which he is also aware: "one of the unseen world, that is, of death; one of the spirit—the devouring ocean of evil—and might I not have added yet another, encompassing and silencing all the rest—that of truth!" (208). It is at the convergence of such physical and metaphysical shores that he and his family discover the artist Percivale. He has transformed a jagged, rocky island into Dante's Purgatorial mountain, upon which Beatrice leads the poet ever higher. In his late twenties, Percivale (his first name "Charles" is only used twice) is of noble and ancient English blood, though when teasingly asked if he is "a descendant of Sir Percivale of King Arthur's Round Table," he replies that he "cannot count quite so far back" (249). It is quickly established that Percivale is a fervent admirer of *The Divine Comedy* and of *Modern Painters*, and he wrestles deeply with questions of life, death, and the divine: "the mere romantic [he] never had much taste for" (327).

Both pastorally and personally, Walton is drawn to this exceedingly chivalrous young man who is fluent in Italian and a student of the Pre-Raphaelite school. He would willingly mentor Percivale on his pilgrimage. However, much to his chagrin, Percivale and Walton's spiritually struggling daughter Winnie are clearly romantically drawn to each other.[27] While Walton had no issue acting as a knight to his wife Ethelwyn in their own courtship, rescuing her in both body and soul, he does have an issue with Percivale being the gallant savior of his daughter. Percivale is still on his own spiritual journey: not yet a Christian, let alone a Galahad. In discussions over this dilemma (most pointedly after Percivale physically rescues Winnie from plunging over a cliff), Ethelwyn challenges Walton. Now in partnership with him, as his Spenserian Una, she reminds him that he himself was struggling in his faith-journey when they fell in love and that still the two of them are progressing—although now together—yet far from any final state of sanctification. Ethelwyn implies that Walton might be a bit jealous in his desire that *he* be the knight who rescues his daughter. She suggests that perhaps Winnie and Percivale might be of assistance to each other if they journey together in their search for truth, each so driven in their "Holy Longing" for something more. Walton concedes, but continues to struggle with allowing another to be his daughter's champion.

Walton and Percivale must resolve their tensions and physically work together once they are at Tintagel (Arthur's birthplace), for there they carry the chivalric invalid Constance up a dangerously steep path into the castle ruins, so that she might look out upon the shining seas. The image they create as they share their burden echoes that of a painting by Percivale, in which a dying knight is carried by his squires "on the edge of a steep descent" (*Seaboard* 614). As mentioned above, this painting is based on an actual work of art, executed by MacDonald's friend Arthur Hughes, titled both *Knight of the Sun* and *Morte D'Arthur*. The subject is a devout knight whose dying wish is to see the setting sun, the inspiration of the insignia borne on his own personal heraldry ("Review" 374).[28] Not till long after the event with Connie does Walton see Percivale's

---

27 Although *Winnie* is sometimes used as a nickname for variants of Guinevere, MacDonald is very clear that in this situation *Winnie* is an abbreviation of the name *Ethelwyn*: the daughter being named after her mother.

28 On the frame, Hughes had inscribed half a stanza from MacDonald's poem "Better Things": "Better a death when work is done, / Than earth's most favoured birth" (ll. 45–46). The remainder of the stanza, the last in the poem, is: "Better a child in God's great house / Than the king of all the earth."

painting; upon viewing it, he calls it "a grand picture, full of feeling—a picture and a parable" (*Seaboard* 615). Percivale's gallant conduct throughout the Tintagel adventure goes a long way toward persuading Walton to relinquish his grip as Winnie's prime protector. Walton's final release is made when Percivale risks his life in order to rescue some strangers in peril of drowning in the stormy sea (see chapters 38 and 39).

These characters, Winnie and Percivale, struggle with doubt, but they *are* in pursuit of the truth. They are "reverent doubters" (a term MacDonald used for agnostics in whom he identified integrity), seeking to serve without pneumatological assurance or eschatological hope (*Antiphon* 326). They may not be as secure as Walton, or even Constance, in their sense of Truth or Home, but they quest onward nonetheless, and—as Walton eventually indicates—are perhaps even more to be admired for doing so, for in their quest they seek to serve without expecting reward. It is a chivalry for which MacDonald the author has much respect, and, as he shows in the relationships here, one that can teach much to the confident Christian. This particular trilogy—*Annals of a Quiet Neighbourhood*, *The Seaboard Parish*, and *The Vicar's Daughter*—has many such reverent and honest doubters who teach and pastor even the minister. The service-oriented lives of these characters in realistic novels model the attitude of "knights" as Anodos had come to understand the appellation by the end of his journey in Fairy Land. In time, the shared quest of Winnie and Percivale does result in their release from what Walton sees as spiritual confinement, but that is in another book, and both reader and father have to relinquish assurance and wait.

In keeping with the broader understanding of knighthood communicated in *Phantastes*, Walton also explicitly acknowledges some of the social reform issues being argued in England's Parliament even as *Seaboard Parish* was published. He discusses particular forms of societal confinement to which the women in his lifetime are bound. Like MacDonald, Walton is a suffragist, and while he struggles with whether he would "like to see any woman [he] cared much for either in parliament or in an anatomical class-room," he clearly states that that is her decision to make—not his or that of any man (*Seaboard* 291). Consistent throughout the text are reminders to the reader that Una and Beatrice both have occasion to be rescuers and guides to the Redcross Knight and Dante (physically, emotionally, and spiritually), just as Ethelwyn—now Walton's helpmeet and partner—rescues him repeatedly from inner turmoil (jealousy, impatience, willfulness). Both Walton and Anodos learn that while they will sometimes be rescuers, they will also have to be rescued at times, and may even have to simply accept that the rescuing is not always theirs to do. In both novels, the successful knights are those who become socially progressive, working as partners with, being educated by, and at times even being dependent upon both women and persons of lower social status. For Walton, this list of partners also includes persons with different beliefs.

The Seaboard Parish is a modern and "realistic" contrast to the fantastical peregrinations of *Phantastes*. The change in genre helps to emphasize MacDonald's endeavor to usurp an ever-growing, romanticized notion of knighthood. Informed not only by the literature of early English Romance, but also of the older Holy Romance, MacDonald's message is for his modern audience, regardless of gender or class. *Phantastes: A Romance for Men and Woman* was written at the beginning of a fad, before it became a national obsession, and MacDonald engages in the new trend in a manner that calls his readers to a better knowledge of their own heritage. In doing so, the novel challenges readers to reconsider their definition of knighthood and their understanding of truly English chivalry. A reader who expects *Phantastes* to be a fashionable tale in which the gallant knight saves the damsel-in-distress and wins the glory will be disappointed, perhaps even frustrated. The reader is asked instead to accept numerous concepts subversive to popularized Victorian medievalism: that chivalry and valour are gender- and class-neutral, both for those who give and those who receive; that patience, preparation, and waiting are necessary acts of service; that not all good deeds are rewarded or even successful; that saving the girl does not equal winning the girl (nor marriage to a damsel or finding the grail equal the adventure's end); and that the true chivalric quest never ends.

In *Phantastes*, Arthurian Faerie is the Secondary World in which Anodos is fostered for a life of knighthood in his Primary World: it is in Faerie that "by being a squire first, the servant of one, he learned to rise to the higher rank, that of servant of all" (*Seaboard* 94). His struggles to emulate the Repentant Knight within that world return him to his own earthly responsibilities once he finally comprehends the True Quest. Self-revelatory peregrinations lead him out of himself and back to his responsibilities of service in his earthly home. He is left with a longing, a *Sehnsucht*, for "something too good to be told" (*Phantastes* 321). This longing will inform the service Anodos must practice in preparing his panoply: service "more honourable because it [is] harder" (*Seaboard* 94). No longer needing to be a triumphant hero, he recognizes the true gallantry of being "nothing but a doer of his work" (*Phantastes* 287) in the place where he is.

His peregrinations are more specific than those of the characters in *Seaboard Parish*, yet even without the explicit definition of *knight* that the modern *Seaboard Parish* contains, that second Arthurian novel serves to strengthen MacDonald's argument. Regardless of age, even with "tottering old legs," Walton knows that one must be "ever ready ... to go with [a] brave heart to do the work of a true man" (*Seaboard* 5). He is reminded by Ethelwyn, his own Una, that knights need not be young, that a knight works best in company, and that truth-finding and servanthood are not gender-specific endeavors. In observing the integrity of young Charles Percivale, the well-travelled Walton is also reminded that a knight need not have his life sorted in order to do good: it is in doing good that he will come closer to Truth. Being a truth-searcher—a servant of goodness and of others—nears a Percivale to a Galahad. Aptly, one of Walton's own most frequent teachings in the pulpit and in conversation is that even when one is "conscious of a desire after honour," lessons must often be relearned and death-to-self repeated (*Cumbermede* 50): *perigrinatio* is life-long.

In these two tales so different in genre, MacDonald responds to the renewed fascination with Arthurian myth in his contemporary culture. Fortified by his own privileged education from—and relationships with—other medieval scholars, his creative engagements with these ancient stories remind his readers that behind this new trend lies their own rich literary and historic past. He challenges the misconstrued notion of modern English chivalry that manifests as a paternalistic *noblesse oblige* or a shallow gallantry and that feeds common tropes such as damsels-in-distress and gallivanting knights; he shows how little they have to do with the truly English definition of *knight*. An etymologically accurate understanding of the word demands that it cannot be unrelated to a conscience of social reform, whether that involves issues of suffrage, class, education, or theological orientation. MacDonald is not hesitant to challenge patterns in the old stories either: for him, literature is a conversation. He defies the convention of the "solitary knight," incongruent as it is with the English definition of *cniht*: as all four of his "knights" progress in their journeys, it becomes evident that not only the novices but also the experienced adventurers have benefitted from and been changed by their respective engagements.

Although Malory's Percival (the version with which the majority of MacDonald's readership was most familiar) achieved a type of union with God upon completing his quest and became a hermit, MacDonald's Anodos is returned to his family and home responsibilities to continue enacting nobleness of deed. The Repentant Knight for whom Anodos was squire likewise never ceases questing. Although his armor indicates he is like Galahad in spirit, and though he even has his lady, he continues to serve others. The journey's end is not his to decide; if he ceases to serve, he ceases to be a knight. For a truly English knight, the quest cannot end in this life. The wait for a happy ending will be long—an Arthurian *Sehnsucht*—but both Anodos and Walton know that "a great Good is coming" (*Phantastes* 323). Death to self is a continuous battle, whether for young Anodos and the artist Percivale, or the elder Walton and the well-travelled Repentant Knight. Anodos was once eager to be a knight who fights evil through deeds of valiance, yet the mentor he comes to admire is one who proves that the true quest is discerning whom to serve and how, and then doing so. For MacDonald, every reader has the potential to be such a knight: an adventurer choosing how to venture.

To stand in the ruins of Arthur's birthplace, as do the Waltons and Percivale, is to be reminded that England's heritage is mythic. When MacDonald, the predecessor of the Inklings, writes, "it was a world of faery; anything might happen in it," he is not describing another world. Rather, it is his own nineteenth-century Britain. He continues:

> Who, in that region of marvel, would start to see suddenly a knight on a great sober warhorse come slowly pacing down the torrent of carmine splendour, flashing it, like the Knight of the Sun himself in a flood from every hollow, a gleam from every flat, and a star from every round and knob of his armour? (*Lossie* 108)

Despite his connections with early medieval revivalism, MacDonald also empathizes with the popular interest in Arthurian legend as mythic inspiration; he encourages neither forgetting nor reverting to the past, but rather the development of new perceptions informed by attention to that past. He believes in a place "where the borders of national, cultural, and mythological identities overlap"; utilizing his literary training, he seeks to meet his readers there (Bryden 1). For MacDonald, "every door and staircase [in this world is] invested with the excitement and mystery of a spiritual romance," and he is eager to show how England's own literature and language give access to that romance.[29]

When he first began to write, the Arthurian revival was only beginning: Tintagel was not yet a tourist shrine, Tennyson's first *Idylls* were not yet published, and his own poem on the Sangreal was of the first of its kind. MacDonald responded simultaneously to a cultural hunger for identity and a cultural need for reform by reintroducing that culture to its roots, engaging the spirit of the age with its own ancient tales of transformation. In so doing, he crafted new mythopoeic art that continues to compel. By shifting the angle, calling his readers back to their own identity, and enabling them to converse with voices of their own past, he evoked the mythic into their "here and now." Rather than simply riding the trend, MacDonald enticed

---

29   This particular quotation is from a *New Witness* review by Frances Chesterton. Greville MacDonald, son of George, copied it into a letter to his publisher, Stanley Unwin, on 6 April 1924.

his readers to look deeper, challenging them to claim their identity and accept the inherent responsibilities. His desire was for England's would-be gallants to discover "that noble deeds had yet to be done, and therefore might be done" (*Cumbermede* 321); for his readers to commence a peregrination of their own. *Phantastes* and *Seaboard Parish* are his invitations. Long after the Victorian trend had faded, half a century later, the invitation still appealed to a young C. S. Lewis when he happened upon the journey of Anodos and then was given *The Seaboard Parish* by his friend Arthur Greeves. And so the conversations of Arthurian inheritance and challenges of chivalric reform continued: from Anodos to Reepicheep, Winnie to Orual, and on; a long—but never solo—pilgrimage of service.

Works Cited

Bloom, Harold. *Classic Fantasy Writers*. NY: Chelsea House, 1994. Print.

Broome, Frederick Hal. *The Science-Fantasy of George MacDonald*. Ph.D. Diss. U of Edinburgh, 1985. Print.

Bryden, Inga. *Reinventing Arthur: The Arthurian Legends in Victorian Culture*. London: Ashgate, 2005. Print.

Burstyn, Joan N. "Education and Sex: The Medical Case against Higher Education for Women in England, 1870–1900." *Proceedings of the American Philosophical Society* 117.2 (1973): 79–89. Print.

Carlyle, Thomas. *The Carlyle Letters Online*. 2007. carlyleletters.org. Web. November 2014.

Chesterton, G. K. *In Defense of Sanity: The Best Essays of G. K. Chesterton*. San Francisco: Ignatius Press, 2011. Print.

Digby, Kenelm Henry. *The Broad Stone of Honour: Goefridus*. London: Wyman & Sons, 1877. Print.

Gillies, Mary Ann. *The Professional Literary Agent in Britain, 1880–1920*. Toronto: U of Toronto P, 2007. Print.

Gould, Sabine Baring. *The Vicar of Morwenstow, R. S. Hawker*. London: Henry S. King, 1876. Print.

Hale, Amy. "The Land Near the Dark Cornish Sea: The Development of Tintagel as a Celtic Pilgrimage Site." *Journal for the Academic Study of Magic* 2 (2004): 206–25. Print.

Jeffrey, David L. *A Dictionary of Biblical Tradition in English Literature*. Grand Rapids, MI: Eerdmans, 1992. Print.

Jenkins, Elizabeth. *The Mystery of Arthur*. NY: Coward, McCann, and Geoghegan, 1975. Print.

Jeffrey Johnson, Kirstin. "*Rooted In All Its Story, More Is Meant Than Meets the Ear*: A Study of the Relational and the Revelational Nature of George MacDonald's Mythopoeic Art." *North Wind* 30 (2011): 85–134. Web. www.snc.edu. 26 February 2016.

Landlow, George. "*The Art-Journal*, 1850–1880: Antiquarians, the Medieval Revival, and the Reception of Pre-Raphaelitism." *The Pre-Raphaelite Review* 2 (1979). 71–76. Print.

"The Late Professor A. J. Scott." *Scotsman* 19 January 1866. Print.

Lewis, C. S, ed. *George MacDonald: An Anthology*. London: Geoffrey Bles, 1946. Print.

——. *The Collected Letters of C. S. Lewis*. Ed. Walter Hooper. 3 vols. San Francisco: Harper San Francisco, 2004–07. Print.

Lewis, Warren. *Letters of C. S. Lewis*. Ed. W. H. Lewis. NY: Harcourt, Brace & World, 1966. Print.

MacDonald, George. *Annals of a Quiet Neighbourhood*. London: Kegan Paul, Trench, Trübner, n.d. Print.

——. *A Dish of Orts*. Whitefish, MT: Kessinger, 2004. Print.

——. *England's Antiphon*. London: MacMillan, 1868. Print.

——. *An Expression of Character: The Letters of George MacDonald*. Ed. Glenn Sadler. Grand Rapids, MI: Eerdmans, 1994. Print.

——. *Lilith*. 1895. Whitehorn, CA: Johannesen, 1995. Print.

——. *Marquis of Lossie*. Vol. 2. London: Hurst & Blackett, 1877. Print.

——. *Phantastes: A Faerie Romance for Men and Women*. London: Smith, Elder, 1858. Print.

——. *The Poetical Works of George MacDonald*. London: Chatto & Windus, 1893. Print.

——. "The Sangreal: A Part of the Story Omitted in the Old Romances." *Good Words* 4 (1863): 454–55. Print.

——. *The Seaboard Parish*. NY: George Routledge & Sons, 1876. Print.

——. *The Vicar's Daughter*. Kila, MT: Kessinger Publishing, 2004. Print.

——. *Wilfrid Cumbermede: An Autobiographical Story*. Vol. 2. NY: Charles Scribner, 1872. Print.

MacDonald, Greville. *George MacDonald and His Wife*. London: Allen & Unwin, 1924. Print.

——. Letter to Stanley Unwin. 6 April 1924. MS. Greville MacDonald Papers. Marion E. Wade Center, Wheaton College. Wheaton, IL.

Matthews, David. "Scholarship and Popular Culture in the Nineteenth Century." *A Companion to Arthurian Literature*. Ed. Helen Fulton. Oxford: Wiley-Blackwell, 2009. 355–67. Print.

"New Books: *Malcolm* by George MacDonald." *Wingfold* 42 (2003): 25–26. Print.

Raeper, William. *George MacDonald*. Tring, Hertfordshire, UK: Lion Publishing, 1987. Print.

"Review of 'Knight of the Sun.'" *Athenaeum* 20 September 1873. 374. Print.

Roberts, Leonard. *Arthur Hughes: His Life and Works*. Woodbridge, Suffolk, UK: Antique Collectors' Club, 1997. Print.

Ruskin, John. *The Winnington Letters: John Ruskin's Correspondence with Margaret Alexis Bell and the Children at Winnington Hall* (1969), 109–10. London: Allen & Unwin, 1969. Print.

Staines, David, trans. *The Complete Romances of Chrétien de Troyes*. 1990. Bloomington and Indianapolis, IN: Indiana UP, 1993. Print.

Tolkien, J. R. R. "On Fairy-Stories." *Essays Presented to Charles Williams*. Ed. C. S. Lewis. London: Oxford UP, 1947. 38–89. Print.

17

Camelot Incarnate: Arthurian Vision in the Early Plays of Charles Williams

Bradley Wells

While long acknowledged for his unique Arthurian poem cycle, *Taliessin through Logres* and *The Region of the Summer Stars*, and his posthumously published commentary on the history and significance of the Arthurian legend, "The Figure of Arthur" (1948), the full reach and impact of "the Matter of Britain" upon the other writings of Charles Williams has not been fully appreciated.[1] Not only was Arthur there from the beginning, but the mythology of Camelot is inseparable from Williams' overall literary and theological vision.

To fully appreciate the nature and scope of Williams' Arthuriad, one must understand his unique vision of what he termed "The City." This theological, literary, and imaginative vision of an ideal co-inhered City emerged alongside Williams' re-imagining of the Arthurian myth and fed into all his creative work, particularly his plays. Indeed, a study of Williams' early dramatic writings including his Masques shows how his Arthurian vision and his theology of the City are interconnected, even co-inhered, and how he was able to realize this Arthurian vision of the City on stage by embodying its incarnational truths in the physical domain of performance.

---

1   All subsequent references to *TtL* and *RSS* come from Charles Williams, *Taliessin through Logres, The Region of the Summer Stars, Arthurian Torso* (Grand Rapids, MI: Eerdmans, 1974.)

Williams' Theology of the City

Williams' notion of the City is not unlike Augustine's "City of God" in that at its center is a sense of community and unity that implies the rejection of the self in favor of the other.[2] It is also, in one sense, the Heavenly City of Revelation: "the holy city … coming down from God out of heaven."[3] The influence of the theologian Duns Scotus is also detectable in his adherence to the Athanasian vision of this City made "not by conversion of the Godhead into flesh: but by taking of the Manhood into God" (qtd. in Medcalf 28). Williams draws upon all these traditional Christian notions of the City but also appropriates them in a unique way within his broader co-inhered Arthurian vision.

His City is fundamentally paradoxical. It is concurrently natural and supernatural, physical and spiritual, real and ideal, ordered and chaotic: "These images, making altogether one greater image, show the City both ideally and actually (and even historically), in schism and in concord, as in heaven and as on earth" (Williams, "Image" 92). Yet, ironically, it is this sustained tension in the City that facilitates its capacity to be also "woven into unity" ("Image" 93). For Williams, the City must be a place of order. As C. S. Lewis recalled: "On many of us the prevailing impression made by the London streets is one of chaos; but Williams, looking on the same spectacle, saw chiefly an image—an imperfect, pathetic, heroic, and majestic image—of Order" (qtd. in Ridler xlvii). For Williams, this sense of divine majestic order existed even in the most seemingly mundane activities of daily urban life. Indeed, it is in these moments that the most profound truths can be accessed and the true City experienced.

According to Williams, this metaphysical order evident in the smallest daily act should also be extended to the broader socio-political sphere, and he came to express this belief through his model of a hierarchical republic. According to his biographer, Alice Hadfield, this conjunction had early origins. Williams

> saw the *res publica* … as a balance between equality and hierarchy …. He slowly created for himself over the years a synthesis in which all men and women were equal and yet different within their hierarchies of excellence and distinction, in which above political equality everyone's distinctness was embodied in the single person of the monarch, as everyone's personal equality and distinctness was held in Christ. (Hadfield, *Exploration* 21–22)

Such "equality and distinctness" can be detected in his early poem "Celestial Cities," which encapsulates his passion for being a citizen subject to, but co-inhered with, both secular and divine authority, here embodied in the young Lord Mayor of London as Christ in Sarras:[4]

---

2   Flora Liénard contends: "Williams chose to prefer the Augustinian version of the City as the ideal for human harmony" (73). Williams acknowledges his debt to Augustine when he writes: "'Fuimus ille unus' [Augustine] said; 'we were in the one when we were the one,'" in a discussion about "the principle of inevitable relationship" (*Dove* 69).

3   Revelation 21:2. See Hockley's discussion of this notion of the City.

4   According to Arthurian Legend, the island Sarras is where the Holy Grail was brought on its way to Britain.

When our translated cities
Are joyous and divine,
And through the streets of London
The Streets of Sarras shine,

...

When we shall hear—how gladly!—
The general shout declare
That up Cheapside his pageant
Conveys the young Lord Mayor,
When all applause salutes him,
Man chosen among men,
By proof of former friendship
Known to each citizen. (lines 1–4, 13–20)

This vision of the ideal city is the same as that discovered by Taliessin when he reaches the closely structured and finely ordered city of Byzantium where "the streets repeat the sound of the Throne" (*TtL*: "The
Vision of the Empire" l. 4) and "its citizens [are] as diverse in structure and function as the parts of the
human body, yet as precisely coordinated as a geometrical diagram" (Shideler 9). Such a hierarchical
republic seems paradoxical, but it is part of what Williams describes elsewhere as the "great exchange of
duty" whereby "the classless Republic is a republic of hierarchies, and each hierarchy is the flashing out
of ranked equalities" ("A Dialogue on Hierarchy" 129). For Williams, the City is not a passive intellectual
construct; it is an active, lived reality. This is clearly illustrated in another key element of his theology of
the City: the importance of individual choice.

Choice, or what is also termed "freedom" or "liberty," underpins Williams' vision of the ideal City,
which is not to be simply discovered like a medieval paradise nor inherited as some inalienable democratic
right, but that has to be chosen through asserted human will and action. The true City is one where men
are not immune from decisions, but rather empowered to make them out of their own free will. So, unlike
a medieval escapist paradise or a delusory totalitarian utopia, Williams' City is one that demands constant
choices: "The choice exists everywhere, at every minute, as a fundamental, though that fundamental may have
been accepted, and our business be with the edification of the City upon it" ("The Redeemed City" 103).

Paradoxically, though, true freedom can only be achieved by choosing servitude. This element of his
theology of the City can be detected in an episode from the poem "The Departure of Dindrane" in *The
Region of the Summer Stars*, in which a Greek slave girl struggles in deciding whether to accept the offer of freedom or to stay with the household of Taliessin. In this "masterful analysis of the process by which choice is
made" (Shideler 13), whereby Taliessin refuses to make the choice for her but uses his power and authority
over her to "force" her to make her own choice, she comes to realize the universal truth of the City that
"servitude and freedom were one and interchangeable" ("The Departure of Dindrane" 77). In extending
the principle of individual choice to states, governments and institutions, Williams declares: "The State
itself must be willing continuously to die in order to live" ("The Free Act" 114).

Williams' utopian vision of the City is further distinguished through the operation of the principles of Exchange and Substitution. As one of Williams' favorite poets, John Donne, wrote: "I am no companion for myself …. I must not be alone with myself …. I am the Babylon that I must go out of, or I perish" (qtd. in "The Redeemed City" 107). As Williams explains: "The name of the City is Union; the operation of the Infamy is by outrage on that union. The process of that union is by the method of free exchange" (103). That is, the City is only achieved through the daily offering of oneself to others in the daily moments of existence. For Williams, "The whole effort of imagining the City … is the use of propinquity as a means to neighbourliness, and so to the continual interchange of courtesies of the spirit" ("Image" 101). This interchange within the City is, in effect, an expression of the essential incarnational truth of a co-inhered world where actions are physical embodiments of a spiritual truth:

> What is the characteristic of any City? Exchange between citizens. What is the fact common to both sterile communication and vital communication? A mode of exchange. What is the fundamental fact of men in their natural lives? The necessity of exchange. What is the highest level of Christian dogma? Exchange between men and God, by virtue of the union of Man and God in the single Person, who is, by virtue again of the Manhood, itself the City, the foundation and the enclosure. (Williams, "Anthropotokos" 112)

Here, as elsewhere, Williams' examples of Substitution and Exchange are imbued with a sense of their being able to operate outside the constraints of earthly time. Like William Wordsworth's Nature in *The Prelude*, Williams' City, which is "the proper community of men" ("Image" 94), is intergenerational and timeless. It is a union of "the generations of mankind / Spread over time, past, present, and to come."[5] According to Williams, this is similar to T. S. Eliot's *The Family Reunion*, which "carries within it the poetic hints of the civil union of the living and the dead …. I do not recollect any other modern work which throws so strange a light on the true relationship of the generations, and therefore on the principles of the City" ("Image" 101). This paradoxical fluidity of historical and imaginary time is foundational to Williams' Arthurian framework, where he contorts history to suit his imaginary vision because, as he writes in "Figure," "In a sense, of course, history is itself myth" (264). This can be seen in the earliest of Williams' thoughts on Arthur, such as those contained in his *Arthurian Commonplace Book*,[6] in which he plans to merge various historical periods into the one mythology:

> ? Bring [Ar] Arthur and his surroundings in England [Britain], about A.D. 500, forward + parallel to Charlemagne + his surroundings in France, A.D. 800: so as to obtain the full effect of Islam, in Africa, in Spain. (*Arthurian Commonplace Book* 12)

---

5   William Wordsworth, *The Prelude*. Book 14, ll. 109–10. Qtd. in "Image" 94.
6   Being an unpublished blank bound copy of the Concise Oxford Dictionary with "The Holy Grail" inscribed on the spine and which contains various clippings and handwritten notes. Undated. Catalogued as "Notes on the Holy Grail" in the Bodleian Library, Oxford University. [MS Eng.e.2012].

This sense of the fluidity of time, however, can also have negative implications for those who reject the Way of Exchange[7] and Substitution: "The burden of the guilt of a murder conceived in one generation is carried in another: 'bear ye one another's burdens' is given here a terrible interpretation" ("Image" 101).

Within Williams' vision of the City, then, there is always the lurking potential for "terrible interpretation." For example, the City of London can be a negative place, apparently lacking love. In the novel *All Hallows' Eve,* as Lester and Evelyn walk in the streets of a deserted and dark London lit only by empty houses, Lester is scared of finding herself alone in this new City: "all in a silence she did not know, so that if she yielded to the silence she would not know those other things, and the whole place would be different and dreadful" (77). This risk of the Infamy, however, is tempered by the redemptive potential of choice, and even in this "silence" potential freedom is implied in Williams' evocation of a supernatural timelessness that pervades the eternal City.

An appreciation of these aspects of Williams' theology of the City is essential for an understanding of how his Arthurian vision is realized and embodied in his plays. From his earliest theatrical experiments, Williams wrestles with both his theological ideas themselves and the means by which he can embody those ideas on the stage. The resultant early dramatic writings and masques can be seen as Arthurian mini-cities insofar as they demonstrate how Williams was able to incarnate his theology of the City into the flesh of performance.

Prince Rudolph of Silvania

The earliest known surviving manuscript of an original dramatic work by Williams is found within a hand-written booklet currently housed in the manuscript collection at the Marion E. Wade Center in Wheaton, Illinois.[8] Believed lost until recently,[9] it is a school notebook and appears to contain entries made during the period of Williams' final years at St Albans Grammar School and his first years at University College London, where he took up an Intermediate Scholarship in autumn, 1901.[10] The content of the manuscript relates to an imaginary world created by him and his school friends, called "Silvania," and its hero, Prince Rudolph. Williams' close boyhood friend, George Robinson, recalls how at that time Williams maintained

---

7   Williams often used the expression "The Way of Exchange" interchangeably with the term "Exchange." It was also the title of his pamphlet on the subject.

8   Marion E. Wade Center, Wheaton College, Wheaton, Illinois USA. CW/MS-113 "Prince Rudolph of Silvania." Unpublished. Previously labelled "Ministry at the End of 1902." For an explanation of the change of title, see footnote 12 below. The pages of the manuscript are unnumbered.

9   Anne Ridler notes and laments the apparent loss of these writings: "Of this Gondal country nothing seems to have been recorded in writing" (Ridler xiv).

10 There are no dates on the early entries in this manuscript, but some later entries are dated 1902, while the final few are dated 1903. This would correlate with the period when Williams and Robinson travelled together to London during their first years at University College. However, the subject matter of the material contained in this manuscript correlates to the imaginary world that Williams and his friends invented during their final school years. See Ridler xii–iv.

a sort of running drama concerning one Prince Rudolph (Ruritania, of course, in the background) Princess Rosiland and a Baron de Bracey (!) a comic character in the Falstaff vein. I was usually Rudolph, Charles' sister Edith the Princess and Charles was Baron de Bracey, in which character he showed a ripe sense of humour and power of dramatic portrayal. (Hadfield, *Exploration* 8)

Interestingly, the apparent extension of this "running drama" from school into his early university years shows not only the attraction of the drama of this imaginary world, but also how "college life made comparatively little impression on him and seemed to be no more than an extension of school" (Carpenter 78). What was it about this City of Sylvania that appealed to Williams, and what does it reveal about his early theological and literary vision?

The only existing critique of this manuscript comes from Alice Hadfield who, in recollecting a document misleadingly titled "Ministry at the End of 1902,"[11] makes only general reference to her memory of "a rambling drama, which has hints of things to come" (*Exploration* 8). Indeed, it is difficult to describe this work because, on many levels, it resists easy categorization in a particular genre. Episodic in form but linear in chronology, unlike, say, Tolkien's Middle-earth, Silvania is firmly embedded in the real contemporary world where imaginary characters and situations are located alongside real events and historical figures, including Edward VIII, Tsar Nicholas II, and Kaiser Wilhelm. Similar to the convergent historical and imaginative Arthurian myth planned in his *Commonplace Book* and presented in his Taliessin poems, the form, structure, and subject matter of this work show the seeds of Williams' notion of Co-inherence.

Two items from this collection that warrant particular attention are extracts from two plays purportedly by Silvanian playwrights. These extracts are introduced and contextualized by Williams in an official introductory note that locates them in the second phase of the literature of the Kingdom, "from 1342 to the death of Princess Eleanor (1705): Era of Dramatic and Epic poetry." The first of these plays is titled "The Lamentable, and ever to be mourned history and death of the great and good Prince John II, and of his son, Henry," from which is "reproduced" an extract from Act I Scene 4, set in a "Hall in the Castle." After having carefully rendered the historical credentials of this play, a more supernatural dimension unfolds when we find King John, alone, tormented by the prospect of his imminent death:

> *John:*   Break! Break My Heart!
> The time has come for this white soul to part.
> Could I believe the time had really come

---

11   The title "Ministry at the End of 1902," used by Hadfield and all critics since to refer to the whole workbook, is somewhat of a misnomer. It appears to have been taken from the title that appears on only the first page of the manuscript whose full heading is "Long Live Our Prince. The Ministry at the End of 1902." This title is the specific heading for only the first document in the collection, a relatively short item listing the members of the Ministry from the imaginary government of Silvania in the year 1902. The original cover of the workbook, and presumably its title page, is unfortunately missing from the sole remaining manuscript. Given the breadth and nature of its content, the Wade Center has recently re-catalogued its manuscript as "Prince Rudolph of Silvania."

> That I should hear the dark archangel's drum
>
> Within myself the breath I, stern, would hold
>
> Has my time come? And yet I am not old. (1.4.1–6)

The invocation of the heavenly figure of "the dark archangel" together with the metaphysical question "Has my time come?" imbues these ostensibly individual personal cogitations of King John with a supernatural and universal significance. Similarly, by combining references to natural physical realities such as "breath" and temporal age—"I am not old"—with the more mystical references to "soul" and "heart," as well as the shift in tense, Williams suggests the paradoxical nature of this world that is concurrently natural and supernatural, fixed and malleable, determined and random.

This paradox is further reflected in the internal dilemma of the central character, who is struggling against external forces apparently beyond his control:

> My son a traitor! Can it really be?
>
> Never had he aught but great love to me.
>
> I hurl the thought far from my maddened brain
>
> Yet with persistence it returns again! (1.4.7–10)

Despite the somewhat forced rhyme, clumsy rhythm, and derivative pseudo-Shakespearean nature of the verse here, Williams is attempting to convey a genuine sense of the dynamic tension, conflict, and drama between an individual and his world, as between the entire natural and the supernatural worlds. Even in the final couplet where King John contemplates death, he is confronted by the significance of this convergence of natural ("air") and supernatural ("spirit"): "Death would be welcome, yet I do not dare / To let my spirit reach the outer air" (1.4.11–12).

Having established the metaphysical, Williams' next scene purports to recount the more tangible setting of action at a "Field of Battle" (3.2.1). Possibly influenced by his personal study of Shakespeare's *Henry V*, Williams presents his Prince Henry as something of an existentialist who is struggling to reconcile his private desires and public duties. Henry's invocation to his men to fight for three concurrent conceptions, "To me, your country and yourselves be true!" (3.2.6), is compounded by his later invocation of his dead father, that same King John from the previous extract:

> You see my father close beside you stand
>
> Pointing you forward with his trembling hand!
>
> Think how you swarmed around him as he died
>
> And swore for and, when he for vengeance cried,
>
> You vowed revenge, with weapons raised on high. (3.2.9–13)

In having both the living prince and dead king present, Williams effectively invokes both the earthly and spiritual world. This early expression of a type of co-inherence of the natural and supernatural is made authentic and more accessible to the audience by embedding it within a context of the action of the battle itself that ends the scene: "With flashing armour, and with flags of gold! / Show that you're not enfeebled by his loss! / Strike for St Brendan and the Golden Cross!" (3.2.16–18).

While the imagery of this final passage attempts to co-inhere the earthly battle of Prince Henry with the heavenly world of St Brendan and the Golden Cross, it is the drama of the actions on stage, through implicit stage directions ("flashing," "show," "strike"), that resonates with the audience because, like the City, it is through action that these ideas are incarnated into flesh and made real.

Williams' early vision of co-inherence between the natural and the supernatural world takes on a more overtly socio-political dimension in the second play of this manuscript, titled "The Rival Princes." In Perivale's opening description of the "forest glade" (1.4.1), the natural landscape becomes animated and also imbued with supernatural qualities through Williams' deployment of a simile comparing trees to "spirits" that can "hear":

> These gnarled trunks like spirits sent from hell
> To hear our dreadful purpose, and to aid,
> To me appear, so doth a guilty mind
> Turn nature's works to warnings to desist.
> I have a mind Lysander, to return
> And take no further steps with thee as guide. (1.4.7–12)

Like the Arthurian "mysterious forest of Broceliande" ("Figure" 265), which Williams locates in his mythology somewhere between Sarras and P'o-L'u and thereby depicts as representing the threshold between heaven and hell,[12] we find in this passage contrasting emotions of fear ("dreadful purpose") and hope ("aid") that are combined in order to position the audience to reconsider their assumptions about emotional or moral absolutes. Even traditional absolutes such as good and evil are presented as being mutable and subject to perception: "so doth a guilty mind / Turn nature's works to warnings to desist." The resulting theological and emotional tension is further compounded by the accompanying dramatic action contained in the tension of Perivale's fears and doubts in the face of his impending dilemma to choose whether or not "to return."

A further glimpse into Williams' early theology of the City is found in the final scene from "The Rival Princes," which depicts the re-establishment of order when Errion returns to rightfully reclaim inheritance of his father's throne from the conspirators. The spiritual order that accompanies this return to the City is reflected in the social and political hierarchy embodied in the return of the rightful ruler, emphasized by one of the play's very few explicit stage directions: "[Errion] ascends the throne" (4.2.7). This visible re-establishment of hierarchy on stage is notably not at the cost of the community or the "republic" of its individual members, or even the conspirators. As Errion's "freedom" (4.2.4) is assured only in the continuance of the hierarchical order, the conspirators are offered the opportunity to exercise free choice as a means of redemption. This choice must be realized through a penitential act, within an early motif of

---

12   See Williams, "Figure" 265–66, and Lewis, WA 283–84.

Williams' theology of romantic love, whereby they must seek, approach, and kiss a mysterious lady. In this very early depiction of a type of Beatrician encounter, Williams notably balances the sense of imperative "necessity" with a corresponding sense of mutability and subjectivity. The repeated reference to perception and appearance in the phrases "wondrous fair to me, / To some most horrible doth she appear" (4.2.9–10) and "Howe'er this lady shall appear to you" (4.2.13) creates a sense of paradox between the mutability of perception and appearance and the absolutes implied by the accompanying notions of justice and moral truth. A similar paradox lies at the heart of Williams' emerging vision of the City. For now, though, this is a tension that remains unresolved.

These juvenilia give tantalizing hints of what is to come both in regard to Williams' theological ideas and in the way in which he will incarnate them on the stage. In Silvania, we find glimpses of his Arthurian City in its detailed, organized, sophisticated, dynamic, authentic, and coherent world of order, hierarchy, yet equality, where choice is offered within a dramatic sense of ritual, imagery, conflict, and an emerging sense of the co-inherence of the natural and supernatural and expressed through a dramatic dynamic of action and paradox.

The Chapel of the Thorn (1912)

Written for publication rather than performance, Williams' early dramatic poem *The Chapel of the Thorn* contains various significant elements of his evolving Arthurian vision, but the Camelot that Williams creates in this work is more cerebral and literary rather than physical and theatrical.

On one level, there are some clear Arthurian parallels in this imaginary tale about the struggle between a group of Christians and pagans for the control of a holy relic—a thorn from the Crown of Thorns. In her introduction to the recently published work, Sørina Higgins is right to note that the character of Amael, the harp-playing poet and priest of the cult of Druhild, is a prototype for the character of Taliessin from Williams' later Arthurian poetry (Higgins 13). Indeed, there is evidence that Amael foreshadows Williams' later Arthurian figures in being presented as an incarnation figure with Christ-like characteristics who, as the "seed of Adam,"[13] is both human and divine: "I am little dust blown from the temple of the gods" (1.613–14).

Furthermore, Williams characteristically places a physical object at the center of his drama, in this case the sacral item of the Thorn, which operates as provocateur and catalyst for the action in much the same way as the Grail does in Williams' more explicit Arthurian writings (Higgins 11). Visions of an ideal Arthurian city can also be glimpsed in the various extended passages of theological debate between the key characters on each side of the conflict. In these debates between the mystic Joachim, the ecclesiastical Innocent, and the pagan Amael, Williams appears to be working out his own evolving vision of a world that embodies the universal application of the principles of Co-inherence, Exchange, and Substitution. The

---

13 Williams often used this phrase to denote Christ, most notably in his various Nativity plays, including *The Death of Good Fortune* (1939), *The House by the Stable* (1939), *Grab and Grace* (1941) and, in particular, *Seed of Adam* (1936).

characters are unwittingly seeking an Arthurian City, one which encapsulates what Abbot Innocent calls the "folklore of the world" (2.276) and which is embodied in the "flesh and soul ... blood or thought" (2.293–94) of the Incarnation. Here, the principles of Exchange are seen to exist beyond the constraints of earthly time whereby a character such as Joachim can bear "the times of twain his brothers, those who died" (1.157) and where "hands pluck at him from their grave" (1.161). Such exchange is supernatural but, more importantly, physical. As Joachim acknowledges later in the play: "Are not these poor folk whom God died for, freed / From any law except Christ's pulse in theirs, / And irregularly his in each one beats" (1.545–47). This clear gesture toward the Incarnational source of all earthly Exchange is further suggested in the opening reference to the Virgin Mary in the simple but compelling words of the woman who says of the "white Christ-lord" (1.8) that "He had a mother" (1.10).

However, Williams' vision of a truly co-inhered world remains ultimately elusive in the text, and the reader is entitled to ask, along with Amael, "What power makes this man dream as if he saw?" (2.357). The vision of a utopian Camelot that co-inheres the temporal and spiritual, such as that offered by the truce between the King Constantine and the Abbot Innocent at the climax of Act I, remain unconvincing, and the reader shares Joachim's skepticism of such a paradox:

> King-abbot, abbot-king!
> Aye: I have waited long until this hour.
> Thine is it ye should swear yourselves allies
> To work a masterdom on soul and flesh,—
> Against man's unity a unity. (1.533–37)

In the end, the Arthurian city presented in *Chapel* remains predominantly intellectual rather than experiential. While foreshadowed and glimpsed in this work, Williams' Camelot was still a little way off, and it is perhaps not surprising that the work concludes somewhat ambiguously. *Chapel* is more poetic than dramatic and, despite experimenting with some elements of his Arthurian city, it would take the subsequent experience of writing specifically for dramatic performance for Williams' Arthurian vision to become more fully realized.

The Masque of the Manuscript (1927)

After the early dramatic and intellectual experiments of his youth, Williams' first major plays written and performed for a wider audience (albeit a select one)[14] were his three masques written while working at Oxford University Press at Amen House in London.[15] Unlike the limited and embryonic "scribblings"

---

14   The audience consisted of colleagues and select friends associated with Amen House. According to Hadfield, "The audience was chosen with a little care for those who would not think it boring and before whom there could be complete unbending" (Hadfield, *Introduction* 72).

15   *The Masque of the Manuscript* (1927), *The Masque of Perusal* (1929) and *The Masque of the Termination of Copyright* (1930). These plays were specifically written to be performed in the library of Amen House, although the third was

of Silvania and experiment of *Chapel*, these masques represent an attempt by Williams to fully incarnate on stage his city of Amen House as an embodiment of the ideal City—a Byzantium, a new Camelot. The playwright adored his working life at the Press and, similar to how he perceived "the Company" in his Arthurian poetry as "a particular image of the Divine city" (Russell 14), he saw the community that existed at Amen House as a physical expression of the heavenly City of God on earth, and by directly paralleling this known world with his imaginary masques he was attempting to realize his vision of the City through the flesh of performance.

His first masque, *The Masque of the Manuscript,* affectionately parodies life at Amen House by tracking the trials and tribulations of a manuscript as it journeys from draft to publication. By setting the performance in the actual library of Amen House, and with no attempt to disguise its surroundings, Williams hopes to make the link between the imaginary and real publishing worlds immediately explicit and thereby facilitate a co-inherence between the two.[16] This reclamation of a secular space for spiritual theatre also represented an early contribution to a key development in the wider English religious drama revival of the early twentieth century, for which Williams would later be lauded as "not only the most original, but also the most exciting of the modern playwrights" (Weales 164). By having his characters refer to and gesture toward various parts of the room throughout the play, Williams appropriates items such as telephones, bookshelves, and chairs as props and imbues them with dramatic potential, thereby blurring the traditional barriers between audience and stage. For example, in a humorous but unsettling scene in which the actor playing the role of Manuscript is physically lifted and placed on an actual bookshelf, the audience witnesses a physicalized exchange between the imaginary and real worlds.[17] By deploying such a device, the set and performance of this masque becomes both symbolic and real, contemporary and universal, a City that co-inheres the natural with the supernatural.

This quasi-sacramental convergence of the natural and supernatural worlds is echoed in the relationship and interplay between the set and the characters. In the opening stage direction, Williams explicitly prescribes the layout of the set, insisting that "Caesar's chair is between the two recesses, but rather more forward; the rest of the spectators are behind him." In addition to this obvious conceit of having the Oxford University Press Publisher, Humphrey Milford, presented as an emperor who reigns over Amen House, there is the theatrical conceit of co-inhering observer and participant into the one person. The "fourth wall" of the theatre being breached, the audience is better prepared for the climactic redemptive scene in which Caesar (Milford) "having signified assent" (page 317) grants final magisterial approval for the publication of the

---

never performed in Williams' lifetime. The first two were privately published by Henderson & Spalding as separate volumes at the time, but all three have since been published in one volume: Williams, Charles. *The Masques of Amen House.* Ed. David Bratman. Altadena, CA: The Mythopoeic Press, 2000. All quotations will be taken from this edition.

16   While no image from the actual performance survives, we do know from an inscription on the flycover of an original copy of the published acting edition of *The Masque of the Manuscript* that "the eastern part ... was used for the stage." See Bodleian Archives: Hadfield Collection Box 2, Book 10.

17   See stage direction on page 49 of *The Masque of the Manuscript.*

Manuscript.[18] The world of the play exchanges with the world of the audience because, for Williams, they are both incarnations of the same universal and eternal City.

The traditional demarcation between the imaginary world of the play and real world of the audience is further eroded by Williams' deployment of music and song in all the masques. The music contributes to the mystical, almost sacramental, nature of the action that invites the audience to transcend the normally prosaic nature of the everyday. In *Manuscript*, immediately following the Introducer's prologue, a song is heard from behind the curtain. Williams specifically chose the professional singer Dora Stevens (the only professional member of the cast) to sing the music that was especially composed by Hubert Foss for the occasion; this choice shows how important this song, "The Carol of Amen House," was to him for the overall success of the play. The song itself is a haunting, even unsettling, melody in a minor key described as "lyrical but chromatic in harmony, and containing a middle section (the third verse) raising the tension and providing contrast by suppressing the movement of the melodic line" (Bratman 162). The transcendental and timeless nature of such music has a liturgical quality that, together with the various repeated rituals of kneeling and bowing throughout the play, is quasi-Anglo-Catholic, even quasi-Rosicrucian,[19] in its ceremony, and it helps contribute to the overall sacramental nature of the performance. Through the music, the library of Amen House is transformed into a place of worship in which the act of publishing a book equates to the celebration of a sacrament.

This elevation of Amen House to the status of a sacred perfect City is echoed in the lyrics: "Beauty arose of old / And dreamed of a perfect thing" (47–48). The City Williams presents here is sacramental and becomes "an outward and visible sign of an inward and spiritual grace"[20] just as "the perfect thing" of the Holy Grail becomes the "visibility of the invisible" in Williams' Arthurian myth ("Figure" 206). In the same way that the Grail in the Arthur legend is made manifest through "the unifying act, perilous and perpetual, universal and individual" ("Figure" 197), here the sacramental City of Amen House is only "seen by the seekers of truth" ("Figure" 69) via individual action within community, even of the most seemingly mundane activities of work: "O'er the toil that is given to do, / O'er the search and the grinding pain" (63–64). After raising this idea of a Community of Exchange, Williams then opens the action of the play with an ordinary scene of Phillida[21] working alone at her table in the library. This simple image is juxtaposed against the Master of the Music's declaration that she is not merely an office worker but, in fact, is a type of "warden" of "celestial defence" participating in supernatural activity associated with the occult:

---

18   The significance of this action by Milford and its importance to the masque is evidenced by the fact that Williams was not willing to leave this scene to chance and took time to prepare Milford by rehearsing the scene prior to the performance.

19   Williams was an active member of A. E. Waite's occultist group, the Fellowship of the Rosy Cross, from 1917 to 1927. See Ashenden.

20   As defined by the Catechism from the Anglican Prayer Book (1662).

21   'Phillida' was one of CW's nicknames for Phyllis Jones, and occurrences of 'Phillida' in this volume are indexed under 'Jones, Phyllis.' [Editor's note]

> Lo, the Library unclosing
> On the sadness of the earth,
> All its occult lore exposing
> To the souls of mortal birth. (71–74)

Such explicitly occultist invocations are on one level consistent with the syncretistic traditions of the masque genre, but their bluntness here also reflects Williams' particular esoteric sympathies and heterodox oeuvre. Such a direct invocation of supernatural forces may be clumsy and would appear to demand much of an audience, but it is certainly intentional.[22] Explicit reference to the occult has the effect of efficiently and quickly elevating earthly activities to more supernatural significance, just as Phillida's opening speech invokes a similar timeless supernatural dimension to her work. Behind her apparent calm exterior lies a frenzied world:

> Here on my watch I sit, and all around
> The ancient masters of the music sound,
> Pythagoreal, spheral; rune and rhyme
> Concordant moving with the face of time
> Against the dark future and the void. (83–87)

This image of the dance, like that from Williams' later novel *The Greater Trumps*, is used to transcend the traditional restraints of time. Phillida's ability to transcend time and place, like Arthur's, is reinforced through an amalgam of historical and geographical allusions from classical Delphic symbols to Renaissance, African and oriental. This creative tension between the past and the present, the imaginary and the real, helps create a seductive paradox and is encapsulated in the earlier oxymoronic phrase "backward-thrusting" (7). Williams thus positions his characters within a unique timelessness whereby they can glimpse a sense of the eternal City. More so than his Arthurian poetry, which merely tells the "story" (Russell 11) of co-inherence, this early play attempts to embody it in incarnate form. This City, while eternal and supernatural, is also real and made actual through physical action.

For example, having been successfully positioned as some kind of mythic protector of the knowledge and truth of mankind throughout history, Phillida then arms herself with physical weaponry when sensing the arrival of a "rash foot" (108) into her mystical world. As the music of a "dance measure" begins (in the stage directions to l. 108), Phillida casts off her librarian pose and "catches up her sword" in a visually striking gesture of epic heroism reminiscent of Arthur and Excalibur. This is accompanied by the physical appearance of the Manuscript on stage; she is searching for fulfilment and satisfaction in the city: "Is this then the place of achievement, the end of waiting, / The portal of freedom, the high city's final ungating?"

---

22 Bosky's suggestion in her footnote that the word "occult" is used here in merely its old meaning of "hidden" or "secret" is unduly apologetic and at odds with the various direct references to the occult later in the play (Bosky 191n73).

(108–09). Like Camelot, this city is both a physical and spiritual place. The Library is described as a physical "place," "house," and "cave," but one that is of "freedom," "peace," "all holy indwelling," and "desire."

It is at this point that Williams gives a more explicit allusion to that ultimate embodiment of physical and spiritual co-inherence: The Incarnation. The Manuscript explains the reason for her arrival: "I was my father's sole delight, / His *dulcis filia*, lass of might" (121–22). Like Christ, the Manuscript has been sent by her father. So, too, the Manuscript is the incarnation of its creator's mind, but it is also seeking a more complete incarnation as a published book. Just as in the clever opening conceit at the start of the play, where Williams links the birth of God (Christmas) with the birth of Milford (his birthday) and with the birth of this Masque as divine acts of incarnation, so all great literary creations are incarnational expressions. A similar conceit is deployed by Williams in his Arthuriad by having Taliessin, the creative poet, experience his incarnational epiphany of the City in Byzantium "on the name-day and birthday of their father the Emperor" (*TtL:* "The Vision of the Empire" 32). Thus, both the Taliessin poems and the Manuscript are in the tradition of Herrick, Wither, Jonson, Milton, and Shakespeare; they are divine acts invoked by the heavens themselves: "Solemn devices have no better thrift / Than that the Athenian craftsmen for a gift / Brought to their Due: as they, so we to ours" (31–33).

Furthermore, Williams links these incarnational images with that of the ultimately redemptive purpose of the Incarnation; namely, the Atonement of Christ. Phillida knows that resurrection and fulfilment (publication) can only come via sacrifice and pain:

> *Phillida:*   Art thou purged as by fire and by water made clean?
> *Manuscript:*   I mean what I say and I say what I mean.
> *Phillida:*   Nine years has thy father revised thee with pain?
> *Manuscript:*   Twice nine on his desk I have patiently lain. (125–28)

Amid the strange amalgam of occultist and orthodox imagery, we find a complex convergence between incarnation—be it childbirth as implied in the nine years (months?)—and redemption—be it through the atonement or purgation of being "made clean" or baptism implied by "water" —and all is presented within a numerology of threes that alludes to the ultimate co-inherence of the Trinity.

This incarnation of draft text into a published book is not without pain or loss. To fully enter the City, the Manuscript must experience real sacrifice. This sacrifice must be individual and genuine. Or as Colin pronounces shortly after his triumphal arrival, parodying *Hamlet*'s Polonius, "So Shakespeare has taught; to your own self be true, / And see that your style is undoubtedly you" (279–80). This Christian paradox, encapsulated in Phillida's maxim that "Nothing at all can live except it die" (320), is illustrated visually in the accompanying scene wherein the other characters ritualistically and physically "pluck and pull" (292) at the Manuscript in order to prepare her for publication. Interestingly, the purgatorial overtones of this "cleansing" are juxtaposed against the pagan tone arising from a frenzied rhythmic verse reminiscent of the witches from *Macbeth.* Both pagan and Christian readings are carried through to the following scene when Manuscript is placed upon the bier, covered by a pall and ritualistically sacrificed.

Here, the allusion to Christ's paradoxical life-giving death through his sacrifice on the cross is echoed in Colin's line: "See from her wounds the deathly life-blood starts" (346), but it is placed beside Colin's catalogue of secular invocations to Odysseus, Connaught, Cuchullain, Lady Persephone, and Dom Galahad during the sacrifice and the ode to Mnemosyne sung by all the company at the end of the play. Williams identifies a similar phenomenon from the Arthurian legend in the episode in which Gawaine experiences an incarnational epiphany during the pageant at the castle of the Fisherman, when he sees "the Grail all in flesh, and he seeth above, as him thinketh, a King crowned, nailed upon a rood, and the spear was still fast in his side" ("Figure" 262). This theological paradox is developed in the dramatic tension in the Masque with the climactic ritualized spectacle of the sacrifice scene, in which we find the divine conceptions of sacrifice and redemption counterbalanced by more earthly and human elements of doubt and humour. At the climax of Manuscript's "conversion," Phillida unexpectedly expresses a poignant and very human moment of doubt: "Ah to what end, by mere good will of thought, / Have I this woman and my sister brought?" (347–48). Even the confident ritual of purgation apparently stumbles in an awkward moment of premature resurrection that gives the audience pause to doubt.

The overall effect of Williams' deployment of these various dramatic and literary devices is to give the audience a sense of a paradoxical but real and accessible incarnational world where natural and super-natural, real and imagined, doubt and faith, pagan and Christian, earth and heaven co-inhere. These are the foundations of the City; of a real accessible City in the physical world that Williams felt was achievable now. Like "the organic body" (TtL: "The Vision of the Empire" 1) of the ideal Arthurian City, rather than being a purely intellectual exercise, the final image of the "lustral cities" (Manuscript 467) reminds the audience that the play itself, like Amen House, represents an experience of that truth. Couched in a syncretistic amalgam of esoteric and pagan spiritualism, Williams has presented his City of Amen House on stage as both an archetype and a specific example of his imagined Christian Arthurian City, and, in doing so, has attempted to re-create and incarnate that spiritual reality into a physical reality. Not bound by didacticism but determined to be humorous and entertaining, The Masque of the Manuscript is genuine in its theatricality and sensitivity to audience, and Williams is thereby able to exploit various masque-genre traditions while experimenting with his own dramaturgy in order to begin to "flesh out" his unique incar-national performance theology.

The Masque of Perusal (1929)

In response to the popular acclaim of his first masque, Williams' decision to write a sequel, The Masque of Perusal, provided him with an opportunity to further test the dramatic possibilities of his literary and theological vision of the City. The play continues on from the plot of its predecessor in that it depicts the process of the sale of a book and its subsequent adoption into the wider field of learning and publica-tion. The result is a play that is no mere "ephemeral delight" (Hadfield, Exploration 68), but an innovative embodiment of "statements of a theology of work" (Exploration 68).

One of these embodied "statements" is what Bernadette Bosky describes as the play's assertion that "it is not blasphemy but truth to say that, like Christ (though on a lesser level), publishing ensures that the

Word is made flesh" (Bosky 29). At times Williams even goes so far in *Perusal* as to place the truth of both on the same level by asserting that words being made flesh on the page carry the same spiritual significance as the Incarnation of Christ himself. By attempting to perform both "truths" on stage, he invokes the experience of the co-inhered truth of the one universal and eternal City that Amen House embodies. To achieve this, *Perusal* extends the scope of Williams' City beyond the words and physical objects of *Manuscript* and expands it into the metaphysical realm of incarnate ideas.

The first hint of this broader vision can be seen in the expanded role of the Introducer, now named Tityrus,[23] in order to become both commentator on, and participant in, the action. It is as if Tityrus has now boldly chosen to exchange with the City himself: "How shall we dare.… / How shall we lay presumptuous hands on heaven / To wring again therefrom what once was given?" (1.1, 5–6). The inversion of the process from the first masque, in which ideas and drafts were turned into a formal printed published book, to one whereby the physical book now achieves its purpose by becoming a spiritual idea, could appear at first to constitute an inverse or reversed incarnation. However, far from being inconsistent, this later journey reflects deeper truths about the co-inherence of the City in which this incarnation of word into thought is both physical and metaphysical. In a passage rich in bodily and sensory imagery, Tityrus speaks for all true poets and dramatists (including Taliessin and Williams) when he declares their incarnational power whereby they can reveal and enact co-inherence:

> *Tityrus*:   … poets have the art
>   To breathe their message in at secret ears
>   Whereby the brain and all the being hears
>   At once, and knows each line and feels each cue. (1.36–39)

And, on cue, Williams then enacts this reality by opening the curtains to a scene of a highly visual spectacle in the form of a tableau. In this part that is reminiscent of a medieval morality scene, he shows his key characters "rigid" in a pose and dress depicting their character, profession, and symbolic role. Dorinda is at her typewriter, Alexis is clutching advertisements, Phillida is putting a book on the shelf of the library, and Colin is looking up a reference. Time and action appear frozen, and it is only upon a musical cue that the image dissolves into the action, whereupon, to emphasize the point, the cast sings a song about the importance of doing and not simply being: "Shall being learn from doing / The being in ourselves?" (1.73–74). Williams evokes a sense of the elevation of apparently mundane work and a banal workplace to more metaphysical and spiritual significance. In this way, the City of Amen House and the individuals who work there are part of the greater supernatural City of the divine realm and therefore have access to all its accompanying possibilities of union and co-inherence.

In such a quirky world, the sight of all characters stopping to genuflect in unison every time the name "Caesar" is mentioned might prompt a humorous response from the audience for seeming anachronistic and absurd in the modern workplace, but it is deployed to emphasize again the hierarchy and rituals inherent

---

23   Played by CW himself. [Editor's note]

in the City. The importance Williams placed on the accuracy of these rituals is evident in the level of detail in his stage directions. The type of genuflection required of the actors is not left to their improvisation; consistent with the level of detailed exactitude required of Anglo-Catholic liturgy, Williams directs them very specifically: "At the name of CAESAR he pauses and everyone genuflects: the head bent, the right hand on the heart, the right leg bent, and the left hand extended backward at full length" (stage direction at 1.112). In a deft balancing act, such rituals are presented as being sacramental in that they point to that "far off gleam or echo of *evangelium* in the real world" (Tolkien 83), but they are also rendered more intimate and personal through the clever use of humor that gives the audience license to share vicariously in the action. In this context, the humorous fracas over the missing book called *Mosaics in the Walls of Saint Sophia* (1.99) and the debate over whether "Imperial pronouns have *no* accusative case" (1.138) mock the pedantic world of publishing but also allude more to the universal and eternal implications of linking this world to Williams' prototype ideal City, Byzantium; the same city which is the prototype for his Arthuriad, that he explicitly chooses to set at a time when "the centre of the Roman *imperium* lay in Byzantium" ("Figure" 263).

The emphasis on such rituals and allusions also shows how *Perusal* is more explicit than *Manuscript* in its projection of a socio-political blueprint for the City, such as when Dorinda bemoans her status in a mock-socialist lament that "We workers are always getting put upon" (1.236), or when Alexis, in a thinly disguised personal acknowledgement by Williams of his sensitivity to critics and reviewers, yearns for a hierarchy of intellect as well as profession:

> These fellows rage and bring injustice down
> To wreck the glad ways of our singing town,
> Till all but the stout-hearted students flee
> From blatant mobs of skilled illiteracy. (1.253–56)

Such blunt references to the real political and social machinations of this actual earthly city remind the audience that Amen House, like all true cities, is both real and imagined, natural and supernatural, myth and truth; just as in Williams' Arthuriad the world is both imagined and, most importantly, also "an actual kingdom and an actual glory: that is, Lancelot has his proper duties to the State" ("Figure" 271).

Toward the end of the play, this hierarchy is explicitly exalted as an ideal and therefore essential characteristic of the City when Phillida proclaims just before the Procession of the Graal:[24]

> Part found by search, part without search inspired:
> You hierarchy, whereby man's best heart,
> Communicated to his outward part,
> Does in the forms and shapes of time prevail,
> Lead forth the ritual and expose the Graal. (2.206–10)

---

24 Williams often used the archaic spelling "Graal" in preference to "Grail."

This projection of a more ordered society is contrasted with the disordered and fragmented society of the dysfunctional publishing house presented in Part 2 of the play. In what appears to be a false city, similar to the "inarticulate" and "headless" empire of P'o-L'u in Williams' Arthuriad (*TtL* "The Vision of the Empire" 160, 181), we find an unsettled and frustrated artist, Thyrsis (Foss), struggling to find truth at work. The fragmented and faltering verse, accompanied by the sound of the guttural noises "grr" (2.29) and "grah" (2.30), together with loud snoring and fractured Latin phrases, challenges the sense of order alluded to in Part 1. This scene of "bestial noises" by characters who "wander to-and-fro" on a "darkened stage" (2.46) while Phillida remains "on a height, blindfolded and chained hand and foot" (2.46) creates an immediate sense of despair and fear as the daily work becomes monotonous, overwhelming, and meaningless.

The deployment of a bodily aesthetic here is an example of how Williams "make[s] use of bodies, corpses and fuse[s] the two with landscape in a particularly modernist way" (Hiley 82), and how he confronts "the spiritual despair of modern life" (Innes 466) and attempts to "stabilize the precariousness of his age" (Marshall 82) by invoking a vision of an ideal bodily incarnational city similar to that depicted in *Taliessin through Logres*: "The crowned form of anatomized man, / Bones, nerves, sinews, / The diagram of the style of Logos" (*TtL*, "Taliessin in the School of the Poets" 93–95). So, by placing this scene after his earlier images of the ideal City, Williams hopes to warn his audience of the dangers of losing sight of the true City and descending into the Infamy of a deceptive and empty parody.

For, amid this parody, cause for hope is found in the pleas of the captive Phillida, who yearns for the true liberation found only in the co-inhered nature of the redemptive City, when she seeks to transcend physical geography ("centre as I am the gate"; 2.71), time ("prophecy ... and the straight"; 2.72), history ("the ending and beginning"; 2.76) and consciousness ("the extreme without and the extreme within"; 2.74). The key to achieving this level of transcendence, we discover, is via Co-inherence or, more specifically, through a type of Substitution. As the Thought realizes: "I make my oath to find and set thee free; / But O thereafter do even so for me!" (2.77–82). While there is an element of self-interest in this type of projected offer of reciprocal *caritas*, there is also a clear acknowledgement of a dependence upon others to help save or, at least, relieve a burden. This sense of Substitution is echoed in the following line from Phillida, who knows that "Thou canst not trouble the enchanted sloth: / Thou canst not wake her—thou nor I—but both" (2.103–04). Here is a clearer statement of the principles of Exchange that are needed in order to liberate "both" Phillida and the Thought from the enemies of the City.

It is at this heightened point in the drama that Williams invokes one of his central images of selfless sacrifice when the Thought asks the fundamental question by which all action is to be judged: "What serves the Graal?" (2.117). This is the same question that Percival critically fails to ask at the castle of the Fisher King (see "Figure" 249) and the same question that lies at the heart of Williams' entire Arthuriad, where the Grail "is the central matter of the Matter of Britain" ("Figure" 267). Like the sword of truth, this question cuts through the illusions and distractions of a false city and presents an alternative vision of the ideal redemptive City. For Williams, "The Graal (whose centre is everywhere ...) is to some a test, to some fruition, to some union, to some torment" (*Commonplace Book* 70). Thus, at the invocation of the Graal, some (like Alexis) fall: "Alas, I fail. I care for nothing but the sale" (2.117–18), while others scramble to rationalize with empty clichés of "things half-understood, of things half-taught" (2.123).

The risk of such responses is clear in the selfishness and pride that underpins such rejection of the Way. Even the Thought is momentarily tempted and forgets the selfless maxim of Exchange: "Teach? Shall I teach the world? O happy dream! / Am I indeed much wiser than I seem?" (2.141–42). The veracity of this delusion goes beyond the poetry and is then incarnated physically on stage by having the Thought "fiercely" (2.178) break from Colin's hypnotic and seductive litany of clichés, until even he capitulates and "collapses on top of Alexis" (2.183) in light of the divine truth reached beyond the dark glass. Colin laments: "Alas I fail: / Reflections and remembrances through me pass, / But only darkly and as in a glass" (2.180–82).[25] This liberating truth is incarnated in a physical way on stage with the subsequent action of the Thought who "rushes" (*Perusal* 2.182) to liberate Phillida from her chains, and then Dorinda "leaping to her feet" (*Perusal* 2.198) to immediately acknowledge these "qualities of action" (2.199), thus showing the union of word, thought, and deed in the true City.

It is at this point in the drama that the action climaxes with what Williams calls "The Procession of the Graal" (2.211). By this highly visual and aural ceremony, the playwright hopes to stimulate the audience's senses, intellect, and spirit and show how the deeper truths of the Incarnation can be realized through the Affirmation of Images. In this scene, Williams attempts to incarnate the central "achievement of the Grail" (*Commonplace Book* 3) and the entire Arthurian myth, whereby there is "the reconciliation of inner and outer, of liberty & authority—etc: reconciliation of body & soul" (*Commonplace Book* 3). Each item of the "Hallows of the Graal" (inkpot, pen, type, paper, periodicals) that is carried in procession on stage becomes an affirmed image of the Incarnation. Dorinda says: "As without, ah so within, / As below, ah so above; / To its incarnation kin" (2.211–13).

Furthermore, the incarnational truth of this *via affirmativa* is conveyed through an incarnational process of staged theology. Even the subtle transition in the song—where the final lines of each verse build from a more passive apprehension of "shine" and "lo" to the more demonstrative active substitutionary deed of "bear"—reflects this incarnational transformation from word into action. In this scene, Williams successfully co-inheres the language, action, theatricality, sounds, music, lights, action, and dialogue to incarnate his ideal City on stage and show how the traits of this universal City are shared by the city of the Masque; the city of Amen House; the Arthurian City; and the eternal, universal, heavenly City. The play is in this sense Camelot incarnate, or as Tityrus describes it in the final speech: "the outward motion of the inward Graal" (2.297).

The Masque of the Termination of Copyright (1930)

The last of Williams' Amen House masques, *The Masque of the Termination of Copyright*, was completed in 1930 but was never published or performed "owing to various hindrances."[26] This final masque concerns the

---

25 "For now we see through a glass, darkly; but then face to face: now I know in part; but then shall I know even as also I am known." (1 Cor. 13:12).

26 Williams wrote on the cover of his manuscript for this play: "The Masque was written for production in Amen House, but owing to various hindrances was never presented." See Wade CW/MS-413.

rediscovery and re-publication of a neglected book, and it is a more brutal, earthy, and, at times, astringent play that begins to probe the fleshier aspects of his Arthurian vision of the City. This play is also darker than its predecessors, because, while it continues the theme of the joy and humor found within a community of workers at a publishing house, it also depicts the more dysfunctional and violent world of a type of anti-City.[27] The results are mixed: Williams by this time has pushed the boundaries of the masque form to the point where it can barely accommodate the demands of his expanding theological vision.

The characters in *Termination* remain the same as in the previous masque, albeit with even more expanded roles for Williams as Tityrus[28] and Foss as Thyrsis and also the notable addition of the character of Perigot, "the Herald of the Gods" (95). Unlike the Introducer from the previous masques, Perigot is a more complex character, who operates in the play as narrator, guide, participant, and exemplar. It is Perigot, for example, who initiates the main dramatic action by bringing the plight of the Book to the attention of the Muses upon whom "her future life, her freedom, waits" (114). Perigot's subsequent decision to leave the Muses' heaven and disguise himself in order to seek out the Book both propels the action and embodies a supernatural phenomenon akin to a form of incarnation: "here must I cover my divinity / And shroud myself in earth" (192–93). Like Dante's descent into the Inferno, Perigot's incarnation upon the earth will be costly, painful, and sacrificial:

> In diverse shadows of the Unity
> Amid the apes of freedom, the false glee
> That fills the infernal semblances of truth,
> I pass, in watchful judgement and great ruth,
> To pluck from hell what hell may never keep. (196–200)

The audience finds a dystopic world where the once "enskied" (108) Muses are now fallen, pathetic and petty people working in squalid surroundings. It is a city in decline. Alexis, "in his shirt-sleeves, puffing at a horrible pipe, is leaning against the side" (*Termination* 105) and is reading the horseracing form-guide while arguing with Dorinda, who bemoans his laziness and is resentful of her role as the only breadwinner.[29]

---

27 Hadfield describes Williams' personal experience of both joy and despair at this time: "The joy, the new wonder, the perfect end are there within, for he knew that these were true, sure and lasting, however one's own experience of them had been true, destructive and fleeting" (*Exploration* 68).

28 Tityrus even expresses some of Williams' own personal views, including his desire for commercial writing success, seen in the lines "Who knows? —another century view / Shall we not live in other centuries too?" (16–17) and "Ah, did not holy Milton hope for fame?" (157). Also, Williams' affection for Amen House and its publisher, Humphrey Milford, can be seen in Tityrus's rhetorical question, "What other Caesar could our thoughts divine?" (41).

29 This reference may reflect the fact that Charles was sensitive to his and his wife Michal's anxiety over the fact that at this time the Williams home relied on only the one income.

At the centre of this corrupt and decaying world is the character of Phillida, who represents both the extremity of such infamy and, paradoxically, the best hope of redemption. Phillida is the subject of verbal abuse and slander from the likes of the dominating bully Dorinda:

> *Dorinda*:   Where is Phil?
> What that girl does besides make up her face—
> And the way she does it is a fair disgrace;
> It isn't as if she ever had any looks—
> And she muddles up different leaves from different books. (231–35)

Phillida is also the victim of physical abuse. After merely expressing sympathy for Colin's poetry, Dorinda responds by "swooping on [Phillida], shaking her, knocking her about generally, and at last throwing her into a corner" (*Termination* 324). The portrayal of such physical violence on stage between characters whose actors are recognizable from their previous role in Amen House demonstrates the extent to which the original ideal City has steadily declined to become a perversion of its true principles. As physical exchange is an essential element of the City, so physical perversion is a sign of the corruption and decay of a false city.

Significantly, it is here, where this infamy is most felt, that the source of redemptive hope can be found. It is the simple but sincere Phillida who offers hope. Like many of Williams' heroes, she is not a perfect character. She is frustratingly simple-minded, can over-react, has poor expression, and is prone to ignorant misinterpretation; but in all this she is acutely human and therefore ultimately divine. She, like Guinevere, embodies a spiritual truth whereby "The body of the beloved appears vital with holiness: the physical flesh is glorious with sanctity—not her sanctity, but its own" ("Figure" 239). As Shideler notes of Williams' Arthuriad: "nothing can be truly loved until it is known, known concretely and carnally with bodily hands and brains and the sturdy acts of the disciplined and liberated imagination" (Shideler 14). A Beatrician vision of sorts, it is precisely this authenticity and honesty that gives Phillida an insight beyond that of her co-workers and finds a way of redemption beyond the infamy of this perverted anti-city and toward the true City of Exchange and Co-inherence.

Finally, after successfully finding the Book, Perigot celebrates and makes an extraordinary offer to grant to each of the members of the publishing house their "heart's delight" (518). While Alexis asks, "what's going to win the three o'clock?" (533), Dorinda asks, "What's the surest thing to stock and sell?" (543), and Colin asks, "What word will one figure show?" (553), Phillida hesitates: "Well—and how do I know what I want?" (564). Having thus built the tension, Williams has Perigot prompt once more before Phillida gives her climactic response. It is as profound as it is simple: "A little happiness and joy and peace" (566).

This is the key to the City. As "the other three slip away" (570), Perigot describes a vision of paradise where true happiness, joy, and peace can be found. It is an image of Williams' City, a paradoxical co-inhered world that is neither heaven nor earth: "less and more than either" (572) but "between" both (571). It is a type of Logres, located between the heaven of Sarras and the hell of P'o-L'u but simultaneously intersecting with both. Like Arthur's Logres and Taliessin's Byzantium, it is an image of community: "There Caesar is and there are Caesar's friends" (581), of mutual Exchange: "until once adoring and adored" (584), and of order: "within the imperial and general mind" (586). It is a place of physical incarnation: "there beauty into being slowly draws" (576) and of physical work and occupation: "there toil of spirit learns" (578).

Having projected this image of community, Williams ends the play with an embodiment of that image in physical form by way of a return to Amen House. Signalled by the singing of the Carol of Amen House, the final scene completes the process begun with the first masque as the audience is brought back to the everyday machinations of daily life at the publishing firm. Having returned from the world of the Muses, we find the characters appear once again as the workers of Amen House. The privileged jokes at the Press about Hubert Foss' extensive travel, the reminder of the "rule" of Humphrey Milford, and the expert details of the professional publishing process all reappear and are reminiscent of the opening scenes from the first masque. Order is restored, and the natural world returns; the co-inhered supernatural City also restored, wherein even the simplest action such as Phillida's handwriting is an incarnational act of divine significance: "And in the good time of the perfect end / Me of this charge may their high grace acquit. / Here at my work, here on my watch I sit" (866–68).

Williams' dramatic worlds of Silvania and Amen House are thus all Arthurian worlds in that they express and embody the principles of the City. Not only did Williams' evolving Arthurian vision feed directly into these plays, and not only was he able to express his understanding of the co-inhered nature of the Arthurian myth through these plays, but their very construction and performance consolidated and developed that vision. As mini-Arthurian cities themselves, these early plays are all places of order, choice, timelessness, exchange, and substitution. Most importantly, they are incarnational worlds where universal truths are actualized and "made flesh" through a unique bodily aesthetic of performance where the natural and supernatural, the physical and spiritual, the real and the imagined, and history and myth all co-inhere.

Works Cited

Ashenden, Gavin. *Charles Williams: Alchemy and Integration*. Kent State UP, 2008. Print.

Bosky, Bernadette. Introduction. *The Masques of Amen House* 1–30.

Bratman, David. "Hubert J. Foss and the Music of the Masques." *The Masques of Amen House* 159–64.

Carpenter, Humphrey. *The Inklings: C. S. Lewis, J. R. R. Tolkien, Charles Williams, and Their Friends*. Boston: Houghton Mifflin, 1978. Print.

Hadfield, Alice Mary. *An Introduction to Charles Williams*. London: Robert Hale, 1959. Print.

——. *Charles Williams: An Exploration of His Life and Work*. Oxford UP, 1983. Print.

Higgins, Sørina. Introduction. *The Chapel of the Thorn: A Dramatic Poem*. By Charles Williams. Berkeley, CA: Apocryphile Press, 2014. 5–38. Print.

Hiley, Margaret. *The Loss and the Silence: Aspects of Modernism in the Works of C. S. Lewis, J. R. R. Tolkien and Charles Williams*. Zurich: Walking Tree Publishers, 2011. Print.

Hockley, Raymond. "In the City and Under the Mercy." *Theology* 79.668 (1976). 97–104. Print.

Innes, Christopher. *Modern British Drama: The Twentieth Century*. Cambridge UP, 2002. Print.

Lewis, C. S. "Williams and the Arthuriad." *Taliessin through Logres, The Region of the Summer Stars, Arthurian Torso*. Grand Rapids, MI: Eerdmans, 1974. Print.

Liénard, Flora. "Charles Williams' City against J. R. R. Tolkien's 'Green World.'" *Charles Williams and His Contemporaries*. Ed. Suzanne Bray and Richard Sturch. Newcastle-Upon-Tyne: Cambridge Scholars Publishing, 2009. 69–83. Print.

Marshall, Ashley. "Reframing Charles Williams: Modernist Doubt and the Crisis of World War in *All Hallows' Eve*." *Journal of Modern Literature* 30.2 (2007): 64–85. Print.

Medcalf, Stephen. "The Anathasian Principle in Williams' Use of Images." *Rhetoric of Vision*. Ed. Charles A. Huttar and Peter J. Schakel. London: Bucknell UP, 1996. 27–43. Print.

Ridler, Anne. Introduction. *The Image of the City and Other Essays*. By Charles Williams. London: Oxford UP, 1958. ix–lxxii. Print.

Russell, Mariann. "Elements of the Idea of the City in Charles Williams' Arthurian Poetry." *Mythlore* 6.4 (1979): 10–16. Print.

Shideler, Mary M. Introduction. *Taliessin through Logres*. By Charles Williams. Grand Rapids, MI: Eerdmans, 1974. 5–17. Print.

Tolkien, J. R. R. "On Fairy-Stories." *Essays Presented to Charles Williams*. Ed. C. S. Lewis. London: Oxford UP, 1947. 38–89. Print.

Weales, Gerald. *Religion in Modern English Drama*: Philadelphia: U of Pennsylvania P, 1961.

Williams, Charles. *All Hallows' Eve*. London: Faber & Faber, 1945. Print.

——. "Anthropotokos." *Image* 110–13.

——. *Arthurian Commonplace Book* (as "Notes on the Holy Grail"). MS. Eng. e. 2012. Bodleian Library, Oxford University. Oxford, UK.

——. *The Chapel of the Thorn: A Dramatic Poem*. Ed. Sørina Higgins. Berkeley, CA: Apocryphile Press, 2014. Print.

——. "Celestial Cities." *Divorce*. London: Oxford UP, 1920. 30–31. Print.

——. *The Descent of the Dove: A Short History of the Holy Spirit in the Church*. London: Longmans Green, 1939. Print.

——. "A Dialogue on Hierarchy." *Image* 127–31.

——. *Divorce*. London: Oxford UP, 1920. Print.

——. "The Figure of Arthur." *Taliessin through Logres; The Region of the Summer Stars; Arthurian Torso*. By Charles Williams and C. S. Lewis. Grand Rapids, MI: Eerdmans, 1974. 189–245. Print.

——. "The Free Act." *Image* 113–15.

——. *The Image of the City and Other Essays*. 1958. Ed. Anne Ridler. Berkeley, CA: The Apocryphile Press, 2007. Print.

——. "The Image of the City in English Verse." *Image* 92–102.

——. *The Masques of Amen House*. Ed. David Bratman. Altadena, CA: The Mythopoeic Press, 2000. Print.

——. *The Masque of the Manuscript*. MS. 1927 Hadfield Collection, Box 2 Book 10 (uncatalogued). Bodleian Library, Oxford University. Oxford, UK.

——. *The Masque of the Termination of Copyright*. 1930. CW/MS-413. Marion E. Wade Center, Wheaton College. Wheaton, IL.

——. "Prince Rudolph of Silvania." CW/MS-113. Marion E. Wade Center, Wheaton College. Wheaton, IL.

——. "The Redeemed City." *Image* 102–10.

——. *Seed of Adam and Other Plays by Charles Williams*. Ed. Anne Ridler. London: Oxford UP, 1948. Print.

——. *Taliessin through Logres, The Region of the Summer Stars, Arthurian Torso*. Grand Rapids, MI: Eerdmans, 1974. Print.

——. *The Way of Exchange*. London: James Clarke, 1941. Print.

18

"Any Chalice of Consecrated Wine": The Significance of the Holy Grail in Charles Williams' *War in Heaven*.[1]

Suzanne Bray

Although he enjoyed a certain reputation and relatively good sales during his lifetime, Charles Williams is today relatively unknown to the general public. However, according to Jean-Pierre Deloux, his work includes "some of the most important and unusual contributions to fantastic literature" (i) in the twentieth century. Deloux is referring here to Williams' seven novels, of which the first to be published, *War in Heaven*, remains popular, with three different editions currently available in English.[2] Williams' first novel, *Shadows of Ecstasy*, did not at first find a publisher, so the author started a new project, finding inspiration both in crime fiction and in some of G. K. Chesterton's themes and narrative tricks. The resulting novel, which David Llewellyn Dodds calls "a detective novel about the Grail" (Dodds 4) and Deloux a "metaphysical thriller" that is also "the story of a symbolic quest for spiritual power, represented by the sacred cup which is said to have contained Christ's blood" (vii), started off his career in fiction.

However, this was not the first time Williams had shown interest in the Holy Grail. A large Commonplace Book,[3] "entitled *The Holy Grail* and which covers the years 1912–1920" (Versinger 502), contains newspaper

---

1   An earlier version of this chapter was published in French as «'N'importe quel calice': La signification du vase sacré dans La Guerre du Graal de Charles Williams», *Le Graal : Genèse, évolution et avenir d'un mythe*, Dirs. Danielle Buschinger, Florent Gabaude, Marie-Geneviève Grossel et Jürgen Kühnel et Matthieu Oliver; Amiens: Presses du Centre d'études médiévales de Picardie (2014), 63–73.

2   As of October 2014.

3   Toward the end of his life, Williams entrusted the file to Anne Ridler. It is currently in the Bodleian Library, Oxford.

cuttings, copious notes, and everything he could find which "might have some connection, however vague, with the subject" (Versinger 502–03). Williams assembled it to help him write a full cycle of Arthurian poems.[4] In the book are "a number of ideas which, later developed, were his own contribution to the great Arthurian myth" (Ridler lix).

Williams' interest in the Holy Grail (or Graal, as he often called it) came, at least in part, from his involvement in the Fellowship of the Rosy Cross, led by the Roman Catholic author and occultist A. E. Waite. Williams was initiated into the order on 21 September 1917 (Willard 269), at the autumn equinox, and he left ten years later. According to Barbara Newman, "Williams remained active for … a decade, attaining a high level of initiation and frequently serving the fellowship as an officer" (4). He served, in fact, as Master of the Temple for two six-month periods in 1921 and 1924 (Gauntlett 16). According to Aren Roukema, members like Williams, who "had reached the level of successful mystical experience … were tasked with expressing the inexpressible" (36), which Waite believed could be done "through interaction with symbols that could express all but the most intimate aspects of the Secret Tradition" (36). The group's "beliefs apparently involved, as a principal symbol, the Holy Graal" (Carpenter 82), and a rapid overview of Williams' writings confirms Sørina Higgins' remark that "the ideas and the knowledge he gained there continued to influence his writing throughout his life" (82). It also reveals the way in which Waite's book *The Hidden Church of the Holy Grail* (1909), which presents the history of the Grail legend and Waite's own particular and distinctly alchemical understanding of this, enabled Williams to find an interpretation of the myth which would be relevant to his contemporaries.

To grasp the nature and originality of Williams' approach to the Grail in *War in Heaven*, three main issues need to be examined. First of all, *War in Heaven* reveals its full meaning when examined in the context of the Fellowship of the Rosy Cross. More specifically, the ideas behind Williams' novel become clearer if seen together with the writings of some of the movement's members in the period preceding its composition and also with those popular theories of the Grail in the areas of both literary studies and anthropology that they were trying to counter. Secondly, an examination of the role of the Grail and its knights in the novel shows the extent to which the holy cup is portrayed not only as a sacred relic, but equally as an active force playing a decisive role in its own destiny and in that of the people with whom it comes into contact. Finally, analysis of *War in Heaven* is essential when evaluating Williams' originality and the value of his contribution to the Grail myth, his conviction both that it was possible to overestimate the importance of the relic and that the message of the Grail was not for a spiritual elite, but for all believers.

During the period when he started to write about the Grail, Charles Williams and those who shared elements of his spiritual vision were dissatisfied with the way the chalice was perceived in Britain. This was partly on account of the occult revival of the 1890s, but also as a result of the appearance of Comparative Religion as a field of academic study and of the interest generated by T. S. Eliot's bestselling poem *The Waste Land* (1922), which, according to Linda Ray Pratt, "belies the Grail's traditional values" (307). Williams was "well aware of the rich diversity of the Grail tradition" (Ashenden 112), including the hermetic and

---

4   Williams never finished the project. Just over thirty poems were published during Williams' lifetime in *TtL* and *RSS*.

folklore elements, and he regretted the absence of a serious, up-to-date Christian interpretation of the source material. In his Commonplace Book, "you find numerous references to [James] Frazer, to Jessie Weston and also to the study of foreign civilizations" (Versinger 506) from all parts of the world. Frazer's famous twelve-volume study, *The Golden Bough*, published between 1911 and 1915, was an immensely successful bestseller and considerably influenced the way the Grail was perceived in Britain, even though Frazer never actually mentions it. It also provided tacit support for the more pagan interpretations of the Grail's origin and significance. In addition, Jessie Weston, who claimed to be "an impenitent believer in Sir J. G. Frazer's main theory," made the link between his work and the Grail explicit, asserting that "it is only in the recognition of this one-time claim of essential kinship between Christianity and the Pagan Mysteries that we shall find the key to the secret of the Grail." For the general public, the main point of Weston's study appeared to be "the sexual symbolism of the story, notably the grail and the lance, which can be interpreted as symbols of the female and male genitalia" (P. Lewis).

Williams strongly disagreed with these fashionable theories, which he felt missed the whole point of the Grail stories. He also thought that the general public had accepted them rather too uncritically. In his opinion:

> Such a great work as *The Golden Bough*, for example, was too easily supposed to have proved what it had never meant—or should never have meant—to prove. Its hinted thesis that all religion arose from a desire to encourage the annual harvest was generally thought to have explained satisfactorily how the harvest came into existence at all, and its multitude of gods conditioned by magic were identified with a Godhead unconditioned except by its own Will. (*Dove* 223)

For Williams, the main problems with this type of interpretation are that it is openly syncretistic, mixing up elements from different belief systems which are normally incompatible, and that it requires the reader to ignore the obvious Christian and Eucharistic meaning of the Grail legends:

> There has been much controversy about them—vessels of plenty and cauldrons of magic—and they have been supposed by learned experts to be the origin of the Grail myth. That, in the Scriptural and ecclesiastical sense, they certainly cannot be … the Grail entered Europe with the Christian … faith. It came from and with Christ. ("Figure" 23)

In this passage, Williams echoes A. E. Waite's declaration that the "mystery in chief of the faith in Christ … is the only real concern of the Holy Graal" (Waite 38). Without the Last Supper, the Crucifixion and the Resurrection, the Grail, for Williams, is just like any other vessel.

In addition to disagreeing with the way many authors of the day understood the origins and meaning of the Grail, Williams was equally dissatisfied with many of the best-known literary works on the subject and, in particular, with Alfred, Lord Tennyson's famous cycle of narrative poems, *The Idylls of the King* (1859 to 1885). In a critical article published in April 1941, Williams admits that he felt "a vague disappointment" ("The Making of *Taliessin*" 179) when he read Tennyson's poetic texts about the Grail relics. He continues:

I am not attacking Tennyson as a poet; I am only saying that in this particular respect his treatment of the Sacred Lance as a jumping pole left a good deal to be desired ... it was clear that the great and awful myth of the Grail had not been treated adequately in English verse. (179–80, 187)

The religious significance of Tennyson's relics is notably absent, which, to Williams, meant that the poet had missed the point of the story.

When it came to prose depictions, Williams was less critical. He appreciated certain attempts by his own contemporaries to evoke the mythical and the Christian elements of the legends at the same time. Waite's *The Hidden Church of the Holy Grail* is more of a historical study with some passages of literary criticism than a work of the imagination; however, Williams approved of Waite's desire to "place the story in a living tradition" (Willard 270). Williams also agreed with Waite that "the history of the Holy Graal becomes the soul's history, moving through a profound symbolism of inward being" (Ridler lxv). At the same time, it was obvious that Waite's voluminous tome, destined principally for those with a specialist interest in the subject, was not going to interest the general public.

Before Williams wrote his first novel, two other Christians with esoteric interests whom Williams knew personally, Evelyn Underhill and Arthur Machen, had decided to include the Holy Grail in their works of fiction and, going against the majority movement of the time, include overtly Christian elements in their stories.

Several aspects of Evelyn Underhill's third novel, *The Column of Dust* (1909), met with Williams' approval. In 1904, Underhill joined the Order of the Golden Dawn, where Waite was Grand Master at the time. This hermetic movement, which Waite had reformed in order to accentuate the mystical rather than the magical elements, was the predecessor of the Fellowship of the Rosy Cross. Underhill left the Order a few years later, after her conversion to Christianity in 1907, but continued to use much of the Order's imagery in her writings. In her novel, as Glen Cavaliero has pointed out: "the Grail itself is presented, according to the theories of [Arthur] Machen and A. E. Waite, as the focus of a secret religion" (58). The main character, Constance, an ordinary young working woman, gets lost in the hills and finds a chapel where the Holy Grail is kept hidden from the world. When its keeper dies, the Grail is entrusted to Constance. She is supported by a group of intercessors called the Helpers of the Holy Souls, whose rite, according to Thomas Willard, "was broadly inspired by Waite's ideals and may have owed details to his fellow initiate Arthur Machen, to whom the novel was dedicated" (280). Certain critics, including Willard and Cavaliero, consider that the idea of a new Grail community for the twentieth century that Williams evoked in *War in Heaven* was originally inspired by Underhill's tale, although both novelists may equally have taken the idea from A. E. Waite. However, even if Williams thought that "*The Column of Dust* has a superb theme" and "possibilities of wit, terror and sublimity" (Introduction to *Underhill* 10), he admitted that he was disappointed by the novel, as "its literary effect is less than exciting" (10), principally on account of the author's poor use of imagery.

The second one of Williams' contemporaries, once again both a practicing Anglican and an initiate, to bring the Grail into his works of fiction was Arthur Machen, a personal friend of both Underhill and Waite. Arthur Machen joined the Hermetic Order of the Golden Dawn in October 1899 and followed

Waite in all the divisions of the movement during the following decade. In his 1904 novella *A Fragment of Life*, the hero, a simple office worker, leaves London for the Welsh hills where he was born and receives a glorious vision of the Grail. However, Machen's most elaborate portrayals of the Grail come in *The Great Return* (1915) and his best-known work, *The Secret Glory* (1922), where the chalice plays a central role in the plot and transforms either an individual or a whole community.

In *The Great Return*, those who are open to its influence are aware of "odours of paradise" (19), hear beautiful music, and notice mysterious people they have never seen before—elements that are also present in *War in Heaven*. Another common feature between the two works may be found in the healing powers of the Grail. In Machen's story, Olwen Phillips is cured of tuberculosis, while in Williams' novel, Barbara Rackstraw regains her sanity thanks to the Cup. In addition, both women feel that they are dreaming at the moment they are healed, and they discern a level of spiritual reality that they have never known before. *The Great Return* and *War in Heaven* both end with a Grail Mass.

The Secret Glory is a much more ambitious work and, according to Richard Stanley, it represents "a sustained attempt to resituate the quest [for the Holy Grail] in a contemporary context." The protagonist, Ambrose, goes to Asia in order to take the Grail to "a certain hidden sanctuary" where the people know how "to hide its glories forever from the evil world," and which probably represents the kingdom of Prester John, a character who had rarely appeared in English literature since the Renaissance, although the publication of John Buchan's eponymous novel in 1910 had somewhat revived interest in the legends surrounding him. Like Williams' Kenneth in *War in Heaven*, Ambrose becomes a Christian martyr and, through this sacrifice, is said to have "achieved the most glorious Quest and Adventure of the Sangraal" (Machen, *The Secret Glory*).

It is therefore clear that Williams' decision at the end of the 1920s to put the Holy Grail into a novel was not entirely original, but rather one more attempt to bring a Christian vision of the relic to the reading public. Like Underhill and Machen, Williams was strongly influenced by Waite, although he did not always agree with him and at the time of writing had recently ceased to take part in the activities of his order. However, like Waite, he wanted to show that the Grail was part of a living tradition with a message that was still valid. While he certainly hoped that his major contribution to the Arthurian tradition would come through the cycle of poems he had already started to write, *War in Heaven* provided a more popular means by which Williams could communicate his ideas. In order to do so, he both borrowed from his contemporaries and clearly demonstrated where he differed from them.

As in several others of Williams' spiritual thrillers, the plot of *War in Heaven* focuses on what happens when, by chance or intention, a breach appears in the frontier between our material world and the spiritual domain. Barbara Newman observes that every time "the veil between worlds is torn," spiritual powers are enabled "to invade mundane reality and wreak havoc until they can be contained by characters who willingly surrender to the Divine" (6). *War in Heaven* is the first of Williams' novels to follow this pattern and, from beginning to end, "the thing that controls everything … is the Holy Grail" (Howard 79). It is, as Karl Heinz Göller asserts, "the centre of the entire myth, and therewith the *raison d'être* of Williams' work" (122).

In *War in Heaven*, the Grail, which has been forgotten for centuries in a rural English parish church, is found, thanks to research undertaken by the cynical, atheist scholar Giles Tumulty. The chalice is described as containing a certain power, which does not come from its essential nature, but from everything "that has been stored in the Grail through its presumed use at the Last Supper and in its subsequent uses to hold the Blood of the Eucharist" (Hill 19). It is also a gateway between different levels of spiritual reality and is perceived by the characters, and in particular by the evil ones, as "being able to open the centres of Evil just as much as those of Good" (Deloux vii). Mark Morrisson even likens it to "a radioactive atom," noting that Williams' descriptions of the Grail as a "storehouse of power," "encompassed" by "radiations" and with a "material centre" that can be "dissipated," may be taken as much from the world of atomic science as from that of religious mysticism (Morrisson 18, 141). In fact, the nature of this power is never very clearly defined and "the line dividing religion and magic is really very thin" (Deloux v). Gavin Ashenden notes this confusion and remarks that Williams does not explain "the distinction between the power that the Graal contains latently within it, the power of the Godhead released, and the power that Gregory seeks union with" (107). However, this ambiguity adds to the suspense of the plot.

Throughout the novel, the Grail acts as an agent of revelation "judging everyone simply by being itself and by calling forth responses from the characters which reveal the sort of people they are" (Howard 79). As Williams states in his Commonplace Book: "The Grail ... is to some a test, to some fruition, to some union, to some torment" (Versinger 515). From the moment the Grail is discovered, a struggle begins between "those who wish to use it and those who only seek to preserve it" (Cavaliero 67); one could call them the attackers and the defenders. Gregory, one of the trio of attackers, at first seeks to dominate and control the Grail, which is, as Glen Cavaliero observes, "an absurdity" (62). He wants to use it for a black mass, to see the future and to increase his personal power. The two others are more inclined to destroy it for, as Manasseh, another attacker, sees it, the power of the Grail may be a great constructive force for the servants of God and for that reason "to destroy this [cup] is to ruin another of their houses" (WiH 144). However, they let Gregory persuade them. They decide to keep the Grail and intend "to destroy earth and heaven through it" (212), thus bringing about a nihilistic apocalypse and defeating God's purposes forever.

What the three villains do not perceive is that the Grail is not a neutral tool in their hands. When he is near the Grail, Gregory can make out "a curious smell ... more like ammonia than anything else; a sort of pungency" (63), but he does not realize that the Grail is reacting to his presence and rejecting him. In the same way, when Gregory enters the room "the Grail shuddered forward in a movement of innocent distaste" (118). At the end of the story, it is the Grail itself that puts an end to their plans and ensures the victory of the powers of Good. Supporting its efforts is a group of three new knights of the Grail, who only seek to protect the sacred vessel against its attackers, even if only the Archdeacon seems to have any real understanding of what is happening. Like the original Arthurian knights, but unlike Waite, Underhill, or Machen's knights, Williams' trio is completely open about what they are doing. Rather than using the Grail for their own interests, the three defenders are ready to make personal sacrifices for it—Kenneth, the employee, risks losing his job, the Archdeacon his parish, and the Duke of the North Ridings his reputation. These three twentieth-century men take on the identities of the three knights who, in Malory's version of the legend, successfully completed the Grail quest. By choosing to follow Malory instead of Tennyson, where only Galahad achieves the Grail, Williams reaffirms his conviction that the Grail myth is at the same time "the tale of the mystical way; but ... also the tale of the universal way. It is not ... only for the elect;

it is for all" ("Figure" 84). Not only the saintly, mystical, celibate knight is holy enough to succeed, but equally the single man with strong family ties who struggles to do right and the man who works hard and has to deal with the world's wealth.

The Archdeacon is a natural choice for Galahad on account of his obvious holiness. His first name is Julian, and his spirituality, in addition to his deeply rooted faith that all things work together for good for those who love God, create, as Gavin Ashenden has noted, "a clear link between the Archdeacon and Mother Julian" (103), the medieval English mystic. The Duke, who is a poet and, while he remains single and chaste, seeks to write a sonnet that "reflects the lady" (WiH 96) in his thoughts, takes on the role of Percival. Kenneth, even though he is also single, represents Bors who, like him, was obliged to look after the affairs of this world. While the Archdeacon's identity as the new Galahad remains constant throughout the novel, up until the moment when he leaves this world with the chalice during the final Grail mass, the roles played by the two others vary. At the end, it is Kenneth who dies and the Duke is left, like Bors in Malory's text, to return into the everyday world and tell the families and friends of his two fellow knights what has happened to them.

From another perspective, the three virtuous characters personify "three different strands of the tradition" (Ashenden 112) of the Grail quest in England throughout the ages, representing between them all those English believers who have loved and served the Grail and its Master. The Duke represents the English Roman Catholic tradition:

> He was aware of a sense of the adoration of kings—the great tradition of his house stirred within him. The memories of proscribed and martyred priests awoke; masses said swiftly and in the midst of the fearful breathing of a small group of the faithful. (WiH 135)

On the other hand, Kenneth understands the Grail via the English literary tradition:

> He approached the idea of the sacred vessel ... through exalted poetry and the high romantic tradition in literature. This living light had shone for so long in his mind upon the idea of the Grail that it was now a familiar thing. (100–01)

Yet Kenneth's approach is not exclusively literary. As an Anglican Christian, like Williams, he also has a good knowledge of the Scriptures and the Gospel stories of Jesus, and the disciples are connected in his imagination with the knights of the Holy Grail:

> Liturgical and romantic names melted into one cycle—Lancelot, Peter, Joseph, Percivale, Judas, Mordred, Arthur, John Bar-Zebedee, Galahad—and into these were caught up the names of their makers—Hawker and Tennyson, John, Malory and the medievals. They rose, they gleamed and flamed about the Divine hero, and their readers too—he also, least of all these. (136)

The placing together of the names of the two traitors, Judas and Mordred, as well as the two pure, mystical young men, John and Galahad, is certainly not a coincidence. Williams presents the original disciples around the table of the Last Supper, devoted to Christ, and the Arthurian Knights of the Round Table, devoted to the Grail, as very similar communities, with their saints and sinners, as well as their roles to play in the history of salvation.

The Archdeacon, who has a closer and more direct relationship with the Grail than his two companions, finds "no such help in the remembrances of kings or poets" (137). The Grail supremely represents for him "the chalice offered at every altar" (137), for he seeks Christ in the Grail rather than the relic for its own sake:

> But in accord with the desire of the Church expressed in the ritual of the Church the Sacred Elements seemed to him to open upon the Divine Nature .... Never so clearly as now had he felt that movement proceeding, but his mind nevertheless knew no other vision than that of a thousand dutifully celebrated Mysteries in his priestly life; so and not otherwise all things return to God. (137)

For this reason, the Archdeacon sees no value in the Grail except that which it receives from the Christian tradition and from obedience to Christ, who uses it in order to enable believers to know and to experience the abundant life promised in the Gospel. Like Williams, he is a high church Anglican, with a strong attachment to the Eucharist and a mystical streak. As Williams approves of Malory's decision to present the Grail as attainable by men from all walks of life, so the Archdeacon sees the highest value of the Grail in the rite that is not reserved for some hermetic elite, but offered to all men, every Sunday, in their parish church.

In the battle that rages around it, the Grail is not passive, but shows its own preference for the three knights and in particular the Archdeacon. When he is in the presence of the Grail (unlike Gregory, who is confronted with a disagreeable smell), Julian is greeted by "a note of gay and happy music" (50). When he gazes at it, he becomes aware of "some slight movement—toward which he was impelled" (117–18) and knows that the chalice wants to join him, as if it knows to whom it truly belongs and who is most fully aware of its intentions. The Grail moves toward the Archdeacon's hands. The clergyman realizes what is happening, grasps the cup, and runs. Later on, even when the Grail is calm and seems to be "as dull as the furniture about it" (180), the Archdeacon remains "conscious of that steady movement of creation flowing toward and through the narrow channel of its destiny" (180) and, therefore, the reader too is made aware that the chalice is, in some way, alive. Moreover, during the nocturnal attack on the Grail, only the Archdeacon notices that "the Graal itself was the centre—yet no longer the Graal, but a greater than the Graal. Silence and knowledge were communicated to him as if from an invisible celebrant" (141) with whom he can be in communion.

The identity of this mysterious celebrant is ambiguous. Williams uses capital letters for some of the pronouns referring to him, which may indicate that Christ himself is present. Yet the principal person in the novel to be identified with the Grail is Prester John. Williams' inspiration here comes from the numerous legends about Prester John, which were well-known in Europe at the time the first Grail poems were written (Silverberg). Sticking closely to the texts, Williams' Prester John is both priest and king. John speaks in the novel about seventy kings who eat at his table, a statement similar to that found in the letter received by Emmanuel of Constantinople in 1165, purportedly from Prester John.[5] In addition, the child Adrian sees in the Grail a scene that probably represents the doctor Philip, Pope Alexander III's special messenger, handing a letter to Prester John. John claims in a mysterious fashion that he is "the Graal and the Keeper of the Graal" (*WiH* 189), "the prophecy of the things that are to be and are" (245). During the Grail Mass, Williams gives a capital letter to the pronouns describing John, creating a certain confusion between the Keeper of the Grail and Jesus Christ, who seems at one point to replace him at the altar, or at least to preside through him. In the same way, the Grail stands for Christ himself when John declares to Kenneth, adapting Christ's words from the Cross to the penitent thief: "For you I have no message, except the message of the Grail: 'Surely I come quickly. Tonight thou shalt be with Me in paradise'" (203, quoting Rev. 22:20 and Luke 23:43). Equally, when the Archdeacon lifts the Grail, he feels he is holding at the same time "the Mystery and the Master of the Mystery" (141).

Like the Grail, Prester John is what Sørina Higgins calls "a catalyst of self-revelation" (85). Each character is aware of having met him before. Gregory immediately "became conscious that he actively disliked the stranger, with a hostility that surprised him with its own virulence" (154), while little Adrian, in his innocence, welcomes him at once as a friend. For all the adult characters on the side of the angels, Prester John brings back good memories of times when they were particularly close to God. It is also Prester John, at the end of the novel, who pronounces the judgment of God on each one, a judgment that is equally his own:

> You who have sought the centre of the Graal, behold through me that which you seek, receive from me that which you are. He that is righteous, let him be righteous still; he that is filthy, let him be filthy still. I am rejection to him that hath sought rejection; I am destruction to him that hath wrought destruction; I am sacrifice to him that hath offered sacrifice. Friend to my friends and lover to my lovers, I will quit all things, for I am myself and I am He that sent me. (246)

The Duke will be saved because he loved the Grail, but Gregory too will in the end find salvation, although he will first be hanged for the murder he committed, for, as Prester John tells him: "You have sought me and no other" (246)—a reason that resembles that given by Aslan to Emeth in C. S. Lewis' *The Last Battle* many years later (156). Here too the reader is uncertain if Gregory has really sought the Grail, Prester John, Jesus Christ, or all three.

However, even if Williams joins Waite, Underhill, and Machen in his desire to accentuate the Christian dimension of the Grail quest and to place it in a living tradition that would still be relevant in the twentieth century, he does not share their perception of the sacred vessel itself. For Waite, for example, the Grail "is the most precious of all relics for all Christendom indifferently, for, supposing that it were manifested at this day, I doubt whether the most rigid of Protestant sects could do otherwise than bow down before it" (10).

Machen almost certainly shares this conviction as, during the church service in *The Great Return*, the members of the very evangelical parish of Llantrisant (where the vicar considers that using incense is a

---

5   In the original text, there were seventy-two kings; see "The Letter of Prester John."

Catholic abomination) most surprisingly kneel and then "fall down flat on their faces" (57) in front of the altar with the Grail. Constance too, in *The Column of Dust*, kneels down before the Grail and worships it (139).

On the other hand, Williams clearly indicates that such an act, while entirely comprehensible, is based on an error of understanding. When the three Grail knights are in London, the Duke gets the chalice out of his safe. "In a minute the Duke, crossing himself, knelt down before it. Kenneth followed his example" (*WiH* 135). Straightaway, the Archdeacon, who represents both holiness and wisdom in the novel, stands up. In fact, right from the start, the Archdeacon shows he has a very different attitude to the Grail not only from his adversaries, but also from his colleagues. For this new Anglican Galahad, while fully aware of the Grail's power, believes: "In one sense … the Graal is unimportant—it is a symbol less near Reality now than any chalice of consecrated wine" (37). This attitude can also be seen when he promises not to offend the Catholic Duke by using the Grail to celebrate Communion. As far as the Archdeacon is concerned, "a liqueur glass would do as well" (138); the power of the Eucharist resides in the presence of Christ at the rite he himself initiated, rather than in the chalice used to hold the wine.

However, the Archdeacon is aware that "a great many people might attach a good deal of importance" (41–42) to the Grail, and above all, that the relic "was not perhaps so important as Rome would inevitably tend to make it" (178). This refusal to venerate an object, even a powerful object of great historical importance, comes from the Archdeacon's faith in Christ as the Master of the Grail and from his certainty that, when the time is right, "He shall dispose [of it] as He will" (180). Or indeed, as Thomas Howard expresses it, that "the Omnipotent Love will look after its relics" (100). For this reason, when the defenders of the Grail are invited to hand it over to their enemies in exchange for Barbara's sanity, the Archdeacon does not hesitate, saying: "I would give up any relic, however wonderful, to save anyone an hour's neuralgia—man depends too much on these things" (184).

In contrast, Martin, the keeper of the Grail and Underhill's spokesman in *The Column of Dust*, considers that "the body is nothing after all; only a little heap of dust, wrapped round to hide the soul" (160). Williams' hero actively opposes this view and has a well-developed theology of the Incarnation, honoring the human body, which Christ himself hallowed when he came down from heaven and took on flesh. Far from despising his own body, the Archdeacon even practises fencing to keep it fit.

In his article "Notes on the Arthurian Myth," Williams writes about Galahad: "I doubt whether he is concerned even with the quest; he is only aware of the End" (177), or the union of all things in Christ that the Grail may hasten. This is clear in the relationship between the Archdeacon and the chalice, which seems to help bring to tangible reality all that the priest had been living for a long time by faith through the sacraments. From the very start of the story, whenever he holds the Grail, the Archdeacon is aware of a change that comes over him:

> He became again as in all those liturgies a part of that he sustained; he radiated from that centre and was but the last means of its progress in mortality. Of this sense of instrumentality he recognized, none the less, the component parts—the ritual movement, the priestly office, the mere pleasure in ordered, traditional, and almost universal movement. (50–51)

It is as if the Grail helps him to fully live out his role as priest and celebrant, enabling him to experience the sacrament as it should always be experienced but, perhaps, rarely is.

In the same way, at the end of the novel, during the Grail Mass, "the thoughts with which he approached the Mysteries faded; the Mysteries themselves faded. He distinguished no longer word from act; he was in the presence, he was part of the Act which far away issued in those faint words" (253). A few minutes after the consummation of that union, a voice (the Grail's? Prester John's? Christ's?) calls him, his soul departs with the Grail, and it is finished. As Williams explains:

> What then is the Achievement of the Grail ... to live in the world where the Incarnation and the Sacrament (single or multiple) happen. It is more: it is in some sense to live beyond them, or rather ... to be conscious of them as one is conscious of oneself, Christ-conscious instead of self-conscious. The Achievement of the Grail is the perfect fulfilment of this. ("Figure" 79)

In this Achievement during the celebration of the Eucharist, Williams brings the reader, as Gavin Ashenden observes, "into an altogether wider dimension that incorporates space and time, spirit and matter ... drawing together ... all things into union with the Godhead" (113). Unlike Machen, whose Grail Mass is celebrated in Welsh and whose celebrant makes "no attempt to perform the usual service" (Machen, *Great Return* 56), Williams allows Prester John to celebrate a normal Anglican Eucharist, while at the same time including all those who are present. The Catholic Duke, who stands in the doorway because his church does not allow him to take part in Protestant services, hears the Mass in Latin and becomes aware of the communion of saints present in the church. Barbara, however, hears the familiar words of the Anglican liturgy. All those present, including Barbara's agnostic husband, see a "vision of creation" (*WiH* 255), perhaps even of the new creation, which swathes the Grail like a robe, revealing the presence of the Creator.

If Williams' Grail is not, in itself, more important than any other chalice, it is the catalyst for numerous transformations and enables each individual soul to be revealed. Its presence in the world places a small community of people, good and bad, on the road to salvation. Through it, the eschatological aspects of the Eucharist and the communion celebrated in that sacrament with the ultimate and divine reality pass from the realm of faith to that of direct experience. And, for Williams, unlike many of those who preceded him, that experience is not reserved for Galahad; it equally concerns modest employees, housewives, children, agnostics, and even former villains. It does not concern, principally, members of esoteric fellowships, secret religions, or seekers after hidden truths: "It is the universal way ... it is for all" ("Figure" 84).

Works Cited

Ashenden, Gavin. *Charles Williams: Alchemy and Integration*. Kent State UP, 2008. Print.

Carpenter, Humphrey. *The Inklings: C. S. Lewis, J. R. R. Tolkien, Charles Williams, and Their Friends*. Boston: Houghton Mifflin, 1978. Print.

Cavaliero, Glen. *Charles Williams: Poet of Theology*. Eugene, OR: Wipf and Stock, 1983. Print.

Deloux, Jean-Pierre. "Introduction to Charles Williams." *La Guerre du Graal*. Paris: Terrain Vague, 1989. i–ix. Print.

Dodds, David Llewellyn. Introduction. *Arthurian Poets: Charles Williams*. Arthurian Studies 24. Ed. David Llewellyn Dodds. Woodbridge, Suffolk: The Boydell Press, 1991. Print.

Gauntlett, Edward. "Charles Williams, Love and Shekinah." *The Charles Williams Quarterly* 126 (2008): 8–29. Print.

Göller, Karl Heinz. "From Logres to Carbonek: The Arthuriad of Charles Williams." *Arthurian Literature* 1 (1981): 121–73. Print.

Higgins, Sørina. "Is a 'Christian' Mystery Story Possible? Charles Williams' *War in Heaven* as a Generic Case Study." *Mythlore* 30:1/2 (2011). 77–90. Print.

Hill, Victor E. "The Christian Vision of Charles Williams." *The Charles Williams Quarterly* 131 (2009): 5–17. Print.

Howard, Thomas. *The Novels of Charles Williams*. Eugene, OR: Wipf and Stock, 1991. Print.

"The Letter of Prester John." Celtic Literature Collection. www.maryjones.us. Web.

Lewis, C. S. *The Last Battle*. 1956. London: Fontana Lion, 1983. Print.

Lewis, Pericles. "The Waste Land." *Introduction to Modernism*. Cambridge UP, 2007. 129–51. *The Modernism Lab*. Yale University. modernism.research.yale.edu. Web. 9 March 2014.

Machen, Arthur. *The Great Return*. 1915. North Hollywood, CA: Ægypan Press, 2011. Print.

——. *The Secret Glory*. NY: Alfred A. Knopf, 1922. *Project Gutenberg*. Web. 9 March 2014.

Morrisson, Mark S. *Modern Alchemy: Occultism and the Emergence of Atomic Theory*. London: Oxford UP, 2007. Print.

Newman, Barbara. "Charles Williams and the Companions of the Co-inherence." *Spiritus: A Journal of Christian Spirituality* 9.1 (2009): 1–26. Print.

Pratt, Linda Ray. "Subversion and Revival of a Tradition in Tennyson and T. S. Eliot." *Victorian Poetry* 11 (1973): 307–21. Print.

Ridler, Anne. Introduction. *The Image of the City and Other Essays*. By Charles Williams. 1958. Berkeley, CA: Apocryphile Press, 2006. ix–lxxii. Print.

Roukema, Aren. "A Veil that Reveals: Charles Williams and the Fellowship of the Rosy Cross." *Journal of Inklings Studies* 5.1 (2015): 22–71. Print.

Silverberg, Robert. *The Realm of Prester John*. Athens, OH: Ohio UP, 1972. Print.

Stanley, Richard. "Pan's People." *The Guardian* 30 October 2004. theguardian.com. Web. 9 March 2014.

Underhill, Evelyn. *The Column of Dust* (1909). London: Hardpress Publishing, 2010. Print.

Versinger, Georgette. *Charles Williams, sa vie, son œuvre*. Professorial thesis. Paris: Université de la Sorbonne Nouvelle, 2004. Print.

Waite, Arthur Edward. *The Hidden Church of the Holy Graal: Its Legends and Symbolism Considered in Their Affinity with Certain Mysteries of Initiation and Other Traces of a Secret Tradition in Christian Times*. 1909. NY: Cosimo Classics, 2007. Print.

Weston, Jessie. *From Ritual to Romance*. 1920. *Project Gutenberg*. Web. 9 March 2014.

Willard, Thomas. "Acts of the Companions: A. E. Waite's Fellowship and the Novels of Charles Williams." *Secret Texts: The Literature of Secret Societies*. Eds. Marie Mulvey Roberts and Hugh Ormsby-Lennon. NY: AMS Press, 1995. 269–302. Print.

Williams, Charles. *Arthurian Commonplace Book* (as "Notes on the Holy Grail"). MS. Eng. e. 2012. Bodleian Library. Oxford, UK.

——. *The Image of the City and Other Essays*. 1958. Ed. Anne Ridler. Berkeley, CA: The Apocryphile Press, 2007. Print.

——. Introduction. *The Letters of Evelyn Underhill.* 1943. London: Darton, Longman and Todd, 1991. Print.

——. "Notes on the Arthurian Myth." *Image* 175–79.

——. *The Descent of the Dove: A Short History of the Holy Spirit in the Church.* London: The Religious Book Club, 1939. Print.

——. "The Figure of Arthur." *Arthurian Torso.* Ed. C. S. Lewis London: Oxford UP, 1948. 5–90. Print.

——. "The Making of *Taliessin*." *Image* 179–83.

——. *War in Heaven.* 1930. Grand Rapids, MI: Eerdmans, 1991. Print.

19

The Acts of Unity: The Eucharistic
Theology of Charles Williams' Arthurian Poetry

Andrew C. Stout

The sacramental cast of Charles Williams' literary vision has been well attested.[1] The notion that human loves, human persons, and human bodies communicate the divine is the very foundation of his theology of romantic love. However, in addition to an inherent sacramentality, Williams' work also displays trenchant insights into the nature of the particular sacrament of the Eucharist. His unique contribution to eucharistic theology has been suggested by Gavin Ashenden in his excellent book *Charles Williams: Alchemy and Integration*. Commenting on *War in Heaven*, Ashenden observes that

> Williams provides an extraordinary Eucharistic theology that transcends the conventional lines of argument that fall into categories of symbolism, real presence, or transubstantiation. Instead we are moved into an altogether wider dimension that incorporates time and space, spirit and matter, in a sense of the drawing together of all things into union with the godhead through, in this case, the Grail. (Ashenden 113)

I would like to pick up this suggestion and draw out the eucharistic theology in Williams' work, looking both to his explicit statements about the sacrament in his theological and literary essays and to his mythic depiction in the Arthurian poems. I will place Williams' positions in these works within a historical theological framework, with an eye toward their potential for ecumenism. These reflections will provide a picture of the Eucharist that avoids the pitfalls of so much of the Church's sacramental theology. Williams'

---

1 Anne Ridler observes: "One may consider Charles Williams as above all a great exponent of the Affirmative, the Sacramental, Way, in the canon of Christian writing; one of the few who have written of it with a full understanding of its relation to the Negative, or Mystical, Way" (ix). Also see McLaren and Ware.

unique metaphysical perspective offers a distinctive theory of Christ's presence at the altar, giving a robust account of the nature of that presence while avoiding overly narrow speculations on the mechanics of the transformation of the elements. He recognizes and gives full expression to the social and unitive character of the sacrament. As we shall see, Williams' contribution to the Church's reflection on the memorial of Christ flows from a life that centered itself on participation in the eucharistic mystery.

Another noted feature of Williams' work is the influence of the occult, particularly through his involvement with A. E. Waite's Rosicrucian group, the Fellowship of the Rosy Cross. Waite's *The Hidden Church of the Holy Graal* (1909) was a major influence on Williams. Waite charts the literary history of the Grail romances and discusses the existence of a "Secret Church" that exists within the official Church. This Secret Church observes the rite of the Grail Mass, a rite that is "the declared pageant of the Eucharist .... its demonstration in the transcendent mode" (Waite 494). Waite does not view the Grail Mass as a replacement for the official Church's Eucharist, but he understands the doctrine of transubstantiation and the practice of the reservation of the host as "the nearest approaches to the idea of the arch-natural Eucharist" (637). Williams also sees transubstantiation as something of an approximation of a more fundamentally mysterious presence in the Eucharist. This structure of a mysterious rite that reveals the true nature of the eucharistic presence makes its way into Williams' Arthurian poems. In fact, "Taliessin at Lancelot's Mass," which I will discuss more thoroughly, is best understood as a kind of picture of the Grail Mass that Waite speaks of in cryptic terms.

While Waite's influence is undeniable, and the legitimacy of Williams' synthesis of occult and Christian themes and practices remains a significant area of research in Williams scholarship, it is equally clear that Williams works within the framework of orthodox Christian theological concepts. I hope to show that his appropriation of Grail imagery does not compromise his contribution to sacramental theology, but rather, that it imaginatively generates new possibilities for a thoroughly orthodox understanding of Christ's presence in the Eucharist.[2]

Eucharistic Center

Because he was a devout Anglo-Catholic, it is natural that the Eucharist was the center of Williams' spiritual life. For Williams, that which is spiritual or supernatural encompasses all of life, allowing for no simple dichotomies between spirit/matter or natural/supernatural. Accordingly, the centrality of the Eucharist can be seen in the entire scope of Williams' life, including the details of his personal life and the themes of his writings. Alice Mary Hadfield, his friend and biographer, notes the sustained and practical devotion to the Eucharist that spilled over into his imaginative life: "Charles went almost every Sunday to the Eucharist. It was the centre of his thought and so of his life. He never tired of meditating on it" (212). She

---

2   A recent article by Roukema combs the rituals and meeting minutes of the Fellowship of the Rosy Cross to show how Williams' novels and poetry need to be reinterpreted as literary embodiments of the group's ceremonies. For more on the way that hermetic practices inform and shape Williams' thought and fiction, see Stout, "It Can Be Done."

interprets the concerns of his life from his earliest years to his death in terms of sacramental and Arthurian themes as she speaks of his confirmation in the Church of England:

> Charles now entered the sacramental life, as the young men of Arthurian history entered the Castle of the Grail. They failed, one after another, to ask 'What serves the Grail?' or 'What purpose does the Grail serve?' because they were overcome by mystery, their own reactions, or inattention. Already to Charles, history and today, other worlds and himself, were all of one life, and he was concerned about its meaning. What was eating and drinking the bread and wine for? Why was it started? How did it work? How did it preserve your body, or your soul? This exploring mind worked in him all his life and the theme of the Eucharist was the subject of the book he was planning to write after *The Figure of Arthur*, left unfinished by his last illness in 1945. (Hadfield 11)

Hadfield articulates Williams' deferential attitude toward the gracious mystery of the sacrament and his understanding of the Eucharist in mythic terms. This conditions Williams' understanding of the sacrament and sets the trajectory for his expression of the purpose of the eucharistic celebration and of Christ's presence at the altar.

Williams saw himself primarily as a poet, and contemporary evaluation of his work has borne this out. Beyond the cult following of his novels, most critics who undertake a serious evaluation of his literary output acknowledge that his Arthurian poetry is his most significant contribution, both for the originality of his handling of the legends and for the skill and maturity of expression evidenced in their composition. All of his writings, whatever their genre, bear the mark of a poetic mind that sees form and beauty of expression as an essential component of accuracy and evaluation. He was a serious theologian, and this is never more evident than when he tackles the issue of the eucharistic presence in his theological writings like *The Descent of the Dove*. Yet even here, where historical and doctrinal accuracy are more explicit components of his agenda, the issue of the eucharistic presence is still spoken of in allusive and suggestive terms. Williams attempts to draw some explicit parameters for an original and innovative understanding of the Eucharist in his theological essays, and I will look at those shortly. But it is in *Taliessin through Logres* and *The Region of the Summer Stars* that we see his fullest depiction of the eucharistic mystery and the joining of the heavenly and earthly realms that manifests the presence of Christ to his Church. In this sense, Williams' poetry must be understood as a mode of serious theological engagement. To say that he makes a serious contribution to eucharistic theology is to acknowledge that Williams is, perhaps above all else, a eucharistic poet.

An Anglican Context

Williams' eucharistic theology must be situated within the context of the Anglo-Catholic stream of the Church of England in the first half of the twentieth century. Williams offers a poetic vision of Christ's presence in the Eucharist that is unique and that goes a long way toward reconciling some of the tensions between traditional theories of the eucharistic presence. However, Williams' discomfort with the terminology of transubstantiation, his attempt to revive patristic ideas about the Eucharist, and his emphasis on the irreducibly social character of the sacrament are all impulses that can be located within broader discussions of the Eucharist within the Anglican church of Williams' day.

With regard to transubstantiation, the 1938 report of the Commission on Christian Doctrine, entitled *Doctrine in the Church of England*, observes a current within Anglicanism among theologians who were influenced by the Oxford Movement, a nineteenth-century High Church movement lead by Edward Pusey and John Henry Newman that advocated for a fuller expression of apostolic traditions in the Church of England. They adhere to the objective nature of Christ's presence in the rite, but they maintain a certain ambivalence toward the terminology of transubstantiation: "Some of them are content with the use of traditional language to express [the real presence]; but others, especially in recent years, have felt the need for some restatement of it designed to remove traditional objections; and various suggestions for such restatement have been made."[3] Williams displays precisely this kind of ambivalence toward transubstantiation, alternatively making use of and dismissing the term. His particular approach to the Eucharist does not take the form of an explicitly defined position. However, taken as a whole, Williams' poetic rendering of the real presence might function as an alternative to transubstantiation.

The report looks back to the early centuries of the Church as an era when the mystery of the real presence was particularly valued. It discerns two major stages in the history of eucharistic doctrine. The first was a stage of grateful reception of the mysterious presence of Christ: "For about eight hundred years the attempt to understand and to express precisely how the Gift is given, and to provide an account of the Gift in its various relations, was quite subordinate to a thankful recognition of the reality of the Gift itself." This was followed by "a stage of definition and controversy, beginning in the ninth century, and marked by attempts at precision" (163). This stage included the definition of transubstantiation in 1215 at the Fourth Lateran Council, and it would come to fuller expression in Reformation debates about consubstantiation, spiritual presence, and Zwinglian memorialism. As a whole, the Anglican tradition has taken its cues from the former stage, and the report notes that

> perhaps the strongest and most characteristic tradition of Anglicanism is to affirm such a real presence of Christ in the Eucharist as enables the faithful communicant both to receive His life as a spiritual gift and to acknowledge Him as the giver, while at the same time the affirmation is combined with a determination to avoid as far as possible all precise, scholastic definitions as to the manner of the giving. (170–71)

This impulse is characteristic of Williams' account of the development of the Eucharist. He also appeals to a time prior to scholastic definitions when the real presence was just as strongly maintained, but the mystery of that presence was also more pronounced.

---

3   *Doctrine in the Church of England* 169. Williams was familiar with this report and held it in high esteem. He included selections from it in *The Passion of Christ* and *The New Christian Year*, two volumes of devotional reading that he compiled.

The report is marked throughout by an emphasis on the social character of the eucharistic rite. Aside from questions of the mechanics of the real presence, it characterizes the Eucharist as "a corporate act of the Church toward God, wherein it is united with its Lord, victorious and triumphant, Himself both Priest and Victim in the Sacrifice of the Cross" (161–62). Similarly, Charles Gore, an important Anglo-Catholic theologian of the early twentieth century, draws out the essentially social and corporate nature of sacramental rites in *The Body of Christ*. After observing a Protestant tendency to oppose the idea of spiritual blessing being delivered by material means, Gore articulates a "sacramental presupposition" that must be in place to properly understand the doctrine of the real presence:

> The communication of this spiritual life [of Christ's] to us by means of a material and social cer-
> emony is quite analogous to the whole of what we know about the relation of the human spirit to
> bodily conditions, about the relation of the individual to the society, and about the principles of
> the pre-eminently human and social religion of the Son of Man. (47)

Williams certainly reflects this interest in the social character of the Eucharist. In his explicitly theological works, he views the Eucharist as a way of charting and enacting the history of Christendom.[4] In his Arthurian poems, the fate of Logres is tied up in the fate of the Grail, and he uses the Grail as a means to reveal the sacramental nature of the social order.

As these sources show, Williams is well situated within the sacramental context of the Church of England in the early twentieth century.[5] Within that context, his intellectual and aesthetic orientation was consistently Anglo-Catholic. Williams' parish church, St. Silas the Martyr in Kentish Town, London, was and remains one of the most distinctly Anglo-Catholic parishes in the Church of England.[6] While Williams'

---

4   In a review of a book on "the Liturgy of the Church of England as it was received by the Anglican Divines of
    the seventeenth century," Williams notes how the tradition has put the Eucharist at the center of its social
    theory, noting that "the sacred City could not be built by everyone raising his own little pile of bricks. Men
    were to be part of it, and so only it of them. The Eucharist, which was the centre and consummation of all
    the Rites, was the union of the City" ("The Liturgy" 122).

5   It has also been noted by Ralph that Williams displays a substantial understanding of the nuances of
    sixteenth-century eucharistic debates. Ralph cites some lines from the verse play *Thomas Cranmer of Canterbury*
    in which Williams compresses complex "theological argument into a few lines, with little context" (218).

6   Understanding the heavily Anglo-Catholic context of St. Silas the Martyr and the formative effect it must
    have had on Williams' imagination is important for grasping the imagery of the mass in his Arthurian
    poems. An essay on the architect Ernest Charles Shearman offers some liturgical background:
    > That Shearman was working at St. Silas for Anglo-Catholic clients cannot be overstated, for
    > that relationship directly shaped the overall form of the church and its sundry appointments.
    > Broadly speaking, within the liturgies of the Anglo-Catholic branch of Anglicanism, there are two
    > predominant sources of inspiration in liturgical matters. These sources govern a wide range of
    > elements, from the inclusion or exclusion of genuflections at specified points in the liturgy to altar
    > appointments, iconography, and vestiture. The two major sources are the pre-Reformation English
    > medieval church on the one hand, and post-Reformation Rome on the other hand. At St. Silas, the
    > source of inspiration is significantly drawn from the latter. (Row 351)

eucharistic views can be identified within the theological climate of his day, he contributes a distinct ontological rationale for the real presence.

Real Presence and the Metaphysics of Co-inherence

Williams' theology of the Eucharist rests on a unique metaphysical perspective. The idea of co-inherence is the metaphysical basis for his understanding of Christ's presence and the Church's participation in the sacrament. What Williams is trying to maintain is a view of Christ's presence that holds to the reality of that presence but that also eschews the traditional language of transubstantiation to describe its mysterious quality. He is attempting to return to a patristic reticence to explain the eucharistic mystery. He achieves this through a reappropriation and development of the patristic term "co-inherence," to produce what I will call an "ontology of co-inherence."

Co-inherence is a (perhaps *the*) governing principle of Williams' thought. It is a principle that is derived from the Christian faith, but that speaks of the interconnectedness of the created order in a way that is recognizable to anyone. The trinitarian definitions of the Church "declared not merely that the Father and the Son existed co-equally, but that they existed co-inherently—that is, that the Son existed *in* the Father and that the Father existed *in* the Son" ("The Way of Exchange" 149). This co-inherent life is extended to the Church: "The same preposition was used to define our Lord's relations with His Church: 'we in him and he in us'" (149). The pagans, however, also recognized the inevitable reliance of individuals on one another, and today our even more highly specialized divisions of labor reinforce this truth. We cannot escape the obvious truth that "The whole natural and social world depended, then as now, on some process of exchange" (149). If the trinitarian relationship of exchange and co-inherence is what lies behind and gives life to the created order, then we should expect to see these characteristics defining every part of the reality that we experience.

Though evidenced in our daily experience and established in the doctrines of the Church, co-inherence comes most clearly into view in the celebration of the Eucharist: "The great Rite of this (as of much else) within the Christian Church is the Eucharist, where the co-inherence is fully in action: 'He in us and we in Him'" (154). This is the angle at which Williams approaches the fraught question of the real presence of Christ in the Eucharist. He employs co-inherence as a principle of the ontological makeup of the universe to explain how Christ is present in the sacrament. By doing this, Williams attempts to recapture something of the patristic sense of mystery that he claims surrounded the Eucharist prior to the Fourth Lateran Council and the climax of the medieval eucharistic controversies in the definition of transubstantiation.[7] Prior to this:

---

7   Stevenson notes the possible objection that an Anglican appeal to a patristic sense of mystery in formulations of the eucharistic presence could be a kind of cop-out. He defends the legitimacy of this appeal on the part of the Anglican divines, claiming that "Far from the intellectual bankruptcy of taking refuge in the idea of mystery, these men were asserting and affirming mystery as something irreducible in itself and the essential reality pervading the sacramental action and its effects—*the mystery of the Eucharist*" (McAdoo and Stevenson 19, emphasis original).

in those earlier centuries the central Mystery of Ritual, the Eucharist itself, had rather been accepted than discussed. From the days of St. Paul the holy celebrations had continued, and the presence of Messias been acknowledged. But argument had been small. The nature of the change had not been defined, nor had the means or moment of the change been settled. (*Dove* 113)

With this definition, the doctrine of the real presence was raised to the status of dogma, along with the triune nature of God and the dual nature of Christ, which Williams sees as a positive development. However, with this elevated status came the difficulty of formal definitions, and Williams is clearly not entirely comfortable with the terminology of transubstantiation. According to Williams' understanding, transubstantiation requires that the body of Christ displace the elements of bread and wine. He notes, "I'm a little inclined to agree that if there is nothing but He there, there is hardly a sacrament" (qtd. in Hadfield 212). By examining the sacrament as a rite that reveals, in a concentrated way, the co-inherent nature of the created order and of the Christian faith, Williams seeks to offer a subtler,[8] and ultimately a more broadly suggestive, account of the presence of Christ in the Eucharist.

Williams' meditations on the co-inherent nature of the Eucharist reveal a number of different dimensions to the ritual meal. First, we see that Christ and the Church co-inhere in one another. As noted above, the act of the Eucharist reveals that the Church has been ushered into a participation with Christ that reflects the participation of the three members of the Godhead within each other. Christ draws his Body, the Church, into participation with Himself by both offering and constituting the sacramental meal: "There, visible but hidden, perfect under either species, were the subtlety, the glory, the agility, the impassibility. They were there for sacrifice and communion. The True Priest (hidden in wafer and in wine) offered them, and generously permitted the Church and City a participation in His Act" ("Figure" 204). It is Christ's act of atonement and substitution that affects the Church's reconciliation to God, but in the eucharistic meal the bread and wine become the means by which that atonement and substitution are accomplished in the Church. By reenacting the Last Supper, the Church participates in an act initiated by Christ. It was not enough that Christ, through his own actions on the cross, accomplish the reconciliation of humanity, but He continues that act into our own time and beyond by institutionalizing a ritual meal for us to participate in: "The whole act is Christ's and is imparted to those who are also His. But now, as he had commenced the Act, and indoctrinated the theology, He was said to have directed the ritual" ("Figure" 205).

---

8   Williams claims that "Only the most subtle theologians can adequately discuss the Nature of that Presence." He certainly counted Aquinas in this group, and yet, with reference to St. Thomas, maintained that a sufficient account of the eucharistic presence has yet to be offered: "The answers are lofty and sublime, but we yet await the genius who can make those high speculations vivid" (*Dove* 113–14). Williams' Grail poetry can rightly be seen as his own attempt to make the speculative "vivid."

Second, we see in the Eucharist that matter and deity can co-inhere in one another.[9] Williams notes that in the early centuries of the Church, the Eucharist "was used, as well it might be, as an argument against the Gnostic doctrines of the unreality of matter and of the evil of the flesh" ("Figure" 197). As the conviction that Christ both offered and was offered in this act grew, so did the conviction that the elements contained or offered Christ's real body. Following the definition of transubstantiation in the Fourth Lateran Council, the feast of Corpus Christi was established in 1264:

> The co-inherence of matter and Deity as a presence became as liturgically glorious as it was intellectually splendid, and the performance of the dramatic Mysteries and Miracles celebrated in many places through a long summer's day the Act in the present sacrament as well as in history and in the soul. It was organized and exhibited. (*Dove* 119)

It is part and parcel of Chalcedonian orthodoxy that both divine and human natures are united in the person of Christ. By acknowledging that God, who is a spirit, can co-inhere with the matter of bread and wine, the dogma of the divine and human natures of Christ is defended and continually reenacted.

Finally, and most crucially, the Eucharist reveals the co-inherence of time with eternity.[10] Though the Incarnation brought together humanity and divinity in the person of Christ, the healing of the rift between the heavenly and earthly realms was yet to be fully manifested. Temporal history continued after the ascension of Christ, and the early Church therefore had to come to grips with the fact that Christ's heavenly session did not usher in the end of that history. Time had to be reconciled with eternity. According to Williams, the early Church "had been fixed on the elements which, being the veil, were in some sense rather the mystery beyond … the great Rite soared to its climax in the eternal, and yet communicated the eternal to time" (*Dove* 114). Williams quotes Gregory the Great, who says that in the sacrifice of the Eucharist "things lowest are brought into communion with the highest, things earthly are united with the heavenly, and the things that are seen and those which are unseen become one" (114). The Eucharist became the means by which the Church experienced and participated in the reality of heaven. Christ took His human status with Him into the presence of the Father existing in eternity, and through continuing to celebrate

---

9   Horne draws out the importance of co-inherence to Williams' Christology. In doing so, he also notes the source through which Williams identifies co-inherence as a patristic concept:
> While this vocabulary of substitution and exchange, emphatically used by Williams, might suggest a more immediate union between the natures than was propounded at Chalcedon, which would lead in the direction of the confusion of natures, monophysitism is avoided by the use of the complementary concept of co-inherence. The divine and human natures of the incarnate Lord do not merge into one another, are not confused, they co-inhere. Williams had been very impressed by G. L. Prestige's essay on co-inherence that concluded his study *God in Patristic Thought*; Williams found his own theological sensibility confirmed by that work. (Horne 117)

10   In a chapter on Williams' Arthurian poems, Cavaliero states that "The co-inherence of time and eternity is of the essence of his poetic vision; and systematic exploration is the matter of his theology. As Williams practised them, the two disciplines are complementary" (*Poet* 125).

the meal that Christ shared with His disciples, the Church is drawn up into the presence of the ascended Christ. History had not yet come to a close, but the eternal was made present to the Church in the midst of history as Christ is presented in the Eucharist. In the Eucharist, Christ, ascended to eternity, co-inheres with the temporal congregation of the Church.

This presence of Christ through the Eucharist is no mere mental remembrance on the part of the Church. The view that the meal is simply a commemoration of Christ's work is associated with the Swiss Reformer Ulrich Zwingli—this is far from Williams' position. As mentioned above, he is pleased with the fact that Christ's real presence has been raised to the level of dogma with the doctrine of transubstantiation, but he is not satisfied with the Aristotelian terms in which transubstantiation has been defined. Christ is present physically in the Supper, yes, but it is the mysterious ability of the eternal to co-inhere with the temporal that accounts for this physical presence. This constitutes a new ontological basis on which to begin thinking about how Christ is truly present in the Eucharist. In his Arthurian poetry, Williams begins to give expression to what this presence might look like.

Real Presence through Co-inherence in the Arthurian Poems

The Grail at the Center

Williams' two volumes of Arthurian poetry, *Taliessin through Logres* and *The Region of the Summer Stars*, are unique and important contributions to the development of the Arthurian myths. Their most distinctive feature is the central role that the quest for the Grail plays, both thematically and organizationally. The organization of the Arthurian myths around the central theme of the Grail was a conscious strategy on Williams' part. Though he drew inspiration from both Malory and Tennyson, he claimed that "the great and awful myth of the Grail had not been treated adequately in English verse" ("The Making of *Taliessin*" 180). He understood such an emphasis to be a recovery of a medieval sensibility. As Williams states the primary tension of the story, "The problem is simple—is the king to be there for the sake of the Grail or not. It was so the Middle ages left it; but since then it has been taken the other way. The Grail has been an episode" ("Figure" 267). To recognize the Grail's centrality is to recover the central theme of the mythology: "Logres then must be meant for the Grail …. This indeed must be the pure glory of Arthur and Logres …. It is the central Matter of Britain. We may, if we choose, reasonably and properly refuse it, but we can hardly doubt that if we do we shall have no doubt a consistent, but a much smaller myth" ("Figure" 267). By making the Grail central, Williams revealed that the Arthurian stories are not simply cultural artifacts, but that they form a complete mythology with broad social and theological application.

The central place of the Grail is well attested to in the literature that discusses Williams' handling of the Arthuriad. While earlier versions of the myths focused on Arthur's kingship or the romance of Lancelot and Guinevere, Williams brought the quest for the Grail and its spiritual power to the forefront. Elizabeth Brewer notes that Williams, like Malory before him, does not simply retell a series of stories; rather, he absorbs and reshapes the existing tradition. "The Grail is of course Charles Williams' real subject, though for Malory it was only incidental …. Naturally, therefore, the selection of characters and the parts that they play in Williams' cycle were controlled by the focus on the Grail" (Brewer 102). McClatchey connects the central place that the Eucharist played in Williams' life to the place of the Grail in his writing. He notes that "the artistic center of Charles Williams' imaginative writings is the Mysteries of the Holy Eucharist, that is, the Bread and Cup of the Lord's Supper or Communion ... he has presented the world with a new Grail hero from the very nature of his poetic development of the tradition."[11] The Eucharist and the Arthurian myths are entwined in Williams' imagination, creating a unique emphasis on the spiritual power and determinative role of the Grail in the story of Logres.

With the Grail at the center, Williams shapes the Arthurian myths in such a way as to draw out their social and political implications.[12,13] Williams conceives of Logres, or Britain, as the western-most outpost of the Byzantine Empire. The various parts of the Empire, the "organic body," are laid out early in *Taliessin through Logres* in the poem "The Vision of the Empire," and those parts of the organic body are mapped out and overlaid with the figure of a female body in the book's frontispiece. Logres is the head of the Empire, Gaul or France the breasts, Rome the hands, Byzantium the navel, and Jerusalem the loins.[14] As the head, Logres has the potential to establish the full unity of the Empire through Arthur's reign. He is to bring order to Logres by establishing a court at Camelot that embodies the principals of co-inherence and exchange. Williams, commenting on Robert de Boron's thirteenth-century version of the myth, notes how the developing myth of the Grail took on a closer association with the Eucharist:

> The first table ... had been established by Christ himself; the Second by Joseph of Arimathea, at the bidding of Christ himself; the Third was to be by Uther, at the bidding of Merlin. This alternation gives the myth a new stress, for the idea of a spiritual relationship is immediately present, circles of sanctity. The Apostolic company is the first institution; the company of true believers the second; the third is the chivalry of the Table ... Logres and the Grail are to come together, and the king is to preside at the union.[15] ("Figure" 258)

---

11   McClatchey 51. For more on the way that Williams' Arthuriad differs from another major Arthurian writer (Tennyson), see Schneider.

12   The City is a major theme in Williams' work. See his essays "The Image of the City in English Verse," and "The Redeemed City" in *Image* (92–102, 102–10). David Llewellyn Dodds notes: "Williams set himself to show the proper relation of 'the Republic' and the Grail. As suggested above, there is no radical opposition in the poetry between earthly and heavenly. Instead, the universe and especially human society, reflect in their interrelatedness the co-inherent 'community' of the Persons of the Trinity" (Introduction 11).

13   For more on Williams' doctrine of the City, see Benjamin Utter's chapter in this volume, "What Does the Line along the Rivers Define?" (12) and Andrew Rasmussen's, "Beatrice and Byzantium" (14). [Editor's note]

14   Williams lays out the rationale for interpreting earthly and geographical realities according to the image of the human body in "The Index of the Body," in *Image* (80–87). As Williams explains in the essay, part of the rational is the sacramental unity of the spiritual and physical realms.

15   Even here, in recounting the development of the medieval Grail romances, Williams' own understanding of the Eucharist's centrality is shaping his interpretation. Barber notes this of the Grail romances: "If the Grail owes much to the popular devotion to the Eucharist, and to the debates and images surrounding it,

Williams discerns a sort of eucharistic typology that informs the developing Grail narrative. Christ's celebration of the Last Supper sets the pattern for proper table fellowship and for rightly ordered social relationships. Williams incorporates this typology into his own cycle of poems, creating a Logres that is intended, through a demonstration of a social order defined by co-inherence, to bring unity to the Empire.

That task, however, is marred from the beginning, as the knight Balin, in an attempt to protect himself, wounds King Pelles, the keeper of the Grail, with another relic: the spear that pierced the side of Christ. This Dolorous Blow brings division to Logres and will eventually result in a civil war between Arthur and Mordred. This division can be healed only by the Grail itself. Galahad therefore, the champion of the Grail, takes on a greater importance in the myth. In Williams' imagination, Galahad "is not exactly Christ, but rather man's capacity for Christ, or—to avoid dogma—let us say, for divine things" ("Notes on the Arthurian Myth" 176). The restoration of the divided kingdom is envisioned as "Galahad comes to Camelot, and the Sacred Graal, i.e. the reunion of all things, is seen in a vision" (177). As Karl Heinz Göller expresses it:

> The centre of the entire myth, and therewith the *raison d'être* of Williams' work, is clearly the Grail. The poet sees the union of the world of Arthur with that of the Grail less as a legendary or historical phenomenon, and far more as a complex symbol of the union of Empire and Christendom, that is to say as a symbol of the Ultimate Epiphany, the Second Advent of Christ. (Göller 465)

For Williams, the Arthurian myth is a symbol of Christendom. It gives mythic form to the situation of the Church in the time between Christ's first and second advents. By placing the Grail at the center of that mythic structure, and by emphasizing the role that it plays in reconstituting the lost unity of the social order, Williams imbues the Grail with an explicitly eucharistic function. Arthur fails to serve the Grail and to embody co-inherence, destroying the fellowship of his Round Table, and ultimately Logres, by his self-absorption. The Grail can only finally be achieved by Galahad, who is willing to ask: "What serves the Grail?" His quest is characterized by co-inherence and substitution, and this allows him to achieve the Grail and to participate in the co-inherent universe that it creates.

Williams' focus on the Grail and its significance for the social order is an essential part of what sets his Arthuriad apart from those of other major Arthurian writers. This emphasis is a product of the fact that his image of the Grail is informed by a eucharistic typology grounded in the practice of Christ, the historical development of the Eucharist, and the development of the Arthurian myths. His emphasis on the Grail's shaping of the social order also reflects the specific concerns of the Anglican church of his day.

We will turn now to see how these particular concerns are reflected in the eucharistic imagery of two particular poems in Williams' Arthuriad. The final poems of each cycle, "Taliessin at Lancelot's Mass" and

---

Grail and Eucharist are by no means one and the same. The Grail is both more and less than the central icon of the Mass, beginning as a mysterious container for the Host, and ending as a transcendent vehicle for the highest of all visions" (147). The Grail and the Eucharist are not identical for Williams either, but the symbolism has coalesced. The grail represents the ultimate union of heaven and earth in Christ's *Parousia*, while the Eucharist is the ritual meal that mediates a partial fulfillment of that union in history.

"The Prayers of the Pope," depict celebrations of the Mass. While there are eucharistic allusions throughout the cycles, these poems are particularly rich with imagery that combines Williams' distinct ontology of co-inherence with his inherently social understanding of the Eucharist. From this basis, Williams is able to offer a perspective on Christ's presence in the eucharistic rite that avoids the pitfalls of the traditional theories of the eucharistic presence.

"Taliessin at Lancelot's Mass"

As *Taliessin through Logres* comes to a close, it has become clear that Logres has failed to fulfill its role as the unifying head of the Empire. Mordred has rebelled against Arthur and broken the unity of the Round Table and of Camelot. Though Arthur has failed to put the Grail at the center of his kingship, Galahad, along with Percivale and Bors, has entered the castle of Carbonek, achieved the Grail, and sailed to the heavenly city of Sarras. Galahad's service to the Grail has achieved some measure of healing in Logres in the aftermath of the rebellion and the Grail quest, as seen in the ending of "The Last Voyage":

> In Logres the king's friend landed, Lancelot of Gaul.
> Taliessin at Canterbury met him with the news
> of Arthur's death and the overthrow of Mordred.
> At the hour of the healing of Pelles
> the two kings were one, by exchange of death and healing.
> Logres was withdrawn to Carbonek; it became Britain. (120–25)[16]

Though Arthur failed to bring union to the Empire in his life, his death has a substitutionary quality, making possible the healing of Pelles and restoring a degree of peace to the land. However, with the transference of Galahad and the Grail, the union of Sarras and Camelot has not been achieved. The mythic kingdom of Logres is now simply historic Britain.

In "Taliessin at Lancelot's Mass," Taliessin, the king's poet, encounters Lancelot at Carbonek, the castle where the Grail had been housed:

> I came to the altar when dew was bright on the grass;
> he—he was not sworn of the priesthood—began the Mass.
> The altar was an ancient stone laid upon stones;
> Carbonek's arch, Camelot's wall, frame of Bors' bones. (1–4)

Lancelot begins to conduct his Mass on the site that connects Sarras and Byzantium, heaven and earth. Still clad in armor and dappled with blood, but with his weapons laid down, Lancelot's "hands were bare as Lateran's to the work of our Lord" (8). As he conducts the ritual, the recently shattered unity of the Round Table begins to be spiritually reconstituted as "In the ritual before the altar Lancelot began to pass; / all

---

16   All quotations from the poems come from *Arthurian Poets: Charles Williams*, edited by David Llewellyn Dodds.

the dead lords of the Table were drawn from their graves to the Mass" (9–10). This reconciliation begins to take place among all the broken figures of Camelot. Even the slain Arthur, through the substitution of Guinevere in exile, becomes present at the Mass, demonstrating a sacrificial deference that he failed to demonstrate during his life:

> Out of the queen's substitution the wounded and dead king
> entered into salvation to serve the holy Thing;
> singly seen in the Mass, owning the double Crown,
> going to the altar Pelles, and Arthur moving down. (17–20)[17]

At Lancelot's Mass, the living and the dead relate to one another through acts of exchange and substitution. The realms of spirit and matter co-inhere, and in this way, the union that failed in Camelot is now made manifest as an arch-natural reality through the Mass.

Taliessin and his Company are present at this Mass, and they observe the coalescence of living and dead. The Company joins in the arch-natural chorus at the Epiclesis, the invoking of the Holy Spirit that transforms the eucharistic elements:

> Then the Byzantine ritual, the Epiclesis, began;
> then their voices in Ours invoked the making of man;
> petal on petal floated out of the blossom of the Host,
> and all ways the Theotokos conceived by the Holy Ghost. (33–36)[18]

At the point of the transformation of the Host, the ultimate co-inherent mystery is enacted—deity and humanity co-inhering in the person of Christ. As the Incarnation is celebrated, the constellation of events that made this co-inherent mystery possible is also celebrated. The combined voices of the dead lords of the Round Table and the members of Taliessin's Company invoke the creation of man. The Virgin Mary is honored in her role as *Theotokos*, or God-bearer. The petals that float out of the Host at the moment of transformation—and this is where the obscurity of Williams' poetry makes interpretation difficult—seem to

---

17   Scarf writes about the nature of kingship in Williams' writing, and he notes the way that the Eucharist redeems Arthur's failed kingship: "Williams believes that, because of the Fall, King Arthur cannot emulate Christ *as* king. Through the benefits of the passion remembered in the Eucharist, anamnesis, the king is able to be reconciled to God, and redeemed from the failure that the Fall inevitably brought about and enter, like Christ into his royal Glory" (32).

18   This poem displays a sacramental character, not only in its conceptual content, but in its form and execution. Commenting on this stanza, Bradbury notes that these poems create "the experience of seeing the Arthurian world in brief flashes, rather than as a sustained panorama .... These flashes allow for the realisation of aspects of reality which lie beyond the reach of normal language. The more of the poetry one reads, the more these images coalesce around referents beyond the world of sensation" (43). For more on the sacramental nature of Williams' Arthurian poetry, see Cavaliero's "Charles Williams and the Arthuriad: Poetry as Sacrament."

allude to Christological and Marian rose symbolism. Mary is commonly associated with the rose, and the five wounds of Christ were sometimes represented in medieval piety by the five petals of a rose. Following the prophetic imagery of Isaiah 11, Christ has been depicted as the "bloom" from the stump of Jesse.[19]

This ritual enactment of the Incarnation "exposes" or reveals both the hidden unity of the Empire and the greater unity of Byzantium and Sarras:

> We exposed, We exalted the Unity; prismed shone
> web, paths, points; as it was done
> the antipodean zones were retrieved round a white rushing deck,
> and the Acts of the Emperor took zenith from Caucasia to Carbonek. (37–40)

The divided zones on the Empire were momentarily unified around the "white rushing deck" of the ship that carried Galahad to Sarras with the Grail. Galahad achieved what Logres as a whole could not; but in his wake, a glimpse of the unity that was intended for Logres was revealed. Now, as the Mass is celebrated, Galahad appears over the altar, and the reconstituted Round Table ascends with Galahad at the head:

> The Table ascended; each in turn lordliest and least—
> slave and squire, woman and wizard, poet and priest;
> interchanged adoration, interdispersed prayer,
> the ruddy pillar of the Infant was the passage of the porphyry stair. (45–48)

The "Infant," Galahad as a type of Christ, has forged a pathway for communion between Byzantium and Sarras, just as Christ unified heaven and earth through the Incarnation and the Crucifixion. This pathway required the shedding of blood, as symbolized in the blood red of "ruddy" pillar and the "porphyry" stair that connect heaven and earth. The unity of the spheres is mediated by the Eucharist, and the Round Table, now functioning as the type of "egalitarian hierarchy" that it was always intended to be, ascends to the heavenly city in Galahad's wake.[20]

The ultimate and definitive co-inherence of Sarras and Byzantium through the fulfillment of Logres as a model of exchange is frustrated in the departing of the Grail for Sarras. Christ's *parousia*, the promise of Logres, is delayed. It is through the Mass that this co-inherence is experienced in part and through which the promise of the Grail is carried on. We see here a "frustrated co-inherence" as the Grail departs, and we are left with the Eucharist to provide the sign and partial experience of the union of heaven and earth.[21]

---

19 See the traditional carol of German origin: "Lo, How a Rose E'er Blooming."

20 The Eucharist celebration in "Castra Parvulorum," the final chapter of Williams' novel *War in Heaven*, depicts the co-inherent nature of the sacrament as deceased members of the community become visible, and those present receive supernatural insight into their future. The past and future co-inhere in the present as the supernatural nature of the universe is displayed through the Eucharist.

21 Moorman picks up on the particular significance of the Mass in this poem as he notes that "what should have been accomplished in the ordinary life of Logres can be effected only after the failure of the kingdom

"The Prayers of the Pope"

In "The Prayers of the Pope," the scene is no longer Logres but Rome, the "hands" of the anatomical Empire. The poem "represents a turbulent, eventful crescendo of historical events and developments which lead to the final catastrophe—the downfall of the realm and the dissolution of Taliessin's fellowship" (Göller 493). The poem takes the form of a meditation on the *Magnificat* as Pope Deodatus prepares to celebrate the Eucharist:

> Over the altar a reliquary of glass held
> an intinctured Body; the Pope waited to pass
> to sing his tri-fold Eucharist; meanwhile he prayed
> alone in the candled shroud of the dark. (8–11)

The Pope has heard reports of the conflict among Arthur, Lancelot, and Mordred. The division of this civil war has brought disorder to Logres:

> Against the rule of the Emperor the indivisible
> Empire was divided; therefore the Parousia suspended
> its coming, and abode still in the land of the Trinity.
> Logres was void of Grail and Crown, but well
> had Mordred spelled his lesson from his father King Arthur. (145–49)

Mordred has cast Logres and the Table into in-coherence, and social disintegration has spread throughout the Empire as rulers and governors turn from service of the Emperor to tribalism. With the passing of the Grail, the Empire has ceased to look "for the perfect Parousia" (43), despairing of Christ's coming. This breakdown of the social order is a result of the failure to live according to co-inherence, as, "Frantic with fear of losing themselves in others / .... / They rejected the City; they made substitutes for the City" (47, 51). Mordred has replaced the lords of the Table with pagan chieftains, and wizards, the seers of the heathen, are performing rituals of necromancy. Invoking pagan deities, they raise an army of corpses, "the poor, long-dead, decomposing / shapes of humanity" (106–07). The tentacled grip of P'o-l'u, the land to the south of Byzantium under the chaotic reign of the Headless Emperor, spreads and threatens to overwhelm the Empire.

In the midst of the violent division of the Empire, a note of hope resounds. In one scene, Taliessin addresses his Company, releasing them from the vows that have held his "household" together. If Logres was meant to function as the ideal City, demonstrating co-inherence for the whole Empire, then the Company, centered on the lieutenancy of Taliessin, was meant to be the model of co-inherence to which

---

and within the operation of the Mass. All is reconciled and exchanged in the final moment, but the grail has departed, the 'parallels,' symbols of order, 'desecrated'" (75–76). In the Mass, culminating in the Eucharist, a social order is enacted that cannot yet be known in Logres.

Logres itself looked.[22] With the lords of the Table dead, save Lancelot, Taliessin sends the Company out into the broader Empire:

> "Therefore now We dissolve the former bonds—"
> the voice sounded, the hands descended—"We dissolve
> the outer bonds; We declare the Company still
> Fixed in the will of all who serve the Company,
> but the ends are on Us, peers and friends; We restore
> again to God the once-permitted lieutenancy;
> …
> We restore it to God in each singly and in all.
> Receive it in God." (187–96)

The scene moves back to the Pope, who prays for the disbanded Company. "Keep thy own for thyself" (212), he petitions, further asking:

> let them then
> go into every den of magic and mutiny,
> touch the sick and the sick be healed, take
> the trick of the weak devils with peace, and speak
> at last on the coast of the land of the Trinity the tongue
> of the Holy Ghost. (226–31)

The Pope charges the Company in exile with practicing co-inherence within the now divided and paganized empire. Like the first-century Christians, they are to act as ambassadors of co-inherence and substitution in an antagonistic empire.

The Pope passes from his meditation on the *Magnificat* to the Eucharist proper. As he does so, the hope that he expresses for the Company's capacity to continue to act as agents of co-inherence is reflected in the ritual that he performs:

> The Pope passed to sing the Christmas Eucharist.
> He invoked peace on the bodies and souls of the dead,
> yoked fast to him and he to them,
> co-inherent all in Adam and all in Christ. (300–03)

---

22   See "The Founding of the Company," in *RSS*. The real-world model for Taliessin's Company was Williams' own informal group of followers, the Companions of the Co-inherence. For more on how Williams and his company engaged in the practice of substitution, see Newman.

It is in the Eucharist that co-inherence becomes explicitly demonstrated. At the altar, past and present, visible and invisible co-inhere in the Pope's ritual act. The living and the dead are brought into the presence of Christ through this extension of his saving work. At the moment of "the junction of communion" (310), the moment that the elements of the Eucharist are transformed, Christ acts as a substitute through the person of the Pope. At that moment,

> he offered his soul's health for the living corpses,
> his guilt, his richness of repentance, wealth for woe.
> This was the Pope's prayer; prayer is substance;
> quick the crowd, the thick souls of the dead,
> moved in the Pope's substance to the invoked Body,
> the Body of the Eucharist, the Body of the total loss,
> the unimaged loss; the Body salvaged the bodies
> in the fair, sweet strength of the Pope's prayer.
> The easement of exchange led into Christ's appeasement
> under the heart-breaking manual acts of the Pope. (310–20)

Through the Pope's substitutionary mediation at the altar, Christ is made present.[23] The army of reanimated corpses "stopped, dropped, disintegrated to dust" (322); they are put back to rest in order to await their true resurrection at the time of Christ's *parousia*. The Empire is still broken, and the promise of the Grail still goes unfulfilled; however, the downward spiral has been broken:

> … consuls and lords within the Empire,
> for all the darkening of the Empire and the loss of Logres
> and the hiding of the High Prince, felt the Empire
> revive in a live hope of the Sacred City. (324–27)

Though the Grail is gone and the *parousia* delayed, the hope of the Grail is mediated through the Eucharist. Sarras and the Empire are not yet united, but the reality of that union can be experienced in part through participation in the Mass. Just as each act of Communion brings worshipers, living and dead, into the

---

23   Ridler draws out the co-inherent nature of the poem's Eucharist celebration:
    It is a most difficult poem to grasp, because it has to express, in the sequential form of poetry, happenings which require to be held simultaneously in mind. It is the same difficulty that we are in when we use the words *repetition* or *recalling* for the action of the priest in the breaking of bread—words which tend to separate his action from Christ's sacrifice, made 'once for all' and yet here *happening*. So the Pope's Christmas Eucharist gives us the *happening* of the division and reconciliation, which have been the subject of the whole cycle. (lxvi, emphasis original)

presence of Christ, so the future union of heaven and earth co-inheres in each eucharistic act. Logres failed to achieve that union through the Grail, but its promise remains and is enacted through the Eucharist.[24]

Christendom Unified Around the Eucharist

Williams, in his more scholarly writings, articulates a metaphysic in which time/eternity, humanity/deity, and Christ/Church co-inhere within one another. This view is brought to life in the Arthurian world of the Grail quest. If the traditional questions surrounding the nature of Christ's presence in the Eucharist have dealt with how the physical matter of bread and wine can be transformed into the actual body and blood of Christ, Williams creates an ontological category through which he can explain as well as depict how such a mystery can occur. If the Eucharist is the ultimate rite of a co-inherent universe, then its celebration is able to make present every stage of redemptive history, past and future, in any individual celebration. When bread and wine on any altar are consecrated, that particular celebration will itself co-inhere with the celebration of the Last Supper, the Crucifixion, and the future Marriage Supper of the Lamb. The substance of the elements does not need to be transformed for this to happen, but it does make Christ present in a way that is entirely real. If the universe cannot easily be divided into natural and supernatural, but is rather "arch-natural" in its composition, then Christ's real presence in the ritual cannot be limited by time or space. Instead of offering one more suggestion about how the natural elements can supernaturally become the body and blood of Christ, Williams undermines the metaphysical presuppositions of the traditional eucharistic debates. If Williams' picture of the universe is accurate, then the real presence of Christ comes not through transubstantiation of the elements but through co-inherence of events.

If, for Williams, the Arthurian myth is a symbol of Christendom, then there can be little worse than a Christendom in schism. The Grail is the focus around which Logres and the Empire have the possibility of being unified, and it is around the Eucharist that the divided branches of the Church must seek their unity. Ironically, eucharistic theology has been one of the major issues that has divided and defined the separate branches of the Church. Williams' understanding of Christ's presence in the Eucharist, by recasting the metaphysical underpinnings of the longstanding debates of Western theology, offers the possibility that these divisions might be overcome.[25] Surely this will only happen when, with Williams, we prostrate ourselves before the mystery of the co-inherent sacrament:

---

24 Bray makes the important observation that for Williams, "any sacrament, Christian, satanist or whatever, becomes the present realisation of the spiritual event evoked by the rite" (12). This comment shows that something like the traditional formula of *ex opere operato* ("by the work worked" or "by the very fact of the action's being performed") is present in Williams' thinking.

25 The ecumenical potential of Williams' eucharistic theology extends beyond the Western Church. Ware notes the resonances in Williams' theology with Eastern Orthodoxy. Furthermore, the potential of Grail imagery in articulating a eucharistic theology is picked up by Sergius Bulgakov, an Orthodox contemporary of Williams. Bulgakov's *The Holy Grail and the Eucharist* contains striking parallels with Williams' themes of the co-inherent nature of time and of Christ's presence at the Eucharist.

I will genuflect and adore the Presence, because it seems to me consistent with the general movement that he should so have withdrawn creation into him. On the other hand, I am shy of the arguments; the Rite which culminates in an adorable Mystery of co-inherence will serve for me! (qtd. in Hadfield 212)

There is unlimited ecumenical potential here for the divided Body of Christ if it is willing to ask: "What serves the Grail?"

Works Cited

Ashenden, Gavin. *Charles Williams: Alchemy and Integration*. Kent State UP, 2008. Print.

Barber, Richard. *The Holy Grail: Imagination and Belief*. Cambridge, MA: Harvard UP, 2004. Print.

Bradbury, J. G. "Charles Williams' Arthuriad: Mythic Vision and the Possibilities of Belief." *Journal of Inklings Studies* 1.1 (2011): 33–46. Print.

Brewer, Elizabeth. "Women in the Arthurian Poems of Charles Williams." *Charles Williams: A Celebration*. Ed. Brian Horne. Leominster, UK: Gracewing, 1995. 98–115. Print.

Bulgakov, Sergius. *The Holy Grail and the Eucharist*. Library of Russian Philosophy. Trans. Boris Yakim. Hudson, NY: Lindisfarne Books, 1997. Print.

Cavaliero, Glen. "Charles Williams and the Arthuriad: Poetry as Sacrament." *The Charles Williams Quarterly* 108 (2003): 7–17. Print.

——. *Charles Williams: Poet of Theology*. Grand Rapids, MI: Eerdmans, 1983. Print.

Doctrine in the Church of England: The Report of the Commission on Christian Doctrine Appointed by The Archbishops of Canterbury and York in 1922. 1938. London: SPCK, 1950. Print.

Göller, Karl Heinz. "From Logres to Carbonek: The Arthuriad of Charles Williams." *The Grail: A Casebook*. Ed. Dhira B. Mahoney. NY: Garland Publishing, 2000. 465–504. Print.

Gore, Charles. *The Body of Christ: An Inquiry into the Institution and Doctrine of Holy Communion*. NY: Charles Scribner's Sons, 1901. Print.

Hadfield, Alice Mary. *Charles Williams: An Exploration of His Life and Work*. Oxford UP, 1983. Print.

Horne, Brian. "He Came Down from Heaven: The Christology of Charles Williams." *The Person of Christ*. Ed. Stephen R. Holmes and Murray A. Rae. London/New York: T & T Clark International, 2005. 105–20. Print.

McAdoo, H. R., and Kenneth W. Stevenson. *The Mystery of the Eucharist in the Anglican Tradition*. Norwich: Canterbury Press, 1997. Print.

McClatchey, Joe H. "Charles Williams and the Arthurian Tradition." *VII: An Anglo-American Literary Review* 11 (1994): 51–62. Print.

McLaren, Scott. "A Problem of Morality: Sacramentalism in the Early Novels of Charles Williams." *Renascence* 56.2 (2004): 109–27. Print.

Moorman, Charles. *Arthurian Triptych: Mythic Materials in Charles Williams, C. S. Lewis, and T. S. Eliot*. Berkeley, CA: U of California P, 1960. Print.

Newman, Barbara. "Charles Williams and the Companions of the Co-inherence." *Spiritus: A Journal of Christian Spirituality* 9.1 (2009): 1–26. Print.

Ralph, George. "An Audience in Search of Charles Williams." *The Rhetoric of Vision: Essays on Charles Williams.* Ed. Charles A. Huttar and Peter J. Schakel. Lewisburg: Bucknell UP, 1996. 217–37. Print.

Ridler, Anne, ed. and intro. *The Image of the City and Other Essays* by Charles Williams. 1958. Berkeley, CA: The Apocryphile Press, 2007. Print.

Roukema, Aren. "A Veil that Reveals: Charles Williams and the Fellowship of the Rosy Cross." *Journal of Inklings Studies* 5.1 (2015): 22–71. Print.

Row, Christopher D. H. "The London Churches of Ernest Charles Shearman: St. Silas the Martyr, Anglo-Catholicism and the Modern Gothic Tradition." *Coming About: A Festschrift for John Shearman.* Ed. Lars R. Jones and Louisa C. Matthew. Cambridge, MA: Harvard U Art Museums, 2001. 349–55. Print.

Scarf, Christopher. *The Ideal of Kingship in the Writings of Charles Williams, C. S. Lewis and J. R. R. Tolkien: Divine Kingship Is Reflected in Middle-earth.* Cambridge: James Clarke, 2013. Print.

Schneider, Angelika. "A Comparison of the Treatment of the Grail Legend in Tennyson's Idylls of the King and Williams' Arthurian Cycle." *The Charles Williams Quarterly* 125 (2007): 8–22. Print.

Stout, Andrew C. "'It Can be Done, You Know': The Shape, Sources, and Seriousness of Charles Williams' Doctrine of Substituted Love." *VII: An Anglo-American Literary Review* 31 (2014). 9–29. Print.

Waite, A. E. *The Hidden Church of the Holy Graal: Its Legends and Symbolism Considered in Their Affinity with Certain Mysteries of Initiation and Other Traces of a Secret Tradition in Christian Times.* London: Rebman, 1909. Print.

Ware, Kallistos. "Sacramentalism in C. S. Lewis and Charles Williams." *C. S. Lewis and His Circle: Essays & Memoirs from the Oxford C. S. Lewis Society.* Ed. Roger White, Brendan Wolfe, and Judith Wolfe. Oxford UP, 2015. 53–64. Print.

Williams, Charles. *Arthurian Poets: Charles Williams.* Arthurian Studies 24. Ed. David Llewellyn Dodds. Woodbridge, Suffolk: The Boydell Press, 1991. Print.

——. *The Descent of the Dove: A Short History of the Holy Spirit in the Church.* 1939. Grand Rapids, MI: Eerdmans, 1980. Print.

——. "The Figure of Arthur." *Taliessin through Logres; The Region of the Summer Stars; Arthurian Torso.* By Charles Williams and C. S. Lewis. Grand Rapids, MI: Eerdmans, 1974. 189–245. Print.

——. *The Image of the City and Other Essays.* 1958. Ed. Anne Ridler. Berkeley, CA: The Apocryphile Press, 2007. Print.

——. "The Liturgy." *Image* 121–23.

——. "The Making of *Taliessin.*" *Image* 179–83.

——. "Notes on the Arthurian Myth." *Image.* 175–79.

——. *War in Heaven.* 1930. *A Charles Williams Reader.* Grand Rapids, MI: Eerdmans, 2000. Print.

——. "The Way of Exchange." *Image* 147–154.

Williams, Charles, and C. S. Lewis. *Taliessin through Logres, The Region of the Summer Stars, Arthurian Torso.* Grand Rapids, MI: Eerdmans, 1974. Print.

Conclusion—Once and Future:
The Inklings, Arthur, and Prophetic Insight

Malcolm Guite

There are many senses in which Arthur can be described as *Rex quondam, rexque futurus*: the once and future king. One of those is the way that, whatever might be the case with the historic or the mythic Arthur, the literary Arthur refuses to lie down, but is constantly revived, re-imagined, and set moving through the minds of each new generation. The deep, wide, and persistent engagement with the "Matter of Britain" by writers of the caliber of Williams, Lewis, and Tolkien, writing at the height of their powers, which this book has been exploring, is a case in point. Though all three of these writers were more than capable of making their own imaginary worlds, and two of them did so with unparalleled success, all three were nevertheless drawn again and again to the numinous worlds of Camelot and Avalon and to the intriguing and tragic figure at their heart: Arthur himself, the once and future king. Looking back over the essays in this book, which explore their involvement with the "Matter of Britain" in such depth and variety, can we get a coherent sense of what drew them to Arthur and what they made of him?

If we are to answer this question properly, we must deal at the outset with a serious misconception amongst secular literary historians as to who the Inklings were and what they were about. That misconception is that they were essentially escapist or nostalgic writers who refused to engage with modern reality, especially with the revolutions of literary Modernism, and perversely sidelined themselves into a neo-romantic backwater where they remained irrelevant—if inexplicably but perhaps culpably popular.[1] Meanwhile the "real" "mainstream" of the twentieth century, driven at a philosophical level by Marx, Freud, and Nietzsche, and at a literary level by Eliot, the Bloomsbury group, Joyce, and Beckett, carried on without them, and carried with it the only significant developments of western life and thought. The Inklings are then dismissed as having nothing relevant to say to the modern world because they are assumed never to have really engaged with it, but on the contrary to have retreated into a pseudo-mediaeval fantasy in a prolonged act of intellectual cowardice and refusal.

This patronizing and dismissive view on the part of the literary and academic establishment was dominant even when the Inklings were producing their best work and continued to hold sway until almost the

---

1   See, for example, Shippey's summary of the various dismissive accounts of Tolkien in the Foreword and
     Afterward to *Author*, vii–xxxv, 305–28.

end of the last century, bolstered by a secular-liberal distaste (acknowledged or unacknowledged) for the Christian faith that the Inklings shared, a faith which itself was seen as further evidence of their anachronistic irrelevance. Now for those who held, and hold, this view, the publication of a book detailing the extent of the Inklings' interest in and reworking of Arthurian legend might seem to confirm their worst suspicions, for of all forms of escapist and naïve nostalgia, surely a yearning for Camelot and King Arthur is both the worst and most obvious and hackneyed.

The purpose of this essay is to argue the reverse! First, to show that, far from refusing the challenges of Modernism, the Inklings were dealing with those challenges in a far-reaching and prophetic way, and that the very medium of their response—imaginative literature—was itself an essential part of their message: their prophetic critique of reductive scientism and the hermeneutics of suspicion. Second, to show that the very way they handle and rework the Arthurian material, as is clearly demonstrated in many of the essays in this book, was itself a powerful and helpful response to the deepest currents of modernism, from the terrifying eruption of mechanized warfare and slaughter on an industrial scale during the first World War to the immense questions about the future identity of humanity and basis of society posed by the reductive sciences and developments in genetics and technology, some of which they anticipated in uncanny detail. So before we survey the particular use they make of the Arthurian material, let us offer a response to the charges of evasion, escapism, or irrelevance when it comes to their engagement with the traumas and challenges of the modern world.

By common consensus, the key event that ushered in that modern world was the First World War. It is commonly remarked that the fragmentation, anomie, and constantly probing skepticism of the Modernist agenda, whilst it had some earlier philosophical roots in Nietzsche, Freud, and Marx, was really a profound and natural reaction to the carnage of the Great War; that a naïve optimism about general social progress and a grand narrative of gradual amelioration of human suffering, aided by the spread of "civilization" and religion, was blown to bits, along with so many millions of people, in the carnage of the Western Front. Eliot's line in *The Waste Land*, "these fragments I have shored against my ruins" (431), was taken as the watchword for the whole post-war literary and philosophical effort; there could be nothing but fragments and what Levi-Strauss called "bricolage" after that. But Eliot of course was not in the war, and neither were Woolf or Pound, Joyce or Beckett. The whole Bloomsbury set claimed to respond to a trauma they had not seen at first hand or lived through and to speak for people of whose experience they could have no real conception. By contrast, Lewis and Tolkien, like Sassoon and Owen, were young officers on the Western Front and experienced these things first hand. Lewis himself pointed this out in the trenchant satire of his first "post-conversion" book, *The Pilgrim's Regress*. The hero, John, meets "the Clevers": "'We lost our ideals when there was a war in this country,' said a very young Clever, 'they were ground out of us in the mud and the flood and the blood. That is why we have to be so stark and brutal'" (69). *The Pilgrim's Regress* also makes it clear that Lewis was fully familiar with the philosophical roots of Modernism in Marx, Freud, Nietzsche, and Hegel, all of whose ideas are raised and explored in the course of that narrative.

What influence did the experience of the Great War have on Lewis and Tolkien? Was their allegedly escapist fantasy-writing simply a way of evading or suppressing their experience? Certainly, they experienced trauma, but equally certainly they used imaginative literature not to evade but to deal with, move through, and learn from their experience. Tom Shippey's work on Tolkien, and particularly his book *J. R. R. Tolkien: Author of the Century*, which does so much to locate Tolkien in his twentieth-century context, has clearly shown that Tolkien should be considered (along with Orwell, Golding, Vonnegut and—interestingly—Lewis) as one of the "traumatised writers" who responded deeply to the war. He summarizes these views, helpfully, in the preface to the third edition of *The Road to Middle-earth*, his other great work of Tolkien scholarship. Having listed Tolkien along with the other writers mentioned above, he goes on to say that Tolkien was

> one of a group of … "traumatised authors", writing fantasy but voicing in that fantasy the most pressing and most immediately relevant issues of the whole monstrous twentieth century—questions of industrialised warfare, the origin of evil, the nature of humanity. (xix)

One can see the influence of the war most startlingly in some of the imagery in *The Lord of the Rings*; for instance, consider the passage of the Dead Marshes, where Frodo is drawn to the corpse-lights of the bodies in the pools and craters around him. Also, the desolation before the gates of Mordor and across the plains of Gorgoroth, with its treeless landscape of craters, mud, and poisonous fumes, seems to draw directly on memories of the Western Front. Likewise, there are passages in Lewis' poetry, both in *Spirits in Bondage* (which he wrote directly after the war and published in 1919) and the later narrative poem *Dymer*, that recall the horrors of the Great War.[2] But, as we shall see, Lewis and Tolkien do more than simply record these impressions of the devastation of war; rather, they seek, in a recovery of heroic narrative, to test how far a right understanding of heroism might be restored to us after the senseless waste and abuse of so much personal courage on the killing fields of France. They sought to get beyond the understandable despair of Wilfred Owen's "Dulce et Decorum Est," which rejects every call to heroic sacrifice as essentially a lie, and to ask, through their stories of Frodo, the children in Narnia, and (as we shall see) in Arthur, whether a chastened and renewed heroism is possible.

But Shippey is also right to observe that it wasn't simply the direct trauma of the Great War that was addressed and explored in Tolkien's fantasy. He deals with many of the other "most pressing and immediate issues" of the twentieth century—and indeed, we might add, of the twenty-first. We read the legendarium now in an era of ecological crisis, of global warming, and of anxiety about aging and body-image; we read it in an age when reductive materialism has broken everything into minute parts but can give no account of the luminous whole—and we find that every one of these issues and concerns is addressed in Tolkien's work! Further, he addresses these issues not by giving us trite formulae or pat answers, but by giving us profound emblems and symbols with which to discern and deal with our dilemmas.

Much of this is adumbrated in the conversation in *The Fellowship of the Ring* between Gandalf and Saruman when Saruman reveals his hand: "'White!' he sneered. 'It serves as a beginning. White cloth may be dyed. The white page can be overwritten; and the white light can be broken.'" Gandalf says: "And he that breaks a thing to find out what it is has left the path of wisdom" (*LotR* 2.2; 272). That strikes me as one of the wisest statements written in the twentieth century. Wordsworth, of course, described the same thing earlier:

---

2   See my essay on Lewis' poetry in *The Cambridge Companion to C. S. Lewis* (294–310).

"We murder to dissect" ("The Tables Turned" l. 28), and Keats spoke of Newton's *Opticks* as an attempt to "unweave the rainbow" ("Lamia" l. 237). Perhaps the entire effort of the Enlightenment was to break everything down, to analyze the brain, to split the atom—and then to believe that reality comprises the broken bits we've got left. But in the process, we have undone the beautiful, magical, imaginative, growing synthesis that originally made an organic whole.

It is not that we should not make analytical distinctions. But if we have only parts and no whole, we have departed from the path of wisdom. Breaking things to find out what they are made of presumes that we have the right to break them, as though they are ours, then put them back together the way we want and control them. It is an essentially mechanistic attitude toward reality. Such an outlook can ultimately lead to seeing and treating people as extensions of machines; it is interesting that Tolkien referred to both the first and second world wars as "the wars of the machines" (*Letters* 111). We take metaphors from objects we have made and apply them to ourselves, speaking of our "memory banks" or saying we are going to "reprogram" people. What a dreadful, dehumanizing thing to say about anybody. A piece of clockwork or computer work is not a good metaphor for a person.

For better metaphors, we can look at the Psalms. One of Tolkien's favorites was Psalm 1:1, 3, which reads:

> Blessed is the man that walketh not in the counsel of the ungodly, nor standeth in the way of sinners, nor sitteth in the seat of the scornful.... And he shall be like a tree planted by the rivers of water, that bringeth forth his fruit in his season; his leaf also shall not wither; and whatsoever he doeth shall prosper. (KJV)

Trees are a key image for Tolkien. We might look at the difference in worldview between Saruman and Gandalf. Gandalf related to and actually loved the Hobbits; he said: "Hobbits really are amazing creatures, as I have said before. You can learn all that there is to know about their ways in a month, and yet after a hundred years they can still surprise you at a pinch" (*LotR* I.2; 72). Gandalf displayed humility toward those whom he was sent to serve. He delighted in them—often in the midst of perfectly proper exasperation. When the Hobbits spoke to him, he discerned what they were saying, as in that moment when a frightened Frodo notes about Gollum: "What a pity that Bilbo did not stab that vile creature, when he had a chance!" And Gandalf replies: "Pity? It was Pity that stayed his hand .... My heart tells me that he has some part to play yet, for good or ill, before the end; and when that comes, the pity of Bilbo may rule the fate of many—yours not least" (*LotR* I.2; 68–69). Gandalf's approach was long-term. It was about seed-sowing and fruit-gathering. By contrast, Saruman, to borrow a phrase from the Psalm again, "sat in the seat of the scornful." He despised the Hobbits, despised Gandalf.

Again and again Tolkien's mythos invites us to confront, rather than to evade, the reality of death. Tolkien's idea of an alliance between Elves and Men allows him to explore ideas of mortality, contrasted with immortality, alongside one another and—in particular—to explore the notion that for mortal men death itself is the gift of Ilúvatar that can be accepted graciously and made blessed. The Ring represents a challenge to that grace and humility. There is a key moment in which Gandalf talks about the supposed longevity given to the wearer by the Ring, which is one reason mortal men desire it. He says: "A mortal,

Frodo, who keeps one of the Great Rings, does not die, but he does not grow or obtain more life, he merely continues, until at last every minute is a weariness" (*LotR* 1.1; 56). That is put in a homelier way by the hobbits when Bilbo says: "Why, I feel all thin, sort of stretched, if you know what I mean: like butter that has been scraped over too much bread" (*LotR* 1.1; 41).

Many people in the twenty-first century, even more so than when these words were written, will recognize that sense that we spread ourselves thin. We make a false choice. We can mistake endless iteration of minutes for fullness of life. And there is the challenge. The way we are now is characterized by cosmetic surgery; endless extensions of life by more and more elaborate, expensive, and invasive medical interventions; the assumption that we must keep going, even though, in Gandalf's phrase, "every minute is a weariness"—this motif in a supposedly escapist fantasy seems both prescient and pressing. The story of Théoden presents a recovery from such protracted, drug-ridden senility. Gandalf comes and gets him out of his wheelchair, so to speak, takes him for a walk, and says: "Come and live." It could be argued that Gandalf shortens Théoden's life. But, at his death, Théoden says: "I go to my fathers. And even in their mighty company I shall not now be ashamed" (*LotR* 5:6; 117–18). He fulfills the heart of who he was. It is a picture of life and death altogether different from the modern geriatric mentality that seeks mere continuance of bodily life at all costs.

But perhaps the single most prophetic element in *The Lord of the Rings* is the fact that it reverses the usual quest narrative, the quest to acquire a magic treasure, and becomes instead what our century most needs: a story of self-emptying and doing without. Tolkien had the complete range of Icelandic myths at his disposal, and he played with those elements beautifully in making his own myth. But he made a radical reversal, which was entirely right for his century and for ours. What we have in *The Lord of the Rings* is a glorious epic of letting go. It is about a quest to let go of something, to accept that we do not need something, to drop the Ring into the fire and be set free of destructive possession. I cannot think of a more necessary story for us today. We need to find a way of living life to the full that leaves behind our consumer culture, that does not entail the use of credit cards five or six times a day to validate our existence. We have replaced our sense of what it is to be human with the bleak affirmations of consumerism, the mere ring of the cash register.

If Lewis and Tolkien were deeply responsive to the Great War as the crisis that began the twentieth century, then Charles Williams, the other Inkling whose work is deeply engaged with the Arthurian material, was even closer to the literary, artistic, and philosophical circles of the Modernist movement. He was a friend of T. S. Eliot, who deeply admired his work and saw that it was published and republished by Faber. Indeed, it was Williams who organized the first meeting between Eliot and Lewis, who had been famously antagonistic to one another in print. The meeting was not a success, but later Eliot and Lewis reconciled and became friends, for (as I have argued in *The Cambridge Companion to C. S. Lewis*) they had a great deal in common. In his role as a proofreader, copy editor, and eventually assistant editor at Oxford University Press, Williams was exposed to all the currents of contemporary thought and had a hand in shaping the intellectual climate through his editorial advice and insights. Indeed, it was at Charles Williams' initiative and insistence that a translation of Kierkegaard's *Philosophical Fragments* and many of Kierkegaard's other works were first published in English, with an enormous and lasting influence on philosophy, theology, and poetry (Hadfield, Introduction 124–26; cf. Paulus). Likewise, Williams' own approach to writing poetry underwent a revolution, in both style and content, as a direct result of his work in helping to edit the poems of Gerard Manley Hopkins (a transformation very similar to that effected in the poetry of Williams' friend and contemporary W. B. Yeats by the influence of arch-Modernist Ezra Pound). Of course, there was a profound difference between the Inklings and the High Modernists in what they had to say about the crises and challenges of the twentieth century—and that difference is already beginning to make Tolkien seem more relevant to the twenty-first century than Joyce or Pound—but there can be no question that the Inklings were as concerned and engaged with these as the Modernists.

So, having shown that the Inklings were as much engaged with their own century as their contemporaries, as much concerned with discerning and addressing its failings as other modern writers who are praised for their "realism," let us now turn to the way the Inklings handled the Arthurian legends and see if through their retellings they are also advancing a prophetic rather than a nostalgic agenda.

The first thing to say is that the whole history of Arthurian literature is itself a history of the appropriation and retelling of old stories for new purposes, to bring out new insights or emphases that arose in the world and generation in which the story was being retold, not the one in which it was set. Holly Ordway's useful survey of the history and relations of the prime Arthurian sources makes this clear. Geoffrey of Monmouth has a very different agenda from Chrétien de Troyes, and Malory's context, in the endless bloodlettings and betrayals of fifteenth-century England, also accounts for his desire both to glimpse the ideals of the Round Table and also to narrate the tragedy of its destruction from within. What makes the Inklings' own appropriation and reshaping of the Arthurian material so fascinating is that we know how deeply aware they were, as medieval scholars, of the pre-history of their sources. Their knowledge of the ways in which the stories had already been shaped and changed and the purposes for which those changes were made in one sense gives them license and precedent for the extensive changes and developments they in turn choose to make. Readers of this book will have seen how extensive, original, and effective these were, but it is worth highlighting some of them again in this conclusion.

Let us start with Charles Williams and particularly with his fascination with the grail legend. Suzanne Bray has offered us a thorough survey of the significance of the Holy Grail in Williams' *War in Heaven* (in chapter 18 above). This novel is not only a pointer to Williams' powerful Eucharistic theology, but also to the freedom and originality with which he handled the myth. Rather than taking us back into the original setting of the grail stories, Williams gives us a contemporary setting in which, nevertheless, the pattern of the ancient narrative still emerges. So, as in Malory, there are three grail knights, but in Williams' narrative they are three modern characters who only discover and assume their roles in the course of events. This technique, in which mundane events are gradually aligned with an underlying mythic pattern that gives them meaning, owes a lot to Williams' modernism and has parallels (though with great differences of tone) with *Ulysses* and *The Waste Land*. But there is more to it for Williams; for of course the Eucharist itself is for him a mundane event that is transfigured by the fact that it conforms to an underlying mythic pattern and meaning, as time and again the particular partakes in and co-inheres with the transcendent. He writes in *War in Heaven*:

But in accord with the desire of the Church expressed in the ritual of the Church the Sacred
Elements seemed to [the Archdeacon] to open upon the Divine Nature …. Never so clearly as
now had he felt that movement proceeding, but his mind nevertheless knew no other vision than
that of a thousand dutifully celebrated Mysteries in his priestly life; so and not otherwise all things
return to God. (137)

Bray's insights are further amplified and illuminated in Stout's account of the Eucharistic theology of
Charles Williams (chapter 19); its particular relevance for this chapter, which seeks to show that the Inklings
used the Matter of Britain to engage with their times rather than to retreat from them, is that at the heart
of his theology (and so of his handling of the grail material) are Williams' notions of co-inherence, substitution, and exchange. For Williams, the Matter of Britain and the Arthurian tales, especially those that
concern "the Graal," as he called it, can never be simply about the past. At the heart of the Eucharist,
manifested in the grail, is Christ's supreme act of substitution and exchange, in which he stands in for
us and receives our pain, sorrow, and mortality in exchange for his glory and life; we in turn, receiving
that life, are enabled to bear and transfigure the pain of others into glory. He does this, always, for all
times and all places, in the same "eucharistic" moment. These ideas are perhaps most fully worked out
in Williams' non-Arthurian novel *Descent into Hell*, but they are condensed and embodied supremely in his
Arthurian poetry. They are summed up so well in the passage from the final poem of *The Region of the Summer
Stars*, "The Prayers of the Pope," in which the young pope passes from his meditation on the Magnificat
to begin the Christmas Eucharist:

> The Pope passed to sing the Christmas Eucharist.
> He invoked peace on the bodies and souls of the dead,
> yoked fast to him and he to them,
> co-inherent all in Adam and all in Christ. (300–03)

For a poet for whom all humanity is always co-inherent in both Adam and Christ, the contemplation
of any moment in history can never be a retreat into the past but must rather be a summons to a deeper
understanding of the present moment of exchange; "for History," as Williams' friend T. S. Eliot wrote,
"is a pattern / Of timeless moments" (*The Four Quartets*, "Little Gidding" 5.21–22).

These ideas are already well explored in the essays on Williams in this book, but it is worth noticing,
in this concluding chapter, one of the many other places in Williams' Arthurian poetry where his handling
of the story speaks directly to the issues of our own time. For me the most striking of these is a passage
in his poem "Bors to Elayne: On the King's Coins" about money as a medium of exchange, a real and
fair exchange of goods and labor, rather than a detached end in itself, whereby it becomes not a means of
exchange but a means of robbery and exploitation. Williams, writing in the thirties and forties after the
great crash, was only too aware that money had become an end instead of a means of exchange; he knew that
when it becomes an end, it becomes terrible. The following passage is, I think, remarkably prophetic and
has a great deal to do with what is going on now, with the creation of complex financial instruments, the

packaging and trading of high-risk loans that became so "toxic" as to bring the monetary system itself to the brink of self-destruction. Williams describes in the poem how Arthur is advised to set up and mint coins that bear the image of a dragon; he is Arthur Pendragon, so it is the King's image on the coin. Williams shows the excellence and usefulness of money as a medium of exchange:

> They laid the coins before the council.
> Kay, the king's steward, wise in economics, said:
> "Good; these cover the years and the miles
> and talk one style's dialects to London and Omsk.
> Traffic can hold now and treasure be held,
> streams are bridged and mountains of ridged space
> tunnelled; gold dances deftly across frontiers.
> The poor have choice of purchase, the rich of rents,
> and events move now in a smoother control
> than the swords of lords or the orisons of nuns.
> Money is the medium of exchange."

But Taliessin, the poet, also prophesies what would happen if the "dragons" no longer served the kingdom, the city, or the web of our exchange, but instead became dragons of greed themselves:

> Taliessin's look darkened; his hand shook
> while he touched the dragons; he said, "We had a good thought.
> Sir, if you made verse you would doubt symbols.
> I am afraid of the little loosed dragons.
> When the means are autonomous, they are deadly; when words
> escape from verse they hurry to rape souls;
> when sensation slips from intellect, expect the tyrant;
> the brood of carriers levels the good they carry.
> We have taught our images to be free; are we glad?
> are we glad to have brought convenient heresy to Logres?" (54–74)

What starts as a proper medium of exchange quickly easily becomes "a convenient heresy." For if Money stops being simply a medium of exchange and becomes autonomous, it becomes completely destructive. Then, while the poet and the steward Kay are arguing, the Archbishop speaks:

> "Might may take symbols and folly make treasure,
> and greed bid God, who hides himself for man's pleasure
> by occasion, hide himself essentially: this abides—

that the everlasting house the soul discovers

is always another's; we must lose our own ends;

we must always live in the habitation of our lovers,

my friend's shelter for me, mine for him.

This is the way of this world in the day of that other's;

make yourselves friends by means of the riches of iniquity,

for the wealth of the self is the health of the self exchanged.

What saith Heracleitus?—and what is the City's breath?—

dying each other's life, living each other's death.

Money is a medium of exchange." (75–89, emphasis original)

There are three things going on here: first, an acknowledgement of the economic convenience and benefit of money; second, an acknowledgement of how destructive the exchange of money can become when the "means become autonomous" and therefore "deadly"; and finally, the Archbishop's intervention, saying effectively: "The only way to prevent or to recover from the deadly amoral 'autonomy' of a financial system is constantly to recall and recover the difference between means and ends, constantly to remind ourselves that there is no autonomy but only a mutual interdependence, constantly to remember that 'the everlasting house of the soul is always another's. We must lose our own ends; we must always live in the habitation of our lovers."

In the midst of this "Arthurian" poem, there is a revolutionary and timely message, relevant to something right at the core of Christian faith, to the way we live and the way we love. Far from retreating into some costume-clad nostalgia, Williams is offering a prophetic and profoundly Christian critique of economics that seems even more relevant now than it was when he wrote it.

If we turn from Williams to Tolkien—the publication of whose fragment of an epic, *The Fall of Arthur*, has itself prompted this reconsideration of Arthur and the Inklings—we can also see how much he was writing from his own times into ours, shaping and reshaping the material so that it speaks directly to our own lives and conditions. Of course, we must bear in mind that we only have a fragment and not the whole of Tolkien's intended poem; nevertheless, we can see something of the way he is working. Here, Taylor Driggers' reading of *The Fall of Arthur* as a post-World War One text (chapter 10) is extremely helpful. He points out how, from the outset, Arthur's war-like adventure, urged on by Mordred's false rhetoric, is not at all glamorized, as it is, for example, in Geoffrey of Monmouth. Rather, it is subverted and exposed as folly. He also makes the interesting suggestion that Tolkien is deliberately subverting the nineteenth-century readings of Arthur, particularly Tennyson's, because he was conscious of how much the language of noble battle and chivalry had itself first been exploited and then betrayed in the propaganda that drove recruitment to the Great War. He makes this clear in this crucial passage of his essay: "Here again we have a subtle subversion of Victorian versions of the tale; whereas in Tennyson's version Arthur subdues an untamed landscape to establish his control over humanity's animalistic nature, here the effect is much more bleak and foreboding" (Driggers page 270 above).

Driggers goes on to note:

> Just as the war signified for Britain a destruction of older values and ideals in favor of an imper-
> sonal, destructive, and mechanistic society, Tolkien suggests that the "long glory" Arthur experi-
> enced during his reign and the ideals he established have now been destroyed. This is given even
> greater significance by the fact that Arthur's reckless war leaves Mordred, the embodiment of
> modern cynicism, free to assume the throne in Arthur's absence. While it would be rash to assume
> that this situation is a direct allegory or "veiled rewrite" of World War I—which Shippey calls "an
> exercise with almost no point" (*Author* 167)—it is nonetheless applicable to the cultural landscape
> Tolkien inhabited. (Driggers 273)

Indeed, one might go further and point out that just as Tolkien would later embody those aspects of the
modern world he most wished to critique in the machinations and machinery of Saruman, so in the figure
of Mordred he embodies and exposes as self-serving folly the whole Nietzschean "will to power" and the
notion of the Superman who sees himself as beyond good and evil and so above loyalty (see *FoA* 2.147–53).
As Driggers comments on this passage, though without mentioning Nietzsche:

> The chief conflict in *The Fall of Arthur*, therefore, seems to be one between medieval community and
> the modern individual's will to dominate, which Tolkien would later symbolize through the insidi-
> ous power of the Ring in *The Lord of the Rings*. (Driggers 270)

Tolkien, of course, abandoned the poem, but Driggers shows clearly how some of its prophetic or critical
motifs are taken up into *The Lord of the Rings*.

It is possible, of course, to regard the Arthurian material entirely as a branch of Faërie. We will return
at the end of this chapter to Tolkien's insights, in "On Fairy-stories," into the positive role of Recovery,
Escape, and Consolation in mythopoeic narrative. However, his own handling of the Arthurian material, at least in the fragment we have, is not Faërie Romance but much closer to grim Anglo-Saxon epic,
inflected with great pathos and an elegiac undertone (on the topic of Elegy, see chapter 8, "The Elegiac
Fantasy of Past Christendom in J. R. R. Tolkien's *The Fall of Arthur*" by Cory Lowell Grewell). In the end,
Tolkien's Arthurian poem stands not as a glorification but as a critique of battle and conquest.

Finally, let us turn to Lewis and consider the extent to which Arthurian motifs and narrative in his
work constitute a prophetic engagement with Modernity. As Brenton D. G. Dickieson's paper on intertextuality in Lewis' Arthuriana (chapter 3) makes clear, Lewis had a lifelong engagement with the "Matter
of Britain," ranging from early infatuation with the tales that led to Lewis calling his best friend Arthur
Greeves (Arthur!) "Galahad," through writing a long narrative poem on Launcelot and taking up explicit
Arthurian narrative in a modern context in *That Hideous Strength*, to the reworking and re-imagining of many
Arthurian themes and motifs in the secondary world of Narnia. In the Narniad, of course, there are no
explicitly Arthurian references, as Arthur does not exist in that world. Nevertheless, the stories and images
drawn from Malory re-emerge—and this is the topic of Jon Hooper's article, "'Lilacs Out of the Dead
Land': Narnia, The Waste Land, and the World Wars" (chapter 11). However, the material of most interest

here, at least because it draws together explicit references to the works of both Tolkien and Williams, is the emergence of Arthurian matter in *That Hideous Strength*.

That Hideous Strength has often been referred to as "a Charles Williams novel by C. S. Lewis" (Green and Hooper 174), and it is true that Williams' influence is extensive. It might even be the case that, whereas the Ransom of the first two novels is to some degree modeled on Tolkien, the Ransom of the third novel is more modeled on Williams himself, particularly in his transformative effect on others and his ability to make disciples.[3] The most obvious point of connection, particularly when it comes to the Arthurian strand, is that, like *War in Heaven*, the novel is set in the modern, immediately contemporary world, in this case after the second world war (the novel was in fact first published in 1945). Like *War in Heaven*, it concerns the emergence of a company (here explicitly called Logres) that fulfills the Arthurian pattern (like Williams' three "knights of the grail") in a contemporary way. Lewis goes further, by a turn in the plot in which Merlin himself is revived and becomes a living link between the original court of Arthur and the new Logres, the company of St. Anne's-on-the-Hill, centered around Ransom, who has become, for his own time and ours, "The Pendragon." By this device, Lewis is able to bring the ancient, mythopoeic worldview and modern, atomizing, machine-driven reductivism face to face with one another. This encounter, in Lewis' narrative, is deeply informed by his understanding of Owen Barfield's ideas about the evolution of consciousness. This is more than literary game-playing; serious issues are at stake, as Lewis makes clear in the preface: "This is a 'tall story' of devilry, though it has behind it a serious 'point' which I have tried to make in my *Abolition of Man*" (*THS* 7).

The Abolition of Man is the book in which Lewis most seriously and consistently engages what he regards as the deep evils and deadly tendencies inherent in amoral reductivism and moral subjectivism, which, together with the untrammeled will to power and the exploitation of science, could indeed bring about the abolition of man. What are we to make of *The Abolition of Man*? In a letter of 1955, twelve years after its publication, Lewis said of this little volume, "it is almost my favourite among my books but in general has been almost totally ignored by the public" (*CL* 3:566–67).

In some ways, *That Hideous Strength* was an attempt to reframe those ideas in a fictional format that would find a wider readership. For Lewis, the concept of Arthur and Logres becomes a place from which to re-assess and critique contemporary Britain; indeed, he comes up with the beautiful idea of a kind of moral "haunting"; that "Britain" is in some sense always haunted by "Logres," the vision of what it might have been or might yet be. There is not space here to go through the many levels at which Lewis' critique works or the many areas of modern life which it probes, but one of the most important is that in which the figure of Merlin plays a key role in our relation to nature and the way we do our science. In the novel, Merlin wants to awaken the soil of England, all its woods and fields, and return to a more animistic, personalised relationship, but Ransom hesitates and feels this may not still be legitimate. In *The Abolition of Man*, though, Lewis does in fact suggest that we need just such a return or recovery, and asks us to "imagine a new natural

---

3   See the chapters in this volume by Dickieson and Huttar, and also Charles Huttar's article "How Much Does *That Hideous Strength* Owe to Charles Williams?" *Sehnsucht: The C. S. Lewis Journal* 10 (2015): 19–46. [Editor's note]

philosophy, or regenerate science." He says that a true science would treat all elements of creation with respect, honoring their natures while studying them. Science would not lose its soul while it gained knowledge (see *Abolition* 47). This is the approach represented by Merlin in the novel. As Dimble says:

> Merlin is the reverse of Belbury. He's at the opposite extreme. He is the last vestige of an old order in which matter and spirit were, from our modern point of view, confused. For him every operation on nature is a kind of personal contact, like coaxing a child or stroking one's horse. After him came the modern man to whom nature is something dead—a machine to be worked, and taken to bits if it won't work the way he pleases .... In a sense, Merlin represents what we've got to get back to in some different way. (*THS* 352–53)

Both these books were written in the nineteen forties, before the current ecological crisis, before the emergence of ideas like the Gaia hypothesis or "deep ecology," but one can see how the writings of this group (once thought naïve, "escapist" and backward-looking) anticipated and can inform contemporary debate and exploration. Indeed, it would be good, in conclusion, to remind ourselves of Tolkien's radical rereading of the charge of "escapism" in the great passage on "Recovery, Escape, and Consolation" in "On Fairy-stories." There, he talks of just such a "recovery" of deeper vision in relation to nature as Lewis speaks of and in almost the same terms:

> the story maker who allows himself to be free with nature can be her lover and not her slave. It was in fairy stories that I first divined the potency of the words, and the wonder of the things, such as stone, and wood, and iron; tree and grass; house and fire; bread and wine. (OFS 59–60)

Tolkien famously takes the word "escapism" and flings it back in the teeth of his accusers: "Why should a man be scorned, if, finding himself in prison, he tries to get out and go home? Or if, when he cannot do so he thinks and talks about other topics than jailers and prison walls?" (OFS 60). He then goes on to show that the person who has "escaped" and imagined a better place can reveal the prison for what it was and set a course that others may follow to freedom.

In the one direct and playful reference to King Arthur in the Narniad, Lewis refers to the return of King Peter to Narnia in the reign of Prince Caspian as being like the return of Arthur to England: "When the Pevensie children had returned to Narnia last time for the second visit, it was (for the Narnians) and as if King Arthur had come back to Britain, as some people say he will. And I say the sooner the better" (*VDT* 15). Lewis the author steps out from the narrative for a moment and plays with the idea of Arthur as *Rex quondam, rexque futurus*; just as, in *That Hideous Strength,* he imagined a succession of "Pendragons" of whom Ransom is the latest, who in some sense keep the vision of Logres alive. Whichever way one might choose to imagine a return of Arthur, the contents of this book make it clear that, for the Inklings at least, he had never really gone away. Furthermore, it is clear that he is also in some sense "Rex"; in the Story of Arthur, in both his rise and fall, in both the forming and the betrayal of the Round Table, the Inklings found material not only for escape and consolation, but most profoundly, for recovery: a recovery of vision that they believed to be vital for their own generation and that has proved to be prophetically relevant for ours.

Works Cited

Bray, Suzanne, and Richard Sturch, eds. *Charles Williams and His Contemporaries*. Cambridge Scholars Publishing, 2009. Print.

Green, Roger Lancelyn, and Walter Hooper. *C. S. Lewis: A Biography*. NY: Harcourt Brace Jovanovich, 1974. Print.

Guite, Malcolm. "Poet." *The Cambridge Companion to C. S. Lewis*. Ed. Robert MacSwain and Michael Ward. Cambridge UP, 2010. 294–310. Print.

Hadfield, Alice Mary. *An Introduction to Charles Williams*. London: Robert Hale, 1959. Print.

Lewis, C. S. *The Abolition of Man*. London: Geoffrey Bles, 1946. Print.

——. *The Collected Letters of C. S. Lewis*. 3 vols. Ed. Walter Hooper. London: HarperSanFrancisco, 2004–07. Print.

——. *The Pilgrim's Regress: An Allegorical Apology for Christianity, Reason and Romanticism*. Glasgow: Collins, 1933. Print.

——. *That Hideous Strength: A Modern Fairy-Tale for Grown-Ups*. 1945. London: The Bodley Head, 1969. Print.

——. *The Voyage of the "Dawn Treader."* 1952. London: William Collins, 1974. Print.

Paulus, Michael. "From a Publisher's Point of View: Charles Williams' Role in Publishing Kierkegaard in English." Bray and Sturch 20–41.

Shippey, Tom. *J. R. R. Tolkien: Author of the Century*. London: HarperCollins, 2000. Print.

——. *The Road to Middle-earth*. Expanded ed. London: HarperCollins, 2005. Print.

Tolkien, J. R. R. *The Fall of Arthur*. Ed. Christopher Tolkien. London: HarperCollins, 2013. Print.

——. "On Fairy-stories." *Tree and Leaf*. London: HarperCollins, 2001. 59–60. Print.

——. *The Lord of the Rings*. 1954–55. 2nd ed. Boston: Houghton Mifflin, 1965. Print

——. *Tree and Leaf*. London: HarperCollins, 2001. Print.

Tolkien, J. R. R. *The Letters of J. R. R. Tolkien*. Ed. Humphrey Carpenter. Boston: Houghton Mifflin, 1981. Print.

Williams, Charles. *Arthurian Poets: Charles Williams*. Arthurian Studies 24. Ed. David Llewellyn Dodds. Woodbridge, Suffolk: The Boydell Press. 1991. Print.

Bibliographies

Arthurian Sources

This bibliography contains citations for all non-Inklings Arthurian works referenced throughout the volume. Editions are those used by the various chapter-writers throughout the text, which means that there are multiple editions listed of some of the works, and no attempt has been made to list first editions.

Alliterative Morte Arthure. Trans. Valerie Krishna. *The Romance of Arthur: An Anthology of Medieval Texts in Translation*. Ed. James J. Wilhelm. NY: Garland Publishing, 1994. 491–527.

"Aotrou Nann Hag Ar Gorrigan." *Barzaz-Breiz: Chants Populaires de La Bretagne*. Ed. Théodore Hersart de la Villemarqué. Vol. 1. 2nd ed. Paris: A. Franck, 1846. 40–45.

Chrétien de Troyes. *Arthurian Romances*. Trans. William W. Kibler and Carleton W. Carroll. London: Penguin, 1991.

——. *The Complete Romances of Chrétien de Troyes*. Trans. David Staines. 1990. Bloomington and Indianapolis, IN: Indiana UP, 1993.

Eliot, T. S. "The Waste Land." *Selected Poems*. London: Faber & Faber, 1976.

Geoffrey of Monmouth. *The History of the Kings of Britain*. Trans. Lewis Thorpe. NY: Penguin, 1966.

——. *Vita Merlini*. Trans. Basil Clarke. Cardiff, U of Wales P, 1973.

Gerald of Wales. "The Tomb of King Arthur." Trans. John Sutton. *The Camelot Project: A Robbins Library Digital Project*. U of Rochester, 2001.

——. *The Journey Through Wales and The Description of Wales*. Ed. and trans. Lewis Thorpe. 1978. NY: Penguin, 2004.

Gildas. *The Works of Gildas. Old English Chronicles*. Ed. J. A. Giles. London: George Bell and Sons, 1901. 293–380.

The High History of the Holy Grail. Trans. Sebastian Evans. *Camelot On-line*.

King Arthur's Death: The Middle English Stanzaic Morte Arthur *and* Alliterative Morte Arthure. Ed. Larry D. Benson. Rev. Edward E. Foster. TEAMS Middle English Text Series. Kalamazoo: Medieval Institute Publications, 1994.

Lancelot-Grail: The Old French Arthurian Vulgate and Post-Vulgate in Translation. Ed. Norris J. Lacy. 9 vols. Cambridge: D. S. Brewer, 2010.

Laȝamon. *Laȝamon's "Arthur": The Arthurian Section of Laȝamon's "Brut" (lines 9229–14297)*. Ed. and trans. W. R. J. Barron and S. C. Weinberg. Essex: Longman Group UK Limited, 1989. Rpt. U of Exeter, 2001.

——. *Laȝamon's Brut: A History of the Britons*. Trans. Donald G. Bzdyl. Binghamton, NY: Medieval and Renaissance Texts and Studies, 1989.

——. *Laȝamons Brut, or Chronicle of Britain*. Ed. and trans. Sir Frederic Madden. Vols. 2 and 3. London: The Society of Antiquaries of London, 1847.

The Mabinogion. Trans. Jeffrey Gantz. NY: Penguin, 1976.

Machen, Arthur. *The Great Return*. London: The Faith House, 1915.

——. *The Secret Glory*. London: Martin Secker, 1922.

Malory, Sir Thomas. *Works*. Ed. Eugène Vinaver. Oxford: Clarendon Press, 1947.

Map, Walter. *La Quest del Saint Grael*. Ed. F. J. Furnivall. London: Roxburgh Club, 1864.

Marie de France. *The Lais of Marie de France*. Ed. and trans. Robert Hanning and Joan Ferrante. Grand Rapids, MI: Baker Academic, 2008.

Navigatio Sancti Brendani Abbatis from Early Latin Manuscripts. Ed. Carl Selmer. Publications in Medieval Studies 16. U of Notre Dame P, 1959.

Nennius. *Nennius: British History and the Welsh Annals*. Arthurian Sources 8. Ed. and trans. John Morris. London and Chichester: Phillimore, 1980.

——. *Nennius' History of the Britons*. *Old English Chronicles*. Ed. J. A. Giles. London: George Bell and Sons, 1901. 381–416.

The Quest of the Holy Grail. Trans. W. W. Comfort. Old French Series. Cambridge, Ontario: In Parenthesis Publications, 2000.

The Saga of Hrolf Kraki. Trans. Stella M. Mills and E. V. Gordon. 1933. Marcellus, MI: Nodens Books, 2012.

Sir Gawain and the Green Knight. Ed. and trans. William Vantuono. 1990. Rev. ed. U of Notre Dame Press, 1999.

Sir Gawain and the Green Knight. Trans. Simon Armitage. NY: Norton, 2007.

Stanzaic Le Morte Arthur, King Arthur's Death: Alliterative Morte Arthure and Stanzaic Le Morte Arthur. NY: Penguin, 1988.

Steinbeck, John. *The Acts of King Arthur and His Noble Knights*. NY: Farrar, Straus, and Giroux, 1970.

Tennyson, Alfred. *Idylls of the King*. Ed. J. M. Gray. 1983. NY: Penguin, 1996.

——. *The Poetic and Dramatic Works*. Boston: Houghton, Mifflin, 1898.

Trioedd Ynys Prydein: The Welsh Triads. Ed and trans. Rachel Bromwich. 1961. 2nd ed. Cardiff: U of Wales Press, 1978.

Underhill, Evelyn. *The Column of Dust* (1909). London: Hardpress Publishing, 2010.

Von Eschenbach, Wolfram. *Parzival*. Trans. A. T. Hatto. London: Penguin, 1980.

Wace. *Arthurian Chronicles: Roman de Brut*. Trans. Eugene Mason. *The Internet Archive*.

Wolfram von Eschenbach. *Parzival; And, Titurel*. Trans. Cyril W. Edwards. Oxford UP, 2006.

Works by the Inklings

This bibliography contains citations to first editions of all works by C. S. Lewis, J. R. R. Tolkien, Charles Williams, and Owen Barfield referenced throughout the volume, as well as works by others who attended meetings of "The Inklings" (according to Appendix A, "Biographical notes," in Humphrey Carpenter's The Inklings*)—even though such a rigid definition of an "Inkling" is admittedly problematic—and also by George MacDonald and G. K. Chesterton., whose direct influence on the Inklings and creative similarities have often been noted (and who otherwise would not fit into these three bibliographies).*

Barfield, Owen. "Ballade." www.owenbarfield.org.

——. "Either : Or." *Imagination and the Spirit: Essays in Literature and the Christian Faith Presented to Clyde S. Kilby.* Ed. Charles A. Huttar. Grand Rapids, MI: Eerdmans, 1971. 25–48.

——. *Eager Spring.* Barfield Press UK, 2009.

——. *History in English Words.* London: Methuen, 1926.

——. *Night Operation.* Barfield Press UK, 2009.

——. *Owen Barfield on C. S. Lewis.* Ed. G. B. Tennyson. Middletown, CT: Wesleyan UP, 1989.

——. *Poetic Diction: A Study in Meaning.* London: Faber & Gwyer, 1928.

——. *The Quest of the Sangreal.* TS. Dep. c. 1101. ml#barfield.C.1. Bodleian Library, Oxford University. Oxford, UK.

——. *Romanticism Comes of Age.* London: Anthroposophical Publishing, 1944.

——. *Saving the Appearances: A Study in Idolatry.* London: Faber & Faber, 1957.

——. *Speaker's Meaning.* London: Rudolf Steiner Press, 1967.

Barfield, Owen, and C. S. Lewis. *Mark vs. Tristram: Correspondence between C. S. Lewis & Owen Barfield.* Cambridge: Lowell House Printers, 1967. Cf. Lewis, *CL* 2:780–86.

Bennett, J. A. W., ed. *Essays on Malory.* Oxford: Clarendon Press, 1963.

Bennett, J. A. W., and Douglas Gray. *The Oxford History of English Literature: Middle English Literature: 1100–1400.* Oxford: Clarendon Press, 1986.

Cecil, David. "Oxford's Magic Circle." *Books and Bookmen* 24.4. (1979): 10–12.

Chesterton, G. K. "The Ballad of King Arthur." *Collected Poetry*, Part 1. *The Collected Works of G. K. Chesterton* 10. San Francisco: Ignatius, 1994. 531–533.

——. *The Ballad of the White Horse.* London: John Lane, 1911.

——. *Charles Dickens.* NY: Dodd, Mead, 1911.

——. *The Collected Works of G. K. Chesterton.* San Francisco: Ignatius, 1986–2012. 27 vols.

——. *The Defendant.* NY: Dodd, Mead; London: R. Brimley Johnson, 1902.

——. *The Everlasting Man.* London: Hodder & Stoughton, 1925.

——. "The Grave of Arthur." *Collected Poetry*, Part 1. *The Collected Works of G. K. Chesterton* 10. San Francisco: Ignatius, 1994. 542–543.

——. "King Arthur: Myth and History." *Illustrated London News 1920–22. The Collected Works of G. K. Chesterton* 32. San Francisco: Ignatius, 1989. 502–06.

——. "Modern Elfland." *Collected Poetry*, Part 1. *The Collected Works of G. K. Chesterton* 10. San Francisco: Ignatius, 1994. 233–234.

——. "The Myth of Arthur." *Collected Poetry*, Part 1. *The Collected Works of G. K. Chesterton* 10. San Francisco: Ignatius, 1994. 555–556.

——. *The Napoleon of Notting Hill*. London: The Bodley Head, 1904.

——. *Orthodoxy*. London: The Bodley Head, 1909.

——. *A Short History of England*. *The Collected Works of G. K. Chesterton* 20. San Francisco: Ignatius, 2001.

——. *What's Wrong with the World*. London: Cassell, 1910.

Green, Roger Lancelyn. *King Arthur and his Knights of the Round Table*. London: Puffin, 1953.

Green, Roger Lancelyn, and Walter Hooper. *C. S. Lewis: A Biography*. New York and London: Harcourt Brace Jovanovich, 1974.

Lewis, C. S. *The Abolition of Man*. London: Geoffrey Bles, 1946.

——. *All My Road Before Me: The Diary of C. S. Lewis 1922–1927*. Ed. Walter Hooper. London: Harvest, 1991.

——. *The Allegory of Love: A Study in Medieval Tradition*. London: Oxford UP, 1936.

——. "The Anthropological Approach." *English and Medieval Studies: Presented to J. R. R. Tolkien on the Occasion of his Seventieth Birthday*. Eds. Norman David and C. L. Wrenn. London: Allen & Unwin, 1962. 219–23.

——. "*Arthuriana: Arthurian Literature in the Middle Ages: A Collaborative Study*, ed. R. S. Loomis." *Image and Imagination* 217–22.

——. *Christian Reflections*. Ed. Walter Hooper. Grand Rapids, MI: Eerdmans, 2003.

——. *The Collected Letters of C. S. Lewis*. 3 vols. Ed. Walter Hooper. NY: HarperCollins, 2004–07.

——. *The Collected Poems of C. S. Lewis*. Ed. Walter Hooper. London: HarperCollins, 1994.

——. *The Dark Tower and Other Stories*. Ed. Walter Hooper. London: Fount, 1977.

——. "De Descriptione Temporum." Inaugural Lecture from the Chair of Mediaeval and Renaissance Literature at Cambridge University. Cambridge: Cambridge UP, 1954. *Internet Archive*. archive.org. 12 July 2014.

——. *The Discarded Image: An Introduction to Medieval and Renaissance Literature*. Cambridge UP, 1964.

——. *Dymer: A Poem*. London: J. M. Dent and Sons, 1950.

——. *English Literature in the Sixteenth Century, Excluding Drama*. Oxford History of English Literature 3. Oxford UP, 1954.

——. *Essay Collection and Other Short Pieces*. Ed. Lesley Walmsley. London: HarperCollins, 2000.

——. *Fern-seed and Elephants: And Other Essays on Christianity*. Ed. Walter Hooper. Glasgow: Fontana, 1975.

——. *The Four Loves*. NY: Harcourt Brace Jovanovich, 1960.

——. *God in the Dock: Essays on Theology and Ethics*. Grand Rapids, MI: Eerdmans, 1970.

——. "The Gods Return to Earth." 1954. www.theonering.com.

——. *The Great Divorce*. London: Bles/Centenary Press, 1945.

——. *The Horse and His Boy*. London, Geoffrey Bles, 1954.

——. *Image and Imagination*. Ed. Walter Hooper. Cambridge UP, 2103.

——. Introduction. *Selections from Laȝamon's Brut*. Ed. G. L. Brook. Oxford: Clarendon Press, 1963. vii–xv.

——. *The Last Battle*. London: The Bodley Head, 1956.

——. *The Lion, the Witch and the Wardrobe*. London, Geoffrey Bles, 1950.

——. *The Magician's Nephew*. London: The Bodley Head, 1955.

——. *Mere Christianity*. London and New York: MacMillan, 1952.

——. *Miracles: A Preliminary Study*. London: Bles/Centenary Press. 1947.

——. *Narrative Poems*. Ed. Walter Hooper. New York and London: Harcourt Brace Jovanovich, 1969.

——. *Of Other Worlds: Essays and Stories*. Ed. Walter Hooper. NY: Harcourt, Brace, and World, 1967.

——. *Of This and Other Worlds*. Ed. Walter Hooper. London: Collins, 1982.

——. *On Stories: And Other Essays on Literature*. Ed. Walter Hooper. San Diego, New York, London: Harcourt, Brace & Company, 1982.

——. *Out of the Silent Planet*. London: The Bodley Head, 1938.

——. *Perelandra*. London: The Bodley Head, 1943.

——. *The Pilgrim's Regress: An Allegorical Apology for Christianity, Reason and Romanticism*. Glasgow: Collins, 1933.

——. *A Preface to* Paradise Lost. Oxford UP, 1942.

——. *Present Concerns*. Ed. Walter Hooper. San Diego: Harcourt, Brace, Jonavovich, 1986.

——. *Prince Caspian*. London, Geoffrey Bles, 1951.

——. "The Quest of Bleheris." MS. Eng. lett. c. 220/5. Bodleian Library, Oxford University. Oxford, UK.

——. *Rehabilitations and Other Essays*. London/New York: Oxford UP, 1939.

——. *The Screwtape Letters*. London: Geoffrey Bless, 1942.

——. *Selected Literary Essays*. Ed. Walter Hooper. Cambridge: Cambridge UP, 1969.

——. *The Silver Chair*. London: Geoffrey Bless, 1953.

——. *Spenser's Images of Life*. Ed. Alastair Fowler. Cambridge UP, 1967.

——. *Spirits in Bondage: A Cycle of Lyrics*. 1919. Ed. Walter Hooper. NY: Harcourt Brace Jovanovich, 1984.

——. *Studies in Medieval and Renaissance Literature*. Ed. Walter Hooper. Cambridge UP, 1998.

——. *Studies in Words*. Cambridge UP, 1960.

——. *Surprised by Joy: The Shape of My Early Life*. London: Geoffrey Bles, 1955.

——. *That Hideous Strength: A Modern Fairy-Tale for Grown-Ups*. London: The Bodley Head, 1945.

——. *That Hideous Strength*. c. 1943–44. MS. CSL/MS-119/B, Marion E. Wade Center, Wheaton College. Wheaton, IL.

——. *They Asked for a Paper: Papers and Addresses*. London: Geoffrey Bles, 1962.

——. *Till We Have Faces: A Myth Retold*. London: Geoffrey Bles, 1956.

——. *The Voyage of the "Dawn Treader."* London, Geoffrey Bles, 1952.

——. *The Weight of Glory and Other Addresses*. London: SPCK, 1942.

——. "Williams and the Arthuriad." *Arthurian Torso*. Ed. C. S. Lewis. London: Oxford UP, 1948. 91–200.

——, ed. *Essays Presented to Charles Williams*. Oxford UP, 1947.

——, ed. *George MacDonald: An Anthology*. London: Geoffrey Bles, 1946.

Lewis, C. S., and Owen Barfield. *Mark vs. Tristram: Correspondence between C. S. Lewis & Owen Barfield*. Cambridge: Lowell House Printers, 1967. Cf. Lewis, *CL* 2:780–86.

Lewis, Warren. *Letters of C. S. Lewis*. Ed. W. H. Lewis. NY: Harcourt, Brace & World, 1966.

MacDonald, George. "The Sangreal: A Part of the Story Omitted in the Old Romances." *Good Words* 4 (1863): 454–55.

——. *A Dish of Orts*. Whitefish, MT: Kessinger, 2004.

——. *An Expression of Character: The Letters of George MacDonald*. Ed. Glenn Sadler. Grand Rapids, MI: Eerdmans, 1994.

——. *Annals of a Quiet Neighbourhood*. London: Kegan Paul, Trench, Trübner, n.d.

——. *England's Antiphon*. London: MacMillan & Co, 1868.

——. Letter to Stanley Unwin. 6 April 1924. MS. Greville MacDonald Papers. Marion E. Wade Center, Wheaton College. Wheaton, IL.

——. *Lilith*. 1895. Whitehorn, CA: Johannesen, 1995.

——. *Marquis of Lossie*. Vol. 2. London: Hurst & Blackett, 1877.

——. *Phantastes: A Faerie Romance for Men and Women*. London: Smith, Elder, 1858.

——. *The Poetical Works of George MacDonald*. London: Chatto & Windus, 1893.

——. *The Seaboard Parish*. NY: George Routledge & Sons, 1876.

——. *The Vicar's Daughter*. Kila, MT: Kessinger Publishing, 2004.

——. *Wilfrid Cumbermede: An Autobiographical Story*. Vol. 2. NY: Charles Scribner, 1872.

Tolkien, J. R. R. *Beowulf: A Translation and Commentary together with Sellic Spell*. Ed. Christopher Tolkien. Boston: Houghton Mifflin Harcourt, 2014.

——. *Beowulf and the Critics*. Ed. Michael Drout. Tempe, AZ: Arizona Center for Medieval and Renaissance Studies, 2002.

——. *The Book of Lost Tales*. The History of Middle-earth 1–2. Ed. Christopher Tolkien. 2 vols. Boston: Houghton Mifflin, 1984.

——. *The Children of Húrin*. Ed. Christopher Tolkien. Boston and New York: Houghton Mifflin, 2007.

——. *The Fall of Arthur*. Ed. Christopher Tolkien. Boston: Houghton Mifflin Harcourt; London: HarperCollins, 2013.

——. *Farmer Giles of Ham*. London: Allen & Unwin, 1949.

——. *The Hobbit*. London: Allen & Unwin, 1937.

——. "The Lay of Aotrou and Itroun." *The Welsh Review* 4.4 (1945): 254–66.

——. *The Lays of Beleriand*. The History of Middle-earth 3. Ed. Christopher Tolkien. Boston: Houghton Mifflin, 1985.

——. *The Legend of Sigurd and Gudrún*. Ed. Christopher Tolkien. Boston and New York: Houghton Mifflin Harcourt, 2009.

——. *The Letters of J. R. R. Tolkien*. Ed. Humphrey Carpenter. Boston: Houghton Mifflin, 1981.

——. *The Lord of the Rings*. London: Allen & Unwin, 1954–55.

——. *The Lost Road and Other Writings*. The History of Middle-earth 5. Ed. Christopher Tolkien. NY: Random House/DelRay; Boston: Houghton Mifflin, 1987.

——. *The Monsters and the Critics and Other Essays*. Ed. Christopher Tolkien. London: Allen & Unwin, 1983.

——. *Morgoth's Ring*. The History of Middle-earth 10. Ed. Christopher Tolkien. Boston: Houghton Mifflin, 1993.

——. "On Fairy-Stories." *Essays Presented to Charles Williams*. Ed. C. S. Lewis. London: Oxford UP, 1947. 38–89.

——. *The Peoples of Middle-earth*. The History of Middle-earth 12. Ed. Christopher Tolkien. Boston: Houghton Mifflin, 1996.

——. *The Return of the Shadow*. The History of Middle-earth 6. Ed. Christopher Tolkien. Boston: Houghton Mifflin, 1988.

——. *Roverandom*. Ed. Christina Scull and Wayne G. Hammond. Boston: Houghton Mifflin, 1998.

——. *Sauron Defeated*. The History of Middle-earth 9. Ed. Christopher Tolkien. Boston: Houghton Mifflin, 1992.

——. *The Silmarillion*. Boston: Houghton Mifflin, 1977.

——. *The Story of Kullervo*. Ed. Verlyn Flieger. London: HarperCollins, 2015.

——. *The Tolkien Reader*. NY: Ballantine, 1966.

——. *Tolkien on Fairy-stories: Expanded Edition with Commentary and Notes*. Ed. Verlyn Flieger and Douglas Anderson. London: HarperCollins, 2008.

——. *Tree and Leaf*. London: HarperCollins, 2001.

——. *Unfinished Tales of Númenor and Middle-earth*. Ed. Christopher Tolkien. Boston: Houghton Mifflin, 1980.

Tolkien, J. R. R., trans. *Sir Gawain and the Green Knight, Pearl, Sir Orfeo*. Boston: Houghton Mifflin, 1975.

Tolkien, J. R. R., and E. V. Gordon, eds. *Sir Gawain and the Green Knight*. Oxford: Clarendon Press, 1925.

Williams, Charles. *All Hallows' Eve*. London: Faber and Faber, 1945.

——. *Arthurian Commonplace Book*. MS. Eng. e. 2012 (as "Notes on the Holy Grail"). Bodleian Library, Oxford University. Oxford, UK.

——. *Arthurian Poets: Charles Williams*. Arthurian Studies 24. Ed. David Llewellyn Dodds. Woodbridge, Suffolk: Boydell & Brewer, 1991.

——. *The Chapel of the Thorn: A Dramatic Poem*. Ed. Sørina Higgins. Berkeley, CA: Apocryphile Press, 2014.

——. "Charles Williams on *Taliessin through Logres*." CW/MS-2, CW/MS-166, CW/MS-415. Marion E. Wade Center, Wheaton College. Wheaton, IL. Rpt. *Poetry Review* 32 (1941), 77–81. Rpt. *Gnomon* 1 (1965), 37–45.

——. *Collected Plays*. London: Oxford UP, 1963.

——. *Descent into Hell*. London: Faber & Faber, 1937.

——. *The Descent of the Dove: A Short History of the Holy Spirit in the Church*. London: Longmans, Green, 1939.

——. *Divorce*. London: Oxford UP, 1920.

——. *The Figure of Beatrice: A Study of Dante*. London: Faber & Faber, 1943.

——. *He Came Down from Heaven*. London: Heinemann, 1938.

——. *Heroes and Kings*. London: Sylvan Press, 1930.

——. *The Image of the City and Other Essays*. Ed. Anne Ridler. London: Oxford UP, 1958.

——. Introduction. *The Letters of Evelyn Underhill*. London: Longmans, 1943.

——. *Many Dimensions*. London: Victor Gollancz, 1931.

——. *The Masque of the Manuscript*. MS. 1927 Hadfield Collection, Box 2 Book 10 (uncatalogued). Bodleian Library, Oxford University. Oxford, UK.

——. *The Masque of the Termination of Copyright*. 1930. CW/MS-413. Marion E. Wade Center, Wheaton College. Wheaton, IL.

——. *The Masques of Amen House*. Ed. David Bratman. Altadena, CA: The Mythopoeic Press, 2000.

——. *To Michal from Serge: Letters from Charles Williams to His Wife, Florence, 1939–1945*. Ed. Roma A. King. Kent State UP, 2002.

——. *Outlines of Romantic Theology; with Which Is Reprinted, Religion and Love in Dante: The Theology of Romantic Love*. Ed. Alice Mary. Hadfield. Grand Rapids, MI: Eerdmans, 1990.

——. "Prince Rudolph of Silvania." CW/MS-113. Marion E. Wade Center, Wheaton College. Wheaton, IL.

——. *Poems of Conformity*. London: Oxford UP, 1917.

——. *The Region of the Summer Stars*. Editions Poetry London, 1944.

——. *Seed of Adam and Other Plays by Charles Williams*. Ed. Anne Ridler. London: Oxford UP, 1948.

——. *Shadows of Ecstasy*. London: Gollancz, 1933.

——. *Taliessin through Logres*. London: Oxford UP, 1938.

——. *The Way of Exchange*. London: James Clarke, 1941.

——. *Three Plays*. London: Oxford UP, 1931.

——. *War in Heaven*. London: Faber & Faber, 1930.

——. *Windows of Night*. London: Oxford UP, 1924.

Williams, Charles, and Lois Lang-Sims. *Letters to Lalage: The Letters of Charles Williams to Lois Lang-Sims*. Kent State UP, 1989.

Wrenn, Charles Leslie. *A Study of Old English Literature*. NY: Norton, 1967.

Wrenn, C. L., and Norman David, eds. *English and Medieval Studies: Presented to J. R. R. Tolkien on the Occasion of his Seventieth Birthday*. London: Allen & Unwin, 1962.

Secondary Studies

Here are citations for sources that examine either the Arthurian legends, the works of the Inklings, or both. This includes most of the scholarly works on either Arthurian literature or the writings of the Inklings referenced throughout the volume. They have been chosen because they either are cited by more than one chapter or have been deemed by the editor to be significant for this field of study. Articles in periodicals are generally listed here; articles contained in essay collections, however, are not listed individually unless there is one article of significance in an otherwise unused volume.

Aeschliman, Michael D. *The Restitution of Man: C. S. Lewis and the Case Against Scientism*. Grand Rapids, MI: Eerdmans, 1998.

Alcock, Leslie. *Arthur's Britain: History and Archaeology* AD *367–634*. Harmondsworth: Penguin/Pelican, 1973.

Archibald, Elizabeth, and Ad Putter, eds. *The Cambridge Companion to the Arthurian Legend*. Cambridge UP, 2009.

Armstrong, Dorsey. "Postcolonial Palomides: Malory's Saracen Knight and the Unmaking of Arthurian Community." *Exemplaria* 18.1 (2006): 175–203.

Ashe, Geoffrey. *Camelot and the Vision of Albion*. NY: St. Martin's Press, 1971.

——. *The Discovery of King Arthur*. Garden City, NY: Anchor Press, Doubleday, 1985.

——. *Mythology of the British Isles*. North Pomfret, VT: Trafalgar, 1990.

Ashe, Geoffrey, et al. *The Quest for Arthur's Britain*. NY: Praeger, 1968.

Ashenden, Gavin. *Charles Williams: Alchemy and Integration*. Kent State UP, 2008.

Ashley, Mike. *The Mammoth Book of King Arthur*. London: Robinson, 2005.

Barber, Richard. *The Holy Grail: Imagination and Belief*. London: Penguin, 2004; Cambridge, MA: Harvard UP, 2004.

Barczewski, Stephanie. *Myth and National Identity in Nineteenth-Century Britain: The Legends of King Arthur and Robin Hood*. Oxford UP, 2000.

Barrett, Justin L. "Some Planets in Narnia: A Quantitative Investigation of the *Planet Narnia* Thesis." *VII: An Anglo-American Literary Review* 27 (2010): 1–18.

Barron, W. R. J. *The Arthur of the English: Arthurian Literature in the Middle Ages*. 2 vols. Cardiff: U of Wales Press, 1999.

Baswell, Christopher, and William Sharpe, eds. *The Passing of Arthur: New Essays in Arthurian Tradition*. NY: Garland, 1988.

Battis, Jes. "Gazing Upon Sauron: Hobbits, Elves, and the Queering of Post-Colonial Optic." *Modern Fiction Studies* 50.4 (2004): 908–26.

Bennett, J. A. W., ed. *Essays on Malory*. Oxford: Clarendon Press, 1963.

Bennett, J. A. W., and Douglas Gray. *The Oxford History of English Literature: Middle English Literature: 1100–1400*. Oxford: Clarendon Press, 1986.

Bethlehem, Ulrike. *Guinevere, a Medieval Puzzle: Images of Arthur's Queen in the Medieval Literature of England and France*. Diss. Universität Bochum, 2001. Heidelberg: Winter, 2005.

Biddle, Martin. "The Painting of the Table." *King Arthur's Round Table: An Archaeological Investigation*. Ed. Martin Biddle and Sally Badham. Woodbridge: The Boydell Press, 2000. 425–74.

Blamires, Harry. "Against the Stream: C. S. Lewis and the Literary Scene." *Journal of the Irish Christian Study Centre* I (1983): 15.

Blaxland-de Lange, Simon. *Owen Barfield: Romanticism Come of Age: A Biography.* Forest Row, UK: Temple Lodge Publishing, 2006.

Bosky, Bernadette. Introduction. *The Masques of Amen House.* By Charles Williams. Ed. David Bratman. Altadena, CA: The Mythopoeic Press, 2000. 1–30.

Boughton, Brenda. "The Role of the Slave in Charles Williams' Poetry: A Talk Presented to the Charles Williams Society's Annual General Meeting on 11 May 1991." *The Charles Williams Society Newsletter* 61 (1991): 7–20.

Bradbury, J. G. "Charles Williams' Arthuriad: Mythic Vision and the Possibilities of Belief." *Journal of Inklings Studies* 1.1 (2011). 33–46.

Bray, Suzanne, and Richard Sturch, eds. *Charles Williams and His Contemporaries.* Cambridge Scholars Publishing, 2009.

Bromwich, Rachel, ed. *Trioedd Ynys Prydein: The Welsh Triads.* Cardiff: U of Wales, 1961.

Brown, Clay. *C. S. Lewis and Postmodernism: Areas of Convergence and Divergence.* Ph.D. Diss. Trinity Theological Seminary, 2005.

Bryden, Inga. *Reinventing Arthur: The Arthurian Legends in Victorian Culture.* London: Ashgate, 2005.

Buckman, Ty, and Charles Ross. "An Arthurian Omaggio to Michael Murrin and James Nohrnberg." *Arthuriana* 21.1 (2011): 3–6. *Project Muse.*

Burns, Marjorie. *Perilous Realms: Celtic and Norse in Tolkien's Middle-earth.* 2005. 2nd ed. Toronto: U of Toronto Press, 2008.

Burrow, John. *A History of Histories: Epics, Chronicles, Romances and Inquiries from Herodotus and Thucydides to the Twentieth Century.* NY: Alfred A. Knopf, 2008.

Byrne, Aisling. "The King's Champion: Re-Enacting Arthurian Romance at the English Coronation Banquet." *English Studies* 94.5 (2013): 505–18.

Caldecott, Stratford. "Tolkien's Elvish England." *The Chesterton Review* 31.3 (2005): 109–23.

——. *Secret Fire: The Spiritual Vision of J. R. R. Tolkien.* London: Darton, Longman, and Todd, 2003.

Carpenter, Humphrey. *The Inklings: C. S. Lewis, J. R. R. Tolkien, Charles Williams, and Their Friends.* Boston: Houghton Mifflin, 1978.

——. *Tolkien: A Biography.* Boston: Houghton Mifflin and NY: Ballantine, 1977.

Carter, Susan. "Galadriel and Morgan le Fey: Tolkien's Redemption of the Lady of the Lacuna." *Mythlore* 25.3/4 (2007): 71–89.

Cavaliero, Glen. "Charles Williams and the Arthuriad: Poetry as Sacrament." *The Charles Williams Quarterly* 108 (2003): 7–17.

——. *Charles Williams: Poet of Theology.* Eugene, OR: Wipf and Stock; Grand Rapids, MI: William B. Eerdmans, 1983.

——. Introduction. *Letters to Lalage: The Letters of Charles Williams to Lois Lang-Sims.* By Lois Lang-Sims and Charles Williams. Kent State UP, 1989. 1–14.

Cavendish, Richard. *King Arthur and the Grail: The Arthurian Legends and their Meaning.* NY: Taplinger, 1978.

Chambers, E. K. *Arthur of Britain*. London: Sidgwick & Jackson, 1927.

——. *The Oxford History of English Literature: English Literature at the Close of the Middle Ages*. Oxford: Clarendon Press, 1945.

Chance, Jane, ed. *Tolkien the Medievalist*. Routledge Studies in Medieval Religion and Culture. NY: Routledge, 2003.

Chance, Jane, and Alfred K. Siewers, eds. *Tolkien's Modern Middle Ages*. Basingstoke: Palgrave Macmillan, 2005.

Christopher, Joe R. "Mount Purgatory Arises near Narnia." *Mythlore* 23.2 (2001): 65–90.

——. "C. S. Lewis' Lost Arthurian Poem: A Conjectural Essay." *Inklings Forever* 8 (2012). 1–11.

——. "John Heath-Stubbs' *Artorius* and the Influence of Charles Williams." *Mythlore* 48–50 (1986–87): 56–62, 51–57, 51–57.

Collingwood, R. G., and J. N. L. Myers. *Roman Britain and the English Settlements*. Oxford: Clarendon Press, 1936.

Como, James T., ed. *C. S. Lewis at the Breakfast Table*. NY: Harvest, 1992.

Croft, Janet Brennan, ed. *Tolkien and Shakespeare: Essays on Shared Themes and Language*. Jefferson, NC: Walking Tree, 2007.

——. *War and the Works of J.R.R. Tolkien*. Westport, CT: Praeger, 2004.

Cross, Tom Peete, and William Albert Nitze. *Lancelot and Guenevere: A Study on the Origins of Courtly Love*. 1930. NY: Phaeton, 1970.

Crowley, Cornelius P. *A Study of the Meaning and Symbolism of the Arthurian Poetry of Charles Williams*. Ph.D. Diss. U of Michigan, 1952.

Curry, Patrick. *Defending Middle-earth: Tolkien: Myth and Modernity*. NY: Houghton Mifflin, 2004.

Curtis, Jan. "Byzantium and the Matter of Britain: The Narrative Framework of Charles Williams' Later Arthurian Poems." *Quondam et Futurus: A Journal of Arthurian Interpretations* 2.1 (1992): 28–54.

——. "Charles Williams' 'The Sister of Percivale': Toward a Theology of 'Theotokos.'" *Quondam et Futurus: A Journal of Arthurian Interpretations* 2.4 (1992): 56–72.

Deloux, Jean-Pierre. "Introduction to Charles Williams." *La Guerre du Graal*. Paris: Terrain Vague, 1989. i–ix.

Dickerson, Matthew T. *Following Gandalf: Epic Battles and Moral Victory in* The Lord of the Rings. Grand Rapids, MI: Brazos Press, 2003.

Dickerson, Matthew T., and Jonathan D. Evans. *Ents, Elves, and Eriador: The Environmental Vision of J. R. R. Tolkien*. U of Kentucky, 2006.

Dickieson, Brenton D. G. "The Unpublished Preface to C. S. Lewis' *The Screwtape Letters*." *Notes and Queries* 60.2 (2013): 296–98.

Dodds, David Llewellyn, ed. and intro. *Arthurian Poets: Charles Williams*. Arthurian Studies 24. Rochester, NY: Boydell & Brewer, 1991.

——. "*The Chapel of the Thorn*: An unknown dramatic poem by C. Williams." *Inklings Jarbuch* 5 (1987): 133–52. Rpt. in *Chapel of the Thorn*. Ed. Sørina Higgins. Berkeley: Apocryphile Press, 2014. 123–39.

——. "Charles Williams, Arthurian Commonplace Book." Unpublished introduction.

Doughan, David. "An Ethnically Cleansed Faery? Tolkien and the Matter of Britain." *Mallorn* 32 (1995): 21–24.

Downing, David C. "'The Dungeon of his Soul': Lewis' Unfinished 'Quest of Bleheris.'" *VII: An Anglo-American Literary Review* 15 (1998): 37–54.

——. "C. S. Lewis Among the Postmodernists." *Books and Culture* November/December 1998.

——. *Into the Region of Awe.* Downers Grove, IL: InterVarsity Press, 2005.

——. *Planets in Peril: A Critical Study of C. S. Lewis' Ransom Trilogy.* Amherst, MA: U of Massachusetts Press, 1992.

Driggers, Taylor. "Modern Medievalism and Myth: Tolkien, Tennyson, and the Quest for a Hero." *Journal of Inklings Studies* 3.2 (2013): 133–52.

Duriez, Colin. *The A–Z of C. S. Lewis: An Encyclopedia of His Life, Thought, and Writings.* Oxford: Lion Books, 2013.

——. *Tolkien and C. S. Lewis: The Gift of Friendship.* Mahwah, NJ: Paulist Press, 2003.

Edwards, Bruce L., ed. *C. S. Lewis: Life, Works, and Legacy.* 4 vols. Westport: Praeger, 2007.

Edwards, Raymond. *Tolkien.* Robert Hale, 2015.

Eggers, John Philip. "The Weeding of the Garden: Tennyson's Geraint Idylls and *The Mabinogion*." *Victorian Poetry* 4.1 (Winter 1966): 45–51.

Ekman, Stefan. *Here Be Dragons: Exploring Fantasy Maps and Settings.* Wesleyan University Press, 2013.

Eliot, T. S. "The Significance of Charles Williams." *The Listener* 19 December 1946.

Ellis, Jim. "Kenilworth, King Arthur, and the Memory of Empire." *English Literary Renaissance* 43.1 (2013): 3–29.

Enright, Nancy. "Tolkien's Females and the Defining of Power." *Renascence Essays on Values in Literature* 50.2 (2007): 93–108.

Escobedo, Andrew. "The Tudor Search for Arthur and the Poetics of Historical Loss." *Exemplaria* 14.1 (2002): 127–65.

Fenster, Thelma S., ed. *Arthurian Women: A Casebook.* Garland Reference Library of the Humanities. Vol. 1499. NY: Garland Publishing, 1996.

Fenwick, Mac. "Breastplates of Silk: Homeric Women in *The Lord of the Rings*." *Mythlore* 21.3 (1996): 17–23, 50.

Filmer, Kath, ed. *Twentieth-Century Fantasists: Essays on Culture, Society and Belief in Twentieth-Century Mythopoeic Literature.* London: Macmillan; New York: St. Martin's, 1992.

Fimi, Dimitra. "'Mad Elves' and 'Elusive Beauty': Some Celtic Strands of Tolkien's Mythology." *Folklore* 117.2 (2006): 156–70.

——. "Tolkien's '"Celtic" Type of Legends': Merging Traditions." *Tolkien Studies* 4 (2007). 51–71.

Finke, Laurie A., and Martin B. Shichtman. *King Arthur and the Myth of History.* Gainesville: UP Florida, 2004.

Finn, Richard J. "Arthur and Aragorn: Arthurian Influence in *The Lord of the Rings*." *Mallorn: The Journal of the Tolkien Society* 43 (2005): 23–26.

Flieger, Verlyn. "J. R. R. Tolkien and the Matter of Britain." *Mythlore* 87 (2000): 47–59.

——. *A Question of Time: J. R. R. Tolkien's Road to Faërie.* Kent State UP, 1997.

——. *Splintered Light: Logos and Language in Tolkien's World.* 1983. 2nd ed. Kent State UP, 2002.

——. "The Fall of Arthur by J. R. R. Tolkien." Tolkien Studies 11.1 (2014): 213–25.

——, ed. *Green Suns and Faërie: Essays on J.R.R. Tolkien.* Kent State UP, 2012.

——, ed. *The Story of Kullervo* by J. R. R. Tolkien. London: HarperCollins, 2015.

Flieger, Verlyn, and Douglas A. Anderson, eds. *Tolkien on Fairy-Stories: Expanded Edition with Commentary and Notes.* London: HarperCollins, 2008.

Fredrick, Candice, and Sam McBride. *Women Among the Inklings: Gender, C.S. Lewis, J.R.R. Tolkien, and Charles Williams.* Contributions in Women's Studies 191. Westport, CT: Greenwood Press, 2001.

Fulton, Helen, ed. *A Companion to Arthurian Literature.* Chichester, West Sussex: Blackwell, 2009.

Fussell, Paul. *The Great War and Modern Memory.* NY: Oxford UP, 1975.

Gaertner, Christopher Bennett. *The Interplay of Logos and Tao in Tolkien's* The Lord of the Rings *and its Chinese Translations.* Master's thesis, Southwest Jiaotong University, 2007.

Garth, John. "'The Road from Adaptation to Invention': How Tolkien Came to the Brink of Middle-earth in 1914." *Tolkien Studies* 11 (2014): 1–44.

——. *Tolkien and the Great War: The Threshold of Middle-earth.* NY: HarperCollins and Boston: Houghton Mifflin, 2003.

——. "Tolkien's Unfinished Epic: 'The Fall of Arthur.'" *The Daily Beast* 23 May 2013.

Gauntlett, Edward. "Charles Williams, Love and Shekinah." *The Charles Williams Quarterly* 126 (2008): 8–29.

Glyer, Diana Pavlac. *The Company They Keep: C. S. Lewis and J. R. R. Tolkien as Writers in Community.* Kent State UP, 2007.

——. "'We are *All* Fallen Creatures and *All* Very Hard to Live With': Some Thoughts on Lewis and Gender." *Christian Scholar's Review* 36.4 (2007): 477–83.

Goebel, Stefan. *The Great War and Medieval Memory: War, Remembrance and Medievalism in Britain and Germany, 1914–1940.* Cambridge UP, 2007.

Goller, Karl Heinz. "From Logres to Carbonek: The Arthuriad of Charles Williams." *Arthurian Literature* 1 (1981): 121–73.

GoodKnight, Bonnie. *Scene from "Imram."* Mythlore 4.2 (1976): 1–2.

Goodrich, Peter H. "Saracens and Islamic Alterity in Malory's 'Le Morte Darthur.'" *Arthuriana* 16.4 (2006): 10–28.

Goodrich, Peter H., and Raymond H. Thompson, eds. *Merlin: A Casebook.* NY: Routledge, 2003.

Gordon-Wise, Barbara Ann. *The Reclamation of a Queen: Guinevere in Modern Fantasy.* Westport, CT: Greenwood Press, 1991.

Gossedge, Rob. "'The Old Order Changeth': Arthurian Literary Production from Tennyson to White." Ph.D. Diss. Cardiff U. 2007.

Green, Roger Lancelyn, and Walter Hooper. *C. S. Lewis: A Biography.* New York and London: Harcourt Brace Jovanovich, 1974.

Grewell, Cory. "'It's All One': Medievalist Synthesis and Christian Apology in Owen Barfield's Studies of Meaning." *Journal of Inklings Studies* 3.2 (2013): 11–40.

——. "Medievalist Fantasies of Christendom." *Journal of Inklings Studies* 3.2 (2013): 3–10.

——. "Neomedievalism: An Eleventh Little Middle Ages?" *Studies in Medievalism* 19 (2010): 34–43.

Grimaldi, Angela. "Owen Barfield's Marginalia in Sir Thomas Malory's *Le Morte d'Arthur.*" *Renascence* 63/1 (2010): 55–82.

Guite, Malcolm. "The Inklings: Fantasists or Prophets?" St. Edward King and Martyr, Cambridge, UK. November 2011.

Hadfield, Alice Mary. *Charles Williams: An Exploration of His Life and Work.* Oxford UP, 1983.

——. *An Introduction to Charles Williams.* London: Robert Hale, 1959.

Haldane, J. B. S. "Auld Hornie, F. R. S." *Modern Quarterly* 1 (1946): 32–40.

Hale, Amy. "The Land Near the Dark Cornish Sea: The Development of Tintagel as a Celtic Pilgrimage Site." *Journal for the Academic Study of Magic* 2 (2004): 206–25.

Halsall, Guy. *Worlds of Arthur: Facts and Fictions of the Dark Ages*. Oxford UP, 2013.

Hanks, D. Thomas Jr. "'A Far Green Country Under a Swift Sunrise': Tolkien's Eucatastrophe and Malory's *Morte Darthur*." *Fifteenth-Century Studies*. Vol. 36. Eds. Barbara L. Gusick and Matthew Z. Heintzelman. Rochester, NY: Camden House, 2011. 49–64.

Hannay, Margaret. "Arthurian and Cosmic Myth in *That Hideous Strength*." *Mythlore* 2.2 (1970): 7–9.

Higgins, Sørina. "Arthurian Geographies in Tolkien, Williams and Lewis." *The Bulletin of the New York C. S. Lewis Society* 45.4 (2014): 1–8.

——. "Double Affirmation: Medievalism as Christian Apologetic in the Arthurian Poetry of Charles Williams." *Journal of Inklings Studies* 3.2 (2013): 59–96.

——. "Is a 'Christian' Mystery Story Possible? Charles Williams' *War in Heaven* as a Generic Case Study." *Mythlore* 30:1/2 (2011). 77–90.

——, ed and intro. *The Chapel of the Thorn*. By Charles Williams. Berkeley, CA: Apocryphile Press, 2014.

Higham, N. J. *King Arthur: Myth-Making and History*. London, New York: Routledge, 2002.

Hilder, Monika B. *The Gender Dance: Ironic Subversion in C. S. Lewis' Cosmic Trilogy*. NY: Peter Lang, 2013.

Hiley, Margaret. *The Loss and the Silence: Aspects of Modernism in the Works of C. S. Lewis, J. R. R. Tolkien and Charles Williams*. Zurich: Walking Tree Publishers, 2011.

Hiley, Margaret, and Frank Weinreich, eds. *Tolkien's Shorter Works*. Zurich, Jena: Walking Tree, 2008.

Hill, Victor E. "The Christian Vision of Charles Williams." *The Charles Williams Quarterly* 131 (2009): 5–17.

Hooper, Walter. *C. S. Lewis: A Companion and Guide*. NY: HarperSanFrancisco, 1996.

——. "The Lectures of C. S. Lewis in the Universities of Oxford and Cambridge." *Christian Scholar's Review* 27.4 (1998): 436–53.

Hopkins, Lisa. "Female Authority Figures in the Works of Tolkien, C.S. Lewis, and Charles Williams." *Mythlore* 21.2 (1996): 364–66.

Horne, Brian. "He Came Down from Heaven: The Christology of Charles Williams." *The Person of Christ*. Ed. Stephen R. Holmes and Murray A. Rae. London/New York: T & T Clark International, 2005. 105–20.

——, ed. *Charles Williams: A Celebration*. Leominster, UK: Gracewing, 1995.

Howard, Thomas. *The Novels of Charles Williams*. Eugene, OR: Wipf and Stock, 1991.

Huttar, Charles A. "'Deep lies the sea-longing': Inklings of Home." *Mythlore* 26.1–2 (2007): 5–27.

——. "How Much Does *That Hideous Strength* Owe to Charles Williams?" *Sehnsucht: The C. S. Lewis Journal* 10 (2015): 19–46.

——. "What C. S. Lewis Really Did to 'Cupid and Psyche.'" *Sehnsucht: The C. S. Lewis Journal* 3 (2009): 33–49.

Huttar, Charles A., and Peter J. Schakel. *The Rhetoric of Vision: Essays on Charles Williams*. Lewisville: Bucknell UP, 1996.

Ingham, Patricia Clare. *Sovereign Fantasies: Arthurian Romance and the Making of Britain*. Philadelphia: U of Pennsylvania P, 2001.

Ingledew, Francis. *Sir Gawain and the Green Knight and the Order of the Garter*. U of Notre Dame P, 2006.

Jenkins, Elizabeth. *The Mystery of Arthur*. NY: Coward, McCann, and Geoghegan, 1975.

Jensen, Todd. "Tolkien and Arthurian Legend," *Beyond Bree* (1988): n.p.

Karlson, Henry. "Vox Nova At The Library: Owen Barfield's *Eager Spring*." *Vox Nova: Catholic Perspectives on Culture, Society, and Politics*.

Kaufman, Amy S. "Guenevere Burning." *Arthuriana* 20.1 (2010): 76–94.

Kelly, A. Keith, and Michael Livingston. "'A Far Green Country': Tolkien, Paradise, and the End of All Things in Medieval Literature." *Mythlore* 27.3/4 (2009): 83–102.

Kennedy, Edward Donald. *King Arthur: A Casebook*. London: Routledge, 2013.

Kilby, Clyde. *Tolkien and the Silmarillion*. Chicago: Harold Shaw Publishers, 1976.

King, Don W. *C. S. Lewis, The Poet: The Legacy of his Poetic Impulse*. Kent State UP, 2001.

——. "Lost but Found: The 'Missing' Poems of C. S. Lewis' *Spirits in Bondage*." *Christianity and Literature* 53.2 (2004): 163–201.

——. *Plain to the Inward Eye*. Abilene, TX: Abilene Christian UP, 2013.

King, Roma A. *The Pattern in the Web: The Mythical Poetry of Charles Williams*. Kent State UP, 1990.

Kocher, Paul H. *Master of Middle-earth: The Fiction of J. R. R. Tolkien*. Boston: Houghton Mifflin, 1972.

——. *Reader's Guide to the Silmarillion*. NY: Houghton Mifflin, 1980.

Korrel, Peter. *An Arthurian Triangle: A Study of the Origin, Development and Characterization of Arthur, Guinevere and Modred*. Leiden: E. J. Brill, 1984.

Kreeft, Peter. *The Philosophy of Tolkien*. San Francisco: Ignatius Press, 2005.

Lacon, Ruth. "On *The Fall of Arthur*: Pre-Publication Speculation By a Longtime Student." *Tolkien Library* 20 March 2013.

Lacy, Norris J., ed. *The Arthurian Encyclopedia*. NY: Garland, 1986.

——, ed. *The Fortunes of King Arthur*. Cambridge: D. S. Brewer, 2005.

——, ed. *Lancelot-Grail: The Old French Arthurian Vulgate and Post-Vulgate in Translation*. Vol. 3. NY: Garland, 1993–96.

Lacy, Norris J., and Geoffrey Ashe. *The Arthurian Handbook*. New York, London: Garland, 1988.

Lagorio, Valerie M., and Mildred Leake Day, eds. *King Arthur through the Ages*. NY: Garland, 1990.

Lindop, Grevel. *Charles Williams: The Third Inkling*. Oxford UP, 2015.

Lindskoog, Kathryn. *The C. S. Lewis Hoax*. Portland: Multnomah Press, 1988.

Lobdell, Jared. *The Scientifiction Novels of C. S. Lewis: Space and Time in the Ransom Stories*. London: McFarland, 2004.

——. *The World of the Rings: Language, Religion, and Adventure in Tolkien*. Chicago and La Salle, IL: 2004.

Loconte, Joseph. *A Hobbit, a Wardrobe, and a Great War: How J. R. R. Tolkien and C. S. Lewis Rediscovered Faith, Friendship, and Heroism in the Cataclysm of 1914–1918*. Nashville, Thomas Nelson, 2015.

Loewenstein, Andrea Freud. *Loathsome Jews and Engulfing Women: Metaphors of Projection in the Works of Wyndham Lewis, Charles Williams, and Graham Greene*. NYU Press, 1993.

Loomis, Roger Sherman. *Celtic Myth and Arthurian Romance*. NY: Haskell House, 1967.

——. *The Development of Arthurian Romance*. Mineola, NY: Dover Publications, 2000.

——. *Wales and the Arthurian Legend*. Cardiff: U of Wales Press, 1956.

——, Ed. *Arthurian Literature in the Middle Ages: A Collaborative History*. Oxford UP, 1959.

Lupack, Alan. *The Oxford Guide to Arthurian Literature and Legend*. Oxford UP, 2005.

Lutton, Jeannette Hume. "Wasteland Myth in C. S. Lewis' *That Hideous Strength*." *Forms of the Fantastic: Selected Essays from the Third International Conference on the Fantastic in Literature and Film*. Ed. Jan Hokenson and Howard Pearce. Contributions to the Study of Science Fiction and Fantasy 20. New York; Westport; London: Greenwood Press, 1986. 69–86.

MacDonald, Greville. *George MacDonald and His Wife*. London: Allen & Unwin, 1924.

——. *The Religious Sense in its Scientific Aspect*. London: Hodder and Stoughton, 1904.

MacSwain, Robert, and Michael Ward, eds. *The Cambridge Companion to C. S. Lewis*. Cambridge UP, 2010.

Mahoney, Dhira B., ed. *The Grail Casebook*. New York, London: Garland, 2000.

Malone, Kemp. "Artorius." *Modern Philology* 22 (1925): 367–74.

——. *The Historicity of Arthur*. Urbana: U of Illinois, 1924.

Markale, Jean. *Merlin: Priest of Nature*. Trans. Belle N. Burke. Rochester, VT: Inner Traditions International, 1995.

Marshall, Ashley. "Reframing Charles Williams: Modernist Doubt and the Crisis of World War in *All Hallows' Eve*." *Journal of Modern Literature* 30.2 (2007): 64–85.

Martin, Thomas L. "Merlin, Magic, and the Meta-fantastic: The Matter of *That Hideous Strength*." *Arthuriana* 21.1 (2011): 66–84.

Matarasso, P. M. Introduction. *The Quest of the Holy Grail*. Trans. P. M. Matarasso. Harmondsworth, Middlesex: Penguin, 1969. 11–12.

McClatchey, Joe H. "Charles Williams and the Arthurian Tradition." *VII: An Anglo-American Literary Review* 1 (1980): 51–62.

McCleary, Joseph. *The Historical Imagination of G. K. Chesterton: Locality, Patriotism, and Nationalism*. NY: Routledge, 2009.

McGrath, Alister. *C. S. Lewis: A Life*. Carol Streams: Tyndale House, 2013.

——. *The Intellectual World of C. S. Lewis*. Oxford: Wiley & Sons, 2014.

McGuire, Ian. "Epistemology and Empire in 'Idylls of the King.'" *Victorian Poetry* 30.3/4, (1992): 387–400.

McKusker, Paul. *C. S. Lewis and Mere Christianity: The Crisis That Created a Classic*. Carol Stream: Tyndale, 2014.

McLaren, Scott. "A Problem of Morality: Sacramentalism in the Early Novels of Charles Williams." *Renascence* 56.2 (2004): 109–27.

Merriman, James Douglas. *A Study of the Arthurian Legend in England between 1485 and 1835*. UP Kansas, 1973.

Moorman, Charles. *Arthurian Triptych: Mythic Materials in Charles Williams, C. S. Lewis, and T. S. Eliot*. Berkeley, CA: U of California P, 1960.

Morris, Rosemary. *The Character of King Arthur in Medieval Literature*. Bury St Edmunds: St. Edumundsbury Press, 1982.

Moynihan, Martin. "C. S. Lewis and the Arthurian Tradition." *Inklings Jahrbuch fuer Literatur und Aesthetik* 1 (1983). 21–41.

Myers, Doris T. *Bareface: A Guide to C. S. Lewis' Last Novel*. Columbia: U of Missouri P, 2004.

——. "Brave New World: The Status of Women According to Tolkien, Lewis, and Charles Williams." *Cimarron Review* 17 (1971): 13–19.

——. *C. S. Lewis in Context*. Kent State UP, 1994.

Newman, Barbara. "Charles Williams and the Companions of the Co-inherence." *Spiritus: A Journal of Christian Spirituality* 9.1 (2009): 1–26.

Noble, Peter. "Arthur, Anti-Fascist or Pirate King?" *Quondam et Futurus* 3.3 (1993): 46–54.

Nutt, Alfred. *Studies on the Legend of the Holy Grail.* London: D. Nutt, 1888.

Olsen, Corey. *Exploring J. R. R. Tolkien's* The Hobbit. NY: Houghton-Mifflin, 2012.

Parry, John Jay. "The Historical Arthur." *Journal of English and Germanic Philology* 58 (1959): 331–35.

Pearce, Joseph. *Tolkien: A Celebration: Collected Writings on a Literary Legacy.* San Francisco: Ignatius Press, 2001.

Pearsall, Derek. *Arthurian Romance: A Short Introduction.* Oxford: Blackwell, 2003.

Petitpas, Harold. "Chesterton's Metapoetics." *Renascence* 23.3 (1971): 137–44.

Phelpstead, Carl. *Tolkien and Wales: Language, Literature, and Identity.* Cardiff: U of Wales Press, 2011.

Poe, Harry Lee. "C.S. Lewis Was a Secret Government Agent." *Christianity Today* 10 December 2015.

Pratt, Linda Ray. "Subversion and Revival of a Tradition in Tennyson and T. S. Eliot." *Victorian Poetry* 11 (1973): 307–21.

Rateliff, John D. "The Fall of Arthur." *Sacnoth's Scriptorium* 23 May 2013.

——. "The Lost Letter: Seeking the Keys to Williams' Arthuriad." *Mythlore* 34.1 (2015). Email correspondence with Sørina Higgins. 7 September 2015.

——. "'That Seems to Me Fatal': Pagan and Christian in *The Fall of Arthur.*" Unpublished. Email correspondence with Sørina Higgins. 19 June 2015.

——. Introduction. *Eager Spring.* By Owen Barfield. Barfield Press UK, 2009. ix–xiii.

Rawls, Melanie. "The Feminine Principle in Tolkien." *Mythlore* 10.4 (1984): 5–13.

Reichenbach, Bruce. "C. S. Lewis and the Desolation of Devalued Science." *VII: An Anglo-American Literary Review* 4 (1983): 14–26.

Reid, Margaret J. C. *The Arthurian Legend: Comparison of Treatment in Modern and Mediæval Literature.* Edinburgh: Oliver & Boyd, 1938.

Reilly, R. J. *Romantic Religion: A Study of Owen Barfield, C. S. Lewis, Charles Williams, J. R. R. Tolkien.* Great Barrington, MA: Lindisfarne Books, 2006.

Reynolds, Patricia, and Glen H. GoodKnight, eds. *Proceedings of the J.R.R. Tolkien Centenary Conference, Keble College, Oxford, 1992. Mythlore* 21.2; *Mallorn* 30. Milton Keynes, U.K.: Tolkien Society; Altadena, CA: Mythopoeic Press, 1995.

Rhŷs, John. *Studies in the Arthurian Legend.* Oxford: Clarendon Press, 1891.

Rich, Janet Bubar. *Exploring Guinevere's Search for Authenticity in the Arthurian Romances.* Lewiston, NY: Edwin Mellen, 2012.

Ridler, Anne, ed. and intro. *The Image of the City and Other Essays* by Charles Williams. London: Oxford UP, 1958.

Roukema, Aren. "A Veil that Reveals: Charles Williams and the Fellowship of the Rosy Cross." *Journal of Inklings Studies* 5.1 (2015): 22–71.

Rovang, Paul. *Malory's Anatomy of Chivalry: Characterization in the Morte Darthur.* Lanham, MD: Fairleigh Dickinson UP, 2015.

Russell, Mariann. "Elements of the Idea of the City in Charles Williams' Arthurian Poetry." *Mythlore* 6.4 (1979): 10–16.

Ryan, J. S. "Uncouth Innocence: Some Links between Chrétien de Troyes, Wolfram von Eschenbach and J. R. R. Tolkien." *Inklings Jahrbuch fuer Literatur und Aesthetik* 2 (1984): 25–41.

Saklatvala, Beram. *Arthur: Roman Britain's Last Champion*. NY: Taplinger, 1967.

Sammons, Martha C. *A Far-off Country: A Guide to C. S. Lewis' Fantasy Fiction*. Lanham, MD: UP of America, 2000.

Sarot, Marcel. "The Cardinal Difficulty for Naturalism: C. S. Lewis' Argument Reconsidered in Light of Peter van Inwagen's Critique." *Journal of Inklings Studies* 1.2 (2011): 41–53.

Sayer, George. *Jack: A Life of C. S. Lewis*. 2nd ed. Wheaton, IL: Crossway Books, 1994.

Scarf, Christopher. *The Ideal of Kingship in the Writings of Charles Williams, C. S. Lewis and J. R. R. Tolkien: Divine Kingship Is Reflected in Middle-earth*. Cambridge, UK: James Clarke, 2013.

Schakel, Peter J., and Charles A. Huttar, eds. *Word and Story in C. S. Lewis*. Columbia, MO: U of Missouri Press, 1991.

Schneider, Angelika. "A Comparison of the Treatment of the Grail Legend in Tennyson's *Idylls of the King* and Williams' Arthurian Cycle." *The Charles Williams Quarterly* 125 (2007): 8–22.

Schwartz, David. *The Third Spring: G. K. Chesterton, Graham Greene, Christopher Dawson and David Jones*. Washington: Catholic U of America P, 2012.

Schwartz, Joseph. "The Theology of History in *The Everlasting Man*." *Renascence* 49.1 (1996): 57–66.

Schwartz, Stanford. *C. S. Lewis on the Final Frontier: Science and the Supernatural in the Space Trilogy*. Oxford UP, 2009.

Scull, Christina, and Wayne G. Hammond. *The J. R. R. Tolkien Companion and Guide*. 2 vols. Boston, New York: Houghton Mifflin, 2006.

——. The Lord of the Rings: *A Reader's Companion*. Boston and New York: Houghton Mifflin, 2005.

Shideler, Mary M. *The Theology of Romantic Love: A Study in the Writings of Charles Williams*. Grand Rapids, MI: Eerdmans, 1962.

——. Introduction. *Taliessin through Logres*. By Charles Williams. Grand Rapids, MI: Eerdmans, 1974. 5–17.

Shippey, Tom. *J. R. R. Tolkien: Author of the Century*. Boston: Houghton Mifflin; London: HarperCollins, 2000.

——. "Medievalisms and Why They Matter." *Studies in Medievalism* I (2009): 46–54.

——. *The Road to Middle-earth*. Boston: Houghton Mifflin, 1982.

Simpson, Roger. "King Arthur in World War Two Poetry: His Finest Hour?" *Arthuriana* 13.1 (2003). 66–91.

——. *Camelot Regained: The Arthurian Revival and Tennyson, 1800–1849*. Cambridge: D. S. Brewer, 1990.

Slack, Anna, ed. *Doors in the Air: C. S. Lewis and the Imaginative World*. Vitoria, Spain: Portal Editions, 2010.

Starr, Nathan Comfort. *King Arthur Today: The Arthurian Legend in English and American Literature 1901–1953*. Gainesville: U of Florida P, 1954.

Stimpson, Catherine R. *J.R.R. Tolkien*. Columbia Essays on Modern Writers. Vol. 41. NY: Columbia UP, 1969.

Stone, Brian. Introduction. *Stanzaic Le Morte Arthur*. King Arthur's Death. Trans. Brian Stone. NY: Penguin, 1988.

Stout, Adam. "Grounding Faith at Glastonbury: Episodes in the Early History of Alternative Archaeology." *Numen* 59 (2012): 249–69.

Stout, Andrew C. "'It Can be Done, You Know': The Shape, Sources, and Seriousness of Charles Williams' Doctrine of Substituted Love." *VII: An Anglo-American Literary Review* 31 (2014). 9–29.

Sturch, Richard. "Charles Williams as Heretic?" *Charles Williams Quarterly* 136 (2010): 7–19.

Tolhurst, Fiona. *Geoffrey of Monmouth and the Feminist Origins of the Arthurian Legend.* NY: Palgrave Macmillan, 2012.

Vale, Juliet. *Edward III and Chivalry: Chivalric Society and Its Context, 1270–1350.* Woodbridge, Suffolk: Boydell Press, 1982.

Van Leeuwen, Mary Stewart. *A Sword between the Sexes? C. S. Lewis and the Gender Debates.* Grand Rapids, MI: Brazos, 2010.

Vaninskaya, Anna. "'My mother, drunk or sober': G. K. Chesterton and Patriotic Anti-imperialism." *History of European Ideas* 34 (2008): 535–47.

Versinger, Georgette. *Charles Williams, sa vie, son œuvre.* Professorial thesis. Paris: Université de la Sorbonne Nouvelle, 2004.

Waite, A. E. *The Hidden Church of the Holy Graal: Its Legends and Symbolism Considered in Their Affinity with Certain Mysteries of Initiation and Other Traces of a Secret Tradition in Christian Times.* London: Rebman, 1909.

Walker, Mark. Introduction. *Geoffrey of Monmouth's Life of Merlin.* Stroud, Gloucestershire: Amberley, 2011.

Walsh, Chad. *The Literary Legacy of C. S. Lewis.* NY: Harcourt Brace Jovanovich, 1979.

Walters, Lori J., ed. *Lancelot and Guinevere: A Casebook.* Garland Reference Library of the Humanities. Vol. 1513. NY: Garland, 1996.

Ward, Michael. *Planet Narnia: The Seven Heavens in the Imagination of C. S. Lewis.* Oxford UP, 2008.

Warren, Michelle R. "Making Contact: Postcolonial Perspectives through Geoffrey of Monmouth's *Historia Regum Britannie*." *Arthuriana* 8.4 (1998): 115–34. JSTOR. 14 October 2014.

Wendling, Susan. "Charles Williams: Priest of the Co-inherence." *Inklings Forever* 5 (2006).

West, John G, ed. *The Magician's Twin: C. S. Lewis on Science, Scientism, and Society.* Seattle: Discovery Institute Press, 2012.

Weston, Jessie L. *From Ritual to Romance.* London: Cambridge UP, 1920.

——. *King Arthur and his Knights: A Survey of Arthurian Romance.* London: David Nutt, 1899.

Wheeler, Bonnie, and Fiona Tolhurst, eds. *On Arthurian Women: Essays in Memory of Maureen Fries.* Dallas, TX: Scriptorium Press, 2001.

Wheeler, Bonnie. "Grief in Avalon: Sir Palomydes' Psychic Pain." *Grief and Gender: 700–1700.* Ed. Jennifer C. Vaught. NY: Palgrave Macmillan, 2003. 65–80.

White, Paul Whitfield. "The Admiral's Men, Shakespeare, and the Lost Arthurian Plays of Elizabethan England." *Arthuriana* 24.4 (2014) 33–47.

White, Roger, Brendan Wolfe, and Judith Wolfe, eds. *C. S. Lewis and His Circle: Essays & Memoirs from the Oxford C. S. Lewis Society.* Oxford UP, 2015.

Wilhelm, James J., ed. *The Romance of Arthur: An Anthology of Medieval Texts in Translation.* NY: Garland Publishing, 1994.

Willard, Thomas. "Acts of the Companions: A. E. Waite's Fellowship and the Novels of Charles Williams." *Secret Texts: The Literature of Secret Societies.* Eds. Marie Mulvey Roberts and Hugh Ormsby-Lennon. NY: AMS Press, 1995. 269–302.

Williams, Peter. *C. S. Lewis vs the New Atheists.* Milton Keynes: Paternoster, 2013.

Williams, Rowan. *The Lion's World: A Journey into the Heart of Narnia.* Oxford and New York: Oxford UP, 2012.

Wilson, A. N. *C. S. Lewis: A Biography.* NY: Norton, 1990.

Wood, Ralph. "The Lady with the Torn Hair Who Looks on Gladiators in Grapple: G. K. Chesterton's Marian Poems." *Christianity and Literature* 62.1 (2012): 29–55.

Zemmour, Corinne. "Tolkien in the Land of Arthur: The Old Forest Episode from *The Lord of the Rings*." *Mythlore* 24 (2006): 135–63.

Zimbardo, Rose A., and Neil D. Isaacs, eds. *Understanding* The Lord of the Rings: *The Best of Tolkien Criticism.* Boston and New York: Houghton Mifflin, 2004.

About the Contributors

Suzanne Bray is Professor of English Studies at Lille Catholic University in the north of France. She specialises in the history of religious ideas in Britain in the twentieth century and in the interaction between literature and theology. She has published extensively in English and French on C. S. Lewis, Dorothy L. Sayers, Charles Williams, and other twentieth-century Christian authors. She has also edited several volumes of critical essays, the most recent in English being *Dimensions of Madeleine L'Engle: New Critical Approaches* (McFarland 2017). She is a lay reader in the Church of England.

Chris Butynskyi holds a Ph.D. in humanities from Faulkner University's Great Books Honors College. His dissertation examines the historical context of tradition's relationship with the modern age and its survival through individuals like the New Humanists and the Inklings. Publications on this topic have appeared in *The Chesterton Review, The University Bookman*, and *The Journal of Faith and the Academy*. He is a Lecturer of European History (largely cultural and intellectual) at Eastern University. He lives in Macungie, PA, with his wife, Tricia, and their two children: Chase and Molly.

Brenton D. G. Dickieson (@BrentonDana) holds a B.A. from Maritime Christian College and an M.C.S. from Regent College and is a Ph.D. Candidate at the University of Chester. Brenton is Adjunct Professor in Theology at Maritime Christian College, Sessional Professor at the Centre for the Study of Christianity and Culture at the University of Prince Edward Island, and Instructor in Spiritual Theology at Regent College. Brenton consults in higher education, does freelance speaking and writing, and is the author of the popular Faith, Fantasy, and Fiction blog *A Pilgrim in Narnia*. Using his biblical studies background, Brenton investigates the worldview-rooted speculative universe-building projects of the Inklings. In his doctoral research, Brenton has turned specifically to how C. S. Lewis' (sub)creation of fictional worlds helps in spiritual formation, theological exploration, and cultural criticisms. Brenton lives with his wife Kerry and their son Nicolas in the almost-fictional land of Prince Edward Island.

Taylor W. Driggers holds a B.A. in English Literature from Messiah College and an M.Sc. in Literature and Modernity from the University of Edinburgh. He serves as the International Student Representative on the General Council for the Student Christian Movement and is also on the editorial staff for *Movement* magazine, the organization's official publication. A long-time admirer of the Inklings, Taylor is primarily interested in how their work anticipates postmodernism's rejection of modern realism and its subsequent turn toward rediscovering pre-modern spiritual and artistic practices. His current Ph.D. study at the University of Glasgow examines Derrida's desert theory of religion as a framework for understanding feminine religious expression in the works of C. S. Lewis, Angela Carter, and Ursula K. Le Guin. Taylor is greatly indebted to Crystal L. Downing and Amy Burge for their guidance and support during the writing of his contribution to this volume.

Christopher Gaertner holds a B.A. in Communication Studies from the University of North Carolina at Chapel Hill and an M.A. in Linguistics and Applied Linguistics from Southwest Jiaotong University, Chengdu, China. His Master's thesis in his concentration on Chinese and Western Comparative Language and Culture is entitled "The interplay of Logos and Tao in the Chinese Translations of Tolkien's *The Lord of the Rings*." He and his wife Leah have lived in China for fifteen years and have three young children, with whom he loves to play baseball and read stories by the Inklings. Chris has enjoyed culture-fusing endeavors in China, from writing and playing music for American-Chinese folk-rock fusion bands, to playing and coaching American football, to organizing arts festivals for marginalized communities. You can check out his band at www.facebook.com/chrisgaertnermusic.

Cory Grewell is an Associate Professor of Literature at Patrick Henry College in Purcellville, VA, where he teaches courses in Western Literature, Early British Literature, and the Inklings. He holds a Ph.D. from Northeastern University and has published scholarly work on contemporary medievalisms, Shakespeare, and Owen Barfield. His scholarly interests are in the areas of medieval and Renaissance English Literature, especially Renaissance drama; the works of the Inklings, particularly Owen Barfield; and the perennial interplay between Christianity and Literature. He also has related interests in detective fiction and the literary iteration of the hero throughout Western history. Dr. Grewell resides in Reston, VA with his wife and two sons.

Malcolm Guite (www.malcolmguite.com, @malcolmguite) is a poet and priest, working as Chaplain of Girton College, Cambridge. He also teaches for the Divinity Faculty and for the Cambridge Theological Federation and lectures widely in England and North America on Theology and Literature. He is the author of several volumes of poetry and books of theology and aesthetics. He contributed the chapter on Lewis as a poet to the *Cambridge Companion to C. S. Lewis* (Cambridge UP, 2010) and another entitled "Yearning for a Far-Off Country" to *C. S. Lewis and his Circle*, published in 2015 by Oxford University Press. He is also a musician and librettist, was the inaugural Artist in Residence at Duke Divinity School in September 2014, and was "Visionary in Residence" at Biola University in March 2015.

Sørina Higgins (www.SorinaHiggins.com, @SorinaHiggins, @Oddest_Inkling) is the Chair of the Department of Language and Literature at Signum University and a PhD candidate, Teacher of Record, and Presidential Scholar at Baylor University. Her interests include British and Irish Modernism, the works of the Inklings, Arthuriana, and magic. She holds an M.A. from Middlebury College's Bread Loaf School of English, where she wrote about *Sehnsucht* in the works of C. S. Lewis. She wrote the introduction to a new edition of Charles Williams' *Taliessin through Logres* (Apocryphile, 2016) and edited *The Chapel of the Thorn* (Apocryphile, 2014). As a creative writer, Sørina has published two books of poetry: *Caduceus* (2012) and *The Significance of Swans* (2007).

Jon Hooper discovered the academic works of C. S. Lewis while researching a dissertation on John Gower's *Confessio Amantis* as an undergraduate, though it was several years before he turned to Lewis' fiction. He recently completed an M.A. in Medieval Studies as a mature student, for which he wrote a dissertation on Lewis and the medieval worldview entitled *"A Taste in Universes": C. S. Lewis and the Medieval Model of the Cosmos*. He publishes Inklings-inspired fiction under the pen name Frederick Hilary, and his stories have been published in *The Mythic Circle*, *New Fairy Tales*, and *Cabinet des Fees*. His fiction website is located at http://frederickhilary.weebly.com.

Alyssa House-Thomas holds an M.A. in Language and Literature from Signum University, where she is on staff. She also earns cash by grading secondary school examinations, just as her favorite Inkling did at one point in his career. "Tolkien's Guinever" is Alyssa's second published article and represents a working version of her thesis for Signum University, supervised by Dr. Verlyn Flieger. Alyssa's scholarly interests include the fiction of J. R. R. Tolkien, Old and Middle English literature, and Old Norse literature.

Charles Huttar, Professor of English Emeritus at Hope College, has published extensively on Lewis, Williams, Tolkien, and Barfield (as well as a variety of other subjects, especially in medieval and early modern literature and art). He graduated from Wheaton College (A.B.) and Northwestern University (M.A., Ph.D.) and taught for eleven years at Gordon College before moving to Hope. He is the editor of *Imagination and the Spirit* (1971), a festschrift honoring Clyde Kilby, who founded the Wade Center. He coedited *Word and Story in C. S. Lewis* (1991, 2007) and *The Rhetoric of Vision: Essays on Charles Williams* (1996), both of which received the Mythopoeic Society's Scholarship Award. His photographs of Lewis and Tolkien have also been published. His primary book project currently is a study of the mythography of metamorphosis in C. S. Lewis' writings. He is a founding member and past president of the Conference on Christianity and Literature.

Yannick Imbert is professor of apologetics at the Faculté Jean Calvin (Aix-en-Provence, France). He regularly publishes articles on Tolkien and the Inklings, as well as on other cultural issues. Tolkien was the subject of his Ph.D. work at Westminster Theological Seminary, with a dissertation entitled *"Who Created the Stories Anyway": A Reformed Perspective on Tolkien's Theory of Faërie*. He has written and edited books on apologetics, philosophy and more recently, transhumanism. He is a cofounder and regular contributor to the cultural apologetics blog *Visio Mundus*.

Jason Jewell (www.westerntradition.wordpress.com, @WestTradition) is Professor of Humanities at Faulkner University, where he chairs the Department of Humanities and directs interdisciplinary M.A. and Ph.D. programs (www.studyliberalarts.org). He received a B.A. in history and music from Harding University, an M.A. in history from Pepperdine University, and a Ph.D. in humanities from the Florida State University. He is the Associate Editor of the *Journal of Faith and the Academy* (faithandtheacademy.wordpress.com) and serves on the editorial board of *Libertarian Papers* (libertarianpapers.org) and of the *Christian Libertarian Review* (libertarianchristians.com). He is also an Associated Scholar of the Ludwig von Mises

Institute. His most recent publication was a collection of essays for *Christian Faith and Social Justice: Five Views* (Bloomsbury Academic, 2014). He lives in Montgomery, Alabama, with his wife and their seven children.

Kirstin Jeffrey Johnson (www.kirstinjeffreyjohnson.com) is an independent scholar based in the Ottawa Valley, Canada. Her doctorate at the University of St. Andrews, Scotland, considered *The Relational and Revelational Nature of MacDonald's Mythopoeic Art.* She has tutored students in Inklings studies in Oxford and lectures internationally on MacDonald, the Inklings, and Theology and the Arts. Dr. Jeffrey Johnson has published numerous articles on these subjects in academic journals, essay collections, magazines, and online venues. She is on the Advisory Board of the Inklings journal *VII: An Anglo-American Literary Review*, *sits on the Committee of the George MacDonald Society, and is* an associate member of the Inklings Institute of Canada. She also chairs the Linlathen Project and is a regular contributor to *ArtWay* journal. She is currently co-writing a book on the literary and social legacy of A. J. Scott, and her book *Storykeeper: The Mythopoeic Making of George MacDonald* is forthcoming.

J. Cameron Moore is Assistant Professor of English at Spring Arbor University in Spring Arbor, Michigan, where he teaches World Literature, Twentieth-Century British Literature, and Composition. His fields of interests include Chesterton, theological aesthetics, Irish literature, and Arthurian literature. He is currently working on a project that considers the place of beauty in Chesterton's fiction and poetry. His recent publications have appeared in *Arthuriana*, *Renascence*, and *ANQ*. Cameron is also the president of the Spring Arbor Chesterton Society.

Holly Ordway (hollyordway.com) is Professor of English and faculty in the M.A. in Apologetics at Houston Baptist University; she holds a PhD in English from the University of Massachusetts Amherst. She is the author of *Not God's Type: An Atheist Academic Lays Down Her Arms* (Ignatius, 2014) and *Apologetics and the Christian Imagination: An Integrated Approach to Defending the Faith* (Emmaus Road, 2017). Dr. Ordway is also a published poet and the Charles Williams Subject Editor for the *Journal of Inklings Studies.* Her academic work focuses on the writings of the Inklings, especially C. S. Lewis and J. R. R. Tolkien. Her current book project is *Tolkien's Modern Sources: Middle-earth Beyond the Middle Ages* (forthcoming from Kent State University Press, 2019).

Andrew Scott Rasmussen (@andysrasmussen) is a Ph.D. student of English Literature and Rhetoric at Baylor University. His research interests include Early Modern British literature, urban rhetoric, and the civic intersection of theology, politics, and literature that emerged in the short-lived English Republic. He is also particularly interested in the works of Charles Williams and the other Inklings. He has presented at the Conference on College Composition and Communication, the Thomas R. Watson Conference, and the Southern Conference on British Studies, among others.

Benjamin Shogren is an alumnus of the Templeton Honors College of Eastern University with a B.A. in Philosophy. He lives with his wife Stephanie in Pennsylvania, and welcomes questions and comments on his chapter at benshogren.inklingsandarthur@gmail.com.

Andrew C. Stout (@ThomasACStout) holds an M.A. in Information Science and Learning Technologies from the University of Missouri, and he works in the Paul and Helen Schnare Library at St. Charles Community College. He earned a B.A. in Philosophy at Lindenwood University and an M.A. in Theological Studies at Covenant Theological Seminary. His articles have appeared in the journals *Religion and the Arts, VII: An Anglo-American Literary Review,* and *Pro Ecclesia.* In addition to his continued interest in Inklings studies, his research interests include ecumenism, sacramental theology, and the relationships among theology, literature, and technology.

Benjamin D. Utter (@liberapertus), a naturalized Narnian, received his M.A. in English from Wake Forest University and is currently a doctoral candidate at the University of Minnesota. He recently moved with his wife and daughter to Little Rock, Arkansas, where rock climbing, triathlon, and choral music provide delightful alternatives to working on his dissertation, tantalizingly close to completion, on the theology of sin and the idea of the hero in later medieval English literature.

Bradley Wells recently completed his Ph.D. in English Literature at the University of Sydney, Australia, where he also taught. His thesis was on the collected plays of Charles Williams; he has been invited to present at various literary, theological, and philosophical conferences and has written extensively on Williams and the other Inklings. He was appointed Hunter Baillie Fellow at St. Andrew's College and Vice Master of Wesley College at The University of Sydney. He is currently Head of English at Malvern College UK, but he is particularly proud to be a founding and ongoing member of The Sydney Inklings.

Index

Made in the USA
Las Vegas, NV
12 October 2024

96695622R00313